HUMAN RESOURCE MANAGEMENT IN IRELAND

FIFTH EDITION

**Patrick Gunnigle,
Noreen Heraty & Michael J. Morley**

Published in 2017
by the Institute of Public Administration
57–61 Lansdowne Road
Dublin 4
Ireland
www.ipa.ie

© Patrick Gunnigle, Noreen Heraty & Michael J. Morley 2017

Design and print origination by OK Graphic Design, Dublin
Cover design by Identikit Design Consultants
Printed by W & G Baird, Antrim

All rights reserved. No part of this publication may be reproduced or transmitted in any form or by any means, electronic or mechanical, including photocopying, recording or any information storage and retrieval system, without permission in writing from the publisher.

British Library cataloguing-in-publication data
A catalogue record for this book is available from the British Library

ISBN: 978-1-910393-17-8

Contents

Foreword	*v*
Acknowledgments	*vii*
1. Human Resource Management in Ireland: An Introduction	1
2. Contextualising Human Resource Management in Ireland	24
3. Strategy, Human Resource Management and Performance	51
4. Human Resource Management and the Labour Market	84
5. Human Resource Planning, Recruitment and Selection	104
6. Motivation and Work Design	133
7. Managing Rewards	165
8. Managing Performance	190
9. Workplace Learning and Development	212
10. Employment Relations: Institutions and Actors	244
11. Employer and Management Approaches to Employment Relations	282
12. Employment Relations Practice	297
13. Employment Law	325
Bibliography	351
Index	382

Foreword

I very much welcome this new edition of *Human Resource Management in Ireland* from three leading academics from the University of Limerick. Ireland, indicative of the global trend, has faced and will continue to face unprecedented change and unpredictability in our economy and in our workplaces. At a point in time, there is a need to capture, analyse and reflect on the progress and trends and on how HRM in Ireland has been responding. This excellent publication presents insights, from a combination of research and practice, to show how HRM in Ireland is developing, and dealing with, the current employment and organisational challenges.

The book's content reflects the changing nature of work and HRM practices globally. It takes account of the effects of social and demographic change, globalisation and technology on workplaces and on HRM. It highlights the increasing emphasis on individualisation in the workplace and the personalisation of the employment relationship, particularly in an increasingly diverse workforce.

Throughout *Human Resource Management in Ireland*, the authors reflect the integrated nature of people management in organisational operations and performance, not solely the perspective of the HR function. They highlight the role and contribution of HRM in enabling organisations to fulfil their strategic objectives through leading and engaging with senior management, and they address how successful HRM practices are dependent on line management.

The more specialist HRM function has a role to both administer, increasingly supported by technology, and deliver effective HRM policy and practices. This revised edition highlights the breadth of HRM influence across the employment life cycle, from recruitment, development, reward, performance, to the complex management of employment relations.

CIPD, the professional body for HR and people development, believes the changed labour market in Ireland, with unemployment down to 6 per cent in 2017 compared to a peak of over 15 per cent five years before, and the changing nature of work, has exposed skills shortages at a national level. The profession's response will serve to highlight the significant contribution of HRM to attracting, developing and retaining the right skills to operate in a changing world.

With the volatile external environment and the nature of work and jobs changing rapidly, *Human Resource Management in Ireland*, now in its fifth edition, from the thought leading authors, Patrick Gunnigle, Noreen Heraty and Michael J. Morley of the University of Limerick, is a very valuable resource for practitioners and students of HRM. It excellently captures the ongoing developments in HRM and provides a resource to help demonstrate HRM's contribution to improved workplaces, organisations and society.

Mary Connaughton, Chartered FCIPD
Director, CIPD Ireland

Acknowledgments

In helping us complete this text, we would like to acknowledge the help and contribution of a number of organisations and individuals who provided data and assistance, particularly the following:

- Brian Sheehan, Colman Higgins and Andy Prendergast, *Industrial Relations News* (IRN). We are indeed very fortunate to have such a magnificent source of up to date information and independent analysis as IRN.
- Marianne Doyle, Membership and Communications Manager, Chartered Institute of Personnel & Development (CIPD) Ireland.
- Jane Brophy and Paula Butler, Local Government Management Agency.
- James Connington, Cedric Chau and Edwin Maguire, Institute of Public Administration.
- Professor Bill Roche, University College Dublin.
- Professor David Collings, Dr. Edel Conway and Dr. Margaret Heffernan, Dublin City University.
- Dr. Jimmy Donaghey, Warwick Business School, and Dr. Brian Harney, Dublin City University, for their learned advice and respective contributions on the employment relations and HR strategy sections.
- Mike Crowley, HR Director, Pfizer Ireland Pharmaceuticals.
- Maria Ryan, University of Limerick, for her specific assistance on HR analytics.
- Dr. Gerard McMahon, Dublin Institute of Technology.
- Alan O'Leary, Services Industrial Professional Technical Union (SIPTU).
- Ruth Gill, Gill.
- Labour Market Section, Central Statistics Office.
- Gillian Chamberlain and Barbara Nestor, Irish Business & Employers Confederation (IBEC).
- Michael McDonnell, Chairman, UTS HR Group and former Managing Director of the Chartered Institute of Personnel and Development in Ireland.
- Professor Aidan Kelly, University College Dublin and Shenzhen Business School, who provided the initial encouragement for developing an Irish HRM textbook many years ago.

We also wish to thank Dr. Michelle O'Sullivan, University of Limerick and board member of the Workplace Relations Commission for her advice and assistance on legislation and employment/industrial relations institutions. We thank UL colleagues Drs. Jonathan Lavelle and Jean McCarthy for comments on earlier versions of the text. We also wish to acknowledge the support of Mary Connaughton, Director of the Chartered Institute of Personnel and Development in Ireland, in writing the Foreword to this new edition.

Various colleagues at the University of Limerick were most helpful and supportive of our efforts – Drs. Christine Cross, Juliette MacMahon, Sarah MacCurtain, Sarah Kiernan, Caroline Murphy and Claire Hartnett, who all contributed in various ways, not least through their own research and publications. We also wish to thank our business studies librarian, Peter Reilly, and all the library staff at UL.

Finally, we would like to mention the contribution of staff in the Institute of Public Administration, especially Richard Boyle, Hannah Ryan and Michael Mulreany and also the work of our indexer Geraldine Begley. We must also acknowledge the immense support and expertise provided by our ever-patient editor, Aoife Barrett of Arcadia Publishing Services.

PG, NH, MM, 2017

1
Human Resource Management in Ireland: An Introduction

People are the lifeblood of organisations. An organisation's workforce is one of its most potent and valuable resources. Consequently, the extent to which an organisation's workforce is managed effectively is a critical element in improving and sustaining organisational performance. Indeed, it is widely argued that effective workforce management is one of the pivotal factors that characterise high-performing organisations (Boxall 2012; Tiernan and Morley 2013). However, the challenge of workforce management is one of the most difficult aspects of organisational management. This difficulty largely stems from the fact that people are inherently different. Managing an organisation's workforce means dealing with people who differ physically and psychologically. This is the essence of *Human Resource Management* (HRM) – that aspect of organisational management concerned with the management of an organisation's workforce.

This chapter explores the nature of HRM in practice and identifies key Human Resource (HR) activities within organisations. It focuses on variation in organisational practice in HRM, thereby acknowledging the evident differences that exist between organisations in terms of their approach to HRM.

THE NATURE OF HRM

During discussions with a class of mature students taking an introductory HRM course, several class members indicated that they didn't have 'HRM' in their organisations since they had 'no HR department'. The notion of HRM as being the exclusive responsibility of HR specialists is a common, if flawed, conception. HRM is concerned with the management of an organisation's workforce. On this basis, it is primarily a *generalist* management function, and therefore an integral part of the work of everyone with managerial responsibilities. HRM encompasses all policies and practices related to workforce management. Therefore, all organisations have important HRM responsibilities, with the deployment, development, motivation and reward of employees representing core areas of HR activity.

Of course, HRM can also be understood as a *specialist* management function. In this conceptualisation, certain HR activities are seen as the responsibility of HR specialists whose remit is to develop and deploy their organisation's HR strategies, policies and practices. However, even where a specialist HRM function exists, *line management* will continue to play a pivotal role in operational day-to-day HR activities (e.g. recruitment or on-the-job training), as well as potentially contributing at a more strategic level (e.g. HR policy implementation).

The principal role of the specialist HRM function is to provide adequate assistance, advice and administrative support. It may sometimes play a more executive role, by taking direct responsibility for certain activities. Common examples might include collective bargaining with trade unions or approving decisions on workforce promotions.

This conception of HRM in *generalist* and *specialist* terms is important. It recognises that HRM is a key responsibility of all managers, at all levels in the organisation's hierarchy. It also recognises that in some – primarily larger – organisations, HRM specialists are employed to undertake particular aspects of HR practice. It is useful to consider the respective roles of three critical layers: top/senior management, line management and the specialist HR function.

At the highest level of organisational decision-making, top/senior management have ultimate responsibility for developing the organisation's approach to HRM. In many larger firms this may entail articulating a particular HR philosophy and related HR strategies. Senior management may comprise the owner or manager of a small retail store or the top management team in a multinational company.

At an operational level, HRM primarily involves *line management* undertaking the day-to-day operational activities of HR: communicating with employees, monitoring performance, handling employee queries or grievances and so forth. As noted above, larger organisations generally have a *specialist HRM function*. This involves the employment of one or more HR practitioners, who together might constitute a HR department. The primary role of the specialist HRM function is normally to deliver HR services and assistance to management and employees, and, at a more strategic level, to devise and execute the organisation's HR plans and policies. In so doing, the HR function may also undertake specialist tasks and provide advice and guidance to line and senior management.

HR ACTIVITIES

If we accept that HRM is concerned with the management of an organisation's workforce, it is clear that the range of HR activities that may be undertaken is extensive. Many of these are basic activities, common to all types of organisation, such as recruiting and rewarding workers. Certain HR activities may only be appropriate in particular organisational contexts and may require more specialist skills, such as the administration of job evaluation schemes or negotiating collective agreements with trade unions. Other HR activities may be more optional in character, relating to preferred managerial approaches or styles, such as the operation of profit-sharing schemes or the establishment of employee assistance programmes.

Since the range of HR activities and the ways they may be undertaken is vast, it is clear that the nature of HRM may differ considerably between organisations. At a generic level, however, we can identify critical HRM activities that are shared by almost all types of organisation (cf. Personnel Standards Lead Body 1993; Taylor and Armstrong 2014) (see Table 1.1).

Table 1.1 Key HRM activities		
1.	*Strategy and organisation*	Contributing to organisational strategy, organisation structure and processes; influencing culture and values; developing personnel/HR strategies and policies.
2.	*Employee resourcing*	Human resource planning; recruitment and selection; deployment; termination of employment.
3.	*Employee development*	Training and development; management development; career development; performance management.
4.	*Reward management*	Selection of reward strategies; administration of pay and benefit systems.
5.	*Employment relations*	Collective bargaining, employee involvement and participation; grievance handling and discipline administration; aspects of social responsibility; aspects of health, safety and welfare; employee services.
6.	*Employment and personnel/HR administration*	Administration of employee records; policies and practices; working conditions; HR information systems (HRIS).

THE IMPACT OF SCALE

A useful approach in considering the nature of HRM practice is to reflect on the extent and variation of HRM activities as organisational scale (numbers of employees) increases.

In *smaller organisations* responsibility for all HR matters invariably rests with line management (Gunnigle and Brady 1984; MacMahon 1996; Cooper and Burke 2011; Harney and Nolan 2014). For obvious financial and structural reasons, these organisations would not normally employ HR specialists. Nevertheless, effective HRM remains a vital consideration. Since payroll may often be one of the largest ongoing costs in small firms, performance and profitability can frequently be increased by better human resource utilisation. In fact, poor recruitment or inadequate training can have a disproportionately more negative impact on smaller organisations than on their larger counterparts, where the effects of bad HR decisions may be more diluted. Of course, HRM practice is rendered potentially simpler in small firms due to the scale of operations, which eases the burden of communications and reduces the level of administrative support required. In the majority of small companies, HRM will be concerned with basic activities essential to the effective running of the organisation. For such organisations, key HR activities might incorporate:

- Human resource planning.
- Recruitment and selection.
- Training and development.
- Reward management.
- Employment relations.
- Health, safety and welfare.
- HR systems/administrative support.

When we consider larger organisations, we find that increased scale normally renders HRM practice more complex. Generally, there are a greater range of HRM activities which in turn may increase the scale of HR service delivery and related administration. HRM in larger organisations also tends to be characterised by greater formality and sophistication in HR policies and procedures. Many larger organisations deploy a specialist HR department with responsibility for co-ordinating HR practice and activities, and providing adequate services and administrative support. Such specialist departments may simply comprise one or two individuals with general responsibility for HR matters. Alternatively, bigger organisations may have much larger HR departments, comprising some combination of HR specialists, HR generalists and administrative support staff, as illustrated in Figures 1.1 and 1.2, which contain examples for HR structures from large private and public sector organisations, respectively (also see Tables 1.7 and 1.8 on page 20).

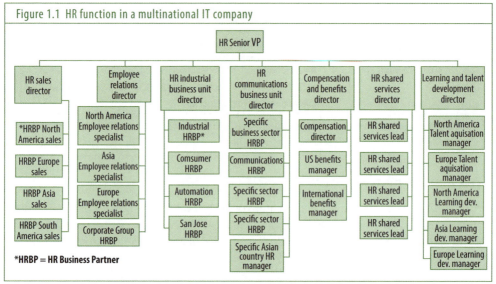

Figure 1.1 HR function in a multinational IT company

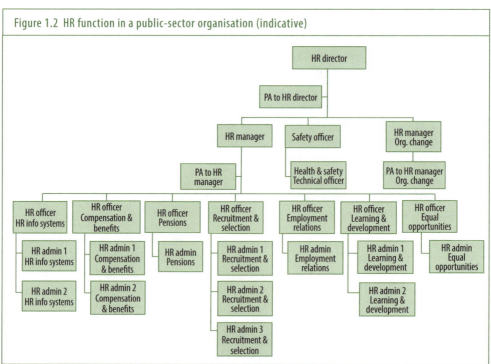

Figure 1.2 HR function in a public-sector organisation (indicative)

It is clearly evident from these two examples, that increases in the size and complexity of organisations lead to higher levels of specialisation and formalisation in HR practice and the execution of HR activities. You will also find that, as scale increases, the HR function may assume responsibility for a larger range of activities. However, the strategic responsibility of top/senior management in shaping the overall HR approach, and of line management in carrying out a range of operational HR tasks, should remain intact. As noted earlier, the specialist HR function normally operates in an advisory capacity. This means that its primary role is to provide advice, assistance and services to line management (at all levels) in undertaking their HR responsibilities.

STRATEGY, POLICY AND PRACTICE IN HRM

The study of *business strategy* has achieved ever increasing prominence, as organisations seek to adapt to a rapidly changing business environment. Business strategy is concerned with policy decisions affecting the entire organisation, the main objective being to optimally position the organisation to deal effectively with its environment. Strategic decisions are long-term in character, affect the future nature of the organisation and serve to guide subsequent decision-making across a variety of management functions, including HR. From an HRM perspective it is widely argued that strategic decision-making should incorporate HR considerations. This way organisations can establish and articulate a corporate HR philosophy and develop a complementary and coherent set of HR strategies and policies (Beer *et al.* 1984; Tiernan and Morley 2013; Taylor and Armstrong 2014).

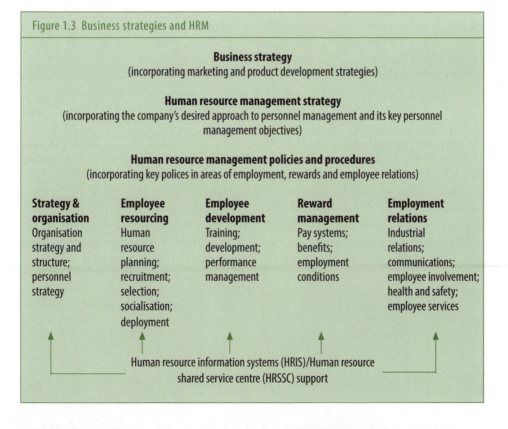

Figure 1.3 Business strategies and HRM

In recent years, the HRM literature has increasingly focused on improving the alignment between HRM and overall business strategy. This literature is largely posited on the argument that more optimally aligning business strategy and HR strategy can contribute to improvements in an organisation's performance ('the bottom line') (Huselid 1995; Boxall and Purcell 2011). Many commentators have identified HRM as a neglected area of strategic management and consequently one with a potentially crucial role to play in the more effective implementation of business strategy (Fombrun *et al.*1984; McGrath and Geaney 1998; Monks and McMackin 2001). The potential link between business strategy, HRM strategy and HR activities, is illustrated summarily in Figure 1.3 and explored in greater detail in Chapter 3.

HRM STRATEGY

An HRM strategy incorporates an organisation's basic philosophy, overall approach and long-term objectives in managing human resources. It forms the basis for the organisation's subsequent development of more explicit HR policies and procedures in critical areas of workforce management, such as recruitment, training and reward management, and their deployment in practice.

Responsibility for developing HR strategy rests primarily with top management, aided, as appropriate, by the specialist HR function. HR strategies are often expressed in the form of general statements outlining critical organisational beliefs and values concerning HRM. Table 1.2 outlines examples of such statements from two companies. These examples are explicit indications of particular espoused organisational strategies in HRM. However, in practice, many companies do not have such explicit statements. A 2008 survey of the *Business and Finance* list of top 1,000 Irish organisations found that 46 per cent (over four in ten) of respondent firms had a written HR strategy, while 43 per cent reported a HR presence at board level (Heffernan *et al.* 2008). Of the latter, however, almost a quarter reported having little involvement in business strategy development.

A more recent *Chartered Institute of Personnel and Development* (CIPD 2017) study of HR practices in Ireland found a similarly patchy picture of HR's strategic role in organisations, with 45 per cent of respondents reporting a lack of senior management understanding of HR's strategic contribution and 36 per cent, over one third, indicating that HR did not play a strategic role within their organisation.

Much of this research tends to be based on larger firms (i.e. those with fifty or more employees). Clearly the incidence of formal HR strategies is likely to be much lower among smaller organisations. Does this imply that these organisations do not have an HR strategy? This is a difficult question to answer definitively. Virtually every organisation has a philosophy and broad approach, however basic, regarding how it views and manages its workforce. While this may not necessarily be written, it can be inferred from how employees are treated and rewarded in the organisation. In such situations, the organisation's HR philosophy is implicit rather than explicit in nature.

Table 1.2 Statements of corporate beliefs in HRM

Company 1: Key beliefs in managing people
- To treat each employee with dignity, as an individual.
- To maintain an open atmosphere where direct communications with employees affords the opportunity to contribute to the maximum of their potential and fosters unity of purpose.
- To provide personal opportunities for training and development to ensure the most capable and most efficient workforce.
- To respect senior service.
- To compensate fairly by salary, benefits and incentives.
- To promote on the basis of capability.

Company 2: Core values and beliefs about how employees should be managed (selection)
- *Employment*: Employees are recruited and promoted on merit and we believe in maximum openness in competition and appointments. We respect our employees and value each as an individual. All employees have equal opportunity for development and advancement according to their qualifications, abilities and the needs of the business. We seek to use individual talents and skills to the best advantage of the person and the company.
- *Pay and conditions*: We have pay and conditions of employment designed to attract the right people, motivate employees, stimulate quality work and reflect performance, while taking account of national economic circumstances and policy. We try always to be fair and equitable in the treatment of individuals and in responding to their needs.

HRM POLICIES

Of course, broad HR strategies and related HR statements expressing corporate beliefs and values are likely to be ineffective unless they are implemented in the day-to-day practice of HRM. In reality there may often be a disconnect between the apparent intent of HR strategies and statements and HRM practice on the ground. For example, in Table 1.2, an employee might find that in spite of the explicit statement committing to 'maximum openness' in job appointments, this strategy may not always be carried out in practice, with some appointments being made without any prior knowledge or any communication from HR.

To try to effectively bridge the gap between espoused beliefs and workplace practice, organisations may develop HR policies in key activity areas of HRM, such as recruitment, rewards and employment relations. The primary role of such policies is to guide line managers in the execution of their HRM responsibilities. They also act as an important yardstick for workers in outlining the standards and approaches they should expect from the organisation, and the norms the organisation expects from its workforce. Examples of HR policy statements are outlined in Table 1.3 on the next page.

Table 1.3 HRM policy statements (indicative)

Company 1: Policy statement on promotion and development
This company encourages everyone to prepare for career enhancement through its educational assistance and training programmes. It is our policy to promote from within whenever suitable and experienced candidates are available.

Company 2: Policy statement on employment equality
It is our policy to ensure that all employees are afforded equal treatment irrespective of their sex, marital or parental status, race or religion. This company ensures equal access to employment, training, development and promotion solely based on essential job requirements and the individual's ability and fitness for work.

Company 3: Policy statement on pay and employment conditions
It is our policy to provide pay and terms of employment which are competitive with the top quartile of comparable firms in our industrial segment.

Company 4: Policy statement on employee relations
We seek to develop good relations with employees and their trade unions. Where difficulties arise, the company will seek to resolve these quickly and as close to the workplace as possible. The company is committed to adherence to agreed procedures in the resolution of employee relations difficulties.

HRM PROCEDURES

Policy statements, therefore, establish guidelines and sometimes limits within which managers, supervisors and team leaders can execute their various operational HRM responsibilities. To further aid managers and workers in the implementation of HR policies, organisations may develop HRM procedures, comprising detailed statements on various aspects of HR. These procedures normally embrace detailed statements covering a range of operational HR activities, some examples of which are outlined in Table 1.4. The specialist HR function normally plays a key role in developing HR policies and procedures. It also provides support and direction to line managers in their implementation of procedures, through advice, guidance and administrative assistance.

Table 1.4 HRM procedures (indicative)

Company 1: Procedure on educational assistance
To help personal development and maintain the company's competitive position, all relevant educational courses or parts thereof, which have been successfully completed and are appropriate to your career will be paid for by the company. All such courses must be approved, prior to the commencement of the course, by your department manager and the Human Resource Manager in order to be considered for reimbursement. Application forms are available from the Human Resource Department.

Company 2: Procedure on probationary period
The first six months of your employment will be considered a probationary period. During this time, your supervisor will assess your suitability for the job. He/she will sit down with you and discuss your performance after one month, after three months and, again, after six months service. You will be given every opportunity and assistance to make a success of your new position. Within this time the company shall have the sole and absolute right of deciding on your suitability for continued employment. Your employment may be terminated by the company at any time during this period without recourse to the disciplinary or grievance procedure.

HRM POLICY CHOICE: VARIATIONS IN STRATEGY, POLICY AND PRACTICE IN HRM

The preceding discussion alluded to the fact that, in practice, there is an immense variation between organisations in their approach to workforce management. This is manifested in the wide variety of differing HR approaches and related HRM strategies, structures, policies and procedures between organisations. The variation may be attributed to the differential impact of factors in the external or internal environment of organisations.

While many of these differences are due to external environmental factors, such as consumer sentiment or sectoral trends, Purcell (1987) identified *strategic choice* (as exercised by senior management) as the key factor explaining differences in organisational approaches to HRM. Strategic choice in this context addresses the extent to which management (i) possess; and (ii) exercise choice in developing their HRM strategies, policies and procedures. This implies that senior management possess some room for manoeuvre, and while environmental factors may constrain the range of choice, they retain considerable power in making decisions on 'appropriate' HR approaches and policies. Senior management can therefore use their resources and power to make strategic choices, which both influence environmental factors and effect particular management approaches or 'styles'. Thus, organisational approaches to HRM are often evaluated in terms of the interplay between environmental factors, managerial ideology and values, and strategic choice:

> Choice should be viewed as both a cause and consequence of environmental influences, that is, management have some influence over the kind of markets in which they choose to operate, and in some cases over the structure of the market itself, as well as having some choice over the way in which they respond to environmental pressures.
> Marchington and Parker (1990: 99)

THE CONTEXT FOR CHOICE: EXPLAINING VARIATION IN ORGANISATIONAL APPROACHES TO HRM

To identify and explain variations in organisational approaches to HRM it is necessary to examine the interplay between a diverse range of external and internal factors that influence and constrain managerial choice and practice in the sphere of HRM. Key factors impacting on organisational approaches to HRM relate to the external environment, such as product and labour markets. It is argued that changes in environmental conditions influence decisions on business strategy and, ultimately, HRM. Such decisions will be conditioned by managerial values and beliefs, and constrained by historical factors and 'custom and practice' in HRM. Figure 1.4 on the next page presents a framework for evaluating variation in organisational approaches to HRM. This framework is further discussed below.

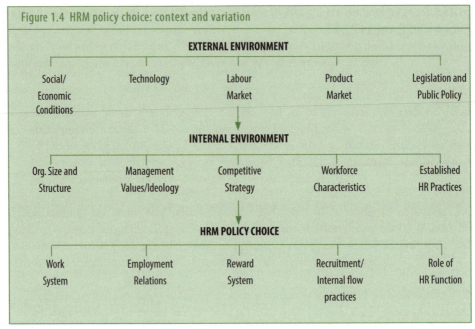

Figure 1.4 HRM policy choice: context and variation

The External Environment

In evaluating contemporary developments in HRM, there is general agreement that the main forces for change originate outside the domain of HRM and stem from developments in the broader business environment, particularly the impact of globalisation, technology and trade regulation. These changes are outlined in Table 1.5 and impact upon both the public and private sectors.

Table 1.5 Competitive pressures impacting on HRM
• Globalisation of competition.
• Improved communications and transport infrastructures.
• Greater liberalisation of international trade.
• More intense price competition.
• Competitive strategies based on quality, product innovation and price.
• Diffusion of new production techniques to improve performance.
• Greater competition from emerging economies.
• Mergers and acquisitions.
• Increased product and service customisation.
• Pace of technological change.
• Demographic change (e.g. ageing population, low birth rates, etc.).

Developments in the international business environment have particularly significant implications for Ireland because of our high level of dependence on multinational investment and international trade (see Chapter 2 for greater detail). Increased competitive pressures have focused attention on cost, product innovation and quality as factors impacting on competitive positioning. These in turn may create a 'flexibility imperative', where companies have to be increasingly responsive to consumer demands on areas such as customisation and after-sales support.

These competitive challenges impact both the public and private sectors. EU-level initiatives to reduce or eliminate state monopolies in sectors such as air travel have detrimentally impacted on national flag carriers. In Ireland, for example, deregulation in the airline industry meant that the former national airline, *Aer Lingus*, faced increased competition from low-cost carriers, most notably *Ryanair*, which has quickly grown to become one of Europe's largest airlines (Creaton 2007; O'Sullivan and Gunnigle 2009). Resultant restructuring in *Aer Lingus* led to significant changes in HRM, including reductions in headcount, changes in work practices and rosters, and changes to its reward systems (Harrington et al. 2005). *Aer Lingus* ultimately transitioned from the public to the private sector, being floated on the Irish and London Stock Exchanges in 2006. It was taken over by *International Airlines Group* (IAG), the parent company of *British Airways* and *Iberia*, in 2015. EU deregulation initiatives in sectors such as electricity and telecommunications have similarly impacted on HRM in other state-owned or formerly state-owned companies in Ireland, notably *Eir* (formerly the state-owned telecommunications company *Telecom Éireann*) and the *Electricity Supply Board* (ESB).

Trends in the socio-economic context, such as *levels of economic performance* and *cultural norms and values*, can greatly influence business strategy and management practice. Economic performance and public policy, as manifested in levels of economic activity, state intervention and approaches to organised labour, clearly impact on HRM. In Ireland, we saw that while economic activity remained depressed for much of the 1980s, the country then experienced an unprecedented economic boom, from the late 1990s until the onset of the global financial crisis (GFC) or 'great recession' as it has now become known. Strong economic growth during the boom years led to high levels of business activity across almost all sectors of the economy. Consequent labour shortages and pressures for increased output were just two of the dimensions of economic growth with important implications for HRM. In contrast, the great recession, accompanied by dramatic increases in unemployment and depressed consumer demand, greatly altered the HR landscape. HR activity became focused on downsizing, cost reduction, productivity enhancement and organisation restructuring (see Chapter 2 for greater detail on these developments).

Broader *social changes* in areas such as education, living standards and class mobility, also exert significant influence on HRM. For example, higher levels of educational attainment will help improve the quality of the labour force but may concurrently lead to increased employee expectations with regard to rewards, working conditions and opportunities for personal development.

Developments in *technology* are another key external environmental factor impacting on organisational approaches to HRM. Technology, seen in generic terms as the equipment used to perform particular tasks, and the way in which work is organised, has a major influence on approaches to workforce management (Beer et al. 1984). Guest (1987) identified 'technological/production feasibility' as a requisite condition for the successful implementation of more 'strategic' HRM approaches, suggesting that large-scale investment in short-cycle, repetitive, assembly-line technology mitigates against the job design and autonomous team-working principles characteristic of 'strategic' HRM (also see Chapters 2 and 3 for greater detail). Technology also affects cost structure, and consequently impacts upon important aspects of HRM, such as reward systems.

Boxall and Purcell (2011) suggest that in labour-intensive sectors, where wage costs are high, organisations may be more constrained in developing employee-oriented 'soft' HRM styles. However, in capital-intensive sectors, where labour constitutes a small proportion of total costs, organisations may have greater scope to adopt such approaches, incorporating, for example, attractive reward and employee development policies. Technological developments also impact on job content and lead to changes in the competencies required to carry out particular tasks effectively. These issues are addressed in greater detail in Chapter 2 and particularly in Chapter 6 (specifically concerning the issues of work systems and job design).

The *labour market* exerts possibly the most profound influence on HRM, especially in the areas of recruitment, training and reward systems. Looking at the Irish labour market, the most notable development has been the huge growth in employment levels from the early 1990s until the great recession and subsequent crash in economic activity, and the related dramatic growth in unemployment which jumped from less than 5 per cent in 2007 to 15 per cent at the height of the recession. By early 2017 it had fallen back to approx. over 6.5 per cent. An associated and significant development has been the change in the sectoral distribution of employment, encompassing a progressive decline in agricultural employment and growth in industrial and – particularly – service sector employment. This means that in approximately three decades the Irish labour market has oscillated from significant over-supply to very limited labour availability and skill shortages, back again to over-supply during the recent recession, and currently to significant employment growth. Generally speaking, prevailing levels of high unemployment reduce the onus on organisations to 'grow' capacity from within (e.g. by investing more in training and development), to develop HR policies to attract and retain workers, or develop new sources of labour supply. High unemployment also tends to exert downward pressure on wages and fringe benefits. It can also impact on other aspects of HRM, as manifested in reduced labour turnover and greater employer power in employment relations/collective bargaining, whereas low unemployment has the opposite effect. Other notable developments in employment structure include the increased feminisation of the workforce (higher female participation), growth of atypical and more precarious employment forms and changing migration patterns(see Chapters 2 and 4 for greater detail).

Product market performance refers to how an organisation is performing in the market into which it supplies its goods or services. Clearly market performance can significantly impact on strategic decision-making and organisational approaches to HRM. Favourable market performance, as might be indicated by high market share and high margins, allow organisations greater scope to adopt 'soft' HRM approaches, such as high pay and attractive fringe benefits. Thus, organisations that operate from a strong product market position (e.g. high market share, growing market and stable demand) have greater financial capacity to adopt sophisticated HR policies such as employee development, job tenure commitments and elaborate management–employee communications. In contrast, firms with poor market performance (e.g. contracting market share and intense price competition) may have considerably less scope for choice. They may be forced to adopt a more traditional cost reduction and labour control approach. A particular example is provided by high-volume, low-margin garment manufacturers. Some years ago, we witnessed the closure of *Fruit of the Loom*'s operations in Donegal and Derry, and the loss of a huge number of jobs to Morocco's lower cost base (Jackson, 2000). The characteristics of an organisation's product market will be influenced by a variety of factors, such as the cost of entry, nature and intensify of competition, technology and their customers.

There are a number of important aspects of *public policy* that impact on HRM in Ireland, most pertinently in the domains of employment relations and employment law. In regard to industrial/employment relations, the traditional approach of Irish governments was historically rooted in the so-called 'voluntarist' tradition (see Chapters 2 and 10). This meant that the state intervened to only a minimal degree in workplace employment relations, thereby allowing employers and employees (and their representative institutions, particularly trade unions and employer associations) considerable scope to determine the terms of their relationship in regard to pay and benefits, working conditions and the extent of employee involvement and consultation (cf. Hillery 1994). However, this approach has been considerably diluted over recent decades, with greater state intervention in employment relations and with the enactment of an array of legislation dealing with employment issues, particularly individual employment rights, (Wallace et al. 2013). Until the onset of the recent 'recession', successive Irish governments were strong advocates of centralised agreements on pay, and other aspects of social and economic policy, involving negotiations with the main employer and trade union federations and commonly described as 'social partnership' (Wallace et al. 2013). The issue of trade union recognition (i.e. employer willingness to accept trade unions as the legitimate representatives of worker interests and to engage with such unions through negotiations/ collective bargaining) has also emerged as an area of considerable debate, due in large measure to the increasing number of organisations that have chosen to pursue a non-union strategy. This is evident not only among high-profile multinational corporations (MNCs), such as *Intel*, *Google* and *Facebook* but also in a number of indigenous firms, most notably *Ryanair* (cf. O'Sullivan and Gunnigle 2009) (see Chapters 2 and 10 for greater detail on these issues).

In the area of employment law, the period since the 1970s has witnessed the enactment of several important Acts, especially in the area of individual employment rights (e.g. unfair dismissal), and an increase in the volume of legislation dealing with atypical employment forms, such as the *Protection of Employees (Part-Time Work) Act 2001* and the *Protection of Employees (Fixed Term Work) Act 2003*. A particular catalyst behind this trend was Ireland's membership of the European Union (EU) formerly the European Economic Community (EEC). The 1987 Single European Act, aimed at strengthening economic cohesion, placed considerable emphasis on integrating social policy throughout the then EEC (Hourihan 1997). In 1989, a Charter of Fundamental Social Rights of Workers (the *Social Charter*) was signed by all member states, with the exception of the UK. The Social Charter and attendant Social Action Programme comprised forty-nine legally binding directives and recommendations in the broad area of employment law and regulation (see Chapters 10, 11 and 12 on employment relations and Chapter 13 on employment law).

A final important aspect of public policy relates to approaches to industrial development. Since the 1960s, Irish government policy has actively sought to encourage foreign direct investment (FDI) into Ireland. This public policy focus on attracting inward investment from multinational companies has helped shape economic development and

HRM in Ireland (Lavelle et al. 2009). While MNCs have been an important source of innovation in HRM, particularly in the application of new HR approaches in Ireland and in expanding the role of the specialist HRM function, it is also clear that MNCs can act as a source of disruption, particularly in their ability to switch the locus of production/investment and in their increasing trend of trade union avoidance (see Chapter 2 for greater detail on the impact of MNCs on HRM in Ireland).

The Internal Environment

While factors in the external environment may exert a significant impact on management practice and decisions, it is largely factors in the *internal environment* that shape the unique organisational responses to such external factors.

As we have seen earlier in this chapter, *organisation structure and size* are clearly important factors impacting upon HRM. Irish organisations are generally smaller in scale and employ fewer numbers than their counterparts in larger countries, such as the UK or Germany. Numerous studies have noted that the likelihood of trade union recognition and greater specialisation in HRM are positively correlated with organisation size (Cooper and Burke 2011). Management in smaller organisations are also more likely to veer towards a unitarist frame of reference and adopt less formality in HR and employment relations than their larger counterparts (cf. Gunnigle and Brady 1984) (See Chapter 11 for greater detail on managerial frames of reference and their impact on workplace employment relations). In relation to organisation structure, Purcell (1989) argues that top management in large, highly diversified organisations are primarily focused on financial matters, with the consequence that HRM considerations are not a primary concern of corporate decision-makers but are rather a more operational concern of management at the business unit or individual site level. A corollary of this argument is that 'core business' organisations, whose operation relies on a narrow product range, are more likely to integrate HRM issues into strategic planning, whereas highly diversified organisations are more likely to adopt differing HR strategies and policies tailored to the needs of their different constituent businesses and operations.

Several writers identify the locus of HR strategy formulation as a key issue in influencing the nature of establishment-level HRM. For example, Poole (1986: 53) argues that, in the employment relations sphere, the growth of large multinational companies presents management with the opportunity to develop policies at corporate level, 'where they are relatively unrestricted by intervention by government or plant-level agreements with labour'. Of course, the extent of unfettered management prerogative is dependent on public policy, (which may, for example, place constraints on management decisions) and on the relative power of the various parties, especially the balance of power between employers and trade unions.

Managerial values and ideology are also seen as having a major influence on organisational approaches to HRM. Management values and ideology incorporate the deeply-held beliefs of senior management, which help guide decisions on various aspects of workforce management. These are particularly important in interpreting developments in the external and internal environment, and on impacting decisions regarding the organisation's overall approach to HRM. Clearly, all organisations are characterised by particular values and philosophies on workforce management and employment relations. As mentioned earlier, such values/ideology may be explicit in some organisations, as manifested in statements of corporate mission or philosophy. In many others, the values/ideology may be more implicit in nature, and must thus be inferred from management practice on dimensions such as supervisory style, reward systems and communications.

A first instance of the impact of managerial values on HRM can be seen in a number of organisations, where we can identify the pivotal role of influential founders in determining their organisation's corporate values and general HRM approach. Prominent international examples include *Marks and Spencer*, *Hewlett Packard* and *Dell Computers*. The influence of entrepreneurial founders is also evident among indigenous firms with the HRM approaches adopted by organisations such as *Dunnes Stores*, *Superquinn* and *Ryanair* heavily influenced by the values and philosophy of their respective founders and/or chief executives.

A second instance of the impact of managerial values on HRM relates to the notion that managerial ideology is related to broader ethnic and cultural values. Of particular significance is the suggestion that in the domain of employment relations managerial opposition to pluralism (i.e. acceptance that a conflict of interest exists between employers and workers), and especially to trade unions, is characteristic of the value system of American managers. Certain HRM-type approaches that emphasise individual (as opposed to collective) management–employee relations, direct communications and merit-based rewards, are very much in line with this value system (Bendix 1956; Kochan et al. 1986). This interpretation is very significant in Ireland, given its dependence on foreign investment, the bulk of which is American. In analysing the broad links between ideology and management practice, Poole (1986) finds support for the suggestion that managerial ideologies differ between countries, particularly in relation to the achievement of control over labour. In the US context, he argues, the influence of values and ideologies is most obviously manifest in trade union avoidance practices, a pronounced 'unitary' perspective and deployment of sophisticated HRM approaches. Both Poole (1986) and Kochan et al. (1986) note that while managerial preferences have fluctuated over time, many US employers have embraced a non-union approach against a more general trend in the developed world towards tacit acceptance of trade unions.

Looking specifically at the Irish context, we also find that a traditional criticism of business culture in Ireland is that it has not always encouraged enterprise and innovation. This trait was attributed to Ireland's relatively late independence, which created what some have termed a 'dependence mentality'. However, this criticism seems to have been effectively laid to rest over recent decades. Levels of productivity and export performance have increased dramatically, and compare very favourably with international standards. Indeed, various studies have noted the flexibility of the Irish workforce and the relevance of coherent and strong corporate culture formation (cf. Tiernan and Morley 2013) (See Chapter 2 for greater detail on this).

Another internal factor impacting upon HRM is *competitive strategy*, which is concerned with achieving sustainable competitive advantage in a particular industry or industry segment. The notion of competitive advantage is primarily associated with the work of Michael Porter (1980, 1985) and encompasses the means (i.e. competitive strategies) through which competing firms seek to gain market advantage over one another. This is normally achieved by an organisation pricing its products or services more competitively and/or differentiating these from competitors', along some dimension that will make them more attractive for customers, such as added features, or better quality/reliability. Porter argues that an organisation's choice of competitive strategy helps define its overall approach to market competition and thus establishes the context for policies and actions in other key areas of organisational management, such as HRM. In particular, commentators posit that different competitive strategies require specific complementary HRM strategies and furthermore that the HR function and HR specialists have an important role in effectively aligning HRM with competitive strategy (cf. Schuler 1992; Schuler and Jackson 2014). These issues are addressed in greater detail in Chapter 3.

Other important internal factors influencing organisational approaches to HRM include *workforce profile* and *established HRM practices and traditions*. These factors are especially important in impacting upon the efficacy of organisation change initiatives, such as those aimed at developing specific employee competencies. Clearly particular workforces will be characterised by a specific age and skill profile. An ageing workforce may require training in areas such as information technology while a younger workforce may need experiential placements to build understanding of the business. Past HRM practice also affects the viability of certain change initiatives. For example, while many organisations have experimented with job re-design initiatives, the extant evidence indicates that employees may not necessarily react positively to such initiatives (Tiernan and Morley 2013). Rather it appears that employees characterised by a strong desire for achievement, responsibility and autonomy are most positively disposed to, and motivated by, such initiatives (Hackman and Oldham 1980). Such employee characteristics may in turn have been conditioned by past practice in HRM. For example, individual initiative may have traditionally been stifled through restrictive job design and repetitive monotonous tasks. Consequently, it may prove difficult to change the status quo due to work practices and traditions having become deeply embedded over time. These issues are addressed in greater detail in Chapter 6, which deals with employee motivation and the design of work.

KEY AREAS OF HR POLICY CHOICE

The above discussions have indicated the major factors that help explain variation in organisational approaches to HRM. Manifestations of such variation will be evident in key areas of HR policy choice, particularly how work is organised and managed (work system), industrial/employment relations, how pay and benefits are managed (reward systems), recruitment and internal HR flow, and the role and status of the specialist HR function.

THE WORK SYSTEM

The *work system* incorporates the way various organisational tasks are structured, affecting issues such as organisational structure, job design and ultimately how employees experience work. Decisions on the work system are primarily a managerial responsibility. The approach chosen is a valuable indicator of management beliefs regarding HRM.

Traditional approaches to the organisation of work have been dominated by a desire to maintain control over the work process whilst maximising the productive efficiency of the organisation's technical resources. Thus, choices on the organisation of work and the design of jobs were often seen as determined primarily by the technical system. Management's role was to ensure that other resources, including employees, were organised in such a way as to facilitate the optimal utilisation of the technical system. This approach often resulted in bureaucratic structures, elaborate procedures and systems, top-down supervisory control and limited employee involvement. It also encouraged the fragmentation of jobs into simple, repetitive and measurable tasks, which afforded postholders limited autonomy.

In contrast, it appears that the increased emphasis on improving quality, service and overall competitiveness has led to work redesign initiatives aimed at restructuring work systems to increase employee autonomy, motivation and performance (Tiernan and Morley 2013; Walton 1985). Much of this focus has been on restructuring organisations and jobs to give greater scope for intrinsic motivation and employee involvement, through *inter alia*, providing more challenging jobs within a more organic, flexible organisational structure. At the same time, we also find evidence of the adoption of 'harder' approaches as evidenced by job and work design initiatives which seek to tightly prescribe performance targets and objectives, intensify the pace of work and more closely monitor employee performance (Green 2006; Green and Whitfield 2009).

INDUSTRIAL/EMPLOYMENT RELATIONS

A second important area of HR policy choice is *industrial* or *employment relations*. This involves issues such as collective bargaining, communications, grievance handling, dispute resolution and discipline administration. It may also encompass related areas such as health, safety and employee welfare. Traditionally the emphasis in larger organisations focused primarily on collective bargaining between employers and trade unions. However, as noted earlier, we have seen a shift over recent decades towards a more individualistic approach to workforce management and increased trade union avoidance.

The major difference here is that terms and conditions of employment (e.g. pay increases) would be determined by individual contracting (individual worker and management) as opposed to collective bargaining between trade unions and employers. Another important aspect relates to management–employee communications. Differences in managerial approaches in this domain tend to focus on the range of communication mechanisms used and the extent to which these operate in a top-down fashion, vis-à-vis their potential to facilitate upward communications. These issues are further addressed in Chapter 11.

THE REWARD SYSTEM

An organisation's *reward system* is another important aspect of HR policy choice. High or low pay, the range and nature of fringe benefits and the processes used to determine reward levels, provide valuable insights into an organisation's general approach to HRM. Significant considerations in the design of reward systems are the role of pay, the extent to which pay increases are based on measures of employee performance, and the compatibility of the reward system with business strategy and other areas of HR activity, such as recruitment and retention.

In the Irish context, basic pay levels have traditionally been based on the 'going rate' concept, namely that the appropriate pay levels for a particular occupation are largely determined by the 'going rate' paid for that job in other organisations and/or sectors. As previously noted, for almost four decades pay movements in Ireland have, in most instances, been determined at national level through centralised agreements. The outcomes of these agreements applied to almost all unionised employees but also influenced pay determination in non-union firms, acting as benchmark for pay movement. However, in non-union firms, and especially among managerial and professional categories, pay movements are often linked to periodic performance reviews. An interesting trend in the Irish context is the growing utilisation of performance-related pay (PRP) based on formal reviews (appraisals) of individual employee performance (Lavelle *et al.* 2009). However, decisions on pay movements in individual firms will invariably be informed by comparisons with pay trends in other comparable organisations or sectors. The area of reward and reward management is addressed in Chapter 7.

RECRUITMENT AND INTERNAL HR FLOW PRACTICES

This is another important area of HR policy choice as, in addition to recruitment and selection, this area also incorporates the management and deployment of workers once they have taken up employment and incorporates key HR issues such as induction/socialisation, training and development, succession planning, appraisal and career progression. This area of HR activity is crucial in ensuring organisations have the required numbers of employees with the right skills and knowledge to meet the strategic needs of the organisation. In Ireland, we have witnessed some important developments over the recent past. As mentioned in the 'external environment' section, strong economic growth and high levels of job creation from the late 1990s until 2008 meant that firms found it increasingly difficult to fill vacant positions. This encouraged employers to place a greater emphasis on sourcing and retaining labour as sourcing new recruits from the external labour market was proving particularly challenging. It also led to increased 'poaching' of employees, particularly in areas of the labour market characterised by skill shortages. However, the onset of the 'great recession' dramatically altered the prevailing pattern, with high unemployment leading to ample levels of labour supply in most occupational categories. A further important issue in the domain of recruitment and internal HR flow practices concerns the relative organisational emphasis on using either internal or external labour market sources, i.e. whether vacancies are normally filled from the current pool of workers within the organisation or by sourcing labour (new recruits) from outside the organisation. These issues are addressed in Chapters 4 and 5.

The Specialist HR Function

A particularly significant aspect of HR policy choice concerns the role of the specialist HR function. While it is argued that an essential feature of 'strategic' HRM is that major responsibility for HR is assumed by senior and line managers (Beer *et al.* 1984), we know that many HR activities are coordinated and supported by a specialist HR function and its constituent HR practitioners. Guest (1987) notes the existence of a 'well-established professional structure' of HRM whereby 'professional' HR specialists undertake responsibility for a range of HR issues and possess valued expertise in core HR areas such as selection, training, pay and employment relations. The historical evolution of HRM and the HR function is considered in greater detail in Chapter 2.

It would seem that the issue of whether HR issues are best managed by a specialist HR function or by line managers is a matter of emphasis since, in larger organisations, both will be involved in various aspects of HRM practice. For example, the 'professional' HRM model involves a major role for the HR function in handling HR activities, with a heavy reliance on systems and procedures, particularly in areas such as recruitment, selection and employment relations. Guest (1987) argues that this approach is most appropriate in stable, bureaucratic organisations. On the other hand, we have already noted that contemporary approaches place more emphasis on the role of line management in operational HR activity and greater top/senior management involvement in developing HR strategies and policies. Recognising the variations that may occur in the organisational role played by the HR function, Tyson and Fell (1986) identified three broad typologies of the HR function, as outlined in Table 1.6 (also see Tyson 1987).

Table 1.6 Typologies of specialist HR function		
1.	Administrative and support	In this typology HRM is a low-level activity operating in a clerical support mode to line and senior management. It is largely responsible for personnel/HR administration and welfare provision.
2.	Systems/reactive	In this typology HRM is a higher-level function with a key role in handling employment relations (particularly interaction with trade unions) and in developing policies and procedures in other core areas of HRM. However, the role is largely reactive, dealing with the HR implications of business decisions. This typology incorporates a strong 'policing' dimension, where the HR function is focused on securing adherence to agreed systems and procedures.
3.	Business manager	In this typology, HRM is a top-level management function involved in the development and implementation of strategic HR policies designed to facilitate the achievement of business goals. HRM considerations are recognised as an integral component of corporate success and the HR Director is a member of the top management team and fully involved in strategic decision-making. Routine HR activities are delegated to a lower level, allowing senior HR practitioners scope for strategic involvement.

Source: Adapted from Tyson and Fell (1986).

Early Irish studies by Shivanath (1987) and Monks (1992, 1993) investigated the nature and operational characteristics of the HR/personnel function in Irish organisations. In relation to the *administrative and support* typology, Shivanath's (1987) work found that the great majority of Irish HR practitioners were not limited to this role. While HR departments were, of necessity, concerned with routine clerical and administrative tasks, these were generally delegated, allowing senior practitioners to deal with higher order and arguably more strategic matters. The description of the HR practitioner in the *systems/ reactive* typology seemed most accurately to reflect the then roles of the majority of Irish practitioners. Employment relations was identified by the bulk of respondents as the most crucial area of their work. The studies also found that the *business manager* typology, where the role of the senior HR practitioner was more strategic in nature, was found to characterise a number of Irish organisations.

More recently we have seen greater focus on HR delivery or the way in which the HR function is structured to provide various services to employees and other managers. Swift's (2012) review of literature in this area identifies two dominant approaches to HR delivery.

The first mode is the traditional 'single team' HR Function, comprising of some combination of HR generalists (e.g. HR manager(s) and HR officers or equivalent), HR specialists (e.g. dealing with compensation and benefits or employment relations) and HR administrative support, commonly located onsite and thus generally available to service users. CIPD data (2011) suggests that this remains the most common mode of HR delivery being particularly popular among small and medium-sized enterprises (SMEs). A UK study identified a typical HR function as comprising twelve people (namely a HR director, three HR managers, three HR officers, one HR supervisor and four HR assistants) for a workforce of approximately 1,200, largely focused on HR administration but also engaged in some more strategic activities (Crail 2006). A more recent CIPD study (2017) on HR practices in Ireland found that most HR departments in Irish organisations employed between one and five people, largely comprising HR generalists (see Tables 1.7 and 1.8).

Table 1.7 Size of the HR function in Ireland	
Size (number in HR function)	**%**
1–5	54%
6–10	13%
11–30	15%
31–50	6%
51–100	6%
100+	6%

Source: CIPD (Ireland) 2017.

Table 1.8 HR roles in Ireland	
Most common HR role (within HR function)	**%**
HR generalist	63%
HR business partner	46%
HR shared service	31%

Source: CIPD (Ireland) 2017.

The second more contemporary – yet still evolving – mode of HR delivery is based on Ulrich's (1997) widely used 'three-legged stool model' of (i) HR business partners, (ii) HR shared service centres (HRSSCs); and (iii) HR 'centres of excellence' (see also, Ulrich *et al.* 2007). The ultimate aim of this model was to shift the HR role from a predominant focus on HR administration to a focus on strategy. This model is outlined in Figure 1.5.

Figure 1.5 Ulrich's 'three-legged stool' model of HR delivery

Source: Adapted from Ulrich 1997 (also see Ulrich, Younger and Brockbank 2008).

In his book *Human Resource Champions*, Ulrich (1997) proposed this model as a way of restructuring the HR function and HR delivery, moving away from the traditional model to one centred on three key areas:

1. **Business partners (also known as generalists or strategic partners)**: these are senior HR practitioners whose primary role is to work with business leaders and line managers, to effect HR strategy formulation and especially implementation. These practitioners are generally located in the business unit and therefore are available to work with mangers in that unit. An argued benefit of HR business partnering is that it allows HR practitioners to play a more strategic role, focused on business needs and objectives.
2. **HR shared service centres (HRSSCs)**: this refers to the provision of standardised transactional and administrative HR services for a range of business units/divisions in an organisation. These are essentially 'back-office' type arrangements related to HR issues such as recruitment, training and development, payroll, attendance/absenteeism and general advice and direction on routine HR-related issues (please see Chapter 2 for further detail). These arrangements are most common in larger private sector organisations but are also attracting considerable interest in the public sector. In 2012, for example, the Irish government moved to establish a HRSSC for the civil service (Department of Public Expenditure and Reform 2012).
3. **Centres of excellence (also known as centres of expertise)**: this relates to the deployment of a small group of HR experts with specialist knowledge and skills in specific domains of HR. Their role is to help enhance competitive advantage through high level HR interventions in specific areas of strategic import such as managing talent, employee engagement, reward management or employee learning (Armstrong and Taylor 2014). Their expertise is generally provided to business partners or, on occasion, directly to line managers. These centres normally characterise larger organisations and their services may be located at a corporate, regional or national basis (Swift 2012).

As alluded to above, the original Ulrich (1997) model has been posited as a means of improving efficiencies in the delivery of standardised HR services and concurrently releasing higher level HR practitioners to engage in more strategic activity, in liaison with line and top management. However, the model has also attracted substantial criticism. While a detailed analysis of these criticisms is beyond the scope of this text, it is useful to summarise some of the most important issues raised.

First, it appears that the take-up or practical application of Ulrich's three-stool model has been limited. A 2007 UK study found that less than a fifth (18 per cent) of organisations had implemented all three legs of the Ulrich model (CIPD 2007; Armstrong and Taylor 2014). However, almost half of the organisations reported implementation of two stools (47 per cent), with business partnering (29 per cent) being the most commonly applied dimension.

A second and arguably more important criticism is that, contrary to the view of its advocates, the Ulrich model, and particularly business partnering, has not enhanced the strategic role or contribution of HR practitioners (Pitcher 2008; Pritchard 2010).

This resonates with a third criticism that the Ulrich model has led to a 'fragmentation' of the HR function and HR service delivery which has, in turn, raised related concerns regarding confusion around HR roles and boundaries, division of HR responsibilities and accountability (Gratton 2003).

In response, Ulrich has suggested that flaws in implementation of his model, and a lack of understanding by those involved, have mitigated its effectiveness (Roberts 2014). The model is no 'silver bullet' to address all of the challenges facing HR. Rather the broad advice suggests that application needs to be tailored to the specific needs of the business and to its organisational context (Orion Partners 2015). Any initiatives in adjusting HR delivery must also consider the capacity of HR practitioners to adequately carry out the differing HR roles which characterise the Ulrich model. The various roles of the HR function are considered throughout this text.

CONCLUSION

There is little doubt that approaches to HRM have changed over time and that the field is constantly evolving. We have also seen that the main underlying sources of change lie outside HRM and relate to broader changes in the business environment, specifically globalisation and a concomitant increase in competitive pressures.

In the Irish context, we find evidence of both 'continuity and change' in HRM. The continuity dimension is evident in that core HRM activity areas (recruitment, selection, training, etc.) have remained more or less constant. We can similarly note continuing demand for a specialist HR function in organisations. However, we can concurrently identify important areas of change in HRM. Thus, while the core areas of HRM have remained fairly constant, practice within specific areas (e.g. recruitment and selection) has undergone considerable change. In Ireland, as elsewhere, these changes have been driven by political, economic and social developments, such as globalisation, technology and related structural changes in the distribution of employment, particularly growth in the services sector, cycles of positive and negative economic growth, and changes in demographics and migration patterns.

Given the variety of external and internal factors impacting on HRM discussed in this chapter, and the differing ways organisations may seek to respond to these influences, it is hardly surprising to find considerable variation in HRM practice across organisations. The following chapter, which deals with the historical evolution of HRM, develops many of these themes.

2
Contextualising Human Resource Management in Ireland

This chapter provides an historical overview of the field of Human Resource Management (HRM). Its objective is to situate HRM in Ireland within a national and international setting, and thus allow an evaluation of HRM in the context of broader historical and contemporary developments in the field. It also explores the concept of *human resource management* as a distinctive approach to workforce management which emerged in the US in the 1980s. It contrasts this new approach with what was then viewed as 'traditional' personnel management and assesses the implications for HRM practice in Ireland and beyond.

THE HISTORICAL DEVELOPMENT OF HRM

EARLY DAYS: THE EMERGENCE OF THE HUMAN RESOURCES (HR) ROLE

The origins of what we now term HRM lie in the dramatic changes brought about by the industrial revolution, which had its roots in eighteenth-century Britain, later spreading to Europe and North America (see Niven 1967). A principal catalyst was the growth of the 'factory system', whereby owners of capital employed large numbers of wage labourers to produce standardised goods in larger quantities for bigger markets. Such developments had dramatic effects on the organisation of work. From the owner's perspective, the new factory employees required direction, equipment had to be maintained, production controlled and goods distributed and sold. These requirements incorporated many of the key elements of modern management: the need to plan, organise, direct and control the use of equipment, capital, materials and workers within organisations.

The early phase of industrial society, however, was characterised by extremely poor working conditions for the bulk of the new 'factory' labour. Workers themselves could do little to improve their position as they had virtually no economic or political power. It was not until the growth of organised labour through the trade union movement, and of political influence resulting from mass enfranchisement, that the concerns of workers could effectively command the attention and action of employers and, governments.

We can point to two important developments in the late nineteenth and early twentieth century which critically impacted upon the development and evolution of HRM, particularly in regard to the emergence of the specialist HR function. These were (i) the welfare tradition; and (ii) scientific management.

The Welfare Tradition

The genesis of modern HRM is generally traced back to what has become known as the 'welfare tradition', which initially developed in a few large companies in Britain during the late nineteenth and early twentieth centuries. In the early stages of industrialisation many factory owners regarded their labour force in instrumental terms. Working conditions were poor and employees enjoyed few of the benefits we now associate with employment, such as sick pay, pensions or even basic health, safety and welfare provision (Niven 1967). The welfare tradition refers to a series of voluntary initiatives undertaken in certain companies to improve the conditions of factory workers, particularly in relation to pay, working hours and health and safety.

This phase is particularly important in the development of HRM as it was characterised by the appointment of welfare officers who are seen as the forerunners of the modern HR practitioners. Welfare officers first emerged in mainly Quaker-owned firms in the food and confectionery industry in Britain in the late 1800s. Formally known as the Religious Society of Friends, Quakers are a Christian group that originated in England in the middle of the seventeenth century and, influenced by their religious beliefs, these progressive employers undertook various initiatives to improve working conditions in their factories. A common aspect of this approach involved the appointment of so-called welfare 'secretaries' or 'officers'. In Ireland, the early 1900s saw the initial appointment of welfare secretaries or officers in a handful of Irish companies, such as *Jacobs* and *Maguire & Paterson* in Dublin (Byrne 1988; Monks 1997).

The First World War added some impetus to the welfare movement in Britain because of the need to accelerate factory production. However, large-scale unemployment and depression in the post-war period meant that pro-worker initiatives in the area of welfare were abandoned in many organisations. In 1919 the Welfare Workers' Institute, founded in Britain in 1913 as the Welfare Workers' Association, had a membership of 700. By 1927, when it had been renamed the Institute of Industrial Welfare Workers, its membership had fallen to 420 (Farnham 1984).

Despite such oscillation in the significance of welfare, its influence on contemporary HRM practice is enduring. Welfare has been inextricably linked with a 'caring' approach to employees, dealing with issues such as working conditions, health and safety, and wellbeing. This is very much in evidence in modern HRM practice in areas such as counselling, employee assistance programmes, and occupational health and safety provision.

The welfare tradition has, however, also been a source of some confusion about the position of the HR practitioner in the managerial hierarchy. Early welfare workers, mostly female, largely occupied a semi-independent organisational position, with employees the main beneficiaries of their work (Monks 1997). This led to a perception of welfare workers as a kind of 'intermediary' between employers and employees. However, it is patently apparent that modern HR practitioners generally seek to operate as an integral part of the management team, primarily representing employer interests.

Scientific Management

Another important early influence on the emergence of HRM was the advent of Scientific Management (Taylor 1911, 1947) and what became known as 'Taylorism'. As the welfare tradition succumbed to economic depression, Taylorism, and its associated notions of labour efficiency, became an increasingly popular managerial approach. By the early years of the twentieth century, improvements in technology coupled with increases in company size and complexity led many employers to investigate new ways of improving industrial performance. In the US, F.W. Taylor led the way by pointing to the efficiency and profitability benefits to be gained through greater standardisation of work systems and methods.

Based on his research at the *Bethlehem Steel Company* (1900–11), Taylor encouraged employers to adopt more systematic approaches to job design, employment and payment systems (Taylor 1947; Tiernan and Morley 2013). Such scientific management approaches became widely adopted in both the US and Britain in the inter-war years. Particular emphasis was placed on job analysis, time and motion studies, and the creation of incentive bonus schemes, thereby extending the work of the emerging HR function.

Scientific Management led to a shift in the emphasis of HR away from the employee-oriented, 'caring/do-gooding' agenda of the welfare tradition towards the more managerial 'efficiency/profitability' agenda of the work study officer. From the HR perspective, the spread of scientific management placed greater weight on the careful selection and systematic training of employees. Associated with this trend was an increased attention to job design, working conditions and payment systems. HR often also assumed responsibility for much of the research and administration required to underpin such initiatives.

Despite extensive criticism, the principles of Scientific Management had, and continue to have, a profound impact on management practice. Probably its most significant legacy is the notion that work *planning* (seen as a management task) should be separated from work *doing* (seen as a worker task). This separation delineated the primary role of management as that of establishing work standards, procedures and methods. These approaches to work organisation were dominated by a desire to maximise the productive efficiency of the company's technical resources. Management's role was to ensure that all organisational resources, including employees, were organised in such a way as to facilitate the optimal utilisation of the technical system.

This efficiency-oriented approach, based on 'Taylorist' principles, has been a characteristic of employers' approaches to job design since the early years of the last century. It advocated the breaking down of jobs into simple, repetitive, measurable tasks requiring skills that could be easily acquired through systematic job training. Taylorism helped improve efficiency and promoted a systematic approach to selection, training, work measurement and payment. However, it is also seen as the source of many of the problems associated with industrial work, such as high levels of labour turnover, absenteeism and low levels of employee motivation (see, for example, Mowday *et al.* 1982; Steers and Mowday 1987). Indeed, the growth of the behavioural science movement (discussed in the next section) can be traced to the 'downsides' of Scientific Management and to suggestions that improvements in organisational effectiveness might also be achieved through greater attention to workers' needs and, particularly, by providing workers with more challenging jobs and an improved work environment.

THE BEHAVIOURAL SCIENCE MOVEMENT

The emergence of the behavioural sciences provided a major impetus to HRM by establishing a body of knowledge to underpin many aspects of HR work such as selection, training, motivation, employment relations and reward systems. It also served to focus attention on many of the problems associated with the organisation of work in the large factories of the new industrial era, such as worker monotony and low morale.

The emergence of the behavioural science movement is most commonly associated with the work of Elton Mayo (1933, 1945) and Roethlisberger and Dickson (1939). Harvard Professor Mayo came from a Taylorist tradition and his research initially focused on the impact of working conditions on productivity, including alterations in lighting levels. Mayo's studies, conducted at *Western Electric*'s Hawthorne Works in Chicago, using a control group (for whom lighting conditions didn't change) and an experimental group (who were subjected to changes in lighting levels), found that changing working conditions had little impact on productivity or worker satisfaction. In fact, productivity increased among both groups – where lighting levels altered and where levels were unchanged. Mayo and his research team concluded that the employees worked harder, not because of working conditions or self-interest, but rather because they were part of a group selected to participate in an important 'experiment' and thus felt more committed individually, and as a group, to their work roles (often termed the 'Hawthorne effect').

Mayo's work suggested that employee behaviour and performance was influenced by a complex combination of motivation, individual needs and group dynamics, in addition to working conditions and rewards. This research thus highlighted the influence of social factors, group dynamics, and employee motivation on both individual performance and organisational effectiveness. Although this work has been the subject of methodological criticisms (cf. Carey 1967), it has had an enduring influence on management practice, particularly in the sphere of HRM. Its major contribution was possibly the stimulation of interest in applying behavioural science principles to the study of organisational and worker behaviour. Subsequent research on the application of the behavioural sciences to the study of organisations has helped inform our understanding of organisational functioning and, particularly, of workers' motivation. Indeed, much of the subsequent research in this field has focused on investigating employees' motivation and attempting to reconcile employers' and workers' needs through appropriate organisation structures, work systems, and managerial styles. We consider this literature in Chapter 6, which deals with employee motivation and the design of work.

INDUSTRIAL/EMPLOYMENT RELATIONS AS A KEY HR ACTIVITY

A concurrent and especially significant development affecting the nature of HRM, and the role of the emerging HR function, was the growing significance of industrial relations, now often termed 'employment relations' (see Chapter 10). The importance of an industrial relations emphasis in HR work can be traced back to the growth of the factory system and the attempts by workers to organise into trade unions and seek improvements in pay and working conditions.

In Ireland, the trade union movement had become well established in industries in the major cities of Dublin, Belfast and Cork by the early 1900s (McNamara *et al.* 1988). The emergence of a 'new unionism', primarily focused on organising unskilled workers, was a particularly important development during this period. The growth in its influence was most visibly manifested in the activity of Jim Larkin and the *Irish Transport and General Workers' Union* (ITGWU). A period of conflict between employer and worker interests came to a head in the 1913 Dublin Lockout, involving some 20,000 workers and numerous Dublin employers (Yeates 2000). The dispute, which lasted five months, centred around the workers' right to organise into trade unions and thereby advance their claims for higher pay and better working conditions. Although the unions were ultimately unsuccessful in achieving these aims, the Dublin Lockout represented a seminal moment in Irish labour history and in the development of industrial relations in Ireland. The ideas of trade union recognition and collective action were firmly established and would characterise management–worker relations over subsequent decades.

Trenchant employer opposition to Irish trade unions gradually gave way to a reluctant acceptance of their role and legitimacy. Roche and Larragy (1989) estimate that union membership rose from 110,000 in 1914 to 250,000 in 1920, leading Roche (1997: 54) to label this period the 'first phase of rapid mass union membership growth in Ireland'. An important outcome of this turbulent period was that it served to accelerate the organisation of employees into trade unions and employers into employers' associations and thus placed an increased emphasis on industrial relations as an important aspect of workforce management (Wallace *et al.* 2013).

The period from the early 1920s saw a reversal in the fortunes of Irish unions. Membership fell in the face of economic recession. This reflected developments in Britain where economic depression after the First World War saw a re-emergence of autocratic management styles. A combination of factors, particularly low pay and poor working conditions, contributed to high levels of industrial conflict, culminating in the General Strike of 1926 in Britain. During this period workers and their trade unions became increasingly suspicious of management motives in introducing welfare initiatives in the workplace. Trade unions became quite anti-welfare, viewing it as an employer strategy to prevent workers from joining trade unions.

A related factor contributing to the growth in emphasis on industrial relations was the nature of collective bargaining between employers and trade unions (Wallace *et al* 2004). During the Second World War Irish wages were controlled under the Emergency Powers Orders. The rescinding of these orders in 1946, combined with the establishment of the Labour Court that same year, marked a new era. This was initially manifest in the negotiation of a general pay increase for unionised employees constituting what became known as the first *wage round* (see Nevin 1963; O'Brien 1989). A wage round was essentially a period of intensive collective bargaining between employers and trade unions, occurring at regular intervals and resulting in a similar general wage increase for unionised employees.

The nature of collective bargaining in the immediate post-war period had important implications for the development of HRM in Ireland. Growth in the size and complexity of organisations demanded greater specialisation and knowledge in workforce management, particularly in industrial/employment relations. In the public sector and among some larger private companies these needs were achieved through the establishment of specialist 'personnel' departments, whose key activity was industrial relations (Barrington 1980; O'Mahony 1958). By the 1960s, levels of unionisation among manual workers had increased significantly and shop stewards were emerging as important players in regard to workplace-level industrial relations (Roche and Larragy 1989; Marsh 1973). This was accentuated by a growth in white-collar unionisation in Ireland from the 1960s (Kelly 1975). Indeed the 1960s was characterised by a marked increase in the levels of industrial conflict, placing an increasing focus on industrial/employment relations.

A further development contributing to the growing significance of industrial relations as a critical concern in HRM was the onset of the *national wage agreement* 'era' in 1970. The negotiation of the first national wage agreement in 1970 marked a transformation from the rather unclear system of wage rounds, which had existed since the end of the Second World War. An important effect of national wage agreements was to move major pay bargaining issues away from the level of the workplace/enterprise. This development was initially seen as freeing management from complex negotiations with trade unions and giving them more certainty in strategic planning. However, the reality was somewhat different. At a time of relative economic prosperity and substantial growth in union membership, the key workplace role for trade unions, namely pay bargaining, was removed. With the expectation that pay increases would be derived by means of national agreements, trade unions increasingly focused their attention on matters that could be negotiated at local (workplace) level such as working conditions, pay anomalies and productivity issues. Indeed, far from eliminating local bargaining, national agreements merely changed their focus, and the period saw the negotiation of various types of productivity agreements at workplace level. These became an important means by which trade unions could gain pay increases above the stated maxima laid down in national wage agreements. The emphasis on industrial relations therefore continued to expand during the national wage agreement era.

For the HR function, industrial or employment relations remained a priority with HR ('personnel') practitioners heavily involved in workplace bargaining with trade unions throughout this period. Industrial harmony was the objective, and personnel/HR specialists, through their espoused negotiating, inter-personal and procedural skills, had responsibility for its achievement. Increased industrial unrest from the mid-1960s to the end of the 1970s served to confirm industrial relations as a key concern of employers. It gave the emerging HR function a central management role. HR departments, whose major responsibility was industrial relations, were established in many medium-sized and larger organisations. The Donovan Report on industrial relations in Britain (1968) was also influential in encouraging collective bargaining, the adoption of comprehensive industrial relations procedures and greater managerial specialisation in industrial/employment relations.

Increased government intervention from the 1970s has also had a significant influence on the HR function. As discussed above, this was particularly evident in the area of centralised pay bargaining. The 1970s also witnessed the introduction of an unprecedented wave of *employment legislation*, which had an important impact on the roles of HR practitioners. This legislation primarily focused on extending the individual employment rights of workers, in areas such as dismissals and equality. Key legislation approved in this period included the *Unfair Dismissals Act 1977*, the *Anti-Discrimination (Pay) Act 1974*, the *Employment Equality Act 1977*, and a number of redundancy Acts. Clearly, organisations had to come to grips with this legislation and much of the responsibility for doing this was assumed by the HR function. HR practitioners were expected to provide expert advice and guidance on the new legislation and to oversee its implementation in the workplace.

THE MULTINATIONAL INFLUENCE

The attraction of foreign direct investment (FDI) by multinational companies (MNCs) has been a cornerstone of Irish government policy for six decades. This policy has been demonstrably successful, with Ireland considered the European Union's most FDI intensive economy (Barry and O'Mahony 2005). *IDA Ireland*, the semi-state agency vested with primary responsibility for the attraction and retention of FDI, has played a key role in stimulating economic development. There are now approximately 1,200 *IDA Ireland* assisted foreign MNCs in Ireland and in 2016 employment in these companies reached a record high of 187,000 (IDA Ireland 2016). It is worth noting that these figures relate to *IDA Ireland* assisted MNCs only and thus is likely to understate the scale of FDI activity, as many MNCs operating in Ireland do not benefit from IDA assistance, e.g. MNCs in the retail, hospitality, construction and consultancy sectors (cf. Lavelle *et al.* 2009).

The significance of the FDI sector to the Irish economy is reflected in the fact that foreign-owned MNCs account for 50 per cent of manufacturing employment (CSO 2014). This substantially contrasts with an average of 19 per cent across EU member states (Barry and O'Mahony 2005).

The 1990s witnessed a three-fold increase in FDI inflows into Ireland, with a five-fold increase from the US (Organisation of Economic Co-operation and Development (OECD) 2000). It is reported that MNCs contributed approximately 55 per cent of manufactured output and a staggering 75 per cent of industrial exports throughout the 1990s (O'Higgins 2002; Tansey 1998). However, Ireland's economic circumstances changed dramatically with the onset of the global financial crisis, resulting in a seismic shift from an economy with high economic growth (up to 2007) to negative growth from 2008 to 2010 and slow recovery thereafter. The global recession led many MNCs in Ireland to engage in cost saving and restructuring. In certain circumstances this led to divestment, most notably in the case of *Dell Computers* who moved their manufacturing activities from Ireland (Limerick) to Poland, with a loss of approximately 2,000 jobs. However, concurrently, some MNCs increased employment over the recessionary period and many new MNCs have been attracted, particularly internet-based firms such as *Google*, *ebay*, *Dropbox* and *Facebook*.

The key areas of MNC activity from 2010–2014 are outlined in Table 2.1, while the profile of multinationals in Ireland by ownership is summarised in Table 2.2. The United States is clearly Ireland's largest source of FDI, with US MNCs accounting for almost half of all foreign-owned firms in the country and employing more than 125,000 people.

The main factors explaining Ireland's success in attracting mobile inward FDI over the years include our comparatively low level of tax on company profits, grants and related incentives, labour quality and supply, and particular aspects of the Irish business environment (Jacobsen and Andreosso 1990; Lavelle *et al.* 2009). Both Barry (2004) and Gunnigle and McGuire (2001) point to the critical significance of Ireland's low corporate tax regime in attracting US FDI. Labour supply and quality have also been identified as a positive influence in attracting FDI, particularly the comparatively young age profile of the Irish labour force and the relatively high level of educational attainment. High levels of labour flexibility and a comparatively less regulated industrial relations system and HR environment also emerge as factors favourably impacting on FDI, as does the use of English as a first language, and Ireland's membership of the EU (Barry 2004; IMI 2013).

Table 2.1 Foreign direct investment by sector: employment in IDA assisted companies 2010–2014

Sector	2010	2012	2014
Pharmaceuticals	22,344	22,413	23,371
Computer, electronic and optical equipment	15,698	16,296	18,022
Medical/Dental instruments and supplies	22,363	24,474	25,455
Metals and engineering	11,207	11,505	11,619
Miscellaneous industry	6,670	6,420	6,363
International and financial services (including software)	68,346	78,083	89,658
Total	**146,628**	**159,191**	**174,488**

Source: IDA Ireland Annual Reports.

Table 2.2 Foreign direct investment by ownership: number of firms and total employment 2010–2014

	2010	2012	2014
USA	491 (99,772)	531 (111,661)	632 (125,579)
Germany	99 (9,694)	95 (9,950)	99 (11,399)
UK	94 (6,807)	103 (6,804)	104 (6,737)
France	43 (3,770)	43 (4,339)	54 (5,525)
Rest of Europe	167 (12,350)	160 (12,691)	169 (14,661)
Rest of World	91 (6,575)	101 (7,340)	137 (10,587)

Source: IDA Ireland Annual Reports.

Given the significance of MNCs in Ireland it is hardly surprising that they have significantly impacted on HRM and indeed on management practice more generally. MNCs have been to the fore in developing comprehensive policies and practices across various aspects of HRM, and in giving a greater impetus to the role of the specialist HR function (HR department). A particularly important legacy of MNC investment has been the diffusion of new HR practices and techniques in areas such as selection testing, training methods, reward systems and communications. We have evidence, for example, that MNCs have also been associated with innovation in areas of high-performance work systems (Mooney 1988), performance-related pay (Gunnigle et al. 1998) and in enhancing the status of the specialist HR function (Gunnigle 1998a). In the industrial/employment relations sphere, US-owned MNCs have been to the fore in avoiding trade union recognition in their Irish facilities. This practice appears to have taken root in the early 1980s and has become increasingly commonplace since then (cf. Gunnigle 1995).

The influence of inward FDI has also had an important spill-over effect in enhancing the managerial capability and technological knowhow of Irish managers as a result of their experience of working in foreign-owned MNCs (McDonnell *et al.* 2014). Geary and Roche (2001: 124) observed that domestic (Irish) firms were 'increasingly introducing new HR practices most often associated with MNCs', while Begley *et al.* (2005) identified the role of US MNCs in expediting the training and development of a strong cadre of Irish managerial talent. Indigenous firms may often 'buy in' talent with experience of working in foreign MNCs, thus enabling knowledge transfer and providing a platform for cross-fertilisation of practices that may not be typical of these domestic organisations (McDonnell *et al.* 2014).

Overall it would appear that MNCs have helped to develop managerial capacity and have specifically contributed to establishing HRM as a more central aspect of management practice in Irish organisations. The impact of MNCs on HRM in Ireland is considered throughout this text.

EDUCATION AND THE HUMAN RESOURCE PROFESSION

Another important factor which contributed to the growth and expansion of the HR role was a progressively greater emphasis on the professional education of HR practitioners, especially since the 1970s. Clearly, greater specialisation in the HR sphere required commensurate growth in the education and training of HR specialists. Alongside Ireland's economic progress, many of the newer multinational and larger indigenous organisations emphasised the appointment of qualified and experienced HR practitioners. While the origins of formal courses on aspects of HRM can be traced back to the 1940s, the most significant developments took place from the 1960s onwards. The establishment of *AnCO** (An Chomhairle Oiliuna) as the national training agency in 1967 added impetus to the development of the HR role through increased emphasis on training and development.

In the 1970s, the first courses leading to membership of the then *Institute of Personnel Management*, now the *Chartered Institute of Personnel and Development* (CIPD), the professional body for personnel and HR practitioners, were offered at centres in Dublin and Limerick. Since then, a variety of full and part-time undergraduate and postgraduate programmes have been established at most universities and a large number of other institutes of higher education. In 2016, courses leading to various categories of membership of the CIPD were available at seventeen centres throughout the Republic of Ireland. We also find that courses in HRM, industrial and organisational psychology and/or employment relations form part of most undergraduate programmes in business and related disciplines. There are also a number of specialist HRM Masters' programmes on offer, while HRM is generally a core module in Master of Business Administration (MBA) programmes in Ireland. Thus we have seen a progressive increase in the formal education of HR practitioners, which has served to enhance the status and competencies available across the broad field of HRM.

* In 1988 AnCo was replaced by FÁS (An Foras Áiseanna Saothair), as the national training and employment authority under the terms of the *Labour Services Act 1987*. The roles of two other state agencies, the National Manpower Service and the Youth Employment Agency, were also subsumed into FÁS.

This growth in HR education occurred in parallel with growth in membership of the CIPD in the UK and Ireland. Its headquarters are located in the UK, with an Irish branch office located in Dublin. Its forerunner was the *Welfare Workers Association* founded in the UK in 1913, and it then operated for many years as the *Institute of Personnel Management* (IPM). It became the *Institute of Personnel and Development* (IPD) in 1994. The 'IPD' nomenclature was itself a derivate, resulting from the merger of the IPM with the *Institute of Training and Development* in the UK. The IPD was subsequently granted a Royal Charter in 2000, in acknowledgement of its role as the primary management association in the field of HR. This resulted in yet another title change to the *Chartered Institute of Personnel and Development* (CIPD) reflecting its ascension to Chartered status. Membership of the CIPD in the UK and Ireland was reported as 135,000 in 2014. CIPD membership in the Republic of Ireland, now spread across seven regional branches, increased from a base of just fourteen members in 1937, to passing the 1,000 mark in 1987 and peaking in 2008 at 6,642 members. Membership then declined during the recession, falling to 5,265 members in 2013. In 2016 the CIPD in Ireland had 5,243 members.

RETRENCHMENT AND RE-DEFINITION OF HRM IN THE 1980s

In evaluating the historical development of HRM in Ireland, it is clear that increased industrialisation, foreign direct investment and general economic activity since the 1960s have contributed to the establishment of HR as a discrete management function. By the late 1970s, the HRM role was firmly established in most of the larger Irish organisations. HR, or 'personnel' departments, as they were generally termed, operated as a distinct management function with responsibility for a reasonably well-defined range of HR activities, with particular focus on employment relations.

However, the 1980s heralded a period of major change for HRM. A depressed economic climate, together with increased competitive pressures, led to a slump in business activity for much of the decade. These developments helped change both the focus of HRM and the nature of HR activities. Competitive pressures combined to set new priorities, forcing the HR function to act under tighter cost controls and to undertake a wider range of activities (Tyson 1987; Monks 1992). The recessionary climate reduced the need for many hitherto 'core' activities such as recruitment and, particularly, industrial/employment relations. The harsher economic conditions of the 1980s dramatically changed the employment relations environment. An economic context characterised by redundancies and high unemployment significantly altered the bargaining environment, with adverse consequences for trade unions. Increasingly employers sought to address issues such as payment structures and levels of wage increases, the extent of demarcation and restrictive work practices, and generally to reclaim managerial prerogative, which they felt had heretofore been eroded by trade unions.

Restrictive trade union legislation in Britain and hard-line management approaches in many firms indicated a more belligerent approach to dealings with trade unions. This was reflected in adverse outcomes for trade unions in strikes by miners in the UK and by air traffic controllers in the US in the early 1980s. Trade unions were in retreat and membership began to fall in many developed economies. In Ireland trade union membership fell significantly throughout the 1980s and industrial unrest also declined from the highs of the 1970s (see Chapter 10 for further detail).

At the same time, increased market competition forced many organisations to seek new means of establishing competitive advantage. One apparent source of such improvements lay in the better utilisation of human resources. Some organisations began to investigate different approaches to workforce management, particularly in areas such as work organisation and job design, reward systems, employee relations and training and development.

However, the most widely debated development over the period was the emergence of what became known as *human resource management*. In this text we use the term 'human resource management' (HRM) in a generic fashion to encompass all aspects of workforce management in organisations. HRM has indeed become the umbrella term for what was formerly known as 'personnel management'. From an academic perspective, HRM has also become the umbrella discipline encompassing research and education in the fields of employment relations, personnel management, organisational behaviour and human resource development. However, this was not always the case.

The term 'human resource management' only came into popular usage in the early 1980s. In its initial conception, HRM essentially referred to the development of a more integrated and strategic approach to workforce management. It had its roots in the US, which has traditionally been receptive to the application of organisational psychology and behavioural science principles in an attempt to improve organisation performance (Beaumont 1993; cf. Harney *et al*. 2014 for insights on the Irish context).

We now consider this phenomenon.

THE DISTINCTIVE CONCEPT OF HRM AS IT EMERGED IN THE US IN THE 1980S

While we use the label *human resource management* as a generic term to encompass that aspect of organisational management that is concerned with the management of an organisation's workforce, it originally entered the management vocabulary as a term to describe a distinctive and seemingly novel approach to workforce management. The conception of *human resource management* as a distinctive approach to workforce management and the associated emphasis on a greater role for HRM stems from two contrasting sources in the US literature.

The *first source* emanates from the 'human resource' literature and is based on the 'human capital approach' developed at the Harvard Business School (HBS) (Beer *et al*. 1984, 1985). This focused on the individual employee as the key organisational resource that management must nurture and develop to maximise the employee's potential and organisational contribution. It encouraged employers to systematically deploy a range of pro-employee HR policies to ensure the attraction, retention and development of committed, high-performing employees. This model is the basis for what is often termed 'soft' HRM (Legge 1995), given its focus on the *human* side of HRM. In this approach management acknowledges that people are one of the organisation's most valuable resources and it deploys coherent policies and practices to make the most of this resource. The HBS model is outlined in Figure 2.1.

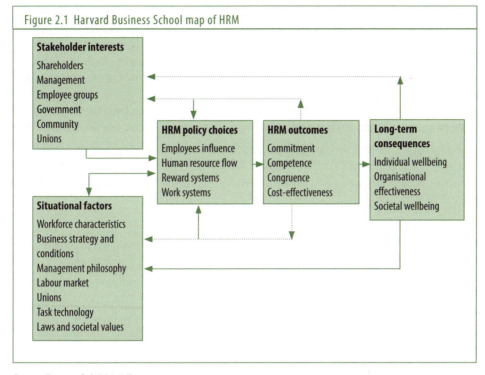

Figure 2.1 Harvard Business School map of HRM

Source: Beer et al. (1984: 16).

The Harvard Business School map presents a broad causal model of the determinants and consequences of HRM policy choices. HRM is viewed as 'involving all management decisions and actions that affect the nature of the relationship between the organisation and its employees – its human resources' (Beer et al. 1984: 1). Thus, those in top management, and particularly CEOs, are seen as having primary responsibility for aligning business strategy and HRM. Four key components comprise the HBS model, namely stakeholder interests, HRM policy choices, HR outcomes and long-term consequences. The central message is that HR outcomes (and ultimately organisational performance) are affected by HRM policy choices relating to (i) employee influence; (ii) HR flow; (iii) reward systems; and (iv) work systems. Each of these policy areas is seen as a key element of strategic choice, which profoundly impacts upon employee behaviour and attitude towards the organisation. Strategic choices in these areas are influenced by broader contextual factors (situational constraints and stakeholder interests). Decisions made in these policy areas are seen as affecting HR outcomes in the areas of employee commitment and competence, congruence of employee and management interests, and on cost-effectiveness. These outcomes are also seen as having broader long-term consequences for individual employee wellbeing, organisational effectiveness and societal wellbeing.

The *second source* of literature advocating increased strategic consideration of HRM comes from broader business strategy literature, particularly the work of Charles Fombrun and his colleagues, often known as the 'Michigan School' (cf. Fombrun et al. 1984). This approach was premised on the idea that organisational performance can be substantially improved by integrating HRM considerations into strategic decision-making to ensure that HR policy and practice complements business strategy. Here the focus was overtly managerial, focusing on the *resource* side of HRM, in aggressively managing labour cost and headcount and more broadly deploying HR policies that yield the best returns in terms of organisational performance. This work became the basis for what was termed 'hard' HRM (Storey 1989).

CONTRASTING HRM AND PERSONNEL MANAGEMENT

The emergence of *human resource management* as a distinctive approach to workforce management drew comparison with 'traditional' *personnel management*. HRM's apparently proactive stance was viewed as a major departure from the traditionally reactive focus associated with established approaches to personnel management.

> The new approaches ... which adopted a managerialist rather than a pluralist stance, the restructuring possibilities, and the reduction in trade union power and influence were the backdrop to what is now perceived as a new paradigm on which to base employment relationships. In the eyes of some commentators, human resource management (HRM) came to represent the new paradigm, and the critical distinction drawn was the notion that HRM placed initiatives on people management at the strategic heart of the business . . . The new flexibility agreements, new working practices, reorganisations, de-layering activities, the flatter organisations, direct communications with the workforce, and stronger corporate cultures . . . could be understood as a new, more coherent approach . . . If this was propaganda, it was propaganda that managers themselves started to believe as the 1980s came to a close.
>
> Tyson, Witcher and Doherty (1994: 7)

Guest (1987) provided a comprehensive comparison between HRM and traditional personnel management (see Table 2.3), identifying seven areas of difference between HRM and personnel management:

1. With HRM, workforce management considerations were fully integrated into strategic decision-making, whereas in the traditional personnel model the 'personnel' input was less and issue-specific.
2. HRM adopted a proactive and long-term orientation, while personnel management was more reactive and short-term in perspective.
3. On the nature of the psychological contract – defined by the CIPD (2016) as the perceptions of the employee and employer as to their mutual obligations towards each other – HRM was seen as focused on eliciting employee commitment, while personnel management was more focused on promoting managerial control over employees.
4. With regard to employment relations, HRM was viewed as essentially unitarist in perspective, seeing no conflict of interests between employers and employees. In contrast, personnel management was seen as grounded in pluralist traditions, acknowledging that an inherent conflict of interest existed between employers and workers. Thus HRM was viewed as primarily focused on relations between (line)

management and the individual worker, while personnel management operated more through collectivist relations between management and employee representatives (normally trade unions).
5. HRM was felt to be more suited to organic, fluid organisational structures, while personnel management was seen as characteristic of more bureaucratic structures.
6. Operational responsibility for HRM was entrusted to line management, whereas with personnel management, primary responsibility vested in the specialist personnel function.
7. The main focus of HRM was on maximising HR's contribution to overall organisational effectiveness, while for personnel management the focus was on the more limited goal of improving cost-effectiveness.

Table 2.3 Traditional personnel management and HRM compared

	Personnel Management	Human Resource Management
Input into strategic management	Issue-specific	Integrated
Time and planning perspective	Short-term; reactive; marginal	Long-term; proactive; strategic
Psychological contract	Compliance	Commitment
Industrial relations	Pluralist; collective; low trust; adversarial	Unitarist; individual; high trust
Organisation structure	Bureaucratic; mechanistic; centralised; formally defined roles	Organic; fluid; devolved; flexible roles
Principal delivery systems	Specialist personnel function	General/Line management
Overall aim	Maximise cost-effectiveness	Maximise HR utilisation

Source: Guest, 1987 (Adapted).

Despite these proposed contrasts between HRM and traditional personnel management, Guest (1987) cautioned that this did not imply that HRM was better than traditional personnel management. Rather, he advocated a contingency approach whereby either a HRM or traditional personnel management approach may be best suited to particular organisational contexts. Notwithstanding this reservation, the development of workforce management since the 1980s has seemingly leant more towards a HRM orientation, with particular emphasis on increasing the HR input into strategic decision-making and on matching business strategy and HRM policy (see Chapter 3).

CONTEMPORARY DEVELOPMENTS

REGRESSION AND RECOVERY – IRELAND FROM THE 1980S TO THE GLOBAL FINANCIAL CRISIS

When we consider the exceptionally high levels of Irish economic growth and employment creation from the early 1990s, it is sometimes difficult to appreciate the pessimism that characterised the Irish economy for much of the 1980s. Economic growth during the first half of the decade was extremely low, inflation rose steadily and the country's fiscal debt became unsustainable. Substantial employment decline was recorded during this period, as unemployment rose to almost 20 per cent, resulting in the resumption of large-scale emigration (Tansey 1998). As public debt and unemployment reached record proportions, the economy became locked in deep recession.

As the 1980s progressed, there was broad political and societal agreement in Ireland that fundamental initiatives were needed to tackle the problems facing the country, but there was limited support for the Thatcherite policies deployed in the UK at the time (Wallace *et al.* 2013). Rather, the government embraced fiscal rectitude, with severe cutbacks in public expenditure, and social partnership, the twin strategies designed to turn the economy around. These initiatives, together with a serendipitous confluence of favourable developments in both the domestic and international economy, contributed to a remarkable transformation in Ireland's economic fortunes. Indeed, the Irish economy recovered to such an extent that by the late 1990s it was widely heralded as a model of effective economic management. Expansive growth characterised this period. From the mid-1990s to the turn of the millennium, GDP growth rates averaged over 9 per cent a year, almost four times the EU average. Ireland had become the OECD's fastest growing economy with levels of economic performance at or above the levels of the world's high-growth economies. Employment grew apace. In 1986 unemployment levels were 18 per cent, almost one in five. By 2004 the equivalent figure was over 4 per cent, or less than one in twenty.

Industrial/employment relations played a key role in this transformation. In 1987 the first of a series of centrally negotiated accords (the *Programme for National Recovery 1987–91*) was agreed by the 'social partners', principally government, employers and trade unions. A further seven social partnership agreements were concluded up to 2008. While opinion varies on the relative contribution of centralised bargaining to Ireland's economic transformation, there is general consensus that the social partnership agreements played an important role. In particular, they are seen as having achieved low wage inflation (Tansey 1998; Walsh 1999), reductions in personal taxation and low levels of industrial conflict (Roche 1997a, 1997b).

From a broader HRM perspective, the arrival of the 'Celtic tiger' brought very different challenges. Probably the most pressing of these concerns was the attraction and retention of workers. Rapidly falling unemployment levels, combined with increased demand for labour, made for a very tight labour market. Employers came under greater pressure to compete for labour and develop innovative ways of retaining employees. Related issues included pressures from workers and trade unions for better reward packages. The period also witnessed increased activity in training and development and in reward systems, as organisations sought both to enhance the capacity of their workforce and to improve performance and competitiveness.

Changes in the structural distribution of employment have important implications for HRM (see Chapter 4 for greater detail). The transformation from a comparatively poor and under-developed economy to one characterised by industrial expansion and strong economic growth involved major changes in the structural distribution of employment. This primarily involved a progressive decline in agricultural and traditional industrial employment, and a dramatic rise in employment in the service sector, particularly in private services. In 1926 agriculture accounted for 54 per cent of total employment while the equivalent figure is now just over 5 per cent. Thus, Ireland has followed a predictable pattern of economic development whereby employment in the primary sector (agriculture, fishing, etc.) is generally superseded by industry (including manufacturing, construction, etc.), which in turn is superseded by employment in services. By far the most striking development in the sectoral distribution of employment in Ireland has been the progressive growth in employment in the service sector, which, for example, increased by a staggering 70 per cent between 1993 and 2004.

The HR implications of these changes are addressed throughout this text. Of particular note is the associated increase in the variety of employment forms, higher levels of female participation and greater ethnic and cultural diversity in the workforce. There is little doubt that growth in employment in the service sector has led to an increased diversity in employment forms, specifically in atypical or non-standard employment (i.e. any form of employment that deviates from a full-time, permanent format). This includes self-employment, temporary and part-time work, and emerging modes such as zero-hours and 'if and when' contracts (O'Sullivan *et al.* 2015). Growth in atypical employment is generally linked to employer demands for greater flexibility and to cost pressures in specific sectors, notably in hospitality but also more recently in health care (specifically in areas such as home care, where this work is increasingly contracted out via standard tendering processes). From an industrial relations perspective, many of these areas of the service sector have also proved difficult contexts for trade unions to organise collectively.

Other HR implications of these developments in the Irish labour market are addressed later in this text, notably changing migration patterns (see Chapter 4), learning, training and development (see Chapter 9) and related repercussions for employment relations (see Chapters 10, 11 and 12).

HRM IN THE 'GREAT RECESSION'

By the turn of the millennium a number of developments, particularly the so-called *dot.com* downturn and the aftermath of 9/11 (2001), impacted on the Irish economy. Given Ireland's reliance on FDI, especially by American MNCs, it was predictable that these events would have important knock-on effects here. The period immediately after 2001 saw a fall in FDI into Ireland and increasing economic difficulties for some MNCs operating in Ireland. However, the impact was primarily concentrated on the information and communications technology (ICT) sector, where the level of job losses and company closures increased in 2001 and 2002. These included the closure of both *Motorola* and *Gateway*'s Dublin plants, involving a loss of almost 1,700 jobs. Indigenous ICT firms suffered particularly badly and some of the prominent casualties included *Ebeon* and *Baltimore Technologies*. IDA Ireland (2003) estimated that employment in the ICT sector fell by over 5 per cent in 2002, which represented quite a creditable performance in the circumstances.

More significantly, much of Ireland's economic growth post-2001 was based on high levels of consumer spending and a huge construction and real estate boom, fuelled by reckless lending by the banking sector. This partially, and temporarily, masked a progressive fall in competitiveness. The 2000 *IMD World Competitiveness Report* ranked Ireland as the fifth most competitive world economy, achieving particularly strong scores in areas such as education, government and technological capacity. Successive reports charted the progressive decline in Ireland's competitive standing to an all-time low of twenty-fourth in 2011. Ireland's ranking has since recovered, being listed as the sixteenth most competitive world economy in 2015, and climbing up to seventh in 2016.

In September 2008, Ireland became the first eurozone country to enter recession (CSO, 2008). Output as measured by gross domestic product (GDP) which had grown by 6 per cent in 2007 (to peak at €189 billion) fell by 5 per cent in 2008, 9 per cent in 2009 and 3 percent in 2010, before increasing by almost 2 per cent in 2011 (CSO 2012). At the same time unemployment increased substantially, from 4.6 per cent in 2007 to almost 6 per cent in 2008. It then doubled in 2009 to 12 per cent, peaking at 15 per cent in 2012, before falling back to just under 14 per cent in 2013 (CSO 2014). By early 2017, unemployment had fallen to 6.5 per cent.

The recession in Ireland has been described as the costliest since the Great Depression of the 1930s, in terms of its detrimental financial impact and the economic and social devastation reeked, while the Irish banking crisis was ranked among the world's 'Top 10' worst banking catastrophes (Laeven and Valencia 2012).

It is clearly impossible to address all of the implications for HRM in this section, and indeed some repercussions are currently unfolding as Ireland and the rest of the world grapples with the challenge of recovering from the huge downturn in economic activity wrought by the recent recession. Consequently, in this section, we summarily document some of the more apparent HRM implications.

The first and most obvious is that, as during the 1980s, much HRM activity in organisations during the recession focused on cost reduction, including organisational restructuring and, in many cases, downsizing. This embraced a range of related activities such as managing redundancies/layoffs and/or outsourcing programmes, but also implementing measures to protect employment (somewhat) such as redeployment, overtime bans, wage cuts or freezes, benefits reduction, sabbatical/unpaid leave, recruitment bans and enforced shut-downs (Dobbins 2008). In unionised firms this often involved in-depth negotiations and so called 'concession bargaining' (Roche and Teague 2015). Where redundancy programmes were deployed, the HR function generally assumed responsibility for managing the process. An indicative snapshot of the types of HRM activity prevalent in organisations during the great recession is outlined in Table 2.4.

Table 2.4 HRM in the great recession	
Aer Lingus	'Leave and return' plan whereby employees take a lump sum severance payment and leave the company before returning on reduced pay and conditions; lower entry pay rates for new employees, voluntary redundancies and changes in working conditions. Trade union led.
AXA	Voluntary redundancies, early retirement, new pay scales and a revamped profit share scheme. Agreed with trade unions.
Bausch and Lomb	Voluntary redundancies and short time working for remainder of staff. Agreed with trade unions.
Coca-Cola	Outsourcing of distribution and warehousing, involving redundancies for relevant staff. Trade unions opposed.
Independent News and Media	Series of new working time arrangements and pay cuts. Trade unions opposed.
Dell Computers	Loss of approximately 3,000 jobs through off-shoring and internal restructuring. Non-union company (but led to creation of employee representative association).
Dublin Airport Authority	Redundancies, a pay freeze and 'Employee Recovery Investment Contribution' (ERIC) scheme, providing for a 'repayment of savings' to employees if strict profit targets are achieved. Trade unions opposed.
Element Six	Short-term working with voluntary and, possibly, compulsory redundancies. Trade unions opposed.
Kingspan	Reduction in shift premium, elimination of 11 per cent 'flexibreak', abolition of an incremental scale for clerical staff, removal of profit-share scheme, reduction in overtime rate and a pay freeze. Trade unions opposed.
Pfizer	Closure of one of its plants. Trade unions opposed.

Source: Dobbins 2008; European Restructuring Monitor 2010; Farrelly 2010; Gunnigle *et al.* 2013; reports from *Industrial Relations News*.

Turning to specific HR activities, the great recession heralded a sea change in regard to recruitment and selection, especially when compared to the 'Celtic tiger' era. Then the booming economy and effective full employment created widespread labour shortages, but in contrast the recession created a very loose labour market, with an abundant supply of labour across many categories of employment. Related changes included a substantial decline in employee turnover. For example, one large medical devices firm reported a fall in employee turnover from an average of 20 per cent during the Celtic tiger years to approximately 4 per cent in 2010 (cf. Gunnigle *et al.* 2013). Learning, training and development (LT&D) was another victim of recession as firms cut back on expenditure in this area. A particular case in point was the extensive decline in induction and other basic training, resulting directly from the dramatic decline in recruitment.

As noted earlier, pay negotiations and pay movement in Ireland have generally been determined through centralised agreements, either bipartite (employer associations and trade unions) or tripartite (primarily employer associations, trade unions and government). This latter process of 'social partnership' lasted from 1987 until the onset of recession in 2008. Indeed, 'social partnership' was one of the first major institutional casualties of the great recession. At the onset of recession a prevailing national agreement was in place: *Towards 2016: Review and Transitional Agreement 2008–2009*. This agreement was concluded in September 2008 and provided for a 6 per cent pay increase over twenty-one months. As recession quickly deepened, the country's largest employer body, *Irish Business and Employers Confederation* (IBEC) abandoned social partnership. The government concurrently withdrew in 2009 and deployed unilateral actions, notably pay cuts and the introduction of the Universal Social Charge (effectively more personal taxation), which in tandem with other measures 'spelled the end of the low-tax model on which the wage restraint of Irish social partnership was based'. (Wallace *et al.* 2013: 297). The government had also unilaterally introduced a public sector pension levy earlier that year.

Looking at the immediate aftermath of the onset of the global financial crisis (2008–2010), it appears that the great majority of private sector employers implemented pay freezes, with only a small minority conceding any element of pay increase (Regan 2013). On closer examination of pay trends we find that unionised MNCs were disproportionately represented among the comparatively small cadre of firms that bucked the overall trend of pay freezes or cuts and implemented pay increases (Gunnigle *et al.* 2013). This was evident in sectors such as pharmaceuticals and medical devices which are generally seen as more 'recession proof' than other sectors (especially some areas of the service sector, such as retail and hospitality, which suffered severely in the face of the collapse in personal consumption). There is limited evidence of extensive pay cuts in the private sector, with employers sometimes preferring to secure savings through reductions in working hours (Bergin *et al.* 2012). However, there were very significant, unilaterally imposed pay cuts for public sector workers, averaging a reduction of 14 per cent (Roche 2013), though some estimates put this as high as 18 per cent (Regan 2013).

More generally, it seems that the recession has contributed to an ongoing decline in trade union density. At the start of the recession in 2007, approximately one-third (32 per cent) of employees were trade union members. The early recession years saw a temporal increase in density to 34 per cent in 2010, but this quickly fell back to 33 per cent in 2011 and has since continued its slide, declining to 27 per cent in 2015 (Walsh 2015). Trade union density tends to be significantly higher in the public sector than in the private sector. Data from the *National Workplace Survey* (O'Connell *et al.* 2010) found that two-thirds of public sector employees were union members (68.7 per cent), while the equivalent private sector figure was a quarter (24.9 per cent). Falling trade union recognition and density, combined with the collapse of social partnership indicates a significant decline in trade union power and influence (cf. D'Art and Turner 2011). While some pockets of strength remain in the private sector, and are more pronounced in the public sector, the recession has presented trade unions with additional challenges, notably losing membership due to job losses and the deployment of concession bargaining, whereby trade unions are forced to surrender or give back previous gains in pay and working conditions, normally in return for securing some level of job security (Roche *et al.* 2015; Mitchell, 1994). Even some highly unionised organisations, many of whom traditionally conceded 'above the norm' terms and conditions of employment, used the rationale of recession to engage in concession bargaining and significantly row back on these terms and conditions (Gunnigle *et al.*, 2013). However, this has not been associated with any widespread offensive on trade union recognition, while unions themselves have tried to respond through more strategic membership drives. This may yield some returns in the recovering economy.

Clearly, the recession has demonstrably impacted on the workplace employment relations 'climate' with some managers reporting a greater willingness among – and arguably pressure on – employees to accept changes in working conditions (e.g. greater flexibility), as part of organisational efforts to protect business and employment. However, there may also be an element of opportunism in management behaviour as firms sometimes used the guise of recession to push through workplace changes (Gunnigle et al. 2013). The fact that trade unions were in a weak bargaining position rendered them less capable of resisting such management action, a point also illustrated above regarding the inability of trade unions to prevent widespread pay freezes or cuts. Employers seem to have also accelerated moves to change benefit schemes, particularly pension plans and profit-sharing arrangements, most notably manifested in attempts to shift from 'defined benefit' to 'defined contribution' pension plans*. While this phenomenon predates the recent global financial crisis, it again provides an example of a trend which gathered significant traction during the recession.

The recession placed a question mark over the efficacy and suitability of particular HR techniques. A case in point is performance-related pay/performance by results systems. In the banking sector, for example, the performance of senior managers on metrics such as the size of the 'loan book' and quarterly growth in business activity formed the basis for decisions on the distribution of additional financial rewards. It would appear that too little attention was paid to the quality of the 'loan book' and related growth, as demonstrated by the extent of bad loans among many major banks and financial institutions.

A final consideration is the impact of recession on the HR function. A traditional view regarding the impact of recessions on HRM was largely negative, positing that HR considerations are likely to be side-lined as organisations prioritise survival and bottom line financial and operational concerns. In contrast, a contemporary viewpoint is that recession provides an opportunity for HRM to play a more strategic role in addressing the challenges a financial crisis creates (Ulrich 2007; Brockett 2010). To date it appears that the evidence is equivocal and arguably best captured by Roche and Teague (2012: 1333) who found that HR managers in Ireland were both 'business partners and working the pumps', in both responding effectively to organisational challenges presented by the recession and by helping line managers deal with related operational challenges.

---

* Defined Benefit Pension: A defined benefit (DB) scheme fixes the benefit in advance – usually as a proportion of the member's earnings when they retire. For instance, a DB scheme might provide a retirement pension of 1 per cent of earnings for each year an employee was in that scheme. If an employee retired after forty years, that employee would receive a pension of 40 per cent of their pre-retirement earnings. In a DB scheme, the benefits are fixed and the contributions must be adjusted from time to time to make sure that the correct amount is being accumulated to provide for them. It is usual in a DB scheme for the member's contribution rate to be fixed and for the employer rate to increase or reduce as needed, though in some DB schemes both employer and employee contribution rates change from time to time.

Defined Contribution Pension: A defined contribution (DC) scheme has a set contribution for both the employee and the employer. For example in many DC schemes, the employer and the employee will each contribute 5 per cent of the employee's earnings, or 10 per cent in total. These contributions are invested on behalf of each scheme member. The retirement benefits for each member depend on how much money has been built up by retirement and so it is not possible to know in advance what pension benefits a member will receive.
Source: www.welfare.ie

Broadly speaking we can identify two potentially contrasting developments for the HR function. On the one hand, it appears that the HR function has acted as an important delivery agent for organisational responses to the impact of the recent recession. One need only summarily review the main types of organisational responses to see that much, if not most, of the re-structuring activity engaged in falls within the domain of HR, including downsizing, reductions in working time, lay-offs, pay cuts/freezes, concession bargaining and related changes in reward systems and working conditions. Thus the global crisis would appear to have helped bring HR to centre stage, in addressing key strategic challenges facing multinationals, most notably pressures to reduce costs and enhance productivity. However, this role generally took a reactive form in addressing immediate organisational challenges, with little or limited emphasis on strategically aligning their responses with long-term business strategies or goals (cf. Roche 2001; Harney et al. 2014). On the other hand, we also find evidence of increased 'hard' metric evaluation of HRM structures and performance, and reductions and rationalisation in regard to the scale and organisation of the HR function. For example, in 2010 a leading financial institution reported a 25 per cent cut in HR headcount and a large pharmaceutical company experienced a 20 per cent cut (cf. Gunnigle et al. 2013). An important complimentary dimension here is the increased application of information technology in HR administration, as manifested in HR Information Systems (HRIS) and HR Shared Service Centres (HRSSCs). These developments are often associated with a reduction in numbers employed in conventional HR departments. Both of which are considered later in this chapter.

In evaluating the overall impact of the great recession for HRM, we find little support for the proposition that when times get tough organisations tend to jettison putative 'softer' areas of managerial activity such as HR. Indeed the Irish experience provides limited evidence of any widespread diminution in the role and status of the HR function *vis a vis* that of other management functions or of any substantial change to the status quo that pertained before recession. Rather it appears that the HR function played a critical, if largely reactive, role in 'delivering' organisational responses to recession. This was apparent in arguably vital areas such as restructuring, downsizing and changes in terms and conditions of employment which were generally orchestrated by the HR function and resulted in financial benefits for organisations. In undertaking this role of delivering apparently 'hard HRM' responses to recession, the HR function adopted an archetypal 'conformist innovator' role (cf. Legge 1978; 2005) in providing operational HR responses to improve the bottom line. This role demonstrated HR's contribution on orthodox business metrics such as those focused on operating costs and operational efficiencies.

However, this did not mean that 'soft HRM' was abandoned. Rather, as Roche (2011) demonstrates, organisations concurrently deployed hard and soft HRM practices. The former focused on reducing direct costs and the latter on maintaining employee motivation and commitment in the face of recession, using various forms of communications and employee engagement. This combination of responses is captured in Figure 2.2.

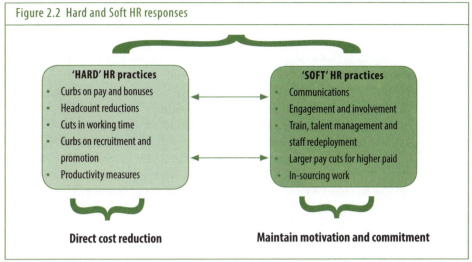

Figure 2.2 Hard and Soft HR responses

Direct cost reduction — 'HARD' HR practices
- Curbs on pay and bonuses
- Headcount reductions
- Cuts in working time
- Curbs on recruitment and promotion
- Productivity measures

Maintain motivation and commitment — 'SOFT' HR practices
- Communications
- Engagement and involvement
- Train, talent management and staff redeployment
- Larger pay cuts for higher paid
- In-sourcing work

Source: Roche (2011: 33).

HR GOES TECHNICAL?

Fittingly, in a world where much of our daily lives are influenced by technology, particularly the internet and social media, our final area of focus is the impact of information and communication technology (ICT) on HRM and its evolution. Since the reach of ICT is multi-dimensional and ubiquitous, we have chosen to focus on two key areas where the impact on HRM is arguably most apparent, namely (i) the use of ICT in helping deliver HR services; and (ii) the use of HR analytics to help inform HR decision-making.

THE USE OF TECHNOLOGY IN THE DELIVERY OF HR SERVICES

As previously discussed, the impact of the great recession caused changes in the mode of delivery of HRM, linked to drives for organisational efficiency and aptly captured in the following quote from the HR director of a large US MNC in the pharmaceutical sector (Gunnigle, Lavelle and Monaghan 2013: 226) on the challenges facing HR:

> ... as part of this cost agenda, people in [US HQ] have said "... hang on a second we are not just squeezing production ... and engineering, we need to start squeezing you". They are moving to the centres of excellence model which is driving redundancies in HR. I had eight people working for me when I started ... now there's me and one other ... there were [HR] redundancies, about 20 per cent. If you have a HR issue, it's gone to Shared Services ... It [the HR function] has been stripped down to the bare bones. It has thrown up a huge challenge ... and behind all this is cost – to drop the numbers, push more work back to the line, drive specialisation ...

While the recent recession may well have accelerated the pace of rationalisation in the scale and operation of the HR function, the principal drivers relate to a shift in the mode of delivery of HR services, and especially to an increased provision of HR shared service centres (SSCs) (see Chapter 1). HR SSCs normally refer to the provision of a common HR services platform (e.g. for payroll, employee benefits or recruitment) for a range of operating units or divisions of an organisation. The HR SSC 'model' may differ, depending on whether the platform is provided internally, outsourced or indeed 'off-shored'. In practice, this model generally means that employees using HR SSCs (e.g. on payroll issues) must do so remotely, by phone or email, as opposed to the traditional on-site model which provided the option of face-to-face interaction with HR specialists. In effect, HR SSCs often operate in the form of call centres.

This growth of HR SSCs was a phenomenon identified in a large scale survey of HRM in MNCs in Ireland, conducted just before the onset of the recession (cf. Lavelle et al. 2009). There is general consensus that HR SCCs, often combined with other applications of ICT in the workplace, certainly help streamline HR delivery and leverage economies of scale to improve cost-effectiveness and most probably enhance bottom line performance. Indeed, centralised HR shared service provision represents one of the three key elements in David Ulrich's (1997) widely applied 'three-legged stool' model of HR best practice (the other two being 'business partnering' between senior HR practitioners and line management, and the development of 'centres of excellence' in specialist areas of HR, e.g. in compensation and benefits (see Chapter 1 for greater detail, particularly on the configuration of the HR function).

HR SSCs and related changes in the configuration of HR service delivery are viewed in many quarters as a positive and strategic development, putatively aligning business and HR objectives and generating added value. The implementation of this model, however, can cause difficulties for HR including prioritising the need for efficiency over 'employee care' and concerns about privacy (Ulrich et al. 2008). Other potential downsides include reduction in HR headcount on the ground, and substantial decline or elimination of face-to-face interaction between employees and HR practitioners. While these may be difficult to quantify in financial terms, they again highlight the role of HR in managing 'contradictions of capitalism' in instances where the interests of workers and management are potentially at odds (Legge 2005). Indeed, greater emphasis on 'best practice' through greater HR SSC delivery potentially begs the question 'best' for whom – management or workers? Our analysis indicates that decisions on what constitutes 'best practice' are invariably managerially driven with limited attention afforded to employee preferences or voice (Marchington and Grugulis 2002).

An associated, and increasingly pervasive, development is the use of HR Information Systems (HRIS) for the storage and sharing of HR data. This normally takes the form of software (e.g. *PeopleSoft* or *SAP HR*) and is used for data entry, tracking and the data information needs of the HR function, such as those related to personnel records, payroll and training. HRIS can also be used to monitor policy implementation and performance and to facilitate communications on such matters. In multinational companies (MNCs) for example, HRIS can provide corporate management with access to HR data across their international subsidiaries and enable comparison of site performance on HR metrics, such as productivity and headcount. A study of the utilisation of HRIS among MNCs in Ireland found that over half of all MNCs here (54 per cent) reported the use of HRIS on an international basis (Lavelle, et al. 2009) and that levels of usage were steadily increasing.

HR ANALYTICS

Many argue that so-called 'HR Analytics' or the application of complex 'big data' mining to HRM may be the area where ICT exerts its greatest impact on HRM (CIPD 2013). Marler and Boudreau (2017: 15) define HR analytics as 'a HRM practice that is designed to provide managers with information that connects HRM processes to employee attitudes and behaviour, and ultimately to organizational outcomes'. However, as we have seen above, HRM and HR practitioners have not traditionally been associated with a quantitative orientation. As a management consultant quoted in the *Financial Times* (Pritchard, 2011: 1) observed: 'HR people tend not to be very analytical; they don't do numbers'.

Building a HR analytics team is therefore a major challenge, as companies require employees with a strong mix of business knowledge, HRM and technical skills (Ryan 2016). This challenge is also highlighted by Ulrich and Dulebohn (2015: 202):

> Many HR professionals went into HR to avoid the quantitative side of business. But it is no longer possible to sidestep data, evidence, and analytics that bring rigor and discipline to HR. Statistics is the foundation for HR analytics and needs to be become *de rigueur* for HR professionals going forward.

Conspicuously, the most frequently cited reason that HR Analytics is not more widely adopted is the shortage of analytically-skilled HR professionals (Marler and Boudreau 2017).

However, the availability of large masses of electronic data means that HR practitioners, like most other management functions, are increasingly entreated to use 'big data' to garner both operational improvements and increase their strategic impact. The term 'big data' applies to very large, and often unstructured, data sets that may be analysed computationally to identify patterns, trends, and relationships, particularly relating to human behaviour and interactions. It is seen as an additional source of data to that stored on conventional HRIS. For example, data stored on HRIS might normally include basic records and employment history (hiring, promotion, transfer, etc.) together with data on demographic profiles, knowledge, skills and qualifications, performance reviews, training and development and so forth. 'Big data' can then provide additional information garnered largely from the internet, email and smartphones. For example, additional biographic information, locational data, browsing patterns, electronic calendars, communications and networking patterns. In effect, HR analytics enables the development of various metrics (sophisticated statistics) with which to identify and evaluate employee behaviour and ideally to improve an organisation's performance (cf. Edwards and Edwards 2016). These lofty aspirations have led the CIPD (2013) to describe HR analytics as a 'must have' for the HR profession, while Taylor (2011, 1) postulated that 'the face of HR in a growing number of organisations is a portal rather than a person'.

In regard to specific aspects of HRM, it would appear that an important future opportunity for HR is to engage big data and HRIS to better manage and develop talent (Ryan 2016). It is postulated that returns on investment in this area are likely to be substantial, since decision-makers have traditionally struggled to make sound decisions in the area of talent management, due in part to inadequate data regarding person-opportunity (job) fit (Russell and Bennett 2015). Furthermore it would seem that the capabilities of HR analytics can now enhance performance across key talent segments and thereby improve organisational capacity to resource future talent needs (Ryan 2016). This would concur with the work of Angrave *et al* (2016: 5) which found that almost all of the major management consultancies have now developed product lines which seek to provide client firms with 'the skills and know-how to implement integrated talent management suites (ITMS)'. Such ITMS come in the form of software platforms which aggregate and share talent data across multiple HR activities and claim to provide users (e.g. line managers, HR practitioners) with better information leading in turn – it is argued – to improved decision-making (Bersin 2017). These integrated talent management suites are a comparatively recent development, provided by a relatively small number of key suppliers such as *Oracle* (with its 'Taleo Talent Management Suite'), *IBM*, *SAP* and *Workday* (Angrave *et al.* 2016). Research in the area of talent management conducted by Deloitte *Bersin by Deloitte Talent Analytics Maturity Model* 2017 argues that organisations broadly progress through four stages in building big data talent management capacity, from a relatively basic operational and reactive stage to a highly advanced predictive analytics stage as outlined in Figure 2.3.

Figure 2.3 Talent Analytics Maturity Model (Bersin by Deloitte)	
Bersin's Talent Analytics Maturity Model	
Level 1: Operational Reports	Using data primarily for ad-hoc, operational reports. An example would be reporting on 'average time to fill', but not really using the data for anything in particular. 56% of organisations are at this level.
Level 2: Advanced Reports	Using data to keep a pulse on trends and goals. For example, creating a visual that shows 'average time to fill' per month over the past two years against a defined goal. This provides insight on 'performance' over time, but it doesn't tell us why or how to improve. 30% of organisations are at level 2.
Level 3: Proactive Analytics	This is when data is finally used to solve problems and make decisions. One example would be piloting a new recruiting tool and using data to decide whether the tool delivered what it promised to deliver. Only 10% of organisations are at this level.
Level 4: Predictive Analytics	Organsiations at the highest level of maturity are able to use data to predict future talent outcomes. For example, creating a forecast that indictaes how many open roles to expect next year, how much it will cost to fill them, and how many recruiters will be needed. Only 4% of organisations have mastered this level.

Source: www.bersin.com/Lexicon/details.aspx?id=15392. Copyright © 2017 Deloitte Development LLC.

A concern in the sphere of HR analytics, however, relates to the quality of the data upon which decisions are predicated. It would seem that data used is often inconsistent, unclean (and possibly incorrect), out of date and located in multiple locations, resulting in a lack of unique insights from HR analytics (cf. Tonidandel *et al.* 2015). Although IT should normally be an enabler of HR analytics, this often depends on the quality and accessibility of the data and capabilities of an e-HRM software system (Marler and Boudreau 2017).

Returning to the argued ubiquitous diffusion of HR analytics and related implications for HRM, a recent analysis conducted by David Angrave and colleagues (2016) provides for somewhat more sober reflection. This work takes issue with the more optimistic narratives on the capacity of HR analytics to positively impact on HR's strategic contribution, or more broadly to significantly improve organisational performance. Rather, they argue that progress in the domain of HR analytics is being hindered by a lack of understanding of its nature and functioning among HR practitioners. They further argue that this problem is compounded by the HR analytics 'industry' itself and its emphasis on products and tools which often come up short in delivering performance improvement or enhancing the strategic value of HR and which may in fact negatively impact on various facets of organisational life. This line of argumentation is aptly captured by Angrave et al. (2016: 1):

> Unless the HR profession wises up to both the potential and pitfalls of [HR] analytics, [it] . . . is likely to have a number of negative consequences for the HR profession itself, for workers and for organisations. Specifically, there is a risk that analytics will further embed finance and engineering perspectives on people management at boardroom level in ways that will restrict the strategic influence of the HR profession. It may also damage the quality of working life and employee well-being, without delivering sustainable competitive advantage.

The essential conclusion of Angrave and his colleagues' work is that, contrary to popular rhetoric, HR practitioners are 'behind the curve' when it comes to the application of HR analytics and big data. Indeed the authors argue that a lack of understanding of HR analytics stems from two perspectives. Firstly, HR practitioners do not possess an adequate grasp of HR analytics but, secondly, the analytics 'experts' do not adequately understand HR. This intersection means that investment in HR analytics is failing to deliver the promised benefits, in terms of organisational performance and strategic impact.

We might add in conclusion that HR analytics is very much a new frontier and its application in organisations is at a comparatively early stage and continually developing. It certainly carries the potential to imbue HR with a harder, quantitative edge that might enhance its overlap with, and impact on, strategic management. It thus concurs with Ulrich and Dulebohn's contention (2015: 202) that 'with HR analytics, line managers and HR professionals can better justify, prioritise and improve HR investments'. On the other hand, there is a danger that it may facilitate a shift in focus away from HR and people management toward a greater 'number crunching' orientation and development of metrics. This approach may often lack relevance and sometimes be potentially damaging to work and working lives. As Rasmussen and Ulrich (2015: 239) conclude:

> At best, HR analytics provides input for management discussions that can elevate the decision quality, but there is rarely a straight line from data and analysis to action.

Overall, the impact of ICT on HR is indeed one of the areas where evolution is continuing apace and its impact remains unclear.

CONCLUSION

The various historical developments, both national and international, addressed in this chapter should help to contextualise our understanding of the diverse dimensions of HR work, the role of HR practitioners and the operation and influence of the HR function itself. It should allow us to more deliberately consider each major area of HR activity, such as management of HR flows, work systems, performance management, reward systems, training and development and employment relations. In so doing, we can also identify the influence of key phases in historical evolution of HRM on contemporary HR practice in Ireland, and beyond.

In our latter discussion on the role of HR analytics we chose not to focus on the application of ICT to specific HR activities. For example, the use of social media in recruitment and selection, or of e-learning in training and development. Rather we address these issues in the relevant chapters on these topics.

In the next chapter we consider the area of HRM strategy, with particular emphasis on the impact of HRM on organisational performance.

3
Strategy, Human Resource Management and Performance

Over the past three decades strategic HRM has emerged as one of the sub-fields of HRM, along with 'micro' and 'international' HRM (Lengnick-Hall et al. 2009). Batt and Banerjee (2012) argue that, as a movement, strategic HRM essentially shifted the unit of analysis from individual employees and HR functions to the organisation as a whole, directing research away from employee attitudes and wellbeing to the broader field of firm performance.

The strategic positioning of the HR function and its impact on organisational performance and competitiveness is a central focus in both the practitioner and the academic literature. On the HR practice front, for example, the 2017 Chartered Institute of Personnel and Development (CIPD) Survey of HR Practices in Ireland (Connaughton and Staunton 2017) reported that 45 per cent of respondents believed that there was an ongoing lack of understanding of the strategic role of HR by senior management, while some 36 per cent believed that HR was not playing a strategic role within the organisation. These results point to an underlying concern among HR professionals in Ireland about the overall positioning of the HR function as a strategic partner. On the academic front, the debate on the relationship between strategy, HRM and performance has been characterised as a road that is now 'well-travelled' (Wright and Ulrich 2017). There is little doubt that it incorporates a substantial body of literature which is characterised by areas of both consensus and disagreement.

At its broadest level, the term strategic HRM is used by professionals to signal their belief that effective HRM contributes to business effectiveness (Jackson et al. 2014). It involves the development of a strategic corporate approach to workforce management, whereby HR considerations become fundamental to strategic decision-making, as organisations seek to establish a corporate HR philosophy and strategy that complements their business strategy (Fombrun et al.1984; Buller and Napier 1993; Guest 1987; Mayrhofer et al. 2000; Purcell 2004). Coined as a 'matching' process by Boxall (1992), and often alluding to the messages advanced in the resource-based view of the firm (Barney 1995), the core objective of strategic HRM is the alignment of business strategy, organisational configuration and HR policies and practices – to achieve competitive advantage. A recent review and mapping of the HRM field (Markoulli et al. 2017) reveals a substantial collection of work focused on strategic HRM and the relationship between HRM systems and performance. Within the domain area, the main corpus of work is in documenting the key approaches developed to understand the relationship between HRM and performance, how policies either support or contradict firm strategies, how

HR practices affect a firm's ability to change and adapt and the criticality of the social and human capital base of the firm, as a determinant of overall performance. Though complex, it is a literature that is now well established and one that clearly illustrates the strategic potential and significance of HRM to all organisations (Boxall and Purcell 2008; Wright and Ulrich 2017). Part of the complexity arises from the fact that much of the literature in the field is either normative (written mainly by those in consultancy roles) or conceptual (written by academics) with relatively few attempts to integrate both streams satisfactorily (Beattie and McDougall 1998). Similarly, Ferris et al. (1999) point to the gap between the science and the practice of HRM in this area. They refer to Buckley et al. (1998: 1), who characterise the hiatus between the two streams of literature as 'a disconnect', noting that:

> It is a disconnect in that scientists and practitioners seem to have segregated along these lines. This is a relatively recent phenomenon because until the relatively recent past, the study of HRM was problem driven (e.g. the Hawthorne studies are a shining example of significant scientist/practitioner collaboration). Our zest to develop a theory of HRM may have been instrumental in driving a wedge between scientists and practitioner . . . managers are relatively familiar with the research in HRM, but they fail to see many practical implications coming from said research.

In spite of the enormous amount of research conducted on HRM in the interim, things have not changed much for the better. Rynes et al. (2007: 987) note that 'the gap between HR science and practice is so persistent and pervasive that some have despaired of its ever being narrowed'. Recent calls have come again to rebalance strategic HRM enquiry to include working with managers (Cascio 2015). Batt and Banerjee (2012) argue that the hunt for validating the HR-performance link, prevalent in American research, may prove problematic as the 'current field of strategic HR is limited in its ability to explain HR patterns, practices and performance because its theoretical assumptions and empirical focus do not fit the changing reality of global economic activity'. Additional calls have also been made for more longitudinal research, as scholars are still unable to fully answer some core questions about the relationship between HRM and performance (Guest 2011). Thus, despite an extensive and growing body of literature addressing the concepts of strategy and a strategic approach to HRM, consensus as to the substance, nature and implications of these concepts has not been achieved. In seeking to establish the link with overall organisational performance, scholars have been urged to be more explicit in their work about the level and type of performance they are predicting in their models (Lepak and Shaw 2008). They have been exhorted to advance the theoretical understanding of the 'black box' in strategic HRM research, in order to capture the many complexities at play (Jiang et al. 2013).

While a great deal has been achieved in unearthing aspects of the relationship between HRM and performance, there are also voices that call for the exercising of some caution in assuming any automatic connection between HR strategies and organisational performance (Paauwe 2009). This is particularly the case in light of ongoing methodological limitations in research concerned with the HRM–performance link (Wall and Wood 2005), coupled with modest progress in developing theory that adequately captures the precise mechanisms by which HRM impacts performance (Way and Johnson 2005; Fleetwood and Hesketh 2008; Chadwick and Dabu 2009). In addition, it has been argued that there is an over reliance on knowledge areas and perspectives pertaining to the internal dimensions of organisations, to the neglect of external, contextual dimensions (Kaufman 2012).

This chapter considers several aspects of the debate on linking decisions in the HRM sphere with broader decisions on business strategy, and focuses on the link between HRM practice and organisation performance. It introduces the concept of strategic management and discusses strategic decision-making and HRM. It examines dominant theoretical perspectives vested in 'best fit' versus 'best practice' models, along with theoretical developments and looks at the cumulative evidence on aspects of strategic HRM to date.

THE CONCEPT OF STRATEGIC MANAGEMENT

There is an extensive literature on the notion of business strategy, much of which can prove somewhat perplexing. Numerous writers dealing with managerial and business decision-making have used the term 'strategy' to describe a particular set of choices, taken over a period of time, to achieve prescribed business objectives (see Carter et al. 2008). Thus, *strategic management* is concerned with policy decisions affecting the entire organisation, with the overall objective being to best position the organisation to deal effectively with the environmental contingencies it faces. This concept of strategic management implies that in an organisational setting there is a hierarchy of decision choices and that critical decisions on business strategy will direct more specific operational decisions on shorter-term matters.

Most evaluations of strategic management have attempted to identify the various components of the strategy concept, and the levels and types of strategy that can occur – namely corporate, business and functional levels. *Corporate-level strategy* is essentially concerned with the question, 'What businesses should we be in?'. *Business-level (competitive) strategy* addresses the question, 'How do we compete in a given business?'. Finally, *Functional-level strategy* focuses on how the activities of particular functions (such as HRM) come together to support the business-level strategy. These different strategy levels are illustrated in Figure 3.1.

Figure 3.1 Levels of strategic decision-making

CORPORATE STRATEGY
(what business should we be in?)

BUSINESS/COMPETITIVE STRATEGY
(how to establish and sustain competitive advantage)

FUNCTIONAL STRATEGY
(contribution of various functional parts of the organisation, e.g.:
Marketing
Operations/Production
Finance
HRM)

In addition to identifying different levels of strategy, it is useful to distinguish between strategy process and strategy content. On the one hand, *strategy process* concerns the activities involved in the formation of a strategy, including analysing competitors and scanning the environment to identify threats and opportunities. *Strategy content*, on the other hand, refers to the actual policies chosen by the organisation and the methods and activities used to implement these policies.

While these distinctions help to clarify the concept of strategic management, there remains some difficulty in relation to analysing the strategy concept in such a way that it reflects the reality of organisational life. For example, there is an inherent assumption that an organisation's strategy is formed after key organisational leaders have formally analysed all relevant information, developed a number of possible options and rationally chosen the option that will likely maximise organisational performance. Consequently, it is often assumed that implementing these strategic policies is not problematic because there is goal congruity between the parties, with the expectation that decisions made by top/senior managers are expected to be followed, with little or no resistance, by individuals and groups at lower levels in the organisation.

Some of these assumptions, however, run contrary to evidence on the realities of actual practice in regard to organisational decision-making and implementation, as demonstrated by the pioneering work of Mintzberg (1978, 1987). He introduced the distinction between *'realised'* and *'unrealised'* strategies, and between *'intended'* and *'emergent'* strategies. *'Deliberate'* strategies are those that are both intended and realised in the organisation. This is the concept of business strategy that appears most frequently in the literature. In addition to deliberate strategies, there may be intended strategies that for some reason fail to be implemented. These are *'unrealised'* strategies. Finally, according to Mintzberg, realised strategies may 'emerge' without the conscious intentions of the strategists. These are termed *'emergent'* strategies. This categorisation therefore goes beyond that of a deliberate strategy (in the sense of the traditional planning-oriented view of the term) to that of an emergent strategy, which is conceived of as patterned responses that may not have been planned by the actors and may develop in an incremental and opportunistic manner. Strategies can therefore develop in an organisation without being consciously intended. Indeed, Mintzberg suggests that for a strategy to have been intended exactly as realised would be a 'tall order'.

A further advancement of this argument comes from the 'strategy as practice' perspective (Jarzabkowski and Spee 2009). This arose from an underlying dissatisfaction with the conventional rational approach which, it is argued, failed to capture the social complexity and multiple levels of action surrounding the successful implementation of strategy. In an effort to capture and explain how strategy making is assisted or constrained by organisational and social practices (Vaara and Whittington, 2012) the strategy-as-practice movement focuses on the 'doing' of strategy, asking: 'Who does it?, 'What do they do? and 'How do they do it?'. In this way it directs attention to the multiple activities of a broader range of actors who actually constitute the strategy process and seeks to give expression to the dynamic and messy nature of strategic organisational decision-making.

STRATEGIC DECISION-MAKING AND HRM

Despite these complexities, we have seen an ever-increasing emphasis on strategic management as organisations strive to address an increasingly turbulent and competitive business environment. Indeed, the impact of the 'great recession' has served to make strategic management more rather than less important (Rumelt 2009). We noted earlier that strategic management is concerned with long-term policy decisions affecting the future of the organisation. Yet strategic management is not simply about deciphering the routes to competitive advantage; it also concerns how such advantage can be realised and sustained (Cunningham and Harney 2010). Strategic decision-making therefore incorporates strategy formulation, strategy implementation, evaluation and control; it emphasises the monitoring and evaluation of environmental opportunities and constraints, as well as the strengths and weaknesses of the organisation. Corporate, business/competitive and functional strategy represent different levels of strategic decision-making. Each level involves decisions that are strategic in nature.

Boxall and Purcell (2003) emphasise this point by differentiating between *upstream* and *downstream* strategic decisions. Upstream, or first-order, decisions concern the long-term direction and nature of the organisation. Downstream, or second-order, decisions deal with the implications of upstream decisions for organisational structure. HR policy choices are made in the context of downstream strategic decisions on organisational structure. Such choices are strategic in nature since they establish the basic approach to workforce management. However, Purcell's argument suggests that HR policy choices are third-order strategic decisions since they will be heavily influenced by first- and second-order decisions, and by broader environmental factors (see Figure 3.2).

Figure 3.2 Upstream and downstream strategic decision-making

		UPSTREAM	
FIRST-ORDER		Long-term direction of the firm	E
		Scope of activities, markets, location	N
			V
SECOND-ORDER		Internal operating procedures	I
		Relationships between parts of the organisation	R
			O
			N
			M
THIRD-ORDER		(e.g.) Strategic choice in HRM	E
			N
			T
		DOWNSTREAM	

Using British data, Purcell examined how trends in first- and second-order strategy, particularly diversification and decentralisation, affect management decision-making.

He identified the growth in size and influence of the diversified organisation as giving greater prominence to decision-making at the corporate level. In this business form, portfolio planning is commonly used to evaluate the performance of constituent business units, aid resource allocation, and investment/divestment decisions. In the portfolio planning approach to corporate strategy, the organisation is seen as a collection of different businesses that should pursue different strategies to suit particular market conditions. This implies that different functional strategies, including HRM, need to be applied at the business unit level to suit particular business strategies. Key decisions on resource allocation (first-order decisions) are taken at corporate level and it is the responsibility of business unit managers to deal with the implications of such decisions and make appropriate operational decisions to satisfy corporate requirements. Thus, first-order decisions, while not necessarily incorporating HRM considerations, significantly influence HR policy and practice within particular business units.

This somewhat pessimistic view of HR's influence on the strategy process has been counterbalanced by other work, particularly from US scholars. In particular, commentators have argued that the influence of HR considerations on strategy development has increased and that the distinction between corporate, competitive and HR strategy has blurred (Barney 1991; Ulrich 1997; Pfeffer 1998a, 1998b; Snell 2005). For example, as Snell (2005) and others have argued, against the backdrop of increased competition and globalisation, many of the traditional sources of competitive advantage, such as barriers to entry (e.g. monopolies), technology and access to capital, have become less important, with the result that HR and HR processes can emerge as key sources of competitive advantage. Thus, rather than viewing HRM as acting in response to a given strategy being cascaded down the organisation, this perspective holds that HR can play a key role in informing and crafting strategy in the first place, through fully understanding all aspects of the business and finding its place as a strategic partner.

Overall, though perspectives may vary and the challenges of precisely what constitutes the 'black box' of strategic HRM remain, there is little doubt that the relationship between HRM and performance has become a dominant issue in the field. Indeed, identifying the means and extent to which firms can leverage HR capacity to impact positively on performance has become the essence of strategic HRM. A large number of landmark studies have examined the relationship between HR practices and selected measures of performance, such as profits, sales and quality (Ichniowski 1992; Huselid 1995; MacDuffie 1995; Snell and Youndt 1995; Wright and Snell 1998; Godard and Delaney 2000; Guest et al. 2003). We can categorise much of this work into two 'schools', namely (i) the 'best fit' (or contingency) school; and (ii) the 'best practice' (or universalistic) school. We now consider each in turn.

'BEST FIT' OR CONTINGENCY APPROACHES TO HRM

The essence of the 'best fit' or contingency approach is that the optimal HR strategy is one that 'fits' or matches the organisation's overall business strategy. The primary emphasis is on achieving 'vertical' fit (i.e. the chosen HRM approach should complement the overall business strategy). Harvard academic Michael Porter's work on competitive strategy provided much of the basis for subsequent research on linking HR strategy with business or competitive strategy (Porter 1980, 1985, 1987, 1990). The research on competitive advantage focuses primarily on identifying those factors that allow an organisation to differentiate its product or service from its competitors to increase market share. Porter argues that the focus of strategic decision-making should be on the development of appropriate competitive strategies at the level of individual business units. *Competitive strategy* is concerned with achieving sustainable competitive advantage in particular industries or industry segments. Price and quality are common mechanisms by which organisations attempt to achieve competitive advantage. Porter's key legacy has probably been his three generic strategies for achieving competitive advantage – namely *cost leadership, differentiation* and *focus* (Porter 1985).

1. *Cost leadership* involves positioning the organisation as a low-cost producer of a standard 'no frills' product or service, for either a broad or a focused market (e.g. *Ryanair, Lidl, Aldi*. To succeed with a cost leadership strategy it is suggested that the firm must become the cost leader and not one of several firms pursuing this strategy. Cost leadership requires an emphasis on tight managerial controls, low overheads, economies of scale, and a dedication to achieving productive efficiency.
2. A *differentiation* strategy requires that an organisation's product or service becomes unique in some dimension that is valued by the buyer, to the extent that the buyer is willing to pay a premium price (e.g. *Nike, Intel*). The basis for a differentiation strategy may be the product or service itself or other aspects, such as delivery or after-sales service.
3. The third generic competitive strategy, *focus*, involves choosing a narrow market segment and serving this through either a low-cost or a differentiation focus (e.g. *Aston Martin*).

Porter's approach is essentially contingency-based: a particular organisation's choice of competitive strategy (cost leadership, differentiation or focus) is seen as determining the context for downstream policies and actions in each key functional area, including HRM. Thus, each generic strategy warrants different skills and requirements for success. Of particular significance from an HR perspective is the need to match HR practices in areas such as recruitment and selection, compensation and benefits and employment relations with the chosen competitive strategy. He further contends that different organisational cultures are implied in each strategy and that HR policy choice is a key influence in establishing and maintaining 'appropriate' corporate cultures. For example, in the *differentiation* strategy, it is suggested that culture might serve to encourage innovation, individuality and risk-taking, while in *cost leadership*, culture might encourage frugality, discipline and attention to detail.

In line with contingency theory, Porter argues that there is no such thing as a good or bad culture. Rather, he suggests that culture is a means of achieving competitive advantage and should match the competitive strategy: culture is a means to an end, not an end in itself. Consider, for example, the low-cost airline sector where both *Southwest Airlines* (a pioneer in this field) and *Ryanair* pursue a no-frills approach but yet are decidedly different in terms of organisational culture. *Southwest* is unionised and extremely customer-focused, while *Ryanair* remains non-union and on the customer services front it has historically pursued a minimalist approach but in recent years it has begun to turn around its reputation in this area.

For the past three decades, numerous authors have developed models of 'best fit' strategy–HRM linkages. While some of these have focused on the link between an organisation's stage of development (growth, maturity, decline, etc.) and HRM, by far the most influential have been those focused on promoting fit between the firm's competitive strategy and HRM. We now briefly consider some of the most established best-fit HRM models.

SCHULER'S 'STRATEGY – EMPLOYEE BEHAVIOUR' MODEL

Some of the most extensive work on matching business strategy and HRM has been conducted by Randall Schuler and his colleagues in the US. This work suggests that business strategies are most effective when they are systematically co-ordinated with HRM practices. Of particular note is the suggestion that the key focus of HRM should be to develop employee behaviours that 'fit' the organisation's chosen competitive strategy (Schuler 1987, 1989; Schuler and Jackson 1987a). Employing Porter's generic competitive strategies, this approach argues that firms should deploy HRM policies and practices that develop and reinforce employee behaviours best suited to achieving the chosen competitive strategy (cost leadership, differentiation or focus) Thus, for a chosen competitive strategy to be successful, it has to be supported by particular patterns of employee behaviour, which can be shaped by the organisation's HR strategies, policies and practices: see Figure 3.3.

This model identifies three alternative HRM strategy types *accumulation*, *utilisation* and *facilitation*, each designed to develop and reinforce particular employee behaviour patterns to facilitate the achievement of the chosen competitive strategy:

- Firms following a *focus* competitive strategy require an 'accumulation' HRM strategy, which emphasises careful selection based on personality rather than technical fit, and an emphasis on training, egalitarian pay structures and lifetime employment.
- Organisations following a *cost leadership* competitive strategy require a HRM 'utilisation' strategy, based on selecting individuals on the basis of technical ability and emphasising cost minimisation in terms of training, and so forth.
- Organisations following a *differentiation* strategy require a 'facilitation' HRM strategy, focused on the ability of individuals to work together via cross-functional work teams and the use of job rotation and career planning to help foster a collaborative work climate.

FOMBRUN'S 'STRATEGY IMPLEMENTATION' MODEL

Also espousing of the 'best fit' approach, Fombrun *et al.* (1984) developed a model linking strategy, organisation structure and HRM. Suggesting that the integration of HRM considerations into strategic decision-making represented 'a true frontier' in workforce management, they cautioned that while many organisations wish to include HR issues in strategic decision-making, the traditional approach has been to consider these issues only after strategic decisions have been taken. They also observed that often the major emphasis in strategic planning has been on strategy formulation, with very little thought being given to strategy implementation, sometimes resulting in the failure of strategic planning at the operational level (Pfeffer and Sutton 2006).

Figure 3.3 Linking business strategy and HRM

BUSINESS STRATEGY	HR STRATEGY	DESIRED EMPLOYEE BEHAVIOURS		HRM POLICY AND ACTIVITY FOCUS
Cost leadership	Utilisation	Relatively repetitive and predictable behaviour	Recruitment	Explicit job analysis Mostly internal recruitment/labour market focus
		Mostly short-term focus High concern for quantity Moderate concern for quality	Appraisal	Short-term focus; individual criteria; results-oriented criteria
			Rewards	Hierarchical pay; few incentives
		Major emphasis on results	Training and Development	Narrow career paths; limited training
		Comfortable with stability	Employee Relations	Little employment security; low employee participation; 'traditional' industrial relations
Differentiation	Facilitation	Long-term focus	Recruitment	Implicit job analysis; external recruitment/labour market focus
		Creative job behaviour High level of independent co-operative behaviour	Appraisal	Long-term focus; process and results criteria; some group criteria
		Moderate concern for quality	Rewards	Egalitarian pay; numerous incentives
		Moderate concern for quantity	Training and Development	Broad career paths; extensive training
		Equal concern for focus and results Tolerance of ambiguity	Employee Relations	High employee participation; co-operative labour management relations; some employment security
Focus	Accumulation	Relatively predictable and repetitive behaviour Long-/medium-term focus	Recruitment	Explicit job analysis; some external recruitment
		High concern for quality Moderate concern for quantity	Appraisal	Long-term focus; process and results criteria; Some group criteria
			Rewards	Egalitarian pay; numerous incentives
		Concern for process and results	Training and Development	Broad career paths; extensive training and development
		Commitment to organisation goals	Employee Relations	High employee participation; co-operative labour management relations; some employment security

Source: Adapted from Schuler (1987, 1989, 1996); Schuler and Jackson (1987a and b).

This lack of attention to strategy implementation is seen as a major challenge to organisations, and provides a potentially central role for HRM in ensuring that employees work to make strategies happen. Thus, a central plank of the Fombrun *et al.* model is that HRM plays a crucial role in effective strategy implementation, providing the key to implementing strategic choice and to achieving better alignment between strategic direction and HRM policy and practice.

The model proposed by Fombrun and his colleagues posits strategic management consideration of three key issues (Fombrun *et al.* 1984):

1. *Mission and strategy*: identification of an organisation's purpose and its plan for how this can be achieved.
2. *Formal structure*: for the organisation of people and tasks to achieve mission and strategy.
3. *HRM systems*: recruitment, development, evaluation and reward of employees.

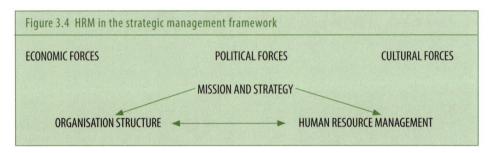

Figure 3.4 HRM in the strategic management framework

This framework, represented in Figure 3.4, differs from traditional approaches to strategic management by incorporating HRM considerations as an integral component of strategic decision-making. Fombrun *et al.* (1984) further suggest that an organisation's HRM approach tends to reflect managerial assumptions about employees and 'appropriate' workforce management practices. Fombrun (1986) identifies four key aspects of organisational approaches to workforce management that give valuable insights into the managerial approach to employees:

1. *The nature of the psychological contract*: This may range from, at one extreme, a managerial perspective that views employees in instrumental terms and emphasises high levels of control of both employees and the work environment to, at the other extreme, an approach that sees employees as able and instinctive beings who should be afforded challenging and meaningful work in an agreeable work environment.
2. *Level of employee involvement*: Organisational approaches may vary from those with high levels of employee involvement in decision-making to those where decisions are solely a management prerogative.
3. *Internal/external labour market*: This addresses the relative emphasis on internal versus external recruitment and related differences in emphasis on employee development.
4. *Performance evaluation*: This factor addresses the relevant managerial emphasis on group versus individual performance evaluation.

Fombrun further argues that HRM systems need to become more flexible so as to 'fit' strategic choice. Four key areas of HRM are identified where management should ensure their respective approach fits the chosen competitive strategy: (i) selection/promotion/placement; (ii) appraisal; (iii) rewards; and (iv) employee development. His model evaluates each of these in relation to its strategy fit.

MILES AND SNOW'S 'STRATEGY – HR FIT' MODEL

A third model in the 'best fit' competitive strategy tradition was advanced by Miles and Snow (1978; 1984). They advanced three generic strategy types, namely 'defenders', 'prospectors' and 'analysers':

- *Defenders* seek stability by producing only a limited set of products directed at a narrow segment of the total potential market.
- *Prospectors* are almost the opposite of defenders; their strength is in finding and exploiting new product and market opportunities.
- *Analysers* try to capitalise on the best of both other strategy types as they seek to minimise risk and maximise opportunity for profit. The strategy here is to move into new products or new markets only after viability has been proved by Prospectors.

Miles and Snow suggest that these three basic types of strategic behaviour can be associated with particular HRM configurations, as outlined in Figure 3.5.

Figure 3.5 Linking business strategy and HR policy

	STRATEGIC TYPE		
	DEFENDER	PROSPECTOR	ANALYSER
PRODUCT and MARKET STRATEGY	Limited, stable product line Predictable markets	Broad, changing product line Changing markets	Stable and changing product lines Predictable and changing markets
RESEARCH and DEVELOPMENT	Narrow; product improvement	Broad; new product development	Focused; 'second to market'
MARKETING	Sales emphasis	Market research emphasis	Extensive marketing campaigns
HR STRATEGY	Maintenance	Entrepreneurial	Co-ordination
RECRUITMENT and SELECTION	'Make'; internal	'Buy'; external	'Make and Buy'; mixed
MANPOWER and PLANNING	Formal, extensive	Informal, limited	Formal, extensive
TRAINING and DEVELOPMENT	Extensive; skill building	Limited; skill acquisition	Extensive; skill building

	STRATEGIC TYPE		
	DEFENDER	PROSPECTOR	ANALYSER
APPRAISAL	Process-oriented; identify training needs; individual/group performance evaluation	Results-oriented; identify staffing needs; corporate/division performance evaluation	Process-oriented; identify training and staffing needs; individual/group/divisional performance evaluation
REWARDS	Based on level in hierarchy; internal equity; pay-oriented	Based on performance; external equity; incentive-oriented	Mostly based on level in hierarchy; internal and external comparisons; pay and incentive-orientated

Source: Adapted from Miles and Snow (1984).

Combining academic insights with observations from practice, they draw upon three specific case study examples to illustrate strategy–HR 'fit', namely a Defender (*Lincoln Electric*), a Prospector (*Hewlett Packard*) and an Analyser (*Texas Instruments*).

In *Defender* organisations, the emphasis is on building the organisation's HR capacity through recruitment at entry levels and internal promotion. The key HR activities are: selection, placement, training, development, appraisal, and ensuring a fit between the reward system and job design. Defender organisations are characterised as lean and hard-working, and demand predictable, planned HR policies and regular maintenance of these policies.

Prospector organisations experience rapid change, demanding considerable HR redeployment. The major HR focus is on sourcing and deploying high-quality personnel. The HR management objective is entrepreneurial, acquiring and developing critical staff. There is little opportunity for long-term planning or sophisticated HRM techniques.

In *Analyser* organisations, the emphasis is on developing appropriate organisational structures and management approaches with the HRM focus on co-ordinating policies and allocating personnel optimally across the organisation.

CRITICISMS OF 'BEST FIT' APPROACHES

Despite the advances that models have brought, there remain numerous criticisms of 'best fit' approaches. First, and most significantly, commentators point to the lack of sophistication in identifying and describing 'strategy' (Ferris *et al.* 1999; Boxall and Purcell 2000). Ferris *et al.* (1999: 387) find that linking HRM with business strategy remains 'troublesome', principally because of the measures of strategy used in the studies to date. In their review, they plausibly note that:

> Recent conceptual pieces have been critical of researchers in this area, suggesting that they have incorporated antiquated notions of firm strategy. Most studies have utilised

such typologies as those of Porter (1980) or Miles and Snow (1978). These generic categorisations have little in common with the realities of the modern competitive environment with which organisations are confronted. First, categorisations are exclusive, assuming that organisations pursue a certain strategic goal while ignoring other strategic concerns. Second, they depict the competitive environment, and consequently organisational strategy, as being static instead of dynamic.

In light of this, Ferris *et al.* suggest that future tests of the HRM–strategy relationship must view strategy along a broader continuum involving a wider range of strategic factors and must conceptualise it as a dynamic, rather than as a static, phenomenon. Finally, they suggest that the almost exclusive focus on deliberate or intended strategy, to the detriment of the emergent or realised strategy, remains problematic. It, they suggest, represents a 'flawed reality' in the context of the omnipresent unstable, dynamic environments that we have all become accustomed to.

This suggests that the assumption of a necessary fit between HRM and strategy may not hold (Paauwe 2004). Indeed, some have argued that a rigid 'fit' between strategy and HRM may actually hinder the innovation and flexibility often considered necessary for strategic success (e.g. Dyer and Erickson 2005). In their quarter-century review of HRM 'best fit' authors, Schuler and Jackson (2005: 14) themselves note the need to move from mechanistic and static views of HRM towards approaches which explore how HRM systems evolve and change in accordance with their dynamic context.

A further conceptual difficulty with 'best fit' approaches is the reality that some of the most successful organisations are those that compete simultaneously on each of the competitive strategy dimensions, namely low cost, high quality and innovation. A plausible Irish example is *Dunnes Stores*. Once heralded as one of the 'kings' of low cost ('Dunnes Stores' better value beats them all!'), the company now competes much more aggressively across a range of other dimensions, particularly on quality and product range. In the past, such firms would have been viewed as 'stuck in the middle' and consequently doomed to failure. However, organisations are now encouraged to compete on the basis of *both* low cost *and* differentiation (Kim and Mauborgne 2009).

It would also appear that the 'best fit' literature overestimates the extent of management prerogative in choosing the most 'appropriate' HR policies and underestimates contextual influences on outcomes. Boxall and Purcell (2000) note the need for organisations to comply with prevailing traditions and legal requirements. For example, a particular organisation's preferred HR approach may be to avoid trade unions and collective bargaining, but local tradition and legislation may require them to engage in this activity. Similarly, particular labour or product market conditions may force organisations to employ policies that they would not ideally choose, or indeed that do not 'fit' with their business strategy. For example, labour shortages among particular employee categories may lead some organisations to provide special incentives and HR policies to attract and retain such employees, even though such polices may be out of line with their preferred HR approach and with policies pertaining to other employee categories.

'BEST PRACTICE' OR UNIVERSALISTIC APPROACHES

'Best practice' or universalistic approaches involve the identification of the 'best way' of undertaking a particular management function and ensuring that this 'best way' is applied in all instances, regardless of context (Gooderham et al. 2004; Boxall and Purcell 2000; Brewster et al. 2000). With regard to HRM, it posits that if organisations adopt a set of best HR practices they will reap returns in terms of enhanced performance:

> Proponents of the universalistic [best practice] perspective . . . contend that there is one 'best' way to manage human resources in firms. In this stream of work . . . [HRM] is viewed as the implementation of a set of high-performance work practices . . . to motivate and facilitate worker contribution to organization success.
>
> Harrell-Cook (2002: 33)

The 'best practice' school thus rejects contingency approaches ('best fit') and encourages organisations to adopt particular HR practices in areas such as employee selection, rewards, development and involvement. The primary emphasis is on achieving 'horizontal' fit, i.e. ensuring that practice across different HR areas (e.g. selection, training, rewards, etc.) is consistent and complementary.

While best practice HRM is most often associated with the work of Pfeffer (1994, 1998a, 1998b) (see discussion below), its roots can be traced back somewhat further. The Harvard Business School (HBS) model (Beer et al. 1984) encouraged top management teams to deploy a set of 'pro-employee' policies in four key areas of HRM (reward systems, HR flow, work systems and employee influence/involvement), suggesting that this would yield both tangible benefits for the organisation (high commitment, enhanced competencies, better employment relations and greater cost-effectiveness), and long-term benefits in terms of employee wellbeing, organisational effectiveness and societal wellbeing. This model has formed the basis for what is sometimes termed 'soft' HRM, whereby senior management recognise that people are the organisation's 'most valuable' resource and deploy a set of employee-oriented policies to nurture and develop this resource (Walton 1985b). Similarly, Arthur (1992, 1994) found that HR approaches focused on increasing employee commitment (i.e. high levels of training and employee participation, good rewards and decentralised decision-making) led to higher performance, while HR approaches focused on control, efficiency and reduced employee discretion were associated with high labour turnover and poor performance.

The upsurge in interest in the idea of 'best practice' HRM is led in large measure by Pfeffer's (1994, 1998a) identification of 'best' HRM practices which, he argues, can enhance performance (e.g. higher profits, greater sales, etc.) regardless of the basis upon which firms seek to compete. He further contends that the benefits can be even more pronounced when complementary sets of HR practices ('HR bundles') are used together. Pfeffer identifies seven specific HRM practices, which, when used together, he argues, will lead to higher revenue, increased profits and market value and organisational survival (see also Huselid 1995; Pfeffer and Viega 1999). These seven key HRM practices are outlined in Table 3.1.

Pfeffer's work draws on a comparatively small number of case studies to establish his argument that HRM practice leads to superior organisational performance and sustained competitive advantage. This work has also been closely linked with the concept of high-performance work systems (HPWS) and with the work practices and HR policies used in a number of 'high-tech' US companies (see Walton 1985a; Lawler 1986). Pfeffer's approach might be best labelled as a 'pure' best practice perspective (universalism), and it differs from the more empirical HPWS studies by Arthur (1992, 1994) and others. While Pfeffer's work is essentially prescriptive, arguing that a standard set of HR practices should be adopted by firms in general, many of the HPWS studies considered the impact of strategy and other organisations in their search for an optimal 'bundling' of HR practices.

Table 3.1 Pfeffer's seven key HRM practices

1. *Employment security*	Viewed as fundamental to securing employee commitment, ensuring employees continue to contribute to improved productivity, promoting long-term thinking and generally underpinning the other HR practices.
2. *Targeted selection*	Focus on selective hiring of outstanding people to ensure the organisation has the competencies to build effectiveness and performance.
3. *Workplace teams and decentralisation*	Utilisation of self-managed teams and decentralisation in decision-making. This is viewed as an important means of pooling ideas and process improvement and also as a way of reducing layers of hierarchy.
4. *High pay contingent on organisational performance*	Focus on 'above the norm' compensation and performance-related rewards to 'incentivise' superior performance.
5. *Employee training*	Strong focus on training to ensure employees have the capability to deal proactively with workplace challenges.
6. *Reduction of status differentials*	Emphasis on developing an egalitarian workplace and removal of status differentials (e.g. differing benefits such as healthcare or differing control mechanisms such as 'clocking in'). Seen as important in promoting a more open management style.
7. *Business information-sharing with employees*	Focus on sharing business and financial information. Seen as important means of developing employee commitment and trust. Provides employees with adequate context for decision-making in teams.

A precise definition of an HPWS is difficult to come by, but it is based on the premise that organisation performance can be improved through the implementation of co-ordinated bundles of particular practices, notably employee participation, team-working and communications, that when combined develop high levels of employee commitment, involvement and flexibility.

One of the more influential of the HPWS studies is that of Huselid (1995), whose work points to a positive causal link between particular 'bundles' of HR practice and organisation performance (as measured by productivity, employee turnover and financial performance). The essence of Huselid's work is that particular 'high-performance' HR practices (including comprehensive employee recruitment and selection procedures, 'incentive' compensation and performance management systems, and extensive employee involvement and training) impact positively on the bottom line. Drawing on data from a large-scale survey of US firms, Huselid (1995: 667) found a strong positive relationship between high-performance work practices and firm performance:

> Prior work in both the academic and popular press has argued that the use of High Performance Work Practices will be reflected in better firm performance. This study provides broad evidence in support of these assertions. Across a wider range of industries and firm sizes, I found considerable support for the hypothesis that investments in such practices are associated with lower employee turnover and greater productivity and corporate financial performance.

These findings are quite emphatic. Huselid (ibid. 667) finds evidence of strong and positive linkages between HR practice bundles and organisation performance. Indeed, he goes on to calculate the dimensions of such linkages and argues that the 'magnitude of the returns for investments in high-performance work practices is substantial':

> A one standard deviation increase in such practices is associated with a relative 7.05 per cent decrease in turnover and, on a per employee basis, $27,044 more in sales and $18,641 and $3,814 more in market value and profits, respectively. These internally consistent and economically and statistically significant values suggest that firms can indeed obtain substantial financial benefits from investing in the practices studied . . .
> Huselid (1995: 667)

Attempts to better demonstrate the linkage between HRM and organisational performance have consumed much of HRM research in the period since Huselid's work. To illustrate this point, a subsequent meta-analysis using data from 92 studies, covering over 19,000 organisations, found that 20 per cent of the utility available from predicting performance differences between organisations was attributable to HPWS (Combs et al. 2006). However, others are more sceptical: Paauwe and Boselie (2005: 74) argue that 'there is little or no convincing empirical evidence that coherent and consistent [HR] systems or bundles automatically lead to higher performance'. This leads us on to some of the key criticisms that can be directed at universalistic or best practice approaches.

CRITICISMS OF 'BEST PRACTICE'

A first and important criticism of best practice approaches is the problem of definition. As alluded to above, there is no uniformly agreed definition which poses challenges to the building of an evidence-based body of knowledge. While there may be some broad agreement that high-performance work systems 'enhance employees' skills, commitment and productivity in such a way that employees become a source of competitive advantage' (Datta et al. 2005:135), one finds contradictory prescriptions as to the precise mix of practices actually involved (see Becker and Gerhart 1996; Combs et al. 2006). For example, there are different views on whether the degree of emphasis on individual performance-related pay is consistent with a corresponding emphasis placed on teamwork (Arthur 1994; Huselid 1995; Pfeffer 1994). Some authors emphasise the use of internal promotions (e.g. Huselid 1995; Pfeffer 1994), while others argue that this leads to a more inflexible HR system and greater bureaucracy, intense unionisation and lower levels of productivity (Arthur 1994; Ichniowski et al. 1996).

Second, there is little consensus on how HRM should be measured (e.g. indices, scales, clusters), while much best practice research suffers from a number of methodological flaws (see Lewin 2001). Of particular note is the over-sampling of manufacturing (and consequently a potential under-representation of the services sector), over-reliance on snapshot surveys and the limited number of longitudinal and case-based studies. A notable exception in this latter regard is MacDuffie's study of the impact of HR policies on performance in the international automobile sector (MacDuffie 1995; Pil and MacDuffie 1996). Yet even here, reworking of the original data has questioned whether key findings should have been interpreted as supportive of a universal argument or instead exhibit significant 'contextual interactions' (Porter and Siggelkow 2008: 51). Other concerns relate to difficulties with the particular measures of organisation performance used (see below) and concerns about direction of causality: is it that certain HRM practices lead to organisational success or that organisational success gives firms the wherewithal to deploy certain HRM practices? Finally, it appears that many of the best practice studies, such as Huselid (1995), rely on single or, at most, two respondents. More often than not, this tends to be the HR practitioner. However, Purcell (1999) and others suggest that HR specialists have neither 'detailed knowledge about competitive strategies nor the proportion of sales which are derived from these strategies', and argue that 'considerable caution is needed when interpreting conclusions from these quantitative studies' (Marchington and Wilkinson 2005: 93). Similarly, Gerhart (2007: 558) cautions that low inter-rater reliabilities can mean that the HR practice scores a researcher obtains for a particular organisation, depend more on the particular persons completing the survey than on what practices are actually used in the organisation.

Third, if deep-set concerns remain over the measurement of HRM, this is also true of the dependent variable typically used in such studies, namely organisational performance. We noted earlier the impact of Huselid's work, which found that certain ('high-performance') HR practices had a predictable and demonstrable impact on bottom line measures of organisation performance, namely financial turnover, sales, market value and profitability. However, in comparing performance along these dimensions there is a risk of ignoring the sector-specific nature of turnover and performance (e.g. retail vs. pharmaceuticals). Moreover, case study evidence from the UK on the impact of HRM on performance found that none of the HR directors interviewed was particularly concerned about demonstrating any links between HR interventions and profitability or shareholder value (Purcell 2004).

This finding is not as remarkable as it may first appear. Measures such as profitability are lag indicators and can be impacted upon by numerous factors, many of which are beyond the realm of management control, such as currency movements, commodity prices and developments in the international economy and international affairs. One might consider, for example, the impact of 9/11 or the *dot.com* downturn on Irish enterprises in the tourism and ICT sectors. Purcell (2004: 17) argues that the connection between HRM and such lag measures is 'too stretched or distant with too many other variables' influencing profitability for it be a useful measure. However, this finding did not mean that these managers were not concerned with the impact of HR on performance – quite the contrary. They paid considerable attention to the role HR played in improving performance, but did so using 'lead indicators', which focused on more immediate measures of HR performance. Three principal measures were used: (i) labour market measures such as labour turnover, labour retention, absenteeism and accident rates; (ii) employee satisfaction measures, which were often linked to opinion survey findings; and (iii) operational measures, such as down time, scrap levels, time delays and customer retention. These present a more proximate and direct measure of the impact of HRM on performance.

Fourth, best practice or HPWS research focuses exclusively on 'high-involvement' (people-centric) approaches, with little or no consideration of the role and impact of 'low-involvement' (structure-centric) work systems (Lawler, 2008). This is all the more surprising given widespread international evidence that increasing demands are being placed on employees, and that employer power and prerogative in the workplace is on the rise.

Finally, Posthuma et al. (2013) argue that we need a fuller mapping of the factors affecting alignment of HPWS practices, suggesting that several questions arise including, for example, in what contexts do organizations adopt different system architectures for different employee cohorts (e.g. core employees vs. contractors and temporary employees), and when and how do these different architectures matter?

Overall, there is little doubt that the best fit and best practice streams of research discussed above have done much to invigorate HRM as an area of strategic significance (Wood 1999). Nonetheless, as we have seen, research samples are typically drawn from large, well-known organisations, so that it is difficult to generalise across organisations and contexts. In the first instance, it is not immediately obvious that the benefits yielded from high-performance work systems will necessarily outweigh the costs associated with their introduction (Cappelli and Neumark 2001). Second, research examining specific contexts, e.g. smaller organisations (Harney and Dundon 2006), or specific types of worker, e.g. highly skilled professionals (Chasserio and Legault 2009), has found that sophisticated HRM practices may not always be viable or even necessary. Moreover, even if realised in practice, the logic of 'best' practice or 'best' fit appears problematic as it implies standardisation, with organisations converging by having the same practices in place (Delbridge and Whitfield 2007). However, it has long been recognised that employers may deliberately deploy unique employment practices as a distinctive means of product market competition (Brown 2008). To date, such considerations have largely been neglected as much HRM research has been consumed by a desire to robustly *demonstrate* HRM's performance effects. Yet while this quest may have been necessary to better establish the field of HRM, it is hardly sufficient to advance *understanding* (Purcell and Hutchinson 2007; Harney 2009). What is required is deeper theoretical explanation and insights into the actual processes by which HRM impacts performance. This involves incorporating the key aspects of human agency which may determine the nature and extent of HRM practices that are introduced and the manner in which they are implemented (Harney and Jordan 2008). More recent models have, by moving beyond the best practice/best fit argument, begun to address this task.

BEYOND BEST FIT AND BEST PRACTICE: BROADENING THE HR-ORGANISATIONAL PERFORMANCE DEBATE

While criticisms of HRM's links with strategy and impact on bottom line performance are well founded, such work has nevertheless advanced knowledge in this key area. For example, although there has been some considerable criticism of Huselid's work (see Purcell 1999), and while one might justifiably harbour reservations about some of the findings on the impact of HRM practices on bottom line performance – especially the apparent precision of the financial benefits outlined above – an important contribution of the work of Huselid and others is that it demonstrates the potential for performance improvement to be gained from using particular 'bundles' of HR practices. This contribution should not be overstated however. While research points to the potential performance benefits that may accrue from investment in HR, such benefits are not universally applicable. Work by writers such as MacDuffie (1995) and Marchington and Grugulis (2002) suggests that 'best practice' HRM may lead to performance improvements only under certain conditions. For example, where employees have specific and much-needed skills/knowledge that take time to develop and nurture, and where the rewards for such HR investment outweigh the costs:

> Innovative human resource practices are likely to contribute to improved economic performance only when three conditions are met: when employees possess knowledge and skills that managers lack; when employees are motivated to apply this skill and knowledge through discretionary effort; and when the firm's business or production strategy can only be achieved when employees contribute such discretionary effort.
>
> MacDuffie (1995: 199)

As alluded to earlier, a related and important implication of this work is that it is the *linkage* between different HRM practices that is important, rather than the implementation of a specific and isolated HR practice. Thus, it is the so-called 'bundling' of HR practices that have the potential to yield gains in organisational performance (Subramony 2009). As Guest (1998: 65) comments:

> One thing is clear from all of the research: there is no value in investing heavily in specific practices. Performance-related pay, psychometric tests in selection or extensive training will not in themselves bring bottom-line results. The key lies in having the right 'bundle' of practices and the challenge for personnel managers is to find it.

However, Becker *et al.* (1997: 43) warn about the adoption of possible 'deadly combinations' that may develop within organisations when HR practices are utilised that:

> ... might well make sense in isolation but when evaluated within the context of other HRM practices deployed throughout the firm are a recipe for disaster. Simple examples can be found in firms that invest in sophisticated performance management systems only to adopt compensation policies that provide for little meaningful economic distinction between high and low performing employees; or firms that encourage employees to work together in teams, but then provide raises based on individual contributions.

Boxall and Purcell's (2003, 2008) work on linking HRM to business performance broadens the debate to address some of these caveats: see Figure 3.6. This starts by positing two broad goals for business organisations: (i) securing viability with adequate profitability; and (ii) achieving some form of sustained competitive advantage. It follows that organisations will seek to use their human and other resources to achieve these business goals. In the HR sphere, Boxall and Purcell (2003: 8) identify three 'critical HR goals' or 'performance domains', namely: (i) labour productivity; (ii) organisational flexibility; and (iii) social legitimacy. They argue that an 'outstanding mix of outcomes' in all three domains makes for 'superior performance in HRM' and (most likely) sustained competitive advantage.

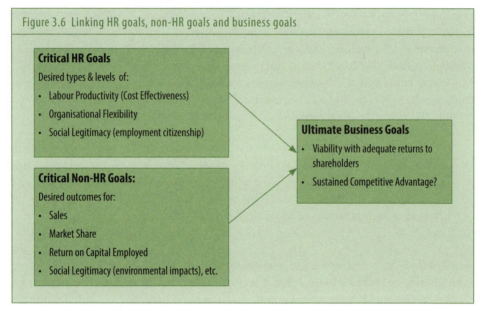

Figure 3.6 Linking HR goals, non-HR goals and business goals

Source: Boxall and Purcell (2003: 7).

CRITICAL HR GOALS

1. **Labour productivity** – the value of labour outputs in relation to the cost of labour inputs. This domain represents the key measure of cost-effectiveness and the 'touchstone against which every new HR policy ought to be evaluated: will it make labour more productive and will its costs, or the investment it implies, be justified?' (Boxall and Purcell 2003: 8). Such evaluation applies both at the level of individual HR practices (e.g. evaluating the costs and benefits of introducing a particular HR intervention, such as formal performance appraisal) and in regard to the organisation's overall approach to HR (is the overall approach giving adequate returns in terms of productivity?). As mentioned earlier, expensive 'soft' HRM approaches (high levels of rewards, training, etc.) may be appropriate for organisations in capital-intensive 'high-tech' environments where labour represents a low proportion of overall costs. A particular example relates to certain organisations in the pharmaceutical sector in Ireland that are involved in the production of premium-price drugs, where it is critical to maintain continuity of supply (e.g. *Pfizer, Merck*). The opposite may be the case among many small organisations acting as sub-suppliers to major multinationals

or in sectors characterised by intense price competition, where labour represents a high proportion of total costs (e.g. clothing manufacture). Reflecting this importance, labour productivity has been increasingly incorporated as a key element in more sophisticated studies exploring HRM's impact (Datta et al. 2005; Guthrie et al. 2009).

2. **Organisational flexibility** – an organisation's capacity to change. Here, Boxall and Purcell (2008) distinguish between two types of flexibility: 'short-run responsiveness'; and 'long-run agility'. Short-run responsiveness incorporates functional (ability to deploy personnel across a range of different job tasks), numerical (ability to take on and shed labour in line with business demand) and financial (ability to link wages to the labour market context and to evaluations of individual performance) flexibility. Long-run agility refers to an organisation's ability to cope effectively with developments in the business environment. This is an altogether more 'woolly' but nevertheless critical HR concern, addressing the extent to which organisations have the capacity to deal with changes in the environment (see also Dyer and Ericksen 2005). There is clearly great potential for conflict between short-run responsiveness and long-run agility. For example, organisations may shed key personnel during a business downturn and consequently lose valuable knowledge and skills that may be required to deal with longer-term changes in its competitive environment.

3. **Social legitimacy** – while the previous two HR performance domains focus on bottom line performance, Boxall and Purcell (2008) argue that organisations must also concern themselves with their standing as an employer, or what they term 'employment citizenship'. This will focus in large measure on how organisations behave with regard to prevailing social norms and government regulation of employment practice and conditions (Boon et al. 2009). However, 'employment citizenship' is only one element of social legitimacy, which also embraces other aspects of social standing – the impact on the environment and general corporate social responsibility. This is in line with Elkington's (1997) concept of a 'triple bottom line' – namely that organisations must be concerned with their performance with reference to financial, environmental and social criteria. It also resonates with Kaplan and Norton's (1996) 'balanced score card', which identifies three key stakeholders in organisations, namely shareholders, customers and employees. Similarly, Paauwe (2004: 3) argues that assessment of HRM should not just be about economic rationality but also about relational rationality manifest in efforts to achieve fairness and legitimacy. In Ireland and internationally, it is clear that firms vary in their approach to employment citizenship. While some clearly aspire to become 'employers of choice' in their particular region or labour market, others will seek to comply minimally or to apply standards below those provided for by legislation or social norms.

Boxall and Purcell's work illustrates the importance of 'bundling' HR practices, as mentioned earlier. Seeking to improve performance in a key domain (e.g. labour productivity) is likely to involve interventions across a number of HR activity areas, such as training, motivation or rewards. However, it is clear that performance in other domains (e.g. flexibility) will require interventions in some similar areas (e.g. training). Thus, the co-ordination of HR interventions represents a key challenge in ensuring HR contributes to organisation performance.

A related and critical consideration raised by Boxall and Purcell (2008: 20) is the inevitability of what they term 'strategic tensions' in regard to HR performance. They identify three major areas where these may arise, namely labour scarcity, motivation and change. Strategic tensions in these areas help capture the power and politics or 'structured antagonism' (Edwards 1986: 5) inherent in the operation of the employment relationship.

To perform well with regard to labour productivity and flexibility, one would expect an organisation to attract and develop highly skilled and competent employees. However, certain categories of employee may be in scarce supply, for example highly qualified information technology or healthcare workers. As a result, they may be forced to compete aggressively for such labour. Inevitably, some will be more successful than others. In Ireland, you will often find that certain large, successful multinationals have the financial resources to provide rewards, training and other incentives necessary to attract such staff. However, others, particularly smaller organisations, may not have such capacity and consequently suffer from problems of labour quality and retention:

> The goals of securing reasonable productivity . . . and building some capacity for development . . . are seriously compromised if the firm cannot make competitive job offers. It then struggles to build capabilities . . . In the extreme, the tension associated with labour scarcity can become a full blown 'capability crisis', compromising productivity and profitability and threatening the firm's reputation and viability.
>
> Boxall and Purcell (2003: 14)

The second area of strategic tension, worker motivation, addresses potential trade-offs between employer (and managerial) interests *vis-à-vis* employee interests. Addressing such tensions often falls within the area of employee relations, and what has been termed the 'wage–effort' bargain. It addresses how employers and workers behave towards each other in the workplace: Will employees work to the best of their ability and deliver on criteria such as productivity and flexibility? Will employers provide satisfactory working conditions and an environment that ensures a favourable work experience for employees?

We find numerous examples of situations where such aspirations are not met. For instance, there is considerable evidence that demands on employees in many organisations have grown over recent decades, notably regarding increasing workloads and intensification in the pace of work (Wilkinson *et al.* 997; D'Art and Turner 2002; Heffernan and Dundon 2004). A key area where conflicts of interest often arise is the distribution of profits, with employees seeking a greater share based on their contribution to performance, and employers seeking to satisfy other 'constituencies', notably shareholders, senior management and the need for re-investment.

The third and final area of strategic tension in HR identified by Boxall and Purcell (2003) relates to organisation change. They specifically note, first, the potential for conflict between improving performance in regard to productivity and flexibility, and second, the need to achieve a balance between the long-run and short-run capacity of the organisation to deal with change. The former issue was raised in Chapter 2 pertaining to our discussion of some of the paradoxes in the concept of HRM as it developed in the USA in the 1980s. There we noted that attempts, for example, to ensure numerical flexibility may detrimentally impact the organisation's capacity to improve productivity.

A common means of achieving numerical flexibility is to employ a higher proportion of workers on a temporary or contract basis, allowing the organisation to lay off such workers more easily. However, the more tenuous nature of such contracts, and the higher level of labour turnover entailed, increases the difficulty in achieving the levels of workforce competency and commitment necessary to deal with longer-term competitive challenges:

> ... suppose a firm decides to place most of its operating staff on temporary contracts to provide for short-term flexibility ... This reduces the level of fixed cost but is likely to create problems with employee turnover ... Over time, the firm is likely to find that it fails to build the kind of learning process that underpins long-term growth.
>
> Boxall and Purcell (2003: 17)

Of course, those that utilise only permanent contracts can face the opposite challenge. In periods of slack demand, the costs of maintaining full employment may become unsustainable and threaten the financial viability of the organisation. Achieving a balance between these competing tensions is clearly the key – but difficult – challenge for organisations and their HR specialists.

HR AND PERFORMANCE: BROADER CONTEXTUAL AND CONFIGURATIONAL EFFECTS

Moving beyond models of linkages between HRM and organisation performance, we now consider some research evidence which has sought to more broadly landscape contextual effects on the relationship between HR and performance and how different HR combinations or configurations may be appropriate for different categories of employees. On this side of the Atlantic, John Purcell and colleagues at the University of Bath have advanced our understanding of contextual influences. Their work for the Chartered Institute of Personnel and Development (CIPD) has involved case study analyses of the association between HR policies and performance outcomes. It provides some important broader insights into the impact of HRM on firm performance (Hutchinson and Purcell 2003; Purcell et al. 2003; Purcell 2004; Purcell and Hutchinson 2007). This research draws on two important ideas in the literature: (i) the *resource-based view of the firm* (RBV) and its implications for HRM; and (ii) the idea of *discretionary employee behaviour* and how this can be 'triggered'.

RESOURCE-BASED VIEW OF THE FIRM (RBV)

Resource-based view of the firm (RBV) focuses on the link between strategy and an organisation's *internal resources* (physical, capital and human). In the RBV, the sources of competitive advantage are the valuable, and sometimes intangible, resources and competencies within an organisation, such as skill pools, reputation and networks. Clearly human resources have the potential to be one such source. However, to provide sustained competitive advantage these resources must meet a number of criteria, notably: (i) they must add positive value; (ii) they must be rare; (iii) they should be inimitable, or extremely difficult to imitate; and (iv) it should not be possible for competitors to substitute them with another resource (Wright and McMahon 1992). High-quality human capital can be considered to satisfy the above criteria for creating and sustaining superior performance and competitive advantage (Takeuchi *et al.* 2007: 1070).

Drawing on some of the insights provided by the RBV, Purcell and his team's case study investigations explore what they term 'HR advantage'. In so doing they employ Boxall's (1996) distinction between *human capital advantage* and *organisation process advantage*, namely the idea that both people and processes can aid organisational performance. Thus, it is important not only to choose, develop and reward people effectively but also to deploy effective systems and ways of working (e.g. supervisory style, mechanisms for involvement and participation, etc.). Stiles and Kulvisaechana (2003) make a similar distinction in cautioning that identifying and developing human capital is not in itself sufficient to achieve competitive advantage. Rather, they argue that organisations must also possess strong social capital and organisational capital (see Figure 3.7).

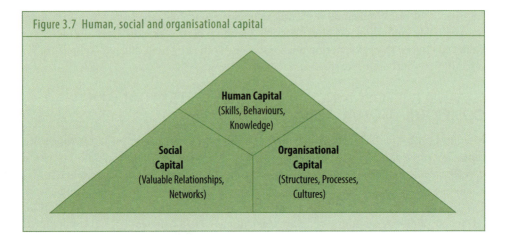

Figure 3.7 Human, social and organisational capital

DISCRETIONARY EMPLOYEE BEHAVIOUR

Discretionary employee behaviour relates to the need to identify how workers could, and why workers should, be encouraged to work at levels of performance above and beyond what might be considered average or acceptable:

> We argued that something must persuade, induce, cajole, or encourage employees to do more or do things better or more innovatively both individually and in working with others than they otherwise would, or were doing in the past. This extra behaviour was discretionary in the sense that it is neither compulsory, nor could be forced. It had to be given.
>
> Purcell (2004: 3)

Consequently, a key challenge for management is to facilitate or 'trigger' such behaviour. The work of Applebaum *et al.* (2000) contends that worker performance is dependent on three key factors: worker *ability* (A), worker *motivation* (M), and adequate *opportunity* (O) to perform. This is generally expressed by the equation:

$$P = f(A, M, O), \text{ where } P = \text{Performance}$$

Thus, superior worker performance is most likely to occur where workers have: (i) the requisite ability ('They *can do* the job because they possess the necessary knowledge and skills'); (ii) the requisite motivation ('They *will do* the job because they are adequately incentivised'); and (iii) an adequate and supportive working environment ('e.g. functioning technology and the opportunity to be heard when problems occur') (Purcell 2004: 4).

University of Bath – People and Performance Model

Using the P = f (A, M, O) equation, Purcell and his University of Bath team identified some eleven HR policy areas that they considered important in impacting on performance (see Figure 3.8). They used this model in examining each of their twelve case studies, a number of which were selected because of their reputation as innovators in HRM.

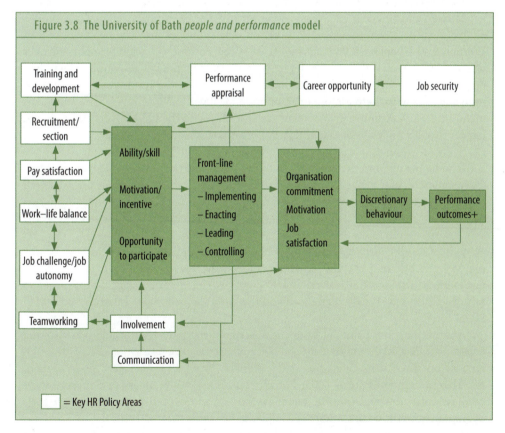

Figure 3.8 The University of Bath *people and performance* model

The first key finding was that a clear and shared sense of an organisation's *mission*, *values* and *culture* was important. This was termed the 'big idea' or 'a clear sense of mission underpinned by values and a culture expressing what the organisation is and its relationship with its customers and employees' (Purcell 2004: 7). It was seen as a key element to 'inform and enthuse' HR policy and practice and that it might be different in different organisations. For example in *Jaguar* the big idea was 'quality', while in *Selfridges* it was being 'friendly, aspirational and bold'. Six of the twelve companies studied had a 'big idea' and all of these reported higher levels of organisation commitment, a factor widely considered critical in contributing to performance (*see* Applebaum *et al.* 2000; Barney 1997; Coyle-Shapiro *et al.* 2004).

A second important finding of the University of Bath research was the critical role played by *front line managers* (FLMs), e.g. supervisors, team/section leaders and so forth, in bridging the gap 'between espoused and enacted policies' and thus in 'bringing HR policies to life' (Purcell 2004: 11; see also Hutchinson and Purcell 2003):

> . . . the really important finding was that the employees' experience of HR policy and practice was strongly mediated by the way front line managers (FLMs) sought to implement a given policy, their enthusiasm in doing so (what we call 'enacted') and their wider role in leading a team or section and in controlling things like quality, lateness and absence.

We noted in Chapters 1 and 2 how this role has become even more important over recent years due to (i) the greater emphasis on returning more HR responsibilities to line managers; and (ii) the fact that the employment relationship has become increasingly individualised (e.g. there is more focus on individual performance reviews, development mentoring, etc.). Again, it was a worker's relationship with their FLM which was found to impact strongly on levels of commitment, job satisfaction and motivation:

> The higher employees rate FLMs in terms of the way they manage people: the more committed and satisfied those employees will be and the higher their levels of (self reported) job discretion.
>
> Hutchinson and Purcell (2003: 14)

A study of a call centre operating in Ireland likewise finds support for the critical role played by FLMs. In particular, in this context team leaders were seen to act as key mediators in the implementation of HR practices, ameliorating some of the negative aspects of how HRM was experienced and the nature of work tasks (Harney and Jordan 2008).

Another important finding from the Bath University team's research was that the *impact of HR policies varied between different occupational categories*. Their research focused on three such categories: 'professionals', 'front line managers' and 'workers' (cf. Hutchinson and Purcell 2003; Purcell *et al.* 2003). A summary of the preferences of these categories and the HR factors positively and negatively impacting on their commitment to the organisation are summarised in Table 3.2 and Box 3.1.

The final important finding from the University of Bath research was that *dissatisfaction with existing policies is a more powerful demotivator than an absence of policies*. The clear message here is that if management are to employ a particular HR policy it is critical to get it right.

Table 3.2 HR policies positively and negatively linked to organisation commitment

	Positive	Negative
Professional workers	• Communication • Reward/recognition • Appraisal • Effort • Relationship with managers • Career opportunity	• Poor management leadership • Lack of job challenge • Unsatisfactory work–life balance • Poor employee relations climate
Front line managers	• Relationship with manager • Career opportunities • Work–life balance • Openness • Job security	• Low job satisfaction (esp. career opportunities) • Dissatisfied with training • Lack of openness
Workers	• Communication • Rewards and recognition • Openness	• Dissatisfied with career opportunities • Poor job security • Low job satisfaction (job challenge and influence)

Box 3.1 Different HR bundles for different occupational categories

Professionals want excellent communication about all aspects of the business with good rewards and recognition for good work. They want to know how well they are doing, enjoy working hard but need to get on with their boss and want some hope of career progression whether in the firm or in their profession. What seems to destroy commitment is poor leadership and a lack of respect from managers, boring work, lack of support to help them achieve a work–life balance, no opportunity to gain more money through better performance, and working in a place with an 'us' and 'them' atmosphere.

Front line managers: What is really important is having a good positive working relationship with their boss and senior managers generally. This includes being able to talk about problems (openness). If they feel secure in their jobs, find the firm helps them achieve a work–life balance and they believe they are not stuck forever in their current job they are more likely to be positive about their employer and show commitment. What destroys commitment is where front line managers find little job satisfaction, have inappropriate or no training and cannot talk about personal problems with their managers.

Workers value communication, want praise and reward (we were often told in answer to a general question about what else the organisation could do to encourage people to improve their performance 'if only someone would say thank you sometimes') and to work in an open environment, able to discuss grievances and personal problems. The destroyers of commitment were working in boring jobs with little opportunity to influence how the job was done, feeling insecure and the lack of any hope for future betterment or change.

Source: Purcell (2004: 16–17).

HR CONFIGURATIONS AND STRATEGY

In the US, several studies have examined the impact of different bundles of HR practices on performance, with the goal of identifying HR 'configurations' that are both internally consistent and aligned with the organisation's strategy and environment (Becker and Huselid 1998; Edwards and Wright 2001). This perspective suggests that 'best fit' and 'best practice' approaches do not necessarily conflict, but can be employed concurrently, albeit at different levels of the HR system (Becker and Gerhart 1996; Arthur and Boyles 2007). First, it posits that different organisations require different 'configurations' of HR practices to meet their specific needs. Second, it suggests that different HR configurations may be used for different employee categories within the same organisation. As we will see below, commentators such as Snell (2005) argue that more costly 'best practice' approaches may be used for highly 'valued' categories (e.g. research and development personnel), while a more cost-controlled and 'minimalist' HR approach may be used for certain other categories (e.g. general operators).

The 'configurational' approach fits neatly with the resource-based view of the firm (Barney 1995), which argues that a properly developed HR system can bring a unique and somewhat invisible asset to an organisation, making it difficult for competitors to imitate. Much of the work using the RBV has focused on developing *human capital*, specifically in identifying and developing *knowledge stocks* and *knowledge flows* (Conner and Prahalad 1996; Lepak and Snell 1999, 2002).

Knowledge stocks are the codified knowledge that an organisation possesses, such as cumulative experience and contextual information, expert insights, intelligence on competitors, business and process knowledge and so forth.

Knowledge flows incorporate the way knowledge grows, travels and is stored within organisations – from, and to, management, between staff, through planned interventions (e.g. training, projects, directives), and through common sources (e.g. data or knowledge bases. HR research has sought to identify the means by which HR strategy and policy can guide the process by which organisations develop and deploy human, social, and organisational capital to enhance competitiveness (Lepak and Snell 1999, 2002; Snell 2005).

While acknowledging that the 'people are our most important asset' mantra is quite hollow in light of the historical evidence, and that HR remains a low-priority activity in many organisations, Snell (2005: 2) argues that the distinction between HR and competitive strategy has currently begun to blur:

> If the competitive potential of a firm rests in its intellectual activities, then what people know and how they behave become the *sine qua non* of strategic management. In other words, neither the formation nor implementation of strategies can be separated from how people are managed.

As a consequence, Snell (2005: 3) suggests that HR may act as a 'catalyst for strategic capability'. This means that HR is no longer something that comes after, and needs to accommodate, strategic planning, but rather that:

> . . . strategic planning is now increasingly viewed as resulting from the capabilities available through a firm's human resources. In this era of competitive potential, HR is perhaps becoming more important for propelling strategy than ever before. And we are seeing the first instances where heads of HR are being promoted to CEOs of companies.

However, he also cautions that assuming this new position poses particular and significant challenges for the HR community. First, he points to the *complexity of managing human assets*. In particular, he argues that much of the work on developing 'best practice' HR interventions has tended to view an organisation's workforce as one large monolith to be addressed by generic HR practices, rather than as comprising different groups and individuals for whom differing HR approaches may be appropriate (cf. Lepak and Snell 1999, 2002). This resonates with the 'configurational' perspective outlined above, and also with Boxall and Purcell's (2003) argument that different bundles of HR practices may be appropriate to different occupational categories.

Second, Snell (2005: 3) argues that *HR strategy needs to extend beyond a focus on human capital* to incorporate consideration of other knowledge-based assets which are significant 'for organizational learning, innovation, and strategic capability', and that we need to explore their links with strategy. Rather than assuming that one single HR system is appropriate for all of an organisation's workforce, Lepak and Snell (1999) advocate what they term an 'HR architecture', which demonstrates how an organisation's portfolio of human capital differs and suggests differing HR strategies and modes of employment contract for different employee categories. Initially, their architecture was based on the premise that a firm's human capital may be evaluated on two dimensions, namely its *strategic value* and its *uniqueness*. The *strategic value* dimension is mainly grounded in the RBV, while the *uniqueness* dimension is based on transaction cost economics. As the *strategic value* and *uniqueness* of human capital varies among different types of employees, so too, it is argued, should the types of HR systems and employment contracts deployed. Using the dimensions of human capital *strategic value* and *human capital uniqueness*, Lepak and Snell (1999) propose four HR configurations: commitment; collaborative; productivity/market-based; and compliance (see Figure 3.9 and Box 3.2).

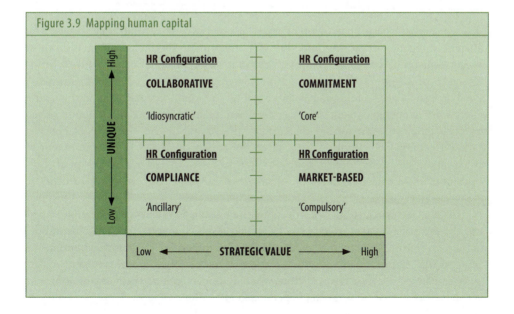

Figure 3.9 Mapping human capital

> **Box 3.2 Four HR configurations**
>
> *Commitment* (high uniqueness, high strategic value). This approach is deemed appropriate for 'core' employees who possess high levels of skills and knowledge and who are of high strategic value to their organisation. The HR mode proposed is a classic 'soft' HRM configuration (internal labour market/employee development/high commitment focus). The focus is on attracting and developing the 'best' and ensuring a positive work experience and reward structure to ensure they are committed and stay with the organisation.
>
> *Collaboration* (high uniqueness, low strategic value). In contrast, one may also find employment ('idiosyncratic') categories or individuals who possess highly specialised skills and knowledge and skills that are critical to the organisation but that provide little value to the customer (e.g. information technology specialists). Here, Lepak and Snell (1999) advocate human capital 'alliances' and a variable range of HR systems. While we find a strong emphasis on recruitment and selection, the overall HR approach will depend on how difficult it is to find such people, and whether their input is required over the long or short term. Where the relationship is short term, there may be little or no scope for employee involvement, but where it is more long term there will likely be a much greater focus on their immersion into company culture and eliciting their commitment and involvement in decision-making.
>
> *Market-based* (low uniqueness, high strategic value). Here the argument is that where qualified ('compulsory') workers are available in the labour market it makes sense for management to recruit such people directly as opposed to incurring unnecessary expenditure in developing these resources internally. From an HR perspective, there is an emphasis on good selection but less focus on employee development, involvement and retention. Indeed, turnover among such categories may provide the organisation with the numerical flexibility in dealing with changes in the business environment.
>
> *Compliance* (low uniqueness, low strategic value). This approach is deemed appropriate among ('ancillary') employment categories, which are necessary but who add little value to customers and who can be easily sourced from the external labour market. The organisation focus is on acquiring such workers at the lowest costs, and once recruited, to engage in minimal levels of HR investment. Thus, while basic recruitment and reward practices will be in place, there is little or no emphasis on employee involvement or development. The mode of employment relationship is one characterised by compliance. Workers are expected to follow clear rules and procedures and achieve pre-ordained standards.

This approach suggests that different types of employment contract may be used for different categories of worker and that HR investment should be directed at those categories most likely to create competitive advantage for the firm. Empirical investigation has shed further light on the utility of this HR architecture (Snell 2005; see Figure 3.10). Based on a study of 148 firms, Lepak and Snell (2002) found that each cell in the matrix differs in terms of employment modes, employment relationships and HR practices. Their approach employed two further dimensions: the nature of the employment contract (either predominantly 'relational' (soft) or 'transactional' (hard)); and the extent to which employees were 'internalised' into the organisation (secure employment, high levels of employee development) or 'externalised' (contract or casual employment, no employee development).

This analysis suggests that categories with a high strategic value tend to be 'internalised' into the organisation (secure employment, high levels of employee development, etc.) and tend to have commitment-based 'relational' connections to their organisations. A similar pattern applies to many 'idiosyncratic' employee categories. In contrast, ancillary contract employee categories had transactional connections to their organisation and were largely managed using a compliance-based HR system.

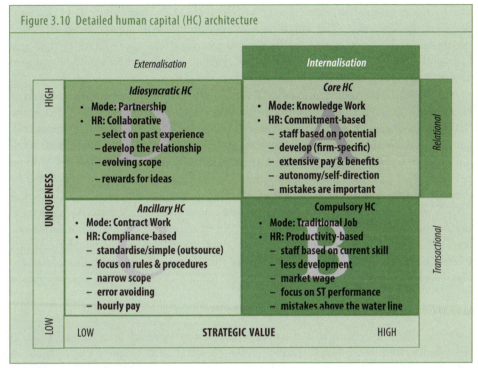

Figure 3.10 Detailed human capital (HC) architecture

Source: Snell (2005: 6).

While a key proposition from this research is that different employees and employee categories possessing different portfolios of human capital tend to be managed in different ways, one should not 'pigeon-hole' particular jobs or skill portfolios. It all depends on how particular employees are viewed and used within the organisation:

> No job or skill area is inherently associated with one cell in the matrix or another. In fact, a skill set such as sales, production, or engineering could show up in any one of the cells depending on how it is used strategically. This is a critical point for HR strategy: A particular type of human capital may be core for one firm, but ancillary for another. It all depends on how the firm competes.
>
> Snell (2005: 6)

A further area of investigation concerns how differing combinations of these four HR configurations impact on organisation performance. A study by Lepak et al. (2003) examined their impact on two measures of performance, namely 'return on equity' and 'market to book' (i.e. the market value of a firm divided by capital invested). The results indicated that organisations that used both core and contract workers had higher levels of performance than those that used only one or neither of these employment modes.

While greatly enhancing understanding of how HRM might differ within and between organisations, one of the key limitations of Lepak and Snell's work is that it largely isolates decisions about how people are managed from the broader institutional context (e.g. labour markets, labour market institutions and other regulative mechanisms), which may restrict or inform the parameters within which HRM and more general management decisions may be made. The key drivers in their frameworks appear to be economic variables, with less appreciation for the notion of strategic tensions or social legitimacy as highlighted by Boxall and Purcell and others (Paauwe 2004), and previously mentioned above.

An area occupying the attention of HRM researchers concerns opening the 'black box' between HRM practices and organisational performance. Theoretically grounded in the RBV and social exchange theory, research has begun to explore the notion of climate as a key mediator through which HRM performance effects take place (Heffernan et al. 2009; Takeuchi et al. 2007). More sophisticated approaches explore the multi-level linkages between HRM practices at organisation level, social climate and employee outcomes by drawing on data from multiple managerial and employee-level respondents (Cafferkey 2007; Takeuchi et al. 2009), in an effort to reduce common method bias and strengthen the overall theoretical and empirical base. Moreover, in addition to traditional organisation-level performance measures such as profitability and sales, dependent variables frequently include measures of innovation and creativity which have a more direct line of sight to HRM interventions.

CONCLUSION

Strategic HRM has grown to a situation where it now occupies a substantial place in the HR literature more broadly and represents a key line of enquiry for a significant cohort of scholars. However, there is little doubt that this is a complex area, built upon diverse literatures, beset by definitional disagreements and characterised by empirics derived from differing notions of what should be measured, what is worth measuring, or indeed how it should be measured. In this chapter we have sought to explore core aspects of this literature and unearth some of the linkages between business strategy, HRM and organisation performance. It will be evident to the reader that, conceptually and empirically, some difficulties remain. Nonetheless, some significant progress has also been made in better discerning strategy–HRM–performance links and the signs are that this will remain a significant line of enquiry in the years ahead.

In the Irish context, there has been more limited investigation of these issues, although work by researchers at Dublin City University and the National University of Ireland Galway goes some way towards providing important insights on the experience of strategic HRM in Ireland (Monks and McMackin 2001; Conway 2004; Conway and McMackin 1997; Heffernan and Dundon 2004; Heffernan et al. 2009; Cafferkey 2007). At a macro-level, recent national surveys have found a low to moderate uptake of sophisticated HRM approaches (Guthrie et al. 2009; Heffernan et al. 2008), echoing previous research findings from Ireland (Gunnigle 1995; Roche 1999) and elsewhere (Blasi and Kruse 2006; Kersley et al. 2006). Other researchers are addressing an important gap in the field by exploring how employees experience HRM practice, and the impact of HRM practice on employee attitudes and commitment (Conway and Monks 2008; Harney et al. 2009; Heffernan 2004). At the same time, there is an Irish literature which takes a healthy critical stance in exploring the possible motives and beneficiaries of both HRM research and practice (Cullinane and Dundon 2006; Harney 2007; Lavelle et al. 2009).

In evaluating developments, we often run the danger of confusing prominent exemplars of 'soft' HRM with the widespread pervasiveness of such approaches. As we have seen, much of the evidence and support for strategic HRM emanates from the US. However, the context of such developments in the United States is considerably different from Ireland and it seems inappropriate simply to extrapolate from the American experience and infer similar trends here. HRM research is very much supply-side driven and still has to address demand-side explanations for the relatively limited diffusion of HRM practices (Kaufman 2010a, 2010b). Part of this may come from an understanding that what constitutes best practice may vary across time and place (Delaney and Godard 2001; Keegan and Boselie 2006). Differences in cultural and political traditions, industrial and employment structure, employment relations institutions and practice are just some of the unique factors influencing approaches to HRM in the Republic of Ireland. As Gooderham *et al.* (2004: 17) suggest, 'clearly the practice of HRM cannot be divorced from its institutional context'. In recognition of this, Ansari *et al.* (2010) expand the notion of fit to encompass dimensions such as technical fit, cultural fit and political fit, while Boon *et al.* (2009) refer to 'institutional fit'.

The next chapter deals with one of the key contextual/institutional backdrops for HRM practice, namely the labour market.

4
Human Resource Management and the Labour Market

We have seen from the first three chapters that human resource management is focused on developing appropriate strategies and policies to allow the organisation to effectively utilise its human capital. Organisational performance hinges on this human capital. Ehrenberg and Smith (2016) note that organisations make complex decisions daily about what goods or services to produce, where they should produce them, what volume of them to produce and who best to employ to do all of this producing. Underpinning all of these complex decisions are literally thousands of discrete decisions relating to hiring, compensating, developing, and terminating the organisation's labour force – its human capital. Our discussion on Ireland during the recession in Chapter 2 serves as a sharp reminder that HRM policies and decisions are contextually bound, i.e. they are both enabled and constrained by the macro external environment in which the organisation operates. One critical component of this environment concerns the labour market to which HR policies and practices are directed, and from where it derives its human capital.

This chapter examines the operation of HRM in the context of the labour market. Broad perspectives of labour market functioning are scrutinised and the implications of these for HRM are discussed. These perspectives provide a basis for explaining why individual organisations vary the nature of their human resource policies and practices in line with the prevailing climate in which they find themselves operating. Core features of labour market operations are next outlined and, finally, a summative account of key features of the Irish labour market in 2017 is presented.

PERSPECTIVES ON THE LABOUR MARKET AND HRM

Ehrenberg and Smith (2016) describe the labour market simply as the market that allocates workers to jobs and coordinates employment decisions. It represents the context within which the buyers and sellers of labour come together to determine the pricing and allocation of labour services.

Elliott (1990: 3) suggests that, while many different markets exist in a modern economy, the market for labour is probably the most important, since it is from selling their services in this market that most families derive their income and it is where so many people spend the largest part of their waking hours. When not working, many individuals devote a large part of the remaining time (through education and training programmes) to acquiring the knowledge and skills necessary for effective performance in this market. Since HRM is concerned with managing this labour by the most effective means possible, it stands to reason that factors that impact the labour market will also affect the practice of HRM.

The labour market comprises all the buyers and sellers of labour, the buyers being the employers and the sellers being the workers. What is being bought and sold is the individual worker's time for a finite period, during which s/he commits knowledge, skills, competence and experience to the organisation's service – and for which s/he receives a benefit. It has long been recognised, however, that labour markets differ from other markets in the economic system. Marshall (1928) held that labour differs from other commodities because workers are inseparable from the services that they provide i.e they carry their history, their culture, values and their social norms into their place of work. Similarly, Keynes (1936) recognised that the employment relationship differs from other contractual relationships because of its frequently long and indeterminable duration, which provides time for customs and norms, particularly those concerned with fairness, to build up around it. Marsden (1986) further notes that several economists have attempted to develop economic theory in such a way as to take account of these kinds of influence. While accepting that pressures of supply and demand, of competition and of substitution are active in the labour market, customs, social norms, group pressures and institutional rules are also active in shaping wage structures, labour mobility patterns and other aspects of labour market behaviour.

The behaviour of labour markets is complex, and there is no one universal way of best understanding how they operate. A range of different social science disciplines offer us alternative explanations of how and why labour markets behave as they do. For example, on the one hand, labour economics might suggest that the behaviour of employers and employees is best understood as responses to the general incentives of wages, prices, profits and non-pecuniary aspects of the employment relationship, such as working conditions. Industrial or employment relations, on the other hand, asks us to focus more on group activities and interests, the internal dynamics of organisations, social norms and the processes of rule-making both within and outside the organisation, to better understand behaviour. Neither is incorrect: rather, they make alternative predictions about human behaviour under similar circumstances, and stress different causes for that observed behaviour.

It is for this reason that there is no one single theory of or perspective on the labour market, but rather a number of differentiated and often competing approaches. Three of the most prevalent perspectives will be briefly examined here and we will look particularly at how each perspective might help us understand how HRM is enacted.

THE COMPETITIVE MODEL OF THE LABOUR MARKET

At its most basic level, the standard competitive model of the labour market, derived from neo-classical economics, works on the assumption that individuals are rational economic maximisers: that is, we make rational choices to maximise economic benefit to ourselves.

It is assumed that we have a set of preferences and will organise our time and effort so that we will achieve the highest possible rate of return to ourselves. In the context of employment, an individual will weigh up the marginal benefits of working as opposed to not working and thus will take into account factors such as wages, time, leisure and so forth when making the decision to work. In this manner, the equilibrium wage and the associated level of employment are determined by the intersection of labour supply and labour demand. This intersection produces a market-clearing wage with the result that, at that wage, the quantity of labour willingly supplied exactly equals the quantity of labour willingly demanded.

There are a number of key assumptions underpinning the competitive model of the labour market (Marsden 1986; Beardwell and Holden 2001):

- The market is made up of a large number of employers and employees, each with their own set of preferences that are based mainly on wealth maximisation.
- There are no constraints on entry to the labour market – organisations and new workers can enter the labour market at any time.
- Jobs in most organisations can be done by a fairly large number of workers provided they have the appropriate skills – in the most extreme form of this principle (homogenous labour), all jobs can be done by all workers.
- The organisation can be treated as a transfer mechanism between markets – in-house training and work experience are of equal benefit to all firms and are thus transferable.
- The only cost to the organisation of hiring labour is the wage, thus there is no marginal gain in retaining existing workers rather than hiring new ones.
- There is perfect information – all workers and all organisations know the state of the market and are instantly aware of any changes in the market.

In the competitive model, adjustments to changes in product markets or production methods are made through the price mechanism, that is as costs increase, the price of labour decreases. In this way both employers and employees are price takers – organisations will only employ as many individuals as is economically viable, bearing in mind the law of diminishing marginal returns. Workers will choose to work where the cost of not working (or leisure) outweighs the benefits of being employed. In such a scenario, unemployment does not exist since wages are flexibly adjusted in line with labour supply.

HRM from a Competitive Perspective

The competitive model of the labour market assumes that, as organisations face increased competition in their product/service markets, they will continually seek new and better ways of reducing costs. From this perspective, one can argue that the primary goal of HRM is cost minimisation and, particularly, the reduction of labour costs. Given the existence of wage rigidities implicit in the model, one would expect that organisations would seek to reduce such wage rigidities by implementing structures and systems that allow for the more flexible use of labour. There are two particular labour pools associated with the competitive model: the unskilled labour market and the skilled labour market.

Taking the unskilled labour market first, the model assumes certain levels of labour turnover and that wages tend towards the market rate. Since there is a ready supply of unskilled labour available in the external labour market, it is relatively easy and cost-efficient to hire these workers. Furthermore, as these workers do not have specific job knowledge or training, it is assumed that they will only leave the organisation when higher wages are offered elsewhere. For this reason, organisations will accept high levels of labour turnover since it is relatively easy to replace these workers and the costs of replacement are lower than the costs of providing incentives to retain them. In such a scenario, it is unlikely that companies would adopt a 'soft' HRM approach.

The competitive model also envisages a second labour pool of skilled workers, what could be termed the core talent of the organisation. In this instance, structured internal labour markets will exist: since organisations contribute to the costs of training workers to ensure competitiveness, they will have a vested interest in retaining them. In this situation, it is more cost-effective for organisations to develop structured, internal labour markets. This labour market would typically provide employment security, progressive wage increases based on service, and opportunities for internal promotion and development through a talent pipeline, rather than the costly alternative of recruiting and training new workers who might be hard to source.

The competitive model therefore suggests two possible scenarios that HRM might enact. The first scenario envisages a 'no frills' employment strategy, which offers unskilled workers, little if any training, and pays the market rate for labour. The second scenario suggests the development of structured internal labour markets for skilled employment, which may be linked to functional and financial flexibility. In both cases, the primary driver of HRM policies, from the competitive model perspective, is cost minimisation.

THE INSTITUTIONAL MODEL OF THE LABOUR MARKET

Not everyone subscribes to purely economic explanations of labour market functioning. Kaufman (2007), for example, argues that the assumptions of the competitive labour market model are internally contradictory and that a perfectly competitive labour market is a logical impossibility. Alternative suggestions (DiMaggio and Powell 1984) propose that several organisational and institutional factors and social norms have perhaps a greater influence on the behaviour of labour markets than pure labour market economics alone.

The institutional perspective is based on a core assumption that individuals do not behave independently of others. Rather, institutionalists perceive that we formulate choices and preferences with reference to the perceived choices and preferences made by other people around us, or by those with whom we are associated. Similarly, organisations make choices based on the actions of their competitors and other organisations. Indeed, organisations are to some degree constrained by the choices made by other organisations operating in a similar product and service market. This is termed *isomorphism* – the tendency to behave similarly to other organisations. These choices are impacted by various institutional actors within the macro environment who impose both supports for, and regulations around, labour transactions.

Institutionalists place a considerable emphasis on the role of stakeholders with various interests, group norms, customs and collective power in shaping labour market conditions such as wage rigidities, structured internal labour markets and efficiency wages. Transaction choices around work/leisure, and work effort, include more than financial considerations and encompass perceptions about equity and fairness, work–life balance, group cohesion and work norms within the organisation or occupational level.

In addition, goals other than pure profit maximisation may be pursued by organisations, i.e. market share, organisational growth, sustainable development, or a target rate of return on capital present within the organisation. This may require approaches that incur greater costs and investments, but for a longer-term gain.

HRM from an Institutional Perspective

The institutional perspective focuses on the process by which the employment relationship is regulated and, in particular, highlights the role played by various stakeholders and interest groups in the development of employment strategies and policies. While the competitive model focuses particularly on cost reduction, the institutional model is more concerned with reducing inefficiencies in the utilisation of labour. Specifically, it suggests that the stakeholders in the labour process play a significant role in determining labour efficiency and advocates the use of various HRM policies that seek to alter the nature of power within organisations. In practice, then, the institutional approach could perceive the central role of HRM as being to develop a unitarist perspective of the firm, whereby policies are introduced that seek to co-opt employees into the managerial vision of the organisation. One might therefore expect some elements of 'soft' HRM to be in evidence (such as employee involvement, performance-related pay, extensive talent management strategies, culture development initiatives, single union agreements, etc.) in exchange for greater flexibility and productivity agreements.

Two HRM scenarios are possible within the institutional framework – the first might involve the co-opting of unions in order to secure agreement through participative decision-making; and the second might result in greater individualising of the employment relationship, perhaps as a means of marginalising trade union power and influence, or indeed circumventing a perceived need for trade union membership at all. In any event, the dominant ethos espoused by the institutional model suggests a focus on modifying existing power structures to improve efficiencies, through changing existing norms and behaviour patterns.

THE RADICAL MODEL OF THE LABOUR MARKET

The radical approach is based on the traditional class struggle between workers and capital as reflected in the work of, among others, Marx and Engels. Within a social exchange paradigm, Marxism has been concerned with the conditions under which the working class could develop sufficient unity and consciousness to challenge, and then replace, capitalism. Here capitalism is essentially viewed in pejorative terms. Thompson (1983), for example, argues that the capitalist labour process is subject to a number of identifiable tendencies, whose critical features are deskilling, fragmentation of tasks, hierarchical organisation, the division between mental and manual work, and the struggle to establish the most effective means to control labour. Similarly, Braverman (1974) argues that deskilling is an inherent tendency of the capitalist labour process and that Taylorism, or scientific management, was an effort to relieve workers of their job autonomy and craft knowledge. Thus, the radical perspective envisages an inevitable conflict between workers and managers (as the owners or representatives of the owners of production), where the division of labour is perceived as a means of constraining workers' power, while greater specialisation of tasks serves to subordinate the worker.

From this perspective, workers' capacity to resist exploitation and alienation lies in the development of collective representation through trade union organisation. Resistance to specialisation and standardisation is not limited to the jobs that workers do but rather extends to forms of work organisation and work structuring that are seen to segment the workforce and workforce solidarity. Hence the adoption of elements of workforce flexibility that result in the creation of core and periphery labour markets is seen as a covert managerial technique to exploit labour further.

HRM from a Radical Perspective

The radical approach also focuses on organisational processes of regulating the employment relationship, but it differs from the institutional approach in that it presumes that all managerial activities are geared towards the creation of greater profits at the expense of the workers. In particular, HRM policies are viewed as deliberate means of exploiting labour and weakening the collective power of workers. Within this framework, the adoption of, for example, flexible employment models, is seen to be a tool of a divide and conquer strategy, where management co-opt a select number of core workers (who receive all the attendant benefits of security, learning and development, promotions and incentives), at the expense of the majority, for whom flexibility results in increased work intensification, greater direct control, diminished employment security and possibly lower pay.

The radical perspective views all policies and strategies that seek to individualise the employment relationship as further evidence of management's covert objective to reduce collective resistance. Within such an organisation, the purpose of HRM, from the radical perspective, is not the reduction of costs or inefficiencies, but rather the exploitation of labour through the extension of managerial control over the employment relationship.

We can see then, that different labour market perspectives offer alternative views on the rationale for using particular HRM practices. However, we must be cautious – perspectives, by their very nature, offer but a partial or uni-dimensional view of their subject matter. The truth of the matter is that labour market functioning is altogether more complex than any one of these perspectives might suggest and indeed a single perspective may not be in evidence at all. Rather, it may be the case that organisations function according to the environment they find themselves in and so their HRM approach may reflect both strategic and reactive components. A number of features of an organisation's particular labour market will influence its choices here.

KEY LABOUR MARKET CHARACTERISTICS

It is well recognised that labour markets are complex for there are a number of core 'peculiarities' of labour markets that shape the way they operate in practice. These characteristics subsequently influence or constrain the range of choices available to those engaging and managing human resources.

UNEMPLOYMENT

A notable feature of labour markets is some element of unemployment and, contrary to the presumptions of the competitive model, not all of those who are seeking employment can find it. Labour is not homogenous – rather it is highly differentiated – and so it is a remarkable peculiarity of labour markets that unemployment can exist alongside wage inflation and job vacancies. Even at the height of Ireland's financial crisis, with unemployment running at more than 15 per cent by the end of the 2000s, there were organisations that found it impossible to fill some jobs from within the Irish labour market.

Skill shortages will always be a feature of labour markets and organisations will inevitably face competition in attracting and retaining key skills and talent.

WAGE RIGIDITIES

One of the key presumptions underpinning most competitive models of labour markets is that wages can be flexibly adjusted in line with demand for labour. In other words, it implies that organisations can reduce wages as their demand for labour falls. In practice, we know how difficult this is to implement, as exemplified by the negative reactions to public and private sector wage cuts. In fact, wages are more likely to move upwards more readily than move downwards, and this downward wage rigidity is offered by some economists as a critical explanation for the nature and extent of high levels of unemployment. More often, organisations resort to recruitment freezes (see for example the successive cutbacks and embargoes on recruitment in the public sector in Ireland in recent years), reductions in overtime, and ultimately lay-offs or redundancy as short-term (initially at least) reactions to decreased demand for labour. Wage levels are also externally influenced by social partnership agreements, Joint Industrial Councils, government interventions and so forth (see detailed discussion in later chapters).

SEGMENTED LABOUR MARKETS

Segmented labour markets are not unusual. Neither labour nor labour markets are homogenous. Labour is diverse in all the numerous ways in which people differ overtly (e.g. race, sex, ethnicity and age) and indirectly in terms of orientation, memberships, educational attainment, skills, beliefs, traditions and values, and so forth. So too are labour markets structured into sub-markets according to classifications of jobs and occupations that require different skills and abilities, and where restrictions on the substitutability between different kinds of labour can be seen to exist.

While competition between workers in different sub-markets may be very limited, each sub-market itself remains a zone of competition, in which normal market relationships tend to apply. Cappelli and Keller (2014) describe how workforce segmentation represents a key theoretical development in the strategic human resource management (SHRM) literature, and which holds that organisations should disproportionately invest scarce resources in the individuals or jobs from which they expect the greatest return. It differs from older approaches, which simply assumed that the importance of an individual or job was associated with their position in the organisational chart.

Both human capital theory (Becker 1964) and transaction cost theory (Williamson 1981) offer a useful distinction between what are termed specific or non-transferable knowledge and skills, for which there is no market outside the employing firm, and general, non-specific knowledge and skills that can be applied in any organisational context. Whereas general skills and knowledge can be sold in external labour markets, firm-specific competencies are valuable to one organisation only. From an organisational perspective, investment in general (transferable) skills is therefore less desirable and riskier since these skills are valuable across organisations and so the potential for organisations to lose their investment through labour turnover is greater (employees with transferable skills are highly employable and can easily move from one firm to another).

Snell *et al.* (1996: 65) note that:

> If the types and levels of skills are not equally distributed, such that some firms can acquire the talent they need and others cannot, then (*ceteris paribus*) that form of human capital can be a source of sustained competitive advantage.

This market segmentation can result in the development of a dual labour market, which is generally understood as being divided into two main segments, with limited mobility in between (Lindbeck and Snower 2001), and this dualism results in various forms of employment. At its most basic level, this dualism results in two very distinct types of labour market: a labour market comprising mainly unskilled or casual labour; and a labour market of highly skilled occupational labour. In addition, Elger (2015) suggests that different categories of workers (minority and majority ethnic groups; migrants and non-migrants; men and women) experience contrasting labour market logics and opportunities within these dual or segmented labour markets. In the context of rational choice, individual workers seeking to maximise their net advantages will focus on searching for information about advantages in other firms and on obtaining access to different occupational labour markets through investment in education and training (typically associated with generic and transferable skills). Let us see below how this works in practice.

STRUCTURED INTERNAL LABOUR MARKETS

An internal labour market (ILM) refers to an organisation's internal employment structure. Doeringer and Piore (1971) define ILMs as internal administrative units within which the pricing and allocation of labour are governed by a set of administrative rules and procedures. An internal labour market comprises the sets of generic and transferable skills that exist within the organisation, and these are ordered according to a hierarchical job classification system.

For the most part, where an investment in skills is required, it is reasonable to argue that investment in specific skills, as explained above, is likely to be the preferred option for organisations since these skills are not readily transferable (there is less likelihood that workers will leave the organisation and take this investment in skills with them). High investment in specific skills can thus facilitate the development of highly valuable firm-specific human capital or talent.

The development of structured internal labour markets can thus be seen as one means of managing these competing interests. Here the ILM system of job hierarchies is designed to provide mobility chains or career progression up through the organisation hierarchy. It forms the talent pipeline of the organisation. Formal patterns of progression between jobs are regulated through rules and customs and provide a sense of stability in organisations. Labour mechanisms working within internal labour markets are governed by administrative rules, rather than open market competition, and adjustments within these markets are typically through management-driven techniques such as job evaluation, job design, wage and salary administration and so forth.

In this context, the use of human resource policies can have the cumulative effect of building barriers to labour mobility since accumulated rights are inextricably linked with tenure or length of service with the organisation. New hires can, of course, be 'parachuted' into the organisation where it is felt that new talent is required and it may not be available internally. This can potentially have adverse effects internally where incumbent employees may have expectations of progression that may now be thwarted, thus impacting perceptions of organisational justice and often resulting in a perceived breach/violation of psychological contracts.

Structured internal labour markets can be a useful mechanism of managing the costs of investment in firm-specific skills or human capital. ILMs are seen to determine wage and employment structures different from, but within the constraints set by, competitive market forces. Williamson (1978) argues that the offer of more stable employment and of internal labour market conditions creates a situation in which it is in the workers' own self-interest to promote the longer-term prosperity of the firm and hence to demonstrate greater commitment to the organisation. Investment in specific skills may be of benefit to both organisations and select employees.

It should be recognised, however, that restrictions in employee mobility through developing non-transferable skills may not be in the interests of either the national economy or the individual worker. The national economy trades itself on having a highly skilled and mobile workforce to attract overseas investment, while individual workers are more likely to be interested in the acquisition of more general skills that will improve their employability in the wider labour market.

FLEXIBILITY AND ALTERNATIVE FORMS OF EMPLOYMENT

The notion of labour market flexibility within organisations emerged as a key debate in the HRM literature during the mid-1980s. Set against the backdrop of global recession, many of the arguments for labour market flexibility called for structural changes to both the design of organisations and work, to overcome rigidities and to offset competitive pressures and low productivity; or to manage the shift towards service sector employment (Morley 1994). The basic premise underpinning these arguments was that organisations could pursue two opposing strategies of labour market utilisation, either relying heavily on the external labour market, or favouring internal mobility and the development of multiple skills among existing employees.

The flexibility debate focused on the contribution that various employment strategies might make, both to organisational adaptability and performance and increased opportunities for employees which are seen to be brought about through the development of numerical, pay/cost and functional flexibility.

The flexible firm model (see Figure 4.1), originally advanced by Atkinson (1984), involves a reorganisation of firms' internal labour markets and their division into separate components, in which the worker's experience and the employer's expectations of him/her are increasingly differentiated. This hierarchical restructuring allows radically different employment policies to be pursued for different groups of workers.

Within this framework, the 'core group' is composed of full-time staff, enjoying relatively secure, challenging jobs with good pay and employment conditions. Two sets of 'periphery' worker categories can be created:

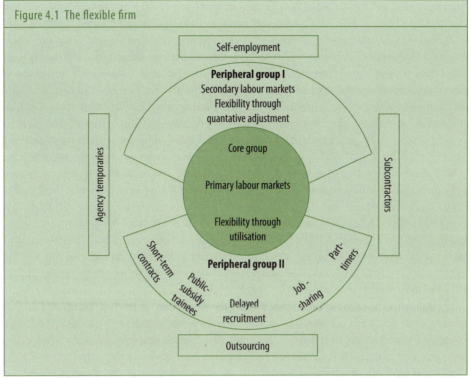

Figure 4.1 The flexible firm

Source: Atkinson (1984).

- The first set is highly skilled, often technical or professional employees who are contracted into the organisation on fixed-term or fixed-purpose contracts and who enjoy relatively good conditions of employment.
- The second set is composed of an amalgam of temporary, part-time and contract groups, with less favourable pay and employment conditions and less job security or fewer training and promotion opportunities.

This flexible firm scenario suggests an attempt by organisations to increase flexibility in three key areas.

1. *Numerical flexibility*, incorporating the use of non-standard employment forms, which allows the organisation to hire and/or shed labour flexibly, in line with business demands.
2. *Financial/pay flexibility*, whereby pay rates are linked to labour and product market conditions and pay increases for individual employees are variable and contingent upon performance.
3. *Functional flexibility*, incorporating multi-skilling, which is defined as the expansion of skills within a workforce or the ability of organisations to reorganise the competencies associated with jobs so that the job holder is willing and able to deploy such competencies across a broader range of skills.

Drawing on the theoretical frameworks of transaction cost economics (Klein *et al.* 1978), human capital theory (Becker 1964; Flamholtz and Lacey 1981), the resource-based view of the firm (Barney 1991) and core competencies (Prahalad and Hamel 1990), Lepak and Snell (2002) proposed a human resource architecture that depicts four particular modes of employee engagement. This architecture is based on the recognition that not all employees possess knowledge and skills that are of equal strategic importance and that top performers contribute disproportionately to firm performance. The issue for organisations is therefore whether to internalise or externalise the employment relationship. *Internalisation* refers to the continual internal development of employees who are felt to possess unique skills and capabilities that are highly valued by the organisation and not readily available from outside it. A strong internalisation focus might be reflected in: jobs that are rather loosely defined to allow for change; provision for extensive learning opportunities including career development and mentoring arrangements; and skills-based payment systems and developmental performance appraisal systems. Indeed, this combination of HRM practices is similar to those depicted in the high-performance work systems literature (Huselid 1995; Lawler *et al.* 1995; Guthrie *et al.* 2002). *Externalisation*, by contrast, refers to a deliberate strategy of sourcing skills and competencies outside the organisation – these skills and competencies are neither unique nor firm-specific and so they are more readily available in the external labour market.

Discussions concerning the manner in which segmentation and differentiated labour market strategies are operationalised at the organisational level have focused on a number of specific observations. Key here is the argument that competitive pressures are forcing organisations to increase their capacity to employ or shed labour more rapidly (numerical flexibility) in order to achieve a better fit between workforce size and fluctuations in the demand for goods and services. Consequently, non-standard employment, in the form of temporary and casual workers, fixed-term contracts, zero-hours contracts, home-working and subcontracting, might be expected to follow. Furthermore, functional flexibility, concerned with the relaxing of demarcation lines and the adoption of broader job descriptions, is seen as a key mechanism for achieving greater organisational adaptability. However, such apparently expedient responses to temporary environmental conditions may well be sustained when the environment changes, as organisations strive to retain the advantages of certain flexibility forms. Eichorst and Marx (2011) note that this chosen path of internal flexibilization, which in many industries is actually based on high skill investments and long-term employment relationships, provides more numerical and wage flexibility to employers and can make standard jobs more cost-attractive. Whether the overall result is more attractive jobs for individual workers is yet to be determined.

Today, while it is not at all clear that employers are deliberately adopting flexible employment practices for the long-term strategic reasons that Atkinson originally identified, there is substantial evidence of increased 'atypical employment' in most OECD countries in the past twenty years. For example, in 2017, just over 21 per cent of total employment in Ireland was part-time in nature, which represents a decrease since 2015, where it stood at 23.3 per cent and is about on a par with the European Union (EU) average of 20 per cent (Eurofound 2016). The growth in part-time work overall may have been an attempt to reduce labour costs during the recession, though most recent CSO figures indicate that growth in employment in Ireland is most likely to be full-time, rather than part-time or fixed term employment. It remains to be seen whether this trend will continue as the economy picks up again.

It is not particularly surprising to note that part-time work remains dominated by females: while the proportion of males employed on a part-time basis has increased significantly since the recession started to be felt in 2007, females in Ireland today are three times more likely to work part-time than are their male counterparts. This can be explained partly by choice, and partly by the nature of the occupation, which may lend itself more to part-time working.

The debate on alternative forms of engagement has been augmented by research agendas dedicated to promoting work–life balance and reducing work–family conflict. Subsumed under the various headings of work–life balance, work–family conflict, flexibility in work arrangements, or family-friendly work practices, the issue of balancing work and non-work aspects has been, and remains a policy priority across many industrialised economies (Hyman and Summers 2004, Steiber 2009; Lyness et al. 2012). Heraty et al. (2008a, 2008b) note that the work–family interface is an area of immense importance, personally, professionally and socially, as increasing numbers of families attempt to juggle work and family commitments and experience underlying difficulties in so doing. Work–family research has tended to focus on the perceived ability (inability) of individuals to control stressors stemming from one or other of the work and family domains. Tension is seen as inevitable.

- At the individual level, tensions in the work–family interface have been seen to affect, *inter alia*, stress and wellbeing, and to lead to reduced spousal and parental effectiveness, decreased life satisfaction and increased psychologically threatening activities.
- In the work and organisational sphere, critical issues include the potential for a negative impact on organisational commitment, job performance, job satisfaction, absenteeism and turnover.
- At the societal level, concerns relate to family disruption and community disconnect, reduced social citizenship and community engagement. In their review of 190 work–family studies, for example, Eby *et al.* (2005: 180) note that, while there is growing evidence to suggest that work and family can positively influence one another, there is far more that points to a negative spillover in terms of work–family conflict. This suggests that it is an area that warrants management focus.

In the Irish context, McGinnity and Calvert (2009) found evidence of lower work–life conflict in Ireland when compared with the other European countries Denmark, Spain, Germany, the Netherlands, France and the UK, but noted that workers in all countries cited long work hours, unsocial working hours and high job pressure as the three key variables impacting work–life conflict.

The work–life balance issue remains high on the European Union policy agenda. For example, the European parliament passed a resolution in September 2016 aimed at creating labour market conditions favourable for work–life balance, while the Women's Rights and Gender Equality (FEMM) committee report (2016) called for improvements to legislation on parental leave and stressed the importance of quality childcare services and flexible forms of work.

PROFILE OF THE IRISH LABOUR MARKET

Among the many commercial attractions of Ireland as a European base are the combination of English as the spoken language, a recognised pro-European outlook, and a well-educated workforce, particularly at the upper end. Over the past decade and more, the Irish workforce has become increasingly better educated, with ever-higher proportions of young people remaining in further education and training. Arguably, these and related labour market characteristics have important explanatory power in accounting for some of Ireland's economic growth throughout the 1990s and up until the mid-2000s. We examine some of the key features of Ireland's current labour market below.

POPULATION

In 2005, Ireland's population crossed the 4 million threshold. In the following twelve years it grew by more than three-quarters of a million people, with Ireland's population standing at 4.75 million people in 2017. This points to a year on year increase in the population for the past fifty years or so, and this growth is attributable both to natural increase (proportionally more births than deaths) and to net migration (more people coming to live in Ireland – inward migration; than those leaving to live elsewhere – outward migration). A few specific features are worth highlighting here. For example, the average age of the population is 37.4 years, while the average family size is 1.7 children, slightly higher than the EU average of 1.5 children (Eurostat 2010), but significantly decreasing over the past fifty years (the average family size in Ireland in the 1960s was four children).

Although Ireland continues to have a relatively young population when compared with other EU countries, the Irish population is starting to age (see Figure 4.2).

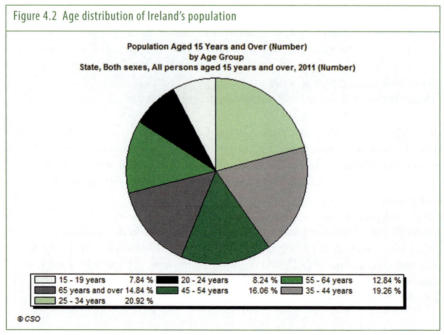

Figure 4.2 Age distribution of Ireland's population

Source: CSO (2017).

As the Irish birth rate continues to decline, there will be an appreciable impact on the dependency ratio (the proportion of the population who are economically dependent on the population of working age, i.e. 15–64 years, which represents the labour force). Census figures show that Ireland's total dependency rate in 2016 was 52.7, which is up from 49.3 in 2011 (CSO 2017). In the time period 2011–2016, the census figures show that the young dependency ratio (those aged 0–14 years) increased by 0.4 points, while the old dependency ratio (those aged 65+ years) increased by 3.0 points. Population projections show this aging of the population will increase over the next twenty years (see Figure 4.3), bringing Ireland into line with the rest of Europe.

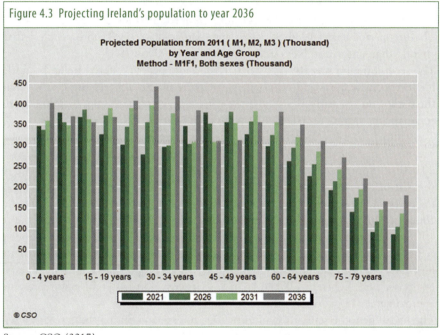

Figure 4.3 Projecting Ireland's population to year 2036

Source: CSO (2017).

This is unlikely to have any impact in the short term but, as the average age of the working-age population moves closer to those aged sixty and over, and with net migration inflows diversifying the characteristics of the active labour market, this will have significant implications for human resources policies, particularly in terms of succession planning, training and retraining, rewards, retention, pensions, and so forth. Moreover, as life expectancy increases such that people can expect to live an average of twenty years' post-retirement (Heraty and McCarthy 2015), we are likely to witness considerable revising of retirement policies, increased bridge employment, encore careers and alternative forms of employment for older workers who may not be interested in retiring at the age of sixty-six.

MIGRATION

Migration, understood here as the difference between emigration from and immigration to Ireland, and the performance of Ireland's labour market are inextricably linked; this relationship has been particularly evident in recent years. Net outward migration has traditionally constituted an integral feature of the Irish labour market. More than 1.2 million people have left Ireland since the foundation of the state in 1921. While the 1970s witnessed a periodical reversal of this trend, net emigration resumed through the 1980s, rising from 9,000 in 1984 to 46,000 in 1989. However, the dramatic economic growth and expansion of employment in the late 1990s changed Ireland from a country of emigration to one of net immigration.

Migration flows since the mid-1980s can be grouped into four key periods.
- The first period spans 1986–90 when approximately 160,000 more people left the country than entered it. Net outflows peaked at 46,000 in 1989.
- The second period was 1991–5, when 1,600 more people entered Ireland than left it. Recession in the world economy, particularly in the US and the UK, stemmed the outflow in the early 1990s, and the commencement of the upswing in the Irish economic environment reduced the numbers migrating abroad.
- The third period represents Ireland's real boom years of 1996–2007. This period witnessed historically large net inward migration. Net inflows averaged about 20,000 per annum until 1999 and increased substantially to more than 40,000 per year thereafter, with a recorded high of more than 57,000 in 2007. Analysis of these migration flows shows that a considerable proportion of the initial net migration comprised Irish citizens who had emigrated some years earlier, and workers from the UK. For example, during the period 1996–2000, 100,000 Irish persons returned to Ireland (accounting for close to half of all immigrants), while UK nationals accounted for nearly one-fifth of inflows. However, the greatest proportion of later immigration comprised both EU (non-UK) and non-EU citizens. Non-Irish nationals represented approximately 14 per cent of the population (CSO 2006).
- The fourth period essentially comprises 2008 to date and during these years we have seen a considerable reversal in migration trends. Net migration between 2011–2016 was 28,558 people which was in stark contrast to net inward migration figures of 115,800 recorded during the census period 2006–2011. However, economic growth from 2015 to 2017 present the possibility of a reversed trend once again for future years.

THE IRISH LABOUR FORCE: EMPLOYMENT AND OCCUPATION TRENDS

A number of key characteristics of Ireland's labour force at the start of 2017 are presented in Table 4.1, which also includes a comparison of where significant changes have occurred.

While aggregate changes in the Irish labour force have, at times, been erratic, overall labour force participation rates have remained relatively consistent in recent years. In 2017, Ireland's participation rate was 60.2 per cent. While most of the increases in the labour force in the 1990s resulted from increased 'domestic labour' supply, supplemented by net immigration, since 2000, we can see that increased participation levels are accounted for principally by immigration: during this time, approximately 25 per cent of the growth in the labour force was accounted for by immigrant, non-Irish-national workers. In 2016, Ireland's labour force grew by some 25,000 people.

Table 4.1 Key labour market indices Ireland				
Indices	Latest 2017	Highest	Lowest	Unit
Population	4.75	4.75	2.97 (1926)	Million
Retirement Age	66	66	65	Years
Labour Force Participation Rate	60.2	64.1	57.0	per cent
Employment Rate	65.6	69.8	58.3	per cent
Full Time Employment	1595.00	1769.50	1251.40	Thousand
Part Time Employment	444.90	461.10	247.70	Thousand
Unemployment Rate	6.4	17.30 (1985)	3.7 (2000)	per cent
Long-Term Unemployment Rate	4.20	9.50	1.20	per cent
Youth Unemployment Rate	13.9	31.2	6.2 (2008)	per cent
Labour Costs	81.10	122.10	78.50	Index Points
Minimum Wages	1563.25	1563.25	944.71	EUR/Month
Wages in Manufacturing	839.32	857.16	37.03	EUR/Week
Productivity	141.90	141.90	69.00	Index Points

Source: www.tradingeconomics.com/CSO 2017.

Employment rates (representing those in the labour force who are employed) are rising in Ireland. The overall employment rate in 2016 was 65.6 per cent among persons aged 15–64 years, just under the EU-28 average of 67.1 per cent. This increased employment was mainly in full-time rather than part-time employment, and among employees rather than the self-employed sector. The largest rates of increase were recorded in the construction, professional, scientific and technical activities sectors.

The unemployment rate measures the number of people actively looking for a job as a percentage of the labour force. Leaving aside the historic high of 17.2 per cent in 1985, and the recent high of 15.2 per cent in January 2012, unemployment rates in Ireland have fallen year-on-year since 2012. In March 2017, the seasonally adjusted unemployment rate in Ireland was 6.4 per cent (CSO 2017) numbering 141,400 people and the lowest it has been in almost ten years. The corresponding unemployment rate among the EU-28 countries at the end of 2016 was 8.2 per cent, with highs in Greece and Spain (22.6 per cent and 18.9 per cent respectively), and a lowest rate of 4.0 per cent in the Czech Republic and Germany. The unemployment rate for males was 6.9 per cent and 5.8 per cent for females, while youth unemployment was 13.9 per cent – the lowest it has been since July 2008.

In occupational terms, we can see that Ireland's labour force profile is becoming increasingly professionalised. Table 4.2, on the next page, provides a breakdown of the employment distribution across the various NACE economic sectors (NACE is the European Industry classification system) within the EU.

Table 4.2 Population aged 15 years and over (number) by occupational group and census year

Occupation	2011
Corporate managers and directors	120,505
Other managers and proprietors	50,904
Science, research, engineering and technology professionals	78,768
Health professionals	88,906
Teaching and educational professionals	98,016
Business, media and public service professionals	88,091
Science, engineering and technology associate professionals	38,606
Health and social care associate professionals	21,709
Protective service occupations	26,697
Culture, media and sports occupations	29,727
Business and public service associate professionals	114,421
Administrative occupations	184,819
Secretarial and related occupations	41,833
Skilled agricultural and related trades	89,292
Skilled metal, electrical and electronic trades	92,744
Skilled construction and building trades	103,978
Textiles, printing and other skilled trades	62,090
Caring personal service occupations	96,216
Leisure, travel and related personal service occupations	48,373
Sales occupations	132,447
Customer service occupations	22,833
Process, plant and machine operatives	84,322
Transport and mobile machine drivers and operatives	83,414
Elementary trades and related occupations	51,522
Elementary administration and service occupations	150,208
Other/not stated	197,596
All occupational groups	2,198,037
Unemployed – looking for first regular job	34,166
Total in labour force	**2,232,203**

Source: CSO (2017).

Across the EU, higher proportions of people are employed in what is termed professional work, comprising scientists, engineers, business and IT specialists, managers and in market services occupations such as research, consultancy, accounting, marketing and legal services. In the most recent SOLAS occupational forecasting report, Behan

(2014) proposes that employment growth will be highest for professional and skilled trades occupations. Particularly strong growth is predicted in construction, STEM (science, technology, engineering and maths), IT and in legal and business professions. The scaling back of proportionate employment in traditional manufacturing (arising from technological changes and labour capital substitution) and in agriculture is set to continue. This trend will increasingly alter the occupational profile of the labour force – professional work (which tends to be associated with high-tech skills/high-qualification based) is growing, while more traditional work (craft-skilled/low-skilled/low-qualification based) is in demise. Ireland's sectoral and occupational employment trends mirror what is happening across Europe, with continuing predictions of job growth in services sectors and in areas requiring some level of formal qualification.

The increasing professionalisation of jobs will affect participation in education and training, as individuals are challenged to upskill for future employment. Table 4.3 presents a summary of the European labour market in 2016 which is useful for comparing with the Irish labour market as discussed here.

Table 4.3 Portrait of the European labour market 2015

Workforce becomes more female and gender segregation still common: Between 2005 and 2015, the employment rate of people aged 15–64 in the EU28 rose – from 63% to 66%. Largely, this is due to the increased participation of women in the labour market. However, the female employment rate is still 11 percentage points below that of men. Moreover, gender segregation remains very high and takes multiple forms.

Ageing of the workforce: As well as becoming more female, the workforce has got substantially older: the proportion of people in employment who are aged 50 years or over has increased markedly – from 24% to 31% over 10 years. At the same time, there has been a continuous decline in the proportion of younger workers (aged under 35): from 35% of the workforce in 2005 to 30% in 2015.

Rise in part-time employment: The proportion of part-time workers in the workforce rose from 18% in 2005 to 20% in 2015. Part-time working is much more common among women, 33% of women working part time as against 10% of men.

Sectoral growth and decline: The three largest sectors are commerce and hospitality (accounting for 19% of the workforce), other services (18%) and industry (17%). Health and education constitute 11% and 8%, respectively, of total employment; however, although smaller, these two sectors (along with other services) have been growing in relative terms, whereas industry and construction are in relative decline.

Employed on indefinite contract is still the norm: The majority (66%) of the EU28 workforce holds an indefinite contract, 11% have a fixed-term contract, and 8% have either another type of contract or hold none. Some 15% of the workforce is self-employed. This picture is little changed since 2000.

Self-employment a preference for many: A majority (59%) of self-employed workers in the EU28 report that they became self-employed out of preference; 20% said they had no other alternative for work; and 16% cited a combination of these two factors.

Source: Eurofound (2016), *Sixth European Working Conditions Survey – Overview report*, Publications Office of the European Union, Luxembourg.

Recent figures released by Eurostat (2017) indicate that although women represent approximately half of all employed persons in the EU, they continue to be underrepresented amongst managerial occupations. Ireland ranks among the top five countries for women in managerial positions where 43 per cent, or just over two out of every five managers in Ireland is a woman – the EU average is 35 per cent. Despite having one of the highest proportion of female managers in Europe, Ireland's female managers earn almost 16 per cent less than their male counterparts, signalling that the managerial gender pay gap is significant, though lower than the EU average of 23.4 per cent. In simple terms, this indicates that across the EU female managers earn on average 77 cents for every euro a male manager makes per hour.

PARTICIPATION IN EDUCATION

The Irish education system has undergone significant change from the early 1960s onwards. In recognition of the fundamental value of a good education system to the economic and social development of a nation, free second-level education was introduced in 1966, and compulsory schooling was extended from fourteen to fifteen years of age.

Following the publication of the 'White Paper on Education (1995)', which echoed a persistent concern regarding the general suitability of the Leaving Certificate cycle for all students, a decision was taken to restructure the Leaving Certificate programme into three components: the established Leaving Certificate programme; the Leaving Certificate Applied Programme; and the Leaving Certificate Vocational Programme. However, the majority of senior cycle students continue to follow the mainstream Leaving Certificate programme, which retains an emphasis on general academic education and continues to prepare students for entry to the labour market or to third-level education.

Participation at third level is determined by a points system based on Leaving Certificate examination results and, while entry to some programmes of study is more difficult in terms of the number of points required, in general demand for third-level education exceeds the limited supply of places available at third-level institutions. The total number of full-time students at third level has increased significantly over the last number of years, to the extent that approximately 67 per cent of students who complete secondary school education progress to third-level programmes, At the start of 2017, 47 per cent of people in employment in Ireland had a third-level qualification.

A number of factors have contributed to this general upsurge in participation. These include the provision of post-Leaving Certificate courses; the abolition of fees for undergraduate students in publicly funded third-level colleges in 1995, which provided wider access to third-level education, greater investment in education and, of course, an increased number of third- and fourth-level places and programmes of study on offer.

Recent years have been marked by increased expenditure on education, coupled with greater numbers in education and higher participation rates more generally. The changing occupational profile can be seen to have had a significant effect on participation rates, as qualifications are seen as the route to professional occupational work. Young people are staying in the education system for longer, across all levels of education. In a comparison of those who have completed third-level education in the OECD countries (OECD 2015), Ireland compares positively with many of its EU counterparts, with considerably more people likely to complete third-level education in Ireland than in many other OECD countries.

The benefits of education have been well established over the years. Tansey (1998) noted that each step up the educational ladder yields a significantly positive rate of return in terms of higher lifetime earnings, thus the benefits of increased educational attainment are spread across the whole of the economy, in terms of increased productivity, increased employment and a widened tax base for the state. Data from the OECD serves to confirm that those with higher-level qualifications are consistently more likely to be in employment across all OECD countries. For example, the OECD *Education at a Glance* report (2015), showed that over 80 per cent of tertiary-educated adults are employed; the comparable figure for those with second-level education is 70 per cent and is less than 60 per cent for those who have not completed second-level schooling. Moreover, adults with a third-level education earn an average of 60 per cent more than adults who have completed secondary schooling only. Education and earnings are thus positively linked, and so the earnings advantage of increased education would appear to outweigh the costs of acquiring it. This link is also evidenced in successive Irish labour force surveys, which suggest that individuals who possess no post-primary qualification are up to six times more likely to be unemployed than are those with a third-level qualification. In the case of those who do find employment, the remuneration they receive is very often far lower than those with higher qualifications. If we factor in the most recent occupation forecasts for Ireland (Behan 2014), we can see that occupations predicted to grow the most are those that are most closely linked with third-level educational attainment. The overwhelming evidence is that employment rates and earnings increase as an adult's level of education and skills increases; highlighting that labour markets around the world consider a diploma or degree as the primary indication of a worker's employability.

We should also note that while many of the benefits of education can be quantified in economic terms, there are other important outcomes associated with improved educational attainment. In particular, factors such as high levels of social cohesion and integration are important benchmarks for modern societies in which all citizens use learning to become more effective participants in democratic, civil and economic processes.

This chapter has sought to provide some insight into how labour markets function and how this might likely shape the nature of HRM in organisations. The Irish labour market has undergone considerable change in recent years and the demographic profile of the Irish population is favourably disposed towards high labour market participation for many years to come. Participation in education is rising and the level of educational attainment among the labour force is high by OECD standards. The occupation profile has seen a huge surge in professional work that requires higher-level educational qualifications, while projections of occupational trends over the next few years (Behan, 2014) suggest that unskilled and semi-skilled jobs will continue to be displaced and that educational attainment and qualifications will increasingly become the criteria upon which employability is determined. There is thus a considerable danger that those who drop out of the education system before completing their formal education will become increasingly marginalised and unemployable.

As business becomes increasingly knowledge-based, there is considerable pressure on organisations to ensure that their internal capability can match external environmental requirements. The onus is increasingly being placed on the HR function or practitioner to ensure that the firm's labour pool has both the skills and abilities to meet organisational requirements, and furthermore, the capacity to deal with possible changes that the external environment might demand.

The following chapters explore these and other issues in greater detail.

5
Human Resource Planning, Recruitment and Selection

Having the best and most talented (i.e. most effective) people working for them is obviously a key priority for organisations today. This makes the ability to attract, hire, develop and retain these most talented and capable individuals one of the most important determinants of an organisation's long-term effectiveness (Breaugh 2013; Dineen and Soltis 2011). Talent is now in fashion and the term talent management appears to have subsumed what was traditionally considered to be simply good HRM practices (Lewis and Heckman 2006). We are constantly reminded that the 'war for talent' is on and that organisations must look to their talent pipelines and engage in talent management, to ensure that they are prepared to meet the challenges that face them. Cappelli and Keller (2014) describe talent management as a practitioner-generated term covering a range of long-standing practices that aim at getting the right person in the right job, at the right time and cite Gallardo-Gallardo et al.'s (2013: 291) assertion that 'talent can mean whatever a business leader or writer wants it to mean'.

Irrespective of the label attached to having the best calibre employees within organisations, there is no doubt that organisations face increasing pressure to improve their existing HR processes and systems. Breaugh (2013) notes that the most fundamental issue an employer faces is deciding on the type of individuals to target for recruitment. Once this decision is made, an organisation needs to determine the method to use to reach these individuals, the recruitment message to convey, and the type of recruitment strategy to adopt. Morley (2007) notes that the priority in many organisations has shifted away from conventional models primarily based on matching knowledge, skills and attitudes (KSAs) for defined jobs towards hiring for organisational compatibility. This 'search for good-fit' (Heraty and Morley 1998; Morley 2007) involves achieving a fit between an individual's personality, beliefs, values and expectations and the organisation's espoused culture, norms, values, and expectations. Arguably, then, selecting individuals based solely on their technical knowledge and skills is no longer sufficient to ensure effective job performance, and employers are seeking people who have good inter-personal and communication skills, good development potential, and who can easily settle into and remain within the organisation.

Poor fit is costly in more than just monetary terms, as Sandico and Kleiner (1999: 132) remind us:

The obvious bad hires are the ones who leave the job soon after they are hired. Other poor hires are not as apparent because the problem does not become noticeable until later: they are the clock-watchers, the incapables who get their work done by others, or the marginal workers who have found a way to beat the system. These are the 'false positive' employees – the people who were hired but should not have been.

Phillips and Gully (2015) suggest we can think about recruitment both from the organisational level, where the key focus is on employer branding and identifying talent, as well as at the unit or team level which is all about fit. This person–organisation fit is especially important during the recruitment and selection process wherein the concern is as much about finding the best organisation to work for as it is about finding the best job. Establishing this fit is a challenging task for human resource management, and in this chapter we review the initial phases that establish exactly what kind of 'fit' is required, i.e. the processes of human resource planning, recruitment and selection. Getting this element right is critical because the calibre of those who are selected into the organisation will have consequences for how all other aspects of HRM are enacted later.

THE PURPOSE OF HUMAN RESOURCE PLANNING

Accepting that human resources are potentially the most valuable resource available to an organisation is one thing – dealing with how highly differentiated, complex and unpredictable they are, is quite another! Failure to place human resources in the right areas of the business, at the right time, and at the right cost, can result in serious inefficiencies across the organisation. It stands to reason, then, that HRM can only be truly effective where human resource actions and activities are linked with strategic business issues or priorities.

At its most basic level, human resource planning is concerned with ensuring that the organisation employs the right quantity of people with the KSAs that are required for effective organisational functioning – both now and for the future. This is no easy feat however. Planning is difficult at the best of times, and in periods of economic uncertainty when organisations may not even know if they will be in business three months down the line, it can become almost impossible. Cappelli (2008) argues that anticipating human capital needs and setting out plans to meet them may require new solutions to account for increased market uncertainty, particularly from labour markets.

Despite the challenges and its imprecise nature, a number of key benefits arise from effective HR planning including:
- Being able to identify potential shortfalls or surpluses of labour and organise to address them before they become a significant problem.
- Having a consistent overview of the talent and skills that exists in the organisation and how to make the best use of them.
- Ensuring the adherence to employment equality principles and regulations across the workforce.

Good HR planning helps to avoid poor hiring decisions.

THE HUMAN RESOURCE PLANNING PROCESS

Human resource planning is based on the idea that a balance needs to be achieved between both the supply of, and demand for, human resources. Demand for labour is derived from corporate plans, while labour supply is either internal – from current employees within the internal labour market; or external – from potential employees in the external labour market. In the first three chapters of this text, the discussion included how external factors impact upon organisational functioning (such as government policies, economic considerations and product market conditions) and how business planning can be linked with HRM to make it more strategic. In Chapter 4 particular labour market considerations that affect how HRM operates were outlined; while Chapter 13 details aspects of the legislative environment that directly affect the employment relationship. These are some of the key issues that influence HRM decisions and so, rather than reiterate the discussions of these chapters here, it is suggested that you take some time to read through them so that you have a better understanding of how they affect the human resource planning process.

A model of the human resource planning process is depicted in Figure 5.1.

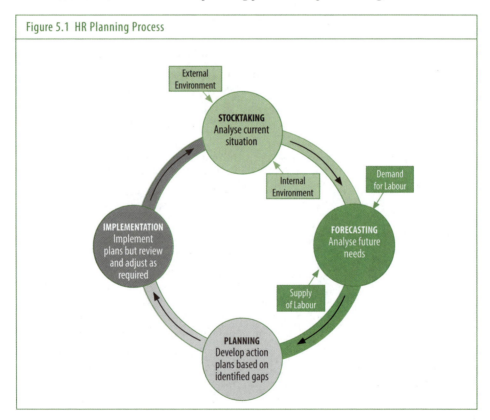

Figure 5.1 HR Planning Process

The planning process outlined in Figure 5.1 identifies four key stages in the human resource planning process: 1. stocktaking; 2. forecasting; 3. planning; and 4. implementing. These stages are interlinked in a cycle and represented in a circular fashion here to indicate the flow from one stage to the next cycle of planning. As indicated earlier, a preliminary step in developing human resource plans involves the identification of clearly defined organisational objectives, which indicate strategic purpose and direction. These may then be supplemented by more detailed operational plans that outline the role of each function in facilitating the achievement of strategic goals. Some changes to plans are inevitable, however, and plans will have to be flexibly adapted as organisational requirements dictate (e.g. responding to external product market fluctuations, or skills shortages in the labour market).

STAGE 1: STOCKTAKING

Stocktaking involves analysing current human resources, i.e. developing an accurate human resource profile of the existing workforce. Specifically, the organisation needs to gather details on the current skills' mix of its workforce in terms of education level, training level, job knowledge and functional ability. Information of this kind should be readily available from existing HR records, additional data from employees' application forms, performance reviews and job descriptions. In addition, job analysis data will indicate the knowledge and skills required for each job type, while organisational charts will present talent pipelines or career pathways within the organisation. Analysis of these various data sources will provide the organisation with a rich database of information that allows it to evaluate both existing human resource capability and potential for development.

STAGE 2: FORECASTING

The forecasting stage of the human resource planning model involves forecasting both the supply of labour and the demand for labour. This is probably the most difficult aspect of human resource planning, because it requires the organisation to make predictions about how many employees will be required for the future (demand analysis based on past trends and likely future business functioning); and to determine where future employees are likely to be sourced (supply analysis). Planning, by its nature, relies heavily on past experience and the development of certain hypotheses concerning the future, and given the mercurial nature of the business environment, it is hardly surprising that forecasting either demand for, or supply of, labour is highly speculative at best. It is a useful process, however, for it forces organisations to be ever vigilant to market conditions and customer expectations and to be more prepared to meet the inevitable changes that they are likely to encounter.

FORECASTING DEMAND FOR LABOUR

Demand for labour can only be forecast with any degree of accuracy in the very short term: while most managers will be aware of their current requirements, the issue of predicting requirements for the future is far more problematic. However difficult the process, and imprecise the results, some forecasting is nonetheless required in order that the organisation can make better informed decisions. Here, organisations can look to data on their recent trade and production trends, demand for their product/service, technology changes and innovations, capital investment plans, market strategies, acquisitions, divestments, mergers, product diversification and so forth. For example, identifying new potential markets, or changes in the type of work being undertaken, will impact on demand for particular knowledge and skills, while identifying the skills mix of particular towns or regions will feed into location decisions. Coupled with these factors, an organisation's demand for labour will also be affected by the profile of the external labour market, legislative provisions around business and employment, the prevailing economic climate, and the range of flexible choices available to organisations in terms of the type of employment required.

FORECASTING SUPPLY OF LABOUR

Internal Supply

The forecasting of internal labour supply constituted the central preoccupation of human resource planning throughout the 1960s and 1970s and resulted in the development of a number of mathematical models to predict labour attrition in a given time period. Cappelli and Keller (2014: 313) highlight that uncertainty on the supply side arises from difficulties in predicting both skills and competencies needed in the future. If the competencies needed in the future change dramatically, a talent pool that looks robust now may look deficient at a later date. Organisations cannot control the future availability of skills and competencies within the labour market and the increased tendency to poach experienced candidates from competitors has created retention concerns across occupational levels, which adds further complication to any estimates of internal supply.

Three key supply indices in particular provide some helpful indicators for organisations: 1. Labour turnover; 2. Absenteeism; and 3. Age profile of the workforce.

1: Labour Turnover

In any given year, it is expected that a certain number of people will inevitably leave the organisation and will need to be replaced, in order to maintain production or service. This is known as natural wastage or attrition and is typically referred to as labour turnover. Employees may leave an organisation for many reasons, such as retirement, better opportunities elsewhere, dissatisfaction with the job, unrealistic/unmet job expectations, incapacity, redundancy, or dismissal. The prospect of being able to predict a rate of labour turnover is an important aspect of human resource planning. Having an expected level of turnover can aid in predicting future labour requirements and allows the organisation to benchmark a 'norm' for itself. If the organisation finds it is losing particular groups of employees, it can look at better ways of improving retention rates, particularly for those employees whom the organisation has a vested interest in retaining (i.e. those who are efficient and/or highly knowledgeable of the organisation, with valuable tacit knowledge, those who are difficult to replace, or those in whom the organisation has invested considerable training). Allen *et al.* (2010) caution against an over-reliance on historic turnover rates to predict future exit rates because voluntary turnover is often unavoidable and can therefore introduce a large degree of error into these predictions.

Having some indication of labour turnover, however imprecise, is a good place to start when considering any HR planning activities. One of the simplest methods of calculating wastage is through a turnover analysis:

$$\frac{\text{Number of employees who leave in one year}}{\text{Average number employed in the past year}} \times 100 = \%$$

Turnover rates will clearly vary within industries, within organisations, and even between departments and jobs, and so it is impossible to establish an 'acceptable' rate of annual turnover. Turnover can be almost static in some organisations (i.e. none), or seemingly alarmingly high in others (i.e. close to 50 per cent). Turnover is not always undesirable however. Some time ago, Beardwell and Holden (1997) suggested that a turnover rate of 25 per cent is perfectly respectable in modern large-scale organisations and allows for movement through the organisation, but that anything approaching 30–35 per cent should give some cause for concern. While the turnover index has the advantage of being easy to calculate, and gives some indication of whether losses are high or low, it is a relatively crude measure, because it does not provide details about the types of employee who are leaving, or in which departments most losses are occurring.

A calculation of the labour stability index can provide additional information about labour turnover. This stability index is calculated as:

$$\frac{\text{Number of employees with more than one year's service}}{\text{Total number employed one year ago}} \times 100 = \%$$

The stability index provides details on whether the organisation is retaining experienced employees since it calculates and emphasises those who stay with the organisation. However, indices alone will not provide specific details on why the organisation is experiencing particular levels of wastage, thus many organisations use the 'exit interview' to help explain turnover. The purpose of this interview is to gather information on why an employee has chosen to leave the organisation. It may ask the employee to rate the organisation against a list of predetermined criteria, such as attractiveness of reward package, satisfaction with job, supervisory arrangements, opportunities for learning and development, and so forth. Combined with turnover and stability indices, the information received from the exit interviews can provide some useful indicators of potential problems that need to be addressed.

A recent CIPD report on HR practices in Ireland (Connaughton and Staunton 2017) revealed that 50 per cent of respondents had experienced increased voluntary employee turnover over the previous two years. Almost half of responding organisations (44 per cent) indicated that they expect turnover to be a significant feature of the workplace for the foreseeable future, thus highlighting the need to put resourcing and retention strategies at centre-stage for HR today.

Many years ago, Hill and Trist (1955), in conjunction with the Tavistock Institute (UK), conducted a number of landmark studies of labour turnover and developed what has become known as the 'survival curve' (see Figure 5.2 on the next page). The evidence from their studies suggested that the propensity to quit employment is highest during the early stages of employment but this tapers away as employees settle down in the organisation.

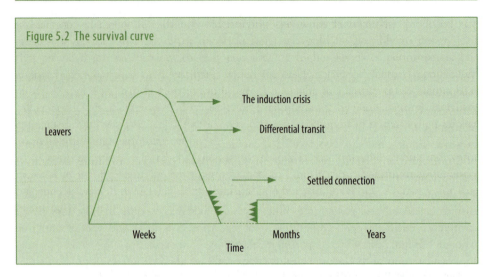

Figure 5.2 The survival curve

Hill and Trist explained the survival curve in terms of a social process that involves three distinct phases. The first phase they labelled the '*induction crisis*', at which time wastage/turnover is very high. Many reasons have been cited for the existence of the induction crisis and generally it is thought to be associated with some of the following:
- New employees find that the job is not what they imagined it would be, i.e. they have unmet expectations – perhaps as a result of the job advertisement and/or selection interview.
- New employees find that they are unhappy with some aspect of the work environment, i.e. they find it difficult to adjust to or settle into working in the organisation.
- Some new employees find alternative work elsewhere that is perceived to be more attractive, i.e. they may have applied for a number of jobs and take the first they are offered until something more 'suitable' comes along.

The period of time covered by the induction crisis can vary considerably between organisations and between job categories, and in some cases can last up to two years. However, it is generally assumed to reach its peak after the first six weeks of employment.

The second phase is termed the '*differential transit*' where, as the employee begins to feel more comfortable in their position and settles into company life, the likelihood of suddenly leaving begins to decrease.

The final stage is called '*settled connection*' and Hill and Trist (1955) suggest that employees who remain with the organisation for this period of time tend to be viewed as 'quasi-permanent'. At this stage, there is a perceived greater incentive in an employee staying with the organisation, rather than leaving to go elsewhere.

The survival curve is indicative only though, and so should not be relied on too much – it does not take into account the individual's personal motivations, career expectations, or non-work variables that may influence the decision to stay with or leave the organisation. Survival curves may also become shorter and have to be re-imagined in accordance with the age of the new entrant. For example, the generational literature (Parry and McCarthy 2017; McCarthy et al. 2014) suggests that individuals at various stages in their life cycle have a range of values and expectations that impact what they seek from the employment relationship. For younger generations, the tendency to 'job hop' is normal, and new careers built in the market, rather than within organisational boundaries, is becoming the new norm – this point is discussed in further detail in Chapter 9.

2: Absenteeism

When forecasting the likely number of people who will be required over the next period, the second key supply index organisations take account of is their current levels of absenteeism and likely future trends. Absenteeism is taken to mean all absence from work other than paid holidays. Seminal work by Steers and Rhodes (1978) suggests that, among other things, an employee's attendance at work is a function of two particular variables: ability to attend and motivation to attend. Ability to attend is chiefly affected by illness or some incapacity that prevents an employee from attending work – in most cases this is involuntary (unplanned) absenteeism. Motivation to attend, on the other hand, is explicitly linked with the employee's feelings about the organisation and the job itself, and describes whether the employee feels a pressure to attend work (see Figure 5.3).

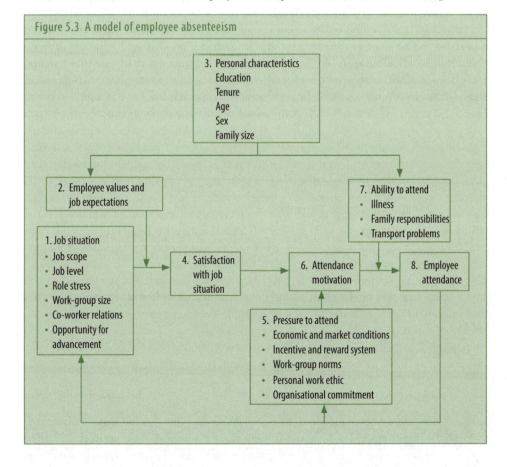

Figure 5.3 A model of employee absenteeism

Steers and Rhodes found a clear correlation between absenteeism trends and labour turnover trends. For example, when employees are unhappy with their work situation (for whatever reason) and would like to leave but are unable to find alternative work, absenteeism rates tend to increase. However, when alternative work is more readily available, absenteeism rates decrease and labour turnover becomes more frequent. In extreme recessionary times, both turnover and absenteeism are reduced as people are less likely to risk their jobs.

At the organisational level, information on absenteeism is typically gathered from attendance files, time records, medical files and other HR data. The most common formula used to calculate absenteeism is as follows:

$$\frac{\text{Total absence (days/hours) in a particular time period}}{\text{Total possible time (days/hours)}} \times 100 = \%$$

This index calculates the percentage of the total time available in a specified period that has been lost because of absence. Absenteeism costs organisations in terms of paying workers for work not done, in paying for substitute workers, in downtime due to inexperience or increased stress levels resulting from one worker doing the work of two.

Eurofound (2010) suggests that average rates of absence across Europe are between 3 per cent and 6 per cent of working time, with a reasonable estimate of the cost as about 2.5 per cent of GDP. A report in 2014 by Ireland's Small Firms Association (SFA) provides a breakdown of absenteeism rates whereby for large businesses, the average absenteeism rate is 2.34 per cent or 5.4 days, whereas in businesses with less than 50 employees the rate is 2.06 per cent or 4.7 days. It estimates that the direct cost to small business with sick pay schemes is over €490 million, but, if all costs are taken into account (including replacing staff, paying overtime and medical referrals, loss of productivity and the time spent managing absence) then the overall cost is close to €1 billion per year. Recent data from the CSO (2015) Irish health survey shows that 24 per cent of respondents reported that they were absent from work due to health problems and the average number of days lost was 5.6. The age group with the highest percentage of absenteeism from work is the 25–34 age group (37 per cent). Although it is almost impossible to quantify the full costs of absenteeism in Ireland, some estimates put them in the region of €2 billion per annum.

It is clearly important, therefore, that organisations maintain accurate records of absenteeism and plot absenteeism on a regular basis to discover any upward trends. High levels of absenteeism might point to inconsistencies between human resource activities and thus might require an organisation to rethink its strategy in respect to, for example, selection, supervision, job design, learning and development, performance appraisal and management, discipline, or rewards. It may also have implications for the operation of the code of conduct and disciplinary procedures within the organisation.

3: Age Profile of the Workforce

The third supply index that an organisation could examine is the age distribution of each category of employee. This is a useful index that can be used to identify imminent retirement patterns, plan recruitment drives, and construct career and succession pathways for those with future potential within the organisation.

Mapping the age structure of a workforce provides important timeline opportunities for the organisation to plan around. A predominantly 'mature' age profile would trigger requirements for retirement planning and phased exit. Depending on the organisation, it may also offer the possibility of bridge employment to retain valuable knowledge and skills and it could prompt a recruitment drive to fill the jobs of those about to retire. A predominantly 'middle-aged' workforce might indicate potential (or existing) bottlenecks in the succession and promotion system, which, if unresolved, can create dissatisfaction and may lead to costly turnover problems. An age distribution that is heavily weighted at the younger end might have implications for knowledge mix and talent management bottlenecks if they stay within the organisation. As already indicated, the notion of the linear organisation career might not be attractive for increasingly mobile younger workers, who may be more interested in developing their employability through a series of jobs and organisations.

In theory, having a balanced mix of ages across the organisation makes it easier to structure and develop the internal talent pool, and optimise the sharing of valuable tacit knowledge from expert to novice. This rarely occurs in practice, however, and is inadvisable since the deliberate selecting (or not selecting) of job applicants based on age constitutes discrimination and is unlawful. However, organisations must take note of the age demographic because effectively managing a multi-generational workforce is challenging since employees of different ages may have different values and expectations that are reflected in workplace behaviours, and sometimes conflicts (McCarthy and Heraty 2017).

EXTERNAL SUPPLY

Any forecasting of external labour supply must take into account external labour market trends and the changing demography of the labour force which were discussed in Chapter 4. In terms of human resource planning, the organisation will be particularly interested in, for example: current levels of unemployment (most especially in its local geographic area); the changing structure of the work force and its effects on recruitment and supply (i.e. the increasing number of labour market entrants with third-level education will impact on recruitment, expectations and reward); the trend towards flexible employment choices and the importance of work–non-work balance; and the current levels of education and training provision that determine the skills mix of the external labour market. HR data analytics, or big data mining, is becoming a feature of the HR role in organisations today, in an attempt to better link HR strategies with business projections and trends. At the individual level, key data on qualifications, interests, and values are readily shared on social media outlets such as Facebook and LinkedIn, so it is becoming easier to identify potential sources of talent outside the organisation. Combined, these factors determine the outcome of the essential 'make or buy' question: Is it more effective to source prospective employees outside the organisation ('buy' decision), or should the organisation develop its own internal labour market ('make' decision)?

STAGE 3: PLANNING

Once the organisation has forecast likely demand for, and supply of, labour it can then estimate whether there are any imbalances between the two, that is, whether the organisation is faced with a labour shortage or a labour surplus. Where a shortage exists, or is predicted to occur, the organisation can decide to plan for recruitment or retraining as appropriate. A labour surplus requires that an organisation make plans for redundancy, redeployment, retraining, or perhaps lay-offs or short-time working. Regardless of the particular options open to it, the organisation's eventual decision will have consequences for the general nature of employee relations, the structuring of work, the reward package offered, and the structure of its internal labour market. For this reason the organisation needs to carefully weigh the attendant costs and benefits of whichever strategy it decides to pursue.

STAGE 4: IMPLEMENTATION

On completion of the human resource plan, the organisation operationalises its decision and the cycle is once again set in motion. Since both internal and external environments are subject to considerable change over time, it is advisable that human resource plans be monitored and reviewed on a regular basis and amended or redirected as required. The human resource planning process identifies a range of options that are available to an organisation depending on whether it forecasts a shortage or surplus of labour occurring in the future.

The remainder of this chapter explores the process of recruitment and selection as a response to a perceived shortfall in required human resources.

RECRUITMENT AND SELECTION

The recruitment and selection process is essentially concerned with finding, assessing and engaging new employees. As such, its focus is on matching the capabilities and inclinations of prospective candidates against the demands and rewards inherent in a given job. As has been noted in earlier chapters, the HRM literature consistently argues that the profitability, and even the survival, of an organisation depend upon the calibre of the workforce and that human resources represent a critical means of achieving competitiveness. Bringing the best human resources into the organisation is therefore a key stage in developing this effective workforce.

Interest focuses on identifying the recruiting sources that are most likely to yield high-quality employees and the selection methods that best predict future job performance. Organisations can be said to deal with two different kinds of uncertainty – uncertainty about job demands and uncertainty about candidates' suitability. Job analysis seeks to cope with the first, while selection deals with the second. Montgomery (1996: 94) highlights this notion of matching as the key to job success:

> Think back in your career and ask yourself, of all the people you know who failed in a job and were terminated, how many of them failed because they lacked the right educational degree, the right job experience, or the right industry background? In all likelihood, most of them failed because of inadequate interpersonal skills, an inability to communicate, or because they just didn't fit in with the culture; in other words – bad chemistry!

There are two distinct phases involved in this matching process: recruitment, which is concerned with attracting a group of potential candidates to apply for a given vacancy;

followed by selection, or the process of choosing the most suitable candidate from a pool of candidates identified through recruitment. A simple flow diagram of the recruitment and selection process is outlined in Figure 5.4.

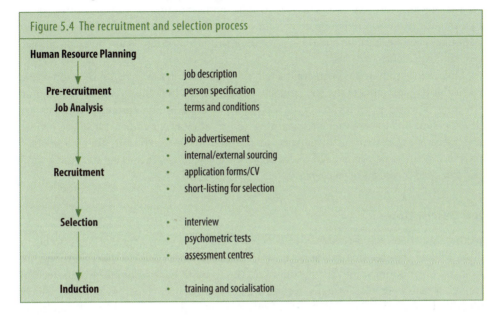

Figure 5.4 The recruitment and selection process

Human Resource Planning

Pre-recruitment
Job Analysis
- job description
- person specification
- terms and conditions

Recruitment
- job advertisement
- internal/external sourcing
- application forms/CV
- short-listing for selection

Selection
- interview
- psychometric tests
- assessment centres

Induction
- training and socialisation

Breaugh suggests (2013) that it is useful to conceptualise much of what occurs during the recruitment process as reflecting an attitude formation/change process that involves individuals forming an impression of what working for an organisation would be like.

THE JOB ANALYSIS PHASE

When an organisation makes the decision to fill an existing vacancy through recruitment, the first stage in the process involves conducting a comprehensive job analysis. This may already have been conducted as part of the human resource planning process, particularly where recruitment is a relatively frequent occurrence. Traditionally job analysis has been described as the process of identifying, not only the knowledge and skills that are required for a particular job, but also the types of attitude and behaviour that are needed. Both Sanchez and Levine (2001) and Morgeson and Dierdorff (2011) point to the danger of focusing solely on job analysis as if each person only has one job, arguing that roles at work are becoming increasingly 'boundaryless'. Since organisations require a more grounded understanding of what makes work a successful experience overall, it is suggested (Fine and Cronshaw 1999; Meyer *et al.* 2010, Sanchez and Levine 2014) that job analysis be considered to perform three key functions:
1. Provide information about specific tasks, i.e. *work behaviour*.
2. Provide information about the characteristics or attributes of people performing such tasks, i.e. *worker attributes*.
3. Provide information about the context within which work activities are performed, including the situational opportunities and constraints that influence behaviour, i.e. *work context*.

There are a number of ways of conducting a job analysis that can vary from asking the current job holder to detail all aspects of the job (via questionnaire, check-list, diary), having someone observe the job-holder performing the job over a period of time, or interviewing the job holder to get a fuller understanding of the different aspects that might not be so easily apparent from outside the job. Each method has particular advantages and limitations and the choice in organisations often comes down to relative cost and expediency.

Once a job analysis has been conducted, the organisation has a clear indication of the particular requirements of the job, and where that job fits into the overall organisational structure. The job analysis can also be used in decisions relating to promotion and career development, for job transfers, for learning and training programmes, for salary review, and for work restructuring initiatives. In the first instance, though, the job analysis provides the information needed to develop the *job description*, the *person specification* and the *terms and conditions of employment*.

Job Description

In the past, there was a tendency to couch job descriptions in vague or loose terms to allow for any changes that might occur in the main job purpose over time. Furthermore, in many organisations, job descriptions were discussed in general terms at the selection interview but were not formally recorded or written down. This practice has largely dissipated in recent years as a result of statutory requirements that all employers furnish their employees with written details of the terms and conditions pertaining to their employment, or refer such employees to where their job details are specified (e.g. company handbook or noticeboard). For this reason, organisations are careful to develop job descriptions that are up to date, complete and inclusive of most job requirements. While job descriptions vary according to job classification or type, they typically conform to a relatively set framework (see Figure 5.5).

Figure 5.5 Elements of a job description

- Job title
- Department
- Location
- Reports to
- Purpose
- Main tasks
- Liaison and main contacts
- Staff responsibilities
- Special features
- Rewards and conditions

The **job description** is essentially a broad statement of the purpose, scope, duties and responsibilities that are attached to the job, and as such is the basis for the contract of employment. Furthermore, since job advertisements normally detail the job description, it is critically important that organisations have a precise understanding of the nature of the job vacancy and that this realistic preview of the job then be used to attract the most suitable candidates. Russo et al. (1995) suggest that an effective job description could include information on the following:

- *Job identification*: in particular job title, department, division, company name and location.
- *Relationship with others*: notable vertical relationships (supervision and monitoring) or horizontal relationships (liaison with others, co-operation).
- *Job content*: especially the actual tasks of the job, the level of responsibility of the task, frequencies of performance, the importance of the task.
- *Working conditions*: for instance physical environment (noise, heat), social environment (working in a group, night shift), monetary environment (salary, fringe benefits).
- *Performance standards/objectives*: expressed in quantitative terms (i.e. level of output or sales, time limits to be met), or in qualitative terms (i.e. maintenance of a quality standard within a group).
- *Human requirements*: such as physical and psychological characteristics of the job holder/applicant that would comply with the demands of the job (person specification).
- *Other important information*: for example, learning, training and career opportunities, firm's performance in its market (image-related information).

Person Specification

Once the job description has been drawn up, the organisation can then develop a person specification. The person specification essentially describes the *ideal* person for the job, i.e. it provides a detailed description of the qualifications, knowledge, specific skills and aptitudes, experience and personal attributes that are required to do the job most effectively.

The person specification has a number of very important functions in the recruitment and selection process: not only does it describe the person required for the job, it also helps in deciding where the organisation should concentrate its search and advertising efforts, for example level of experience and/or qualification can be used as a guide to whether to advertise nationally or target graduate career fairs. The person specification can also facilitate systematic short-listing and will (should) form the basis upon which selection criteria are determined. The person specification *must* match the job description if it is going to be used to attract the most suitable potential job candidates.

Since, by their nature, person specifications describe the ideal candidate or jobholder, it is important to try to differentiate between characteristics/requirements that are absolutely *essential* to perform the job, and those that are *desirable* (would be useful/good to have but are not essential). In this way an organisation can more easily discount applicants who do not match the essential criteria, and concentrate instead on those who match them best. In the 1950s, both Rodger (1952) and Munro-Fraser (1954) developed categorisations for specifying some personal characteristics that can aid effective recruitment and selection. These included factors such as physical appearance/impact, qualifications, abilities, disposition and interests. Organisations need to be careful with these frameworks, however. First, the research underpinning the development of these frameworks was completed many years ago and at a time when the regulatory environment for employment was considerably different from what it is today. For this reason, these schemes are useful as indicators of *some* categories that can be used, but clearly other categories are neither legal nor appropriate for use today. Organisations must be ever vigilant to ensure that the person specification is not discriminatory in any way (the relevant equality legislation is discussed fully in Chapter 13).

Table 5.1 Job description: Advertisement for Human resources (HR) generalist	
Summary	Reporting to the HR Manager, the HR Generalist is responsible for supporting the HR Function and shadowing experienced HR professionals in providing key human resources administration. This role is responsible for co ordinating HR administration activities and also supports key HR projects and initiatives in a dynamic regulated manufacturing environment.
Requirements	• Relevant Business Related Degree Qualification, ideally in HR • 3 years plus previous HR administration experience in a dynamic, fast-paced working environment an advantage • Proficient in MS Office • Good knowledge of employment legislation • Confident and conscientious with excellent communication skills and attention to detail. Excellent written and oral skills • Can work effectively as a team member and independently • Good research and analytical skills • Highly organised, self-motivated and can pre-empt situations rather than waiting for instruction • High degree of professionalism • Ideally experience in SAP, Success Factors or similar HR information system
Essential Duties and Responsibilities	• Providing a high-quality, accurate and efficient HR administration service within strict timeframes e.g. employee queries, filing and correspondence • Support the HR Business Partner with implementing human resources relevant activities including recruitment, performance management, contract preparation, L&D, etc. • Preparing starter packs for new employees joining the company • Deliver HR induction presentation for new employees and support other HR training initiatives • Tracking all new starter documentation to complete employee file • Creating and maintaining all personnel files with accuracy • Producing standard HR documentation and reports/statistics • Provide HR support on the maintenance and audit of HR Information Systems. • Coordinating the on-boarding process for new employees • Support and participate in the end to end recruitment process • Support the communications regarding employee recognition programme and other general communications • Dealing with day to day HR queries from employees and management in a timely and professional manner • Lead and support key HR projects • Support employee welfare initiatives and social events • Archiving and filing of documentation as required • Compliance to all site Environmental, Health and Safety requirements, training and regulations • Compliance to all local site company policies, procedures and corporate policies • Perform additional duties at the request of the direct supervisor • Act in accordance with the company's Guiding Principles and adherence to the corporate Code of Conduct

Source: www.irishjobs.ie (2017).

So, as indicated, some of the features in the frameworks can be used to build a picture of the type of person required for a particular job. Tables 5.1 and 5.2 present two different job advertisements that appeared on the recruitment website irishjobs.ie in 2017. They demonstrate how job descriptions include elements of both the key tasks required of the job holder, as well as the specific knowledge and skills/qualifications that are considered essential, and desirable for successful completion of the job.

Table 5.2 Job description: Advertisement for Senior HR manager	
Role	This individual will be responsible for managing the European Human Resources team as well as activities for the European locations.
General	XX (*name of company withheld*) has an opening for a Senior Human Resource Manager in Ireland. This individual will be responsible for managing the European Human Resources team as well as activities for the European locations. This is a "hands-on" role with expansive responsibilities that include but are not limited to: talent acquisition strategy, strategic workforce planning, employee development and training, coaching and influencing leaders to drive exceptional business results in a dynamic and changing environment, employee relations, corrective actions and investigations, compliance and audits, updating and managing the HRIS (WorkDay) system with employee information and status changes, extracting data and analytics to support business proposals or decisions; as well as interpreting and ensuring that HR policies and procedures are communicated and adhered to. This position is responsible for maintaining a strong relationship with business groups within these matrixed organizations as well as working effectively with a remote HR teams. This HR professional interacts with all levels of the business and reports to Global Director, Human Resources but maintains a strong dotted line relationship with assigned local unit leaders. The position also holds overall responsibility for ensuring that the Business Unit is complying with company and country programs, policies, and regulations.
Responsibilities	• Manages and promotes the implementation of corporate initiatives throughout the Business Units. • Align as a business partner to the business leadership team, providing critical feedback and suggestions. • Clear communication with corporate HR leadership to align with corporate initiates • Managing talent review process and employee development • Collaborate with Business Unit leaders • Develops, manages, and oversees the recruiting and retention strategy for the region, with a focus on short and long term staffing and increasing the bench strength of the employees within the region. Talent acquisition is one of the primary functions of this position. • Serve as project manager for European HR initiative; Ensures that projects meet expectations and conscious of timeline and follow through. Must possess strong Project Manager Skills. • Manage and support labour relations. • Responsible for aligning training strategy with business direction. Manages overall training efforts in region, ensuring employees are trained in a timely manner, and that they meet the Company training goals. • Supports and manages employee policies, procedures, programs and benefits. • Responsible for handling sensitive employment issues and performance management. • Monitors, and coaches, management styles, practices, and behaviours to successfully drive business results and to optimize employee morale. • Provides coaching, mentoring, and development opportunities to others in the HR community as appropriate. • Initiate Improvements • Partner on future acquisition due diligence and post-acquisition integration projects.

Qualifications	- Bachelor's degree in Human Resources or business related discipline
- CIPD certification preferred
- Strategic mindset with strong business acumen resulting in the ability to connect dots and drive HR agenda with proactive thought leadership
- Excellent communication, organisation and time management skills, as the ability to manage several priorities at once will be required
- High level of flexibility, with strong commitment to success
- Outstanding collaboration and project management skills and enjoy interacting with cross functional teams across the organisation
- Ability to lead change
- Skilled in navigating a highly complex organisation
- Experience managing a team of HR professionals, some of which are in remote locations
- Extensive working knowledge of local Employment Law and familiar with European laws
- Confidence to voice opinions and ideas
- Ability to deliver tough feedback/coaching to all levels of the organisation
- Ability to make independent decisions and manage conflicting priorities in a fast-paced environment
- Able to balance strategy and detail orientation, with excellent organisational and documentation skills
- Ability to be an employee advocate who wants to make a difference in the organization by helping employees, managers and leaders succeed.
- Able to build and sustain relationships at all levels of the organisation
- Demonstrated judgment and strong integrity, compliance and confidentiality
- Prior HR experience in an engineering and/or manufacturing environment preferred
- Experience working in a matrixed organisation preferred
- Highly skilled experience in employee coaching and change management
- 10 years HR experience in progressive roles of responsibility, including practical HR experience and success in the following areas: Talent Acquisition (sourcing and staffing); Management Coaching and Employee Development; Employee Relations and Issue Resolution; Workplace Investigations; Compensation Analysis and Organizational Design/Structure; Reward and Recognition Program administration with focus on employee engagement.
- Willingness and ability to travel 25-50%
- Demonstrated intermediate to advanced skill using Microsoft office tools including Outlook, Word, Excel and PowerPoint with detail orientation and accuracy.
- Ability to meet deadlines and handle multiple tasks/projects simultaneously. Must have outstanding reputation for meeting deliverables with high quality and on-time.
- Must possess strong presentation skills with ability to clearly communicate and interpret company policies to all levels of the organization
- Communicate effectively by telephone, email and in group meetings and discussions

Source: www.irishjobs.ie (2017).

Organisations can go a step further and assign weights to the various criteria outlined. This can be particularly useful in differentiating between two or more candidates who appear to be similarly suitable. A clear focus on the job content will indicate the types of behaviours that are required to do the job, and these behaviours can also be weighted to differentiate between candidates.

In summary, then, a person specification must meet four particular requirements:
1. It must relate to a particular job and thus closely match the job description.
2. It must be specific and detail exactly what is required to complete the job effectively, e.g. 'extensive management experience' gives no indication of the quantity or quality of experience that is deemed necessary to do the job.
3. It must allow the organisation to differentiate between individual applicants, so the specification should ideally be weighted or scaled to facilitate an accurate measurement of individual characteristics.
4. It must allow the organisation to assess whether a candidate meets the specification, i.e. all the characteristics specified must be capable of being measured and assessed. As an example, many person specifications require individuals who are 'highly motivated', yet motivation is inherently difficult to assess, particularly in an interview. We shall return to this later in the chapter.

Terms and Conditions

While often included in the job description, in practice the terms and conditions of employment refer specifically to the effort–reward relationship and so include details on the hours to be worked, methods of payment, job entitlements (holidays, bonuses, allowances) and other attendant benefits. Since terms and conditions are often the most visible attributes of the job, they play an important role in the attraction of suitable candidates. Furthermore, as with person specifications, care must be taken to ensure that the terms and conditions of employment meet the requirements of the various employment law statutes (see Chapter 13 for details on relevant employment legislation).

THE RECRUITMENT PHASE

Once the job analysis stage has been completed, the organisation begins the process of recruitment to attract suitable candidates for the particular vacancy. Lieven *et al.* (2002) noted that the 'war for talent' had led to an increased emphasis on attracting potential employees in what they saw as a very competitive recruitment market. Fifteen years on, competition for talent is still fierce, which gives added urgency that recruitment deliver on the following:
1. To attract a pool of suitable applicants for the vacancy.
2. To deter unsuitable candidates from applying.
3. To create a positive image of the company.

The decision to recruit will normally involve the development of a job advertisement. As we saw earlier, the job advertisement should include the job description, person specification and details of the terms and conditions of employment. If it is completed correctly, it is probably the most effective tool available to meet the three key objectives outlined above. The advertisement itself should be striking enough to be noticed and the key information pertaining to the job should dominate, so that it will attract those who might be suitable for the position.

Perhaps the most immediate decision facing recruiters is whether to recruit internally from those already employed by the organisation, or to source the external labour market. The decision to access the internal labour market brings with it a number of distinct advantages. It is cost-effective, both in terms of eliminating the need for external advertising or sourcing and also in terms of reducing the induction or settling-in period. However, the organisation limits its potential range of candidates by drawing solely from the internal labour market, and often, the introduction of 'new blood' can provide new thinking and stimulate positive change. Table 5.3 outlines a range of recruitment methods available to organisations.

Table 5.3 Choice of recruitment method

Method	Comment
Unsolicited applications	Comprising of CVs or applications that arrive unprompted by any vacancy. Some may be just 'on-spec' and part of a general CV mailing, but others may indicate a potential applicant that views a close fit between his/her values and expectations and those of the organisation.
Internal labour market: Existing employees • Promotions • Transfers • Job rotations	Vacancies advertised internally represent the prospects of career advancement, or job variety opportunities for eligible existing employees. As such they are an important mechanism for maintaining robust internal labour market functioning (as discussed in Chapter 4). Often there may not be suitable applicants within the organisation, but this requires careful managing to avoid impacting morale or engagement levels.
Employee referrals	Having existing employees spread the word about a vacancy can be an inexpensive and highly effective means of recruiting new hires. Such prospective employees are likely to have a good understanding of what the organisation is like and what might be expected of them.
Targeted external labour market: • Schools/college/universities • Employment agencies • Recruitment consultants • Executive search consultants	The decision to recruit from outside the organisation can involve the use of simultaneous recruitment methods, and depends on the nature of the job being recruited for. Targeting school leavers or early graduates through annual recruitment drives and career fairs is a common practice worldwide. Recruitment from those who are seeking jobs is a common strategy – and effective, especially where the labour market is loose due to economic recession. The more senior the position, the more likely the organisation is to hire recruitment/search agencies to help in identifying best applicants.
Direct applications	Direct applications usually arise in response to seeing a job advertised. Advertising through newspapers, jobs boards, and social media is increasingly the norm today – advertisements should be targeted at the relevant audience from which the organisation wants to solicit applications.

Breaugh (2013) suggests that the recruitment methods used can have an effect on the outcomes achieved through the recruitment process. He references two particular hypotheses here. The *realism hypothesis* proposes that persons recruited by certain methods (such as those referred by current employees) are likely to possess a more accurate understanding of what a job within the organisation involves. This can help with the notion of fit, discussed at the start of the chapter, and there is some evidence to support the view that these types of hires perform at a higher level than non-referred hires. The *individual difference hypothesis*, on the other hand, assumes that different recruitment methods bring a job opening to the attention of individuals who systematically vary on personal attributes that are linked to recruitment outcomes. He explains that direct and unsolicited applicants for example, may have greater motivation to work for the organisation since they actively targeted the organisation with no assurance that there was a job opening available.

The choice of recruitment method is mainly determined by the nature of the position being advertised and whether the skills required for the job are in short supply or otherwise. Thus, for entry-level jobs, for example, it may be sufficient to advertise in local papers, on online jobs boards, or to disseminate news of the position by word of mouth. However, where the position requires considerable experience and/or qualifications of a particular type, the organisation might have to consider recruitment at national level or beyond, through social media sites such as LinkedIn Recruiter, the newspaper media, trade and professional journals, or employ the services of recruitment agencies or consultants.

Concomitant with decisions on the choice of recruitment method, the organisation must take account of the application process for vacancies. The most common methods involve the application form or the curriculum vitae (CV). The CV is probably still the most common method of job application and it generally tends to conform to a set standard: name, contact address, contact telephone number/email, education and achievements, employment history, professional associations and references. Most CVs are accompanied by a covering letter that seeks to 'sell' the applicant's suitability for the position. Increasingly, however, organisations use in-house application forms that seek to elicit job-specific information in a uniform fashion that can enable comparisons to be made between separate applications. Application forms elicit much the same information as is generally presented in a CV, but they also require applicants to supply additional information in support of their application. In practical terms this requires the applicant to 'sell' his/her skills and highlight the positive contribution s/he could make to the organisation.

More than ten years ago, a report by the CIPD (2006) suggested that about two-thirds of organisations were using online recruitment through general commercial sites, specialised job sites, chatrooms or newsgroups and company websites. Today, applications are increasingly likely to be web-based or online (especially for graduate positions) since web-based recruitment and early-stage pre-screening of applicants are now common across the world. Online recruitment allows access to a wider range of candidates and is probably more convenient and considerably cheaper than traditional methods.

Screening and Short-Listing

Once applications have been received, organisations must devise means of analysing their contents and applicants' suitability for selection. In this respect the person specification becomes an invaluable tool for identifying suitable and unsuitable applicants.

Dale (1995) suggests that there is an inherent tendency to compare applicants against each other rather than against the job requirements, and the biases of the short-lister provide the underlying rationale that determines suitability. Using the example of a vacancy for an office manager, she identifies a short-listing matrix, based on the person specification, that can facilitate more informed decisions (see Table 5.4).

Table 5.4 Short-listing matrix for position of office manager

Criteria	Candidate			
	1	2	3	4
Attainment				
Successful completion of further education course	Yes	Yes	Yes	Yes
Some job-related management training	Yes	No evidence	No evidence	Yes
Experience				
IT office applications	No evidence	Yes	No evidence	Yes
Customer service	Yes	Yes	Yes	Yes
Staff training and supervision	Yes	No evidence	No evidence	Yes
Record maintenance	No evidence	Yes	Yes	Yes
Abilities				
Communication skills	Untidy application	Yes	Application badly produced	Yes
Leadership skills	Trainer with no supervisory responsibilities	No evidence	No evidence	Yes
Planning and organisation	Poor organisation of information on form	No evidence	Application badly produced	?
Training and instructional skills	Yes	No evidence	No evidence	Yes
Aptitudes				
Customer-focused	No evidence	Yes	No evidence	Yes
Accuracy	No evidence	?	Application badly produced	Yes
Concern for quality	Untidy application	Yes	Application badly produced	Yes
Interests				
Involved with people	Yes	Solitary interests	No evidence	Yes
Learning and self-development	No evidence	Yes	No evidence	Yes

Source: Dale (1995).

The matrix can be used as a means of eliminating applicants who fail to achieve the minimum essential criteria, as set down in the job description and person specification. Individuals are scored according to how well they meet the particular job and behavioural requirements (rather than on how they appeal to the individual doing the short list) and those who score lowest are dropped from the process. The short-listing matrix will only work effectively where there is a well-detailed, measurable job description – incomplete or inaccurate information will render the process largely redundant. Those who score high on the short-listing matrix are deemed more likely to be suitable and they can then be progressed to the next phase, i.e. selection.

THE SELECTION PHASE

Ryan and Polyhart (2014) state that selection is really about two key things, namely what should be assessed, and how should we assess it. The first key concern for organisations, 'what should be assessed?', is generally focused on suitability and trying to predict which candidate will likely be the best match for the job. Over the years the second key concern, 'how should we assess it?' has resulted in the development of a number of tests that try to measure this suitability. However, the selection process is far more about how people perceive each other and the impressions that are made when they meet each other – and it is this human interaction that often determines the selection decision that is made.

There are a number of alternative selection techniques that can be used to determine the suitability of a job applicant. Before these are discussed, however, it is important to understand terms such as 'suitability', 'validity' and 'reliability' as they apply to the selection decision.

- **Suitability** is really about deciding how well the candidate's knowledge, skills and abilities match the job requirements. This essentially comes down to a number of key questions:
  1. *Will the candidate be able to perform the tasks required to an acceptable standard?* Previous work experience, educational attainments, and the skills profile of the applicant should provide a reasonable indication of this work ability.
  2. *Will the candidate be able to develop new knowledge and skills and 'grow' with the job?* An individual's previous history of skills development and educational and learning records can provide some useful indicators here.
  3. *Will the candidate 'fit' into the organisation?* The extent to which an individual will 'fit' into the organisation is almost impossible to gauge, but some inference might be drawn from experiences in previous work environments and questions about expectations.
  4. *Will the candidate work productively and co-operatively?* While past behaviour is not a very reliable predictor of future intent, organisations usually conduct reference checks to get some idea of previous work behaviour.
- **Validity**, in terms of the selection decision, refers to the extent to which the selection method used measures what it is supposed to measure. Thus, can the organisation be assured (in so far as is possible) that there are no intervening factors or biases that are distorting the result that has been achieved?

- **Reliability**, on the other hand, refers to whether the same selection decision reached would again be reached if other individuals made it, that is whether it is consistent.

To illustrate the relevance of both validity and reliability it is useful to take the example of the selection interview. If the interview is a valid selection technique it should predict, with a high degree of accuracy, the expected work behaviour of a job applicant (validity). If it is a reliable selection technique, regardless of who makes the selection decision, the end result will be the same, that is if five managers were independently asked to interview and choose between a number of candidates, they would all choose the same candidate.

There are a considerable number of alternative techniques available that can aid the selection decision, and several research studies on the reliability, validity and utility of these different methods (Terpstra et al. 1999; Guion 2011; Ryan and Polyhart 2014). Guion (2011) contends that many people use specific selection instruments simply because they prefer them, or have always used them, and not because of any empirical evidence of their utility and that, for similar reasons, other selection instruments are never used, despite evidence of their predictive value. Gilliland (1993) suggests that applicants determine the fairness of a method according to:

1. Perceived job-relatedness.
2. Opportunity to demonstrate one's ability.
3. Interpersonal treatment.
4. The propriety of the questions.

Studies have found that the predictive validity of the structured interview is quite high (Campion et al. 1988; Wiesner and Cronshaw 1988); that cognitive ability tests are among the most valid predictors available to organisations; and that work samples and assessment centres are highly valid selection devices (Hunter and Hunter 1984; Reilly and Warech 1993).

Individuals tend to assume that a device that is widely used must be valid and it is perhaps for this reason that the interview continues to enjoy considerable popularity across organisations. For many jobs, organisations utilise a series of interviews, ranging from the initial meeting through to the second and often third interview.

While interviews can either be conducted on a one-to-one basis or be panel-based, the principles under-pinning effective interviewing apply to both (these are discussed in the following pages). Anderson and Shackleton (1993) provide an interesting comparison of some of the more commonly used selection techniques (see Tables 5.5 and 5.6 on the following pages). However, they describe the selection interview separately, since the interview forms the basis of almost all selection decisions, and they suggest that the techniques outlined in Table 5.6 should, in fact, be used to augment the interview decision.

Table 5.5 Different functions of the interview

Interview function	Appropriate stage in selection procedure	Interview functioning	Interviewer's objectives	Interviewer's objectives
1. Mutual preview	Phase I/II, Early stages of selection procedure probably following initial screening of written applications but preceeding administration of main assessment techniques	Informal, open-ended discussion to explain selection procedures and to offer career guidance counselling to interviewee by providing detailed and realistic job preview (RJP)	• To meet and 'set the scene' for applicant • To inform applicant of company's selection procedure	• To establish what will be involved at each stage in selection procedure • To visit company 'on site'. • To obtain preview of job to allow self-assessment and self-selection
2. Assessment	Phase II, one of a battery of candidate assessment techniques	Formal, structured interaction guided by detailed job analysis and pre-formulated strategy	• To record answers to critical incident-type questions. • To probe and feed back results of other selection methods (particularly testing)	• To survive! • To obtain feedback and ensure accuracy of results of other methods.
3. Negotiation	Phase III. Final stage of selection procedure, immediately before or after offer of employment has been made.	Negotiation of outstanding points of difference, both interviewer and interviewee-directed and led.	• To ensure acceptance of job offer. • To facilitate job role transition. • To indentify follow-up personnel procedures	• To discuss contractual and non-contractual terms and conditions. • To facilitate job role transition. • To initiate the job change process.

Table 5.6 Main techniques of candidate assessment

Technique	Description	'Fit' with interview	Contribution to selection system
Psychometric testing	Standardised test of performance attitudes or personality. Major types: • cognitive ability • personality • attitudes and values • career choice and guidance	Can precede or follow inyerview stage. Results can form basis of further interview questions, or interview can be used to feed back test results. Personality tests are particularly useful in this respect and can facilitate probing questions at interview.	*Ability tests* • High predictive accuracy for aspects of cognitive ability. • 'Normed' results allow candidate to be compared with many similar people. Longer-term relevance, i.e. job role may change over time; ability remains relatively constant.

Technique	Description	'Fit' with interview	Contribution to selection system
			Personality tests • Indications of inter-personal or managerial style that can be followed up at interview and/or compared with exercises in an AC. • 'Faking' scales built in to tests may detect high level of impression management and biasing of self-presentation
Work examples	Pre-designed and constructed samples of work performance designed to tap aspects of critical job performance usually monitored and observed by trained experts, who rate candidates on job-relevant dimensions.	Usually following initial interview and often conducted as part of an AC. Can therefore provide dynamic and highly job-relevant data for discussion at follow-up interview stage.	• High predictive accuracy. Directly relevant job tasks as samples of future behaviour. Rated by observers on critical dimensions of job performance, some-times identical to those used for staff appraisal. • If constructed properly can add a sample of directly relevant candidate behaviour on segments of the job itself.
Assessment centres (ACs)	Multiple-method design, usually incorporating testing, interviews and work sample exercises, where candidates are tested by observers on job-relevant dimensions. Can last from one to five days.	Usually the final stage of assessment to reach outcome decisions. Because of cost of running ACs interviews usually conducted as integral part of an AC.	All the above, as well as: • Opportunity to observe candidates over longer period in formal and informal situations. • Multiple assessments by several assessors over several exercises can eliminate some individual biases associated with one-to-one interviews.
Reference letter	Varies from very brief factual check (e.g. 'Did candidate hold this position between these dates, as claimed?') to extensive rating of abilities, personality, and attitude to work.	Commonly used as final check on candidate after conditional offer of employment has been made. Interview can throw up specific issues to be checked with previous employers by reference letter.	• Best used as factual check only. • Most appropriate as final check: references taken up with existing employer before offer of employment will not be popular with candidates!

The Efficiency of the Selection Interview

Over the years, considerable research concerning both the validity and reliability of the selection interview has been undertaken, often with conflicting results (Ryan and Polyhart 2014; Anderson and Shackleton 1993). While well-structured interviews can provide very useful information on the individual's job experience, job knowledge, cognitive ability, and social/behavioural skills that, when combined, can be used to determine person–organisation fit, there are lingering concerns regarding the overall efficacy of the selection interview.

Errors and Biases in Selection

There is considerable evidence to suggest that the process of interviewing is all too often subject to a number of underlying biases and errors that adversely affect the selection decision (Anderson and Shackleton 1993; Dale 1995; Cook 2016). While it is untrue to suggest that all interviews are biased, some of the more common errors and biases that can occur have been identified by Anderson and Shackleton (1993).

- Expectancy effect – interviewers can form either a positive or negative impression of a candidate based on the biographical information from the application form/CV and this tends to have a bearing on all subsequent decisions (often termed 'gut instinct' or 'snap decision').
- Information-seeking bias – based on their initial expectations, interviewers can actively seek information that will confirm this initial expectation.
- Primacy effect – interviewers may form impressions about a candidate's personality within the first five minutes of meeting him/her and tend to be more influenced by what is said early in the interview.
- Stereotyping – stereotypes based on gender, race, family circumstances and so forth can often be ascribed to particular groups of individuals, and decisions subsequently based on these stereotypes may be in breach of the current equality legislation.
- Horns/halo effect – based on information received, an interviewer may rate a candidate either universally favourably or universally unfavourably. Furthermore, negative information tends to be more influential than positive information, and thus, even where there is a balance between positive and negative information, the overall impression will tend to be negative.
- Contrast and quota effects – interviewer decisions can be inherently affected by decisions made about earlier candidates, and pre-set selection quotas. Thus, where a number of candidates have been selected for interview, those who are interviewed later are invariably compared with those who went before them (rather than being assessed specifically against pre-determined criteria).

However rigorous the process, interviewing remains essentially a selective process and thus the interviewer needs to ensure that, as far as is possible, the errors or biases described above are eliminated. The operation of panel interviews or successive interviews can obviate many of the inherent problems associated with interviewing and can facilitate greater validity and reliability in the final decision analysis. Furthermore, attention to effective interpersonal interaction, such as active listening, and attendant non-verbal behaviour; competent questioning; and a facilitative interview environment (free from noise and other distractions) can further ensure that the interview is as productive as possible. Evenden and Anderson (1992) suggest that the choice of questions, and appropriate use of them, can ensure greater balance and flow in the interview itself (see Table 5.7 on the next page).

Table 5.7 Types of interview questions

1. Direct or closed
These have the effect of yielding short answers such as 'yes,' 'no,' or 'sometimes': 'How did you travel?'
Note: They are useful for the purpose of getting facts, but too much use leads to a staccato interview, and a short one if the applicant is nervous.

2. Leading
These lead the interviewee to give the answer the interviewer expects or wants to hear: 'We are always in flux. You do like change, don't you?'
Note: There is no value in this type of question, unless the interviewers have self-deception in mind. Most interviewees would follow the lead.

3. Topic-changing
Moving the interview on to a new topic: 'Thanks for the information on your qualifications. Would you tell me how you chose your career route?'
Note: These questions are helpful in creating a smooth flow during the interview and are important to control your timing as you move through your interview plan.

4. Probing and developing
These enquire more fully into a particular area, or encourage building on an answer already given: 'Why did you say you prefer jobs that involve travel?'
Note: These questions are very important in seeking specific evidence and testing the interviewee's knowledge, experience, feelings and attitudes.

5. Open-ended
These encourage full answers: 'Would you tell me about how you spend your leisure time?' 'Why did you apply for this particular job?'
Note: These types of question are very useful in getting the person talking and involved in the interview. Here the interviewee is given the opportunity to answer at length and to choose what to talk about.

6. Reflecting back
Reflecting back to the person what she/he has said by restating it as a question: 'Promotion is very important to you, then?' 'Are you saying you're frightened by computers?'
Note: These types of question are important in making sure that your understanding of the information supplied is clear and accurate. It also shows that you are listening and interested in what the interviewee is saying.

7. Command questions
These are really statements that act as questions, e.g. 'Tell me about that', or 'Give me an example . . .'
Note: These statements are especially useful in getting the interviewee to provide additional information on specific areas that may be required for the job. They can be quite authoritative in tone, so it's probably best to combine them with other types of question.

Overall: The most effective interview is likely to combine the range of question types and in the appropriate order, thus highlighting the importance of preparing for the interview in advance, and indeed effective training in how to interview.

Testing

The use of selection tests can be used to improve the validity and reliability of the selection process, but should not be used in isolation. Rather they tend to be used in tandem with other selection techniques, such as the interview. While a range of tests is available, the most commonly used tests, for selection purposes, include cognitive ability tests, personality tests and performance or work sample tests.

A range of *cognitive tests* has been designed and standardised; they are primarily used to measure an applicant's capability to perform a job and they have a fairly high predictive ability.
- *Personality tests* are designed to measure personality dimensions such as extroversion, conscientiousness, emotional stability, openness to new experiences and ability to get on with others: while some have high predictive ability, over-reliance on their outcomes is not advised.
- *Performance or work sample tests* require job applicants to perform some of the tasks that make up the job being applied for. They provide a fairly immediate assessment of the skills and abilities of the applicant, e.g. a computer technician asked to diagnose a problem with a server; an artist asked to provide a portfolio or produce a sketch.

PLACEMENT, ONBOARDING AND FOLLOW-UP

When the selection decision is reached, a formal job offer is made to the chosen candidate and the unsuccessful applicants (internal and external) are notified. A letter of offer can constitute a legally binding document since it usually forms part of a legal contract of employment. When the offer has been accepted, it is customary to offer a period of induction or onboarding for the successful candidate, which is designed to facilitate the smooth transition to work in the organisation. Onboarding periods vary from company to company and can last anything from a few hours to as long as three months. It is similarly common to find that the new recruit is 'on probation' for the first three months of employment to determine whether the events work out as expected (this 'probation' period largely depends on the job position and can be as long as twelve months in some cases).

As discussed earlier in this chapter, labour turnover tends to be highest during the initial work period and thus organisations can reduce the induction crisis through a carefully managed socialisation process where the newcomer is given all the information that is needed about how things work, including having someone assigned to informally 'show him/her the ropes'.

RECRUITMENT AND SELECTION IN IRELAND

In this final section we look at recruitment and selection practices in Ireland and here we draw on data from the latest CIPD reports and on the available data from the 2010 Cranet Ireland/University of Limerick Kemmy Business School national survey of HR practices. Specifically, we report on how organisations are managing their recruitment and selection decisions, and look at the methods that are being used to fill vacancies.

Recruitment and selection remains an important feature of organisational life in Ireland, and the survey data reveal that responsibility for recruitment and selection remains a joint responsibility shared between the HR department and other line managers. Only 23.6 per cent of respondents indicated that recruitment and selection were made solely by the HR function, which reflects the trend that started back in the 1990s when HR activities started to be devolved to line functions. While a variety of methods are used to recruit employees in Ireland, a strong reliance on internal labour markets remains in place, though this is being balanced by the use of external agencies and consultancies, particularly for managerial and professional/technical grades. Earlier discussion noted the increased popularity of Internet-based recruitment – however, there is little evidence that it is replacing more traditional forms of recruitment.

In terms of the types of selection methods being availed of, the data confirm what previous rounds of the Cranet survey have consistently shown us – the interview and reference checks remain the most commonly used selection methods in Ireland. What is interesting in the 2010 data, however, is the strong growth in reliance on the reference check, across all categories of employee – the average from previous years of the Cranet survey data was 73 per cent, compared with an average in 2010 of 89 per cent. This reliance on reference checks has always been high in Ireland but it seems to have become increasingly important in recent years. The use of what are considered more sophisticated and reliable selection techniques such as psychometric testing, and testing more generally, are used in a smaller, but growing, number of cases. This appears to be particularly the case for managerial jobs, for example, where the data suggest that about half of all managerial positions are psychometrically assessed as part of the selection process. This is an interesting trend and one that we may see increase since occupational forecasts predict substantial growth in professional work in Ireland over the next number of years.

In a recent survey of recruitment trends across Ireland (2015), Hays recruitment reported that three-quarters of employers who responded were planning to grow their staff number in the following twelve months. The view was that the labour market has become more competitive to the extent that employees were perceived to be increasingly mobile in search of better job prospects and greater rewards. Some 62 per cent of employers have active programmes in place to up-skill their staff, while 30 per cent are redeploying employees whose skill sets are transferable. This picture is reflected in a recent CIPD Ireland report on HR practices in Ireland (Connaughton and Staunton 2017). They reported that 78 per cent of respondents in the public and private sectors experienced skills shortages in the past twelve months, and identified challenges associated with attracting and retaining talent. Recruitment and resourcing remain among the top three priorities for organisations.

In summary, this chapter has focused on human resource planning, recruitment and selection. The nature of the human resource planning process in terms of stocktaking, forecasting, planning and implementation was set down and the benefits of engaging in the human resource planning process were presented. With respect to the recruitment process, job analysis and the general advantages and disadvantages attached to it were outlined. The nature of the job description and the person specification were presented and the importance of outlining the terms and conditions attached to the job vacancy were discussed. The large array of recruitment options available to an organisation and their particular advantages and disadvantages were also presented. The selection options, and errors and biases commonly associated with different approaches were set down. Finally, current practices in Ireland were briefly indicated.

It should be noted, however, that while this chapter has presented a phased understanding of the HR planning and recruitment and selection process, the reality is not so static or linear. Neither is it so predictable. The environment for business is changing so rapidly that organisations and jobs need to be flexible enough to respond to these changes – so the best laid plans may have to be abandoned. This doesn't suggest that planning is a waste of time but rather that plans have to be continuously tailored to fit the circumstances.

6
Motivation and Work Design

Maintaining high levels of motivation and engagement and ensuring a balance in job demands have been, and remain, fundamental aspects of the architecture of human resource management. The ongoing centrality of job design to HR professionals in Ireland was recently reported in the Chartered Institute of Personnel and Development (CIPD) 2017 HR practices in Ireland survey (Connaughton and Staunton 2017). It revealed that for some 57 per cent of respondents, job redesign activity in their organisations had increased over the last two years and 70 per cent reported that they anticipated that job redesign activity would continue to increase over the next two years, partly in response to the desire to secure and enhance employee engagement. This is hardly surprising given that job characteristics have been shown to be one of the predictors of job engagement (Saks, 2006), and job demands that employees tend to evaluate as hindrances have been shown to be negatively associated with engagement (Crawford *et al.* 2010).

The keys to understanding engagement, which has been defined as 'an individual employee's cognitive, emotional, and behavioural state directed toward desired organisational outcomes' (Shuck and Wollard 2010: 103), are motivation and the design of our work. Thus, modern interpretation of motivation is somewhat more all-encompassing than heretofore, expressing various understandings of the individual in context. While Vroom (1964) conceptualises motivation as a process governing choices made by persons or lower organisms among alternative forms of voluntary activity, DuBrin (1978) suggests that motivation centres on the expenditure of effort toward achieving an objective the organisation wants accomplished. Arnold *et al.* (1995), using a mechanical analogy, suggest that the motive force gets a machine started and keeps it going, and argue that motivation concerns the factors that push or pull us to behave in certain ways. Most of the early work on motivation was centred on getting more out of the employee, although many of the theorists were also concerned with finding an answer to this problem that was consistent with the essential dignity and independence of the individual. Motivation theory bases its analysis of employees' performance on how work and its rewards satisfy individual employees' needs.

Numerous theories have been developed over the years to aid management in identifying employees' motives and needs, the most influential of which will be discussed here. In this chapter we explore a selected number of these theories and examine the relationship between the motivational processes they identify – job design and engagement. Motivation lies at the core of job design (Campion 1988) and linking motivation and job design helps to establish the importance of job context in generating positive workplace behaviour. It also helps to avoid the all too common mistaken belief that motivation on its own is the singular determinant of work performance when, in reality, a complex mix of individual and contextual factors are at play.

MOTIVATION: ROLE AND DEFINITION

In 1971 Thomas Fitzgerald, writing in the *Harvard Business Review*, argued that motivation theory does not work and that we should discard the dismal vocabulary of motives, motivators and motivation, and think about becoming a society of persons. His argument was based on the premise that the proposed remedies advanced by prominent motivation theorists were proving somehow to be inadequate; because the significance of the motivation problem had been underestimated, and in some respects misunderstood; and because the problem of employees' motivation is rooted in certain fundamental conditions of society and its solution requires costly and extensive changes in our interdependent, closely linked systems. Truth, he argued, is sometimes damaged in the process of analysis and reconstruction, and concepts can easily become more real than the reality from which they were cut in the first instance.

> When transplanted from the laboratory, the language of motivation may become subtly elitist by suggesting that the employee resembles a captive rodent in a training box equipped with levers, trick doors, food pellets, and electric grids . . . When a man gets up in the morning, we can say that this act is a conditioned response to the stimulus of an alarm, but that doesn't tell us anything important.
>
> Fitzgerald (1971: 12)

Over forty years later, the vocabulary prevails, disseminating concepts such as needs, wants and desires as central aspects of the human condition. However, it is recognised that effective management depends on a knowledge and understanding of human motivation and engagement that goes beyond any 'common sense conventional wisdom' (Litwin and Stringer 1968). While motivation as a concept is a complex phenomenon, frequently drawn upon but often also poorly understood, any management practices that wish to make inroads in this area must be based on systematic knowledge about motivational processes that have *relevance* to the individual and the workplace, and that are dedicated to achieving 'good fit' between the individual, the job, the work group and the organisation in order to ensure a high level of engagement. Managers confronted with organisational problems, such as persistent absenteeism and high turnover, low morale, job dissatisfaction, poor job and organisational commitment and unacceptable quality, productivity and performance, want, as Herzberg (1968) put it, 'the surest and least circumlocuted way of getting someone to do something'.

Motivating the workforce is core managerial work and is an aspect of the managerial portfolio of activities that demands time and attention. It has been the focus of continuous discussion since the emergence of industrial society as a result of the Industrial Revolution. Steers and Porter (1987) advance a number of factors that account for the status of motivation as a central point of interest in management practice:

- First, they suggest that managers and organisational researchers cannot avoid a concern for the major behavioural requirements of the organisation. The necessity of

attracting the right talent and engaging it in such a way as to ensure high performance remains a central concern of the productive process.
- Second, they argue that the all-encompassing nature of the concept itself has resulted in it remaining as a central line of inquiry in management research and scholarship. As a complex phenomenon, motivation impacts upon a large number of factors and any worthwhile understanding of organisations requires a deal of attention to be focused on this bundle of factors and how they combine to create positive or negative outcomes for the employee and the organisation.
- Third, Steers and Porter contend that competitive trends in the business environment, coupled with increased business regulation, have forced organisations to seek out any mechanisms which might improve organisational *effectiveness* and *efficiency*. The ability to direct employees' efforts towards these twin goals of effectiveness and efficiency are seen as crucial.
- Fourth, the issue of technological advancement is another reason for the sustained interest in motivation concerns, which is particularly evident in the job design debate. An organisation must continually ensure that its workforce is able and willing to use advanced technologies to achieve organisational goals.
- A final reason centres on the issue of planning horizons. Taking a longer-term perspective on organisational talent and human capital, in an attempt to build up a pool of well-skilled, engaged employees, has brought the concept of motivation centre stage.

Nevertheless it is an extremely difficult area in which to apply accurate measurement. Furnham (1997: 293) notes that there are major problems in measuring job motivation. Asking people, he notes, is problematic, both because some people find it very difficult to report their motives accurately, as they do not have sufficient insight into themselves, as well as the fact that there are pressures put on people to give socially desirable, rather than truthful, answers. Furnham suggests that it is equally difficult to infer motivation from actual behaviour, 'because although it is true that efficient performance is a function of hard work, it may be impaired by a range of other contextual factors, such as the group norm of production, machine breakdown, or the non-delivery of crucial items'. He goes on to note that:

> Measuring job motivation, involvement and commitment is not very problematic in terms of theory. The major problem lies in either people dissimulating their answers (usually lying about how motivated they are to get the job, and demotivated they are on the job) or not being able to report on their motivational patterns accurately. Motivation is complex and many workers are unable to articulate what features of their job are motivating or not.
>
> Furnham (1997: 295)

However, despite such quantification difficulties, or perhaps because of them, motivation remains a central area of inquiry. The study of motivation at work has been, and continues to be, largely based on analysing employees' behaviour at work, Thus, motivation theory is essentially concerned with explaining why people behave as they do, or why people

choose different forms of behaviour in order to achieve different ends. The concept of motivation is comprised of several key features.
1. Though subject to various external contextual influences, motivation is an internal state experienced by the individual.
2. The individual experiences a motivational state in a way that gives rise to a desire, intention or pressure to act.
3. Motivation brings with it an element of choice, i.e. the individual experiencing a state of arousal as a result of an internal or external stimulus responds through choosing to act in a way and at a level of intensity that they determine.
4. Action and performance are, in part, a function of motivation.
5. Motivation is a multifaceted phenomenon, best characterised as a complex process with multiple elements and the possibility of multiple determinants, options and outcomes.
6. Individuals differ in terms of their motivational state and the factors that affect the motivational state of an individual are variable across time and situations.

In relation to individual factors, it is important that organisations select employees whose motives and work values 'fit' the organisational environment, management approach and reward package. Morley (2007) argues that it is an intuitively appealing concept because of what we know about the desirability of good fit in the key domain aspects of our lives and the positive psychosomatic consequences that can accumulate when individuals perceive good fit between these aspects and their environment. In making a selection decision through an examination of the likelihood of good 'fit' between the individual and the organisation, one is calling attention to one of the central ingredients for success in ensuring a high degree of engagement, motivation and performance.

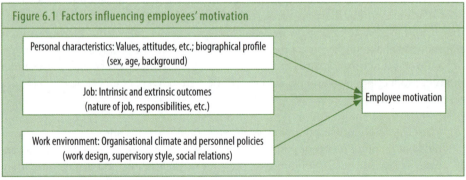

Source: Gunnigle and Flood (1990).

However, in addition to 'good fit', the organisational climate, management style and design of work will also be critical in facilitating good performance, by creating the conditions and opportunities for employees to satisfy their varying needs. Management must be keenly aware of the need to motivate employees through both extrinsic and intrinsic outcomes. Extrinsic outcomes are tangible and visible and include things such as a pay increase or a company car. Intrinsic outcomes relate to the satisfaction of personal wants and desires and include elements such as increased autonomy, responsibility and feedback.

It will be apparent that there is no simple answer to the crucial question: How do you motivate people? Herzberg (1968), in his seminal contribution 'One more time: how do you motivate employees?' published in the *Harvard Business Review*, rather humorously demonstrates the complexity attached to this question:

> What is the simplest, surest, and most direct way of getting someone to do something? Ask him? But if he responds that he does not want to do it, then that calls for a psychological consultation to determine the reason for his obstinacy. Tell him? His response shows that he does not understand you, and now an expert in communication methods has to be brought in to show you how to get through to him. Give him a monetary incentive? I do not need to remind the reader of the complexity and difficulty involved in setting up and administering an incentive system. Show him? This means a costly training programme.

Motivation theory bases its analysis of worker performance on how work and its rewards satisfy the individual employees' needs. The general argument is that if these needs are satisfied, employees will be motivated to work at high-performance levels but, if not, their performance will be less than satisfactory. Of course, as noted earlier, we must remember that motivation is only one factor affecting performance. Other factors, particularly technology, training and individual ability, will have a major influence on performance levels.

A central management concern is how to get employees to perform at the height of their abilities and to be fully engaged. Kahn (1990) views such engagement as a unique and important motivational concept and suggests that it involves the harnessing of an employee's full self, in terms of physical, cognitive and emotional energies, to work role performances. If this can be achieved, management will have gone a long way towards creating a successful organisation. The understanding of human needs at work and the creation of a working environment that satisfies those needs is a key task of senior management.

When discussing motivation theory, it is useful to distinguish between *content* and *process* models of motivation, as they differ in their relative focus:

- Content models focus on the wants and needs that individuals are trying to satisfy or achieve in the situation, or *what* motivates human behaviour. They are dedicated to an exploration of individual needs, wants, desires and aspirations. The content approaches discussed here are the *hierarchy of needs theory*, *ERG theory*, *acquired needs theory* and *dual-factor theory*.
- Process models attempt to show how the external context drives individuals to behave in a particular fashion and how managers can change the situation to better link need satisfaction to performance, or how the content of motivation influences behaviour. The process model examples discussed here are *theory X*, *theory Y*, *expectancy theory* and *equity theory*.

MASLOW'S HIERARCHY OF NEEDS THEORY

More than seventy years ago Maslow suggested that human motivation is dependent on the desire to satisfy various levels of need. Maslow's *hierarchy of needs* is perhaps the most publicised theory of motivation. It seeks to explain different types and levels of motivation, which are important to individuals at different times. It is based on the principle of the existence of a series of needs that range from basic instinctive needs for sustenance and security to higher-order needs, such as self-esteem and the need for self-actualisation. Lower-order or fundamental needs, according to Maslow's theory, must be satisfied before higher-order needs can be set in motion and dealt with.

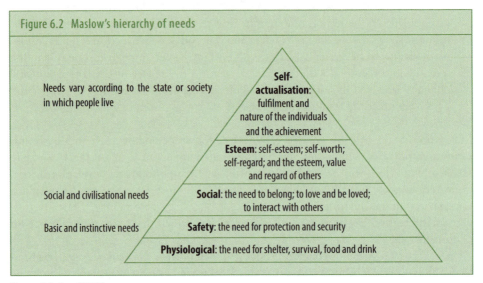

Figure 6.2 Maslow's hierarchy of needs

Source: Maslow (1943).

Maslow suggests that there are five levels of need, ranked in the order shown, as this is the order in which they will likely be activated by the individual in order to satisfy them. The chronological order of needs from the lowest to the highest order is important. First, it suggests that it is the next unachieved level that acts as the prime motivator. Thus, people without the basic necessities of life, such as food and shelter, will be motivated by basic physiological and, later, security needs. Only when these have been satisfied will higher-order needs become important. And then, only when all the lower-order needs are satisfied, do higher level needs act as a motivator – first esteem needs and ultimately self-actualisation.

The second inference arising from this ascending order of needs is that once a particular need category is satisfied it ceases to have a major impact on motivation. Thus, any level of needs only motivates while it remains unachieved. Following its achievement it is the next level in the hierarchy that dominates the individual's priorities.

- *Physiological needs* include such elements as food, shelter, clothing and heat. These basic needs must be satisfied for the person to survive. In modern society it is employment and the income it generates that allows the individual to satisfy such needs.
- *Safety needs* refer to things such as security at home, tenure at work and protection against reduced living standards. Only when physiological needs have been satisfied will the individual concentrate on safety needs.

- *Social or love needs* refers to people's desire for affection and the need to feel wanted. Our need for association, for acceptance by others and for friendship, companionship and love might also be included here.
- *Esteem needs* cover an individual's desire for self-esteem and self-confidence and also one's need for recognition, authority and influence over others.
- *Self-actualisation* refers to the need for self-fulfilment, self-realisation, personal development and fulfilment of the creative faculties (see Figure 6.2).

Hierarchy of needs theory states that a need that is unsatisfied activates seeking or searching behaviour. Thus, the individual who is hungry will search for food and the one who is unloved will seek to be loved. Once this seeking behaviour is fulfilled or satisfied, it no longer acts as a primary motivator: needs that are satisfied no longer motivate. This clearly illustrates the rationale for arranging these needs in a hierarchy. The sequential ascending order implies that it is the next unachieved level that acts as the prime motivator. Need propensity means that higher-order needs cannot become an active motivating force until the preceding lower-order need is satisfied. Self-actualisation is the climax of personal growth. Maslow (1943) describes it as the desire for self-fulfilment: the drive to become more and more what one is, to become everything that one is capable of becoming.

Criticisms of Hierarchy of Needs Theory

Maslow's theory has been the subject of much criticism and it has been argued that as a self-actualisation theory it has failed because Maslow was unable, in principle, to offer an adequate account of the origin and nature of the self and human needs (Geller 1982). First, Maslow's work was based on general studies of dominance in humans and monkeys and, as such, was not directly associated with matters central to the workplace. Arising from this, the theory is extremely difficult to apply because of the elusive nature of the needs identified, particularly in the context of the workplace, and it has proven difficult to test (Wahba and Bridwell 1976). Where it has happened, researchers have also found little support for the concept of exclusive pre-potency. A more realistic scenario is that individuals have several active needs at the same time, which implies that lower-order needs are not always satisfied before one concentrates on higher-order needs.

Another criticism of this approach is that career advancement may be the true factor underlying changes in need deficiencies. Research demonstrates that as managers' advance in organisations their lower-order needs diminish. Simultaneously, they experience an increased desire to satisfy higher-order needs.

Finally, it has also been suggested that the theory attempts to demonstrate an imputed rationality in human actions that may not necessarily exist. The conceptualisation of our needs in such a logical, sequential fashion, while useful as a frame of reference to which we can all compare ourselves, has not resulted in convincing evidence among researchers.

Other inconsistencies that research has thrown up include the fact that needs do not often group together in the ways predicted; the restricting of the concept of a need to a purely biological phenomenon remains problematic; and needs, while often generally described, are done so with insufficient precision.

Overall, Maslow's hierarchy of needs appears to be a convenient way of classifying needs, but it has limited utility in explaining work behaviour. Its primary value has been the fact that it highlights, in a general way, the importance of human needs.

EXISTENCE–RELATEDNESS–GROWTH (ERG) THEORY

ERG theory, as developed by Alderfer (1969, 1972), is grounded in a stronger empirical base than had been achieved by those seeking to verify Maslow's hierarchy. It reduces Maslow's fivefold needs category into a threefold taxonomy. A second major difference, which stemmed from criticisms of Maslow's approach, is that less emphasis is placed on a hierarchical order of lower- and higher-order needs, implying that all needs levels may be influential at the same time. Another important variation is the proposition that an already satisfied lower-order need may be reactivated as a motivator when a higher-order need cannot be satisfied. Thus, an employee who has satisfied basic material and social needs may be concerned with his/her personal growth and development (e.g. promotion). If there is no scope for such development s/he may revert back to a preoccupation with previously satisfied needs (e.g. social or financial). The other implication, referred to above, is that more than one needs category may be important at any one time.

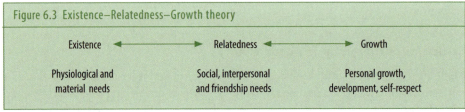

Figure 6.3 Existence–Relatedness–Growth theory

Source: Alderfer (1972).

On reflection, Alderfer's work has been credited with making a number of important contributions to furthering our understanding of human motivation. First, it explicitly recognises the existence of individual differences by establishing that lower-order needs do not necessarily have to be satisfied in all individuals in order for higher-order needs to be focused on and achieved. In this way, it highlights the multiplicity of ways in which employee needs may vary and the importance of management being able to recognise this and respond to it in an appropriate way.

Through its exposition of what is referred to as 'the frustration–regression principle', ERG theory also recognises that if a higher-level need remains unfulfilled, the person may revert to lower-level needs that seem easier to satisfy. It has been argued that the frustration–regression principle inherent in Alderfer's ERG theory has an impact on workplace motivation, such that if growth and developmental opportunities are not available to the employees, they may regress towards relatedness needs, and place a stronger emphasis on satisfying social needs in the workplace, rather than on the task and performance side.

Overall, ERG theory is more consistent with our knowledge of individual differences among people; and has received more empirical support from studies than Maslow's hierarchy of needs.

ACQUIRED NEEDS THEORY

An alternative approach, developed by McClelland (1961), concentrated on identifying motivational differences between individuals as a means of establishing which patterns of motivation led to effective performance and success at work. He distinguishes three basic needs in addition to physical drives:

1. **Need for achievement [nAch]**: Individuals demonstrating a high need for achievement consistently want challenging tasks, demanding responsibility and application. They value success and positive feedback that is related to their performance in completing tasks. They demonstrate a consistent need to excel and thus tend to avoid both low-risk and high-risk situations. In demonstrating task-focused behaviour, they will often express a preference for working on their own or with other high achievers.
2. **Need for power [nPow]**: Individuals possessing a high need for power demonstrate a need for control and authority. This takes two forms – personal and institutional. Those who demonstrate a desire for high personal power typically show a desire to direct others; those who thrive on institutional power are especially satisfied when organising the efforts of others to further broader organisational goals. In the managerial context, it has been argued that while the managerial role clearly demands that the manager directs those whom s/he manages, those with a high need for personal power may become dysfunctional as their focus is on directing others rather than on achieving the company's goals. Managers with a high need for institutional power tend to be more effective than those with a high need for personal power, since they channel their need into accomplishing goals set by the organisation.
3. **Need for affiliation [nAff]**: Individuals demonstrating a high need for affiliation typically express a need for good social and personal relations with people. They demonstrate a consistent wish to be liked and feel accepted by other people. As a result, they tend to conform to the norms of their work group and enjoy the sense of belonging that comes with working as part of this group. They also have a marked preference for co-operation over competition as a model for getting things done. McClelland regarded a strong need for affiliation as a characteristic that could undermine the objectivity and decision-making ability needed to operate effectively in a managerial role.

McClelland suggested that these needs are acquired and developed over an individual's life. Depending on which needs are dominant, these will exert varying positive or negative influences on work performance. People with a high need for achievement tend to have a strong motivation to take on challenging tasks and to do them better. This, combined with a moderate to high need for power and a lower need for affiliation, has been suggested as a good indicator of success in senior management (McClelland and Boyatzis 1982). An important implication of this approach is that, if such needs are acquired, they may be developed through appropriate environmental conditions that facilitate the emergence of the desired needs profile.

DUAL-FACTOR THEORY

Herzberg (1968) was equally concerned about the impact of work and job design on motivation. He saw the key to improving employees' motivation in terms of job satisfaction. Herzberg felt that by identifying the work factors that produced the greatest levels of satisfaction (or dissatisfaction) it would be possible to design jobs that provided job satisfaction, thereby encouraging higher levels of performance. His approach concentrated on identifying which factors ('motivator' factors) contributed most to employees' satisfaction at work. He also sought to identify those factors that influenced levels of employees' dissatisfaction ('maintenance/hygiene' factors). Herzberg concluded that these two sets of factors were inherently different in terms of their impact on motivation and performance.

A central aspect of Herzberg's dual-factor theory is that only by varying motivator factors can management improve performance and motivation. Varying maintenance/hygiene factors will reduce levels of dissatisfaction but will never act as a motivator (see Figure 6.4).

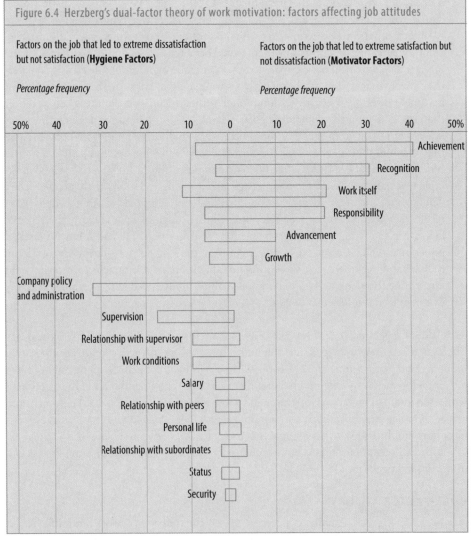

Figure 6.4 Herzberg's dual-factor theory of work motivation: factors affecting job attitudes

Source: Herzberg (1968).

The implication here is that management can only stimulate employees' motivation by designing jobs to incorporate the motivator factors (i.e. jobs that encourage and facilitate responsibility, advancement and recognition). Herzberg believed that high levels of job satisfaction could be achieved by altering job content to allow for personal growth and development, while also ensuring that the job context (pay, working conditions, etc.) was appropriate. This process became known as job enrichment (see below).

Herzberg's approach has gained considerable recognition, particularly for differentiating between the impact of intrinsic and extrinsic factors on employees' motivation. Criticisms have tended to focus on its reliability of application to all types of jobs (not just professional/white collar) and the view of job satisfaction as being almost synonymous with motivation.

MCGREGOR'S THEORY X, THEORY Y

Unlike previous approaches that concentrated on analysing the motivations of people at work, McGregor (1960), in his seminal text *The Human Side of Enterprise*, examined managerial assumptions about employees and the resultant implications of such assumptions for managerial approaches to issues such as control, job design and remuneration systems. He identified two very different sets of assumptions about employees' behaviour and motivation, which were termed theory X and theory Y. Approaches by organisations to workforce management differ considerably and these two contrasting frameworks are useful in helping to analyse and explain management styles. Both classifications represent extreme styles and approaches to people management (see Figure 6.5).

Figure 6.5 Theory X, theory Y

Theory X Assumptions	Theory Y Assumptions
Employees are inherently lazy, dislike work and will do as little as possible. Consequently, workers need to be corrected, controlled and directed to exert adequate effort.	Employees like work and want to undertake challenging tasks. If the work itself and the organisational environment is appropriate, employees will work willingly without need for coercion or control.
Most employees dislike responsibility and prefer direction.	People are motivated by needs for respect, esteem, recognition and self-fulfilment.
Employees want only security and material rewards.	People at work want responsibility. The majority of workers are imaginative and creative and can exercise ingenuity at work.

Source: Gunnigle and Flood.

In practice, organisations may adopt elements of both approaches, but often with a particular leaning that indicates a preference for one or other approach. Traditional autocratic management approaches were clearly based on theory X assumptions.

Despite considerable academic and practical support it would seem that theory Y does not have the whole-hearted backing of many senior managers. Consequently, its application has often been restricted to once-off initiatives designed to deal with particular problems or issues, rather than reflecting a change in corporate approaches to the way employees are managed.

EXPECTANCY THEORY

Most of the approaches discussed above represent attempts to identify a general set of employees' needs, which cause employees to behave in a certain way. The belief is that by identifying such needs, management can provide for their ease of achievement, thus facilitating improved performance. Many of these approaches rank such motives or goals in a hierarchical order, with self-actualisation as the ultimate motivator. However, most managers will probably point out that employees differ markedly in terms of motivation. One may find two employees, similar in terms of age, sex and background, one of whom will strive to achieve high performance levels, undertake additional tasks and so forth, while the other is content to get by doing the minimum acceptable to the organisation.

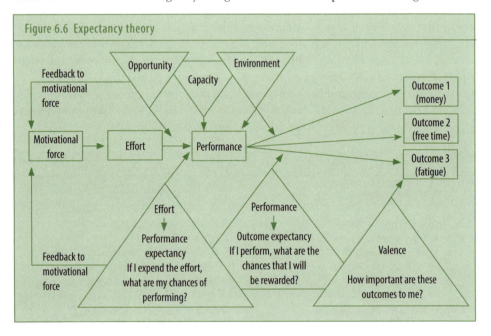

Figure 6.6 Expectancy theory

How does one explain such variations? One approach that avoids attempts to find a definitive set of employees' motives, but seeks to explain individual differences in terms of goals, motives and behaviour, is expectancy theory. Associated with Vroom (1964), expectancy theory focuses on the relationship between the effort put into the completion of particular activities by the individual and the expectations concerning the actual reward that will accrue as a result of expending the effort. Expectancy theory attempts to combine individual and organisational factors that impact on this causal effort/reward relationship.

Broadly, the theory argues that individuals base decisions about their behaviour on the expectation that one or another alternative behaviour is more likely to lead to needed or desired outcomes. The relationship between one's behaviour and particular desired outcomes is affected by individual factors such as personality, perception, motives, skills and abilities, and by organisational factors such as culture, structure and managerial style (the context in which one is operating).

Thus, expectancy theory avoids attempts to isolate a definitive set of employees' motives, but rather seeks to explain individual differences in terms of goals, motives and behaviours. It postulates that employees' motivation is dependent on how the employer perceives the relationship between effort, performance and outcomes. Retrospective commentary on Vroom's work highlights that expectancy theory has evolved somewhat from his early specifications to be articulated as a combination of three factors: *expectancy*, *instrumentality* and *valence*.

1. *Expectancy* is the probability assigned by the individual that work effort will be followed by a given level of achieved task performance (value = 0 to 1). It refers to the perceived probability that a particular level of effort will lead to desired performance levels. If the desired outcome (e.g. bonus pay) demands a given level of performance (production goals), the individual employee must believe that level is achievable or s/he will not expend the necessary effort. (If I tried, would I be able to perform the action I am considering?)
2. *Instrumentality* is the probability assigned by the individual that a given level of achieved task performance will lead to various work outcomes (rewards) (value = 0 to 1). Thus, expectancy theory suggests that employees' decisions on how they perform are based upon their perception of desired outcomes, whether performance targets are achievable and an evaluation of the likelihood that by achieving these targets they will realise their desired outcomes. (Would performing the action lead to identifiable outcomes?)
3. *Valence* is the value attached by the individual to various work outcomes (rewards) (value = –1 to +1). It is thus a measure of the strength of attraction that a particular outcome or reward has for the individual employee. (How much do I value these outcomes?)

The motivational appeal of a given work path is drastically reduced whenever any one or more of the factors approaches the value of zero. Thus, the model suggests that the individual's level of effort (motivation) is not simply a function of rewards. The individual must feel that s/he has the ability to perform the task (expectancy), that this performance will impact on the reward (instrumentality) and that this reward is actually valued (valence). Only if all conditions are satisfied will employees be motivated to exert greater effort in the performance of a job. It is critical that individuals can see a connection between effort and reward and that the reward offered by the organisation will satisfy employees' needs. However, there is no simple formula, since individuals possess different preferences for outcomes and have different understandings of the relationship between effort and reward. They may well be motivated in very different ways.

Among the criticisms levelled at the theory are the difficulties associated with testing it empirically, and the fact that it assumes a type of rationality with respect to how the individual thinks and behaves, which may not exist. This approach suggests that employees will expend a high level of effort if they believe this will result in performance levels that will be rewarded by valued outcomes. These valued outcomes may vary between individuals. One may value money, another promotion, and yet another recognition. However, it is not only the outcome that is important, but also the belief that valued outcomes can be achieved through improved effort and performance.

In relation to the implications of expectancy theory for management, Vroom (1964) suggests that managers must seek to understand the goals and motives of individual employees, and ensure that these are clearly and positively linked to desired performance levels, which in turn are achievable from the employee's perspective.

Expectancy theory does not attempt to identify a universal set of motivational factors. Rather it highlights the importance of a range of potential motivational factors which may be either intrinsic or extrinsic.

EQUITY THEORY

The concept of a fair day's work for a fair day's pay is often utilised to express how the parties to the labour process wish to perceive the employment relationship. Equity theory, sometimes referred to as justice theory, resembles expectancy theory in that it sets down the individual's cognitive process that determines whether or not s/he will engage in the effort–reward bargain within the framework of the social exchange process. Developed by Adams (1965), the equity theory of motivation is based on the comparison between two variables: inputs and outcomes:

- 'Inputs' refer to what the individual brings to his/her employment and includes things such as effort, experience and skills.
- 'Outcomes' describe the range of factors the employee receives in return for his/her inputs, i.e. pay, recognition, fringe benefits and status symbols.

Adams suggests that individual expectations about equity correlation between inputs and outcomes are learned during the process of socialisation in the home or at work, and through comparison with the inputs and outcomes of others. Adams (1965) suggests that individuals can:

- Change inputs, i.e. can reduce effort if underpaid.
- Try to change their outcomes, i.e. ask for a pay rise or promotion.
- Psychologically distort their own ratios by rationalising differences in inputs and outcomes.
- Change the reference group to which they compare themselves in order to restore equity.

Huseman *et al.* (1987) enumerate the core propositions of equity theory as follows:
1. Individuals evaluate their relationships with others by assessing the ratio of their outcomes from, and inputs to, the relationship against the outcome–input ratio of another comparable individual.
2. If the outcome–input ratios of the individual and the comparable other are deemed to be unequal, then inequity exists.
3. The greater the inequity the individual perceives (in the form of either over-reward or under-reward), the more distress the individual experiences.
4. The greater the distress an individual experiences, the harder s/he will work to restore

equity. Among the possible equity restoration techniques the individual might use are: distorting inputs or outcomes; disregarding the comparable other and referring to a new one; or terminating the relationship.

Thus, employees will formulate a ratio between their inputs and outcomes and will compare this ratio with the perceived ratios of inputs and outcomes of other people in the same or a similar situation. If these two ratios are not equal, the individual will take action in an attempt to restore a sense of equity.

Considerable research interest has been generated in testing the relationships advanced by Adams, particularly those relationships that focus on employees' reactions to pay (see Table 6.1). Overall, the research highlights support for Adams' theory about employees' reactions to wage inequities. Mowday concludes that the research support for the theory appears to be strongest for predictions about under-payment inequity. Furthermore, equity theory appears to offer a useful approach to understanding a wide variety of social relationships that may occur in the workplace.

Table 6.1 Equity theory research on employees' reactions to pay

Study	Equity condition	Method of induction	Task	Dependent variables	Results
Lawler (1968b)	Overpayment; hourly	Qualifications, circumstances	Interviewing	Productivity, work quality	Overpaid (unqualified) subjects produced more of lower quality; subjects overpaid by circumstances did not
Lawler, Koplin, Young and Fadem (1968)	Overpayment; piece rate	Qualifications	Interviewing	Productivity, work quality	Overpaid subjects produced less of higher quality in initial work session; in later sessions subject's perceived qualifications and productivity increased; the need for money was related to productivity for both groups
Lawler and O'Gara (1967)	Underpayment; piece rate	Circumstances	Interviewing	Productivity, work quality	Underpaid subjects produced more of lower quality and perceived their job as more interesting but less important and more complex
Pritchard, Dunnette and Jorgenson (1972)	Overpayment and underpayment; hourly and piece rate	Circumstances, actual change in payment	Clerical task	Performance satisfaction	Circumstances induction did not result in performance differences for piece rate, but some support was found for hourly overpay and underpay

Study	Equity condition	Method of induction	Task	Dependent variables	Results
					Changes in pay rate supported hourly predictions; some support found for piece rate overpayment prediction but not for underpayment
Valenzi and Andrews (1971)	Overpayment and underpayment; hourly	Circumstances	Clerical task	Productivity, work quality	No significant differences found between conditions; 27% of underpaid subjects quit; no subjects in other conditions quit
Wiener (1970)	Overpayment; hourly	Qualifications, inputs v. outcomes, ego-oriented v. task-oriented	Word manipulation		Outcome-overpaid subjects produced more; input-overpaid subjects produced more only on ego-oriented task
Wood and Lawler (1970)	Overpayment; piece rate	Qualifications	Reading	Amount of time reading, quality	Overpaid subjects produced less, but this could not be attributed to striving for higher quality

Source: Mowday (1987).

WORK DESIGN

The nature of work organisation and design will significantly influence the degree to which work is intrinsically satisfying for employees and determine exhibited levels of motivation. This in turn has consequences for the organisation, in terms of outcomes such as productivity and performance. Parker (2014) highlights the potential impact of work design on both the individual and the organisation. He argues that:

> Work design, or the content and organization of one's work tasks, activities, relationships, and responsibilities, has been linked to almost every end goal that is of concern in an organization – safety, performance, and innovation, to name a few. Work design also matters for individuals; it affects their sense of meaning, their health, and their development.
>
> Parker (2014: 661)

The study of individual tasks in organisations has long been accorded a high degree of importance in organisation and management literature and theory. This remains the case, as it is suggested that individuals may also have a degree of agency in job design where they continuously seek to introduce changes to their tasks and relationships at work.

They do this through 'job crafting', viewed as an active process where employees redefine and reimagine aspects of their jobs in order to increase experienced meaningfulness (Wrzesniewski and Dutton 2001). Investigation in the area has attempted to describe strategies for changing or refining jobs so as to enhance variables such as effort, performance, motivation, satisfaction, commitment, absenteeism and so forth.

Historically the focus in job design has been on results and outcomes (Janson 1979). There is a body of opinion that sees at least some of the roots of the industrial and indeed social problems of modern societies in the nature of poorly-structured work (Kopelman 1985). The central view of the various schools of thought, according to Kelly (1980), is that the organisation of work on the basis of task fragmentation is counterproductive. It is suggested that the situation can be remedied by reversing the division of labour and meeting the social needs of individuals at work, as well as the economic needs of employers. The central issue, therefore, in Lupton's (1976) words, is 'how to design for best fit'.

Over the years the field of job design has been characterised by shifts from one theoretical perspective to another. According to Griffin (1987), the primary shifts have been from task specialisation (e.g. Taylor 1911), to job enlargement (e.g. Walker and Guest 1952), to job enrichment (e.g. Herzberg 1968), to socio-technical systems theory and the quality of working life (QWL) movement (e.g. Cherns and Davis 1975) to high-performance work design (e.g. Hackman 1987; Buchanan and McCalman 1989).

Broadly conceived, work organisational design refers to the way the various tasks in the organisation are structured and carried out, and it reflects the interaction of management style, the technical system, human resources and the organisation's products or services. Davis (1966) defines the process of job design as that which is concerned with the 'specification of the contents, methods, and relationships of jobs in order to satisfy technological and organisational requirements, as well as the social and personal requirements of the job holder'. Concurring with this definition, Table 6.2, on the next page, demonstrates that the reasons that employers restructure jobs are a mix of improving productivity, reducing or eliminating organisational problems and providing satisfying work for employees.

Cherns and Davis (1975) identify three parties with an explicit interest in job restructuring, employees' motivation and satisfaction, and work performance:
- The first party, they claim, is labour, primarily represented by unions and other organised bodies. Unions are seen to be interested in 'the conditions of work, learning and adaptability, reward and satisfaction, and future structures of formal relationships with management'.
- The second party to the process is management; they are interested in the efficient use of their human resources through the development of appropriate work methods.
- The third party is the state. Government is seen to be concerned with matters related to labour and management because of the integral part they play in the successful running of the economy. Manpower planning, training and education, income policy, unemployment and the enhancement of industrial democracy projects are, argue Cherns and Davis (1975), typically regulated by the institutions of the state.

Table 6.2 Reasons for introducing job changes

	Birchall and Wild		Reif and Schonerbek		Total
	Blue-collar	White-collar	Blue-collar	White-collar	
System output					
Productivity	12	9			21
Costs	5	3	21		29
Quality	7	5	13		25
Down time	1				1
Inventories	1				1
Skills	2	2			4
Flexibility	3	3			6
Specialisation			14		14
System changes					
Introduction of automated equipment	2	1			3
Introduction of new plant	3	2			5
Personnel problems					
Labour turnover	6	5		6	17
Absenteeism	4	1			5
Attract labour	1				1
Improve labour relations	2	2			4
Concern for employee					
Worker morale	10	7	15		32
To give meaning to work	4	4			8
Monotony			11		11
Eliminate social problems	3				3
Others	8	3	4	6	21
Total	74	47	78	12	211

Source: Birchall (1975).

The design of individual jobs is seen to impact particularly upon employees since it influences job content, employees' discretion, degree of task fragmentation and the role of supervision. Decisions on the organisation of work are primarily a management responsibility and the particular approach chosen will be a good indicator of corporate beliefs about how employees should be managed and jobs structured, and about the role of supervision. It will also reflect the organisation's approach to many aspects of human resource management, as manifested by attitudes to recruitment, employees' development, motivation, rewards and management/employee relations.

TASK SPECIALISATION

Task simplification, task specialisation and task standardisation have been viewed as the guiding ideas of what is often referred to as the classical approach to job design. Variously referred to as task specialisation, scientific management or Taylorism, the traditional approach to the organisation of work was dominated by a desire to maximise the productive efficiency of the organisation's technical resources. Choices about the organisation of work and the design of jobs were seen as determined by the technical system. Management's role was to ensure that other organisational resources, including employees, were organised in such a way as to facilitate the optimal utilisation of the technical system. This efficiency approach is based on scientific management principles and has been a characteristic of employer approaches to job design since the turn of the century. Jobs were broken down into simple, repetitive, measurable tasks whose skills could be easily acquired through systematic job training.

Figure 6.7 Traditional approach to job design

Characteristics	Outcomes
Bureaucratic organisation structure	Tight supervisory control
Top-down supervisory control	Minimal need for employee discretion
Work planning separated from execution	Work measurement
Task fragmentation	Reliance on rules and procedures
Fixed job definitions	Job specialisation
Individual payment by results	Reduced job flexibility
	Short training time
	Little employee influence on job or work organisation

The rationale for this approach to work and job design was based on 'technological determinism', where the organisation's technical resources were seen as a given constraint and the other inputs, including employees, had to accommodate the technical system. It also reflected managerial assumptions about people at work. Close supervision, work measurement and other types of control indicate a belief about employees akin to McGregor's theory X. It suggests that employees need to be coerced to work productively and that this is best achieved by routine, standardised tasks.

This traditional model of job design has undoubtedly brought positive benefits to many organisations. It helped improve efficiency and promoted a systematic approach to selection, training, work measurement and payment systems. However, it has also led to numerous problems, such as high levels of labour turnover and absenteeism, and low motivation. Thus, short-term efficiency benefits were often superseded by long-term reductions in organisational effectiveness. Many behavioural scientists argued that the effectiveness of organisations could be increased by recognising employees' abilities and giving them challenging, meaningful jobs in a co-operative working environment. The consequence, according to Newell (1995: 22) in her treatise on the 'healthy organisation' was that:

> Taylor had a limited perspective on human needs and motivation. He saw a worker as no different from a machine. With a machine, output depends on the amount of fuel put in. Likewise, with a worker, output was seen to depend on the amount of fuel put in: however, in this case the fuel needed was money. No account was taken of the individual's psychological needs for interesting work with some degree of challenge and autonomy. Nor was account taken of the psychosocial needs of workers for friendship and support. Indeed, Taylor explicitly tried to prevent the formation of work groups, seeing these as a potential threat to managerial control, and so to efficiency.

More recently, the increased emphases on improving quality, service and overall competitiveness have led to the emergence of other schools of thought aimed at restructuring work systems to increase employee motivation, commitment and performance. Much of the focus of the work of the successors to task specialisation has been on the restructuring of jobs to incorporate greater scope for intrinsic motivation. Subsequent schools questioned traditional management assumptions about why employees work. The traditional approach saw employees as essentially instrumental in their attitudes to work. Jobs were seen as a means to an end and it was these extrinsic rewards that motivated employees. Consequently, employers created work systems with closely circumscribed jobs, supervised work and rewarded quantifiable performance.

JOB ENLARGEMENT

Job enlargement and job enrichment as alternative mechanisms of work structuring differ in their relative emphases; the former makes an individual's job 'bigger', while the latter adds some element to the job that is dedicated to increasing the employees' psychological growth. Job enlargement grew from arguments in the 1950s that production methods prevalent at the time created poor working conditions that led to high levels of job dissatisfaction. The proposed solution was job enlargement that centred on combining various activities at the same level in the organisation and adding them to the existing job, the purpose of which was to introduce more variety and less routine work. This assumption was drawn upon by Walker and Guest (1952) in their study of automobile assembly lines. They studied 180 workers and identified six main characteristics of mass production technology: (i) repetitiveness; (ii) low skill requirement; (iii) mechanically paced work; (iv) little alteration of tools or methods; (v) low requirement of mental attention; and (vi) minute sub-division of product. In proposing that the solution to eliminating some of the negative consequences of mass-production technology lay in job enlargement, they generated some debate. The disputed issues centred on meaning and methodology. Walker and Guest viewed job enlargement as 'the combination of more than two tasks into one'. However, this did not in any way distinguish it from 'job extension', which could possibly be nothing more than the addition of more meaningless tasks (Wall 1982).

It has been argued that there is no explicit theory on which the concept of job enlargement can become a model of job restructuring. There is no motivation theory, according to Buchanan (1979), on which job enlargement stands. Aldag and Brief (1979) note that job enlargement experiments did not employ a conceptual framework of how the structuring of jobs should actually be executed. Furthermore, Buchanan (1979) argues that job enlargement studies have largely ignored external variables and people's differing attitudes towards work.

JOB ENRICHMENT

Largely attributed to Herzberg (1968), job enrichment was developed to advance the dual-factor theory of work motivation discussed earlier in the chapter. The job enrichment approach suggested that employees gain most satisfaction from the work itself and that it is intrinsic outcomes arising from work which motivate employees to perform well in their jobs. In 'One more time: how do you motivate employees?', Herzberg establishes the concept of vertical loading as a means of moving away from the addition of 'one meaningless task to the existing (meaningless) one'. Vertical loading, dedicated to the addition of more challenging dimensions to the job, remains the mainstay of job enrichment.

Figure 6.8 Principles of vertical job loading

Principle	Motivators involved
A. Removing some controls while retaining accountability	Responsibility and personal achievement
B. Increasing the accountability of people for their own work	Responsibility and recognition
C. Giving a person a complete natural unit of work (module, division, area, etc.)	Responsibility, achievement, and recognition
D. Granting additional authority to an employee in their activity; job freedom	Responsibility, achievement, and recognition
E. Making periodic reports directly available to the worker rather than to the supervisor	Internal recognition
F. Introducing new and more difficult tasks not previously handled	Growth and learning
G. Assigning people specific or specialised tasks, enabling them to become experts	Responsibility, growth, and advancement

Source: Herzberg (1968).

HACKMAN AND OLDHAM'S JOB CHARACTERISTICS MODEL

In a similar treatise on intrinsic outcomes and job satisfaction, Hackman and Oldham (1980) enumerate three basic conditions necessary for promoting job satisfaction and employees' motivation:
- Work should be *meaningful* for the doer.
- Doers should have *responsibility* for the results.
- Doers should get *feedback* on the results.

This approach suggests that it is the design of work and not the characteristics of the employee that have the greatest impact on employees' motivation. Hackman and Oldham identified five 'core job characteristics' that need to be incorporated into job design to increase meaningfulness, responsibility and feedback.

1. Skill variety: extent to which jobs draw on a range of different skills and abilities.
2. Task identity: extent to which a job requires completion of a whole, identifiable piece of work.
3. Task significance: extent to which the job substantially impacts on the work or lives of others either within or outside the organisation.
4. Autonomy: freedom, independence and discretion afforded to the job holder.
5. Feedback: degree to which the job holder receives information on their level of performance, effectiveness and so forth.

Having identified the factors necessary to promote satisfaction and intrinsic motivation, the next stage is to incorporate these characteristics into jobs through various job redesign strategies. Hackman and Oldham suggest five implementation strategies to increase task variety, significance and identity, and create opportunities for greater autonomy and feedback.

1. Form natural work groups: arrange tasks together to form an identifiable, meaningful cycle of work for employees, e.g. responsibility for a single product rather than small components.
2. Combine tasks: group tasks together to form complete jobs.
3. Establish client relationships: establish personal contact between employees and the end user/client.
4. Vertically load jobs: many traditional approaches to job design separate planning and controlling (management functions) from executing (employee's function). Vertically loading jobs means integrating the planning, controlling and executing functions and giving the responsibility to employees (e.g. responsibility for materials, quality, deadlines and budgetary control).
5. Open feedback channels: ensure maximum communication of job results (e.g. service standards, faults, wastage, market performance and costs).

Figure 6.9 Designing enriched jobs

How does management enrich an employee's job? The following points, which we have just alluded to in the text, are derived from the application of the Job Characteristics Model and they seek to specify the types of changes in jobs that are most likely to lead to improving their motivation potential score.

Combine Tasks: Management should seek to take existing and fractionalised tasks and put them back together to form a new and larger module of work. This effort increases both skill variety and task identity.

Create Natural Work Units: The creation of natural work units means that the tasks that an employee does form an identifiable and meaningful whole. This increases employees' ownership of the work and improves the likelihood that employees will view their work as meaningful and important rather than irrelevant and boring.

Establish Client Relationships: The client is the user of the product or service that the employee works on (and may be an internal customer within the organisation or an external one beyond the organisation). Wherever possible, managers should try to establish direct relationships between workers and their clients. This has the impact of increasing skill variety, autonomy, and feedback for the employee.

> *Expand Jobs Vertically*: Vertical expansion gives employees responsibilities and control that were formally reserved for management. In particular it seeks to close the gap between the 'doing' and the 'controlling' aspects of the job, and it increases employees' autonomy.
>
> *Open Feedback Channels*: By increasing feedback, employees not only learn how well they are performing their jobs, but also whether their performance is improving, deteriorating, or remaining at a constant level. Ideally, this feedback about performance should be received directly as the employee does the job, rather than from management on an occasional basis.

Source: Hackman (1977).

Having proved to be arguably the most popular approach to task design the espoused advantages of redesigning jobs along the lines of Hackman and Oldham's job characteristics model have been summarised thus:

> By redesigning jobs to increase variety, identity, significance, autonomy and feedback, the psychological experience of working is changed . . . individuals experience the work as more meaningful, they feel more responsible for the results, and they know more about the results of their efforts. These psychological changes lead to many improved work outcomes, which have been observed following the redesign of work.
>
> Beer *et al.* (1985: 576–7)

Hackman and Oldham thus argued that changes have positive long-term benefits for both the organisation and the individual employee, such as increased motivation and improved performance. However, their theory also posits that not all workers are expected to respond favourably to job enrichment initiatives (Hackman *et al.* 1975). 'Employee growth needs strength' is considered the most important source of variation in this respect: only those workers with a strong desire for achievement, responsibility and autonomy will be motivated by increased intrinsic satisfaction and hence motivated to perform better (see Figure 6.10). For other employees, these changes may be a source of anxiety and lead to resentment and opposition to job redesign and other changes in the work system.

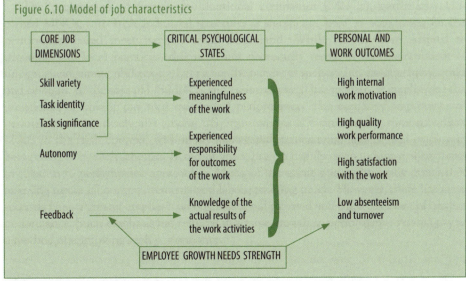

Figure 6.10 Model of job characteristics

Source: Hackman and Oldham (1980).

THE 'QUALITY OF WORKING LIFE' MOVEMENT

While job enrichment has the potential to positively impact on how employees experience work, its focus on job content has certain limitations. Clearly, many factors beyond job content impact on how employees experience work, such as working conditions, employees' involvement and autonomy, work intensity and the nature of supervision. These factors are often referred to as contextual influences on the likelihood of success or failure in the design effort. Giving expression to these contextual issues, the 'quality of working life' (QWL) movement emerged in both Europe, particularly Scandinavia, and in the US during the 1960s and 1970s (see Walton 1973; Skrovan 1983) and has recently been argued to be an early model for evidence-based policy making.

Focusing on the overall quality of employees' experiences in the workplace, it embraces both job design and broader issues such as autonomy, employees' participation, justice, working conditions and job security, as critical factors impacting on the quality of working life. A particular stimulus for the QWL approach was a desire to improve the quality of working life for employees by avoiding what were seen as characteristics of a low quality of working life. Figure 6.11 summarises some of the main characteristics of low- and high-quality working life as identified in the extant literature (see for example Steers and Porter 1987; Schermerhorn et al. 1985; Schuler and Jackson 1996).

Figure 6.11 High- and low-quality working life: indicative characteristics

Low Quality of Working Life	High Quality of Working Life
• Jobs characterised by low levels of task significance, variety, identity and feedback	• Adequate and fair reward systems
• No or little employee involvement	• Safe and healthy working conditions
• Top-down communications	• Opportunity to use personal capabilities
• Inequitable reward systems	• Opportunity for personal growth and development
• Inadequate job definition	• Integration into social system of organisation
• Poor employment conditions/Hire and fire approach	• High labour standards/employee rights
• Discriminatory HR policies	• Pride in relevance and value of work
• Low job security	• Balance between work and non-work roles

Source: Morley et al. (1980).

Beyond the job enrichment initiatives mentioned earlier, the QWL movement seeks to increase employees' influence and involvement in work organisation and job design. Again, this challenges some traditional management assumptions about employees. It involves recognising that employees can, and want to, make a positive input into organisational decision-making. It assumes that such involvement is valued by employees and results in increased commitment, responsibility and performance.

Increased employee influence in work system design also addresses the issue of employee supervision as an aspect of the management role. If employees are to be involved in making decisions about the organisation of work, and responsible for the subsequent execution of such decisions, much of the 'control' aspect is removed from the supervisory role. It necessitates a change in attitude to workforce management. Supervisors become less concerned with monitoring and controlling employees' performance and more involved in advising and facilitating employees in carrying out their jobs. This approach requires high levels of commitment and trust from both management and employees. Management must feel confident that employees have the required competence and will use their greater levels of influence positively and to the benefit of the organisation. Employees must be happy that their increased commitment and sense of responsibility will not be abused or exploited by employers.

There are various mechanisms available to encourage increased employee participation in the design and operation of work systems. Possibly the best-known approach is quality circles. These are small groups of employees and managers who meet together regularly to consider means of improving quality, productivity or other aspects of work organisation. They are seen as having played an important role in the success of Japanese organisations and have been successfully applied in Western economies, including Ireland.

There are numerous other participative and consultative mechanisms that may be established and that can work effectively in the appropriate organisational environment. Creating such an environment has become an important concern for organisations. Past experience in applying various techniques to improve employees' motivation and involvement has demonstrated that these operate best where there is a change in the overall corporate approach. The issue for senior management is how to create a corporate culture whose values, beliefs and practices establish an organisational environment within which employees are highly committed to, and work towards, the achievement of business goals.

HIGH-PERFORMANCE WORK SYSTEMS (HPWS)

Several commentators have suggested that the heretofore limited impact of job design theories is a weakness that needs to be remedied. Buchanan and McCalman (1989) noted that: 'It [job design] has tended to be regarded as an isolated management technique aimed at local organisational problems and at individual jobs, rather than realising that it must form part of the whole company philosophy, through all levels, if it is to be really successful.'

The motive behind high-performance work systems (HPWS) is rooted in the desire and the need to improve the overall competitive position of the organisation. In order to further this, HPWS thinking, as discussed earlier in Chapter 3, centred on the identification of a buttressing set of human resource policies and practices thought to encourage workforce skill and motivation and it has grown in stature since the 1980s.

In its early guise, HPWS was very much associated with the then high-tech companies of the 1980s, and especially those that located in greenfield sites, in attempts to establish a fundamentally different type of organisation and organisation culture. The essence of HPWS appears to lie in the adoption of a culture of continuous improvement and innovation at all levels in the organisation and the implementation of a range of work and human resource practices, to sustain and develop this culture, namely teamworking, quality consciousness and flexibility. They are also felt to reflect an increased management emphasis on developing broadly defined, challenging jobs within more organic, flexible organisation structures, which facilitated involvement and enhanced engagement:

> The high-performance work organisation has a distinctive structure which is designed to provide employees with skills, incentives, information and decision-making responsibilities that will lead to improved organisational performance and facilitate innovation . . . The main aim is to generate high levels of commitment and involvement of employees and managers.
>
> Tiernan *et al.* (1996: 113)

High-performance work systems are thus seen as embracing much more than a change in the nature of jobs. Rather, they appear to embrace fundamentally different assumptions about organisational structure and orientation, so that all aspects of organisational management are altered to embrace a new culture designed to improve performance and responsiveness through developing a more committed, flexible, skilled and engaged workforce.

As noted earlier, a primary driver of HPWS is increased pressure on organisations to improve organisational competitiveness. This indeed may explain its prevalence in high-technology sectors, especially electronics and software, which tend to be characterised by high levels of market volatility and product innovation. In relating the experience of the *Digital Equipment Corporation* as an early exemplar of high-performance work systems in the wave of HPWS initiatives, Perry (1984: 19) notes how the company's Connecticut plant sought to respond to increased competition and product change:

> The goal at the plant was flexibility: the capacity to respond quickly and effectively to an uncertain environment. Traditional ways of handling uncertainty had included the introduction of new procedures, changing the structure, employing more people, and tightening management controls. These strategies simply increased overheads, increased the complexity of the organisation and generated more uncertainty. To deal with these issues, management decided to introduce a more participative style of decision-making, multi-skilled operating teams, an innovative rewards system, and systematic career planning and development. The plant manager's review of these changes revealed: a 40 per cent reduction in product manufacturing time; a sharp increase in inventory turnover; a reduction in the level of management hierarchy to three; a 38 per cent reduction in standard costs; a 40 per cent reduction in overhead and equivalent output, with half the people and half the space.

An important dimension of HPWS entails the development of new or different approaches to the management of employees as well as in regard to the structure of jobs and systems. These themes pervade a number of streams of the literature (Vaill 1982; Perry 1984; Lawler 1986; Buchanan and McCalman 1989). Almost all contributors highlight the need to empower employees in an attempt to make the organisation more effective. While commentators may differ on detail, there is strong support for the use of team-based work systems as a means of developing a highly skilled, flexible and motivated workforce within a leaner, flatter, more responsive organisation structure.

In evaluating the impact of HPWS as a work design initiative Huczynski and Buchanan (1991) identified a number of distinctions between the HPWS approach of the 1990s and the earlier quality of work life (QWL) approach of the 1960s and 1970s:

1. *More strategic focus*: it is argued that the HPWS approach seeks to improve organisational competitiveness through increased flexibility and quality, while the QWL approach primarily concentrated on achieving reductions in absenteeism and turnover.
2. *Focus on performance rather than job experience*: the HPWS approach has a strong focus on performance criteria; increased employee autonomy is seen as leading to increased employee competence and skills, better decision-making, greater flexibility and adaptability and better use of technology. In contrast, the major rationale of the QWL approach was based on improving the job experience of employees; increased autonomy was seen as leading to increased worker satisfaction and a better job experience.
3. *Major change in management style*: the HPWS approach is seen as requiring a fundamental overhaul of management style, requiring major cultural change and redefinition of the role of management, from top management down. The QWL approach appeared to be more limited, involving only a re-orientation in the role of first line supervisors.
4. *Long-term comprehensive strategy*: the HPWS approach is seen as a major change initiative affecting the whole organisation and involving a long-term commitment by all parties. The QWL approach tended to be more of a 'quick fix applied to isolated and problematic work groups' (Huczynski and Buchanan 1991: 86).
5. *Representative of strategic human resource management*: consistent with the argument that the 1980s and 1990s witnessed a move from 'reactive/operational' personnel management to 'strategic' human resource management (HRM), it is argued that HPWS is a key element of strategic HRM, while QWL is more of a personnel administration technique.

Figure 6.12 Organisational characteristics of high-performance, high-involvement work systems

Organisational Structure	Flat and lean Enterprise-oriented Team-based Participative structure; councils, fora
Job Design	Job enrichment Autonomous teams/work groups
Information System	Open flow Work/job focus Decentralised – team/group-based Participatively established goals/standards
Career System	Career tracks/ladders/counselling Open job posting
Selection	'Realistic' job preview Team/group-based Potential- and process-skill-oriented

Training	Strong commitment and investment
	Peer training
	'Economic' education
	Interpersonal skills
Reward System	Open
	Skill-based
	Gain-sharing/share ownership
	Flexible benefits
	All salary/egalitarian
Personnel Policies	Employment tenure commitments
	Participatively established through representative group(s)
Physical Layout	Based on organisational structure
	Egalitarian
	Safe and pleasant

Source: Adapted from Lawler (1982).

It would appear that the optimal means of facilitating workers' influence on the application of new work systems is through some combination of direct and indirect participation. In Ireland, the first prominent examples of organisations that sought to develop HPWS along the lines described above came from the ranks of firms that had previously experimented with such systems elsewhere. These were mostly US high-tech companies such as *Digital, Apple* and *Amdahl*. Subsequently, we saw a greater diversity in the range of companies undertaking such initiatives. One widely quoted Irish example was Bord na Móna (see O'Connor 1995; Magee 1991). Here we find a semi-state company that, by the 1980s, faced severe competitive problems, particularly in relation to (high) costs, (poor) productivity and a pressing need to improve quality, performance and employee relations (Magee 1991). In an attempt to deal with these issues, the company undertook a number of radical initiatives. First, a new multi-disciplinary and team-based management structure was established. The initial challenge was to reduce costs, which was addressed by a major redundancy programme that saw 2,500 workers (out of approximately 5,000) leave the company. After this, management initiated a more fundamental overhaul:

> It was recognised by everyone concerned . . . that cost-cutting through redundancy would not be enough. We had to change our work practices at the same time. We knew that a fundamental restructuring of how we did our business had to be undertaken to create flexibility in adapting to changing markets, to improve productivity and to improve our competitive position. After extensive negotiation, the 'enterprise scheme' was introduced with the full agreement and co-operation of all parties. The Bord na Móna enterprise scheme allows our staff to form their own autonomous enterprise units, which are team-based and where the unit's earnings are directly related to performance and productivity. *Our workers have become their own bosses.*
>
> O'Connor (1995: 116)

The introduction of autonomous work groups meant that instead of working in isolation, the workers became team members. Leaders were selected for these autonomous work groups (AWGs), who then assumed responsibility and authority for the completion of tasks. In addition to the establishment of AWGs, Bord na Móna also reduced the number of levels in the management hierarchy. It seems that the results of these various changes were extremely positive. Edward O'Connor, then managing director of the company, summed up the experience as follows:

> The spirit of enterprise this has brought into Bord na Móna has increased productivity per workers in a way that is truly amazing. Our productivity has increased by 75 per cent. Our people now make their own decisions and take their own risks. The series of work groups or enterprise units that have been set up have different structures, but essentially Bord na Móna supplies them with services and they produce quality peat, at a price that is agreed in advance. These are people who, formerly, did what they were told to do, got paid whether or not peat was produced, whether the sun shone all summer or whether it rained all the time . . . The new work practices and systems we have introduced amount to nothing less than a fundamental restructuring of the organisation.
>
> O'Connor (1995: 117)

More recent survey-based research on the impact of HPWS in the Irish context was undertaken by Flood *et al.* (2008), whose comprehensive study offers multiple insights into the value of taking an integrated HPWS approach to workforce engagement and management. The research is the result of a detailed survey of medium to large companies in the manufacturing and services industries in Ireland which examined the nature of management and workplace practices and their relationship to business performance outcomes.

The research team analysed the data gathered from some 132 companies operating in Ireland to explore a number of alternative models of HPWS. The initial model explored the more common factors associated with HPWS from previous studies, largely referring to strategic HRM in the company. However, the researchers then expanded their analysis to examine factors beyond strategic HRM, including workplace partnership, diversity and equality management, and flexible working systems.

The results of the initial model of HPWS reconfirm results of previous research – that strategic HRM practices, as espoused in the HPWS bundle, are clearly associated with business performance outcomes, including labour productivity, innovation levels and employee wellbeing. The more novel findings relate to the discovery that other factors, including diversity and equality systems, and workplace partnership systems, are positively and synergistically associated with significantly higher levels of labour productivity, workforce innovation, and reduced employee turnover. The results led the research team to advance four particular models of HPWS as outlined in Figure 6.13 on the next page.

Figure 6.13 Models of high-performance work systems in Ireland

	Model 1	Model 2	Model 3	Model 4
	Strategic HRM	Strategic HRM partnership	Diversity and equality systems Flexible work systems	Strategic HRM Partnership Diversity and equality systems Flexible work systems
Labour productivity	Greater use of SHRM associated with increased labour productivity. SHRM accounts for 12.4% variance (p<.01). Statistically significant (p<.01) positive relationship between change of HPWS and change of labour productivity (based on comparison of 2004 and 2006 panel data).	Greater use of SHRM and partnership associated with increased productivity. SHRM accounts for 10% variance. Partnership accounts for 3.9% variance. SHRM partially mediates between partnership and labour productivity.	Diversity and equality system accounted for 6.5% of variance in labour productivity. No significant association between FWS and labour productivity.	Four elements together (SHRM, Partnership, DES, FWS) account for 14.8% of variance in labour productivity. While only SHRM is significant, other three variables are in a positive direction. Total economic value in this sample equates to €44,399 per employee, or almost €12,000,000 in the median-sized company with 270 employees.
Workforce innovation	SHRM associated with greater workforce innovation	SHRM associated with greater workforce innovation (5% of variance). SHRM also mediates relationship between partnership and workforce innovation. Partnership does not have a direct association, but companies with partnership are likely to have greater levels of SHRM.	DES accounts for 7.9% of variance (p<.01). No significant association between FWS and workforce innovation.	Four elements together (SHRM, partnership, DES, FWS) account for 12.2% of variance in workforce innovation. SHRM and DES are significant, while partnership and FWS affects in positive direction. Total economic value in this sample equates to €2,061 per employee, or €556,200 in the median-sized company with 270 employees.

	Model 1	Model 2	Model 3	Model 4
Employee Turnover	SHRM associated with decreased employee turnover.	SHRM associated with decreased employee turnover (4% of variance, p<.01). SHRM also mediates relationship between partnership and employee turnover.	DES accounts for 4.4% variance in employee turnover (p<.01). No significant association between FWS and employee turnover.	Four elements together (SHRM, Partnership, DES, FWS) account for 7.7% of variance in employee turnover. Partnership is significant at 4% of variance explained. Total economic value in this sample equates to retention of up to 2 additional employees in the median-sized company.

Source: Flood et al. (2008).

In this sample of companies, a broad model of HPWS (incorporating strategic HRM, workplace partnership, diversity and equality systems and flexible work systems) was found to be associated with 14.8 per cent of variance in labour productivity, 12.2 per cent of variance in workforce innovation, and 7.7 per cent of variance in employee turnover. In their report, Flood et al. (2008:12) note that:

> While the analyses do not suggest a causal relationship between HPWS and business performance outcomes, they do make important reading for any company that is seeking to build competitive advantage through workplace innovation. They demonstrate a strong business case for building management systems that deal effectively with issues including strategic human resource management, employee involvement and participation, diversity and equality management, and flexible working. Where companies are found to manage these issues more extensively, higher levels of business performance can be demonstrated. Where companies are found to manage these issues in a more cohesive management system, even greater effects are found in terms of business performance.

This Irish research points to the value of thinking about HPWS as something of a step-change from the earlier work and organisational design 'isolated' movements in which it was rooted and emphasises the value of a more integrated approach to understanding the relationship between policy and practice initiatives on a range of fronts, the combination of which make a difference. It was precisely this concern with earlier thinking which became the well-spring for the HPWS movement in the first instance. While adding incrementally to our knowledge about isolated aspects of design or policy, however, it failed to generate insights into how a fuller range of policies and practices might combine in a particular way to distinguish the high-performance organisation.

CONCLUSION

This chapter has explored the principles of motivation and work design. Definitions were set down and the pedigree of both concepts in the management canon were established. In relation to motivation, Maslow's hierarchy of needs theory, ERG theory, acquired needs theory and dual-factor theory were all examined under the umbrella of content approaches to understanding motivation at work. Theory X, theory Y, expectancy theory and equity theory, as process theories of motivation, were also examined. Finally, the importance of work organisation and job design as a critical determinant of employee satisfaction, motivation and engagement at work was presented, and the various schools of thought synthesised.

The issues raised in this chapter are related to broader corporate choices about the nature and role of the organisation. Employee performance will be influenced by a variety of factors relating to both the individual and the work context including the social context of work comprising interpersonal interactions and workplace relationships that are influenced by the jobs that employees perform (Grant and Parker 2009). The work environment is seen as particularly important. As information technology becomes more flexible in its application, employers have possibly greater scope to introduce changes in work organisation. Apart from the necessity for management commitment and positive beliefs about people at work, these changes have broader implications for other HRM policy choices. In particular, it is important that any changes in work organisation complement decisions taken in other HR areas, as demonstrated by the research on HPWS presented above.

Decisions on work organisation and job design represent a critical aspect of HRM in organisations. They influence key areas such as organisational structure, management style, employee motivation, engagement and reward systems. While environmental factors exercise a key influence, top management still retain considerable discretion in making choices on the nature of work systems which impact corporate outcomes. Importantly, the degree of congruence between the work system, job design and employees' needs will be a major influence on the level of engagement and the outcomes secured.

Having reviewed aspects of motivation and the design of work, in the next chapter we turn our attention to the design and management of effective reward systems.

7
Managing Rewards

The essence of an effective reward system essentially involves what Kerr (1995) once coined as 'avoiding the folly of rewarding A, while hoping for B!' Understanding the nature of an organisation's reward system, and its impact upon the strategies and performance outcomes achieved, is a key element of HRM, and in today's competitive, globalised business environment, its importance should not be underestimated.

While the quantity of evidence on the significance of reward policies and practices and their links to organisational outcomes is growing, there have been calls for a stronger evidence base to substantiate such connections (Armstrong et al. 2010). This is largely as a result of the recognition that compensation practices must be relevant in a world where there is increasing competition and awareness of the contribution of the human asset to overall organisational performance. Brown (2014) suggests that contemporary reward management approaches involve a clear focus on core values and principles, a strong basis in evidence and measurement, a greater emphasis on employee engagement through rewards, and improved, and more open, communications of the reward strategy. Thus reward management has become especially important in helping to attract and retain talent and also in influencing engagement, performance and behaviour at work.

Viewed in this way, it becomes obvious that *pay*, *incentives* and *benefits* are of central importance to employees and organisations alike. Subsumed under the label 'reward management' are numerous objectives relating to human resource plans and business strategies, high performance and continuous improvement, the satisfaction of individual needs and wants, cultural maintenance and the promotion of teamwork. High or low pay, the nature of incentives and the range of fringe benefits in existence provide a valuable insight into the corporate approach to HRM.

This chapter explores the concept of reward management. Pay, incentives and benefits as possible components of the overall reward package are defined and the objectives and scope of reward management are examined. During the course of the chapter, it becomes obvious that the management of rewards is more than just direct wages and salaries paid. Additional direct payments, in the form of bonuses and other incentives, are used extensively. A growing cost for many employers is employees' benefits, which represent indirect reward because employees receive the value of the benefits without getting direct cash payments.

The reward package is often one of the largest costs faced by employers, many of whom have labour costs as high as 50 per cent of all operating costs. It will also become clear that although the total cost of a reward system is reasonably straightforward to calculate, the value derived by employers and employees is much more difficult to identify and quantify, hence the call for more evidence-based approaches. In order to help clarify where added value might accrue, the chapter opens by introducing the reader to the debate on pay as a motivator. It then explores issues in the design of an effective reward system and examines the meaning, purpose and methods of job evaluation. Following this, the choice of pay, incentive and fringe benefits that constitute the reward package are presented and examined.

PAY AS A MOTIVATOR

For as long as organisations have existed, rewards have been recognised as a major motivator of employees as well as an important tool and expense for organisations (Werner and Ward 2004). The utility of using pay to motivate and promote performance has been a subject of debate for many years with empirical and theoretical support for both sides of the argument. Most managers instinctively believe that money is a motivator, even though empirical evidence to support this is far from conclusive (Milkovich and Newman 2002; Kelly and Monks 1997; Fowler 1991; Goffee and Scase 1986). Indeed, the failure of different reward systems, in some instances, to fulfil their potential has been attributed to a flawed theoretical base, which in many cases serves to undermine effectiveness by demotivating employees. The academic debate has done little to clarify our thinking; a problem intensified by the fact that empirical evidence has not always established a tangible link between incentive pay and enhanced performance in a consistent manner. Perhaps the key point that may be drawn from the available evidence, both academic and empirical, is that pay is a complex, multi-faceted issue that serves as both a tangible and intangible motivator, offering intrinsic and extrinsic rewards. Thus, the applicability of pay-related incentive schemes across a wide range of organisational contexts is difficult to generalise on and is largely dependent on organisational circumstances and prevailing conditions.

Notwithstanding the reservations expressed about the absolute clarity surrounding outcomes, pay and benefits are increasingly becoming areas of extreme importance in determining the effectiveness of the organisation. In his treatise on how to motivate employees, Herzberg (1968) wrote that a 'KITA', which he suggests stands for a kick in the 'pants', produces movement, but not motivation. Kohn (1993) argues that the same is true of rewards:

> Punishment and rewards are two sides of the same coin. Rewards have a punishment effect because they, like outright punishment, are manipulative. "Do this and you'll get that" is not very different from "Do this or here's what will happen to you."

In the case of incentives, the reward itself may be highly desired, but by making that bonus contingent on certain behaviours, managers manipulate their subordinates, and that experience of being controlled is likely to assume a punitive quality over time. Herzberg has further argued that just because too little money can irritate and demotivate does not mean that more and more money will bring about increased satisfaction or increased motivation.

Pay is important to employees. It provides the means to live, eat and achieve personal or family goals. It is a central reason why people hold down and move between jobs. However, a key question is not the importance of financial incentives as such but whether they motivate employees and engage them sufficiently to perform well in their jobs. Once an employee has been attracted to the organisation and the job, the role of money as a motivator is debatable. Clearly money – or the lack of it – can be a source of dissatisfaction and grievance. However, if the employee is reasonably happy with his/her income, does that income induce him/her to achieve high levels of performance? Many of the theoretical prescriptions suggest that money is important in satisfying essential lower-order needs. Once these are satisfied, it is the factors intrinsic to the job, especially the realisation and fulfilment of one's potential, that are the prime motivators. Others suggest that money is important at all levels and, as expectancy theory indicates, may be a prime motivator where it is a valued outcome and where there is a strong link between effort, performance and the achievement of greater financial reward.

During the 1960s and 1970s many organisational behaviourists emphasised the importance of job enrichment and organisational development and it became somewhat popular to discount the importance of money as a motivator (Biddle and Evenden 1989). The current emphasis on performance, productivity and cost reduction has tended to focus on primary job values such as employment security, benefits and – particularly – the pay package. Most managers will agree that remuneration – especially the money element – has an important role in motivating employees. However, it is only one factor in the total motivational and engagement process. Many people are primarily motivated not by money, but by other factors such as promotion prospects, recognition or the job challenge itself. Not all employees have a generalised set of motives. Rather, an organisation's workforce will be comprised of people with various sets of priorities relating to different situations and work contexts, resulting in differing employee motives and goals. These motives and goals will vary both between employees and with individual employees over time. For example, a young single person may prioritise basic income and free time and the job itself may not hold any great interest. Later, that person, now married and with a mortgage, may be more concerned with job security and fringe benefits such as health insurance and pension.

The literature suggests that there are four key issues that organisations should consider when exploring the extent to which employees are likely to be motivated by pay:
1. Employees must value financial rewards. If people are paid at a very high level, or simply not concerned with financial rewards, higher pay will have little incentive value for employees. At this stage other factors related to the job and work environment must have the potential to motivate employees.
2. If money is a valued reward, employees must believe that good performance will allow them to realise that reward. This suggests that pay should be linked to performance and differences in pay should be large enough to reward high levels of performance. This approach obviously rejects remuneration systems that reward good, average and poor performance equally, such as regular pay increments based on seniority.
3. Equity is an important consideration. Employees must be fairly treated in their work situation, especially in terms of the perceived equity of pay levels and comparisons with fellow employees. They will be keen that rewards (pay, incentives and benefits) adequately reflect their input (effort and skills). Should employees feel they are not being treated fairly on these criteria, performance levels may fall.

4. Employees must believe that the performance levels necessary to achieve desired financial rewards are achievable. The required performance criteria and levels should be clearly outlined and communicated to employees.

Organisations must also ensure that employees have the necessary ability, training, resources and opportunity to achieve such performance levels. Otherwise, employees will either not be able, or else not try, to expend the necessary effort. From the motivational perspective, effective payment systems should:
- Be objectively established.
- Clarify the performance levels required and rewards available.
- Reward the achievement of required performance levels adequately and quickly.
- Ensure employees have the ability, training resources and opportunity to achieve required performance level(s).
- Recognise that financial incentives are only one source of motivation, and design jobs to ensure employees can satisfy other needs through their work (e.g. achievement, challenge).
- Take regular steps to identify employee needs and ensure that these can be satisfied within the organisational environment.

Even where these characteristics are present, success is not guaranteed. For example, an incentive scheme based on production figures may be established to encourage employees to achieve high performance levels. However, unofficial norms established by the work group may dictate 'acceptable' performance levels and ensure these are not exceeded through various social pressures. Equally, this approach may signal to employees that management are clearly in charge and may lessen employee feelings of control and competence, or encourage conflict over the standards set.

It should always be appreciated that, while pay is an important source of employee motivation, it is not the only one. To motivate effectively, financial incentives should be structured in such a way as to highlight the link between effort, performance and reward; adequately reward good performance; and be equitable in the eyes of employees. The remuneration system should be viewed as part of a total motivational process that takes account of individual differences and provides motivational opportunities through additional extrinsic and intrinsic factors, particularly self-fulfilment.

THE SCOPE OF REWARD MANAGEMENT

As with the design of the work system, an organisation's reward system is a powerful indicator of its philosophy and approach to people management. Three aspects of the reward package are worth distinguishing at the outset, namely *pay*, *incentives* and *benefits*.
- Pay refers to the basic wage or salary that an employee receives.
- An incentive refers to the rewarding of an employee for effort that results in higher performance that goes beyond normal performance expectations.
- Benefits refer to indirect rewards, such as health insurance cover and pension entitlements, associated with organisational membership.

In relation to incentive schemes that emphasise differential rewards based on performance as a means of increasing motivation, it is not axiomatic that higher motivation will follow. Such schemes have numerous drawbacks in terms of design, operation and negative side effects. For this and other reasons, many organisations use standard pay rates that do not vary according to performance. In establishing a remuneration system an organisation must weigh up the motivational aspects of a performance-related scheme against its drawbacks, in terms of operational and other difficulties. It must be established in the context of the organisation's strategic needs and workforce profile, and be part of the overall human resource approach encompassing other motivational factors appropriate to the organisation and relevant to the workforce.

An organisation's reward system will typically seek to achieve several core objectives.
- It will seek to play a central role in attracting potential talent into the organisation: in conjunction with the organisation's human resource plan and its recruitment and selection efforts, the reward package and its mix of pay, incentives and benefits, serves to attract employees with the blend of skills, competences and values deemed appropriate by the organisation.
- It will play a central role in retaining valued employees: unless the reward package is perceived as internally equitable and externally competitive, valued employees might potentially leave.
- It will serve to motivate and engage employees: the reward package can assist in the quest for high performance, by linking rewards to performance.
- It will contribute to human resource and strategic business plans. These can take many different forms: for example, an organisation may want to build a rewarding and loyal climate, or it may want to project itself as an attractive place to work so that it can attract the best talent available in the labour market. The reward package can play a central role in the execution of these plans and safeguard success and growth.

Thus, the reward package is important to the organisation because it helps to attract and retain talent and influence performance and behaviour at work. The extent, however, to which reward management actually achieves performance improvements remains somewhat disputed. Concomitantly, it is important to employees because it provides the means to satisfy basic needs and may also allow them to satisfy less tangible desires for personal growth and satisfaction.

TOWARDS AN EFFECTIVE REWARD SYSTEM

Important considerations in the design of an organisation's reward system will be the relative emphasis on extrinsic versus intrinsic rewards, the role of pay and whether it is contingent upon individuals' performance, and its compatibility with the organisation's business goals and other HR policies. This latter issue is particularly significant since the organisation's reward system must complement overall business objectives and other HR policy choices. Decisions on the organisation's cost structure and market strategy will influence the reward strategy. A high-volume, low-cost strategy may constrain the organisation's ability to provide expansive rewards. On the other hand, a product innovation strategy may require a comprehensive reward system that attracts and retains high-calibre talent. The reward system must also 'fit' with other HR decisions.

Recruitment and selection will provide a particular workforce profile and the reward system must cater for their various needs. The reward system also complements HR practices in areas such as employee development and promotion.

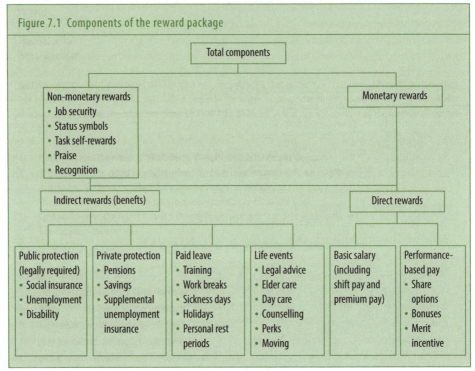

Source: Adapted from Schuler (1995: 384).

The design and implementation of an effective reward system has proved to be a difficult task for many organisations. Beer *et al.* (1985) suggest that many employee grievances and criticisms of reward systems actually mask more fundamental employee relations problems. As extrinsic rewards are a tangible outcome of an employee's relationship with an organisation, they are an obvious target for discontent in the employment relationship. Dissatisfaction with elements of this relationship, such as the supervisory style or opportunities for personal development, may manifest themselves in dissatisfaction with aspects of the reward system. Consequently, organisations experiencing problems with their reward system should examine decisions taken on other HR policy issues, such as selection, employee relations or work design, rather than making piecemeal changes to the compensation package.

Another potential problem of designing and implementing an effective reward system concerns suggestions that pay should be contingent on individual performance. Support for contingent payment systems is based on the concept that it is fair and logical to reward individual employees differentially, based on some measure of performance. While this principle is rarely a source of contention, problems may arise in attempting to develop reliable and acceptable mechanisms for evaluating employee performance. These include the limited criteria used (e.g. work-study), inconsistency of application (e.g. performance appraisal), or bias and inequity in employees' evaluations. A more fundamental issue may be resentment towards the exercise of managerial control via performance measurement and reward distribution, which is inherent in many 'reward-for-performance' approaches.

The literature on rewards systems identifies several core characteristics which should be taken into account when trying to devise and implement an effective system that addresses different stakeholder needs and wants.

- The *level of reward* – at a fundamental level, the reward package must satisfy basic needs for survival, security and self-development.
- *Recognising individuality and individual motivational disposition* – the reward system must be flexible enough to meet the different individual needs of the organisation's employees.
- *Encouraging group effort* – where teamwork and collective effort are desired aspects of the work environment, the reward system has an important role to play in promoting and enhancing this.
- *Promoting internal equity* – rewards must be seen as fair when compared to others in the organisation and criteria for the allocation of rewards should be equitable and clear; these should be communicated and accepted by all parties and applied consistently throughout the organisation.
- *External equity* – rewards must be seen as fair when compared to those offered for comparable work in competing organisations.
- *Stakeholder trust in the reward system* – management and employees must believe in the reward system, with employees accepting that certain rewards will be forthcoming when the relevant criteria are met and management trusting that employees will perform at an appropriate level in return for such rewards.

Thus, the objectives of an effective reward system include: identifying prevailing market trends; balancing individual and group needs with organisational needs and/or constraints; ensuring fairness and equity; inducing and rewarding higher levels of performance, whether individual or collective; and working within the legal framework in the external environment.

DETERMINING THE RELATIVE VALUE OF JOBS

Of primary importance is the establishment of basic pay levels for various jobs. Here again the organisation must be aware of the need to establish pay equity. This initially applies to *external comparisons* with pay levels in other competing organisations. Comparable pay rates influence an organisation's ability to attract and retain the right mix of talent. Suitable comparable organisations should be chosen to maintain pay competitiveness, while keeping wage costs at reasonable levels. Pay levels will be influenced by factors in the broader business environment, including:

- Economic climate: factors such as levels of inflation, disposable income and industrial activity will exert both direct and indirect influences on payment levels by affecting employment levels, demand, consumer price indices and so forth.
- Labour market: the state of the labour market will be influenced by general economic factors. It will also depend on labour supply and demand for certain skills and local

factors such as the level of company closures, emigration and so forth. Information on local and national pay rates can be obtained through wage surveys of comparable organisations.
- Government policy: government will exert considerable influence on pay levels both indirectly (fiscal policy) and directly through what it pays its own employees (state, semi-state sector), national pay guidelines, minimum pay levels (Joint Labour Committees), and legislation (e.g. equal pay).
- Trade unions: through collective bargaining, trade unions will seek to improve or, at least, maintain their members' earning levels. Such claims will generally be based on comparability, differentials and cost of living increases.

Pay levels will also depend on factors relating to the organisation itself. Managerial philosophy and style in managing employees will impact upon approaches to the supervision, development and payment of employees. The organisation's competitive position will influence its ability to reward employees. These factors help determine the organisation's position as a low, high or average payer, which in turn will influence the choice of comparable organisations for pay purposes.

Aspirations for pay equity can be partially satisfied by ensuring that pay rates are competitive in comparison with other organisations. Before this, however, organisations must also strive to maintain *internal equity* in determining differential pay rates for various jobs. The establishment of an internal pay structure involves deciding the relative value of jobs within an organisation and results in the creation of a hierarchy of job grades. The perceived equity of internal job grades will impact upon employees' performance and commitment. Grading can equally be a source of grievance and conflict, which requires careful handling.

Establishing fair and consistent pay rates and differentials between jobs is an important step in developing an effective compensation system. Management will want to ensure that jobs that contribute most to the organisation are rewarded appropriately. They will also be keen to ensure that conflict over pay and job grading is kept to a minimum by establishing an equitable and consistent system for internally grading and evaluating jobs, and determining differentials. The initial stage in establishing the relative worth of jobs is an analysis of job content. This will often be achieved through systematic job analysis that should provide detailed information on the duties, demands, responsibilities and skills of the various jobs in the organisation. Such information may then be used to establish the organisation's grading structure and to decide related pay levels through some method of job evaluation.

APPROACHES TO JOB EVALUATION

Job evaluation is often described as being concerned solely with the techniques used to establish the comparative worth of jobs in an organisation, but it is also, according to Armstrong and Baron (1995), about making decisions on what people should be paid for the work they do. It is a technique for determining the relative worth of jobs in an organisation so that differential rewards may be given to jobs of different worth. It operates by examining job content and placing jobs in a hierarchy according to their contribution to the attainment of the organisation's objectives.

Choosing the correct job evaluation system is critical if the resulting pay structures are to be in keeping with an organisation's structure, style and values. There is no one best scheme. Each organisation needs to assess its own requirements and set these against the range of available methods. Whatever job evaluation scheme is chosen, it will serve several critical purposes, including:
- Providing a balanced basis for the design and maintenance of an equitable, transparent and workable pay structure.
- Assisting in the management of the relativity existing between jobs within the organisation.
- Enabling consistent and fair decisions to be made on grading and rates of pay.
- Establishing the extent to which there is comparable worth between jobs so that equal pay can be provided for work of equal value.

Job evaluation schemes are commonly classified into *non-analytical schemes* and *analytical schemes*. Non-analytical schemes involve making comparisons between whole jobs without analysing them into their constituent parts or elements. Among the main schemes here are *job ranking, job classification* and *paired comparison*. Analytical schemes involve jobs being broken down into a number of critical factors that are then analysed and compared, using a quantitative measure. Among the main analytical methods are *points rating, Hay method* and *competence-based job evaluation*. We now turn to a description of the non-analytical and analytical schemes mentioned.

NON-ANALYTICAL SCHEMES

Job Ranking

Ranking is the simplest method of job evaluation and according to Armstrong and Baron (1995) 'is almost intuitive'. It aims to judge each job as a whole and determine its place in a job hierarchy by comparing one job with another and arranging them in perceived order of importance, their difficulty, or their value to the organisation. No attempt is made to quantify judgments. A ranking table is then drawn up and the jobs thus ranked are arranged into grades. Pay levels are then agreed for each grade. Sometimes a single factor such as skill is used; alternatively a list of factors such as skill, responsibility, complexity and physical demands is used. Armstrong and Baron (1995) list the following advantages and disadvantages of job ranking.

Advantages
- It is in accord with how people instinctively value jobs.
- It is simple and easily understood.
- It is quick and cheap to implement, as long as agreement can be reached on the rank order of the jobs without too much argument.
- It is a way of checking the results of more sophisticated methods to indicate the extent to which the hierarchies produced are 'felt-fair' – but this may simply reproduce the existing hierarchy and fail to eliminate gender bias.

Disadvantages
- There are no defined standards for judging relative worth, and therefore no rationale to defend the rank order – it is simply a matter of opinion.
- Ranking is not acceptable as a method of determining comparable worth in equal-value cases.
- Evaluators need an overall knowledge of every job to be evaluated, and ranking may be more difficult when a large number of jobs are under consideration.
- It may be difficult, if not impossible, to produce a felt-fair ranking for jobs in widely different functions, when the demands made upon them vary significantly.
- The division of the rank order into grades is likely to be somewhat arbitrary. Overall, job ranking as a method of job evaluation is most useful for small organisations with a limited range of jobs to evaluate.

Job Classification

Job classification is more complex than job ranking, in that classes or grades are established and the jobs are then placed into the grades. Thus, it begins, not by ranking jobs, but by agreeing a grading structure. Initially the number of job grades and particular criteria for these grades are agreed, so that for each job grade there is a broad description of its key characteristics. The number of grades is usually limited to between four and eight, between each of which there are clear differences in the demands made by any job in its respective grade. In establishing the grades, benchmark jobs considered to be particularly characteristic of each job grade are chosen, and all other jobs are evaluated, using detailed job descriptions, by comparison with both the benchmark jobs and the criteria for each job grade. Evaluated jobs are then placed in their appropriate grades.

Advantages
- Its simplicity and the ease with which it can be understood.
- It is more objective than job ranking.
- Standards for making grading decisions are provided in the form of the grade definitions.

Disadvantages
- The basis of the job evaluation is either one factor or an intuitive summary of many factors.
- It is difficult to apply to more complex jobs where duties and skills do not fit neatly into one grade but overlap with other grades.
- It may not be able to cater for a wide range of jobs or for senior jobs where grade descriptions have to be very general.
- As it is not an analytical system it is not effective as a means of establishing comparable worth and is unacceptable in equal value cases.

Paired Comparison

More sophisticated than the previous two methods, the paired comparison approach is based on the premise that it is more reasonable to compare one job with another than to consider a larger number of jobs together. The method requires the comparison of each job individually with every other job, until one builds up a rank order of jobs. When a job is deemed to be of higher worth than the one to which it is being compared, it is awarded two points; if it is deemed to be of equal worth it receives one point; if it is found to be of less worth it receives no points. The points are then totalled for each job and a rank order is produced.

The main advantage of this approach is that it is easier to compare one job with another at a time, which results in greater overall consistency. The main disadvantages are that it relies on whole or complete job ranking, which is difficult, and there is a limit to the number of jobs that can be ranked.

ANALYTICAL SCHEMES

Points Rating

Points rating is a widely-used method of job evaluation. It involves breaking down each job into a number of component job factors and then analysing these separately defined factors, which are assumed to be common to all jobs. It is based on the assumption that the degree to which differences in the job factors arise will accurately reflect the actual difference between total jobs.

The selection of the job factors is critical. Benge (1944), who first promulgated the points rating method, suggested that it should be limited to the following five factors, which he believed were the universal factors found in all jobs: skill requirements; mental requirements; physical requirements; responsibility; and working conditions. Each of these job factors may then be broken down into a number of sub-factors, including financial, quality, equipment and materials, training and other. Once the factors and sub-factors have been agreed, point values are then allocated (see Table 7.1).

Table 7.1 Points rating job evaluation

	LEVEL				
Factor	1 Minimum	2 Low	3 Moderate	4 High	**Total points**
Responsibility					
(a) Financial	10	20	30	40	
(b) Quality	10	20	30	40	
(c) Equipment	10	20	30	40	
(d) Training	10	20	30	40	
(e) Other	10	20	30	40	200
Working conditions					
(a) Hazardous	15	30	45	60	
(b) Unpleasant	10	20	30	40	100

In the example shown here, responsibility is twice as important as working conditions, while in relation to working conditions, hazardous conditions get more points than those that are simply rated as unpleasant. The various jobs may then be evaluated and placed in their appropriate grades. This can be done by either taking one factor and evaluating its significance in all jobs under consideration, or taking each job and evaluating it in terms of all job factors. The former approach is recommended as it concentrates on the comparable worth of jobs in terms of a specific factor and this information can be brought together at the end to give a total picture of relative job worth.

Advantages
- It is systematic and analytical in the sense that it compares jobs on a factor-by-factor basis.
- The standards of comparison are clearly defined.

Disadvantages
- It is complex and difficult to understand.
- It can be time-consuming and expensive.
- Although analytical, it still relies on a good deal of subjective judgment.
- It may be impossible to put numerical values on different aspects of jobs, since skills are not always quantifiable in this way, particularly when comparing the skills required by jobs of often disparate demands and responsibilities.

Hay Method

The Hay method or plan is one of the most widely used job evaluation methods in the world and is generally classified as a points-factor rating. Traditionally associated with managerial and professional jobs, it is becoming more widely used for technical, clerical and other positions. The method relies on three primary factors, namely know-how, problem solving and accountability (see Figure 7.2). It combines aspects of points rating and factor comparison. Values are established for each job, using the factors set out in the table, and jobs are compared to one another on each factor. Points-factor schemes of this kind are popular because people generally feel that they work.

Advantages
- The approach is widely accepted.
- Evaluators are forced to consider a range of factors and thus avoid over-simplifications.
- It has a higher level of objectivity than other approaches.
- Many external comparisons are available because of the widespread adoption of the method.

Disadvantages
- The degree of complexity.
- Due to its standardised nature, it may not reflect an organisation's real needs.
- Despite the impression of objectivity, human judgment is required in the process.

> **Figure 7.2 Primary factors in the Hay method**
>
> | PROBLEM-SOLVING (MENTAL ACTIVITY) | KNOW-HOW | ACCOUNTABILITY |
> |---|---|---|
> | The amount of original, self-starting thought required by the job for analysis, evaluation, creation, reasoning, and arriving at conclusions.
Problem-solving has two dimensions:
• The degree of freedom with which the thinking process is used to achieve job objectives without the guidance of standards, precedents, or direction from others.
• The type of mental activity involved; the complexity, abstractness or originality of thought required.

Problem-solving is expressed as a percentage of know-how, for the obvious reason that people think with what they know. The percentage judged to be correct for a job is applied to the know-how point value; the result is the point value given to problem-solving.

Note: The total evaluation of any job is arrived at by adding the points for problem-solving, know-how, and accountability. The points are not shown here. | The total of all knowledge and skills, however acquired, needed for satisfactory job performance (evaluates the job, not the person).
Know-how has three dimensions:
• The amount of practical, specialised or technical knowledge required.
• Breadth of management, or the ability to make many activities and functions work well together; the job of company president, for example, has greater breadth than that of a department supervisor.
• Requirement for skill in motivating people.

Using a chart, a number can be assigned to the level of know-how needed in a job. This number – or point value – indicates the relative importance of know-how in the job being evaluated. | The measured effect of the job on company goals.
Accountability has three dimensions:
• Freedom to act, or the relative presence of personal or procedural control and guidance, determined by answering the question, 'How much freedom has the job holder to act independently?' – for example, a plant manager has more freedom than a supervisor under his or her control.
• Dollar magnitude, a measure of the sales, budget, value of purchases, value added or any other significant annual money figure related to the job.
• Impact of the job on dollar magnitude, a determination of whether the job has a primary effect on final results or has instead a sharing, contributory or remote effect.

Accountability is given a point value independent of the other two factors. |

Source: Schuler (1995).

Competence- or Skill-Based Job Evaluation

Variously referred to as competence-based, skill-based or knowledge-based, the emphasis in this method is on an evaluation of the individual who performs the job and his/her competencies and performance abilities, rather than on job title or grade. Thus, if the previously described job evaluation methods had, at their core, the principle of 'paying for the job', competence-based evaluation has as its central tenet 'pay for the person'. Armstrong and Baron (1995) argue that competence-based job evaluation is growing in importance because much greater significance is now attached to knowledge work in organisations, and more emphasis is placed on flexibility, multi-skilling individuals and team autonomy and empowerment.

Armstrong and Baron (1995) highlight three approaches to developing competence-based job evaluation:
1. Take an existing analytical scheme and modify the factor plan to make it more competence-related by reference to an existing competence framework.
2. Take existing competence frameworks and adapt them to develop a competence-based scheme.

3. Conduct a special analysis of generic and job specific abilities to produce a competency framework and develop a scheme from this analysis.

Among the abilities likely to be examined or considered in any of these approaches are interpersonal and communication skills, reasoning and critical thinking ability, technical and business knowledge, decision-making ability, team-working and leadership skills, resource management capabilities and planning, organising and problem-solving abilities.

Advantages
- It provides a framework for relevant ongoing employee development.
- It can assist in making the organisation more flexible through an ever-expanding focused skill base.
- There is a clear focus on the person.

Disadvantages
- The competence movement has been accused of being vague in its terminology.
- It can be as complex and difficult as any other form of job evaluation.
- It can lead to too much emphasis being placed on the skills and knowledge that the person brings to the job and not enough on the outputs from that job.

Figure 7.3 A comparison of conventional job evaluation and competence-based job evaluation

COMPONENT	SKILL-BASED EVALUATION	JOB-BASED EVALUATION
1. Determination of job worth	Tied to evaluation of skill blocks	Tied to evaluation of total job
2. Pricing	Difficult because overall pay system is tied to market	Easier, because wages are tied to labour market
3. Pay ranges	Extremely broad: one pay range for entire cluster of skills	Variable, depending on type of job and pay grade width
4. Evaluation of performance	Competence tests	Performance appraisal ratings
5. Salary increases	Tied to skill acquisition as measured by competence testing	Tied to seniority, performance appraisal ratings, or actual output
6. Role of training	Essential to attain job flexibility and pay increases for all employees	Necessitated by need rather than desire
7. Advancement opportunities	Greater opportunities: anyone who passes competence test advances	Fewer opportunities: no advancement unless there is a job opening
8. Effect of job change	Pay remains constant unless skill proficiency increases	Pay changed immediately to level associated with new job
9. Pay administration	Difficult, because many aspects of pay plan (training, certification) demand attention	Contingent on complexity of job evaluation and pay allocation plan

Source: Adapted from Schuler (1995).

CRITICISMS OF JOB EVALUATION

Fowler (1996) suggests that job evaluation, once a highly-regarded management tool, has come under fire in recent times. Its critics say that, because it assesses the job rather than the job holder, it fails to recognise the contribution of the individual. It has also

been argued that the detailed job descriptions involved in some schemes serve to inhibit flexibility. Edwards *et al.* (1995) enumerate a number of weaknesses associated with traditional job evaluation.
1. They suggest that it leads to an inappropriate focus on promotion, whereby people are led to believe that a job is more important than the individual in the job.
2. They highlight its inability to reward knowledge workers on the basis that traditional job-based pay systems that reward position in the hierarchy do not work well for knowledge workers whose performance is based on specialised applied learning rather than on general skills.
3. They point to its inability to keep pace with high-speed organisational changes and emergent employee roles.

CHOOSING AND INTRODUCING THE JOB EVALUATION SCHEME

Introducing job evaluation will have a tremendous impact on organisational pay structures and employee relations generally. Therefore, any decisions should only be taken after careful deliberation. The job evaluation scheme needs to be determined primarily by setting the characteristics of different methods against the organisation's circumstances and objectives. In this respect the following questions can prove useful in making an informed choice:
1. What is the main aim of the scheme, i.e. to meet the requirements of pay legislation, or to achieve something more sophisticated?
2. What is the actual number of different jobs to be evaluated?
3. How complex is the pay structure in terms of the mix of incentives and rewards it incorporates?

The introduction of job evaluation can be a complex process and thus it is often useful to seek expert advice and guidance at the initial stages. An expert would usually be responsible for advising on the technical aspects of the scheme and assisting with decisions on the type of scheme to use; the establishment and composition of overseeing committees; the training of job analysts; and communicating the details of the scheme to all concerned.

In relation to participation, it is suggested that, at all stages in the process, staff should be kept adequately informed. It is vital that those who will be most directly affected by the scheme should know its objectives, its content and how it will operate. Middle management and supervisors are critical here. They will play a vital role in implementing the scheme, so it is imperative that they understand it and appreciate their role in its operation.

THE REWARD PACKAGE: PAY, INCENTIVES AND BENEFITS

Determining the worth of a job and setting down basic pay levels are critical aspects of the process of establishing a pay system. Choosing the actual payment system is the other critical aspect. There are numerous options regarding the type of pay, incentives and benefits package an organisation might adopt. Armstrong and Murlis (1998) offer some broad distinctions between the main types of compensation system:

- *Gain-sharing schemes*: the pay of a group of employees is linked to improvements in internal company productivity.
- *Employee stock ownership schemes* (ESOPs): company stock is offered (at a preferential rate) to certain groups of employees.
- *Profit-sharing schemes*: a part of total pay is provided in the form of a share of profits that have accrued over the pay period.
- *Skill-based pay schemes*: payment is made on the basis of job-related skills or competencies.
- *Individual incentive schemes*: employees are rewarded for reaching or exceeding specific established performance criteria. Piece-rate schemes are the most obvious form of individual performance-related pay.
- *Group incentive schemes*: the underlying principles relating to individual schemes are related to team or group incentive plans.

The more common types of payment system are presented below. Statutory and non-statutory benefits available in Ireland are then considered.

FLAT RATE SYSTEMS

Flat Rate Only

A traditional approach to reward, flat rate pay schemes pay a person for the time spent on the job and no incentive is provided for actual performance. They are popular because of their simplicity and ease of administration. They are particularly useful for managerial and administrative jobs where specific performance criteria are difficult to establish. They help attract employees to join the organisation, but their motivational potential in encouraging good performance is thought to be limited.

Annual Hours Contract

As with the flat rate only system, the annual hours contract is based on the premise that an individual is paid for the time spent on the job. However, in this instance, working time is organised on an annual rather than a weekly basis. Thus the annual hours contract will specify the number of hours to be worked in the year rather than the week.

> The basic principle of annualised hours is that instead of defining working time on the basis of the standard working week, e.g. 39 hours, working hours are distributed out over the whole year according to worked out plans.
>
> Gall (1996: 36)

Originally developed in Scandinavia, the annualised hours system, O'Sullivan (1996) noted, was regarded as an important alternative to the standard 39-hour week plus overtime and became increasingly used in Ireland. O'Sullivan cites a number of advantages to be gained from the annual hours contract approach. From the company's perspective, there will often be an improvement in unit costs and productivity, the elimination of large-scale overtime, a closer match between output and demand and a reduction in absenteeism.

From the employee's perspective, the benefits include improved basic pay, stability of earnings and increased leisure time.

The disadvantages cited by O'Sullivan include the necessity to recoup monies owing to the company if an employee leaves during the year; the necessity for re-organisation; and cultural and value changes that are congruent with this approach.

Research from Wallace and White (2007: 14) highlighted that the take-up of annualised hours systems was on the increase. Based on a detailed analysis of reported agreements concluded and additional sources, they identified some fifty-eight organisations operating in Ireland at the time who had introduced such a scheme. A further thirty-nine were identified who were in the process of considering the introduction of annualised hours. Wallace and White also concluded that once such schemes were introduced and began to operate, they were unlikely to be jettisoned. Their analysis pointed to only three organisations that had abandoned such schemes, having earlier introduced them.

Figure 7.4 Methods for calculating the annual hours contract

There are two ways of calculating the contract, which produce the same result:

(1) Standard working week formula
Calendar year:	52.18 weeks (inc. leap year)
Annual leave:	4 weeks
Public holidays:	1.8 weeks
Average working week:	46.38 weeks $\times$ 39 hours
Annual hours:	1,808.82 (net basic working hours)

(2) Annual working formula
In a complete calendar year there are an average of 365.25 days, which comprise 8,766 hours.
Example:
Employee works 39 hours a week.

$$\frac{39 \times 365.25}{7} = 2{,}035 \text{ hours a year}$$

Less annual and public holidays:	2,035
20 days' annual leave:	7.8 $\times$ (20)
9 public holidays:	7.8 $\times$ (9)
	-226.2
Employee available to work:	1,808.8 hours per year

Source: O'Sullivan (1996).

PERFORMANCE-BASED INCENTIVE SYSTEMS

Performance-based pay is a broad term for reward systems where payments are made based on the performance, either of the individual or a team of employees. While performance-related pay systems are a central theme in contemporary HRM, though of note, the use of incentives is not a new phenomenon as performance-related pay schemes have formed a significant part of the traditional remuneration package in many organisations. McBeath and Rands (1989) define performance-related pay 'as an intention to pay distinctly more to reward highly-effective job performance than you are willing to pay for good solid performance', the objective of which should be to develop a productive, efficient, effective organisation.

Kessler and Purcell (1992) argue that the very mechanics of such schemes involve a fundamental restructuring of the employment relationship, which often results in greater managerial control over staff by isolating the individual from the work group and forcing the personalised design and evaluation of work. Support for performance-based incentive systems is based on the concept that it is fair and logical to reward individual employees differentially, based on some measure, or combination of measures, of performance. 'In fact, the principle of [such] pay is so logical that it seems almost ludicrous to criticise it' (Meyer 1975: 39). Since if 'two individuals are performing the same job and one is substantially more effective than the other, the person with the superior contributions should surely be paid more' (Lowery et al. 1996: 27). Bowey and Thorpe (1986) suggest there is a positive correlation between individual performance and incentive payments with improvements in costs and quality. However, they also point to potentially adverse effects on attitudes to work and employee relations.

A continuing problem in such approaches is finding an acceptable mechanism to assess equitable and consistent performance. Otherwise performance-based payments can lead to problems as a result of resentment towards managerial control or inequity and inconsistency in performance evaluation. An important factor seems to be the extent of employee involvement with schemes that require extensive consultation; they have greater chances of success. Armstrong and Murlis (1988) outline six factors that underpin such successful systems.

1. An equitable mechanism for performance measurement incorporating performance appraisal.
2. Consistency of rewards among individual employees.
3. Managerial flexibility to link reward decisions to organisational needs to attract and retain employees.
4. Simple to understand and apply.
5. Good basic compensation package.
6. Clearly defined employee development policy.

It is important that management clearly outline key performance criteria and reward employees accordingly. Employee acceptance will depend on perceived equity in performance evaluation. The system demands a climate of trust and fairness – the main responsibility for whose development lies with management. In this context, performance-based incentive schemes in an organisational environment will be much more likely to fulfil their core functions:

- To ensure an adequate supply of skilled and trained employees in response to fluctuating labour demands. While choice is more repressed in turbulent economic circumstances, individuals making an employment decision will look not only at the terms of employment, but also at the total remuneration package, including variable and incentive pay.

- To elicit from employees, both individually and collectively, performance that reinforces the strategic direction of the organisation. Thus, one of the key underlying assumptions is that pay has the potential to motivate.
- To serve as a vehicle for organisational change.

The growth of performance-based incentive systems in Ireland has been inexorably linked to the broader HRM trend towards relating pay more closely to performance. It is evident that performance-based incentive systems might take a number of forms, and the question facing most organisations is not which type of scheme to pick but rather which combination of methods will be most successful in fulfilling the organisation's strategic goals.

In the section that follows, we provide a description of several variants of 'shorter-term and longer-term' performance-based incentive schemes.

Flat Rate Plus Individual Performance-Based Reward (PBR) System

Many commentators suggest that individually rewarding performance has a strong motivational impact. Payment is related to the employee's contribution and required performance levels; related financial rewards are specified and these are achievable immediately after these performance criteria have been met. Despite the popularity that individual PBR schemes have achieved in the past, they do, according to Appelbaum and Shapiro (1991), potentially have a number of drawbacks.

1. They result in a preoccupation with the task at hand and do not relate individual performance to the larger company objectives.
2. They work against creating a climate of openness, trust, joint problem-solving and commitment to organisational problem-solving.
3. They can divide the workforce into those supporting the plan and those not in favour of the plan, which may create adversarial relationships.

Flat Rate Plus Group-/Team-Based PBR

The greatest problem associated with individual PBR schemes is that they will focus attention and effort in a direction that does not aid the achievement of the strategic goals of the organisation. In recognition of these and related problems, many organisations have turned to group/team bonus schemes. Payment systems that pay a flat rate plus an incentive, based on group/team or sectional performance, are used where it is difficult to measure individual performance or to avoid some of the harmful side-effects of individual-based schemes, while providing some incentive which is related to a measure of performance. Group bonus schemes involve the bonus payments being divided among the members of the team. As with individual schemes, there is a wide range of schemes from which an organisation may choose, but Ost (1990) feels that all incentives based on group or team work are subject to a number of guiding premises:

1. They always have one or more explicitly stated unit or firm-level performance goals that can only be achieved through teamwork.
2. A team-based incentive system always contains a reward component that is contingent on the successful achievement of those goals.

3. The reward must be perceived by the employee as resulting from contributions that s/he has made.
4. The reward must be perceived as a fair reward.
5. The behaviours and the rewards offered must clearly signal what is meant by good performance.

Piecework

Piecework involves payment solely by performance. While it remains popular in specific areas (e.g. seasonal work in agriculture, outworkers) it is unacceptable to many employees and their organisations, since it provides no guarantee of a minimum income to satisfy basic requirements for both individual and societal wellbeing.

Gain-Sharing and Share Ownership Schemes

Gain-sharing and share ownership schemes incorporate arrangements that reward employees for improvements in corporate performance, through profit sharing, share ownership or some other compensation mechanism. Gain-sharing schemes differ from more traditional profit-sharing arrangements insofar as they link rewards based on corporate performance to changes in managerial philosophy and style, which incorporate greater employee influence, involvement and participation. The direct effects of such schemes on employee motivation are believed to be poor because of their weak relationship with individual performance and their lack of immediacy. However, they are seen as having important long-term benefits in increasing employees' participation, awareness and commitment.

Most gain-sharing schemes involve either profit sharing or employee share ownership. Profit sharing is a scheme under which employees, in addition to their normal remuneration, receive a proportion of the profits of the business. Profit sharing may take a number of forms, and it is largely at the discretion of the employer and employees to decide to what measure of profit the incentive should be tied, what percentage should be allocated and how it should be administered to employees.

Employee share ownership or stock option schemes involve the allocation of company shares to employees according to an agreed formula. Interest in Ireland in employee share ownership schemes has traditionally been relatively low. The National Workplace Survey (2009) revealed that approximately 20 per cent of Irish private sector organisations offer some profit sharing, share options or gain sharing scheme to employees. Organisational size was an important determinant of the existence of such schemes with some 26 per cent of organisations with more than 250 employees offering some employee share options. This fell to just 6 per cent of those with 20–49 employees.

Gain-sharing arrangements, incorporating either profit or equity sharing, are generally linked to organisational attempts to increase employee involvement and commitment. Armstrong and Murlis (1988) enumerate a number of the objectives underlying such schemes:
- To encourage employees to identify themselves more closely with the organisation by developing a common concern for its progress.

- To stimulate a greater interest among employees in the affairs of the organisation as a whole.
- To encourage better co-operation between management and employees.
- To recognise that employees have a moral right to share in the profits they helped to produce.
- To demonstrate in practical terms the goodwill of the organisation towards its employees.
- To reward success in businesses where profitability is cyclical.

Competence- or Skill-Based Pay

Competence/Skill-based pay is a payment system in which pay progression is linked to the number, kind and depth of skill that individuals develop and use. The concept is not particularly new. However, it has been revived in the context of 'a move towards person-based pay, rather than job-based pay as the tasks people do at work change so rapidly' (Sparrow 1996). According to O'Neill and Lander (1994), while relatively limited in application, it has been used for years under names such as pay for knowledge, competency pay, pay for skills and multi-skilled pay. While there may be slight technical differences in these terms, they are generally used interchangeably.

Ricardo and Pricone (1996) view skill-based pay as an innovative reward system that promotes workforce flexibility by rewarding individuals based on the number, type and depth of skills mastered. Armstrong (1995) highlights that it involves paying for the horizontal acquisition of the skills required to undertake a wider range of tasks, and/or for the vertical development of the skills needed to operate at a higher level, or the in-depth development of existing skills. In this way competence- or skill-based pay is directly linked to competence- or skilled-based job evaluation described earlier. In terms of operation, there will usually be a basic job rate for the minimum level of skills. Above this level, individuals will be paid for new skills acquired that assist them in performing their job as individuals or members of a team.

O'Neill and Lander (1994) cite four major reasons for the increasing adoption of skill-based pay:
1. The need to develop and maintain productive efficiencies through increased output, often combined with a leaner workforce and fewer levels of supervision.
2. The need to make more flexible utilisation of the existing workforce to cover absenteeism, turnover and production bottlenecks.
3. The need to support new technologies such as computer-aided manufacturing, and new value systems such as total quality management.
4. The need to build higher levels of involvement and commitment, increase team-work, and provide more enriched jobs that provide greater reward opportunities for employees.

Broadbanding

A concept that is closely related to competence- or skill-based pay is broadbanding. Broadbanding has been defined by Tyler (1998) as the elimination of all but a few, usually between three and ten, comprehensive salary bands. It therefore represents a compensation management strategy that involves consolidating several salary grades into fewer, wider pay bands. The bands have minimum and maximum monetary amounts. Stredwick (2000) suggests that broadbanding is a particular response to the competitive global economy in Europe, and that it generates enhanced flexibility. Similarly, Hequet (1995) points to the popularity of broadbanding as an approach to compensation in the US. He cites a study carried out by the American Compensation Association that found that 78 per cent of the 116 respondents used broadbanding. Merrick (1997) notes an increasing trend towards broadbanding in Europe also. Among the reasons for its growth are a trend towards de-layering and flatter organisational structures, along with an increase in knowledge workers across many different sectors.

Overall, it is evident that incentive- or performance-based schemes may take a number of forms and the question facing most organisations is not which type of scheme to pick, but rather which package of methods will be most successful in fulfilling the organisation's strategic goals. Balkin and Gomez-Mejia (1987) highlight a number of issues in implementing incentive schemes which must be addressed: the number of different forms on offer, the relative importance of each form and the proportion of the workforce to which each form may be applicable. The responses to these issues will be determined by the objectives of the performance-based incentive system itself and whether the organisation sees enhanced performance, cost containment or employee retention as the overriding objective of the system.

It must be realised, however, that while performance-based incentive schemes represent a potentially effective tool, they are not a panacea for all organisational ills. Incentive schemes will only fulfil their true potential if existing barriers to individual, group and organisational effectiveness have been removed. Such schemes do not represent a mechanism for compensating wage differentials, nor for overcoming inadequacies in the production system.

Data from the Cranet Ireland/University of Limerick Kemmy Business School national survey of HR practices (Cranet 2010/11) reveal certain trends in performance-based incentive schemes in Ireland. Looking at managerial employees in the first instance, approaches focused on individual performance achievement are the most common incentive scheme in operation, with in excess of 50 per cent of managerial respondents reporting being included in such schemes. The achievement of a bonus based on team performance covers approximately 37 per cent of managers. These are followed by share schemes and profit-sharing approaches, which cover between 20 per cent and 30 per cent of managers in the 2010/11 survey. In the case of professional/technical employees, approximately 50 per cent of organisations responding to the survey report that they are covered by performance-related pay or individual bonus schemes, followed by team bonus schemes (37 per cent) and employee share schemes (23 per cent). In relation to clerical/administrative grades, the data reveal that some 40 per cent are covered by performance-related pay, with other schemes being less common for this grade. Finally, in the case of manual employees, approximately 20 per cent are covered by individual or group-based bonus, with significantly fewer being covered by other incentive schemes. Thus, as is evident from the data, the established practice of differentiating between manual and managerial employees in the application of such performance-based incentive schemes remains very much in evidence. Arguably this may be rationalised in a number of ways.

Table 7.2 Use of incentive schemes in Ireland 2010				
	Management	Professional/ Technical	Clerical/ Administrative	Manual
Employee share schemes	28.2	23.3	19.4	9.7
Profit sharing	23.3	13.6	8.7	3.9
Stock options	22.3	8.7	2.9	1.0
Flexible benefits	23.3	15.5	13.6	8.7
Performance-related pay	57.3	48.5	38.8	23.3
Bonus based on individual goals/performance	60.2	49.9	39.8	20.4
Bonus based on team goals/performance	36.9	32.0	23.3	21.4

Source: Cranet (2010).

A traditional explanation for such treatment has been the difficulty of disaggregating the impact of the individual's effort and performance on effectiveness at the lower echelons of the organisation. Performance-related pay was thus generally considered to be applicable principally to managerial levels. In recent times, this problem has been overcome in many organisations, by assessing the individual within the confines of his/her particular task or job.

A second explanation is the opposition of trade unions, which are often opposed to payments based on individual performance, preferring collective increases achieved through management–union negotiations. In this respect, it has been argued that schemes that operate increases in addition to general salary awards are less likely to cause employee opposition as they operate as a discretionary element, which does not cut across the collective bargaining role of the trade union. In an appropriate organisational climate, performance-based incentive pay can be effectively used to augment negotiated pay and benefit increases and stimulate improved employee and organisational performance.

The penetration of foreign multinational companies (MNCs), particularly US-owned MNCs, into Irish industrial structures is significant here in accounting for the performance-based incentive pay trend in Ireland. While MNCs have adapted to accommodate local practices, this need not necessarily result in an abandonment of foreign management philosophy, but rather the pursuit of such within existing frameworks and customs. In the case of US MNCs, successive research has repeatedly emphasised the prevalence of linking pay to a measure of performance. The perceived importance of performance-related schemes among US organisations is maintained in their subsidiary plants in the Irish context, with many managerial, professional and clerical employees being covered by such schemes. In recent years, Britain has also seen a change of emphasis in relation to performance approaches. Much of the effort was traditionally directed at assessing future labour requirements and labour training needs. However, there has more recently been a greater emphasis on organisational survival and the assessment of current performance. Such emphasis has resulted in a large growth in performance-related pay as a method of improving such performance.

THE REWARD PACKAGE: FRINGE BENEFITS

The nature of fringe benefits provided to employees varies considerably between organisations and they are normally the result of voluntary agreements, either between employees (or their representatives) and management. Some of the more common benefits that are often cited in the literature in this respect include health insurance benefits, pension schemes, sick pay schemes, childcare/crèche facilities, career breaks, company cars and sports and recreation facilities.

In general, fringe benefits (both statutory and voluntary) are estimated to constitute an additional 25–30 per cent on top of basic weekly pay for manual grades. For clerical, administrative and managerial categories, a figure of 15–35 per cent may be appropriate. However, the percentage add-on is primarily related to the level of fringe benefits voluntarily agreed at company level, particularly items such as company cars, pensions, health insurance cover and sickness benefit, and can therefore vary greatly between organisations.

Table 7.3 Use of schemes in excess of statutory requirements, Ireland 2010 (%)

	Yes
Workplace childcare (subsidised or not)	3.9
Childcare allowances	6.8
Career break schemes	41.7
Maternity leave	69.9
Paternity leave	42.7
Parental leave	49.3
Pension schemes	85.4
Education/training break	58.3
Private health care schemes	64.1

Source: Cranet (2010).

Relating to the situation in Ireland, the data from the 2010/11 Cranet national survey reveal that pension, maternity benefit and private healthcare emerge as the most common benefits that employers in Ireland put in place in excess of what is required of them by legislation. Assistance with education and development, parental leave and career break schemes are also reported by a significant percentage of respondents in the 2010/11 Cranet survey. Paternity leave was formally introduced in September 2016 and in excess of 10,500 fathers have availed of the benefit as of April 2017.

This chapter has focused on the area of reward management. An organisation's reward package is seen to consist of pay (base wages), various incentives (performance-related incentives and rewards) and fringe benefits. Organisations will provide various mixes of these three components in order to attract, retain and motivate their employees. While developing an effective reward package can prove a rather difficult task, if the reward package satisfies basic needs as well as being flexible enough to meet individual employee needs and has equity, fairness and trust as its central tenets, it can be effective. Job evaluation is the most common method of determining the relative worth of jobs and a variety of analytical and non-analytical schemes are available. With the exception of skill/competence-based approaches, job evaluation techniques focus solely on the job, rather than on the individual performing it.

Numerous options are available to an organisation in the types of pay, incentive and benefits packages it might adopt. While flat rate systems still prevail, various individual, group and team incentive schemes have grown in popularity in recent years, largely in response to competitive pressures. Additional direct payments in the form of bonuses and other incentives are used extensively.

The cost of employee benefits is also on the increase for many employers. These benefits represent a type of indirect reward because employees receive the value of the benefits without getting direct cash payments. More broadly, the complete reward package is now often one of the largest costs faced by employers, with many organisations having labour costs at or above 50 per cent of all operating costs.

Against this backdrop, the ongoing management of performance is a core aspect of the HR architecture and the next chapter examines various aspects of the nature and the process of performance management.

8
Managing Performance

Managing performance remains the critical underlying function of human resource management. Finding ways of directing, rewarding and motivating employees' performance is challenging since, as we have seen in previous chapters, individual employees may prioritise various aspects within their job and may respond to incentives, directions and instructions differently. Therefore, the management of performance in organisations is perhaps one of the most difficult functions for managers and supervisors, irrespective of the positions they hold.

Aquinas (2011) contends that firms today are not managing employee performance very well. This echoes a growing concern that both performance appraisal and performance management systems may be failing in many organisations (Kluger and DeNici 1996; Pulakos et al. 2015; Barends et al. 2016). We have recently seen a large number of well-known global organisations, including *Accenture, Deloitte, Microsoft, Adobe, Gap* and *Medtronic*, announce that they are moving away from annual performance appraisals in favour of more informal and regular dialogue with employees (Cunningham 2015; Buckingham and Goodall 2015; Crush 2015). They cite a number of concerns including that annual reviews are impractical, costly, time consuming (with estimates that the average manager spends more than 200 hours a year on activities related to performance reviews), and don't yield accurate or timely information. In a recent feature in the *Harvard Business Review*, the *Deloitte* group reported why it has significantly revised its approach to performance management for its 65,000 plus global workforce:

> We tallied the number of hours the organization was spending on performance management – and found that completing the forms, holding the meetings, and creating the ratings consumed close to 2 million hours a year. As we studied how those hours were spent, we realized that many of them were eaten up by leaders' discussions behind closed doors about the outcomes of the process. We wondered if we could somehow shift our investment of time from talking to ourselves about ratings, to talking to our people about their performance and careers – from a focus on the past to a focus on the future.
> Buckingham and Goodall (2015, *Harvard Business Review*, April: 40).

Meriac et al. (2015) note that performance judgments rely on the proper observation, categorisation, and subsequent scaling of behaviours, and this is where issues can and do arise. This echoes earlier concerns by Folger et al. (1992) who argued that some of the biggest problems with current performance management systems are that performance is not measured objectively, or that many of those responsible for measuring performance are not able to do so, or that there is no agreement on what good performance actually is anyway.

The emphasis in this chapter is on exploring different facets of performance management. It identifies the key strengths of having a well-functioning performance management system, and some of the issues and pitfalls inherent in evaluating performance in organisations. It outlines dimensions of the appraisal system and appraisal interview that warrant particular attention, and concludes with an examination of recent developments in the area of performance management practices in Ireland.

THE RATIONALE FOR PERFORMANCE MANAGEMENT

As the term suggest, managing performance is all about determining whether employees are performing their work in the manner required by the organisation. Although there are various interpretations of what might be involved in this assessment, it is important at the outset to differentiate between performance management and performance appraisal. Aguinis (2009: 2) describes performance management as a continuous process of identifying, measuring, and developing the performance of individuals and teams and aligning performance with the strategic goals of the organisation. This involves some shared vision of the purpose and aims of the organisation, so that individual employees understand and recognise their part in contributing to them. DeNisi and Murphy (2017) identify performance appraisal as a formal process, which occurs infrequently, by which employees are evaluated by some judge (typically a supervisor) who assesses the employee's performance along a given set of dimensions, assigns a score to that assessment, and then usually informs the employee of his or her formal rating. Organisations typically base a variety of decisions concerning the employee in part on this rating.

These descriptions suggest somewhat different perspectives on how performance is managed: performance management is an organisation-wide, strategic activity that occurs throughout the year involving practices and interventions aimed at developing and improving performance, while the appraisal is typically a one-off activity (usually interview-based) where a supervisor or managers measures the performance of each of his/her team members/employees. Performance appraisal is thus one component of the overall system, though, as noted by Aguinis (2009), it is also the one that generates the greatest concern and is often perceived as a bureaucratic waste of time.

There are a number of well-established reasons for having an organisation-wide system for managing performance, and the benefits that accrue are distributed between individual employees, their managers and the organisation as a whole. Aguinis et al. (2011) differentiate key benefits for each of these particular stakeholders (see Table 8.1 on the next page).

We can see that the performance management system can have a number of important outcomes. For example, it allows the organisation to monitor whether performance is effective and to take action if it is not. It provides a means of rewarding desirable behaviour and therefore helps build a strong performance culture. It identifies poor performers and prompts early intervention. Evaluations from the appraisal system are used to decide wage adjustments, identify potential talent, and plan learning and development interventions.

Table 8.1 Benefits of performance management

For Employees	For Managers	For Organizations
• Employees experience increased self-esteem. • Employees better understand the behaviors and results required of their positions. • Employees better identify ways to maximize their strengths and minimize weaknesses.	• Managers develop a workforce with heightened motivation to perform. • Managers gain greater insight into their subordinates. • Managers make their employees become more competent. • Managers enjoy better and timelier differentiation between good and poor performers. • Managers enjoy clearer communication to employees about employees' performance.	• Organizations make administrative actions that are more appropriate. • Organizations make organizational goals clearer to managers and employees. • Organizations enjoy reduced employee misconduct. • Organizations enjoy better protection from lawsuits. • Organizations facilitate organizational change. • Organizations develop increased commitment on the part of employees. • Organizations enjoy enhanced employee engagement.

Source: Aguinis, Joo, & Gottfredson. (2011: 505), 'Why we hate performance management – and why we should love it', *Business Horizons*, 54: 503–507.

However, as we review the potential benefits presented in Table 8.1, we come to recognise that these are multiple, and sometimes seemingly incompatible, requirements from the performance management system, and thus it requires a considerable investment from organisations to ensure that the system can deliver these multiple outcomes. The system must be transparent, easy to understand, easy to administer, allow for accurate and unbiased assessments of performance, and provide venues for appeal should employees take issue with some of the judgements. Table 8.2 captures a number of characteristics of the ideal modern performance management system.

Table 8.2 Characteristics of an ideal performance management system

Strategically congruent	Individual goals are aligned with unit and organizational goals.
Contextually congruent	The system is congruent with the organization's culture, as well as the broader cultural context of the region or country.
Thorough	All employees are evaluated (including managers), all major job responsibilities are evaluated, the evaluation includes performance spanning the entire review period, and feedback emphasizes both positive and negative performance.
Practically feasible	Benefits resulting from the system outweigh the costs.
Meaningful	The standards and evaluations conducted for each job function are important and relevant, performance assessment emphasizes only those functions that are under the control of the employee, evaluations take place at regular intervals, the system provides for the continuing skill development of evaluators, and results are used for important administrative decisions.

Specific	There is detailed and concrete guidance about what is expected of raters and ratees, and how they can meet these expectations.
Identify effective and ineffective performance	The system provides information that allows for distinguishing between effective and ineffective behaviours and results, thereby also allowing for the identification of employees displaying various levels of performance effectiveness.
Reliable	Performance scores are consistent and free of error.
Valid	Performance measures include all relevant performance facets and do not include irrelevant ones.
Acceptable and fair	The system is acceptable, and the processes and outcomes are perceived as fair by all participants.
Inclusive	All participants are given a voice in the process of designing and implementing the system.
Open	A good system has no secrets. Performance is evaluated frequently and performance feedback is provided on an ongoing basis, the appraisal meeting consists of a two-way communication process during which information is exchanged, not delivered from the supervisor to the employee without his or her input, and performance standards are clear and communicated on an ongoing basis.
Correctable	No system is 100 per cent error-free. Thus, establishing an appeals process, through which employees can challenge what may be unjust decisions, is an important aspect of a good performance management system.

Source: Aguinis, Joo, & Gottfredson (2011: 506), 'Why we hate performance management – and why we should love it', *Business Horizons*, 54, 503-507.

Lawler (2003) suggests that while managers concur that a performance management system can make a very positive contribution to organisational effectiveness, there is less clarity about what practices make a performance management system effective. Murphy and Cleveland (1991) suggest that the system can only be considered effective if it is perceived to be balanced and equitable by all of those involved in the process.

THE COMPLEXITY OF PERFORMANCE MANAGEMENT

Given the multiple expectations and requirements of the performance management system, and recognising the growing concerns that it does not work well, it is worth taking a closer look at where some of the problems tend to arise. In particular, we isolate three issues for discussion, namely: how we measure performance; what we expect feedback on performance to yield; and how perceptions of fairness impact the performance management system.

MEASUREMENT OF PERFORMANCE

The most contentious issue within performance management concerns making judgements about whether employees are both meeting their performance targets or objectives, and behaving in ways that are required by the organisation. These judgements typically require some means of measuring performance, and, as consistently reported over many years (Kluger and DeNisi 1996; Levy and Williams 2004; Pichler 2012; Meriac *et al.* 2015; DeNisi and Murphy 2017), performance measures are variable and subject to inconsistencies, and may not even be good predictors of performance. We have seen from the discussion on job design and rewards that there are a range of individual and contextual factors that influence individual behaviour and therefore performance. Performance is multi-faceted and influenced by a host of factors that are within, but also outside of, the control of the individual. When considering performance, it is important to differentiate between two important factors which we label here as performance outcomes and performance process. Performance *outcomes* refer to the achievement of the particular job or role tasks that are required, while performance *process* refers to the interactions involved in and around the completion of these job or role tasks. Organisations require that individuals are efficient in completing their work to targets and to schedule, but they also require individuals to work cooperatively with each other, to support each other, be tolerant of diverse perspectives, be inquiring and constantly learning, and to engage with their work in a positive manner – all of these factors create the cultural fabric of the work environment that contributes to the overall work climate. Measuring these latter variables that are captured in process is challenging to say the least.

Murphy and Cleveland (1995) differentiate between objective and subjective performance measures. Objective measures can capture some core aspects of job performance through metrics or hard data. These may include numerical indicators of performance relating to, for example, achieving particular targets set for production, sales, processing, defects and the like. However, they argue that objective measures may be incomplete and often fail to capture aspects of the job that lie behind the actual performance. As objective measures alone are deficient, organisations turn to subjective measures to capture, what they describe as, the complex and wide-range construct of job performance. Performance measures are described as subjective if some judgment is required to assign a grade or a numeric value to the thing being measured. Here they include factors such as citizenship behaviour (helping or supporting co-workers), being proactive, or having positive relationships with others in the organisation.

Campbell and Wiernik (2015) identify some core features of job performance that are required in modern organisations today (see Table 8.3). We can see that measuring these would require a combination of both objective and subjective assessments.

Table 8.3 Dimensions of job performance	
Technical performance	Utilising knowledge and skills to perform core job functions or activities – including technical and interpersonal components
Initiative, persistence and effort	Capturing the range of behaviours that indicate exerting observable effort and drive in the completion of work, including extra-role performance
Communication	Proficiently conveying appropriate and timely information to others – verbally or in written form
Supervisory, management, and/or executive leadership	Including sets of behaviours that involve leading, instructing or structuring the work of others in a hierarchical relationship

Management performance	Facets of the job that relate to obtaining, preserving, or allocating resources to achieve organisational goals.
Peer/team member management performance	Planning, coordinating, problem solving in the absence of hierarchical relationships.
Counterproductive work behaviour	Counterproductive work behaviour – identified as any intentional behaviours, under one's direct control, that are designed to damage or harm others, or have a negative effect on the organisation

Source: Campbell and Wiernik (2015: 53–54)(Adapted).

A number of specific challenges associated with rating performance have been identified, and these are dealt with separately below, under the section on performance appraisal.

FEEDBACK AND PERFORMANCE

At its most basic level, performance management works on the underlying presumption that providing feedback is a positive thing to do, and that individuals are receptive to receiving feedback on their performance. Barends *et al.* (2016) provide three core psychological explanations underpinning performance feedback in the workplace as follows:

- Social comparison theory, first proposed by Festinger (1954), argues that individuals are curious about their own performance, but especially in relation to how they measure up when compared with work colleagues. For this reason, individuals tend to compare themselves with others to decide how well they are doing, and have a strong desire to improve their performance when faced with unfavourable comparative information.
- Feedback intervention theory (Kluger and DeNisi 1996) builds on this social comparison tendency, and suggests that when confronted with a discrepancy between what they wish to achieve and the feedback received, individuals are strongly motivated to achieve higher performance. In this way, if individuals believe that they are achieving lower than most other colleagues, they will be motivated to exert greater effort to improve.
- Equity theory, developed by the work of Adams (1965) (see Chapter 6), explains how employees compare themselves with each other in terms of the 'inputs' they put into performance, and the 'outcomes' they receive. It suggests that high-performing employees will maintain their performance levels when they can see that this is rewarded, and that lower performing individuals receive fewer rewards than they do. It might also encourage lower performing employees to expend more effort to emulate them.

Despite the theoretical explanations, Kluger and DeNisi's (1996) meta-analysis found that although performance feedback generally improves performance, this is not always the case. In fact, feedback actually lowered performance in more than one third of studies they included in their analysis. Smither *et al.* (2005) also reported mixed or inclusive results pertaining to the provision of feedback on performance.

A further point to note here relates to an individual's feedback orientation, that is, what s/he perceives the purpose of feedback to be. Not everyone is open to receiving feedback that highlights areas for improvement or development – some may only want to hear positive affirmation of doing a good job. Additionally, not everyone hears feedback as constructive – they may only hear blame, or fault or that they are a poor performer. Communicating feedback requires skill on the part of the assessor, to ensure that it is provided in a manner that allows the individual to hear it constructively – but sometimes training in providing feedback is not provided, or is overlooked in the assessment system.

PERCEIVED FAIRNESS AND PERFORMANCE

Research on organisational justice over the years has established the centrality of perceptions of fairness in the workplace. Greenberg (1980) proposes that employees make evaluative judgements on three particular aspects:
1. The perceived fairness of outcomes received (distributive justice). This can include ratings that are likely to affect anything from increased money, bonuses, promotions, access to development, projects, travel and so forth.
2. The perceived fairness of the system or procedure that was used to make decisions on outcomes (procedural justice). This mainly refers to the criteria that are used to measure or rate performance, the perceived competence of the person making the judgements, and the opportunity to influence the decision (to have a say).
3. The manner in which outcomes or decisions were communicated to them (interactional justice). This primarily refers to the quality of the feedback and manner in which it was delivered – usually during the performance appraisal interview.

In this way, we can see that employees may react unfavourably to how they are assessed or measured, or how unfavourable ratings or assessments are told to them and therefore employees' reaction to feedback might be every bit as important as the feedback itself. However, it is likely that reactions will not be positive if employees don't believe that the system used to measure their performance is just or accurate. Latham *et al.* (2005) argue that the outcome of many performance appraisals is a decline rather than an improvement in performance because employees believe that they are being incorrectly evaluated, or that the person who is evaluating them is biased or lacks objectivity, or that the feedback they are given is not constructive, or provided in a supportive manner.

Barends *et al.* (2016) contend that there is strong evidence that when a person evaluates another person's performance, systematic errors in judgement occur. Variables such as type and source of measurement, rating method, as well as aspects such as accountability and job complexity, may all affect the accuracy of the performance rating and, as a result, affect the validity and fairness of the appraisal process. They further point to evidence that the purpose of the performance appraisal (administrative versus developmental) strongly affects the way in which raters evaluate and judge a person's performance.

THE PROCESS OF PERFORMANCE MANAGEMENT

As an organisation-wide activity, the process of performance management can be conceptualised as a series of stages that starts with the organisational goals. Individual job objectives and targets are established against the backdrop of these over-riding organisational requirements. Wright and Brading (1992) contend that while the system should have the full commitment of top management, it should not be viewed as a top-down activity. A simple schema of the performance management process is presented in Figure 8.1.

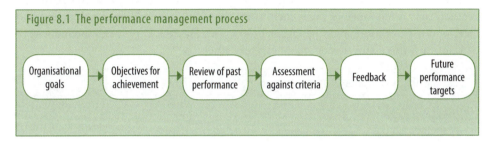

Notwithstanding the issues and tensions associated with actually measuring performance, it is the case that all organisations have some form of performance management in place. At the start of this chapter, we noted that *Deloitte* have decided to move away from an annual appraisal system and replace it with more frequent assessment of employee performance – at the end of every project or once every quarter for long-term projects. Now, they base their evaluation on answers to four key questions which, they believe, are central to making an assessment of whether employees are performing as required. These questions are included in Table 8.4.

Table 8.4 Deloitte's revised performance management approach	
At the end of every project (or once every quarter for long-term projects) we will ask team leaders to respond to four future focused statements about each team member:	
1	Given what I know of this person's performance, and if it were my money, I would award this person the highest possible compensation increase and bonus.	Measures overall performance and unique value to the organization on a five-point scale from "strongly agree" to "strongly disagree".
2	Given what I know of this person's performance, I would always want him or her on my team.	Measures ability to work well with others on the same five-point scale.
3	This person is at risk for low performance.	Identifies problems that might harm the customer or the team on a yes-or-no basis.
4	This person is ready for promotion today.	Measures potential on a yes-or-no basis.

Source: Buckingham and Goodall (2015), 'Reinventing Performance Management', *Harvard Business Review* April.

Most organisations, however, retain the performance appraisal system as part of their overall performance management process. Therefore, we now turn to a review of what performance appraisal entails and the common methods used as part of the appraisal system.

PERFORMANCE APPRAISAL

Performance appraisal is commonplace in organisational life today and virtually every company has an identifiable appraisal system. Performance appraisal can be described as a systematic approach to evaluating employee performance with a view to assisting decisions in a wide range of areas such as pay, promotion, employee development and motivation. The performance management loop (see Figure 8.2) provides the framework within which this systematic appraisal can take place.

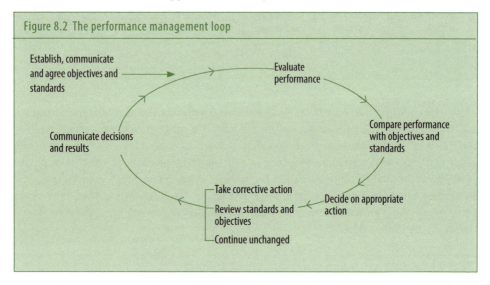

Figure 8.2 The performance management loop

Although some appraisal of performance is likely to occur daily, often very informally, for example through casual meetings, informal discussions between supervisor and staff, team briefings and so forth, it is important to set aside a dedicated time for a formal appraisal. This is necessary because it provides a separate period of time for managers/supervisors and employees to meet together to discuss a range of factors that may be affecting work performance.

The performance appraisal system can be seen to have many interrelated functions, including performance evaluation and target setting, the establishment of work standards, identification of skills gaps and learning needs, improving communications and encouraging motivation and engagement. However, only an effective appraisal system will result in the realisation of many of these outcomes. A number of particular problems are associated with the appraisal system including lack of clarity with respect to what the employee's job fully entails, unclear or unrealistic objectives, poorly-trained or ill-prepared managers/supervisors who are conducting the appraisal, subjectivity within the process, or inaccurate or incomplete data used for determining process outcomes.

At times, measurement becomes the over-riding focus, such that motivational and developmental aspects are given insufficient attention and consideration. Given that the annual appraisal may represent the only formal meeting the manager/supervisor has with staff (on a one-to-one basis), there is a considerable onus on the manager/supervisor to ensure that adequate attention is paid to all aspects of the appraisal process. Adequate preparation in advance of the meeting is critical.

METHODS OF PERFORMANCE APPRAISAL

Many performance appraisal techniques are available to organisations, the most popular of which are described in summarised form in Table 8.5. A number of performance appraisal techniques are examined in closer detail below.

Table 8.5 Performance appraisal techniques

Method	Characteristics	Strengths	Weaknesses
Rating	Appraiser specifies on a scale to what degree relevant characteristics (normally related to job-related behaviour or personality) are possessed by appraisee	Ease of comparison; range in complexity from very simple to very involved, using descriptions of behaviour or performance	Subjective; personality or behavioural traits difficult to measure
Ranking	Appraiser ranks workers from best to worst, based on specific characteristics or overall job performance	Simple; facilitates comparisons	Little basis for decisions; degrees of difference not specified; subjective
Paired comparison	Two workers compared at a time and decision made on which is superior, resulting in a final ranking order for full group	Ease of decision-making; simple	Difficult with large numbers together with weakness attributed to ranking
Critical incident	Appraiser or supervisor observes incidences of good and bad perform-ance. These are used as a basis for judging and assessing or discussing performance	Job-related; more objective	Needs good observational skills; time-consuming
Free-form	General free-written appraisal by appraiser	Flexible	Subjective; difficulty of comparison
Performance or objectives-oriented systems	Appraiser evaluates degree to which specific job targets or standards have been achieved	Job-related; objective; participative	Needs measurable targets; danger of collusion

Method	Characteristics	Strengths	Weaknesses
Assessment centre	Appraisees undergo a series of assessments (interviews, tests, simulations, etc.) undertaken by trained assessors	Range of dimensions examined; objective	Expensive; not necessarily job-specific
Self-assessment	Appraisees evaluate themselves using a particular format or structure	Participative; facilitates discussion; promotes self-analysis	Danger of lenient tendency; potential source of conflict between appraiser and appraisee

Free-Form

The free-form appraisal technique is completely unstructured and essentially involves the appraiser writing a narrative discussion of the employee's performance. While it allows considerable discretion to the appraiser, who is not constrained by set criteria, this discretion can result in some inconsistencies and does not allow for effective comparisons.

Rating

Rating usually involves the appraiser rating the employee's performance and behaviour against a predetermined scale. These ratings, based on a sequential scale, can be made against a series of relatively standard headings that tend to include generalised performance characteristics or particular personality traits.

Rating scales are often used in conjunction with results-oriented schemes, which measure performance against a set of objectives discussed in more detail below. In such cases, rating scales are used to indicate the extent to which an employee was successful in achieving the objectives. Two examples of the use of rating scales in results-oriented schemes are illustrated in Tables 8.6 and 8.7, which contain extracts from performance plans used in a large manufacturing organisation in Ireland.

While rating scales are a convenient means of comparing employees and arriving at an evaluation, they tend to ignore the complex set of variables that determine work performance, and are a highly subjective method of assessment. Furthermore, it is particularly difficult to achieve any great level of consistency with rating scales because, as indicated, they are highly subjective and some appraisers will be more generous than others, while others will be harder on their staff. A further problem associated with both rating and ranking methods concerns the error of central tendency: the tendency to veer towards the mid-point on such scales and so ascribe average values to performance.

Table 8.6 Extract from performance appraisal plan for managers – manufacturing firm

Employee name:
Job title:
Appraiser:
Appraisal period:
Date of appraisal:

Section one: this section outlines the key roles and competencies that managers must demonstrate to perform their jobs effectively. Using the rating scale below, evaluate the extent to which the manager named above demonstrates effectiveness in each of the areas identified. Enter N/A for those areas that are not relevant to the manager's current position.

                                                         Rating

1. Planning   _____
   - manages systems and processes
   - sets measurable goals and targets
   - assigns tasks responsibly

2. Production   _____
   - motivates others positively
   - demonstrates personal commitment
   - facilitates co-operative environment

3. Teambuilding   _____
   - manages conflict
   - facilitates participation
   - develops interaction

4. Coaching   _____
   - develops others
   - communicates effectively
   - understands interaction

5. Innovation   _____
   - divergent thinking
   - challenges processes
   - stimulates change

Rating scale
1. *Negative results, did not achieve objectives*
2. *Mixed results, achieved some objectives*
3. *Good results, achieved most objectives*
4. *Very good results, achieved all objectives*
5. *Strong results, achieved all and exceeded some objectives*
6. *Excellent results, exceeded most objectives*
7. *Outstanding results, exceeded all objectives*

Table 8.7 Extract from performance appraisal form for employees – manufacturing firm

Employee name:
Job title:
Appraiser:
Appraisal period:
Date of appraisal:

Section one: this section outlines the key roles and competencies that employees must demonstrate to perform their jobs effectively. Using the rating scale below, evaluate the extent to which the employee named above demonstrates effectiveness in each of the areas identified. Enter N/A for those areas that are not relevant to the employee's current position.

1. Quality of work: the extent to which the quality of work is accurate and thorough _____
2. Dependability: the extent to which the employee can be relied upon to do a good job _____
3. Judgement: the extent to which the employee makes rational choices _____
4. Organisation: the extent to which the employee can plan and structure work _____
5. Communications: the extent to which the employee can transmit and receive information in a comprehensive manner _____
6. Adaptability: the extent to which the employee can cope with change and uncertainty _____

Rating scale
1. Negative results, did not achieve expectations
2. Mixed results, achieved some expectations
3. Good results, achieved most expectations
4. Very good results, achieved all expectations
5. Strong results, achieved all and exceeded some expectations
6. Excellent results, exceeded most expectations
7. Outstanding results, exceeded all expectations

One means of improving consistency might be to require the appraiser to make a forced distribution of assessment that involves plotting overall evaluation against the normal distribution curve. An example of this might be where, if there are twenty employees in a particular department, the overall distribution of performance should appear as follows: Excellent: 5 per cent, Good: 15 per cent, Average: 60 per cent, Poor: 15 per cent and Unsatisfactory: 5 per cent. While proponents might argue that this type of appraisal puts a rigour and discipline into the performance management system that overcomes managers' all-too-common tendency towards leniency, there is no rule that suggests that work performance or ability should be normally distributed, and to assume it is to ignore the myriad of variables such as culture, production norms, supervisory arrangements and personal motivation that can impact on work performance. These decisions can be difficult to explain, or defend, if queried. An alternative to forced distribution might be the forced choice technique, which seeks to avoid the error of central tendency. Again, appraisers are asked to rate performance against a predetermined scale, but this technique does not have a middle or average value.

Results-Oriented Schemes

Results-oriented schemes are based on the underlying principles of management by objectives (MBO) and include the specification of objectives, participation in agreeing objectives, measurement of performance against objectives, and finally feedback and monitoring.

In the results-oriented system, performance is measured against previously agreed targets or key result areas. As with MBO, there is a particular requirement for targets to be jointly set between manager and employee to ensure commitment to the process and allow for renegotiation as required. Take for example, targets for a salesperson. They might include the total number of sales, number of new customers, number of repeat customers, average size of orders, proportions of different products sold, plus whatever is deemed to be relevant to the organisation (see Table 8.8) In this schema, numerical figures can be put side-by side-with actual performance, and successes and areas for improvement can be straightforwardly determined.

Table 8.8 Performance against previous objectives scheme: sales personnel

Appraisee's name:
Position:
Appraiser's name:
Date:
Length of time in the post (years):

	TARGET	ACTUAL
Number of customers:		
Total value of sales:		
Average value of sale per customer:		
Number of new contacts:		
Number of new customers:		
Proportion of contacts turned into customers:		
Size of territory:		
Number of potential new customers:		

This type of appraisal scheme requires managers to have a comprehensive understanding of the nature and scope of the employee's job and it demands high levels of vigilance in observation, target setting, feedback and future planning. As with all appraisal systems, it is highly dependent on a responsible appraiser.

Although a useful technique, a results-orientated scheme can pose difficulties when the job is subject to considerable variation, or when it is largely dependent on the performance of other jobs. Furthermore, there is a strong emphasis on measurable and quantifiable criteria, which might overshadow more qualitative criteria, such as work behaviour and interaction.

Critical Incident Technique

When jobs are difficult to quantify in measurable terms, the critical incident technique might prove useful. This technique was advanced by Flanagan (1954), who viewed it as a procedure for gathering certain important facts concerning behaviour in defined situations. It involves instances of actual behaviour that constitute job performance at various levels of effectiveness. This technique requires the appraiser to identify three or four critical components of the job, and to write a critical incident report, assessing performance based on how well these tasks were completed (see Table 8.9 for an example).

Critical incident reports detail three important pieces of information:
1. A description of the situation that led to the incident.
2. The actions or behaviours of the focal person in the incident.
3. The results or outcomes of those actions.

Table 8.9 An example of a critical incident report

SITUATION:	A contractor was assigned a project that would involve de-terminating and removing several hundred wires, removing the conduit from the gear, relocating the gear, reinstalling the conduit and wire, and finally re-terminating the wire. The work had to begin at 11.00 p.m. on Halloween and it had to be completed by 7.00 a.m. the following day, which seemed nearly impossible.
ACTION:	The foreman chose seven of the best wiremen employed by the company to do the work. Through skilful planning and hard work, the crew worked through the night without stopping for a break and got the job done on time and with no problems.
OUTCOME:	The customer was extremely impressed that they got such a project completed in such a short period of time with zero errors. As a result, the customer has chosen this contractor to do almost all of its work.

The critical incident technique can be costly to undertake, particularly as it may involve considerable observation, which may generate negative feelings from employees who might feel threatened by the process. When the appraisal takes place on an annual basis, it can be difficult to discuss constructively key incidents that possibly took place several months earlier.

Behaviourally Anchored Rating Scales (BARS)

Behaviourally anchored rating scales (BARS), particularly associated with the early work of Smith and Kendall (1963), were developed to reduce rating errors. They include a number of performance dimensions that represent major requirements of the actual job, such as teamwork. An example of BARS in operation is presented in Table 8.10.

Pulakos (1997) notes that the development of BARS relies on input from job incumbents and/or their supervisors. These stakeholders, referred to as 'subject matter experts' in the developmental process, are charged with the task of providing the detailed information that is necessary to construct the actual rating scales. These scales, Pulakos notes, are the rating dimensions and the behaviours that define different levels of effectiveness for each performance dimension of the job. With respect to how the relevant behaviours are gathered, she highlights that:

> The behaviours are derived from critical incidents [see technique mentioned earlier] ... After the critical incidents are collected from subject matter experts and edited by psychologists, subject matter experts are then asked to sort the critical incidents into

dimensions and rate them on an effectiveness rating scale. Often, a 7-point rating scale is used. The percentage of subject matter experts sorting each incident into a particular dimension and the means and standard deviations of the effectiveness ratings for each incident are computed.

Pulakos (1997: 298)

One of the main advantages of such an approach is that the behavioural anchors settled on for measurement purposes can be particularly effective for generating comparisons. However, the drawback documented in the literature is that those conducting the appraisal often report difficulties in rating the individual's performance to the specific scale anchors that are generated and used in the rating assessment. By way of example, look at the BARS rating scale shown in Table 8.10 and you will get some indication of the potential difficulties that an appraiser might experience in trying to compare the individual's performance to the specific scale anchors illustrated in the table.

Table 8.10 Example of BARS

A.	Continually contributes new ideas and suggestions. Takes a leading role in group meetings but is tolerant and supportive of colleagues and respects other people's points of view. Keeps everyone informed about own activities and is well aware of what other team members are doing in support of team objectives.
B.	Takes a full part in group meetings and contributes useful ideas frequently. Listens to colleagues and keeps them reasonably well informed about own activities while keeping abreast of what they are doing.
C.	Delivers opinions and suggestions at group meetings from time to time but is not a major contributor to new thinking or planning activities. Generally receptive to other people's ideas and willing to change own plans to fit in. Does not always keep others properly informed or take sufficient pains to know what they are doing.
D.	Tendency to comply passively with other people's suggestions. May withdraw at group meetings, but sometimes shows personal antagonism to others. Not very interested in what others are doing or in keeping them informed.
E.	Tendency to go own way without taking much account of the need to make a contribution to team activities. Sometimes uncooperative and unwilling to share information.
F.	Generally uncooperative. Goes own way, completely ignoring the wishes of other team members and taking no interest in the achievement of team objectives.

Source: Armstrong (1995).

360-Degree Feedback

Also known as multi-rater assessment and multi-sourced assessment, 360-degree feedback is an appraisal technique that has gained popularity in recent years and provides a complete multi-dimensional overview of an employee's performance. McCarthy and Pearson (2001) define it thus:

> 360-degree, or multi-rater, feedback is the practice of collecting perceptions of an employee's performance from sources such as subordinates/direct reports, peers/colleagues, and supervisors. What makes 360-degree feedback revolutionary is that the perspectives of many stakeholders are included in the evaluation of an employee's performance and workplace behaviour. In traditional appraisal systems, it is only the observations and opinions of the boss that are considered important and are therefore the only source of evaluation included in the appraisal.

Waldman et al. (1998) suggest that a further key purpose driving the use of 360-degree feedback is the legitimate desire to further management or leadership development, and add that managers probably do not receive as much honest feedback as they need: 360-degree feedback is particularly useful in this regard since it includes information on skills, competencies and work behaviour gathered from multiple sources – records, reports, work colleagues and the individual being appraised. Toegel and Conger (2003), however, caution that the technique was originally designed for developmental purposes, and that its use as an evaluative tool may weaken its developmental potential.

Assessment Centres

For the most part, the assessment centre method is used to identify future potential within the existing pool of employees. A typical assessment centre involves between six and eight participants and lasts from one to three days off the job. Participants are presented with a series of problems, challenges and simulations to determine how they would perform in the target situation. Work-based exercises are used as a key means of identifying performance relevant behaviours, while they are observed by assessors who are specialists in evaluating the behaviour and competencies being assessed. A range of psychometric tests and one-to-one interviews may also form part of the assessment. The final report rates overall performance and details the specific strengths of each participant in addition to identifying aspects for development.

THE APPRAISAL INTERVIEW

Kikoski (1999) suggests that the Achilles heel of the entire performance appraisal process is the annual performance review interview. Specifically, he notes that line managers are under-prepared to handle the interview and reluctant to give negative feedback, leading to a situation where the people being appraised receive incomplete and inaccurate messages about their performance. Some of the principles of effective interviewing were outlined in Chapter 5 (see the section on selection interviews) and many of these have application here.

Of particular importance is the preparation for the interview itself. Most formal appraisal interviews take place once a year, even though there may be ongoing reviews throughout the year. For this reason both managers and employees need to set time aside to think carefully about the appraisal process including:
- The targets that were previously identified.
- Work performance over the period.
- Particular variables that may be affecting successful completion of work tasks.
- The range of developmental opportunities that might have application in developing action plans for the future.

Adequate notice of the appraisal interview is a major consideration in facilitating thorough preparation. An employee needs to determine not only how s/he has performed over the past year but also what his/her main expectations might be, in terms of career and skills development. Equally, the manager needs to be assured that s/he is familiar with all aspects of the employee's performance so that constructive, motivational feedback can be provided. A key 'rule of thumb' associated with appraisal interviewing is to focus on behaviour, which the employee can change if required, rather than personality, which is rather more constant and very difficult to modify. It is in this respect that predetermined key objectives and associated standards and targets come into play.

The appraisal interview is perhaps the most difficult interview that a manager has to conduct, because the twin goals of performance evaluation and motivation facilitation are not necessarily compatible. Evaluation requires a manager to act as 'judge' and yet the developmental aspect demands a more facilitative, 'supportive' approach. When these are combined with the inherent pitfalls that are associated with the interview process (see Chapter 5), the result can often lead to interaction that is stressful and demanding for both the manager and the employee being appraised.

There are three particular interview styles that are often associated with the appraisal interview: the *tell-and-sell* approach; the *tell-and-listen* approach and the *problem-solving* approach.

1. The *tell-and-sell* approach is directive and authoritative in nature and involves the manager telling the employee how s/he has evaluated performance, and then attempting to convince the employee of the fairness of the assessment. This approach is invariably uni-directional, from the manager to the employee, and provides very little opportunity for the employee to participate in the evaluation process. The likely response from the employee is a defensive one, and, where s/he has no input into setting action plans for the future, there is likely to be little commitment to follow-up action. Bearing in mind the key perceived benefits of appraisal outlined earlier, it is unlikely that this approach will facilitate their attainment and thus, it is not recommended as good practice.
2. The *tell-and-listen* approach is similar in some respects to the *tell-and-sell* style, but there is some attempt made to involve the employee in the process. In this approach, the manager again communicates his/her evaluation of performance to the employee, and then actively encourages the employee to respond to the evaluation given. However, given the exigencies of human nature (particularly in respect to being told, rather than being asked), it is unlikely that this approach is any more effective than the first.
3. The *problem-solving* approach is based on the premise that the appraisal process is one that is jointly conducted by the manager and the employee. Here, the manager first asks the employee to discuss his/her performance against agreed targets and to express any problems that might be affecting work behaviour. Rather than being given an evaluation, the employee is free to comment and highlight particular aspects of performance, and the manager provides feedback. This approach advocates that an evaluation be conducted after the interview has been completed and takes account of the contribution made by the employee towards his/her own evaluation.

Once the appraisal interview has been conducted and feedback given to the employee, it is important to ensure that the focus on performance is not neglected until the next interview. The performance management cycle requires a continuous alignment of work targets with key business objectives and thus performance should be reviewed throughout the year. Expectations created at the appraisal interview, in terms perhaps of promotion prospects or learning initiatives, should be acted upon to ensure the motivational aspects of performance appraisal are not disregarded. Above all, however, a genuine commitment to the process of performance management is required of all managers and employees if the process is to be effective.

Pulakos *et al.* (2015) suggest that greater and more regular feedback will improve the overall system of performance management, arguing that more frequent attempts to improve performance are beneficial for employees. In addition, adequate preparation and improved rater training can have a significant impact on the quality of the performance management system (Pulakos and O'Leary 2011), especially where this training helps to develop a common cognitive knowledge structure regarding what constitutes effective performance in the organisation, and how to measure the performance-related behaviours associated with it.

Grote (1996: 137) identifies nine common appraisal errors that retain their significance: contrast effect; first impression error; halo/horns effect; similar-to-me-effect; central tendency; negative and positive skew; attribution bias; recency effect; and stereotyping. Table 8.11, extracted from Grote's (1996) *Guide to Performance Appraisal*, defines and provides an example of each error.

Table 8.11 Common errors in the appraisal process

ERROR	DEFINITION	EXAMPLE
Contrast Effect	The tendency of a rater to evaluate people in comparison with other individuals rather than against the standards for the job.	Think of the most attractive person that you have known. Rate this individual's attractiveness on a scale of 1 to 10. Now think of your favourite glamorous movie star. Re-rate your acquaintance. If you have rated your friend lower the second time around, contrast effect is said to be at work.
First Impression Error	The tendency of a manager to make an initial positive or negative judgement of an employee and allow that first impression to colour or distort later information.	A manager new to a work group noticed one employee, who was going through a divorce, performing poorly. Within a month, the employee's performance had returned to its previously high level, but the manager's opinion of the individual's performance was adversely affected by the initial negative impression.
Halo/Horns Effect	Inappropriate generalisations from one aspect of an individual's performance to all areas of that person's performance.	Jeff was outstanding in his ability to get delinquent customers to pay up. His excellence in this most important area caused his manager to rate him highly in unrelated areas where his performance was actually mediocre.

ERROR	DEFINITION	EXAMPLE
Similar-to-me Effect	The tendency of individuals to rate people who resemble themselves more highly than they rate others.	Carol, a single mother of four small children, had prevailed in her efforts to succeed and had been promoted to manager. She unwittingly rated several women who were also single mothers higher than their performance warranted.
Central Tendency	The inclination to rate people in the middle of the scale even when their performance clearly warrants a substantially higher or lower rating.	Out of an erroneous belief that the law required all companies to treat all employees the same and a conscious desire to avoid confrontation, Harold rated all seven of the employees in his work group as 'Fully Meets Standard'.
Negative and Positive Skew	The opposite of central tendency: the rating of all individuals as higher or lower than their performance actually warrants.	Susan rates all of her employees higher than she feels they actually deserve, in the misguided hope that this will cause them to live up to the high rating that they have been given. Carlos sets impossibly high standards and expectations and is proud of never having met a subordinate who deserved a 'Superior Rating'.
Attribution Bias	The tendency to attribute performance failings to factors under the control of the individual and performance successes to external causes.	Harriet, a manager with a mixture of excellent and mediocre performers in her work group, attributes the successes of the former group to the quality of her leadership and the failings of the latter group to their bad attitudes and inherent laziness.
Recency Effect	The tendency of minor events that have happened recently to have more influence on the rating than major events of many months ago.	Victoria kept no formal records of the overall performance or critical incidents of her work group of twelve people during the course of the year. of the year. When she began writing their appraisal, she discovered that the only examples she could provide for either positive or negative performance had happened in the last two months.

ERROR	DEFINITION	EXAMPLE
Stereotyping	The tendency to generalise across groups and ignore individual differences.	Waldo is quiet and reserved, almost meek – about as far from the conventional cliché of a salesman as can be imagined. His sales record, however, is one of the best in the company. But his boss rated his performance lower than that of other salespeople since he didn't fit the mould, ignoring the results that Waldo had produced.

Source: Grote (1996: 138–9).

PERFORMANCE MANAGEMENT IN IRELAND

Empirical data on performance management in Ireland is relatively scarce. Earlier evidence provided by McMahon and Gunnigle (1994) confirmed performance appraisal as a regular activity in most organisations. Data from the 2010 Cranet Ireland/University of Limerick Kemmy Business School national survey of HR practices provide some more recent evidence on how organisations in Ireland approach and manage performance management issues. The survey focused on three key areas:
1. The existence of an appraisal system for particular categories of employee.
2. The main contributors to the appraisal process.
3. The purpose for which the appraisal information is used.

Data from the survey depict a robust performance management system in operation. Across all categories of employee (managerial/technical/professional/clerical and manual), the use of appraisal systems has grown when compared to previous figures. For example, the data show that more than four-fifths (in excess of 80 per cent) of all managerial and professional/technical employees, and over three-quarters (78.6 per cent) of clerical employees have their performance formally assessed. These figures are up significantly from previous years, where the average percentage use was closer to 61 per cent for managerial/professional grades and 55 per cent for clerical workers (Cranet 2000). By comparison, while formal appraisal seems to be less common among manual workers, its use has also increased from reported figures in that category in previous years – up from 33 per cent in 2000 to 48.5 per cent in 2010. One third of respondents indicate that they operate such a scheme for manual workers.

Turning to the issue of who is involved in this appraisal process, the data portray a relatively traditional picture of involvement and participation. For the most part, those involved are limited to the employee and his/her immediate supervisor. A more senior manager (supervisor's superior) is involved in about a third of companies for all except manual appraisals. There is limited evidence of a 360-degree performance management system in use (involvement of subordinates, peers and customers); there is some evidence perhaps for managerial grades but this is not significant.

As we have seen earlier, appraisal data can be used for many purposes. In the 2010 Cranet Ireland/University of Limerick Kemmy Business School national survey of HR practices, the data suggest that appraisal data is used first and foremost for developmental purposes – either in response to identified knowledge or skill gaps, or as a reward for good performance. Data are also used for planning career moves (again developmental in nature), or as inputs to the workforce planning process itself. The explicit linking of performance with pay was in evidence in more than 50 per cent of cases, indicating perhaps the growing popularity of some performance-related payment systems.

This chapter has provided an overview of the core dimensions of managing and measuring performance, and has focused on some aspects that remain challenging. Reference was made to the performance cycle, and useful detail was provided on the range of appraisal and assessment mechanisms that can be applied. Attention was drawn to critical aspects of appraisal that are especially prone to error and bias. The evidence in 2010 suggests that performance management is an important concern for organisations in Ireland, as demonstrated in the growing utilisation of performance management and appraisal systems for all categories of employees. As Ireland works towards regaining competitiveness and shaking off the current recession, it is likely that organisations will pay more, rather than less, attention to performance management in the years ahead. Moreover, as feedback becomes a more pervasive feature of the everyday life of younger generations, and regular updates on performance become the norm, it may be that performance management systems will undergo more radical overhauling in the years to come. Even if this is the case, we would hold that performance management will retain its critical position in the HRM architecture of the organisation.

Having reviewed critical aspects of managing performance, the next chapter considers the learning and development architecture of the organisation's human resources.

9
Workplace Learning and Development

A nation's standard of living is determined by the productivity of its economy. Thus, creating the conditions for sustained productivity growth is a critical factor for national economies and local organisations alike. The World Economic Forum (WEF)'s Global Competitiveness Report provides an annual assessment of the factors driving productivity and prosperity across 138 countries. It ranked Ireland twenty-third in 2017, and in the top twelve countries in relation to quality of the education system, higher education and training more generally. The *IMD World Competitiveness Yearbook* similarly ranks countries and in 2016 it placed Ireland seventh out of sixty-one countries. Both reports point to positive and continuing improvements in some of the key fundamentals underpinning Ireland's economic growth and development.

Learning capacity lies at the heart of sustainable competitive functioning – Ulrich (1997) describes it simply as the DNA of competitiveness. The recent upsurge in human capital research discussed in earlier chapters lends support to the view that competitiveness is increasingly being built around strong investment in human resources, with learning and knowledge emerging as essential national competitiveness levers (Lam 2003; Hall and Soskice 2001; Fulmer *et al.* 2000). This point is emphasised by the OECD (2010b), which highlights that having a well-skilled workforce is one of the main supports for prosperity and growth in member countries. Competitiveness is clearly on Ireland's national agenda, and there is a strong policy focus on developing the knowledge and skills infrastructure to facilitate economic development.

This chapter examines the nature of workplace learning and development (L&D). It starts with a description of the terminology that is in common use in L&D and which gives an indication of the scope of L&D activities and interventions. Then, adopting a multi-level perspective, it describes how factors at different levels combine to impact the provision and quality of L&D activities generally (see Figure 9.1).

Figure 9.1 Multi-level perspective on workplace learning and development

It outlines the macro context for L&D, arguing that any appreciation of workplace L&D has to be understood against the backdrop of the prevailing institutional and regulatory environment within which organisations are situated, and from which employees are drawn (Tregaskis and Heraty 2017). Next, it presents an organisational-level process view of L&D in organisations, exploring different facets of L&D provision and rationales for their utilisation. Finally, it turns to L&D at the level of the individual and highlights a number of important learning principles, conditions and activities that shape the level and extent of learning that occurs. The chapter concludes with a summary review of current L&D practices in Ireland.

THE TERMINOLOGY OF WORKPLACE LEARNING AND DEVELOPMENT (L&D)

There are several terms in common parlance in the field of L&D: learning, training, development, education, human resource development, competency development, knowledge management, organisational learning, and talent management. Some terms reflect distinctly different concepts; some arise from a particular highlighting of a specific element/s of the field of study, but it is also the case that some of the terms are used interchangeably. For example, useful classifications can be made relatively easily amongst education, learning, training and development, although learning, as a construct, underpins each activity. Meaningful differentiation between some of the other terms is somewhat more problematic as it essentially comes down to a matter of interpretation. Some of these distinctions and interpretations are provided in Table 9.1.

Table 9.1 Description of L&D terms	
Term	**Description**
Education	Education is person-, rather than job-oriented. It refers to the assimilation of knowledge and understanding that can be far broader than the work context within which an individual may operate. When we speak of education, we typically refer to formal programmes of study, many of which are accredited, and which generally occur outside of the workplace.
Learning	Learning is a process through which individuals assimilate new knowledge and skills that results in relatively permanent behavioural changes. It can be conscious or unconscious, formal or informal, and requires some element of practice and experience. Effective learning requires the ability to question habits and methods, and to challenge one's assumptions.
Training	Training focuses on improving capability or capacity to perform and thus has a specific vocational purpose. In workplace terms, training refers to the planned acquisition of the knowledge, skills and abilities (KSAs) considered necessary to perform effectively in a given role or job. Each training intervention requires some change in performance and therefore requires some form of learning to occur.
Development	Development is a broad concept that is future-oriented and is concerned with the growth and enhancement of the individual. In organisational terms, it refers to the acquisition of skills and abilities that are required for future roles in the organisation. In this way, development can be seen as a vehicle for career enhancement (career development), for succession planning, for determining managerial potential (management development) or for reasons of personal development (lifelong learning).

Term	Description
Competencies	Two particular perspectives on competencies exist. The first is a vocational view that separates the job into its various component parts to identify the behavioural characteristics and standards of performance that need to be attained by the job-holder. The second focuses on the nature of the skills and abilities that the individual brings to the job. Organisations are increasingly adopting competency frameworks to help them identify the types of behaviours they wish to promote in order to assist the performance of individuals and organisations.
Human resource development (HRD)	HRD generally refers to the development of a strategic organisational approach to managing L&D at work. It advocates the strategic linking of L&D activities to corporate business objectives and ensuring a central role for line managers in developing employees. It refers to learning at the individual, group and organisational levels to enhance the effectiveness of human resource utilisation.
Knowledge management	Knowledge management refers to an organisational system comprising three central components that are interrelated: skills, cognitions and systems. An organisation's skills include the technical, professional and social expertise of the organisation's members, i.e. the *know-how* of the organisation. Cognitions refer to the information, ideas, attitudes, norms and values shared by the organisation's members, i.e. the *know-why* of the organisation. An organisation's systems include the structures, procedures and policies related to performing tasks, co-ordinating resources and managing external relationships.
Organisational learning	Organisational learning describes an holistic approach to learning and development. The organisation is viewed as a participative learning system, which places an emphasis on the exchange of information, reflection and self-improvement. It promotes continuous development and improvement, a willingness to take risks and a work system that actively facilitates learning at work. Work structures and systems are designed to maximise learning potential.
Talent management	Popularised within the last fifteen years, there remains no uniform understanding of what the term talent management represents. It can be understood to be a strategic approach to succession planning; a broader leveraging of key strengths and talents of all employees within the internal labour pool; or even a re-imagining of HRM in general with an explicit focus on the link between business operations (local and global) and people management. One of the central arguments is that while organisations adopt very sophisticated approaches to sourcing and recruiting key talent, they often then neglect how best to manage that talent to retain it.

In this text, we use the term workplace learning and development in an inclusive manner, to describe deliberate organisational interventions that are used to expand the learning, knowledge sharing, and potential of individuals at work. It is a broader framework than skills acquisition. Workplace L&D is about how, what and where individuals learn, and how an organisation can facilitate this learning. It requires that we understand that individuals can and do learn outside the, often narrow, scope of their job; that an individual's contribution need not be bound within the confines of the job; and that the challenge for organisations is as much about creating work systems that facilitate and capture this as it is about designing effective learning interventions. Workplace L&D also recognises that individual knowledge and skills development are initiated outside of the workplace, and that this development is significantly influenced by the education and learning environment individuals engage with. We examine this macro environment in the next section.

MACRO LEVEL: INSTITUTIONAL AND REGULATORY CONTEXT OF WORKPLACE LEARNING AND DEVELOPMENT

The development of Ireland's national learning and development framework has a long pedigree and occurred through a series of distinct phases that originated with the guild system and controlled apprenticeships around the eleventh century. The rise of industrialisation led to the gradual decline of the guilds throughout Europe in the late eighteenth century. Industrialisation brought with it increased division of labour and mechanisation of work which resulted in a greater structuring of work into particular skills, crafts and tasks, and gave rise to a form of work classification (managerial, technical, clerical and manual) that still exists today. Over time, these categorisations formed the basis for the growing organisation of trade unions around particular groups of workers, i.e. the skilled in craft unions, the semi-skilled and unskilled in general unions, clerical and technical staff in white-collar unions. Throughout the early twentieth century, training was mainly associated with craft apprenticeships, however, and developing this system became the central focus of the earliest initiatives in vocational education and training in Ireland.

In Table 9.2 we present a chronological overview of the various stages of Ireland's L&D infrastructure which traces its development through a series of statutory and institutional reforms, prompted by various political, economic, social and organisational stakeholder interests. The chronological overview demonstrates how the essentially voluntarist nature of the learning and development infrastructure through much of the twentieth century was gradually replaced by greater institutional regulation and state intervention in an effort to stimulate economic growth and increase the knowledge base of Ireland's economy.

Table 9.2 Evolution of Ireland's national learning, training and development infrastructure

Date	Significant Event	Contribution/Commentary
1898	Agricultural & Technical Instruction (IRL) Act	First form of regulated apprenticeship in Ireland; specified that all training should be on-the-job.
1930	Vocational Education Act	Established Vocational Education Colleges (VECs) to provide a nation-wide system of technical and continuing education, with emphasis on vocational education for apprentices. There was no compulsion on the employer to send apprentices on any of the courses organised by the VECs.
1931	Apprenticeship Act	Introduced greater systematic regulation of apprenticeships, with the establishment of apprenticeship committees. They were responsible for regulating apprenticeship training in designated areas and formulating rules governing the length of an apprenticeship, training courses, age limits for entry, educational requirements, wage levels and the number of working hours. Employers were obliged by statute to release apprentices for training courses, providing they were held within three miles of the workplace and took place during normal working hours.

Date	Significant Event	Contribution/Commentary
1959	Apprenticeship Act	Enacted as a result of widespread variation in the standard of apprentice training programmes and, in some cases, abuse of the apprenticeship system. A national apprenticeship board, An Cheard Comhairle, was set up to co-ordinate the apprenticeship system and establish appropriate educational standards governing the release of apprentices to technical colleges, provision of on-the-job training, and establishing a system of examination on the practice and theory of each trade.
Up until 1960	Voluntarism in training	Training was held to be the preserve of joint negotiation between both sides of industry, with the government's role defined in purely advisory and facilitative terms. The Irish industrial sector was largely left to its own devices to provide the skills necessary for its growth and development. Employers, though pressed in some sectors by skill shortages, were prepared to pay the wages necessary to poach the skilled labour they required from their competitors. Trade unions concentrated on consolidating the apprenticeship system, following the logic that maintaining defensive control over conditions of entry led to skilled labour attracting a good price. The principle of voluntarism, and the maintenance of the status quo, appeared to suit everybody.
1960s	Institutional reform to support national training provision	Widespread recognition that the voluntarist approach to training was failing to meet national needs led to institutional reform. There were insufficient skilled workers overall, and the lack of training outside the apprenticeship systems, combined with the narrow content of apprenticeship training itself, resulted in Ireland lagging behind most of its competitors in mainland Europe, in terms of the average skill levels and educational qualifications of its workforce. Government initiatives focused on creating a more open economy with the emphasis on attracting foreign investment to Ireland, prompting interest in vocational and skills training across sectors to support economic expansion. Investment in tourism and agriculture led to the establishment of the Farm Apprenticeship Board in 1963 to provide training for young farmers, and the Council for Education, Recruitment and Training (CERT) in the same period, to handle education and training in the tourism and hospitality sector.
1967	Industrial Training Act	An International Labour Organisation (ILO) report on vocational education in 1962, prompted the Industrial Training Act of 1967 which established An Comhairle Oiluna (AnCo) to assume full responsibility for all industrial training, including apprenticeships. This represented a significant change in government policy, reflecting an interventionist strategy aimed at sweeping away the concept of voluntarism. It also heralded an institutional role for a national training agency. AnCo was funded mainly by the government, but the Act also allowed for the imposition of a levy/grant scheme to underwrite training costs and to heighten awareness of the economic benefits of investment in training.
1970s & 1980s	Recession and revision	Following a period of significant industrial expansion and development, Ireland plummeted into a prolonged recession. Spending on education and training was severely curtailed and consequently, training and development activities were seriously pared back. Rising criticisms of AnCo saw increasing calls for a reform of Ireland's training system to make it more strategic and geared towards industry needs and improving individual employability.

Date	Significant Event	Contribution/Commentary
1987	Labour Services Act	The *Labour Services Act* represented the first attempt in twenty years, at state level, to reform the training system and bring it into alignment with economic objectives pursued by the government. A White Paper on Manpower Policy, published in September 1986, had examined the role of all actors involved in manpower policy, and put forward a number of proposals for action including the amalgamation of national agencies, revision of the levy scheme, modernisation of the apprenticeship scheme and greater focus on management education. This Act provided for the establishment of FÁS (Foras Áiseanna Saothair), one national agency with responsibility for the provision of training and retraining for industry and the management of particular employment schemes to assist in the reduction of unemployment in Ireland.
1988	Galvin report	An advisory committee on management development reported in 1988 that insufficient investment in management education and training was in danger of significantly curtailing organisational performance, and highlighted the urgent need for investment in training and development at all levels of an organisation.
1990s	Repeated stakeholder calls for reform	From the mid-1990s there was a growing recognition that training policy at national level had resulted in a number of inconsistencies and had ill-supported the needs of industry generally. These included the complexity of the National Training agency, with its multiple objectives, both economic and social, coupled with a wide span of activities and programmes. Since the mid-1980s there had been a preoccupation in Ireland with training to reduce mass unemployment (particularly youth unemployment). This, in turn, had switched the emphasis of national training strategies away from the existing business enterprise and its needs and towards the creation of a network of non-business organisations. As a result of this, the value of training for organisational improvement had been diminished in the eyes of many employers. Many of these stakeholder criticisms of the national training system served as the catalyst for a significant change in policy direction through the 1990s and beyond.
1992	Culliton report	Made two specific recommendations about training and development at national level. 1. Institutional reorganisation of FÁS to reflect the distinction between support activities for the unemployed and for industry training. 2. A greater proportion of FÁS resources and activities to be allocated to industry-relevant training directed towards those at work and preparing for work.
1992	Apprenticeship re-examined	Apprenticeship system revisited and reorganised along the lines of competency-based standards.
1993	Employee trade union perspectives on training	The *Irish Congress of Trade Unions* (ICTU) commissioned report, *New Forms of Work Organisation: Options for Trade Unions*, found that Irish firms lagged behind their European counterparts in terms of raising the skill levels of existing employees, and noted specific deficiencies: • Lack of consultation with trade unions on training and development. • Over focus on job-specific training at the cost of personal development. • Tendency of firms to design their training for maximising grant recovery, rather than focusing on the needs of the individuals being trained. *Services, Industrial, Professional and Technical Union* (SIPTU) indicated that the success of the Irish economy was contingent on high levels of skills and knowledge, and that it was the intention of trade unions to press for a highly-skilled and flexible workforce.

Date	Significant Event	Contribution/Commentary
1994	IBEC Analysis of Industrial Training	Identified a number of perceived weaknesses in the national training system: • Employers not involved enough in developing national training policy. • State support for industrial training was insufficient. • Organisations needed to invest more in training and development. • Training provision was overly fragmented.
1997	Government White Paper on Human Resource Development (HRD)	Laid down the state's role in assisting industry to create a learning environment with a view to upgrading the quality of Ireland's human resources. This represented a significant departure from the traditional programme-led interventions approach. Emphasising clear objective-driven solutions, it proposed significant changes: 1. The promotion of investment in the development of skills and knowledge of the workforce. 2. The promotion of gainful employment by helping people to develop their knowledge and skills to their full potential. 3. The achievement of high levels of efficiency, effectiveness and value for money in the delivery of state interventions, which would yield permanent benefits to clients. The White Paper outlined a number of structural and policy-based changes that were seen to be required if the government was to achieve these strategic pillars. Key among them was the re-organisation of FÁS to separate out services to industry from services to support labour market entry/re-entry; the development of a new training networks programme, and the establishment of a Future Skills Identification Group, comprising representatives of business, trade unions, government, state development agencies, and education and training providers, to identify skill needs and make recommendations for the education and training system.
1997	Expert Group on Future Skills Needs (EGFSN)	Following one of the recommendations of the White Paper on HRD, the Expert Group on Future Skills Needs (EGFSN) was set up to investigate and develop national strategies to tackle the issue of skills needs, human resource forecasting and training for business and education in Ireland. Its remit is to identify best practice in enterprise training, both nationally and internationally, and to commission sectoral studies of key skills needs into the future. The EGFSN provides advice to government on skills issues impacting enterprise, through skills benchmarking, strategic skills development by education and training, data collection and analysis labour demand and supply, and influencing and monitoring implementation of key initiatives, and has published a series of reports (see www.skillsireland.ie).
1999	Skillsnet programme	Funded from the National Training Fund (NTF) through the Department of Education and Skills (DES), Skillsnet facilitates enterprise-led training and upskilling programmes for Irish industry. With over 400 networks across industries and sectors, it is tasked with improving the range, scope and quality of training to assist employees in upskilling to meet work-related training needs. Under the Training Networks Programme (TNP) companies from the same industry sectors or geographical regions form a network and co-operate to deliver training programmes specifically designed and adapted to current market requirements (see www.skillsnets.ie for further details).
1999	Qualifications (Education and Training) Act	As directed under this Act, the National Qualifications Authority of Ireland (NQAI) was established by the government in February 2001. A key role for the NQAI is the establishment of a national framework of qualifications (see Table 9.3) to include all awards in Ireland and to provide a mechanism for accrediting prior learning. This Act further provided for the establishment of two national awards councils that would come under the ambit of the NQAI but which are separate and independent from it: Further Education and Training Awards Council (FETAC) and HETAC (the Higher Education and Training Awards Council).

Date	Significant Event	Contribution/Commentary
2000	'Learning for Life' White Paper on Adult Education	Published on foot of a 1997 OECD Adult Literacy Survey that noted that 25 per cent of the Irish population scored at the lowest level of literacy, and that those with low skill levels were among those least likely to avail of any continuing education and training. The White Paper on Adult Education focused mainly on issues surrounding maintaining access to, and participation in continuing education and training throughout life. It called for: • Increased scale and flexibility of existing provision. • Strategic shifts towards adult-friendly policies in existing educational institutions. • Investment in the development of core supporting services, such as guidance and counselling, and childcare. • Increased role and funding for community education.
2000	Task Force on Lifelong Learning	Set up under the Government's National Programme for Prosperity and Fairness to explore core issues surrounding the provision of learning for those in the workplace. Among the recommendations to government were the development of more flexible delivery systems with regard to the opening hours of institutions, the move to modular courses and the potential of open and distance learning.
2001	National Centre for Partnership and Performance (NCPP)	Established by the government to promote and facilitate partnership-led change and innovation in Ireland's workplaces. By building and supporting the case for workplace change and innovation through increased levels of employee involvement and engagement, the NCPP's objective was to contribute to national competitiveness, enhanced public services and a better quality of working life for employers and employees alike. In April 2010, the NCPP was integrated into the National Economic and Social Council (NESC).
2005	Forum on the Workplace of the Future	Formed by the NCPP, at the request of the government, to assess how well Ireland's workplaces were equipped to meet the challenges it might face into the future. Following a lengthy consultation process, the forum reported in 2005 and identified nine key attributes of a successful workplace in the future, concluding that it should be: agile; customer-centred; knowledge intense; responsive to employee needs; networked; highly productive; participatory; continually learning; and proactively diverse. Incorporating these attributes, a National Workplace Strategy was developed, comprising forty-two separate recommendations subsumed under five broad areas for action: 1. Commitment to workplace innovation. 2. Capacity for change. 3. Developing future skills. 4. Access to opportunities. 5. Quality of working life. A high-level implementation group was established to develop and to oversee the institutional arrangements needed for the successful implementation of this National Workplace Strategy.
2007	Management Development Council (MDC)	Established to advise government on the adequacy and relevance of management development provision in Ireland and to promote a co-ordinated approach to building awareness and appreciation in small- and medium-sized businesses for the value of, and need for, upgrading leadership and management skills.

Date	Significant Event	Contribution/Commentary
2010	OECD report on vocational education and training (VET) in Ireland	The OECD (2010b) report highlighted a number of important strengths of the Irish VET system, including a wide range of provision of different types of VET at post-secondary level, comprehensive and integrative National Qualification Framework, and collaboration with social partners through various initiatives. It also identified a number of enduring challenges to be addressed to leverage sustainable human capital competitiveness, including the need to strengthen and widen the apprenticeship system with greater workplace training, improved evaluation of the VET system including providers and closer examination of labour market outcomes.
2013	Further Education and Training Act 2013	Provided for the dissolution of FÁS and the establishment of SOLAS to be responsible for further education and training (FET) in Ireland. Operating under the aegis of the Department of Education and Skills, and in conjunction with the sixteen Education and Training Boards (ETBs), it is responsible for the integration, coordination and funding of FET programmes.
2016	National Skills Strategy 2025	Following a period of consultation in 2016, the government published its national skills strategy for Ireland with a stated aim of future proofing the Irish economy through a long-term skills strategy to ensure everyone can reach their full potential and play an active role in building a better Ireland. Some of the key objectives include: 1. Education and training providers to place a stronger focus on providing skills development opportunities that are relevant to the needs of learners, society and the economy. 2. Employers to participate actively in the development of skills and make effective use of skills in their organisations to improve productivity and competitiveness. 3. The quality of teaching and learning at all stages of education to be continually enhanced and evaluated. 4. People across Ireland to engage more in lifelong learning. 5. A specific focus on active inclusion to support participation in education and training, and the labour market. 6. Support for an increase in the supply of skills to the labour market. A new National Skills Council and a Regional Skills Fora is to be established to facilitate provision of the strategy across regions and monitor/evaluate progress, using identified key national and international skills indicators.

Renewed focus on learning and development in Ireland over the last twenty years has been instigated by demand pressures associated with competitive market functioning, internationalisation and the emergence of skill gaps in certain industries. As with most modern economies, Ireland faces continuing pressures from technological innovations, changing consumption patterns, new ways of working, and global value networks, all of which will influence the nature of the knowledge and skills that will be in demand into the future. Such global pressure highlights the continued importance of training to facilitate national competitiveness and it encourages the delivery of high-quality learning and development as a national priority.

The provision of learning and development services at the macro level has grown considerably in recent years. In addition to the statutory and regulatory bodies identified in Table 9.2, and the main trade unions in Ireland which all have a strong learning remit, four key professional bodies are worth drawing attention to here.

- **Chartered Institute of Personnel and Development (CIPD)** – the CIPD plays a pivotal role in the education and training of Ireland's HRM professionals through an integrated education scheme, delivered by a number of Irish universities, colleges and institutes of technology (ITs). The CIPD also provides information and advisory services to members, arranges conferences, workshops and seminars throughout the year, and publishes regular updates and reports *People Management* in the UK and *CIPD News* in Ireland). (See www.cipd.co.uk; www.cipd.ie for further information.)
- **Irish Institute of Training and Development (IITD)** – the IITD is the professional body for those specifically involved in delivering learning, training and development in business, industry, consultancy and the community. It offers a range of services aimed at supporting and developing training networks and activities throughout Ireland, promoting L&D in the workplace, and providing educationally-accredited (FETAC) courses. It also promotes L&D through its annual National Training Awards. (See www.iitd.ie for further details.)
- **Institute of Public Administration (IPA)** – the IPA is Ireland's only public service development agency focused exclusively on public sector development, and providing a range of services that cater to the particular needs of the public service. It delivers its service through education and training provision, direct consultancy, research and publishing. (See www.ipa.ie for further information on its services.)
- **The Irish Management Institute (IMI)** – The Irish Management Institute (IMI) is a not-for-profit membership organisation dedicated to improving the standard of management practice in Ireland. The IMI delivers a range of executive education programmes and ancillary services to its members. (See www.imi.ie for further details.)

In addition, a considerable range of undergraduate, graduate and post-experience programmes are provided by the various universities, colleges and privately-funded educational establishments throughout the country. A number of institutes have also been established that cater for professional development in select disciplines. The large growth in private sector employment in recent years has also seen a considerable increase in the numbers of consultants who provide expertise in a range of learning and development activities.

Table 9.3, on the next page, lists the main programme types in the Irish education and training system and the corresponding National Framework Qualification (NFQ) level at which awards from these programmes are usually made. It should be noted however that there is considerable overlap between the various categories (e.g. awards at Level 6 on the NFQ span both the further and higher education and training system; the Leaving Certificate award is placed across levels 4 and 5 on the NFQ). In addition, for presentation purposes, all postgraduate awards (e.g. higher diploma, masters, etc.) have been categorised at levels 9/10.

Table 9.3 Mapping Irish education/training to National Framework of Qualifications (NFQ)

Level of Education	Typical Award	NFQ Level
Primary education	QQI Certificate	1/2
Second level education – Junior Cycle	Junior Certificate	3
Second level education – Senior Cycle	Leaving Certificate	4
Apprenticeship, PLC courses, FET	QQI Level 5 Certificate	5
	QQI Advanced Certificate	6
Third level – Higher Certificate or University Diploma	Higher Certificate	6
Third level – Ordinary and Honours Bachelor Degree/ Higher Diploma	Ordinary Degree	7
	Honours Bachelor Degree	8
	Higher Diploma	8
Third level – Master's Degree and Postgraduate Certificates/Diplomas	Postgraduate Diploma Master's degree	9
PhD	PhD	10

What can we take from this review of Ireland's macro L&D environment? Two points are worth highlighting, but first it is advisable to revisit Chapter 4 in tandem with this discussion, in order to get a stronger sense of Ireland's labour market, and the institutional and regulatory environment that shapes it.

1. There is no doubt that L&D is a key issue in Ireland. We have a seen strong investment in, and development of, the infrastructure for L&D in the last number of years. Education and learning are heavily sought by individuals in Ireland as can be seen in the almost full completion rates for senior cycle second-level education (more than 90 per cent); and participation in third-level education that is well above the OECD and EU averages. Arising out of recessionary times, upskilling and reskilling is commonplace and seen as necessary for employment and progression. Our younger-aged labour pool (less than 35 years) is well-educated and increasingly mobile, and actively seeking L&D opportunities in organisations. In consort, this point to a national valuing and established norm of participation in L&D, that carries through into the workplace.
2. Ireland's national infrastructure for L&D could still be improved. Stakeholders have long called for more proactive measures to support industry-based, or organisational level investment in L&D, but progress has been slow in this respect. As skill shortages start to emerge once more, we will see renewed debate on how to further support our national labour market through more targeted investment.

Having established the nature of the enveloping national learning framework, and the economic necessity for a robust L&D infrastructure, we turn now to reviewing L&D at the meso and micro levels.

MESO LEVEL: ORGANISATIONAL PROCESSES OF WORKPLACE LEARNING AND DEVELOPMENT

Effective L&D is a core means of leveraging competitiveness and it is widely accepted now that L&D can deliver sustainable superior performance to organisations (Tregaskis and Heraty 2011). Indeed, Boud and Garrick (1999: 4) cautioned all organisations about the dangers of ignoring learning, arguing that firms put their present and future success at risk if they do so. Almost thirty years ago Porter (1990), in his seminal study on the competitiveness of nations, argued that to sustain competitive advantage an organisation must have a commitment to improvement, innovation and change. The argument is that organisations that improve their capability for learning (through increasing their knowledge, skill accumulation, superior capability and application) are in a better position to compete. Maximising the talents of employees is seen as a source of this sustained competitive advantage and superior business performance (Collings and Mellahi 2009; Farndale *et al.* 2014; Al Ariss *et al.* 2014; McDonnell *et al.* 2017).

Thus, there is considerable responsibility on the organisation's human resource department to ensure that employees are equipped to meet the demands required of them for this competitive agenda.

THE PROCESS OF WORKPLACE LEARNING AND DEVELOPMENT

Superior organisational performance requires that employees can acquire appropriate knowledge, skills, behaviours and values in order to master the complex environment in which they work. The process of L&D is presented here as a series of key stages that commence at the strategic or business level of the organisation and work sequentially down from there. In practice, however, L&D probably occurs much more intuitively and spontaneously than this sequence of activities suggests, but the sequencing is useful to illustrate the interconnected nature of L&D activities. In most organisations planned learning events are converted into training and/or development programmes and so, when we use the term training here (i.e. training policy, training needs analysis, training budget), it is to reflect this operationalisation of work-based learning.

LEARNING/TRAINING PHILOSOPHIES AND POLICIES

A learning/training policy reflects the organisation's philosophy on L&D and governs the priorities, standards and scope of its learning activities. As such it provides the framework within which all planned interventions take place. An organisation's L&D philosophy can be expressed along a continuum where, on the one hand, training is viewed as an expense and occurs only as the need for it arises, and, on the other, employees are seen as a potential source of competitive advantage and so L&D is a central organisational concern. In this respect, all organisations have an L&D policy, whether explicit or implicit. The extent to which organisations develop explicit policies is contextually bound and influenced by a number of factors including:

- Prevailing employment legislation (e.g. equality, health and safety).
- The state of the labour market – whether skilled labour is readily available, or can be contracted in or out.

- Whether there are available resources that can be allocated to L&D.
- Prevailing views on the value of training, particularly at senior and strategic levels.
- The nature of the product or service market.
- The expectations of employees themselves.

Furthermore, organisations can differentiate themselves as 'desirable' employers by providing a range of learning and career development opportunities that are designed to attract and retain the required calibre of employee. Such an approach requires a high level of co-ordination between L&D and the range of other human resource policy choices, such as recruitment and selection, performance management, reward systems and employee relations.

In the extant training literature a myriad of training models have been developed over the years, ranging from the reactive, ad hoc varieties to those that seek to describe training and development in strategic terms. The model adopted by an organisation presents a useful indication of its learning philosophy and thus, the learning/training policy that it will employ. In an organisation that adopts an unsystematic framework, one would expect little integration of employees' considerations into strategic decision-making or broader business issues. The converse holds true for organisations that adopt the more strategic models, where L&D considerations play a critical role in the formulation of strategic business plans.

Once the learning/training policies have been developed the next step involves the organisation in translating these policies into specific objectives for action. At this stage a learning/training plan is drawn up that seeks to merge individual and organisational requirements into a clear course of action. A model of the learning/training process is presented in Figure 9.2.

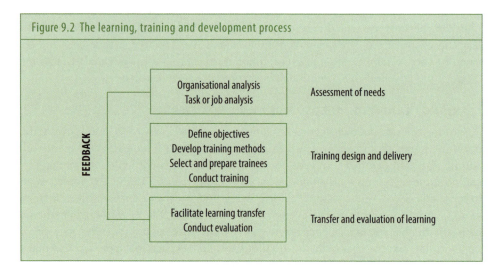

Figure 9.2 The learning, training and development process

The process depicted here presents L&D activities in an orderly and sequential manner: as previously noted, the reality may be quite different in organisations. What is most important to recognise is the interrelatedness of each feature, and how failing to consider certain stages of the process will have consequences for actions later in the organisation.

IDENTIFYING LEARNING/TRAINING NEEDS

The first stage in the L&D process is the identification of learning/training needs, often termed training needs analysis (TNA) or learning needs analysis (LNA). Needs analysis is a central component of the training process, as it ensures that L&D occurs where there is a valid need for it. Many organisations invest considerable resources in L&D, but often fail to examine how effectively these can impact the business bottom line. In an organisational context, a need is a discrepancy or 'gap' between 'what is' and 'what ought to be', i.e. the distance between actual performance and desired/required performance. Thus, LNA refers to any shortfall between current knowledge, skills, attitudes, and so forth, and the level required now, or in the future. This 'learning gap' is represented in Figure 9.3.

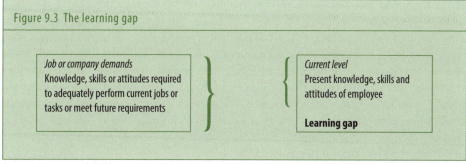

Figure 9.3 The learning gap

Source: Armstrong (1987).

Learning/training needs can be current, for the future, or both. Current needs arise where inconsistencies emerge in the present system and the organisation must act to remedy this situation. This may be linked with the introduction of a new system, or technology, a new approach to job design, or some other change that requires employees to act or behave differently in carrying out their work. It may also be related to opportunities for expanded employee roles, perhaps arising from another employee leaving the organisation. It is often the case that needs analyses can show up just how much know-how resides in one or two employees. It is only when these employees are absent that knowledge deficits begin to surface. Future needs, by contrast, arise from predicting organisational changes that are likely to occur, and considering how they will impact learning requirements. They are prompted by internal and external factors, such as strategy changes in the pipeline, work restructuring, product or service diversification, introduction of new technology, skills inventories matched against future requirements, and so forth. Such needs are usually more developmental in nature, and there can be a temptation to dismiss them and deal only with immediate needs. In such circumstances, however, it is difficult to envisage how L&D can make a strategic contribution to effective organisational functioning.

Needs manifest themselves in a number of ways. Although there is much focus on identifying the needs of individual employees, needs actually occur at three distinct levels: organisational level, job or group level, and individual level. There is a cascade effect at play here, whereby organisational needs highlight needs for particular jobs or groups, and thus, carry implications for individual needs.

As a first step it is recommended that an organisation-wide review of all learning/training needs and requirements is undertaken. Although hugely time-consuming, and expensive to complete, the information arising from this review can significantly influence a range of HR activities including performance management and reward, succession planning, job design and so forth. There are various sources of data that can be used to compile a needs analysis in an organisation. The choice of method to use and information to source is largely dependent on local circumstances. For example, organisations will have to consider how detailed the review needs to be, who should be involved in it, what resources are available to collect and analyse data? Sources of data can come from existing job analyses, HR forecasts, talent pipeline projections, survey, performance reviews, strategic plans, attitude surveys and so forth.

An organisational needs analysis should always include some examination of how the organisation interfaces with the external environment, since this can be a critical factor in determining whether L&D is required. In this instance a first port of call for most organisations is to look at the business strategy and the core objectives that have been identified for the organisation for the next few years. This will give an indication of what changes are likely to occur, especially with respect to any new implementations (products, processes, people) that will be introduced to the organisation – these will usually have some learning dimension to them. Factors in the external environment (legislation, economic policies, taxation issues) will also affect organisational needs as they can influence the way employees do their jobs, how decisions are made and the types of skill and levels of flexibility required.

Organisational needs filter down into more specific division or departmental needs, and these can then be translated into needs at the occupational or job level. For example, the introduction of a new product will immediately impact both the manufacturing department and sales and promotions, in terms of staff, skills, space, and so forth. A comprehensive job analysis provides information about the duties required of, and the responsibilities attached to, various jobs. Here, for example, it is important to identify whether the job description on file is accurate and that it lists relevant knowledge, skills and competency levels for the job in question. This level of needs analysis allows priority areas for individual L&D to be identified, i.e. to isolate the difference between current performance and what is required to do the job effectively, or to do a future identified job.

Needs analysis at the individual level is usually conducted as part of a performance management system – through performance appraisal, 360-degree feedback, or self-appraisal, and should be available from an individual performance development/learning plan.

The value of a comprehensive needs analysis is worth re-stating: it forms the basis for the organisation's investment in learning and development activities and, as such, is the benchmark against which any return on investment can be evaluated. In addition to targeting investment towards its core needs, the process of needs analysis helps to generate consensus and commitment to the principles of continuous learning, and the needs identified feed directly into the design of appropriate learning activities. It can also uncover system anomalies or problem areas that are adversely impacting performance (but may not be learning/training-related) and need attention.

DESIGN AND DELIVERY OF L&D ACTIVITIES

Two key questions arise for organisations during this phase of the L&D process, namely: 'How do we know what we need people to learn?' and 'How will we help them to learn it?' Answering these questions requires attention to four particular activities:
1. Specifying the core learning objectives.
2. Specifying the learning content.
3. Selecting the appropriate learning methods.
4. Structuring the learning event.

The answer to the 'How do we know what we need people to learn?' question is relatively straightforward and can be read from the needs analysis just completed. It is, however, a problematic issue if no needs analysis has been undertaken. Following the needs analysis phase, the organisation can then start to prioritise these needs and in so doing, establish specific learning/training objectives and develop a learning/training plan – at departmental level and for each individual. Thus, for each learning/training event, a set of learning objectives can be identified, for example: 'At the end of this session the learner should be able to/know about/describe . . .'. It is also important to specify what performance standards may be required, e.g. is the learner expected to be completely proficient, or to be more skilled than before the learning/training but still likely to make some mistakes? Three other issues are worth considering:
1. What will the learners expect to achieve from the learning event?
2. How will the learning be transferred to the work context?
3. How will you evaluate whether learning is being used?

Reflecting on these will help in the development of learning content that is designed to fill the learning needs identified and will point to the most appropriate method for delivering this learning. Several of the more commonly used L&D methods are presented in Table 9.4 and, while this table is not exhaustive, it does highlight key characteristics of each approach that merit some consideration.

Table 9.4 Learning, training and development methods

Method	Advantages	Disadvantages
On-the-Job Methods Sitting by Nellie; learn job from co-worker	Inexpensive; natural learning; high transfer of learning;	May pick up bad habits; often time-consuming; feedback may not be supportive/constructive

Method	Advantages	Disadvantages
On-the-Job Methods		
Coaching; supervisor guides and develops employee	Job relevant; facilitates succession planning and employee relations	Adversely affected by time constraints and work pressures; individual attention may be limited
Mentoring; manager guides, counsels and encourages development	Flexible; useful for socialisation, succession planning and management development	Contact may be infrequent; manager may not have the required mentoring skills or be committed to the process
Job rotation; range of placements within company	Relatively inexpensive; provides exposure to many situations; facilitates inter-departmental relations	May be unsettling; may lack direction; may be inconsistent; difficult to monitor
In-house courses	Can be tailored to meet specific organisational needs; range of techniques, i.e cases, projects etc. can be based on real problems	High opportunity costs due to absence from work; participation may be quota based; can become an exercise in head count, i.e. quantity vs. quality of courses
Off-the-Job Methods		
External courses educational/skills-based	Exposure to broader range of knowledge and views; promotes networking; useful for specialised knowledge/skills acquisition	Learning transfer may be difficult; can be very expensive and time-consuming; may raise employee expectations
Workshops, active discussion	Particularly suitable for managers; group-based approach facilitates problem solving; high learning transfer	Requires advance notification and preparation by participants; may be difficult to manage
Computer-based training	Individually focused; self-paced learning; performance is easily monitored; large numbers can be readily trained	Expensive to design; some employees may have a 'phobia' about computers; learning situation is contrived
Open/distant learning	Facilitates career development; useful for self-motivated employees; participants direct pace of learning	Very expensive; high drop-out rate; time-consuming; can be difficult to balance workload and learning
External placements	Provides useful external perceptions; builds external networks; facilitates attitudinal change	Learning transfer may be limited; can be very costly; may be perceived as a 'junket'; difficult to manage and control learning

Source: Adapted from Garavan *et al.* (1995) and Gunnigle and Flood (1990).

Recent developments in technology have had a significant influence on L&D and we are increasingly witnessing the growth of e-learning as a feature of learning design. In essence, e-learning involves delivering learning material electronically through the use of interactive multimedia and often via the Internet, through a web browser. E-learning approaches enable participants to undertake courses at their own pace and at their location of choice, thus offering greater flexibility both to the learner and to the organisation. To ensure greater consideration of factors such as learner support, learning style variations, and particularly the social dimension of learning and sharing knowledge, a blended training approach combining elements of electronic/online and face-to-face is becoming increasingly popular.

The choice of learning method is an important one since it can significantly impact the extent to which any useful learning actually occurs. However, for a variety of reasons, in many organisations the learning method is chosen even before the individual participants are identified. While this may not cause undue concern in some quarters, problems can arise (and the net effect of the learning investment is reduced) when the particular methods chosen are inconsistent with the learning styles and preferences of the trainees. It is important, therefore, to at least give some thought to how individuals do learn, and especially how adults learn best in a work environment (which is, after all, the kind of learning that most concerns organisations).

TRANSFER OF LEARNING

The term 'learning transfer' refers to the extent to which knowledge, skills and abilities acquired during a learning/training session are applied to the actual work situation or to the learning of a new, but related, skill. We can think of transfer in two particular ways.
1. *Lateral transfer* describes the situation where the additional knowledge or skills are building upon existing skills and abilities in the job. In this situation, the learning transfer should be relatively easy since the learner is able to apply what has been learned in training across to their job.
2. *Vertical transfer* is where learners are required to perform in a more effective way, based on earlier training on another task – in other words the learning is accumulating and learners become progressively more effective. Development opportunities in organisations are based on the presumption that learning will be vertically transferred to new roles.

The rate of both lateral and vertical transfer can be variable, however. If the learning represents something new for the employee, and requires a lot of change in what their job entails, or how they do their job, then it is more difficult to transfer and embed.

In some circumstances limited, if any, transfer occurs and this may be as a result of past learning experiences that contradict present practice, or perhaps the learning experience creates inhibitions that impede the acquisition of new skills. An illustration of the former might be where an individual who learns to drive on one side of the road might find it difficult to drive on the opposite side while abroad – and so 'reverts' to earlier behaviour at times, perhaps when they are distracted or stressed. In terms of the latter limit, the particular choice of learning method, style of trainer/facilitation, or indeed the learning situation might, individually or in combination, serve to inhibit the learning process and consequently result in negative learning transfer.

Specific organisational factors can affect learning outcome expectations and the learning transfer. Of particular note is the organisation's pay and promotion policies. Pay/promotions may/may not be perceived as tangible benefit arising from participating in a learning event. Bandura (1986) suggests that learners may believe that they are capable of performing a specific behaviour, but may choose not to do so because they believe it will have little or no effect on their status in the organisation. Both peer group influence and supervisory support are likely to impact the likelihood of learning transfer. Peer interaction can provide positive support and reinforcement not only for learning but also for the application of learning to the job. Good supervisory support increases learner outcome expectations that the learning skills will be valued by the organisation.

We can see that transfer of learning is a critical issue for organisations, since it provides the visible reason for investment in learning and development. However, it should not be considered in isolation of the needs analysis process, and specifically the environment for learning that determines whether learning actually gets used.

EVALUATION OF LEARNING

Evaluation represents the final stage in the L&D process and, while difficult to measure, it does provide information that is critical for effective organisational functioning. Evaluation ensures that control is maintained over the learning process. It allows the organisation to see the impact of any learning, training and development investment, i.e. the cost/benefit ratio to the organisation, as well as the value of the improved performance of those who have undertaken training. Lack of evaluation can result in inappropriate training that is wasteful of both financial and human resources. The difficulty for most organisations, however, lies in identifying a set of measurable criteria that can facilitate the effective evaluation of L&D interventions. This is particularly the case where many of the perceived key benefits of L&D, such as improved morale, increased job satisfaction and improved employee relations, are, by their very nature, difficult to quantify.

Easterby-Smith (1986) outlines three general purposes of learning/training evaluation:
- Summative – testing to determine whether learning was effective and achieved its objectives.
- Formative – qualitative analysis of training as it is occurring, to determine whether improvements or adjustments are required.
- Learning – assessing the extent to which the trainee can transfer the learning acquired back to his/her job performance.

Evaluation requires some sort of systematic measurement of established objectives and both Kirkpatrick (1959) and later Hamblin (1974) propose that learning evaluation can be considered at different levels in the organisation. Their models propose a hierarchy of evaluation levels, where each level requires a different evaluation strategy and is seen as a measure of the progressive transfer and application of training content (see Table 9.5).

Table 9.5 Levels of learning/training evaluation

Level	Description	Methods	Assessment
1. Reaction	Seeks opinions of trainees	Questionnaires at end of training	Easy to collect; subjective; does not evaluate learning or learning transfer
2. Learning	Seeks knowledge, principles and facts learned by trainees before training	Tests, exams, projects, after training is completed	Evaluates level of learning; does not measure impact of learning on job performance
3. Behaviour	Seeks to determine positive changes in behaviour	Observation, measurement before start; after return to job	Objective assessment of impact of training on job performance; can be difficult to assess in some jobs
4. Results	Seeks to determine contribution to organisational objectives	General Indicators (profits, turnover etc.) Specific indicators (absenteeism, accidents)	Evaluates return on investment of training expenditure; difficult to quantify

Workplace L&D, however, is not solely limited to the provision of a number of formal training interventions. It is an ongoing process that spans the individual's lifelong learning experience within the organisation. Development is primarily concerned with developing capabilities and skills for future roles within the organisation, so it is closely related to succession planning and ensuring a vibrant internal labour market. This type of development is variously captured by the literatures on career development, management development and, more recently, subsumed under the term talent management.

We review these important issues in terms of how they impact an organisation's L&D orientation and provision in the next section.

TALENT MANAGEMENT: CAREER MANAGEMENT AND LEADERSHIP DEVELOPMENT

There is little doubt that both organisations and individuals are paying increasing attention to the concept of development across the career lifespan. McDonnell *et al.* (2017) note that manging talent is a popular focus for discussion and debate in both the academic and practitioner literatures. Talent management is used as a general umbrella term Cappelli and Keller (2014) for workforce planning, succession planning, employee development, and career management, or even HRM practices more generally. Gallardo-Gallardo

et al. (2013: 295) suggest that there are two ways of considering talent in organisations: inclusively or exclusively.
- The *inclusive approach* considers all employees to have strengths and capabilities that can potentially create added value for the organisation. Viewed this way – all employees are included in the organisation's talent pool.
- The *exclusive approach* considers that some employees are disproportionately more valuable to the organisation than others, and therefore they alone represent the talent pool that should be invested in.

This differentiation is not purely academic because the approach adopted by the organisation will determine who is afforded L&D opportunities beyond the training required to perform their current jobs. In the discussion on labour market differentiation (see Chapter 4), it was highlighted that segmented internal labour markets can result in different sets of benefits and opportunities for core or valuable employee groups.

The question therefore, is whether everyone is considered talented, or just some people!

CAREER DEVELOPMENT

The exclusive approach to talent management mirrors some of the thinking underpinning many of the traditional models of a career and a career pathway. This traditional career pattern tended to (and still does in many organisations) focus on upward movement through a hierarchy in one (or a small few) organisation/s, with the individual acquiring additional salary and managerial responsibilities along the way. This hierarchical career path is described (Greenhaus and Callanan, 1994; Adamson *et al.* 1998) as a logical sequence of work-related events and experiences, implying development in an upward trajectory. Objective (visible) career success meant reaching the top of the organisation, which reflected their view that the individual was 'valuable'. Individuals who were thus promoted and developed by the organisation were seen as critical resources to be retained.

Accelerated economic change, organisational de-layering and an increase in the use of outsourcing have, however, combined to challenge the traditional perceptions, not only of a job for life, but also of the existence of established, easily identifiable career paths within organisations (Cappelli 2008, Piore 2002, DiRenzo and Greenhaus 2011). The traditional view of a career as essentially managerially based, within a tall organisation hierarchy, and earned through (long) service within one organisation is no longer viable, or even desirable. More contemporary career theories including the boundaryless career (Arthur and Rousseau 1996), the protean career (Hall and Moss 1998) and the career concept model (Brousseau *et al.* 1996) all conceptualise a career as one that can span a variety of organisational settings, and representing, what Davies and Wilson (2002: 299) describe as, 'the long term accumulation of education, skills and experience that an individual sells to an employer or employers, to try to provide the lifestyle that he or she wants for himself or herself and dependents'.

A life cycle perspective is a useful means of looking at careers because it indicates how individuals prioritise different needs, concerns and aspirations as they progress through the various stages of their lives. Now, subjective career success can be as important as objective factors, and individuals prioritise or more highly value opportunities that are not necessarily associated with hierarchical progression, i.e. flexibility (time at work and place of work); better opportunity to balance work/personal lives; meaningful or challenging work; wellbeing and so forth. Greenhaus and Kossek (2014) highlight a number of particular features of the contemporary career and Al Ariss *et al.* (2014) predict trends in talent management that are summarised together below (see Figure 9.4).

Figure 9.4 Talent trends and contemporary careers

Talent trends (Al Ariss *et al.* 2014)
- Global abundance but local scarcity of talent.
- Fewer young people and more older people, many heading rapidly towards retirement.
- More differences across generations at work, as well as similarities (e.g. the need for respect, supportive bosses, and credible, trustworthy leaders).
- More diverse, remote, and virtual workforces with different attitudes toward work.
- New methods of working and new relationships between users and suppliers of talent.

Contemporary career perspectives (Greenhaus and Kossek 2014)
Employees are less likely to:
- Play out their careers in one, or a small number of, organization(s).
- Experience frequent upward mobility within an organization.
- Feel substantial job security.

Employees are more likely to:
- Adjust their timing of retirement to meet lifestyle needs.
- Seek reduced-workload arrangements.
- Telework.
- Make career decisions that accommodate their family or personal circumstances.

Source: Al Ariss, Cascio and Paauwe. (2014: 178); Greenhaus and Kossek (2014: 365) combined.

Careers are increasingly market based, with employees building their career portfolios across jobs, across organisations and across geographic boundaries. Short-term projects, virtual working and technology-enabled roles can create valuable opportunities for mobile individuals to develop tradeable competencies that are highly sought by organisations. Job-matching sites such as LinkedIn and Monster are changing and expanding the ways individuals look for work and companies identify and recruit talent. Independent workers are increasingly choosing to offer their services on digital platforms such as Upwork, Uber, and Etsy and, in the process, challenging conventional ideas about how and where work is undertaken. Such individuals 'sell' their labour to the highest bidder with no expectation of longer-term commitment to any one employer. This can seem like a 'win-win' for both parties. Faced with pressures to reduce costs and be leaner, organisations may be happy to forsake long-term relationships with their employees in favour of short-term more transaction-based ones and thus, buy rather than develop expensive talent. Cappelli and Keller (2014) note that there is some risk attached to this approach, as relying on external hiring to fill strategic jobs can leave employers at the mercy of the labour market, resulting in talent shortfalls and other costs whenever labour markets tighten.

LEADERSHIP DEVELOPMENT

Managerial competence is a central element of an organisation's talent management system and is long established as a means of leveraging organisational performance. Seminal work by Mintzberg (1973) revealed managerial work to be fragmented and disparate, conducted within complex social networks and with short time horizons. Management development was described by Mumford (1986) as an organisation's practice to improve managerial effectiveness, through planned and deliberate learning processes. While theories and models of leadership and management were conceived independently and considered autonomously of each other (and still are by many), there is some evidence that distinctions are blurring (Lunenberg 2011; McGiver et al. 2013). For example, Raelin (2016) suggests that the roles of management and leadership become functionally equivalent when we strip away the individualistic romanticism associated with the expression of leadership.

Leaders and managers are the face of the organisation for their employees. They are involved in daily social exchanges with their employees in which they enact the values and establish the cultural norms around performance and interaction. Their relationships with their employees affects perceptions of justice, satisfaction, support and community, and impacts work effort, performance and retention. The availability and development of managers and leaders, with the requisite combination of technical, social and emotional competencies, is critical for any organisation.

Two divergent approaches to the development of leaders and managers can be taken. The first approach views development as a highly-structured, top-down event, with a strong emphasis on formalised learning programmes and interventions through which all managers must progress in order to advance in their careers. Managers and leaders are identified early through the talent management system and are groomed for future roles within the organisation. A second alternative approach is rather more organic and places greater emphasis on self-development and learning through the everyday experience of managing, collaborating, problem-solving and emulating. Here development is a more iterative and less formalised process – it is still prioritised, though the mechanisms through with development occurs are more varied and broader based.

In an interesting feature in *Forbes* magazine (2012), Myatt argues for a greater focus on development initiatives for managers and suggests that the focus should move away from the notion of training managers for leadership positions and more towards coaching, mentoring and developing them (see Figure 9.5).

Hammond et al. (2017) propose a cross-domain leader development theory that suggests that leaders develop by making cross-domain connections and disconnections between different life roles that they occupy. For example, leaders who have responsible roles or positions in their local communities (in clubs/societies, on boards) can find that there is significant opportunity to leverage those experiences in their work roles, and vice versa. This suggests that leadership and management development is influenced by a variety of life experiences and roles that individuals occupy throughout their lifetime, and that this accumulation of experiences blends to shape the leader's identity and approach to work.

Figure 9.5 Differentiating leadership training from leadership development

Leadership training	Leadership development
Focuses on the present.	Focuses on the future.
Adheres to standards.	Focuses on maximizing potential.
Training is transactional.	Development is transformational.
Focuses on the role.	Focuses on the person.
Focuses on efficiency.	Focuses on effectiveness.
Focuses on problems.	Focuses on solutions.
Training is mechanical	Development is intellectual.
Focuses on the knowns.	Explores the unknowns.
Places people in a comfort zones.	Moves people beyond their comfort zones.
Training is finite.	Development is infinite.

Source: Myatt (2012, www.forbes.com) (Adapted).

MICRO LEVEL: INDIVIDUAL LEARNING AND DEVELOPMENT

Boud and Garrick (1999), in their thorough review of work-based learning, highlighted that learning has moved from the periphery to centre-stage in organisations and that there are few places left for employees at any level who do not continue to learn and improve their effectiveness throughout their working lives. They further suggested that there is no place for managers who do not appreciate their own vital role in fostering workplace learning

The field of individual psychology has informed much of what we know about individual learning. Early behavioural psychologists concentrated on cause–effect models of behaviour (stimulus–response), to demonstrate how learning can occur. Pavlov's experiments with dogs demonstrated how it was possible to prompt a reflexive, involuntary response through classic conditioning. Skinner's (1938) work focused on reinforcement (operant conditioning) and showed how more complex, voluntary behaviours could be shaped through the achievement of a desired reward, or the avoidance of an undesired punishment. In an organisational scenario, the use of praise and encouragement by trainers or line managers can be seen as examples of promoting operant learning. Further work by cognitive theorists focused on the 'thinking' part of human learning and is most closely associated with the process of experiential learning. Kolb's (1984) experiential learning cycle suggests that learning occurs in a sequential or cyclical manner (see Figure 9.6). We experience something new (concrete experience, i.e. new information or knowledge), we reflect on that new experience and try to make sense of it (reflection), we generalise about it (abstract conceptualisation, i.e. what would happen if . . .) and then we test it out (active experimentation, i.e. trying to do something new or adopting a different approach).

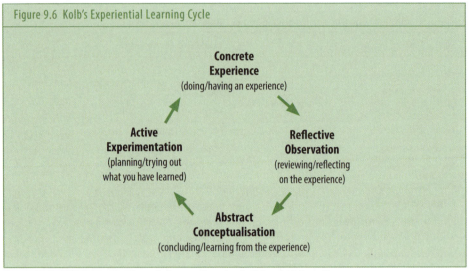

Figure 9.6 Kolb's Experiential Learning Cycle

Source: Kolb (1984) www.simplypsychology.org/learning-kolb.html (Adapted).

The result of this experimentation leads us back to the start of the cycle, where this new result represents the 'something new' or new experience that acts as a catalyst for further learning.

Experiential learning suggests that learners must have time to experiment and try out new ideas if meaningful learning is to take place, i.e. using practice or trial and error. Kolb further suggests that different forms of learning may be triggered at different stages, and outlines distinct learning styles that are associated with each stage in the experiential learning cycle (see Figure 9.7).

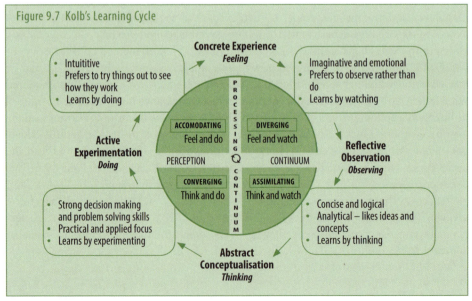

Figure 9.7 Kolb's Learning Cycle

Source: Kolb (1984) (Adapted).

Honey and Mumford (1986) built on Kolb's work and proposed four particular styles of learning that are in the general population. A summary of their work is presented in Table 9.6.

Table 9.6 Honey and Mumford's learning styles	
Learning Style	**Description**
Activist	Activists involve themselves fully and without bias in new experiences. They enjoy the here and now, and are happy to be dominated by immediate experiences. They are open-minded, not sceptical, and this tends to make them enthusiastic about anything new. Their philosophy is: 'I'll try anything once.' They tend to act first and consider the consequences afterwards and they tackle problems by brainstorming. As soon as the excitement from one activity has died down they are busy looking for the next. They tend to thrive on the challenge of new experiences but are bored with implementation and longer-term consolidation.
Theorist	Theorists adapt and integrate observations into complex but logically sound theories. They think problems through in a vertical, step-by-step logical way and assimilate disparate facts into coherent theories. They like to analyse and synthesise. They are keen on basic assumptions, principles, theories models and systems thinking. Their philosophy prizes rationality and logic: 'If its logical its good.' Questions they frequently ask are: 'Does it make sense?', 'How does this fit with that?' and 'What are the basic assumptions?' They tend to be detached, analytical and dedicated to rational objectivity rather than anything subjective or ambiguous. Their approach to problems is consistently logical. This is their 'mental set' and they rigidly reject anything that doesn't fit with it.
Pragmatist	Pragmatists are keen on trying out ideas, theories and techniques to see if they work in practice. They positively search out new ideas and take the first opportunity to experiment with applications. They are the sort of people who return from courses brimming with new ideas that they want to try out in practice. They like to get on with things and act quickly and confidently on ideas that attract them. They tend to be impatient with ruminating and open-ended discussions. They are essentially practical, down to earth people who like making practical decisions and solving problems. They respond to problems and opportunities 'as a challenge'. Their philosophy is: 'There is always a better way', and 'If it works it's good'.
Reflector	Reflectors like to stand back to ponder experiences and observe them from many different perspectives. They collect data, both first hand and from others, and prefer to think about it thoroughly before coming to a conclusion. Their philosophy is to be cautious so they tend to postpone reaching definitive conclusions for as long as possible, until they have considered all possible angles. They prefer to take a back seat in meetings and discussions and enjoy observing other people in action. They listen to others and get the drift of the discussion before making their own points. When they act, it is part of a wide picture which includes the past as well as the present and others' observations, as well as their own.

Source: Honey and Mumford (1982) *The Manual of Learning Styles.*

More recently Fleming and Mills (1992) proposed the VARK model of learning that describe Visual, Aural, Read/write and Kinaesthetic sensory modalities or preferences that are used for learning information.
- Visual (V) learners prefer to take in information through maps, diagrams, charts, graphs, and other symbols.
- *Aural (A)* learners prefer information that is heard or spoken either through lecture, discussion, or conversation (including learning aloud).
- *Read/write (R)* learners prefer information displayed as words, so are most comfortable with reading and writing in all its forms.
- *Kinaesthetic (K)* learners prefer to be informed by experience and practice through demonstrations, simulations, videos and movies of 'real' things, as well as case studies, practice and applications.

Fleming and Mills add that there are seldom instances where one mode alone is used and that all learners combine modes of learning, but just have a stronger preference for one over the others.

Bandura (1986) introduced a social dimension to learning and suggested that many of our experiences are picked up, either directly or indirectly, through observing other people. This social aspect to learning points to the necessity to have a supportive learning environment, which in a work situation would include superior, leader or work colleagues, or (outside work) friends and family.

Each of these theories of learning provides important starting points for L&D systems. If we understand how individuals learn, we can build this into how learning/training courses and development programmes are designed and delivered. In this context of workplace learning, Revans's (1982) ideas on adult learning are worth noting. He suggests that adult learning is *most effective* where adults (learners):

1. Are *motivated* to learn of their own volition and not solely at the will of others – it must be something they want to achieve for themselves, rather than just something that they are required to undertake.
2. Can *identify* themselves with others who may not only share their needs, but who may also satisfy some of these needs – they seek support from their peers and colleagues and learn more effectively with this group support.
3. Can *practice* any new learning in actions of their own design – learning should be more than the acquiring of information but should involve some action where they can see if their learning actually works.
4. Can, within a reasonable lapse of time, attain first-hand knowledge of the results of their trials – they receive *feedback* on their performance which reinforces and further directs the learning.

Arising from much of the theory of individual learning, it is possible to isolate a number of key learning principles that can be applied to the design and delivery of L&D activities and events at work.
- *Motivation to learn* – the employee must want to learn and thus, in order to be committed to the process, must perceive that the learning event will result in the achievement of certain desired goals. There must be some tangible reward, e.g. to be better at performing current job, or more employable for a better job.

- *Involvement of the learner* – the training or learning should be seen as an active rather than a passive process which the individual learner 'owns'. Getting individuals involved in discussing the course content, expectations about what they hope to achieve from it, and seeking opinions and contributions throughout can make the learning more understandable. If they are actively involved in coming up with solutions to problems or thinking up ideas, the learning is more easily internalised.
- *Meaningfulness of the material* – the nature of the training/learning intervention must be seen to be relevant to the employee's work, i.e. it must be something that s/he can use now or will be able to use at some time in the future. Where learning is off-the-job, the use of work problems and case study workshops are a useful means of creating ownership of learning.
- *Reinforcement of learning* – employees should be given an opportunity to practise what they have learned. This facilitates continuous improvement and employees can engage in goal setting to heighten the learning process. In tandem with this, the learning event must allow employees sufficient time both to absorb the material and to practise or test new knowledge and skills.
- *Feedback* – learners need regular and timely feedback on their performance. This feedback should be both realistic and constructive if it is to reinforce desired behaviour, or encourage further learning.
- *Communities of practice* – communities of practice evolve as learners develop a shared history, as well as sets of core values, beliefs, ways of talking and ways of doing things. Since individuals both shape and are shaped by their social contexts, they bring a variety of knowledge, experience and insights to the workplace and they actively learn from each other. They learn to construct shared understandings and can rely on each other for social support. Creating an environment where knowledge is shared and new learning is exchanged can be a powerful mechanism to facilitate and reinforce a workplace learning culture.

There is a danger here of presenting an over-simplification of the learning process. Although it is argued that learning is as natural as breathing, it is also an inherently complex process, and it requires a lot of effort. Work-based learning is particularly complex since individuals at work do not represent an homogenous group. They may share some common attributes, and work within a shared culture, but essentially employees represent a diverse group of individuals who just happen to be working in the same organisation. As such, each individual brings a unique set of experiences and expectations to the learning event that can shape the motivation for learning, the level of learning that takes place and the degree to which the learning becomes a significant aspect of subsequent behaviour.

A number of factors have been found to influence learning including: the employee's age (which affects attitudes, motivations and interests); his/her levels of intelligence and ability (affects preferences for structured vs. unstructured learning events); his/her background and psychological disposition (predetermined perceptions of the value of learning, previous experiences of training/schooling, concerns or anxieties surrounding learning); his/her learning style and preference (for reflective, practical or conceptual approaches); and finally his/her trainability or motivation to learn (affects aptitude for improved performance and expectations of learning outcomes).

An understanding of learning styles is particularly important since the learning/training method chosen by an organisation must take into account the particular learning preferences expressed by individual employees. For example, some individuals may learn more effectively in a structured learning/training environment using concrete examples that they can relate to, whereas others might prefer a more informal, conceptual framework that draws on various scenarios that are not necessarily work-based. Mumford (1986) suggests that a failure to take account of different learning styles can have seriously negative implications for the training process, while Garavan et al. (1995) note that:

1. By the time we reach adulthood, each of us has developed our own method of learning, reflected in a unique and well-established learning style.
2. Trainers also have well-established learning styles and preferences.
3. The more compatible the style of learning with the approach to training adopted, the more likely it is that a positive learning experience will occur.

When deciding on the most appropriate method to use, organisations should take into account the principles of learning discussed earlier, the needs of the employees to be trained, the logistics of L&D that affect every organisation, including available budget, time and expertise resources, physical resources and the number of people requiring L&D. All learning methods have their own particular strengths and can be modified to suit the organisation's requirements. The most important criterion in determining the choice of method is the extent to which it meets the particular objectives that have been established. Once the learning method and targeted learners/trainees have been identified, the organisation then delivers the learning event. Garavan et al. (2003) provide extensive guidelines and tips on how to deliver an effective learning activity, including:

- Allow sufficient time both for preparation and for delivery.
- Introduce the event – identify learning objectives and learners' objectives, and use an 'icebreaker' to help set the tone.
- Alternate theory/information with skill/practice sessions and give constructive feedback throughout.
- Conclude with a review or summary of what has been achieved and pointers for applying the learning in their jobs.

L&D PRACTICES IN IRELAND

The final section of this chapter reviews some evidence on the nature of L&D practices in Ireland. We have seen how institutional actors such as the national educational system, professional associations, government interventions in labour market skill formation and trade unions shape the environment within which organisations do business and ultimately impact on the nature of their L&D activities. The challenge facing Irish organisations, as with their counterparts globally, is to find a way of ensuring that the calibre of their human resources is sufficient to meet the increasing demands being placed on them by market forces.

Data from the 2010 Cranet Ireland/University of Limerick Kemmy Business School national survey of HRM practices provides an important longitudinal overview of L&D

in organisations in Ireland. Earlier data from successive CIPD (Ireland)-sponsored surveys (Heraty and Garavan 2001; Garavan et al. 2003) indicated that the average number of days' training per category of employee was close to 5.5 days per year. Data from the Cranet Ireland 2010 survey suggest that this figure improved somewhat in the intervening years. What is interesting to note is that the gap between employee categories has closed considerably – in earlier rounds of the Cranet survey (1992–2000), it was reported that managerial grades were more likely to receive a greater number of days' training than other grades. Although not a big increase, the impression is that learning and training have remained important considerations during the first two decades of the 2000s, and this may again reflect the increased focus through the decade on sustainable growth through human capital investment (at national and OECD levels).

Despite the level of investment in L&D, it is still surprising to note that just over half of respondents (56.3 per cent) systematically evaluate its effectiveness. This figure is considerably lower than the one reported in the CIPD (Ireland) surveys 2001 and 2003 (where the comparable figure was closer to 75 per cent). The methods used to evaluate effectiveness remain largely unchanged in recent years. In this respect, the data show that the same mix of formal and informal methods tend to be used, although here again we find that the use of more rigorous evaluation techniques such as measured job performance is less pronounced. Evaluation is difficult, as discussed earlier, and this may reflect the fact that organisations are content to focus on more easily quantifiable metrics such as days' training received (which can hardly be counted as evaluation in any real sense), or meeting learning/training objectives. However, feedback from employees and line managers is seen as an important measure of a programme's effectiveness and arguably feedback from these sources is important since it feeds directly into provision. Certification of knowledge and skills is important in Ireland today, and employees are taking an increasing role in deciding the type of learning and training activities they wish to engage in – and focusing increasingly on developing broad sets of knowledge and skills that ensure their employability in the general labour market.

The Management Development Council (MDC) report (2010) on the state of management development in Ireland argued that improving managerial capability can yield significant returns, in terms of better decision-making, better business survival rates and a more skilled workforce. Furthermore, data from McKinsey & Co (2009), comparing management development practices in fourteen countries, suggested that Ireland's performance in management development was lower than it needed to be, as on a range of indicators it averaged between tenth and twelfth among the fourteen countries reviewed.

The latest CIPD survey of HR practice in Ireland (Connaughton and Staunton 2017) reports more positively on the state of L&D in Irish-based organisations. Some 59 per cent of respondents identified talent management as a top priority over the next two years, with some 78 per cent of organisations experiencing skills shortages in the last twelve months. Leadership development was prioritised by just over half of the respondents (51 per cent). In an effort to maintain their talent pool, some 63 per cent of respondents reported up-skilling the current workforce and 57 per cent were increasing the number of development opportunities for employees. The average spend on L&D activities was reported at 3.8 per cent of payroll, with interventions focusing on culture change, systems development/training, technical skills, coaching and mentoring, and performance enhancement.

Finally, the *Deloitte* report (2017) documents the results of a survey on global human capital trends of over 10,000 managers across 140 countries (including Ireland). The data report highly similar trends across countries and provide an interesting perspective on L&D. For example, it identifies the ability to learn and progress as one of the key drivers of a company's employment brand, with more than 80 per cent of the respondents prioritising learning and talent management issues for the next couple of years (see Figure 9.8).

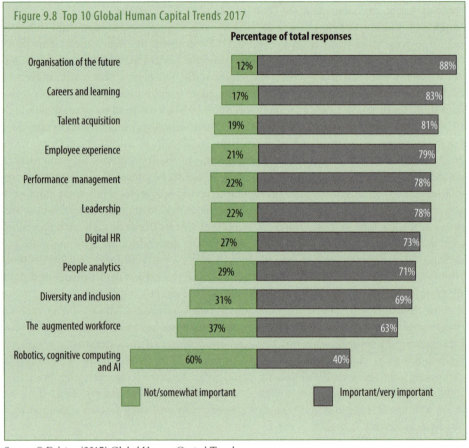

Source: © *Deloitte* (2017) Global Human Capital Trends.

This prioritising of L&D echoes data from Smith and Turner (2016) who reported that some 42 per cent of millennials in their study signalled intentions to leave their employment because they felt they were not learning fast enough. The report further indicates that organisations are shifting to flexible, open career models that offer enriching assignments, projects, and experiences, rather than a static career progression, echoing some of the earlier discussions about changing career pathways.

Interestingly, and somewhat alarmingly for organisations, 42 per cent of surveyed respondents now believe their organisation's employees will have careers that span five years or less. This finding gives added impetus to the continued investment in the internal labour market, and endorses remarks by Gratton and Scott (2016) on how careers need to be reimagined.

In summary, this chapter has presented a multi-level perspective on workplace learning and development to illustrate some of the key drivers and conditions that affect L&D priorities and activities. In so doing, we have argued that, while L&D is presented in a systematic and cyclical nature here, the reality of organisational life means that events rarely run exactly to plan. In fact, given the magnitude of dynamic change in evidence in markets and systems globally, combined with reconceptualisations of careers in organisations, we can see how the landscape of L&D is continually shifting. We would argue, however, that this brings additional requirements, and opportunities, for a strategic focus on L&D, to ensure that the internal talent pool remains competitive and can be used to leverage efficiency gains for the organisation.

10
Employment Relations: Institutions and Actors

'Employment relations is a compelling and complex area of study which involves the interaction of employees, employers, trade unions and government on a regular basis' (Rose 2008: 3). Employment relations disputes, pay talks and legislation governing employment matters have all received vast media attention in the recent past. To understand the nature and significance of what was traditionally called 'industrial relations', but now commonly termed 'employment relations', it is important to understand its historical context (see Chapter 2) and theoretical underpinning. Managing employment relations is one of the most important aspects of the broader HR role in organisations.

This chapter explores the nature of employment relations, describes the Irish institutional context and considers the parties involved in employment relations interactions. It provides a summary overview of relevant legislation pertaining to aspects of employment relations in Ireland but it is worth noting that this chapter is not a legal interpretation thereof. Readers requiring more comprehensive insights can refer to Forde and Byrne (2009), Daly and Doherty (2010), Wallace *et al.* (2013), the relevant Act(s) and/or the Department of Jobs, Enterprise and Innovation. Particular focus in this chapter is also placed on the role of trade unions and state institutions in employment relations. The role of employers and employer organisations is discussed in Chapter 11.

As mentioned above, discourse in this field has traditionally focused on *industrial relations*, a term generally taken to infer a collective approach to managing the employer–employee relations in industrial settings, with emphasis on formal regulation through collective bargaining between *organised* employees and employers. This perspective remains significant as employers, trade unions and government seek to develop processes and agreements at various levels (e.g. enterprise, sectoral or national). However, changes in industrial structure encompassing ever-increasing employment in the services sector, together with the widespread emergence of non-union approaches, now place greater emphasis on (unorganised) employees interacting with employers on an individual as opposed to a collective basis. The concept of *employment relations* (ER) is used here as a generic term to include all employer, employee and state interactions on employment, matters across all sectors of employment. It focuses on the nature of the relationship between the parties to the labour process, embraces both collectivist and individualist approaches and encapsulates state, organisational and intermediary-level arrangements. ER primarily involves the following issues:
- Collective bargaining.
- Communications policy and practice.

- Employee involvement and participation.
- Grievance handling.
- Discipline administration.
- Managing change.
- Aspects of social responsibility.

A critical initial step in grappling with the study of ER in Ireland is an appreciation of the range and nature of the actors and institutions involved in our ER 'system'. The key parties or 'actors' involved in ER include *inter alia* individual workers, trade unions, worker representatives, employers, managers, government and government agencies. The interaction of these parties will be heavily influenced by context, so that economic circumstances, historical and political factors, and developments in technology and markets significantly impact ER practice. Figure 10.1 outlines the main parties involved in ER. The central parties are employers and employees, both of whom may seek to form and use associations to represent their interests (e.g. employer associations and trade unions). The state may also play an important role, particularly in regard to legislation and the provision of conflict resolution agencies.

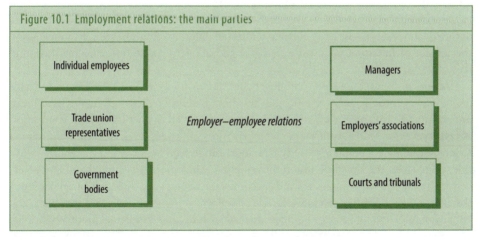

Figure 10.1 Employment relations: the main parties

Source: Gunnigle, Garavan and Fitzgerald (1992).

The respective roles of trade unions and the state are reviewed below, while the role of employers and employer associations is considered in the next chapter.

TRADE UNIONS

As we saw in Chapter 2, the historical development of HRM is inextricably linked to the growth of organised labour through the trade union movement. Indeed, there is evidence of early combinations of workers (mostly craft workers) in Ireland from the late seventeenth and early eighteenth century (O'Connor 1992).

However, the essence of modern trade unionism has its roots in the 'factory system' and the dramatic changes brought about by the Industrial Revolution, beginning in Britain in the eighteenth century and later spreading to Europe and North America. The growth of the factory system heralded a change from a largely peasant society, based on agriculture and craft production, to an industry-based society characterised by new social divisions, where people worked together in much larger numbers and relied on wages for their existence. In the face of often authoritarian management styles and poor working conditions, these new factory workers were poorly positioned, lacking economic or political power. It was not until the growth of organised labour, through the trade union movement, that employee concerns could command the attention of factory owners and management.

Despite Ireland's relatively recent history of industrialisation, trade unions were well established in many industries in Dublin, Belfast and Cork by the early 1900s (McNamara et al. 1988). The development of trade unionism in Britain profoundly influenced events in Ireland. The passing of the *Trade Disputes Act 1906*, often referred to as the 'Bill of Rights for Workers', provided immunity for unions and their members from the offence of civil conspiracy and from defined common law liabilities, and reinforced protection for peaceful picketing (Wallace et al. 2013). However these immunities and protections were only available where trade unions and their members were 'acting in contemplation or furtherance of a *trade dispute*' (*Industrial Relations Act 1990*, [emphasis added]). This renders the definition and understanding of what constitutes a 'trade dispute' critical in determining whether the worker and trade unions involved enjoyed the immunities outlined above. This issue is further addressed later in this chapter, in considering the impact of *Industrial Relations Acts 2000* and *2004* on trade union recognition and collective bargaining.

Increased conflict between employer and trade union interests characterised this period and eventually came to a head in the 1913 Dublin Lockout (cf. Yeates 2000). An important effect of this turbulent period was that it served to encourage the organisation of employees into trade unions and employers into employers' associations. It also served to increase employer emphasis on ER as an increasingly significant aspect of management's role. Over time, the fledgling union movement was reluctantly accepted and employers began to take the initial steps towards accommodating its role. This was often achieved through multi-employer bargaining via employers' associations, and through the employment of 'labour relations officers' to deal with ER and 'personnel' in organisations.

TRADE UNION OBJECTIVES AND LEGAL STATUS

Essentially unions are organisations which aim to unite workers with common interests, while seeking to define those interests, express them, safeguard and advance them through their interactions (particularly collective bargaining) with individual employers, employer associations, government, government agencies and other parties. A trade union's basic strength rests in its ability to organise and unite workers. Through joining trade unions, pluralists would argue that workers provide themselves with the collective means to redress the imbalance in bargaining power that is otherwise perceived to exist between individual workers and employers. While workers may join trade unions for numerous reasons, the most common include a desire to influence pay movement, for protection against management actions and because of an ideological belief in the role that trade unions play in a democratic society (see Turner et al. 2013 for greater discussion).

The Webbs (1920: 1), who wrote the first comprehensive history of trade unions and early collective bargaining, came up with what was a long accepted definition of a trade union as 'a continuous association of wage earners with the objective of improving or maintaining conditions of employment.' Although this definition accurately embraces the workplace role of trade unions, it does not capture their broader societal role in advancing worker interests in the political domain (Salamon 2008). Thus, trade unions may be more appropriately viewed as permanent associations of organised employees whose primary objectives are to:

- Replace individual bargaining by collective bargaining, thereby redressing the balance of bargaining power in favour of employees and reducing management prerogative in employment-related matters.
- Achieve satisfactory levels of pay and conditions of employment and provide members with a range of services.
- Facilitate the development of a political system where worker interests have impact on political decisions, resulting in an economic and social framework which reflects the interests of wage earners.

The main legislation dealing with the formation and operation of trade unions in Ireland is the *Trade Union Acts of 1941 and 1971* and the *Industrial Relations Act 1990*. Trade unions are defined under the *Trade Union Act 1941* as bodies carrying on negotiations for fixing wages or other conditions of employment. This legal definition of trade unions is very broad ranging and extends to employer organisations (Kerr and Whyte 1985). The legislation stipulates that, apart from certain 'excepted' bodies, only 'authorised' trade unions, holding negotiating licenses, are permitted to engage in collective bargaining on pay and working conditions. The legislation also specifies the conditions that a trade union must fulfil before it will be issued with such a licence. A trade union may only be granted a negotiating licence when it registers with the Registrar of Friendly Societies and meets specified criteria, particularly the following:

- At least eighteen months before the date of application for a licence it notifies its intention to make an application to the Minister for Enterprise, Trade and Innovation*, *Irish Congress of Trade Unions* (ICTU) and any trade union of which any members of the applicant trade union are members, and it publishes in at least one daily newspaper a notice of its intention to make an application in the format prescribed in the *Trade Union Act 1971* (Notice of Intention to apply for Negotiation Licence) Regulations, 1972, SI No. 158 of 1972.
- It satisfies the relevant Minister that, both at the date of its application and over the eighteen-month period before the date of its application, it had not less than 1,000 members resident in the state.
- It deposits and keeps on deposit with the High Court, for the eighteen months before the date of its application, a sum ranging from €25,394.76 to €76,184.28 depending on membership numbers as prescribed in the *Industrial Relations Act 1990*, or such sum as the relevant Minister may determine if it is a trade union which has been formed wholly or mainly from two or more trade unions which have amalgamated

---

* The relevant Department is now the Department of Jobs, Enterprise and Innovation, established in 2011. For convenience, we use the terms 'relevant Minister' and 'relevant Department' in the remainder of this text.

and each of which, immediately before the amalgamation, had been the holder of a Negotiation Licence. (It should be noted that financial deposits are not required when a new trade union is formed as a result of the amalgamation of two or more unions. This is in line with a policy orientation of encouraging and facilitating trade union mergers or amalgamations.)

The legislation also provides for the operation of a number of 'excepted' bodies. These excepted bodies are not required to hold a negotiating license to engage in collective bargaining. They include workplace ('staff' or 'house') associations and unions, some civil service associations and teachers' associations (ibid). The most common form of an excepted body would the staff association of a company or organisation. Examples of excepted bodies include the *Irish Hospital Consultants Association* and the *Irish Dental Association*. In Section 6 of the Act of 1941, the expression 'excepted body' 'shall include a body, all the members of which are employed by the same employer and which carries on negotiations for the fixing of the wages or other conditions of employment of its own members (but of no other employees).' A number of organisations which now hold a negotiation licence and operate as a trade union were originally 'excepted bodies', such as the *Irish Nurses Organisation*. The major pieces of legislation governing trade union operation are the *Industrial Relations Acts 1990/2001/2004/2015* and some of their main provisions are considered later in this chapter.

TRADE UNION TYPES

Irish trade unions are normally organised on an occupational basis, i.e. workers tend to join a particular union because of the particular job or trade in which they are employed. Trade unions in Ireland have traditionally being grouped into three broad categories: craft unions; general unions; and white-collar unions. However, it should be noted that it is extremely difficult to categorise unions as 'pure' craft, general or white-collar since many unions deviate on some dimension from a tight definition of their union category. For example, general unions may have white-collar and craft workers in membership, while 'craft' unions may not necessarily operate an 'exclusive' membership system based on the completion of a recognised apprenticeship programme. However, the craft, general, white-collar categorisation provides a convenient yardstick with which to analyse Irish trade unions, as discussed below.

Craft Unions

Craft unions cater for workers who possess a particular skill in a trade where entry is restricted to workers who have completed a prescribed apprenticeship programme or equivalent. Prominent examples of occupational categories which are organised in craft unions are electricians and fitters. Craft unions probably represent the earliest form of union organisation and have their origins in the early unions and combinations that emerged in Britain at the start of the nineteenth century. These craft unions aimed to defend the wages, jobs and working practices of their members. They believed that keeping the supply of labour scarce in that trade offered the greatest strength: controlling entry to the trade was vitally important and often seen as more useful than strike action. These 'model' unions, as they became known, confined their membership to skilled categories such as printers and carpenters who had served a recognised apprenticeship in their particular trade. The first British craft union to organise in Ireland was the *Amalgamated Society of Engineers*, which established branches in the early 1850s (Boyd 1972). While the early craft unions represented a comparatively small proportion of the labour force, the organisation of workers into craft unions was critical in establishing trade unions as legitimate institutions representing worker interests to employers and government.

Craft unions have traditionally sought to protect their trades by ensuring that only full members of the relevant craft union were allowed to carry out particular types of skilled work. This is the basis of the concept of 'demarcation', which relates to the delineation of skilled work among different craft categories. Traditionally, it is suggested that craft unions, by controlling entry to the craft, held considerable bargaining power. This strategy is often criticised as being a source of restrictive work practices and demarcation disputes. Increased mechanisation and consequent de-skilling has had a detrimental impact on the membership and power of craft unions. Indeed some older craft unions have ceased to exist, as their traditional craft was rendered obsolete by developments in technology and work practices.

However, craft unions remain an important part of Ireland's ER landscape. Many of these operate primarily in the construction sector, for example the *Union of Construction Allied Trades and Technicians* (UCATT). UCATT is a UK-based union for construction workers (mainly carpenters, painters and allied trades), representing approximately 15,000 members in Ireland and 120,000 in the UK. Figures from the ICTU suggest that the *Technical, Electrical and Engineering Union* (TEEU) is the country's largest craft union, with over 40,000 members in manufacturing, construction, energy, engineering and electrical contracting. Other examples of primarily craft unions include the *Building and Allied Trades' Union* (BATU), the *Operative Plasterers and Allied Trades Society of Ireland* (OPATSI) and the *National Union of Sheet Metal Workers of Ireland*.

General Unions

In contrast to the craft unions' restrictive recruitment strategies, general trade unions adopt a more open approach, taking into membership all categories of worker, broadly regardless of skill or industry. Despite this open recruitment approach, however, general unions have traditionally catered for semi-skilled and unskilled workers. In more recent years, some general unions have attracted many white-collar and some craft categories into membership.

The origins of general trade unions are rooted in the increased number of unskilled or general workers employed in the large factories and other major organisations that characterised late nineteenth- and early twentieth-century Britain. These new unions tended to be more militant than the more traditional craft unions of the period. They initially organised categories such as general labourers and dock workers and were noted for both their aggressive bargaining style in attempting to improve pay and working conditions for their members, and for their greater political consciousness in attempting to advance working-class interests.

Whereas general unions catering for unskilled workers such as labourers and dockers existed in Ireland from the 1860s, it was not until the early 1900s that they came to play a more active role in Irish industrial and political life. A major development was the establishment of the Irish Transport and General Workers Union (ITGWU), led by Jim Larkin, in 1909. The ITGWU and some other general unions organised categories such as dockers, carters and railway workers and became engaged in a series of disputes, culminating in the 1913 Dublin Lockout. While this dispute initially dealt a severe blow to the general unions, they slowly recovered and reorganised, so much so that by the early 1920s membership had recovered dramatically (Boyd 1972).

General unions are typically the largest union types in Ireland and are commonly found in all types of organisation and industrial sector. The best-known general union in Ireland is SIPTU (*Services, Industrial, Professional and Technical Union*), with approximately 200,000 members in Ireland. This makes SIPTU the country's largest union, accounting for over 30 per cent of the ICTU. SIPTU was created in 1990 as a result of the merger of the then two largest trade unions in the country, ITGWU and the *Federated Workers Union of Ireland* (FWUI).

Other prominent examples of general unions in Ireland are *Mandate* (representing retail, bar and administrative workers) and *UNITE*, another UK-based union with significant membership in Ireland. However, like SIPTU, UNITE also represents large numbers of white-collar workers, a by-product of previous mergers or amalgamations with unions such as *AMICUS* and its predecessor, the *Manufacturing Science and Finance Union* (MSF), both of whom catered for white-collar workers (see below).

White-Collar Unions

White-collar unions cater primarily for professional, supervisory, technical, clerical and managerial categories and experienced significant growth in membership from the late 1960s. In the period 1966–76, white-collar unions increased their membership by 71 per cent, compared with an overall growth in union membership of 30 per cent over that same ten years (Roche and Larragy 1989). Indeed, Donaghey and Teague (2007) argue that white-collar occupations were the most likely to be unionised. The dramatic growth in employment in the services sector (particularly the public sector) was a significant factor contributing to increased white-collar unionisation. However, Kelly (1975) identified other factors that served to increase the propensity of white-collar workers to unionise. In particular, he noted the impact of negative circumstances at work, especially poor job design and quality of working life as important factors encouraging white-collar unionisation. One can also point to changing attitudes of white-collar workers to trade unions, a development accelerated by the emergence of unions designed to cater for the specific needs of white-collar workers. The ITGWU became the first general union to explicitly develop a white-collar section under former TD and Labour Party leader, Pat Rabbitte. Another contributory factor in greater white-collar unionisation was the significant advances in pay and conditions secured by so-called 'blue-collar' unions (i.e. those catering for manual workers), which encouraged hitherto more conservative white-collar workers to unionise. White-collar categories thus represented a relatively 'greenfield' opportunity for union membership drives in the 1960s and 1970s.

In evaluating union membership statistics it is often difficult to differentiate between white-collar and blue-collar workers. However, the major areas of concentration of white-collar workers are the public sector and financial and professional services. Recent figures from the ICTU suggest that the largest public sector unions are:
- Irish Municipal Public and Civil Service Union (IMPACT) – 64,000 members.
- Communications Workers' Union (CWU) – 14,000 members.
- Irish Nurses and Midwives Organisation (INMO) – 40,000 members.
- Civil and Public Service Union(CPSU) – 13,000 members.
- Public Services Executive Union (PSEU) – 10,000 members.

The three main teachers' unions, the *Irish National Teachers' Organisation* (INTO), the *Teachers' Union of Ireland* (TUI) and the *Association of Secondary Teachers Ireland* (ASTI) together account for approximately 68,000 members or around 12 per cent of ICTU membership. Turning to the financial services sector, we find that *IBOA the Finance Union* (formerly the *Irish Bank Officials Association*) accounts for another approximately 16,000 members or just fewer than 3 per cent of ICTU membership.

TRADE UNION STRUCTURE

Turning to the operation of trade unions in Ireland, three different levels may be identified, as illustrated in Figure 10.2 on the next page: (i) workplace level, (ii) branch level; and (iii) national level. Ultimate decision-making authority in a trade union is generally vested in the membership and executed through resolutions passed at the annual delegate conference (ADC). It is the responsibility of the union executive to carry out policy decisions reached at the ADC. The primary role of the trade union official is to carry out the operational aspects of the union's role, servicing the membership through assistance and advice.

The *shop steward* is the key trade union representative in the workplace. Shop stewards are selected by fellow trade union members at elections which normally take place once a year. A shop steward's role is to represent the interests of union members on workplace issues, to liaise with union officials, and to keep members informed about union affairs. Salamon (2000: 209) describes the role of the shop steward as 'an employee who is accepted by management and union as a lay representative of the union and its members with responsibility to act on their behalf in industrial relations matters at the organisational level'. Shop stewards may become involved in workplace bargaining on local grievances or disputes, though on more serious issues their main role is to support the trade union official and provide feedback to the membership. Shop stewards are also employees of the organisation and, as such, must perform their normal job. It should be noted that the *Code of Practice on the Duties and Responsibilities of Employee Representatives* (under the *Industrial Relations Act 1990*) indicates that employee representatives should be afforded 'reasonable' time off to perform their representative duties. Correspondingly, trade union representatives are charged with representing their members in a fair and equitable manner and cooperating with management in implementing agreements.

The *section committee* consists of a group of elected shop stewards. This forum allows shop stewards representing various sections or groupings in the organisation to meet to discuss common problems and decide on policy.

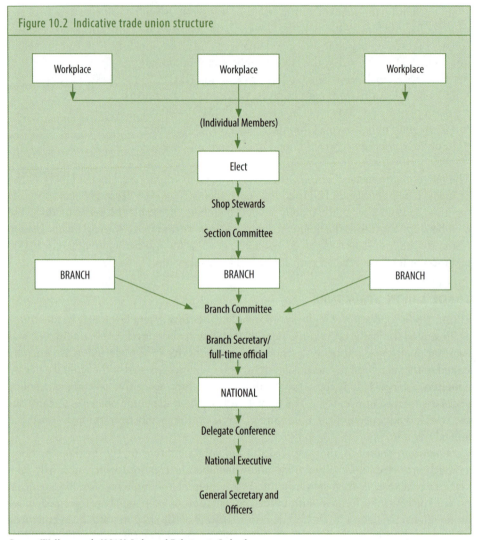

Figure 10.2 Indicative trade union structure

Source: Wallace et al. (2013) *Industrial Relations in Ireland*.

In many trade unions, the *branch* is the basic organisational unit and is commonly organised on a geographical basis (comprising trade union members from several organisations) or establishment basis (McPartlin 1997). In Ireland, a trade union branch normally comprises a group of trade union members from different companies located in the same geographical area. Occasionally, a branch may comprise trade union members from one large organisation. The branch operates as a communications vehicle, disseminating policy and information downwards and membership views upwards. It also plays a key role in managing the internal affairs of the union in a particular region or constituency and strives for improvements in the terms and working conditions of union members.

The affairs of the branch are managed by the *branch committee*. This committee is elected at the annual general meeting of the branch, which is also the forum for electing delegates from the branch to attend the Annual Delegate Conference (ADC) of the union. Both the branch committee and the branch members are served by a *branch secretary*. In larger unions, this individual is normally a permanent employee of the union and thus, described as a full-time branch official, whose role is to administer the affairs of the branch and negotiate terms and conditions of employment of union members with management.

At *national level*, the election of union officers takes place at the *annual delegate conference*. It is here that motions concerning trade union policy are discussed and voted upon. Such motions normally emanate from branch level. If approved by the ADC, a motion then becomes a resolution of the conference and ultimately union policy. The ADC comprises branch delegates and the union's national executive. The *national executive* is responsible for carrying out the decisions of the ADC and appointing branch officials and other union staff. The general officers of the union are usually full-time union employees and normally consist of a general president, a general secretary, a general vice-president and a general treasurer.

The primary source of revenue for trade unions is membership fees which vary across different unions. For example, membership fees in SIPTU (Ireland's largest union) vary from €1 per week, for members earning €127 a week or less, to €4.70 per week, for those earning more than €500 per week, while the membership fees for a registered nurse in the *Irish Nurses and Midwives Organisation* (INMO) costs €299 per year or €5.75 per week.

IRISH CONGRESS OF TRADE UNIONS (ICTU)

The *Irish Congress of Trade Unions* (ICTU) is the central co-ordinating body for the Irish trade union movement. It acts as an umbrella body or confederation for its affiliated member unions on the island of Ireland. It was established in 1959 as a result of the merger between the *Irish Trade Union Congress* (founded in 1894) and the *Congress of Irish Unions* (founded in 1945). This was a very significant merger which helped address a schism in the Irish union movement related in part to ideological and personality issues and also to differences between Irish and British Unions (Wallace *et al.* 2013).

In 2013 there were forty-eight unions affiliated to Congress comprising a total membership of 777,000 – 566,000 in the Republic of Ireland and 211,000 in Northern Ireland (ICTU 2016). There are also thirty-one Trades Councils, representing groups of unions at local/regional level, affiliated to the ICTU Congress covering both the Republic and Northern Ireland. A relatively small number of trade unions are not members of the ICTU. These include the *National Bus and Rail Union* (NBRU), the *Psychiatric Nurses Association* (PNA), the Garda representative organisations and the *Permanent Defence Force Other Ranks Representative Association* (PDForra).

Although Congress acts as the representative of the collective interests of the Irish trade union movement, individual unions retain a large degree of autonomy and the ICTU relies on the co-operation of affiliated unions in promoting its overall goals. ICTU fulfils an extremely important function at national level, representing union views to government and other institutions. Its role in centralised pay negotiations is particularly significant. Along with the other social partners (i.e. government, employer and farming representatives), it is party to national negotiations on pay and other aspects of social and economic policy. Congress is also the vehicle through which trade unions decide on participation in centralised pay bargaining, approve any agreements thus concluded and ensure that affiliated unions adhere to the terms of such agreements. ICTU also represents trade unions on several national bodies and provides union nominees for conciliation and arbitration services.

Ultimate decision-making power within Congress is vested in the biennial delegate council, where delegates from affiliated unions consider various resolutions presented by union delegates and those adopted become ICTU policy. The executive is then responsible for policy execution as well as general administration. A number of important committees operate under the auspices of ICTU: a Disputes Committee deals with inter-union disputes in relation to union membership; the Demarcation Tribunal deals with inter-union disputes in relation to work boundaries; and the Industrial Relations Committee has the particularly important responsibility of granting an 'all-out picket' in industrial disputes. An 'all-out-picket' requires that all union members employed in the organisation with which the dispute exists do not pass the picket, provided that the picket is peaceful, at the place of work of the employer and 'in contemplation or furtherance of a trade dispute'. Furthermore, a secret ballot of all union members must be held and the aggregate majority must be in favour of such industrial action. Individual unions can only sanction a 'one union picket', whereby only members of the union in dispute are obliged not to pass.

TRADE UNION MEMBERSHIP

The historical pattern of trade union membership and density in Ireland is considered below. However, before so doing, we briefly explore the issue of 'union joining'. The reasons why workers might join a trade union (or not) are both complex and multifaceted so we will therefore summarily outline some of the main factors (see Wallace et al. 2013 for greater detail).

WHY MIGHT WORKERS JOIN TRADE UNIONS?

A critical initial consideration is to differentiate between union demand and union supply. Even though workers may wish to join a union (existence of demand), trade unions are not present in many workplaces (absence of supply) and this creates great difficulties for workers who might wish to join a union. As Green (1990) observes, union joining pivots around two important steps, firstly the availability of a trade union and secondly the decision of workers on whether to join a trade union or not. In relation to union availability it is clearly important that unions have access to the workplace and that workers there are afforded the opportunity to join a union (cf. Wallace et al. 2013). Of course, this is often not the case. We know that many organisations do not recognise or deal with trade unions, thus greatly limiting any prospect of union presence in the workplace and of union joining by workers (Lavelle et al. 2009).

Structural factors such as size, sector, occupations employed, and so forth also influence union joining. As noted earlier, union membership tends to be higher in larger organisations and in certain sectors. For example, trade unions have a particularly strong presence in the public sector and also in traditional manufacturing, while union membership has generally been weaker in private sectors.

Changes in the distribution of employment are also influential. For example, the progressive growth in service sector employment and falls in employment in production/manufacturing has detrimentally impacted on trade union membership. Individual characteristics may also be influential. Factors such as gender, age, education and political orientation can all impact on the prospect (or not) of union joining.

In general, union membership tends to be higher among older workers especially those employed on a full-time basis. While traditionally men had higher unionisation rates than women, this is no longer the case in Ireland where 35 per cent of women are union members compared to 32 per cent of men. This change is arguably related to some of the factors discussed above, such as the fall in employment in traditional manufacturing and growth in private services and also to higher levels of female workforce participation. The profile of workers in Ireland who are most likely to be trade unions members is summarised in Table 10.1.

Table 10.1 Which workers are most likely to join Trade Unions in Ireland?

Category	Union membership	
	Highest	Lowest
Employment status	Full-time: 37%	Part-time: 20%
Sector	Public Administration & Defence: 81%	Accommodation & Food Services: 6%
Occupation	Associate Professional & Technical: 50%	Sales: 15%
Size	100+ employees: 50%	9 or less employees: 6%
Age	Age 45–54: 47%	Age 15–19: 4%
Gender	Female: 35%	Male: 32%
Marital status	Married: 41%	Single: 25%
Education	Third-level: 40%	Primary-level or below: 29%
Region	Mid-west: 38%	Mid-East: 30% & Border: 30%

Source: Central Statistics Office (CSO) (2010), Quarterly National Household Survey.

PATTERNS OF TRADE UNION MEMBERSHIP AND TRADE UNION DENSITY IN IRELAND

Important indicators of the role of trade unions in most countries are the levels of trade union membership and density. The most commonly used indicator of trade union penetration is *trade union density*, which gauges the proportion of 'unionisable' workers currently in membership of trade unions. This is normally based on two measures:
1. *Workforce density*: This measures the percentage of the total civilian workforce (i.e. including those employed and those seeking employment) who are trade union members.
2. *Employment density*: This measures the percentage of civilian employees in the labour force (excluding the self-employed, security forces and assisting relatives) who are trade union members.

Figures 10.3 and 10.4 provide an overall picture of trends in trade union membership and employment density in Ireland since the mid-1920s. There are two main sources of data on trade union membership and density in Ireland. Data for the period 1925–1996 are drawn from the membership records from trade unions themselves, while information for more recent years is based on data from the Labour Force Surveys/Quarterly National Household Surveys (LFS/QNHS) conducted since the mid-1990s and administered by the Central Statistics Office (CSO). Three points should be noted regarding these data sources (Roche 2008: 20–1). First, the reliability of union membership data is 'notoriously problematic'. Second, data from the LFS/QNHS are seen as more 'valid and reliable' than those based on returns from trade unions. Third, the LFS/QNHS data consistently point to substantially lower levels of union density than data based on returns from unions themselves.

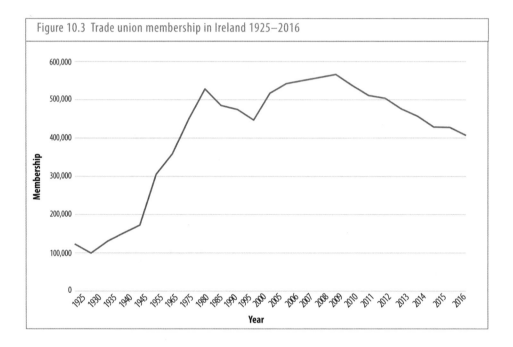

Figure 10.3 Trade union membership in Ireland 1925–2016

This indicates that aggregate trade union membership increased, more or less progressively, from the 1930s right up to the turn of the 1980s. There followed a marked decline in union membership which continued throughout that decade and well into the 1990s. This decline in union membership is principally attributed to cyclical and structural factors: economic depression; increased unemployment; changes in employment structure involving the decline or stagnation of employment in traditionally highly unionised sectors (such as areas of the public sector and 'traditional' manufacturing, e.g. textiles) and growth in sectors traditionally more union averse, such as private services and areas of 'high technology' manufacturing, for example electronics (cf. Roche, 2008). In addition to these factors, it is likely that developments at enterprise level contributed to this decline, most notably changes in management approaches to ER.

However, trade union membership recovered in the late 1990s in line with strong economic growth and a positive business cycle. This pattern continued after the turn of the millennium with union membership peaking in 2008 at 566,000 members. This increase in union membership clearly reflected the very significant growth in employment levels from the late 1990s. The impact of the global financial crisis ('great recession'), however, is evidenced in the dramatic fall in trade union membership in 2009, a pattern that has continued unabated to date (see Chapter 2 for greater detail).

Figure 10.4 Trade union employment density in Ireland 1925–2016

While trade union membership temporarily recovered from the 1980s downturn, the same cannot be said for trade union density. Having reached a high-water mark of approximately 60 per cent at the turn of the 1980s, union density in Ireland has been in progressive decline ever since, with data for 2016 indicating that just under a quarter (24 per cent) of employees in Ireland were trade unions members. These represent lows in union density not witnessed since the 1930s.

In their analysis of the impact of the most recent recession, Roche et al. (2011: 239) concluded that the recession had 'debilitated trade unions', leaving them unable to respond more forcefully to its impact and related employer demands, due largely to the scale of the recession, the collapse of social partnership and employee fears regarding job security (Wallace et al. 2013; Gunnigle et al. 2013). More recently though, we have witnessed a sharp increase in industrial unrest driven by wage demands from trade unions in both the public and private sectors. This may indicate that unions, though severely weakened by recession and other factors, still represent a significant force in ER and in Irish economic and societal life

In comparison to other countries, however, levels of union density in Ireland are not particularly out of line. As illustrated in Table 10.2 on the next page, the level of trade union density in Ireland compares reasonably favourably with union density in a number of European countries and is considerably higher than in the US. However, union density in Ireland is lower than in Belgium and Italy, and considerably lower than in Nordic and Scandinavian countries.

Table 10.2 Trade union density in selected OECD countries 2013/2014

Country	Trade union density (%)
Australia	15.5
Austria	28
Belgium	55
Canada	26
Czech Republic	13
Denmark	67
Estonia	6
France	8
Germany	18
Greece	21.5
Hungary	10.5
Italy	37
Japan	18
Korea (S)	10
Netherlands	18
Norway	52
Spain	17
Sweden	67
UK	25
USA	11
OECD average	**17**

Source: OECD (2016).

TRADE UNION RECOGNITION: LAW AND PRACTICE

While national statistics provide us with an overall picture of trade union density, it is necessary to look at union membership numbers at enterprise level to gain insights into the operational role and impact of trade unions. In this regard, trade union recognition represents a critical barometer of the nature of ER practice within organisations. This is especially the case in Ireland, where there is no mandatory legal procedure for dealing with trade union recognition (see Turner *et al.* 2013 for further detail).

Salamon (2000: 189) describes trade union recognition as the process by which 'trade unions are formally accepted by management as the representative of all, or a group, of employees for the purpose of jointly determining their terms and conditions of employment'. He further identifies trade union recognition as 'perhaps the most important stage in the development of an organisation's industrial relations system … it confers legitimacy and determines the scope of the trade union's role'. By securing recognition, an employer acknowledges the right of a trade union to represent and protect its members' interests in the workplace, and to become jointly involved in regulating key aspects of the employment relationship. As Torrington and Hall (1995: 492) comment, trade union recognition represents 'an almost irrevocable movement away from unilateral decision-making by management'.

LEGAL CONTEXT

Legislative provision to address the mandatory recognition of trade unions by employers in certain circumstances has been to the forefront of the trade union agenda for some time. Unlike the UK or the US, Ireland has no mandatory legal process by which a trade union can secure recognition from a particular employer. This can be partly explained by Article 40.6.1 of the Irish Constitution, which supports the principle of freedom of association. This article provides for the 'right of citizens to form associations or unions' (Constitution of Ireland 1937). The courts have interpreted this to mean that workers have the right to join or not join trade unions.

More significantly perhaps, it also means that employers are free to recognise or not recognise trade unions, as the case may be. In Ireland, therefore, the granting of recognition remains largely an issue to be worked out voluntarily between employers and trade unions and fundamentally pivots on whether or not an employer consents to recognise and bargain with a trade union representing workers in its employment. In addition to data on trade union density, trends in regard to trade union recognition provide another important indicator of trade union penetration. Should this issue lead to a stand-off or dispute between the parties, this would normally be referred to the Labour Court for decision. However, as we will see later, the Labour Court is not a court of law but rather a state agency, which, in industrial relations disputes, provides non-binding recommendations. Specifically in regard to disputes over trade union recognition, the historical approach of the Court has been to recommend in favour of recognition where unions could demonstrate a reasonable level of membership. However – because such recommendations are not legally binding – employers are clearly free to accept or reject them. Indeed, since the early 1980s we have witnessed a pattern of increased employer rejection of recommendations on trade union recognition (cf. Gunnigle *et al.* 2002).

Subsequent trade union demands for legislative provision on mandatory union recognition led to the passing into law of the *Industrial Relations (Amendment) Act 2001*, the *Industrial Relations (Miscellaneous Provisions) Act 2004* and an enhanced *Code of Practice on Voluntary Dispute Resolution*. This legislation allowed trade unions to process cases through the then Labour Relations Commission (now Workplace Relations Commission) and Labour Court, subject to certain conditions being met, namely that it must involve cases where the employer involved does not normally engage in collective bargaining and where the organisation's internal dispute resolution procedures (if any) have failed to resolve the issue in dispute. The substance of such cases must relate to either (i) terms or conditions of employment; or (ii) dispute resolution or disciplinary procedures in an organisation.

In general, the absence of collective bargaining and union recognition were the normal reasons for cases to be triggered under this legislation. While this body of so-called 'right to bargain' legislation did not provide for mandatory union recognition, it allowed trade unions to instigate cases in the Labour Court against organisations that did not engage in collective bargaining. The 2001/2004 Acts and associated codes of practice essentially provided a form of union representation rights for trade union members in non-union firms, but they did not go as far as to bestow union recognition for purposes of collective bargaining. In particular, this legislation provided for extended Labour Court powers in industrial relations cases by allowing trade unions representing workers in organisations which refused to engage in collective bargaining to secure a legally binding order from the Labour Court. Such an order was in regard to specific issues related to terms and conditions of employment, while still prohibiting the Labour Court from ordering that collective bargaining take place (Doherty 2015). In the period from 2004 until 2007 this 'right to bargain' legislation was increasingly utilised by trade unions representing members in what had hitherto been known as 'non-union' organisations (ibid).

The apparent benefit of this legislation for trade unions was effectively scuppered, however, by the Supreme Court's decision in the landmark 2007 case of *Ryanair v Labour Court and IMPACT*. The origins of this case date back to 2004, when the IMPACT trade union, through its branch the *Irish Airline Pilots Association* (IALPA) sought to negotiate with *Ryanair* on behalf of members. In line with its historical stance (O'Sullivan and Gunnigle 2009), *Ryanair* refused to negotiate with the union which then sought a Labour Court investigation under the 'right to bargain' legislation and procedures. In hearing this case, the Labour Court had to first establish whether it had jurisdiction to investigate the issues in dispute since *Ryanair* argued that the conditions necessary for hearing a case under the *Industrial Relations Acts 2001–2004* had not been met. These conditions were that (i) the company [*Ryanair*] did not engage in collective bargaining; and (ii) that their internal dispute resolution procedures had failed to resolve the issues in dispute. However, *Ryanair* argued that the Labour Court could not hear the case given their contention that collective bargaining had taken place through the company's Employee Representative Committees (ERCs). IALPA counter-argued that the ERC was a 'sham', company dominated and could not equate to collective bargaining (Sheehan 2007; Doherty 2015). The Labour Court found that the conditions for hearing the case were met, and agreed with the Union, finding that the ERC was organised and controlled by the company and did not constitute collective bargaining (Wallace *et al.* 2013). *Ryanair* mounted a High Court challenge which upheld the Labour Court decision. *Ryanair* then appealed the High Court decision to the Supreme Court which overturned the High Court decision and found in favour of *Ryanair*. In its 2007 ruling, the Supreme Court found that the Labour Court was mistaken on two counts. Firstly, with regard to the Labour Court decision that a 'trade dispute' existed between *Ryanair* and the IMPACT trade union, the Supreme Court found that the Labour Court erred in its finding that a 'trade dispute' existed under the terms of the *Industrial Relations (Amendment) Act 2001*. It also found that the Labour Court erred in dismissing *Ryanair*'s claim that collective bargaining existed. Here the Supreme Court found that the internal ERCs were 'excepted bodies' within the terms of the *Trade Union Act 1941* and could therefore facilitate collective bargaining. However, it concluded that the Labour Court had not fully investigated this possibility (see earlier discussion on 'excepted bodies' and the legal status of trade unions). The Supreme Court found that an 'excepted body' need not necessarily be a trade union. It declared that such a body can be established by an employer, providing it exhibits a degree of 'independence', has a system of elections and forms part of an internal bargaining system that is 'fair and reasonable' (Sheehan 2007). However, the Supreme Court did not provide further details for the operation of such an internal body or its role in collective bargaining. The judgment also severely criticised the Labour Court's handling of this case and further stated that '. . . as a matter of law, *Ryanair* is perfectly entitled not to deal with trade unions, nor can a law be passed compelling it to do so'. Dobbins's (2007) review of the import of this decision concluded that the case had rendered the 'right to bargain' legislation effectively redundant while D'Art and Turner (2007: 2) expressed astonishment at the Supreme Court decision which they claim 'pre-emptively forbids' the enactment of legislation for trade union recognition.

More broadly the *Ryanair* case has fuelled continuing debate over the meaning of collective bargaining in Ireland and its attendant implications for trade union recognition. In the years after the Supreme Court decision, the trade union movement continued to press for mandatory provision in regard to union recognition and collective bargaining. These issues have recently been addressed through the passing of the *Industrial Relations (Amendment) Act 2015* which significantly alters the ER landscape in Ireland. This legislation extends and amends the preceding *Industrial Relations Acts 2001/2004* in relation to collective bargaining and the power of the Labour Court to make legally binding orders regarding terms of employment against employers who do not have collective bargaining arrangements. It thus provides for some level of collective bargaining in non-union firms which have hitherto refused to so engage. However, it falls short of imposing mandatory collective bargaining or trade union recognition (Doherty 2015; Sheehan *et al.* 2015).

The main import of this legislation is to provide a statutory definition of what constitutes collective bargaining and to outline and clarify the parameters of when a trade dispute can be referred to the Labour Court for a legally binding order. The *Industrial Relations Act 2015* defines collective bargaining as:

> Voluntary engagements or negotiations between any employer or employers' organisation on the one hand and a trade union of workers or excepted body . . . with the object of reaching agreement regarding working conditions or terms of employment, or non-employment, of workers.

This definition delineates collective bargaining as involving voluntary engagements/ negotiations between employers and either a trade union of workers or an 'excepted body', with the purpose of reaching agreement on wages or other conditions of employment. Under this legislation trade unions cannot take claims where the employer engages in collective bargaining with an 'excepted body', a key point of contention in the *Ryanair* case discussed above. In this regard, the Act explicitly requires that the Labour Court consider the extent to which the 'excepted body' is independent and not under the domination and control of an employer. In so doing the Labour Court must consider the establishment, functioning and administration of the 'excepted' body and as Doherty details (2015) take particular account of the following considerations:

1. The manner and frequency of elections of employees.
2. The financing or resourcing of the excepted body.
3. The length of time the excepted body has been in existence and if it has had any prior engagement in collective bargaining during that time.
4. The significance of the numbers involved in the dispute as a proportion of total relevant employees.

The burden of proof in demonstrating the independence of the excepted body and its engagement in collective bargaining lies with the employer. It should be noted that case law under this new 'right to bargain' legislation is currently just emerging with the recent conclusion of a local collective bargaining agreement between the hitherto non-union *Freshways Food* and SIPTU marking an important early example (Sheehan 2016a, 2016b).

As noted earlier, it is anticipated that the new 2015 legislation will provide a mechanism though which workers in non-union firms can seek improved terms and conditions of employment where they can demonstrate shortfalls when comparison is made with terms and conditions of employment among similar comparable firms. However, firms whose pay and conditions are on a par or better than comparable employers are arguably well placed to resist an adverse recommendation should a case be referred to the Labour Court. In investigating cases under the 2015 legislation, the Labour Court is now expected to review pay and conditions of employment in their totality and conduct comparison with both union and non-union firms, including firms outside the state. As Sheehan *et al.* (2015: 2) observe, this may mean that 'trade unions may well find it harder to make a case for improvement in terms and conditions'.

THE MULTINATIONAL CONTEXT

Beyond the legal domain, institutional factors can also significantly impact on ER approaches and practice. Important considerations here include the nature of collective bargaining, management and employer ideologies regarding ER and the role of the state regarding labour market governance and ER practice. In relation to employer approaches to trade unions, we noted earlier (see Chapter 2) that Irish employers grew to accommodate and negotiate with unions particularly after the Second World War and up to the 1980s. More recently, however, we have seen how trade unions have found it increasingly difficult to secure recognition from employers and have encountered greater opposition to union organising, including coercive tactics by employers seeking to resist trade union recognition (D'Art and Turner 2005, 2011).

Multinational companies (MNCs) play a key role in the Irish economy (see Chapter 2) and their influence is particularly evident in the HR/ER sphere primarily regarding management ideology and practice at subsidiary level. The extant research evidence suggests Ireland exhibits a pronounced 'country of origin' effect, manifest through extensive trade union avoidance among US-owned subsidiaries in Ireland since the mid-1980s, and particularly in the IT and financial services sectors (Gunnigle *et al.* 2001; Geary and Roche 2001; Lavelle 2008). Data from a large-scale study of employment practice in MNCs in Ireland (Lavelle 2008) found that Irish, UK and 'other' European MNCs are more likely to engage with trade unions, while US MNCs are far less likely to do so, as illustrated in Figure 10.5. This data indicates that only 42 per cent of US-owned firms recognised unions, compared with 81 per cent of Irish companies. It has been argued that this is due to the 'anti-union sentiment characteristic of the US national business system' when compared with the more pluralist tradition of the Irish system (Lavelle 2008: 58). Indeed, even among long established MNC subsidiaries which recognised trade unions in older sites, we now more commonly find that many of these same companies later established new sites on a non-union basis, a practice known as 'double-breasting' (Gunnigle et al. 2009; Lamare et al. 2013; Lavelle 2008). Greater employer opposition to trade unions is not unique to Ireland, however, and has undoubtedly been a factor in the fall in union density across much of the developed world.

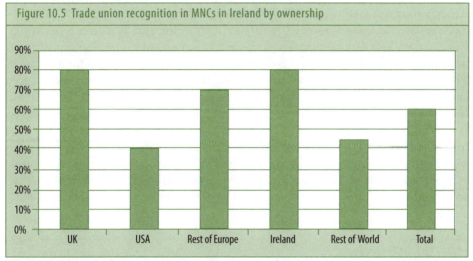

Figure 10.5 Trade union recognition in MNCs in Ireland by ownership

Source: Lavelle et al. (2009).

ALTERNATIVES TO TRADE UNIONS

Before completing our discussion of trade unions, it should be noted that while trade unions have been viewed as the most effective means of representing employee interests in the workplace and beyond, there are a number of alternative approaches (cf. Wallace et al. 2013).

Firstly, workers may deal with employers on an individual basis (*individual bargaining*). This may occur because of the absence of trade unions in the workplace, employer opposition to trade unions or possibly through deliberate choice. For example, individual bargaining may prove attractive to workers who are in a strong bargaining position, especially those in possession of certain skills or knowledge that are highly valued by employers. This may particularly be the case when certain categories of labour are in short supply and workers who possess valued skills can command favourable terms and conditions of employment through direct dealings with employers. Additionally, individual bargaining may be attractive in organisations which generally provide attractive pay and conditions and where management place a high priority on dealing with ER on an individual basis. More generally, however, it is felt that individual workers are at a severe disadvantage in bargaining terms *vis-à-vis* employers, and consequently individual bargaining may not be an optimal approach for most workers. Indeed, this is often posited as a traditional rationale for trade union membership, namely that collective employee representation through trade unions serves to counter-balance employer bargaining power and thus redresses the perceived bargaining disadvantage of individual workers.

Secondly, workers may use work-based *staff associations, works councils* or *employee forums* to represent their interests. Company-based staff associations and similar bodies usually represent employee interests through consultation with senior management on ER issues. Staff associations have traditionally been associated with white-collar grades, particularly professional and managerial categories. These alternative mechanisms for employee representation are generally seen as an improvement on individual bargaining. By joining together, it is argued that workers can present a more united front to employers. An important attraction for employers is the fact that staff associations provide for a modicum of collective employee representation without the introduction of a 'third party' (trade union) into management–employee relations. Employers may also perceive staff associations as less difficult to deal with and less likely to engage in confrontational or adversarial ER approaches. However, work-based staff associations and councils have been criticised because of their lack of independence from the employer. This largely stems from the fact that such associations are often established and resourced by management. Another disadvantage is the absence of an external organisational structure and resources with which to provide bargaining expertise or legal advice. These factors may often combine to limit the bargaining power of staff associations in their interactions with management. Some of the major contrasts between trade unions and staff associations are summarised in Table 10.3. It is important to note that these generalisations may not characterise all trade unions or staff associations.

Table 10.3 Trade unions and staff associations: indicative contrasts

	Trade Unions	Staff Associations
Objectives	Replace individual bargaining with collective bargaining Improve pay and employment conditions Political objectives	Consultative bargaining but less ideological commitment to collective bargaining Improve pay and employment conditions No political objectives
Controlling authority	Union headquarters ICTU plays a strong role	Normally no external authority
Rules/Procedures	Detailed constitution, often with strong political dimension	None or brief constitution; oriented to firm
External resources	Access to external expertise and resources Influence on national issues (e.g. via centralised agreements on pay and other social/economic issues)	None except by contracting in external expertise No explicit means of influence on national issues
Methods/Approach	Collective bargaining	More consultative orientation
Use of sanctions	Prepared to use industrial action, up to and including strikes	Highly unlikely
Member services	May provide range of services	None or very limited

ROLE OF THE STATE

This section considers the role of the state in Irish employment relations. It focuses on the ways through which the state may impact on ER:
1. By providing overall ER policy.
2. As a provider of dispute resolution and wage setting machinery.
3. Through legislation.
4. By its role as a very significant employer.

ER practice in the great majority of medium and large organisations in the Republic of Ireland has traditionally been associated with a strong collectivist emphasis, with relations and interaction between management and employees grounded in pluralist traditions and primary reliance on adversarial collective bargaining. This approach was aptly captured in the following observation by Bill Roche (1990: 22):

> Over a wide range of industries and services, employers and unions have conducted their relations on the basis of the premise that their interests were in significant respects different and in opposition . . . These differences of interest were reconciled on an ongoing basis through what is sometimes known in the academic literature as 'collective bargaining pure and simple'.
>
> Roche (1990: 22)

The 'pluralist tradition' was based on the perspective that employer and worker interests will inevitably come into conflict and that collective bargaining between organised employees (primarily through trade unions) and employers represented the best way of resolving such conflict. It is therefore predicated on reasonably high levels of union density, reliance on collective bargaining to handle ER issues, and ER as a key role of the specialist HR function.

However, we have also seen that, particularly since the early 1980s, developed economies have witnessed what Deery and Walsh (1999: 245) termed 'a secular drift towards individualism and a fracturing of the previously prevailing collectivistic form of industrial relations'. Over recent decades we have also seen considerable change in the environment and practice of ER in Ireland (see Chapter 2). From an employer's perspective, economic recession in the 1980s lessened the emphasis on hitherto core workforce management activities, such as recruitment and, particularly, ER. Trade union membership fell significantly and industrial conflict also declined. At the same time, many companies sought to establish competitive advantage through improvements in quality, service and performance. More recently, as Ireland emerges from the deep recession wrought by the global financial crisis, we have witnessed a resurgence in the ER sphere, most notably in the form of large scale disputes over pay and related matters.

STATE APPROACHES TO EMPLOYMENT RELATIONS IN IRELAND

Before specifically reviewing the Irish context, we briefly consider the broad range of optional policy approaches that governments might pursue in the ER sphere. Crouch (1982) provides a useful framework of four policy alternatives or approaches which may be pursued by the state, namely: (i) market individualism; (ii) liberal collectivism; (iii) corporatism; and (iv) bargained corporatism. Crouch sees these alternative approaches as expressions of the inter-relationship between the dominant political and economic ideology *vis-à-vis* ER, the relative power and autonomy of trade unions and the nature of employment relations (see Table 10.4).

Table 10.4 State approaches to employment relations

Approach	Political Ideology	Trade Unions	Employer–Employee Relations
Market individualism	Laissez-faire	Weak; regulated	Exploitative or paternalistic
Liberal collectivism	Liberal	Strong; autonomous	Voluntarist; free collective bargaining
Corporatism	Corporatist	Weak; regulated	Subordinated; controlled; Trade unions as 'Agents of Control'
Bargained corporatism	Interventionist	Strong; autonomous	Voluntarist; tripartite

Source: Adapted from Crouch (1982) and Rollinson (1993).

The dominant state approach to ER in Ireland at the beginning of the 1900s was market individualism. However, the increased 'collectivisation' of ER, specifically increased worker organisation into trade unions, prompted a change to liberal collectivism or what Roche (1997b) terms 'auxiliary state control'. This is in line with our earlier observation that, traditionally, government approaches to ER in Ireland were grounded in the so-called 'voluntarist' tradition. This is generally taken to indicate an approach in which the role of the state in ER was restricted to the establishment of legislative ground rules and the provision of mediation and arbitration machinery, leaving employers and employers' associations, and employees and trade unions largely free to develop procedures and terms and conditions to suit organisational contexts. Thus, Irish governments tended to adopt a 'hands-off' approach in regard to interactions between employers and workers or trade unions, which were then left comparatively free to engage in collective bargaining and come to their own agreements on issues such as pay increases and working conditions. The state only tended to become involved when conflict occurred (e.g. by providing various conciliation services) or when one party was in a dominant power position (e.g. by laying down basic terms and conditions of employment in a particular industrial sector where trade union organisation was weak: see discussion on Joint Labour Committees below). This approach was largely a historical legacy of the British voluntarist tradition.

In discussing state strategies towards ER in the post-Second World War period, Roche (1989) argues that there has been a drift from auxiliary state control to attempts at greater corporate control, which occurred in two fairly distinct phases. The first phase (1960s) saw trade unions becoming involved in a number of largely consultative bodies, such as the Employer–Labour Conference and the National Industrial and Economic Council. Throughout this period, however, liberal collectivism and 'collective bargaining remained inviolate' with any attempt by the state to intervene in pay determination being perceived as hostile by the trade unions, who used the threat of withdrawing from these consultative bodies as a means of repelling such corporatist advances. Roche suggests that it was during this phase that the strategic and institutional basis for further state intervention in ER and the onset of 'bargained corporatism' was established.

This second phase involved the negotiation of a series of National Wage Agreements and two tripartite National Understandings, beginning in 1970 and continuing into the early 1980s. This period was characterised by greater state involvement in the process of collective bargaining together with trade union participation in the process of government. Liberal collectivism or the auxiliary state re-surfaced for a short period between 1982 and 1986 with a return to decentralised bargaining. However, as noted earlier, 1987 saw the negotiation of the first in a long sequence of national social partnership agreements. This continued right up to the demise of 'bargained corporatism' through the collapse of the last such social partnership agreement (*Towards 2016: Review and Transitional Agreement 2008–2009*) in 2008, in the face of the recession. This sequence of centralised agreements on pay and aspects of economic and social policy also covered issues such as welfare provision, employment creation and tax reform and involved negotiations between the 'social partners' (principally government, trade unions and employers' association but also on occasion other representative groups, such as farming organisations).

Our preceding discussion demonstrates how the approaches of successive Irish governments to ER were grounded in the 'voluntarist' tradition. However, this approach was undoubtedly diluted over the years well preceding the recent recession, particularly through the advent and demise of social partnership, greater legislation on employment matters and, more recently, through greater use of private mediation and arbitration as opposed to the conventional third-party dispute resolution mechanisms provided by the state, such as the Workplace Relations Commission and the Labour Court (cf. Teague *et al.* 2015a). These agencies play a critical role in ER since its adversarial nature means that employer and worker interests will invariably come into conflict on occasion and, as we discuss in greater detail below, it is important to have some form of independent external referral system to help resolve such disputes. While systems vary between countries and our focus is on the Irish context, there are three general forms of independent third party referral in ER (cf. Salamon, 2000; William and Adam-Smith, 2010).

1. *Arbitration* refers to a process for resolving ER disputes through which an independent third party adjudicates on the case and makes a decision thereon, having heard arguments and investigated the positions of both parties.
2. *Conciliation* is a second mechanism where an independent third party works with the conflicting parties in a facilitatory mode to help them reach their own settlement.
3. *Mediation* also involves an independent third party working with the parties in two different ways (Salamon 2000). Like conciliation, mediators work with the parties to help them reach a solution to the immediate issue at hand. In mediation, however, the independent third party does not assume as great an initiative in steering the parties towards a solution. The second differentiating factor is that mediation is viewed as a more long-term intervention strategy, focused, not just on the particular issue in dispute, but also on preventing future conflict (Margerison and Leary 1975).

The line between conciliation and mediation is often confusing. Both are confidential and voluntary processes involving independent third parties assisting parties to resolve a dispute. There are varying opinions on the extent of input or intervention by mediators and conciliators. In Ireland, the Law Reform Commission emphasise the advisory nature of conciliation and the goal of conciliation is for a third party to assist parties to reach a mutually acceptable negotiated agreement (Law Reform Commission 2010). In slight contrast, the Commission emphasises the facilitative nature of mediation and emphasises that the parties attempt *by themselves* to reach a mutually acceptable agreement with the assistance of a third party. Generally speaking, in practice in Ireland, conciliation is often used to resolve an immediate dispute of terms and conditions of employment, while mediation is often used for interpersonal disputes as there is an emphasis in mediation on collaborative bargaining and addressing underlying problems so that parties can develop better working relationships in the future.

DISPUTE RESOLUTION AND WAGE SETTING INSTITUTIONS OF THE STATE*

The passing of the *Workplace Relations Act 2015* and establishment of the *Workplace Relations Commission* was, according to its inaugural Director General Kieran Mulvey 'perhaps the most far-reaching institutional legislative reform in the area of employment and industrial relations in almost 70 years' (Workplace Relations Commission Annual Report, 2016). The Act essentially instigated a comprehensive overhaul of dispute resolution procedures in the country and established the *Workplace Relations Commission* as a 'one-stop shop' for handling employment-related complaints in Ireland. We will now outline and describe the role of the main dispute resolution and wage setting institutions in Ireland and provide some brief commentary on their operation.

THE WORKPLACE RELATIONS COMMISSION (WRC)

The Workplace Relations Commission (WRC) is an independent, statutory body established in October 2015, under the terms of the *Workplace Relations Act*. In line with this legislation, the WRC assumed the roles and functions previously carried out by the National Employment Rights Authority (NERA), Equality Tribunal (ET), Labour Relations Commission (LRC), Rights Commissioners Service. It also took over the first-instance (complaints and referrals) functions of the Employment Appeals Tribunal (EAT), (see Figure 10.6). However, the appeal functions of the EAT have been transferred to the Labour Court which is now the single appeal body for all workplace relations appeals (see discussion on the Labour Court later in this chapter).

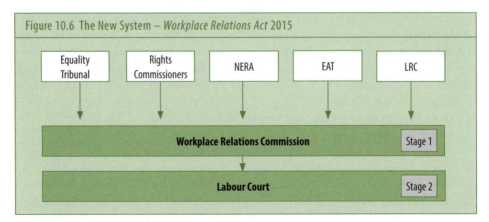

Figure 10.6 The New System – *Workplace Relations Act* 2015

* Data and information on state provided dispute resolution and wage setting institutions in Ireland comes from a variety of sources, primarily the *Workplace Relations Commission*, which includes information on the *Labour Court* (see www.workplacerelations.ie), the Department of Jobs, Enterprise and Innovation (see www.djei.ie) and the *Citizens Information Board* (see www.citizensinformationboard.ie).

The main functions of the WRC are to:
- Promote the improvement of workplace relations, and maintenance of good workplace relations.
- Promote and encourage compliance with the relevant laws.
- Provide guidance in relation to compliance with codes of practice.
- Conduct reviews of, and monitor developments as respects, workplace relations.
- Conduct or commission relevant research and provide advice, information and the findings of research to Joint Labour Committees and Joint Industrial Councils.
- Advise the Minister for Jobs, Enterprise and Innovation in relation to the application of, and compliance with, relevant laws.
- Provide information to the public in relation to employment laws other than the *Employment Equality Act* (information about this Act is provided by the Irish Human Rights and Equality Commission).

The WRC may also provide advice on any matter relating to workplace relations to employers, their representative bodies and to employees, trade unions or other representative bodies of employees. It has specific functions in relation to the resolution of industrial disputes and the implementation of employment laws. As noted earlier, it is now the body to which all industrial relations disputes, and all disputes and complaints about employment laws are presented. Greater detail is available from the WRC website (see www.workplacerelations.ie). It also operates the following services:

1. Advisory Service

The remit of the advisory service of the WRC is to provide advice and assistance on industrial relations to employers, employees and their representatives, develop positive working relationships and mechanisms to solve ER problems, and to generally promote good ER practice in the workplace.

Its various roles include engaging with employers, employees and trade unions to develop effective industrial relations practices, procedures and structures, e.g. in areas such as grievance, discipline, communications and consultation. The advisory service also seeks to facilitate joint management–staff forums to deal with issues of mutual concern (e.g. organisational change or problematic ER issues) and provides training on a variety of ER issues including the implementation of workplace procedures. One of its services is preventative mediation, including advice on grievance procedures and structural change. The WRC publishes codes of practice on topics such as *Grievance and Disciplinary Procedures* and *Procedures for addressing Bullying in the Workplace*. In addition, the advisory service may commission and publish research on contemporary ER themes. Members of the advisory service team are described as independent, impartial and experienced in industrial relations practice and theory. In discussion with the parties concerned, a designated member of the WRC's advisory services may shape confidential assistance to fit the requirements of individual organisations.

2. Conciliation Service

The conciliation service of the WRC is designed to help employers and employees resolve disputes when they have failed to reach agreement during their own previous negotiations. This is achieved by designating an *Industrial Relations Officer* of the WRC as chairperson in meetings between the parties aimed at achieving an agreement. Traditionally the majority of cases referred to the conciliation service are resolved at that level. However, should it fail to facilitate agreement the dispute may be referred to the Labour Court, if the parties so wish.

3. Mediation Service

The mediation service of the WRC is a voluntary process involving the deployment of a *Mediation Officer* and the agreement of both parties to participate and work towards a resolution to the problem at hand. The objective of the mediation service is to provide an alternative to an adjudication hearing in respect of claims involving breaches of employment and equality rights. It seeks to arrive at a solution through brokering an agreement between the parties as opposed to an investigation, hearing or formal decision, and to ensure that the views of all sides are heard and that participants are directly involved in finding an agreed solution. The process is voluntary and either party may terminate it at any stage. Any settlement reached at mediation is legally binding and may be enforced on application to the District Court.

The Mediation Service operates in broad domains, namely dealing with issues related to employment rights and internal workplace ER disputes or disagreements.

- *Employment rights issues:* If an employment rights complaint has been submitted to the WRC by a complainant who has indicated their willingness to engage in mediation, the *Early Resolution Service* (ERS) is generally offered where both parties are agreeable. As part of the mediation service, the ERS normally involves a one-to-one process whereby the ERS contacts the parties by phone and if possible mediates a resolution to the issues in dispute. Where the ERS does not resolve the issue the complaint will normally be referred for adjudication (see below).
- *Internal workplace issues:* The *workplace mediation service* is a confidential service designed to resolve workplace disputes and disagreements, particularly those involving individuals or small groups of workers. These might include interpersonal issues, breakdowns in working relationships or matters related to grievance and/or disciplinary procedures. It is generally preferable that applications for workplace mediation should be made on a joint basis. Workplace mediation involves a Mediation Officer engaging with the parties in dispute and all participants working together to find a mutually agreed solution.

The mediation service operates according to the following principles:
- It is a voluntary process and therefore all parties must agree to participate.
- Anyone who wishes to withdraw may do so at any stage.
- The process is confidential unless the parties agree otherwise.
- It is fast and starts as soon as everyone is available.
- The mediator is impartial.
- The focus is on finding a solution to the issue/dispute which is agreeable to all parties and which will work.
- Participation in workplace mediation does not oblige any party to commit to any further procedure in the event of the problem remaining unresolved.

4. Adjudication Service

The adjudication service investigates disputes, grievances and claims that individuals or small groups of workers make under the employment legislation listed in Schedule 5 of the *Workplace Relations Act* including the *National Minimum Wage Act 2000*, the *Payment of Wages Act 1991* and the *Maternity Protection Act 1994*. Adjudication Officers of the Workplace Relations Commission (WRC) are statutorily independent in their decision-making duties and have a wide range of functions in adjudicating on complaints referred to them by the WRC Director General.

The role of an Adjudication Officer is to hold a hearing at which both parties are provided with the opportunity to be heard and to present relevant evidence. Adjudication officer hearings are held in private. However, some cases may be dealt with by 'written procedure' (i.e. without a hearing). Adjudication Officers do not attempt to mediate or conciliate the case. Parties may represent themselves or choose their own representation, *inter alia*, representation by trade union officials, officials from employer bodies, barristers or solicitors or others that an Adjudication Officers might consider appropriate. After the hearing, the Adjudication Officer will provide a written decision which will be published and communicated to the parties involved. This decision will: (i) declare whether the complainant's complaint was or was not well founded; (ii) require the employer to comply with the relevant provision(s); and (iii) require the employer to make such redress as is just and equitable, including the award of compensation. This decision may be appealed to the Labour Court.

5. Inspection Service

The role of the inspection service of the WRC (formerly operated by NERA) is to monitor employment conditions to ensure the compliance and enforcement of employment rights legislation. WRC inspectors may visit places of employment and carry out investigations to ensure compliance with equality and employment-related legislation. In certain circumstances, the Labour Court may request that a WRC inspector carry out investigations on its behalf. Such investigations involve, but are not confined to, examining books, records and documents related to the employment, and conducting interviews with current and former employees and employers.

In general, WRC inspectors have the following powers:

- To enter, at all reasonable times, any place/work/ premises which s/he has reasonable grounds for believing is being used in connection with the employment of persons, or where s/he believes documents relating to the employment of persons are kept,
- At such premises to inspect and take copies, of any books, documents or records.
- To remove any such books, documents or records and retain them for such period as the inspector considers necessary for the purposes of his/her functions under the *Workplace Relations Act 2015*.
- To require any person at the place of work or premises to give him/her such information or assistance as the inspector may reasonably require for the purpose of their functions under the Act.
- To require any person at the place of work or premises to produce such books, records or documents as the inspector may reasonably require for the purposes of their functions under the Act.

- To examine any person who the inspector believes to be or have been an employer or employee, and to require such person to answer such questions asked relating to the employment, and to make a declaration as to the truth of those answers.

WRC inspectors may on occasion be accompanied by other inspectors from the WRC, the Department of Social Protection, and the Revenue Commissioners or by members of An Garda Síochána. Where breaches of legislation have been found, an inspector may, depending on the section of legislation involved, issue either a Compliance Notice or a Fixed Payment Notice to an employer.

THE LABOUR COURT

The Labour Court was established under the terms of the *Industrial Relations Act 1946*. Over time its role has been significantly altered and amended by subsequent legislation, including the *Workplace Relations Act 2015* which provided for arguably the most profound changes in the role of the Labour Court role since its establishment. The current mission of the Labour Court is to: '. . . find a basis for real and substantial agreement through the provision of fast, fair, informal and inexpensive arrangements for the adjudication and resolution of trade disputes'.

Under the provisions of the Act, the Labour Court now has sole appellate jurisdiction in all disputes. The full list of Labour Court functions are noted below but much of its work involves investigating employment rights and industrial relations cases. Regarding employment rights cases, the Labour Court only hears appeals of decisions of WRC Adjudication Officers, for example, on unfair dismissals or payment of wages. The decisions of the Labour Court on these appeals are legally binding and can be enforced through the District Court. In industrial relations cases, many of these disputes will have used the conciliation service of the WRC but the parties subsequently could not reach a resolution and are voluntarily seeking the assistance of the Labour Court. Typical types of industrial relations disputes are claims by trade unions for increases in pay or disputes between workers and employers over company restructuring. In general, the role of the Labour Court in these disputes is to issue a non-legally binding recommendation setting out the Court's opinion on the dispute and the terms on which it should be settled. Nevertheless, both parties are expected to give serious consideration to the Labour Court's decision even though responsibility for the settlement of disputes ultimately rests with the parties involved. If the dispute remains unresolved after the Labour Court's recommendation, then the parties may decide to engage in further negotiations or they may decide to escalate the dispute, for example, by the trade union deciding on strike action.

STRUCTURE AND FUNCTIONS OF THE LABOUR COURT

The Labour Court currently consists of thirteen, full-time, members – a chairman, four deputy chairmen and eight ordinary members, four each of whom are employer members (nominated by IBEC) and workers members (nominated by ICTU) respectively. The Court normally sits in a division consisting of three members: the chairman (or deputy chairman), an employer member and a worker member. To facilitate the prompt processing of cases the Labour Court generally operates in four separate divisions, although certain issues may require a meeting of the full Labour Court. Hearings are held in the Labour

Court in Dublin and at various venues throughout the country. The eight ordinary members of the court are generally expected to act independently when sitting on the Labour Court and not as representatives of their nominating body. The court members are normally experienced industrial relations practitioners and there is requirement for legal qualifications although some members may not be legally qualified.

The Chairman and the Deputy Chairmen are appointed by the Minister for Jobs, Enterprise and Innovation. The current Chairman is Kevin Foley who was appointed in July 2016. He was previously Deputy Chairman. His predecessor, Kevin Duffy, was formerly Assistant General Secretary of the Irish Congress of Trade Unions (ICTU). The general operation of the Labour Court is supported by an administrative service staffed by civil servants.

The Court has a number of key functions which may be categorised into those focused on (i) general industrial/employment relations matters; and (ii) those relating to the determination of appeals on matters of employment rights.

Industrial Relations

- Investigate trade disputes under the terms of the *Industrial Relations Acts 1946–2015*.
- Investigate, at the request of the relevant Minister, trade disputes affecting the public interest, or conduct an enquiry into a trade dispute of special importance and report on its findings.
- Hear appeals of Adjudication Officer's recommendations/decisions made under the *Industrial Relations Acts 1946–2015*.
- Establish Joint Labour Committees and decide on questions concerning their operation.
- Register Joint Industrial Councils (JICs).
- Investigate complaints of breaches of codes of practice made under the *Industrial Relations Act 1990* (following consideration of the complaint by the Workplace Relations Commission).
- Give its opinion as to the interpretation of a code of practice made under the *Industrial Relations Act 1990*.
- Investigate disputes (where negotiating arrangements are not in place) under the *Industrial Relations (Amendment) Act 2001* as amended by the *Industrial Relations (Miscellaneous Provisions) Act 2004* and the *Industrial Relations (Amendment) Act 2015*.
- Register employment agreements.
- Examine the terms and conditions of employment in a sector pursuant to Section 14 of the *Industrial Relations (Amendment) Act 2015*.
- Grant exemptions from the obligation to pay the remuneration that would otherwise be payable under a Sectoral Employment Order (SEO) pursuant to Section 21 of the *Industrial Relations (Amendment) Act 2015*.

Employment Rights

- Hear all appeals of Adjudication Officer's decisions under the various *Employment Rights and Pension Acts* enactments.

- Issue determinations in regard to certain complaints of the non-implementation of Adjudication Officer's decisions which were lodged with the Workplace Relations Commission before 1 October 2015.
- Hear appeals of Non-discrimination Notices and Substantive Notices issued by the Equality Authority.
- Approve working time agreements under the *Organisation of Working Time Act 1997*.
- Approve collective agreements regarding casual part-time employees under the *Protection of Employees (Part-Time Work) Act 2001*.

As we have seen, the primary role of the Labour Court is to deal with disputes between workers and employers referred to it in accordance with the relevant legislation. An alphabetical list of issues which the Labour Court has dealt with in the past is outlined in Table 10.5.

Table 10.5 Issues dealt with by the Labour Court

Allowances	Annual leave	Computerisation	Contracting out	Demarcation	Discipline
Dismissal	Equal pay	Equal treatment	Equality	Hours of work/ Working time	Interpretation (of scope of Joint Labour Committees/ Employment Regulation Orders)
Lay-off	Leave	Local agreement procedures	Negotiating rights	Overtime	Pay claims
Pay claims under National Agreements	Pay issues	Pensions	Premiums	Productivity	Promotion
Rationalisation	Recruitment	Redundancy	Registered employment agreements	Reorganisation	Sexual harassment
Shift pay	Shift work	Sick pay	Temporary employment	Union recognition	Wage rounds

Source: www.workplacerelations.ie (2016).

WAGE SETTING INSTITUTIONS

As noted earlier, one of the nominated roles of both the Workplace Relations Commission and the Labour Court is to assist *Joint Industrial Councils* (JICs) and *Joint Labour Committees* (JLCs) in discharging their functions. The WRC is responsible for providing advice, information and the findings of research to JICs and JLCs, while a specific function of the Labour Court is to register JICs, help establish JLCs and decide on questions concerning their operation. The Labour Court is also responsible for the registration of JICs, Registered Employment Agreements, Employment Regulation Orders and new Sectoral Employment Orders, many of which impact on pay and employment conditions at sectoral level. We will briefly explain the role of these various bodies below.

Joint Industrial Councils (JICs)

JICs are permanent voluntary negotiating bodies whose task is to facilitate collective bargaining at industry level in certain industrial sectors. While common in many European countries, collective bargaining at industry level in Ireland is confined to JICs (Wallace *et al.* 2013), with councils comprised of representatives of employers and trade unions from within the relevant industrial sector. JICs that fulfil the conditions set out in the relevant industrial relations legislation may apply to the Labour Court for registration and the Court, if satisfied, will place it on the register of JICs. A 'qualified' JIC is described as an association of persons that complies with three general conditions.
1. It is substantially representative of workers of a particular class, type or group and their employers.
2. Its object is the promotion of harmonious relations between such employers and such workers.
3. Its rules provide that if a trade dispute arises between such workers and their employers, a lockout or strike will not be undertaken in support of the dispute until the dispute has been referred to the association and considered by it.

As of 2015, there were five registered JICs covering the footwear, construction, security, contract cleaning and fruit and vegetables (Dublin) sectors. Some other bodies operate in a similar fashion but have not applied for registration with the Labour Court, namely the Electrical Contracting Industry JIC and the State Industrial Employees JIC (Workplace Relations Commission 2016).

Registered Employment Agreements (REA)

Historically, the key role of employer and worker representatives on particular JICs was to come to an agreement on pay and conditions and then register this agreement with the Labour Court. Once registered, the consequent *Registered Employment Agreement* (REA) became legally binding on all workers referred to in it, for example, on all construction workers in the entire construction sector. However, some individual employers in the electrical contracting sector were dissatisfied that they had to abide by the pay and conditions set in a REA and they took a constitutional case against the Labour Court. The employers ultimately won their case in the Supreme Court, with the effect that all pre-existing REAs ceased to have statutory effect from 9 May 2013. The government consequently introduced the *Industrial Relations (Amendment) Act 2015* and this provided for a new system of REAs and Sectoral Employment Orders.

Under the amended Act, REAs are now defined as agreements registered with the Labour Court that relate 'to the remuneration or the conditions of employment of workers of any class, type or group made between a trade union or trade unions of workers and one or more than one employer or a trade union of employers, *that is binding only on the parties to the agreement* in respect of the workers of that class, type or group'. In effect, REAs will now only be used in individual enterprises and not apply to a whole sector.

Sectoral Employment Order (SEO)

A *Sectoral Employment Order* (SEO) may set terms and conditions relating to the remuneration and any sick pay scheme or pension scheme, of the workers of a particular class, type or group in an economic sector and *will be legally binding on all workers in the class/type/group*. The process of creating a SEO begins with a trade union or employer organisation requesting the Labour Court examine remuneration/sick pay/pension scheme for workers in a particular sector. The trade union and employer's organisation must be substantially representative of the workers or employers that the request applies to. Following examination, the Labour Court may make a recommendation to the relevant Minister who, should they accept the Court's recommendation, will then sign a SEO. As noted by Wallace *et al.* (2013), an important benefit of having legally binding pay and employment conditions for a whole industrial sector is that it prevents competition between employers in relation to remuneration and relieves individual employers from the burden of having to negotiate with employees and trade unions on pay and conditions at a company level. The application and implications of SEOs remains to be seen.

Joint Labour Committees (JLCs) and Employment Regulation Orders (EROs)

Joint Labour Committees (JLCs) are statutory independent bodies, comprised of equal numbers of employer and worker representatives appointed by the Labour Court with a chair appointed by the relevant Minister. JLCs determine legally binding minimum wages and conditions for often vulnerable workers in areas or sectors of employment where collective bargaining is poorly established. As of 2015, there were eight JLCs as follows:
- Agricultural workers
- Catering (Dublin and Dún Laoghaire)
- Catering (Other)
- Contract cleaning
- Hairdressing
- Hotels (outside Dublin/Cork)
- Retail, grocery, and allied trades
- Security industry

The role of Joint Labour Committees (JLCs) is to make proposals to the Labour Court for an *Employment Regulation Order* (ERO), with minimum rates or remuneration and conditions of employment. If the Labour Court adopts the proposals, it submits them to the relevant Minister who then decides whether to make an ERO or not. If an ERO is signed, it becomes legally binding on all workers referred to in the ERO.

The terms of the *Industrial Relations (Amendment) Act 2012*, which reformed JLC's wage-setting mechanisms, provide that:
- JLCs have the power to set a basic adult wage rate (and two additional higher rates).
- Companies may seek exemption from paying ERO rates due to financial difficulty/ ability to pay.
- JLCs no longer set Sunday premium rates (a new *Statutory Code of Practice on Sunday Working* is to be prepared by the Workplace Relations Commission).
- When setting wage rates, JLCs will have to take into account factors such as competitiveness and rates of employment and unemployment.

The original JLC system attracted considerable criticism from employer bodies who claimed that, by setting minimum pay rates, JLCs were 'costing jobs' particularly in the context of the severe recession and difficult trading conditions of recent years (Higgins 2011a; Turner and O'Sullivan 2013). Employer bodies such as ISME (Irish Small and Medium Enterprises Association) and IBEC, Ireland's main employer association, have been particularly vocal in their criticisms of JLCs and EROs. In 2011, a fast food employer was successful in their High Court challenge to the capacity of JLCs to set legally binding regulations in the catering sector which resulted in all EROs being suspended (O'Sullivan and Royle 2014). The government subsequently reformed the ERO-setting process in the *Industrial Relations Act 2012* and in 2015 and 2016, two new EROs were established for the security and contract cleaning sectors.

ISSUES AND CHALLENGES

The sentiments expressed below by Angela Black (CEO Citizens Information Board), in welcoming the establishment of the WRC, represent a widely-held view which welcomes the new institutional architecture.

> The National infrastructure to support the employment rights agenda has recently changed for the better. The new Workplace Relations Commission represents a step forward for lay advocacy and less formal access to employment rights. It has reduced and simplified the number of employment rights fora, streamlined timeframes and introduced the single online complaint form. These have all contributed to the creation of a more accessible and user-friendly system.

However, the bringing together of the functions formerly delivered separately by the Labour Relations Commission, the Rights Commissioners Service, the Equality Tribunal, the Employment Appeals Tribunal and the National Employment Rights Authority represents a very significant challenge, the dimensions and implications of which will only become apparent in time. Some of the more salient issues and challenges facing these new institutions might include the following:

- The new institutional framework will need to deliver the putative objectives of fast, efficient, and effective throughput of cases in the face of increased demand for its services, particularly in pressures for better pay and working conditions but will it be able to do this?
- Related to the first point, there is an impending need for some form of coordinated model of pay determination, especially in the public sector.
- There remains much debate around ER in essential services and the possibility of a revision of the *Code of Practice on Disputes in Essential Services* including the prospect of legally binding arbitration (Mulvey, 2015).
- The issue of the jurisdiction of the WRC may be tested given that Article 37 of the Constitution gave 'limited' jurisdiction to institutions outside of the normal court system. However, the new architecture introduced by the 2015 Act gives the WRC jurisdiction to hear cases under more than fifty legislative procedures – whether this is 'limited' or not remains a moot point.

- The mediation process in the new architecture is voluntary and therefore can be by-passed should one or other party object. Will 'bypassing' become commonplace and might it have been more appropriate to have made mediation compulsory.
- Adjudication Officers are vested with extensive responsibility but are not required to have qualifications in employment law – might this create issues in complex cases?
- So-called *Alternative Dispute Resolution* (ADR) procedures and practices have become increasingly popular in many countries, initially among non-union firms but now also in unionised organisations, and thus provide alternatives to conventional state provision of dispute resolution agencies. Examples of ADR practices include open-door management approaches, intensive formal communications, brainstorming and other problem-solving techniques, private mediation/conciliation/arbitration and the like (Teague *et al.* 2011; Teague *et al.* 2015; Wallace *et al.* 2013).

THE STATE AS AN EMPLOYER – EMPLOYMENT RELATIONS IN THE STATE SECTOR

Apart from its legislative and facilitative functions, the state plays a significant role as the country's major employer. In 2016, the public sector (inclusive of the semi-state sector) employed some 386,000 workers (CSO 2016). The pattern of public sector employment in Ireland over an eight-year period from 2008 to 2016 is outlined in Table 10.6. This indicates a substantial decline in public sector employment of approximately 11 per cent between 2009 and 2015, largely caused by the impact of the global financial crisis and its detrimental impact on state finances and the economy in general. The pattern of decline in public sector employment from the end of 2009 contrasts with the period preceding the great recession. For example, in the four years before September 2009 employment in the public sector rose by over 17,000 employees.

Table 10.6 Public sector employment (inclusive of semi-state companies) 2008-2016

	2008	2009	2010	2011	2012	2013	2014	2015	2016
Civil service	41,700	42,200	40,100	44,500	39,700	39,200	38,700	38,100	43,600
Defence	11,200	11,200	10,700	10,300	9,800	9,800	9,700	9,700	9,500
Gardaí	14,900	14,600	14,700	14,300	13,700	13,300	13,000	12,800	12,800
Education	116,100	120,200	113,800	117,700	111,900	110,300	111,200	110,900	112,000
Regional bodies	38,900	38,400	36,700	34,600	33,900	32,100	33,000	32,000	32,700
Health	137,800	137,700	137,400	132,900	128,800	123,600	118,700	119,600	123,100
Semi-state companies	56,400	56,900	53,600	55,100	51,400	49,700	51,200	51,400	52,800
Total	417,000	421,200	406,800	409,400	389,200	378,000	375,600	374,500	386,000

Source: CSO (2016).

Trade unions or staff associations represent the bulk of public sector workers. Indeed, we earlier noted the proportionately higher levels of trade union density in the public sector, with some 87 per cent of workplaces having a trade union presence and an estimated 69 per cent of employees being trade union members (O'Connell *et al.* 2010). This is also a characteristic of public sector employment in many other countries.

While in some areas of the public sector distinctive ER features have developed, as the Commission on Industrial Relations (1981) noted many years ago, ER and HR issues in the public and private sectors are largely similar, and differences that occur are largely in the area of procedural responses (Cox and Hughes 1989).

However, Wallace *et al.* (2013) identify one particularly distinguishing historical feature of public sector ER which is the provision and operation of a variety of internal conciliation and arbitration (C&A) schemes. With regard to the determination of pay and conditions of employment, a notable distinction within the public sector has been drawn between those sector areas subject to agreed C&A schemes, and those which come within the scope of the main agencies involved in dispute resolution in Ireland, currently the Workplace Relations Commission and the Labour Court (cf. McGinley 1997). The government initially agreed to the provision of C&A for civil servants on a temporary basis in 1950, which was made permanent in 1955, and this was followed by schemes for teachers, Gardaí, officers of local authorities, health boards and vocational educational committees (cf. McCarthy 1984; Cox and Hughes 1989). Thus, until relatively recently, public sector C&A schemes broadly covered the civil service (the largest category), Gardaí up to Commissioner level, most teachers, some health workers, the Vocational Educational Committees and officer grades of local authorities. Over the years, we have seen a pattern of trade unions and representative organisations in areas of the public service seeking to abandon their specific C&A schemes in favour of securing access to the LRC (WRC) and Labour Court, e.g. the health service, teachers and more recently Gardaí. Health service and local authorities left the C&A schemes for the LRC (WRC)/ Labour Court over a decade ago, while civil service unions voted to leave in 2008, though this decision has not yet been implemented and – as of early 2017 – there appear to be no immediate plans to progress this matter (cf. Higgins 2008; Prendergast 2014). However, it would appear that Gardaí are likely to leave in 2017 as part of the resolution of their 2016 dispute. The defence forces and primary and second-level teachers still remain within the C&A system. This pattern of seeking to leave C&A schemes is perhaps unsurprising, given Frawley's (2002) observation that the (then) LRC and Labour Court generally adopt what he argues are more flexible and pragmatic approaches when compared to what he terms the inflexibility of C&A schemes.

In terms of their operation, the 'conciliation' stage of a C&A scheme generally comprises a conciliation council, involving equal numbers of employees and employer (management) representatives. The issues deemed appropriate for conciliation include recruitment; discipline; superannuation; annual, sick or special leave and claims relating to pay, allowances, overtime, travelling and subsistence, health and safety, and hours of work. Issues not resolved at conciliation may be referred to arbitration and these generally include pay, allowances, hours of work, overtime and leave entitlements. All of the C&A schemes provide for an Arbitration Board which normally consists of a jointly-agreed chairman (often a Senior Counsel) and representatives from the management and the staff side (McGinley, 1997). Both sides may make detailed written submissions, supplemented by oral submissions, and witnesses may be called as appropriate. The findings of the Arbitration Board are sent to the Minister for Finance and other relevant minister(s), who have one month to either approve the report or submit it to government. Under the terms of Local Authority conciliation and arbitration schemes, the management or employee side have the option of rejecting the arbitration decision. In other public sector C&A schemes the arbitration report can only be rejected by moving a Dáil motion to so reject the report or to amend it, an option which is normally seen as exceptional.

A broader but relevant issue impacting on both ER and HRM in the public sector is the issue of public sector reform. This topic is often captured in debates on *New Public Management* (NPM) which Pollitt and Bouckaert (2004: 8) define as '. . . deliberate changes to the structures and processes of public sector organisations with the objective of getting them to run better'. Of course, public management reform is not a new idea and many developed countries have witnessed a stream of public sector reform initiatives since the 1960s. However, the concept of NPM is generally seen as having initially developed from the early 1990s, with particular focus on (i) maximising efficiency in the use of limited resources to achieve identifiable outcomes/results; (ii) viewing public service users as 'consumers'; (iii) delegating authority and accountability for achievement of defined strategies and objectives; (iv) the breaking up of large public service ministries/departments through the creation of public service executive agencies ('agencification') for service delivery; and (v) using 'quasi-market' mechanisms and outsourcing in securing delivery of public services, e.g. using compulsory competitive tendering, outsourcing of core public services and so forth. (Roche 2013; Vaughan-Whitehead 2013).

These various dimensions of the first cycle of NPM had specific implications for ER and HRM, most notably the greater application of private sector-type practices and associated changes in the expectations of leadership in the public sector. The first cycle of NPM also involved a greater focus on strategic HRM, departure from centralised and standardised HR and ER to more tailored arrangements, linking pay and performance to market conditions, and more generally a reversal of the traditional status quo with the private sector now leading and the public sector following (Brown 2004; Llorens and Battaglio 2010; Micheli *et al.* 2012; Pollitt and Bouckaert 2004; Vaughan-Whitehead 2013). However, the record of the impact of such reform is poor. In commenting on the UK context, Rhodes (1994) observed that much of the reforms undertaken have bred '. . . more cynicism than efficiency and effectiveness with aims and achievements often diverging markedly'. A case in point in Ireland is the *Strategic Management Initiative* (1994–2007) which sought to modernise and increase the effectiveness of the Irish public service, using much of the 'toolkit' associated with NPM, e.g. performance management, performance-related pay, career development and progression systems, workplace partnership and a general emphasis on more strategic HRM (Hardiman and MacCartaigh, 2008). In evaluating the impact of the *Strategic Management Initiative,* Roche (2013: 215) describes this as a 'dismal failure' with 'poorly coordinated HR reforms' having achieved little'. He goes on to outline specific failings of various HR initiatives, describing the New Performance Management and Development System as 'ineffective', the performance-related pay systems as 'poorly managed' and workplace partnership as 'confined in the main to peripheral issues' (ibid: 215).

More recently we have witnessed a second cycle of public sector reform. On this occasion, however, the impetus stemmed not from political or senior civil servant preference but rather from the detrimental impact of the global financial crisis, subsequent recession and the associated need for extensive fiscal consolidation. This issue was discussed at length in Chapter 2 and is considered in some depth in the next chapter, in the context of the series of Public Sector Agreements (2010–2018) deployed since 2010 to help manage public sector cutbacks and general retrenchment in both employment numbers and pay and benefits. The first of these agreements ('Croke Park Agreement' 2010–2014) entailed a three-year pay freeze and some concessions on previously imposed unilateral pay cuts in return for increased efficiencies in the public sector. It also involved some of the staples associated with the first cycle of NPM, particularly changes to the design and delivery of some public services. However, unlike the feeble level of reforms under the *Strategic Management Initiative*, this time the impact was substantial. Roche's (ibid: 215) analysis is quite emphatic, stating that the Croke Park Agreement '. . . delivered more reform than that recorded in the history of the Irish public service'. Over the period 2010–2015, these reforms provided for a managed, but largely peaceful, contraction of the public sector, comprising, *inter alia*, a 10 per cent drop in public sector employment, a decrease of approximately 21 per cent in the annual public service pay bill, and cumulative pay reductions of between approximately 7 per cent and 20 per cent, depending on salary level.

CONCLUSION

This chapter has explored the nature of employment relations and described the Irish institutional context. We have seen that ER is focused on the relationship between the parties to the labour process. These parties or key 'actors' include workers, trade unions, worker representatives, employers, managers and the government/government agencies.

In this chapter, we focused particularly on the role of trade unions and the state in Irish employment relations. The next chapter considers the role of employers and management in ER.

11
Employer and Management Approaches to Employment Relations

This chapter focuses on the role of employers and management in employment relations (ER). It initially considers employers' objectives in ER. The role of employers' associations is then addressed, with particular emphasis on the Irish context. It then outlines the main services provided by employer associations and the relative pros and cons of membership of an employers' association. Finally, the chapter considers management approaches to ER and reviews some contemporary developments in this sphere.

EMPLOYERS' OBJECTIVES IN EMPLOYMENT RELATIONS

The primary concern for organisations operating in a competitive environment is to maximise organisational performance and generate satisfactory returns for the owners and stakeholders of the enterprise. Such returns are often expressed in terms of cost-effectiveness and, for the commercial organisation, profitability. Thus, the primary goal of management is to organise the factors of production, including labour, to achieve these objectives. It is difficult to assess the degree to which employers have specific ER objectives or adopt related workplace strategies (Thomason 1984). Organisations vary greatly and a particular organisation's approach to ER (and HRM more generally) will be influenced by a range of environmental factors such as historical developments and market context and conditions (see Chapter 2). Nevertheless, it is worth considering some general perspectives common among employers. Thomason (1984) identifies the following employer beliefs or objectives in ER:

1. *Preservation and consolidation of the private enterprise system*: This has broader political overtones and relates to the concerns of employers to preserve an environment conducive to achieving business objectives at enterprise level. They will be particularly concerned with principles such as private ownership, the profit motive and preservation of managerial authority and control.
2. *Achievement of satisfactory returns for the owners*: This relates directly to the organisation's primary business goals. For commercial organisations to survive in the long term, satisfactory profit levels must be achieved. Consequently, managerial approaches and strategies will always be influenced by this primary concern. Non-profit-making organisations will be equally concerned with cost-effectiveness and quality.

3. *Effective utilisation of human resources*: An organisation's workforce represents a key management resource and its effective utilisation is central to the management process and organisational success.
4. *Maintenance of control and authority in decision-making*: Employers will strive to ensure effective control and authority in executing their management role, particularly in strategic decision-making. This can manifest itself in relation to trade union involvement. For some employers this could mean a determination to lessen union influence and assert managerial prerogative.
5. *Establishment and maintenance of satisfactory management–employee relations*: Employers will strive to maintain good working relations with employees, but this must be achieved within the operational constraints of the organisation. The scope to provide attractive pay and working conditions will vary according to the organisation's market position and profitability as well as its broader HR philosophy. Fostering employee co-operation and commitment may help contribute to the creation of a stable ER climate. Good employment relations will often be a high priority since it represents an important ingredient in ensuring the organisation achieves its primary business goals, as well as being laudable in itself.

THE ROLE OF EMPLOYERS' ASSOCIATIONS

Employers' associations are organisations of employers established to articulate, represent, defend and pursue members' collective interests and strengthen their position with regard to labour market matters (cf. Traxler 2008; Wallace *et al.* 2012). To help achieve the employer and managerial objectives listed above, employers often combine collectively for purposes associated with employment and labour. This is especially the case in many European countries where employers' associations play a prominent role. In particular, they are seen as a key 'social actor' at national and EU level, specifically in regard to their involvement in the development of EU social policy. This contrasts with the US experience, where 'employers' organisations as a means of advancing employer interests are largely negligible' (Behrens and Traxler 2004: 1).

The major impetus for the growth of employer organisations was the perceived need to react to, and deal with, 'new unionism'. This helps distinguish between employers' associations whose *raison d'être* s to deal with labour matters, and those where trade and commercial reasons are the major focus and which are normally referred to as 'trade associations'. Behrens and Traxler (2004: 1) describe employers' associations as 'bodies designed to organise and advance the collective interests that employers have in the labour market'. They identify three main types of 'business interest associations': (i) *'pure' employers' associations*, which specialise in representing only interests related to the labour market and ER issues; (ii) *'pure' trade associations*, which represent only product market interests; and (iii) *'dual' employers' associations*, which combine the representation of labour market and product market interests. Rose (2008) observes that while employers' associations were established mainly for ER purposes, issues related to commercial activity now feature prominently on the agendas of most such associations. Our focus in this chapter embraces only 'pure' and 'dual' employers' associations. Oechslin (1985) provides a long-standing definition of employers' associations which deal with labour market issues:

... formal groups of employers set up to defend, represent or advise affiliated employers and to strengthen their position in society at large with respect to labour matters as distinct from commercial matters.

A traditional reason why employers formed representative associations was to prevent harmful economic competition with each other, particularly in relation to pay, and to counter the power of trade unions. Another reason for the development of such associations was the increasingly complex nature of collective bargaining and employment legislation. Employers' associations also provide a forum for the exchange of views among employers (Thomason 1984; Traxler 2008). The main role of employers' associations is to represent employers' views in ER, and their objectives may be categorised as political, social, economic and ER (see Figure 11.1).

Figure 11.1 Objectives of Employers' Associations

1. *Political*: To effectively represent employers' views to government, the general public and other appropriate bodies so as to preserve and develop a political, economic and social climate in which business objectives can be achieved.

2. *Economic*: To create an economic environment that supports the free enterprise system and ensures that managerial prerogative in decision-making is protected.

3. *Social*: To ensure any social or legal changes best represent the interests of affiliated employers.

4. *Employment Relations*: To ensure a legislative and procedural environment which supports free collective bargaining and to co-ordinate employers' views and approaches to employee relations matters and provide assistance to affiliated employers.

Employers' associations may assume a significant role in representing the interests of employers on national issues. They provide a mechanism through which governments can solicit the opinions of employers on areas such as labour legislation, and are important vehicles for influencing public opinion on more general political matters. This political role is most clearly associated with the desire to influence broad economic decision-making. Employers' organisations will generally support what could be termed conservative economic policies, which serve to protect the interests of employers and ensure freedom from an excess of state intervention in business. In the area of social policy, the approach of employers' associations will be largely pragmatic. On the one hand, they will generally attempt to prevent, or at least lessen, the effects of protective labour or social legislation, such as legal moves towards extending industrial democracy or information disclosure. On the other hand, they will accept some degree of social and legislative reform provided their perceived effects on the interests of business are not adverse. Employers' associations may contribute to enhancing a country's economic performance by providing 'public goods', including the co-ordination of bargaining with such economic requirements as employment and price stability, or participation in public schemes in areas such as vocational education and training. In their analysis of the role of employers' associations in Europe, Behrens and Traxler (2004: 16) conclude that:

. . . employers' associations play a crucial role in a variety of fields. [They] have an essential function in multi-employer collective bargaining and in bargaining coordination, they pursue political lobbying in a variety of fields, and through their involvement in numerous statutory bodies they participate in shaping various aspects of social and economic life.

The main functions of employers' associations in ER may be categorised into four broad areas:
1. *Exchange of views*: Employers' associations provide a useful forum for opinion exchange and discussion. However, employers may also use associations to develop and agree common policies and strategies in ER.
2. *Lobbying*: Employers' associations provide an important means through which employers can represent their views to government, government agencies and other economic and social institutions as appropriate. For example, they may seek to influence labour legislation and government policy generally so that the position of affiliated employers is adequately protected. In Ireland, this role is executed by the major employers' associations, particularly the *Irish Business and Employers Confederation* (IBEC), in representing business and employers' views. They represent employers' opinions on bodies such as the *National Economic and Social Council*, which was established by the government as a forum for the discussion of the principles relating to the economy; the *Irish Human Rights and Equality Commission* whose remit is to promote and protect human rights; and the *Health and Safety Authority*, which deals with occupational health and safety legislation in Ireland. Employers' associations also provide representatives of employers' interests on appropriate bipartite or tripartite bodies such as arbitration councils, government commissions and international organisations. In Ireland, IBEC plays the lead role in nominating employers' representatives to such bodies as the Labour Court and the Workplace Relations Commission.
3. *Media relations*: Employers' associations represent employers' opinions to the general public on relevant issues such as forthcoming employment legislation and budget submissions. On occasion this may also encompass the dissemination of research conducted by employer associations. These functions are generally achieved through media activity.
4. *Provision of specialised services to members*: A major role of employers' associations is the provision of a range of ER services to their affiliated members (Sisson et al. 1983; Wallace et al. 2012). These services might include help with negotiations (e.g. on pay and working conditions); specialist legal advice in a variety of areas, such as layoffs, dismissal, employment equality and health and safety; education, training and consultancy on HRM practice and approaches.

EMPLOYERS' ASSOCIATIONS IN IRELAND

As indicated above, employers' organisations in Ireland are classified into two categories, namely *employers' associations* and *trade associations*. While both of these are required to register with the Registrar of Friendly Societies, only employers' associations are involved in ER and are required to hold a negotiating licence under the terms of the *Trade Union*

Act 1941. In 2015 there were ten registered employers' associations in Ireland (Registrar of Friendly Societies Annual Report 2015):
- Construction Industry Federation
- Cork Master Butchers Association
- Irish Business and Employers Confederation
- Irish Commercial Horticultural Association
- Irish Hotels Federation
- Irish Pharmacy Union
- Irish Printing Federation
- Licensed Vintners' Association
- Regional Newspapers and Printers Association of Ireland
- Society of the Irish Motor Industry

While the number of employers' associations in Ireland is considerably fewer than their trade union counterparts, there is some considerable diversity in membership composition. For example, in the list above there are examples of traditional masters' associations, industry-based associations, and a general association that is national in scope.

IRISH BUSINESS AND EMPLOYERS CONFEDERATION (IBEC)

The *Irish Business and Employers Confederation* (IBEC) is the largest employers' association in Ireland. Using Behrens and Traxler's (2004) categorisation noted earlier, IBEC is a 'dual' association, which represents business and employer interests in all matters relating to ER, labour and social affairs. It was formed in 1993, as a result of the merger of the then Federation of Irish Employers (FIE) and Confederation of Irish Industry (CII) and has a membership base of some 7,500 organisations. As the country's major representative of business and employers, IBEC seeks to shape public policies and influence decision-making in a way that protects and promotes the interests of its members. Unlike its predecessors, IBEC's role is not confined solely to ER, but rather it also seeks to represent employer interests on all matters of economic and social policy. Historically, one of IBEC's most important functions was its participation in the centralised national pay agreements between 1987 and 2009. A summary of IBEC's services to member organisations is outlined in Figure 11.2.

Figure 11.2 IBEC services

- Industrial relations – advice and representation.
- Employment law – information, advice and representation.
- HR best practice – information and case studies on employee engagement, HR strategy, leadership and diversity amongst others.
- Health and safety – information and support.
- Training and development – programmes on management training, health and safety, equality and environment.
- Management consulting – assistance to organisations to develop leadership effectiveness, enhance employee performance and motivation, carry out investigations into bullying and harassment allegations and audit HR and people-related systems.
- HR networking – a forum for managers and employers to interact on ER matters.
- Online compliance tools – online audits to ensure an organisation's policies meet legislative requirements.
- Sample policies and procedures – on parental leave, annual leave, bullying and harassment and internet usage.
- *HR News* – monthly magazine, research on pay trends, past cases at the Labour Court, etc.

Source: IBEC (2012).

OTHER EMPLOYERS' ASSOCIATIONS IN IRELAND

The *Construction Industry Federation* (CIF) is Ireland's second largest employers' association. Unlike IBEC, which represents employers from a range of industrial sectors, the CIF is essentially an industry-based association dealing with both trade and ER affairs on behalf of employers in the construction industry. Estimates suggest that the CIF has a membership of approximately 3,000 firms, incorporating organisations from all construction sub-sectors, grouped into four categories: general contractors; mechanical and electrical contractors; specialist contractors; and home builders. In the ER sphere, the CIF offers advice, information and support on rates of pay, bullying and harassment, data protection and email usage, and all employment-related matters. It also represents members at the Labour Court and Workplace Relations Commission. The CIF is one of the few employers' associations involved in industry level collective bargaining.

Most of the other employers' associations in Ireland are primarily concerned with trade and commercial issues. However, some also have a strong ER dimension. The *Irish Hotels Federation* (representing some 1000 hotels and guesthouses in Ireland) and the *Licensed Vintners' Association* (representing Dublin publicans) have represented employers interests on respective Joint Labour Committees. While they may also provide some HR advice, these associations generally avoid involvement in enterprise level negotiations with trade unions. *The Society of the Irish Motor Industry* also provides advice and assistance on HRM and ER matters to affiliated members. One of the newest employer organisations is the *Quick Service Food Alliance* (QSFA) founded in 2008 to represent employers in the fast food sector in Ireland. While the QSFA does not hold a negotiation licence, and so does not engage in collective bargaining on terms and conditions of employment, it nevertheless has had a substantial impact in the ER domain. This took the form of a legal challenge by the QSFA against the Catering Joint Labour Committee and the Labour Court, with the QSFA claiming that the authority of the JLC to set minimum pay levels was unconstitutional. The High Court found in favour of the QSFA and deemed that the relevant JLC was unconstitutional, precipitating the introduction of new legislation on Joint Labour Committees (JLCs) and Joint Industrial Councils (JICs) in the form of the Industrial Relations (Amendment) Act 2012 (see Chapter 10, Doherty 2012; Wallace *et al.* 2012).

Chambers Ireland (formerly *Chambers of Commerce Ireland*) is an umbrella body for some sixty business associations encompassing approximately 13,000 firms. Its main function is to lobby the government on issues affecting competitiveness and business. Like the QSFA, *Chambers Ireland* does not hold a negotiation licence and so does not engage in collective bargaining on terms and conditions of employment. However, it provides a 24/7 HR service, now called *Peninsula* (see www.chambers.ie), in response to 'a growing need from our members for skilled advice and guidance in the increasingly complex area of personnel and employment law'. The service is aimed at small employers who do not have specialist HR personnel. Higgins (2005: 6) argues that this development 'appears to be a significant challenge to the services provided by other employer bodies, particularly IBEC'. This is in line with Behrens and Traxler's (2004) finding that competition among employers' associations in Europe is on the increase and that it is most intense in regard to representing small and medium-sized enterprises (SMEs).

The Irish experience certainly bears this out. In 1993, a number of small firms left IBEC to form a separate representative body for SMEs, the *Irish Small and Medium Enterprises Association* (ISME). ISME promotes itself as the only independent representative body for owners of small and medium business in Ireland. Its website (see www.isme.ie) states that 'Uniquely in Ireland ISME is independent of big business, big banks and government and gives voice to the issues facing (SME) owner-managers'. ISME currently boasts a membership of over 10,000 SMEs. Although it not a registered employers' association it too provides a range of HR advisory services to members, similar to those of IBEC and Chambers Ireland. ISME has been particularly active as a lobbyist on economic and social affairs, including on ER/HR matters. It was a vehement critic of IBEC and more generally of social partnership before its demise in 2009.

OTHER EMPLOYER GROUPINGS

An employer body which has had a particularly important influence on public policy discourse in Ireland is the *American Chamber of Commerce* (Amcham) (cf. Wallace et al. 2012). Amcham is the representative voice of American multinational companies located in Ireland and its general mission is to promote a business environment that is attractive to these companies (Amcham 2012). Through a variety of working groups on matters such as taxation, employment law, HRM, and research and development Amcham has developed policy platforms on which to base its lobbying activity. Indeed a study of MNCs in Ireland found that Amcham had a high level of access to senior government officials and that this had influenced the content of Irish laws which transposed EU Directives (Dobbins 2005c; Collings et al. 2008). Collings et al. (2008: 258) argue that 'most of these directives have been enacted along lines which are broadly pro-business and tend to impose the minimal possible restrictions on business and management'. Other policy stances Amcham has presented include the retention of Ireland's low level of corporation tax; that Irish salary structures need to be aligned with EU norms because 'wage costs for manufacturing workers in Ireland exceed that of the OECD average and the US by approximately 20 per cent and this is not sustainable'; and that public sector reform must increase productivity and reduce inefficiencies' (Sheehan 2010). In the area of union recognition and collective bargaining, Amcham has consistently and successfully lobbied the government against introducing compulsory union recognition or collective bargaining involving unions. In 2011, the then President of Amcham, Gerard Kilcommins, said 'that any dilution of the current voluntary model would create a barrier to job creation and could damage our capacity to attract and retain inward investment' (Higgins 2011b).

It is important to note that employers may establish and combine in less formal groupings for purposes associated with ER. Such groups are generally used by employers as a forum for the exchange of views and information on ER/HRM matters. They may also facilitate co-ordination of employers' approaches in dealing with particular ER issues. Such associations may be organised by industrial sector or region and may meet on either a semi-permanent basis or only when a significant issue arises. The *Chartered Institute of Personnel and Development* (CIPD) in Ireland, the major professional association for HRM practitioners, may also act as a forum for representing employers' interests in ER.

EMPLOYERS' ASSOCIATION SERVICES

Our earlier discussion briefly alluded to the range of employment relations services provided by employers' associations in areas such as collective bargaining, research and advice. These services are discussed in greater detail below.

RESEARCH AND ADVISORY SERVICES

Many years ago, in commenting on developments in the UK, Sisson (1983) said that the greatest area of growth in the work of employers' associations was in the provision of research and advisory services. Such services fall into three broad categories: (i) legal, (ii) pay; and (iii) specialist consultancy. The growth of *labour and employment legislation* in Ireland since the 1970s has led to a significant increase in employers' demands for specialist legal advice in areas such as dismissals, employment conditions and employment equality. As we have seen, many larger employers' associations provide a specialist HR and legal advisory service for member companies. They may also publish and disseminate guidelines on legislation for their membership. A more traditional service involves the provision of *information and advice* to members on wage rates and levels of wage increases. Some associations conduct surveys of wage levels and fringe benefits for different occupations and geographical regions, and can consequently provide members with up-to-date information on local, regional and national pay trends and advise on reward issues. Some employers' associations also provide members with specialist advice and assistance, on issues such as performance management, productivity schemes and recruitment.

COLLECTIVE BARGAINING

Historically, one of the most important services provided by employers' associations was assisting employers in collective bargaining with trade unions. Such bargaining might be of a multi-employer (regional, industry or national) or single employer variety. Multi-employer bargaining on an industry or national basis has traditionally meant a key role for employers' associations in representing relevant employers in negotiations on pay and related matters.

In Ireland, employers' associations have been particularly prominent in periods of centralised pay bargaining. IBEC plays a significant role, being the major representative of employers' opinions to the other 'social partners'. In commenting on centralised bargaining Behrens and Traxler (2004: 15–16) observed that '. . . IBEC has seen its role in national bargaining gradually expand under successive social partnership agreements'.

Since 2009 we have seen the locus of collective bargaining move from national to enterprise level. However, employers' associations still play an important role in advising and assisting management in the bargaining process. This role may incorporate co-ordination of policy on pay and employment-related issues; formulating general guidelines for affiliated employers; supplying research data and information for use in negotiations; and providing expert personnel, to either conduct the negotiations or advise and assist local management involved in such negotiations.

A particularly important role for employers' associations in collective bargaining is that of *representing affiliated members* in face-to-face negotiations or during third party referrals. As noted above, they may represent members in enterprise-level negotiations with trade unions. They may also represent employers' interests in industry-level or national-level bargaining. An increasingly significant aspect of this representational role applies to conciliation, mediation and arbitration (see Chapter 10). Here, officials from employers' associations may represent affiliates in tribunal hearings, conciliation meetings and arbitration hearings such as the Labour Court or Workplace Relations Commission.

EDUCATION AND TRAINING

An increasingly important service provided by larger employers' associations relates to the provision of education and training programmes for affiliated members. Such provision is often aimed at keeping member firms *au fait* with current developments in ER and HRM, such as employment law, working conditions and EU-level matters. They may also focus on developing managerial capacity among members' firms by providing training programmes for HR practitioners in areas such as negotiating skills and employment legislation. Employers' associations also provide wider forms of training. IBEC, for example, operates specialist training for its members in the retail industry as part of the *Skillsnet* initiative funded by the National Training Fund.

MEMBERSHIP OF EMPLOYERS' ASSOCIATIONS

In analysing the factors impacting on membership of employers' associations, Thomason (1984) notes the impact of *corporate form*. In particular, Thomason (1984) differentiates between entrepreneurs who essentially own and run their businesses and abstract corporate entities that are run by professional management. The corporate business firm has replaced the older entrepreneurial-type firm as the prevalent type of organisation in membership of employers' associations. Thomason argues that the change in composition of membership from entrepreneurial owner-managers to corporate business firms run by professional management partly explains the changing role of employers' associations.

There is also evidence that *country of ownership* may influence the membership of employers' associations. In Ireland, a study of newly established companies found that US-owned firms were less likely to join employers' associations than other foreign-owned companies (Gunnigle 1995). This may have been related to the corporate approach to trade unions and collective bargaining. Where this involves a preference for non-union status, such organisations may have been reluctant to join an employers' association (Purcell and Sisson 1983; Oechslin 1985), though Lavelle et al. (2009) study of multinational companies (MNCs) in Ireland found that the overwhelming majority (92 per cent) were members of an employers' association, with IBEC (86 per cent of all MNCs) being the preferred choice of these MNCs. MNCs in the manufacturing sector (94 per cent) were marginally more likely to be IBEC members than those in the service sector (90 per cent). This study also found that 96 per cent of unionised MNCs were employers' association members, as compared to 85 per cent of non-union MNCs. This suggests that non-union MNCs also have a high propensity to take up membership of employers' associations. The study found no significant difference in the propensity to join employers' associations among MNCs of different national origin.

The issue of *public sector organisations* becoming members of employers' associations is a relatively recent phenomenon. While initially it might seem incompatible for public sector organisations to join employers' associations (generally viewed as bastions of free enterprise), many public sector organisations, especially semi-state companies, have adopted a pragmatic approach in taking up membership, influenced no doubt by their high levels of unionisation and consequent perceived need for advice and assistance on ER matters. Indeed, the fees paid to employer associations have attracted some considerable controversy, especially in the context of the recent recession. A 2011 review by *Industrial Relations News* (Sheehan, 2011) estimated that IBEC was paid the following fees by state agencies and state-owned organisations: *ESB* €150,000 (2007); *Dublin Airport Authority* €135,000 (2007); *Coillte* €96,000 (2011); *Central Bank* €40,000 (2011) and *VHI* €30,000 (2011).

It has also been argued that an *organisation's size* is an important factor impacting on membership and patterns of utilisation of employers' associations. It is sometimes suggested that small firms have more to gain by joining the associations, for reasons related to cost and resource considerations. When a small organisation becomes involved in formalised collective bargaining it may be particularly attractive to join an employers' association. A small organisation may not be in a position to employ HR specialists, while the owner or manager of such firms may not have either the necessary time or the expertise to handle such matters effectively. Since the cost of joining such an association is generally related to employment size and/or profitability, it may be relatively inexpensive for small firms to join. However, despite the apparent validity of this line of argument, there is no conclusive evidence to support the view that small firms are more likely to join employers' associations (Gunnigle 1995). In fact, the research evidence indicates that employers' associations are not more frequently used by smaller organisations (Daniel and Millward 1983). Indeed, it seems that larger firms are more likely to join and utilise the services of employers' associations and that membership is positively correlated with the organisation's size, trade union recognition, and the existence of a specialist HR function.

Important influences on organisational decisions about whether or not to join employers' associations are the perceived *advantages and disadvantages of membership*. Clearly such perceptions will be influenced by issues specific to the individual organisations, such as management's desired approach to ER. Broader contextual and environmental factors, such as industrial sector, size, product market performance and ownership, will also be influential (Thomason 1984). Table 11.1 summarises some of the generally perceived advantages and disadvantages of employers' association membership. Clearly the relative significance of these will vary between organisations and across industrial sectors.

Table 11.1 Advantages and disadvantages of employers' association membership

Advantages	Disadvantages
Collective and uniform approach	Cost of membership
Advice on ER and trade union matters	Loss of autonomy
Technical/specialist advice and information	Loss of flexibility
Access to skilled negotiators	Comparisons with other firms
Advisory and consultancy services	Greater acceptance of the role of trade unions
Standardised pay and employment conditions	Greater formalisation in ER
On par with regional/industry norms	
Influence on government/national affairs	

The global financial crisis and subsequent recession undoubtedly impacted on employers' propensity to join employers' associations, particularly in regard to cost of membership. However, the recent economic recovery may render this consideration less pertinent.

The range of ER services provided by employers' associations, considered in the preceding section, correlates closely with the perceived advantages of membership of employers' associations (as outlined in Table 11.1). It is therefore appropriate to consider here some reasons why organisations may choose not to join employers' associations.

A common argument for not joining an employers' association is the potential reduction of *managerial autonomy* in decision-making. As in any formal association or club, employers' associations will be keen to ensure that members adhere to commonly agreed polices in areas such as pay and conditions of employment. These policies and related guidelines normally reflect the needs of the general membership. However, it is a decision for the individual organisation to assess whether such norms are appropriate to its particular needs.

The issue of *comparability with other firms* is also an important consideration. By joining an association comprised of numerous other companies, a particular firm's pay and conditions will be compared to the general membership or at least to remuneration levels in other firms operating in the same industrial sector. Trade unions often use the terms of collective agreements struck with some member firms as 'leverage' to secure similar terms with other firms.

Another important consideration is the impact of a firm's desired *ER/HRM 'style'*. As we have seen, the legal definition of employers' associations means that they are, in a legal context, trade unions of employers. Traditionally they have had a preference for dealing with their employee counterparts, trade unions, through collective bargaining. However, it is also clear that many firms now pursue ER 'styles' which seek to avoid trade union recognition. Some of these firms place a strong emphasis on dealing with employees on a more individual basis (Gunnigle et al. 1998; Doherty 2013). For such firms, membership of an employers' association (i.e. a trade union of employers) might well be anathema, or at least inconsistent with a management approach based on direct contact with individual employees.

A more pragmatic reason for non-membership is related to the *cost of membership*, as mentioned above. Normally firms pay the full cost of membership regardless of services used. This contrasts with the situation in relation to the use of management consultants, where firms usually only pay a fee which is related to services used. The subscription fee paid to IBEC is normally based on a company's total salaries/wages paid in a financial year. This can range from a membership fee of approximately €2,000 at the lowest end to a fee of approximately €200,000 for firms with a pay bill in the region of €280 million.

MANAGEMENT APPROACHES TO EMPLOYMENT RELATIONS

While employers' associations clearly play a central role in ER, individual employers are primarily responsible for the development and implementation of ER policies and practices in their own organisations and workplaces. In the remainder of this chapter we address management approaches to ER and pertinent research on this issue.

MANAGERIAL FRAMES OF REFERENCE

In his seminal work, Fox (1968) argues that management approaches to ER are largely determined by the frame of reference adopted by managers. A frame of reference is defined by Thelen and Withall (1949) as the 'main selective influences at work as the perceiver supplements, omits and structures what he notices'. Fox (1968) suggests that a manager's frame of reference is important because:

1. It determines how management expects people to behave and how it thinks they should behave (i.e. values and beliefs).
2. It determines management reactions to actual behaviour (i.e. management practice).
3. It shapes the methods management chooses when it wishes to change the behaviour of people at work (e.g. strategies/policies).

Fox identified two alternative frames of reference to help evaluate management approaches to ER. These were termed (i) the unitarist; and (ii) the pluralist frame of reference. The key features of these two approaches are summarised in Table 11.2.

Table 11.2 Unitarist and Pluralist frames of reference

Unitarist	Pluralist
Emphasises the dominance of common interests. Everyone – management and employees – should strive to achieve the organisation's primary business goals since everyone will benefit.	The organisation is viewed as composed of different interest groups with different objectives but linked instrumentally by their common association with the organisation.
There is only one source of authority (management) and it must command full loyalty.	Management's role is to achieve some equilibrium satisfying the various interest groups and thereby helping to achieve the organisation's goals.
Anyone who doesn't share these common interests and does not accept managerial authority is viewed as a dissenter/agitator.	A certain amount of conflict is inevitable since the objectives of the parties will clash on occasion.
Since dissenters endanger organisational success they must either fall into line, appreciate the overriding importance of corporate goals and accept managerial authority, or risk elimination from the organisation.	Management must expect and plan for conflict so that it can be handled successfully and not endanger the achievement of the organisation's primary objectives.
	Management should not seek to suppress conflicting interests but rather aim to reconcile them in the organisation's interests.

Source: Fox, 1968.

These contrasting frames of reference represent dominant ER orientations that may be adopted by management. In practice, one finds that managers do not strictly adhere to one of these approaches but may adopt different approaches in different situations and/or change their approaches over time. Nevertheless, these frames of reference provide a useful framework for evaluating management approaches to ER at enterprise level. A germane example is Marchington's (1982) analysis of how management approaches in three different aspects of ER (dealing with trade unions, management prerogative and industrial conflict) might differ depending on the particular frames of reference adopted.

In first evaluating *management approaches to trade unions*, Marchington argues that managers holding a unitarist perspective would see no role for trade unions. Rather these managers would generally view unions as encroaching on management's territory, making unreasonable demands, prohibiting change and flexibility and thereby impacting negatively on competitiveness. In effect, trade unions would be viewed as an externally imposed force which introduces conflict into the organisation and prohibits the development of 'good' ER. Furthermore, workers associated with the promotion of trade unionism would be seen as 'disloyal', 'agitators' or 'troublemakers'. In contrast, managers adopting a pluralist perspective would see a legitimate role for trade unions in representing and articulating employees' views in the workplace. They would also accept that employees might have loyalties to groupings other than management.

A second area where Marchington (1982) identified different approaches was in relation to *management prerogative*. Management prerogative refers to areas of decision-making where management see themselves as having sole decision-making authority, i.e. management's 'right to manage and make decisions' (Salamon 2000: 5). Marchington suggests that managers adopting a unitarist frame of reference would be unwilling to accept any diminution of management prerogative as a result of trade union organisation. Rather they would view management as the legitimate decision-making authority. Managers adopting a pluralist frame of reference, however, would acknowledge the legitimacy of other interest groups in the organisation, such as trade unions. They would also accept the need to allow trade unions to play a role in decision-making and, consequently, accept some reduction in managerial prerogative.

The final area where management approaches may differ is in relation to *industrial conflict*. Salamon (2000: 5) notes that the underlying assumption of the unitarist frame of reference is that 'organisational systems exist in basic harmony and conflict is unnecessary and exceptional'. Marchington suggests that managers adopting a unitarist frame of reference would view the enterprise very much along 'team'/'family' lines, with everyone working together to achieve company objectives. In this context, conflict is seen as something of an aberration, only occurring as a result of a breakdown of communications or the work of troublemakers. By contrast, managers adopting a pluralist frame of reference would accept that some degree of industrial conflict is inevitable because the interests of management and labour will clash on occasion. Since the pluralist perspective accepts the legitimacy of conflict, managers adopting this frame of reference will tend to plan for it by, for example, agreeing to grievance disputes and disciplinary procedures. In organisations that operate under a pluralist framework, the role of management is often a balancing act in recognising the legitimacy of the organisation's conflicting interests (Rose 2008).

THE IDEA OF MANAGEMENT STYLES IN ER

Moving beyond Fox's unitarist–pluralist dichotomy, scholars have attempted to develop categorisations of management styles in ER to explain differences in organisational approaches to ER. One of the most widely used management styles typologies is that of Purcell and Sisson (1983), who developed a fivefold categorisation of 'ideal–typical' styles of ER management. Their typology, which was based on differing management approaches to trade unions, collective bargaining and consultation/communications, is outlined in Table 11.3.

Table 11.3 Management styles in employment relations

Management Style	Characteristics
Traditionalist	'Orthodox unitarism': Opposes role for unions; little attention to employee needs.
Sophisticated Paternalist	Emphasises employee needs (training, pay, conditions, etc.); discourages unionisation; demands employee loyalty and commitment.
Sophisticated Modern	Accepting of role for trade unions in specific areas; emphasis on industrial relations procedures and consultative mechanisms. Two variants: (i) *Constitutionalists*: Emphasise codification of management–union relations through detailed collective agreements (ii) *Consulters*: Collective bargaining established but management emphasis on direct contact and communications, playing down formal union role at workplace level.
Standard Modern	Pragmatic approach: Accepting of trade union but no overall philosophy or strategy developed – 'fire-fighting' approach.

Source: Purcell and Sisson (1983).

Despite the attractiveness of management style typologies, it appears that in reality it is difficult to categorise organisations into neat 'ideal–typical' groupings (Deaton 1985; Gunnigle 1995). Using data from some 1,400 UK organisations, Deaton (1985) sought to empirically evaluate the appropriateness of Purcell and Sisson's (1983) typology. He firstly attempted to classify management styles in unionised companies as either 'sophisticated' or 'standard modern'. However, Deaton (1985) found it difficult to distinguish between these two types of management style, suggesting that it is rather tenuous to classify firms recognising trade unions into either of these groupings. Deaton (1985) also attempted to categorise management styles in non-union companies into 'paternalist', 'anti-union', and 'sophisticated paternalists'. Here Deaton (1985) found greater evidence of organisations conforming to Purcell and Sisson's 'ideal–typical' style typologies. He found that 'sophisticated paternalists' and 'anti-union' organisations emerged as 'polar opposites', while 'paternalist' organisations took the middle ground (having some characteristics common to both 'anti-union' and 'sophisticated paternalist' organisations).

Deaton (1985) concluded that attempts to classify firms into a small number of ideal styles were problematic and that, while the distinction between organisations that recognise trade unions and those that do not is crucial, it may not be possible to further sub-divide styles in organisations where unions are recognised. However, Deaton (1985) felt that there was a greater tendency in organisations that do not recognise trade unions to adopt the 'identikit' styles suggested above. Using more anecdotal evidence to examine variations in managerial styles in ER, Poole (1986) suggested that the evidence points to the existence of 'a progressively rich array' of hybrid styles, rather than any convergence towards predominant styles or patterns.

CONCLUSION

This chapter has reviewed the role of employers and employer organisations in ER, placing particular emphasis on the Irish context. It initially considered employers objectives in ER and subsequently examined the role played by employers' associations. Finally, it reviewed the role of management in ER and management approaches and styles at enterprise level.

In the next chapter, we focus more specifically on collective bargaining and related areas of ER practice.

12
Employment Relations Practice

This chapter considers key areas of employment relations (ER) practice, such as collective bargaining, grievance handling, discipline administration and employee participation. It also considers industrial conflict and its resolution. It begins by reviewing the main means through which employers, trade unions and sometimes government interact in ER, namely through collective bargaining.

COLLECTIVE BARGAINING

Collective bargaining refers to the process through which agreements on pay, working conditions, procedures and other negotiable issues are reached between organised employees and management representatives. It therefore provides an orderly mechanism through which the divergent interests of workers and employers can be reconciled, using a process involving negotiation and compromise hence providing a way of dealing with potentially destructive conflict. Its principal feature is that employees do not negotiate with employers individually but rather do so collectively through representatives (normally trade unions, but also staff associations or employee councils/committees) with the result that various aspects of employee's terms and conditions of employment are determined collectively. Collective bargaining has traditionally been seen as the primary means of regulating interactions between unions, employees and employers in Ireland (cf. Wallace *et al.* 2013).

The normal objective and end product of collective bargaining is a collective agreement. However, this objective does not preclude situations in which negotiations break down and some form of industrial action, up to and including a strike, ensues. Collective agreements are frequently regarded as covering two different kinds of arrangements, namely those that deal with *substantive* issues and those that are *procedural* in nature. The scope of substantive agreements may vary widely between organisations, but generally address the 'hard' terms of collective agreements, such as levels of wage increases, hours of work, sick-pay, holidays and so forth. In contrast, procedural issues are concerned with the ways (procedures) in which terms and conditions of employment are arrived at and how differences over the application of agreed terms and conditions are settled. Such procedural arrangements normally prescribe how wage claims, disciplinary issues, grievances, disputes and related matters are to be processed or handled by the parties.

For collective bargaining to operate effectively a number of conditions are necessary:
1. Workers must have the freedom to join together in trade unions which are not in any way under the control or influence of employers – often termed 'freedom of association' (see Chapter 10 for further detail on trade union recognition and the legal definition of collective bargaining in Ireland).
2. Employers must be prepared to recognise and deal with these trade unions for collective bargaining purposes and accept the constraints placed upon their capacity to deal with employees on an individual basis.

As we noted in Chapter 11, the Irish 'system' of collective bargaining is essentially voluntary in nature, meaning that employers and trade unions are free to engage or not in collective bargaining on pay or work-related issues. Any collective agreements reached by the parties are also voluntary and generally binding in honour only. Collective bargaining thus relies mainly on the moral commitment of the participants to adhere to agreements reached.

Argued advantages of collective bargaining include the following (cf. ILO 1975; Donovan 1968; Wallace et al. 2013):
- It serves a dual purpose by providing a means of determining the wages and working conditions for groups of workers, while also enabling employers and workers to define the rules governing their relationship.
- It is seen as more flexible than other methods (e.g. regulation by the state).
- It helps redress the disparity in bargaining power between the individual employee and his/her employer.
- It gives workers an opportunity to participate in decisions on the conditions of employment under which they operate.
- It provides an orderly mechanism for identifying and handling grievances and differences of opinion through negotiation aimed at securing eventual agreement.

According to the International Labour Organization (ILO), freedom of association and collective bargaining are fundamental rights. Both freedom of association and the right to collective bargaining form an integral part of the *ILO Declaration on Fundamental Principles and Rights at Work* (ILO 2016). However, traditional systems of collective bargaining face many challenges including the changing nature of work, political changes and the impact of globalisation. Furthermore, as noted earlier, trade union membership and collective bargaining coverage have also declined in many industrialised economies, including Ireland.

While collective bargaining has been the primary means of managing ER in most industrialised nations, it is not the only method of dealing with issues such as pay and working conditions. Even in countries where it is widely used, such as Ireland, collective bargaining usually operates alongside other mechanisms, such as individual bargaining between employer and employees, regulation by the government (legislation) and the unilateral imposition of terms of employment by management or (more exceptionally) by trade unions. Individual bargaining refers to the situation whereby individual workers negotiate on a one-to-one basis with their employer to arrive at an 'individual contract' that sets outs the terms and conditions of each individual's employment.

LEVELS OF COLLECTIVE BARGAINING

Collective bargaining may take place at different levels as illustrated in Figure 12.1. The most obvious, of course, is bargaining between union and management representatives at the level of the individual workplace or establishment, i.e. *establishment-level bargaining*. However, we also know that many organisations, such as banks, restaurant chains or manufacturing firms, have multiple establishments. Thus, collective bargaining might also take place between unions representing workers from a number of establishments and corporate-level management, i.e. *multi-establishment bargaining*. Both establishment level and multi-establishment level bargaining are focused on a *single employer*. However, employers with common interests may also choose to form employer associations as we seen in the previous chapter. Often these common interests stem from operating in the same industrial sector or geographical region and, consequently, such an employer grouping may seek to bargain with trade unions representing workers in the relevant industrial sector or region, i.e. *multi-employer/sectoral bargaining*. In Ireland, for example, this has occurred in sectors such as the construction industry, where the *Construction Industry Federation*, representing employers, and a grouping of trade unions representing workers in the construction sector, have concluded collective agreements dealing with pay and working conditions for that sector. Until the comparatively recent past, we have also seen that *national-level bargaining*, involving representatives of employers, government and trade unions, operated as the principal means of dealing with pay, in addition to numerous other aspects of economic and social affairs, in Ireland.

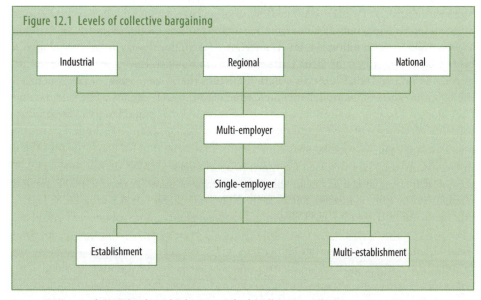

Figure 12.1 Levels of collective bargaining

Source: Wallace et al. (2013) *Industrial Relations in Ireland* (Gill & Macmillan).

This tendency towards so-called 'centralised' bargaining essentially refers to institutionalised, and primarily national-level, negotiations between trade unions (via the *Irish Congress of Trade Unions* (ICTU), employers' associations (primarily the *Irish Business and Employers Confederation* (IBEC) and some other employer associations, government and certain other societal groupings (e.g. farming organisations, and the community and voluntary sector) over wages and various other economic and social issues. Under centralised bargaining, these national-level bodies negotiate agreements, primarily on wage increases, to which their members are expected to adhere. Despite the voluntary nature of such agreements, they traditionally attract high levels of adherence from the parties involved (Teague and Donaghey 2009). Such national-level bargaining normally operates alongside supplementary workplace-level bargaining on company-level issues, such as work practices and productivity.

There are clearly pros and cons associated with collective bargaining on either a single- or multi-employer basis. On the one hand, employers may prefer multi-employer bargaining because it relieves them of the task of periodic wage negotiations and allows them greater scope to devote time to other aspects of organisational management. Also, the standardisation of pay levels and working conditions helps avoid wage competition between employers, thereby regulating an important aspect of the competitive market. On the other hand, multi-employer bargaining can have disadvantages for employers. For example, bargaining on a single-employer basis can allow employers greater capacity to ensure that wage levels and other conditions of employment more closely reflect the particular competitive position of their organisation. This might be achieved by *inter alia* linking concessions on pay or working conditions to union and worker commitments to increase productivity or contribute to other cost reductions in a way that may be more difficult to achieve through multi-employer bargaining.

COLLECTIVE BARGAINING IN IRELAND

Since independence, collective bargaining in Ireland has oscillated between national and establishment or enterprise-level bargaining (including levels in between), with a general trend towards centralised (national) bargaining until the onset of the recession in 2009. From 1970 until 2009 pay determination in Ireland was predominantly handled through some form of centrally bargained agreement between employer associations and trade unions (except for the years 1982–6). Between 1987 and 2009 there were seven tripartite agreements involving unions, employers and government (see Table 12.1). This long period of centralised bargaining came to an abrupt end in 2009 when the prevailing centralised agreement *Towards 2016 – Transition Agreement* was effectively abandoned by the government, which imposed public service pay cuts as one means of dealing with the great recession, and by private sector employers, many of which deployed pay freezes or cuts (see Chapter 2 for greater detail).

Table 12.1 National-level agreements 1987–2009	
Programme for National Recovery	1987–1990
Programme for Economic and Social Progress	1991–1994
Programme for Competitiveness and Work	1994–1997
Partnership 2000	1997–2000
Programme for Prosperity and Fairness	2000–2003
Sustaining Progress	2003–2006
Towards 2016*	2006–2009
(* The agreement collapsed in 2009 – see Chapter 2 for further detail.)	

For the first time in decades, Ireland entered the current period of enterprise-level bargaining in the private sector, while in the public sector a series of agreements were concluded between the government and public service unions as follows:
- The *Public Service Agreement 2010–2014* ('Croke Park Agreement'): In 2010, public service management and unions reached agreement on a 'comprehensive agenda for public service transformation and on a framework for public service pay determination'.
- The *Public Service Stability Agreement 2012–2016* ('Haddington Road Agreement'): It sets out a series of pay and productivity measures to be implemented in the public sector.
- The *Public Service Stability Agreement 2013–2018* ('Lansdowne Road Agreement'): It began the process of reversing pay and implementing pension cuts introduced in the public sector from 2008.

CONTEMPORARY DEVELOPMENTS

The last so-called 'social partnership' agreement, *Towards 2016*, was negotiated in 2005/2006 and sought to cover a much longer time frame than previous agreements, which had usually lasted in the region of three years. *Towards 2016* was designed as a ten-year framework within which the terms for pay agreements for the private sector and the public service would be negotiated roughly every two to three years. The rationale for this long-term focus was related to prospective changes in the profile of Ireland's population in the future. An anticipated large increase in population was expected to put further pressure on services, infrastructure and the environment, and this, combined with other changes in the global market, made a compelling case for taking a longer-term view on policy analysis, formulation and implementation. In its design it also sought to address a number of related issues, including statutory minimum pay; employee financial involvement; partnership at the workplace; workplace learning; pensions; equal opportunities; work–life balance; and the modernisation of the public service.

The first phase of the *Towards 2016* agreement covered roughly twenty-seven months and provided for four sets of pay increases: 3 per cent (six months), 2 per cent (nine months), 2.5 per cent (six months) and 2.5 per cent (six months). The second pay increase of 2 per cent was to be augmented to 2.5 per cent for workers whose weekly pay was at or less than €400 per week. This phase covered the period from June 2006 to September 2008.

The second phase, termed the '*Transitional Agreement*', was negotiated in the context of the ten-year *Towards 2016* social partnership framework. Unfortunately, this agreement was concluded in the same month that the government formally declared the economy had entered recession and that it planned to bring forward the budget to help address the detrimental economic impact of the global financial crisis. In late 2009 IBEC withdrew from the terms of the Transitional Agreement, having failed to agree a suspension of the pay terms with the ICTU. As Sheehan (2009) observed this paved the way for a period of enterprise-level bargaining. By the end of 2009, just 124 companies had paid some element of the pay increases agreed under the Transitional Agreement, according to the specialist weekly journal *Industrial Relations News* (Higgins 2010).

In March 2010, public service unions and the government negotiated a three-year pay freeze and the potential claw-back of some of the imposed pay cuts, in return for increased efficiencies and flexible working arrangements in the public sector. The Public Service Agreement of 2010, referred to as the *Croke Park Agreement*, identified a variety of areas for public sector reform, including redeployment of staff; reconfiguration of the design and delivery of public services; pay and pension policy; mechanisms for resolving disagreements; and, finally, plans to maintain a stable ER climate. As Wallace *et al.* (2013: 298) note, the *Croke Park Agreement* effectively entailed agreement to '. . . no further cuts in core pay in return for large-scale reductions in the number of (public sector) employees and co-operation with change and restructuring'.

The *Croke Park Agreement* was succeeded by two further public sector agreements, firstly the Public Service Stability Agreement 2013–2016, known as the *Haddington Road Agreement* and an extension thereof, the Public Service Stability Agreement 2013–2018 commonly referred to as the *Lansdowne Road Agreement*. A summary of the terms of these agreements is outlined in Table 12.2. Against a background of public sector pay cuts of between 5 and 15 per cent in the 2010 budget, the first public sector agreement of the period, the *Croke Park Agreement*, entailed a government commitment not to impose further pay cuts or layoffs on the public sector. The general pattern in these agreements was initially on freezing pay, increasing working time and workload in return for the acceptance of restructuring and avoidance of compulsory redundancies. More latterly the focus has shifted to embrace some degree of pay restoration, a process which is currently ongoing. This is manifest in the most recent *Lansdowne Road Agreement* which began the process of reversing pay and pension cuts introduced in the public sector since 2008.

Table 12.2 Summary of public sector agreements 2010–2018

Croke Park Agreement	**Haddington Road Agreement**	**Lansdowne Road Agreement**
Public Service Agreement 2010–2014	*Public Service Stability Agreement (2013–2016)*	*Public Service Stability Agreement (extension) (2013–2018)*
• Reduction in numbers (but no compulsory redundancies). • Moratorium on recruitment and promotions. • No further reductions in pay, pensions or layoffs beyond those unilaterally implemented by the government in 2009/2010. • Public sector unions agreed to industrial peace and to cooperate on wide scale public sector reforms aimed at increasing efficiency, flexibility and redeployment, and at reducing cost and headcount. • New pensions scheme (less favourable) for new entrants. • New annual leave and sick pay arrangements for all. • Introduction of binding arbitration for disputes arising from this agreement (this pertained through Haddington/Lansdowne Road Agreement).	• Pay cuts for those earning more than €65,000 (commitment to some reversal in 2017/2018). • Flexibility required on redeployment, performance management, work-sharing and restructuring. • Temporary increment freezes. • Reduction in overtime pay. • Sunday premia pay retained. • Longer working hours. • Protection against compulsory redundancy. • Ongoing commitment to industrial peace and public sector reform.	• Restoration of pay cuts – average payment of €2,000 over three phases to majority of public servants between January 2016 and September 2017. (Pay restoration aimed primarily at low-paid public servants.) • Increase in pension levy threshold to €28,750. • Most public service pensioners will experience restoration up to a value of approx. €34,000. • Continued commitment to industrial peace and public sector reform.

Concurrently, the focus in the private sector has moved to enterprise-level. Here companies engaged in collective bargaining have negotiated local agreements with trade unions, while many non-union companies have decided on pay movements without negotiations with employees. From 2011, the emergence of local pay bargaining, mainly in companies operating in export-oriented sectors (e.g. chemicals, pharmaceuticals, medical devices and food and drinks), reflects a phenomenon not witnessed since the 1980s, and it initially entailed pay increases averaging 2 per cent per annum (Higgins 2011c).

It seems that the extent of local pay bargaining in the private sector increased in subsequent years and entailed greater sectoral coverage, particularly into the services sector (e.g. retail and banking). A standard pay increase of 2 per cent per annum was endured as the accepted norm, but with increasing use of 'add-ons' relating to issues such as permanency (security of job tenure), annual leave and improvements to sick pay, bonus schemes and healthcare (Higgins and Prendergast 2014). Certainly, the 2 per cent per annum average remained the benchmark in 2015, though some companies conceded higher increases in the 2–3 per cent range. By 2016 there were increasing pressures for pay increases substantially above the 2 per cent benchmark that had broadly prevailed from 2011. (Sheehan 2016c). It remains to be seen as to whether the pattern of moderate private sector pay increases endures or whether we will enter a phase of more substantial pay movement in both the private and public sectors (see *Industrial Relations News* for independent up to date information).

ER NEGOTIATIONS

A fundamental element of collective bargaining is the negotiations process. Negotiations in ER involve discussions and interactions between representatives of employers and employees over some divisive issues with the objective of reaching agreement. Walton and McKersie (1965) famously identified two dominant forms of bargaining in ER:

- *'Distributive' bargaining* involves negotiations over pay and conditions of employment, which tend to be characterised as distributive because they involve bargaining or haggling over issues where a favourable settlement for one party means an element of loss for the other. This 'win–lose' approach represents an adversarial model of collective bargaining, where each party pursues its own specific objectives and hopes to concede minimal concessions to the other party. It is most obvious in pay negotiations where concessions by management inevitably represent both a quantifiable cost and a reduction in profits/dividends.
- *'Integrative' (or 'co-operative') bargaining* involves a more joint problem-solving approach, which occurs where both parties are concerned with finding a jointly acceptable solution resulting in benefits for both sides (i.e. a 'win-win' approach).

As we will see below, in practice ER negotiations normally involve some combination of both distributive and integrative approaches.

PHASES IN THE NEGOTIATIONS PROCESS

Formal ER negotiations normally involve one party submitting a claim to, or raising an issue with, the other party and then entering into discussions on this claim or issue. Subsequent interactions generally involve the parties bargaining and haggling over the divisive issues and reporting back to their respective constituents. Such negotiations may conclude either by reaching a mutually acceptable agreement or possibly by a failure to agree, resulting in a breakdown of negotiations. Such an impasse may be addressed through further discussion, use of third party conciliation, mediation or arbitration (see Chapter 10), or the use of sanctions, up to and including industrial action. Whether or not the negotiating process reaches a successful conclusion depends on a number of factors; among the most important are willingness to compromise, bargaining skills (including persuasive abilities) and, ultimately, the balance of power between parties, all of which will influence the final outcome of the negotiations.

It is important to note that negotiating is an ongoing process not limited to one particular issue or time. Consequently, the parties will normally be sensitive to and concerned with the establishment and maintenance of good and stable working relations with each other. The long-term relationship between both parties is often considered more important than the particular issue upon which a single set of negotiations is focused, thus the maintenance of this relationship may take precedence over achieving a short-term 'victory' (Gunnigle *et al.* 1999).

ER negotiations may also occur at a more informal level involving line management and employees and/or their representatives. Such negotiations normally concern more minor and/or individual issues, such as individual grievances or minor disciplinary matters.

The negotiating process itself will generally follow a number of predictable phases, namely (i) preparation; (ii) bargaining; and (iii) follow-up or post-negotiations (see Table 12.3).

Table 12.3 Phases in the negotiations process

Phase	Relevant activities
1. Preparation	Agree objectives and mandate. Assess relative bargaining power. Conduct relevant research. Choose negotiating team/develop skills. Make appropriate administrative and clerical arrangements.
2. Bargaining	*Opening:* Outline case. Expectation structuring. Discover positions/explore other side's case. *Middle:* Offer/Movement/Concession and solution building. Exchange. *Closing:* Final movement(s). Record agreement/disagreement. Clarify details. Agree next steps.
3. Post-Negotiations	Document agreement/disagreement. Communicate. Agree and implement action plans and communicate. Review.

Phase 1: Preparation

As with all types of managerial activity, careful preparation is an important prerequisite for success in ER negotiations. Such preparation requires that negotiators be familiar with the details of the case and have a clear idea of their objectives and mandate before entering the bargaining arena. This means that negotiators should clarify what they want to achieve, both from the collective bargaining process in general, and from each set of negotiations in particular. Specific objectives tend to vary according to the issue at hand and normally involve specific targets, trade-off options and resistance points. Flexible objectives are generally more appropriate than rigid ones, since information may be uncovered during negotiations that can alter the substance of either party's case. It is important that each party's objectives are clearly articulated and approved by constituents, particularly top management on the employer side, and trade union members/representatives on the union side.

A central issue in agreeing negotiating objectives involves establishing a bargaining range, including the limits within which each party is prepared to reach agreement. In practice, this often means establishing an *ideal settlement point*, a *realistic settlement point* and finally a *fall-back position* beyond which a party is not prepared to enter agreement. These various positions are illustrated in Figure 12.2, in the context of hypothetical negotiations on wage increases between a trade union and an employer. Here the process of establishing bargaining parameters facilitates the identification of bargaining objectives, deciding on trade-offs and concessions, and provides a benchmark against which to evaluate progress. In this particular instance, it is clear that agreement between the management and trade union teams is only possible where resistance points (fall-back positions) overlap, that is in the 2–4 per cent pay range (see Figure 12.2). A settlement is not possible outside this range, unless one of the parties alters its position. If this does not happen, the parties will be in conflict over the issue and third party referral or industrial action may be used to help resolve the impasse.

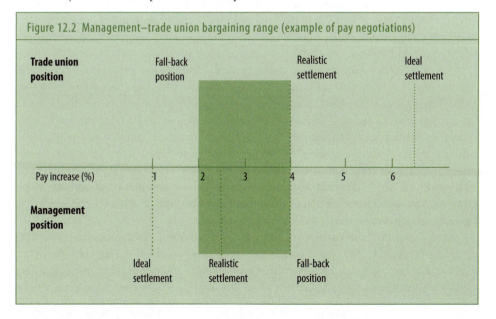

Figure 12.2 Management–trade union bargaining range (example of pay negotiations)

An important aspect of effective preparation for ER negotiations is adequate research. This helps focus negotiations on facts, rather than discussing opinions or value judgments (Fisher et al. 2004; Lewicki et al. 2010). Preparatory research might also incorporate an evaluation of the repercussions of likely settlement options and 'knock-on' effects of different potential outcomes, including industrial action. Effective preparation also involves ensuring that appropriate administrative arrangements are made in relation to timing, location and support facilities. The size and composition of the negotiating team largely depends on the issue(s). It is generally suggested that, except for quite minor issues, a negotiating team should comprise a minimum of two people to facilitate case presentation, record keeping and evaluation of progress (Nierenberg 1968; Fisher et al. 2004). In larger organisations, the HR manager will normally represent management in ER negotiations. However, line managers may often handle more minor issues or assist the HR manager during major negotiations. Personnel from employer associations may also form part of the management team (see Chapter 11).

Phase 2: Bargaining

The typical phases involved in the actual bargaining process are outlined in Figure 12.3, namely (i) opening/outline case; (ii) expectation structuring; (iii) offer, concession, movement; (iv) agreement/disagreement; and (v) close.

The *opening phase* normally involves both parties articulating their respective positions. At this stage both parties normally attempt to find out more about each other's positions and assess the degree to which movement and concession is possible. The next phase involves what is often termed *expectation structuring*, where each party attempts to convince the other of the logic of their own position and their commitment to that position. The parties may also highlight what are seen as deficiencies in the other party's position. Each party to the negotiations thus attempts to structure or influence the other party's expectations and tries to convince them to accept whatever concessions are offered. For example, during pay negotiations employers often refer to factors such as increased competition, or the need for re-investment, in an attempt to reduce employee or union expectations.

The *offer, concession, movement* phase generally follows the process of expectation structuring. This stage normally involves some initial offers and concessions by either party. This is a crucial phase in the overall negotiating process. It is felt that correct timing is absolutely essential in making offers or concessions and it is normally advisable to take some time before making any major concessions. If such concessions are made too early in negotiations, the other party may press for more during subsequent bargaining. Any movement or offer from a team's opening position should be carefully weighed up in terms of its long- and short-term implications. During this phase, adjournments are often used to allow the parties to evaluate their options, consult with others outside the bargaining team and generally evaluate progress to date.

After some time both parties will be in a position to assess the likelihood of reaching *agreement* or, possibly, the extent and implications of a *breakdown* in negotiations. In the event of a breakdown, it is important that neither party walks away from the bargaining table without at least some agreement as to how and by whom communication will be re-initiated. Again, the idea that long-term relations may be more important than the issue(s) at hand is an important principle for both parties to keep in mind. For this reason the parties should be keen to avoid damaging conflict or breakdowns and be prepared to compromise on certain issues for the benefit of that longer-term perspective. Both parties will normally recognise and anticipate the *closing phase* in the bargaining process. This phase normally involves: clarifying and finalising the agreement, issues for further negotiation and agreeing on procedures for interpretation of the settlement or details of breakdown.

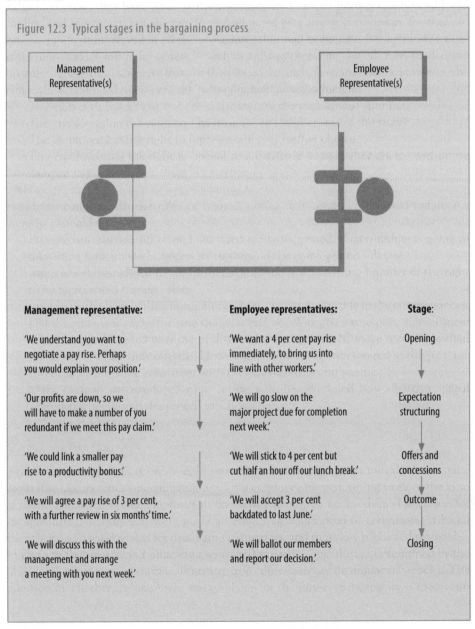

Figure 12.3 Typical stages in the bargaining process

Phase 3: Post-Negotiations

At the end of the negotiations, the parties involved will usually report back on the outcome, the employee or union side communicating it to the workers they represent, and the management team reporting back to senior and, possibly, line management. This post-negotiation phase normally involves reviewing any agreement reached and implementation and communication thereof and a more general evaluation or review of the wider implications of the negotiations and agreement.

INDUSTRIAL CONFLICT

Given the potential differences of interest that can arise on employment matters, it is not surprising that some degree of conflict and industrial action is inevitable in employment relations. Industrial action is defined as work stoppages instigated either collectively and individually by employees and trade unions or by management (Rose 2001: 354). Industrial conflict can take different forms (e.g. strikes, lockouts, sit-ins) and there are varying explanations as to why it occurs.

In the preceding chapter, the pluralist and unitarist frameworks were posited as useful models for explaining ER interactions and industrial conflict (Fox 1968, 1974; Marchington 1982; Wallace *et al.* 2013). In the pluralist framework, organisations are seen as comprising a range of individuals and groups with different interests and priorities. This suggests that the interaction of these competing interests and groups necessitates the development of institutional arrangements to help manage conflicting interests and to achieve a level of bargained compromise that allows the organisation to conduct its normal business. Thus, the pluralist framework accepts that conflict is inherent in organisations because the needs and objectives of various actors or interest groups will clash on occasion.

The unitarist framework provides a different explanation for industrial conflict. Unitarism is based on the premise that organisations are essentially cohesive and harmonious units and that all members of the organisation (management and employees) share common goals. Within the unitarist framework there is only one source of authority, namely management. Thus, management and employees are seen as having the same interests with conflict occurring only as a result of either misunderstandings or the efforts of troublemakers.

As noted earlier, in practice it would seem that some degree of conflict is inherent in ER and that differences will arise between management and workers. These differences are not necessarily harmful and need not necessarily lead to industrial conflict. Indeed, even where conflict does occur it can have some positive effects by, for example, leading to positive changes in management practice. Of course, its impact can also have quite negative implications, for example by damaging trust and thereby potentially damaging future management–worker relations.

Industrial conflict is normally categorised into two broad forms: (i) explicit and organised industrial conflict; and (ii) unorganised and more implicit industrial conflict (Bean 1976; Turnbull and Sapsford 1992: Wallace *et al.* 2013).

- Explicit, overt forms of industrial conflict represent organised and systematic responses and include strikes, lockouts, go-slows and overtime bans.
- Implicit or more unorganised forms include absenteeism, labour turnover and poor performance and may often reflect low levels of employee satisfaction and morale.

A related categorisation of industrial conflict is that which distinguishes between collective and individual conflict. Collective conflict tends to be more organised and explicit involving deliberate and organised action on the part of groups workers and their trade unions, whereas individual conflict largely takes the form of individual grievances on issues of employment rights (under relevant legislation) or more general ER grievances and tends to be more reactive in nature (Rose 2001; Teague et al. 2015b).

STRIKE ACTIVITY IN IRELAND

The most visible way in which workers can engage in industrial conflict is to go on strike. The classic definition of a strike is 'a temporary stoppage of work by a group of employees in order to express a grievance or demand' and is generally attributed to Peterson (1937: 91), though it has been reproduced frequently over the years, most notably by Richard Hyman (1972) in his well-known book *Strikes*. A number of critical factors which may impact on the level and pattern of strike activity have been identified through various studies and include the level of economic activity (business cycle), unemployment (tightness/looseness of the labour market), industrial development, political economy, inflation (earnings) and trade union density and influence (cf. Edwards 1992; Hyman 1972; Kerr 1954). Strike action may also take different forms and arise for a variety of reasons (see Wallace et al. 2013 for greater detail).

In the Irish context, a number of similar critical factors which impact on the level and pattern of strike activity have been identified through various studies and include the level of economic activity (business cycle), unemployment (tightness/looseness of the labour market), industrial development, inflation (earnings), and trade union density and influence (cf. Brannick and Kelly 1983; Brannick et al. 1997; Kelly and Brannick 1990; Teague et al. 2015b). It should be noted, however, that the official Central Statistics Office (CSO) data on industrial disputes do not tell the full story on industrial conflict (Labour Relations Commission 2009). Significantly, disputes are only included in Irish strike statistics calculated by the CSO if they involve a stoppage of work lasting for at least one day and the total time lost is ten or more person days. Clearly, many forms of industrial action may fall outside this definition, such as short sharp stoppages, protests, work to rule and so forth as we will discuss in more detail later in this chapter.

Three key measures are normally used in evaluating the extent of strike activity: (i) strike frequency (number of strikes); (ii) workers involved (number of workers participating in strikes); and (iii) working days lost (number of working days lost due to strike activity). Using these indicators, the pattern of strike activity in Ireland over the period 1922–2016 is summarised in Figures 12.4, 12.5 and 12.6 on the following pages. This evidence indicates a clear upward trend in strike activity in Ireland during the 1960s and 1970s, followed by decline in strikes in the 1980s and generally modest levels of strike activity through the 1990s and to date.

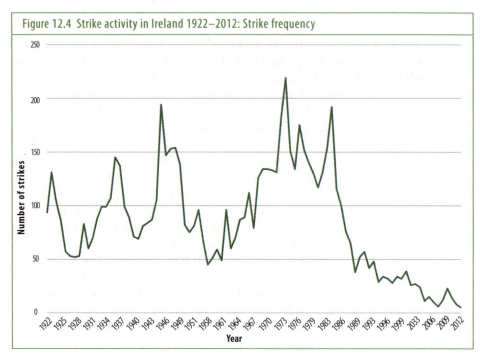

Figure 12.4 Strike activity in Ireland 1922–2012: Strike frequency

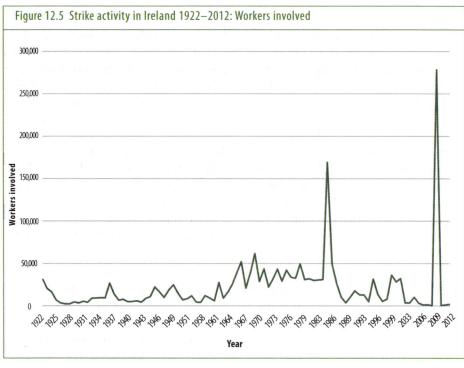

Figure 12.5 Strike activity in Ireland 1922–2012: Workers involved

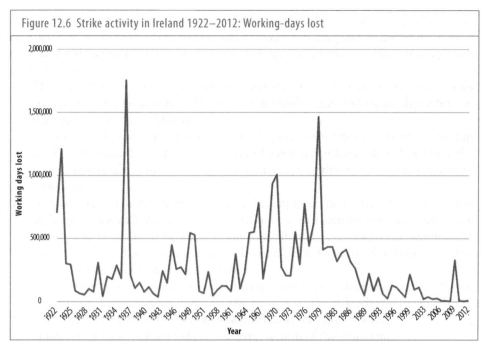

Figure 12.6 Strike activity in Ireland 1922–2012: Working-days lost

In analysing historical trends of strike activity in Ireland, Brannick et al. (1997: 310) found that 'all three indices are broadly pro cyclical with respect to economic changes', meaning that the pattern of strike activity (especially strike frequency or working days lost) rose in times of economic growth and fell in times of economic contraction (cf. Wallace et al. 2013). This cyclical trend can be traced back to the 1920s, a period marked by low levels of strike activity, linked to recession and economic stagnation of the time. Subsequent industrialisation and growth in the 1930s saw increased strike levels and working days lost. The year 1937 remains the record year to date for working days lost (1,754,949) due to strike activity. We then see a sharp decline in strike activity during the Second World War, another period of economic stagnation which also saw the introduction of a *Wages Standstill Order* that imposed an effective freeze on wages (Lee 1989). The lifting of the Standstill Order in the immediate post-war period saw increased strike activity, as various bargaining groups sought pay restoration and pay increases. However, economic depression in the 1950s, combined with high unemployment and widespread emigration, subsequently saw a decline in strike activity. This pertained until the turn of the 1960s when changes in economic policy saw the emphasis move from protection to openness and increased industrialisation, and heralded a decade or more of economic growth (see Chapter 2). This was a period marked by increasing levels of strike activity, a pattern which continued into the 1970s and peaked in 1979 when working days lost due to strike activity reached 1,454,952, the second highest level on record.

Looking at patterns of strike activity, we find a broad decrease in the number of strikes (strike frequency) between 2009 and 2016. The numbers of workers involved and working days lost through strike activity has also remained quite low in this period. The lowest number of working days lost due to strike activity on record (3,695) occurred in 2011. More broadly we can see that the period of recent recession witnessed some of the lowest recorded levels of industrial conflict since 1922 (see Chapter 2). However, 2009 was the exception. That year saw a total of 329,593 days lost, roughly an eighty-fold increase on the previous year. However, the main contributory factor to this huge increase, in both workers involved in strikes and working days lost, was the one-day national public sector strike in November 2009, in opposition to government plans to cut €4 billion in pay and public spending in the budget. This one day dispute accounted for 95 per cent of the workers involved (265,400) and 72 per cent of the working days lost (237,268) due to industrial disputes in 2009.

In their seminal work in the 1980s, Kelly and Brannick (1983) identified two broad trends in strike activity in Ireland, namely the disproportionate effect of large strikes on Irish strike statistics and the different patterns of strike activity between the public and private sectors. In relation to the former, Kelly and Brannick (ibid: 69) note that over the period 1960–79, forty-three strikes (2 per cent of total strikes in the period) accounted for 57 per cent of all days lost due to strike activity and commented:

> Clearly, the Irish strike pattern is extremely sensitive to this comparatively small number of large strikes and it has been an enduring feature over the 20-year period. Indeed should these be removed from the Irish strike quantum the result would be a record which would show a comparatively strike-free nation in terms of workers involved and total man-days lost. This one-strike-major-effect phenomenon had exceptionally disproportionate effects on two of the principal strike statistics (workers involved and working days lost) and if not highlighted can lead to an unrepresentative and inaccurate portrayal of the Irish strike record.

Wallace et al. (2013) have noted the continuance of this trend in more recent years. Their analysis found that in the period 1995–2002, the top two strikes accounted for 75 per cent of all working days lost and 78 per cent of workers involved in strike activity over those years. Similarly, over the period 2003–2011, they found again that just two strikes (2.5 per cent of all disputes) accounted for 75 per cent of working days lost. As mentioned above, the one-day national public sector dispute in November 2009 provides another example of how large strikes can greatly skew Irish strike statistics.

The second key trend identified by Kelly and Brannick (1983) was the contrast in patterns of strike activity between the public and private sectors. The historical pattern of strike activity in both these sectors over the period 1960–2011 is outlined in Table 12.4.

In evaluating historical patterns, Kelly and Brannick (1988) found that the private sector was the most strike-prone sector in the 1960s and 1970s. However, since the 1980s the proportion of strike activity accounted for by the private sector has broadly declined. This development has paralleled a general increase in the proportion of strike activity accounted for by the public sector (see Wallace et al. 2013 for greater detail). However, overall levels of strike activity have declined across the board in recent years (as illustrated earlier in Figures 12.4–12.6), a pattern very much in line with the general international decline in strike activity (Hamann et al. 2013).

Table 12.4 Strike activity in the public and private sector, 1960–2011

Year	Strike frequency (%)		Workers involved (%)		Working days lost (%)	
	Public sector	Private sector	Public sector	Private sector	Public sector	Private sector
1960–1969	18	82	36	64	23	77
1970–1979	18	82	32.5	67.5	38	60
1980–1989	29	71	69	31	38	62
1990–1995	47	53	61	39	27	73
1996–2002	45	55	75	25	59	41
2003–2011	34	66	94	6	74	26

Source: Wallace et al. 2013; 1960–1995 data Brannick et al.(1997); 1996–2011 data CSO.

OFFICIAL AND UNOFFICIAL STRIKES

The relative impact of official and unofficial strikes is another important issue affecting patterns of strike activity. 'Official' strikes are defined as those that have been fully sanctioned by the union executive. Such strikes normally occur after negotiations have failed to resolve the issue and when all due procedures have been exhausted. In contrast, 'unofficial' strikes are those that have not been sanctioned by the trade union. Such strikes tend to be more reactive in nature and may be 'sparked off' by a particular event or incident at workplace level, such as the dismissal or suspension of a worker, unilateral changes in working practices or (alleged) breaches of agreed procedures. Unless subsequently granted official approval by the trade union, unofficial strikes normally last for a shorter time and involve fewer workers than official strikes (Wallace and O'Shea 1987; Wallace 1988a and 1988b).

As illustrated in Table 12.5, while unofficial strikes averaged close to 70 per cent of all strike activity in the 1970s, this fell to just 19 per cent over the period 2000 to 2011. The proportion of working days lost contributed by unofficial strikes demonstrate a similar if less dramatic decline, falling from over 15 per cent in the 1970s to just over 7 per cent in the period from 2000–2011. Arguably this decline is at least partially accounted for by the greater protections afforded to workers by employment legislation enacted over recent decades (e.g. *Unfair Dismissals Acts 1977–2007*).

Table 12.5 Official and unofficial strikes 1976–2011

Time period	Percentage of all strikes which were unofficial	Working days lost through unofficial strikes as a percentage of total
1976–1979	66.8	15.5
1980–1989	42.1	19.3
1990–1999	27.4	6.8
2000–2011	18.7	7.4

Source: Wallace et al. 2013.

OTHER FORMS OF INDUSTRIAL CONFLICT

While strikes – described earlier as temporary work stoppages by employees to express a grievance or demand – are the most visible manifestation of organised collective industrial action, there are numerous other forms of industrial conflict. Below we provide an indicative summary of these other forms of collective industrial action (cf. Salamon 2000; Rose 2001; Wallace et al. 2013).

- *Lockout*: this refers to situations in which the employer denies workers access to their workplace, thus creating a work stoppage. A lockout is generally seen as the employer equivalent of a strike. This form of industrial action is rare in Ireland, although the 1913 Dublin Lockout remains one of the most momentous events in Irish labour and economic history (see Chapter 2).
- *Go slow*: refers to instances where the workers in dispute work at a slower rate and deliver lower than normal levels of performance.
- *Work to rule*: this form of industrial action involves workers operating only in line with a strict interpretation, and to the precise letter, of formal terms and conditions of employment including requiring precise instruction from management regarding the execution of work tasks.
- *Overtime ban*: this involves workers refusing to work outside of normal contractual hours thereby reducing levels of performance.
- *Sit-in*: this refers to instances where workers occupy the workplace and may or may not entail workers continuing to work as normal. It is often used by workers and trade unions as a means of protest against closure or cutbacks and to prevent the removal of plant and equipment by employers.

These alternative forms of industrial action are generally more common than strikes (Wallace et al. 2013) and can provide workers and their trade unions with effective means of achieving bargaining goals, while not entailing the potential hardships of strike action. In particular, actions such as go-slows or overtime bans can place considerable pressures on employers to move towards resolution while not necessarily jeopardising employees' income and job security to as great an extent as with strike action.

As noted earlier, not all industrial conflict is manifest in a collective and organised fashion. One also finds forms of more unorganised and/or individual conflict whereby workers respond to workplace events and management practices by taking certain forms of individual industrial action. Some examples of such actions are featured below.

- *Sabotage* – sometimes termed industrial sabotage, this involves deliberate action aimed at damaging the organisation through some form of action, obstruction or subversion designed to disrupt work flow and lower performance levels. This form of action was historically captured by the term 'throwing a spanner in the works' but may now involve hacking, tampering and other similar types of malicious action.
- *Pilferage* – stealing from the organisation/employer represents a related form of individual action and is sometimes categorised as a counterproductive work behaviour (Anderson et al. 2005).
- *Labour turnover* – where workers leave their job as a form of ER protest.

- *Absenteeism* – whereby workers absent themselves from work as a means of demonstrating their discontent regarding, for example, management action or work practices).

Work by Paul Teague and colleagues has found that one of the most significant trends in industrial conflict in Ireland has been the decline in collective conflict involving trade unions and an increase in conflict related to grievances of individual workers (Teague *et al.* 2015).

CONFLICT RESOLUTION: DEALING WITH DISPUTES IN EMPLOYMENT RELATIONS

At the level of the enterprise, all parties involved in employment relations have an important role to play in conflict handling and resolution. Line managers, employee representatives and workers have a key role in handling disputes and grievances that arise at shop-floor level. Senior management has overall responsibility for the development of strategy and related policies and procedures to effectively handle ER and industrial conflict. Where a specialist HRM function exists, it will normally have responsibility for advising top management on optimal ER strategies and developing appropriate procedures and practices. It may also provide training, advice and guidance to line management in handling workplace ER issues. Trade unions undertake a similar role on the employee side. As emphasised earlier, industrial conflict should not be viewed as having a necessarily negative impact on ER. Rather industrial conflict can have certain positive effects, allowing employees to highlight and pursue issues of concern, and thus facilitate change and development in the nature of an organisation's ER.

Possibly the most widespread response to conflict in the workplace has been the development of joint mechanisms to discuss and resolve issues of difference. This institutionalisation of conflict is primarily characterised by the development of procedures to facilitate conflict resolution, reflects an implicit acceptance that issues of conflict will arise, and is characteristic of the pluralist approach to ER discussed earlier. By creating institutions (such as collective bargaining) and related procedures for handling ER and industrial conflict, the parties involved seek to create a framework through which the parties can interact, argue, disagree and agree, while allowing for the ongoing operation of the business.

A very important facet of workplace ER and industrial conflict involves the handling and management of employee grievances and disciplinary matters. In this regard readers should consult the *Code of Practice on Grievance and Disciplinary Procedures* (Workplace Relations Commission 2006).

HANDLING GRIEVANCES IN THE WORKPLACE

In employment relations, the term 'grievance' is normally used to describe a formal expression of employee dissatisfaction. Given the nature of industrial organisation, it is inevitable that employees, either individually or in groups, will have grievances that they want management to address. The great majority of such grievances normally involve minor issues or complaints related to the immediate work environment. As such, a substantial proportion of these grievances can normally be handled by line management and employees and/or employee representatives. It is widely argued that managers should pay particular attention to effective grievance handling and its contribution to promoting good ER in the workplace (cf. Thomason 1984; Salamon 20010). It is also suggested that management should endeavour to handle employee grievances promptly, since the non-handling of grievances may give rise to frustration which can permeate through to other employees and promote an uneasy working environment in which disputes and poor ER can arise. Some summary guidelines for managers involved in grievance handling are outlined in Figure 12.7.

Figure 12.7 Management checklist for grievance handling

- Management should make every effort to understand the nature of, and the reasons for, grievance.
- All levels of management should be aware of the potentially significant influence that grievance handling has on employment relations and on organisation performance more generally.
- Organisations should have a written policy that sets out an orderly and effective framework for handling employee grievances (see Figure 12.8).
- Line management, particularly first line supervision or team leaders should be aware of their key role in effective grievance handling.
- Management need to be aware of the need for consistency and consider if a precedent is being set in resolving a grievance.

A related and important aspect of grievance handling is the establishment and application of appropriate grievance procedures. Such procedures normally outline the stages and approaches to be followed in handling grievances in the workplace. The main advantages associated with such procedures include:
1. Increased clarity in ER interactions.
2. Prevention of misunderstandings and arguments over interpretation.
3. Easier and better communications.
4. Increased fairness and consistency in application.

An important aim of grievance procedures is to ensure that issues raised by employees are effectively handled and settled fairly and as near as possible to their point of origin. Such aims are based on the premise that – operated effectively – grievance procedures entail a strong preventative dimension in helping thwart the escalation of grievance issues into more serious industrial disputes.

Most problems or complaints raised by employees should, ideally, be handled by the immediate line manager or team leader without recourse to a formal grievance procedure. However, issues that warrant more thorough consideration may be more appropriately handled through a formal and agreed procedure. Grievance procedures should normally be in writing, simple and easy to operate and aim to handle disputes and grievances fairly and consistently. They will generally specify short time limits (normally just a few days) for each phase of the grievance handling process. Formal procedures generally follow an upward path from one hierarchical level to the next. The indicative contents of a typical grievance procedure are outlined in Figure 12.8.

Figure 12.8 Indicative content of a typical grievance procedure

- Clear steps specifying the level at which a grievance should be raised.
- A requirement that the issue should be first discussed between employees and their immediate manager or supervisor.
- Provision for referral to higher levels of management if not resolved.
- A provision for a speedy response and time limits being specified for each stage of the procedure.
- If not dealt with within the specified time, the next stage of the procedure may be invoked.
- A right of employees to be represented by their trade union or an employee of their choice at the various stages of the procedure.
- Provision for referral to a third party if agreement cannot be reached 'in house'. This may be absent in non-union procedures but may still be an option for an employee.
- A 'peace clause', with both parties foregoing the use of industrial action prior to all stages of the agreed procedures being exhausted. Again, this will not be present in non-union companies.

Since it is not always possible to resolve all grievances at local level, it is generally necessary to make provision for referral of issues to an independent third party through conciliation, mediation and/or arbitration. This will normally mean the offices of the Workplace Relations Commission and the Labour Court, especially in organisations which recognise trade unions (see Chapter 10). However, we also noted the growing popularity of so-called *Alternative Dispute Resolution* mechanisms (Teague et al. 2015) which include private mediation/conciliation/arbitration (Teague et al. 2015); discussed in more detail later in this chapter. As also noted earlier, grievance procedures normally contain a provision that no form of industrial action should be taken by either party until all stages of the procedure have been exhausted, and an agreed period of notice has expired before industrial action is initiated. Effectively operated, this ensures that both parties have ample opportunity to settle issues either through direct discussion or, exceptionally, through third party referral.

HANDLING DISCIPLINARY ISSUES IN THE WORKPLACE

Inevitably, situations will also arise in organisations where management may seek to take disciplinary action against employees. Most organisations will seek to establish and maintain what they consider are acceptable rules, standards or norms, in areas such as performance, attendance and behaviour at work. Should employees breach such standards, management will normally seek to take some form of disciplinary action. Such disciplinary action may range from relatively minor advisory caution to more serious forms, such as formal warnings, suspension or dismissal.

An important aspect of discipline administration in organisations is the establishment of acceptable rules and standards and the utilisation of disciplinary procedures to deal with breaches of such rules/standards.

- *Disciplinary rules* set out the standards of acceptable behaviour expected from employees within an organisation and the consequences of not meeting these standards.
- *Disciplinary procedures* constitute the administrative machinery for applying these rules and executing any resulting action.

A critical concern in the area of discipline administration is the legal context within which discipline should be administered in organisations. In particular, the common law concept of natural justice requires that:
1. There should be a basic understanding of what constitutes a transgression, therefore company rules and standards should be clearly outlined and communicated.
2. The consequences of breaching such rules/standards should be clear.
3. Employees not achieving the required standards should be so informed and given opportunity to improve where possible.
4. Employees alleged to have breached discipline should be entitled to fair and consistent treatment, including an opportunity to state their case, have access to representation, and a right to appeal to a higher authority.

These principles, combined with the legislative framework surrounding discipline administration, mean that organisations should have some formal disciplinary procedure in operation, ensure employees are familiar with its contents, and apply this procedure in a reasonable fashion*. The legal context for discipline administration is outlined in Chapter 13. The most significant legislative development affecting discipline administration is the unfair dismissals legislation (1977–2015) which provides guidelines as to what constitutes fair and unfair dismissal, and provides a mechanism for dealing with claims of unfair dismissal, and for deciding upon redress for those found to be unfairly dismissed.

A disciplinary procedure is an important aspect of effective discipline administration. It is suggested that disciplinary procedures serve to establish an explicit *modus operandi* for bringing alleged offences to the notice of employees; allow employees an opportunity to respond to such charges; and facilitate the imposition of disciplinary action as necessary. A critical initial step in establishing a disciplinary procedure is to outline company rules and standards, and the form of disciplinary action associated with breaches of these rules and standards.

The establishment of explicit workplace rules helps ensure consistency in the treatment of employees. Such an outline of rules and standards should indicate: (i) those rules and standards where breaches (gross misconduct) may lead to dismissal or suspension in the first instance (e.g. theft or violence at work); and (ii) those rules and standards where breaches would lead to the operation of a standard disciplinary procedure (e.g. poor timekeeping, absenteeism and poor performance). To facilitate the effective administration of disciplinary procedures the golden rules would seem to be that such procedures are *agreed* between management and employees, are *fair*, are *understood* by management and employees, and are *applied consistently*. A sample disciplinary procedure is outlined in Figure 12.9.

---

* This text provides only a summary overview of the legal context of discipline administration and is not a legal interpretation thereof. Readers requiring more comprehensive insights might refer to Forde and Byrne (2009); Daly and Doherty (2010); Wallace et al. (2013).

Figure 12.9 Sample disciplinary procedure

Preamble
The following disciplinary procedure will be used to deal with all breaches of company rules and standards except where the offences or transgression constitute gross misconduct.

The primary aim of this procedure is to help employees whose conduct or performance falls below company requirements to achieve the necessary improvements. It is desirable both in contributing to company success and the fair treatment of employees. It is company policy to apply this procedure as reasonably as possible and to ensure consistency and order in its application. It will apply to all breaches of company rules or standards not constituting gross misconduct that may typically include, but are not limited to the following:
- Bad timekeeping
- Unacceptable work performance
- Unauthorised absence
- Poor attendance
- Lack of co-operation
- Breaches of safety regulations.

Disciplinary Procedure
1. In the first instance the individual will be asked to attend a counselling interview by his/her supervisor, where the employees' transgression will be made clear, the standard of performance required outlined and the employee orally reprimanded.
2. In the second instance the employee will receive an oral warning at a formal meeting with his/her supervisor and department manager, where details of the misdemeanour and the consequences of further offences will be outlined.
3. In the third instance the employee will receive a final written warning from the HR manager at a meeting with the HR manager, the department manager and, if appropriate, the supervisor. The employee will be informed of the details of the offence, future performance standards required and that further offences will lead to suspension or dismissal.
4. In the last instance the employee will either be suspended without pay or dismissed (depending on the offence). Notice of this will be given to the employee at a meeting with the general manager, when the offence will be outlined both verbally and in writing and the employee advised of his/her right of appeal.

Gross Misconduct
Gross misconduct is conduct of such a serious nature that the company could not tolerate keeping the employee in employment and it is hoped that such instances will not occur. However, for the mutual protection of the company and its workforce, any employee found guilty of gross misconduct may be dismissed summarily. Examples of gross misconduct include:
- Violation of a criminal law.
- Consumption or possession of alcohol or illegal drugs.
- Threats or acts of physical violence.
- Theft from another employee or from the company.
- Malicious damage to company property.
- Falsifying company records (including clock cards).

Before any action is taken the company will thoroughly investigate the case, during which time the employee will be suspended. After such investigations the employee will attend a meeting with company management where s/he will have an opportunity to state his/her case and be advised of his/her right of appeal. Should the company still feel the employee was guilty of gross misconduct s/he will be dismissed and given a letter outlining the nature of the offence and reasons for dismissal.

An important aspect in ensuring procedural fairness and equity in discipline administration is the employee's right to adequate representation (by either a fellow employee or a trade union representative as appropriate). Management should also ensure that full and accurate records are maintained in disciplinary cases.

It is critical to note unfair dismissals legislation places the burden of proof primarily on the employer. Consequently, management must be able to substantiate their case with adequate evidence, both documentary and otherwise. In disciplinary cases there is an onus on management to thoroughly investigate the circumstances and establish the facts of the case. If, after a thorough investigation, management decide that disciplinary action is merited, a meeting is normally arranged with the employee(s) concerned. The purpose of such *disciplinary interviews* is to assess culpability, decide on appropriate action and attempt to effect the desired change in employee behaviour. The disciplinary interview also provides the employee(s) with an opportunity to present their point of view. In disciplinary cases, employees should be given every reasonable opportunity to explain their case.

Only after a full and thorough investigation and disciplinary meeting(s) will management be in a position to decide on appropriate action. Should the investigation and disciplinary meeting point to a need for disciplinary action, management's position should be explained to the employee(s), who should be made fully aware of their shortcomings and management's concern. The precise nature of any improvement required and the means for its achievement should be outlined, as should the consequences of future transgressions. There is an equal onus on management to ensure that employees fully understand the discipline imposed and the right of appeal. After the interview, the details should be accurately recorded and a copy given to the employee(s) concerned (and their representative as necessary). Any commitments entered into should be carried out promptly.

In the longer term, an organisation's full disciplinary process should be reviewed and monitored from a number of viewpoints (e.g. impact on employee behaviour, trends in disciplinary incidents and effectiveness of various forms of discipline). The area of discipline administration should be approached by management in a positive vein with the overall objective being to positively impact and change employees' behaviour. The HR function has an important role to play in establishing disciplinary policy and related procedures and in monitoring their application throughout the organisation. Two key factors, which need to be kept in mind are the need for reasonableness and consistency in undertaking disciplinary action.

DIFFUSION OF GRIEVANCE AND DISCIPLINARY PROCEDURES

Despite the demonstrable importance and utility of grievance and disciplinary procedures and associated 'good practice' in workplace ER, it is perhaps surprising to find that their diffusion is by no means comprehensive. Roche and Teague's (2011) study of some 500 Irish companies found that just 60 per cent had formal written grievance and disciplinary procedures. The presence of such procedures was positively correlated with size (larger firms), unionisation, foreign ownership and location in the manufacturing sector. This lower than might be expected diffusion of standard grievance and disciplinary procedures has been linked to managerial resistance to the formalisation of management–employee relations associated with the operation of these procedures (Wallace *et al.* 2013).

Another explanation relates to workforce profile and competitive pressures on organisations. The use of *Alternative Dispute Resolution* (ADR) approaches has been associated with so-called 'knowledge workers' and a related preference for more innovative conflict management approaches, and perhaps the avoidance of more conventional approaches (Roche and Teague 2011). Increased competitive and cost pressures on organisations may also act as a deterrent to applying conventional ER procedures and encourage a more improvised and ad hoc managerial approach (Colvin 2003).

As noted in Chapter 10, ADR practices have become increasingly popular in many countries, having originated in mostly non-union firms in the US (Stone 1999). ADR was initially posited as a means of solving workplace conflict without recourse to litigation and court appearance, and more generally as a way of improving the overall quality of management–employee relations. As it evolved, the remit of ADR has evolved to embrace workplace conflict resolution through more consensual and less formal approaches (Teague and Doherty 2011).

In the Irish context, Teague and Doherty (2001: 19) argue that the genesis of ADR in Ireland can be traced to multinational companies that located here in the 1960s and 1970s and gradually created what they term was 'a "counterculture" in the areas of union recognition and the use of collective processes to resolve workplace disputes [and] . . . put in place what might be described as a direct engagement model of people management'. They further argue that over time this approach has now gained a reasonable level of legitimacy and diffusion, especially in the private sector. As noted earlier, ADR and the more general direct engagement model prioritises the informal resolution of workplace conflict and is resistant to the involvement of external state-sponsored agencies or individuals in the process of conflict resolution.

As previously mentioned, the most common ADR practices are open door management approaches, intensive communications, use of ombudsmen, brainstorming and other problem-solving techniques and a preference for private mediation/conciliation/arbitration as opposed to state provided services in this area. An indicative listing of ADR practices and comparison with more conventional approaches to conflict resolution in Ireland is provided in Table 12.6.

Table 12.6 Conflict management practices in Ireland		
	Conventional	**ADR**
Conflict involving individuals	Formal written grievance and disciplinary procedures	Open-door policies 'Speak-up' systems Ombudsmen External and internal mediators Review panels of managers and peers Employee advocates Arbitration
Conflict involving groups	Formal written procedures Resort at final stage (when deadlocked) to state agencies e.g. LRC/WRC	Assisted bargaining/mediation Brainstorming Interest-based bargaining Private arbitration Intensive communications surrounding change management

Source: Teague *et al.* (2012: 586).

Open door management is the most widely used ADR practice in Ireland with a reported usage of just over 50 per cent (Teague et al. 2012). This study found that approximately one third of companies studied used formal intensive communications, brainstorming and problem-solving techniques to deal with workplace conflict, while approximately one fifth used external experts. Overall, this evidence points to a reasonable, though not extensive, diffusion of ADR in Ireland.

PARTNERSHIP AND ADVERSARIALISM IN IRISH EMPLOYMENT RELATIONS

Much of the preceding discussion on ER practice, and particularly that concerning collective bargaining, is grounded in what is characterised as 'adversarialism'. The adversarial tradition emanates from the premise that a fundamental conflict of interests exists between management and labour and that such conflict can best be resolved through collective bargaining as to achieve mutually acceptable compromises (Wallace et al. 2013).

The adversarial tradition has attracted considerable criticism, notably regarding the dominance of distributive bargaining and its emphasis on dividing limited resources. It is argued that this approach leads the parties to adopt confrontational positions, believing that any gains can only be made by inflicting losses on the other side. Such critiques often posit integrative/collaborative approaches as a more attractive alternative, with their emphasis on exploring common ground and seeking solutions of mutual benefit for both employers and workers (McKersie 1996). The so-called 'partnership approach' to ER is grounded in such thinking, suggesting that employers, workers and their representative associations should seek to address ER problems jointly and develop mutually beneficial solutions (cf. Kochan and Osterman 1994). Proponents of the partnership approach, encourage employers and trade unions to enter into a set of mutual commitments as follows:
1. Employers recognise and facilitate worker rights to information, consultation and involvement.
2. Workers and trade unions commit themselves actively to productivity improvements.
3. The gains of productivity improvements are shared between employers and workers.
4. Productivity improvements do not result in redundancies but rather employers actively seek new markets to keep workers gainfully employed.

In essence, this mutual gains argument is that workers and trade unions actively pursue, with management, solutions to business problems and work systems in return for greater involvement in business decisions and in the process of work re-organisation. In evaluating the merits of developing such a new relationship with workers and their trade unions, it appears that both sides face some fundamental choices on the nature of management and ER. Should worker/trade union involvement be confined to joint consultation or be extended to joint regulation? From a worker/trade union perspective, do joint consultation initiatives run the risk of remaining essentially 'symbolic', whereby workers/trade unions have no real influence but become associated with decisions where they possess no right to veto? Employers may be equally reticent to enter into joint regulation initiatives because it may delay decision-making and thereby impede 'efficient' management.

EMPLOYEE PARTICIPATION

Partnership approaches to ER are invariably associated with initiatives designed to facilitate greater employee participation. Employee participation may be broadly interpreted as incorporating any mechanisms designed to increase employee input into managerial decision-making. Increased employee participation is an important aspect of many initiatives in the areas of work organisation (Kochan and Osterman 1994).

Employee participation can take place at various levels (Lavelle *et al*. 2010) that range from the relatively basic, such as management informing employees of decisions that affect them, to higher levels involving consultation with employees on certain decisions or joint management–employee participation in the actual decision-making process. These various levels are illustrated in Figure 12.10. These may in turn result in a variety of institutional arrangements to facilitate employee participation, such as suggestion schemes, joint consultative committees, works councils, quality circles and board-level participation.

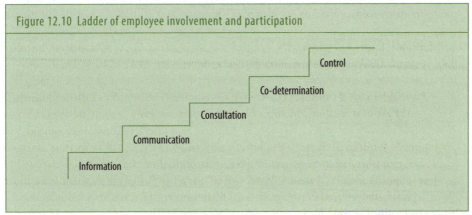

Figure 12.10 Ladder of employee involvement and participation

Source: Marchington and Wilkinson (2000: 343).

We can also point to differences between *direct* and *indirect* forms of employee influence. With the former approach, workers are directly involved in the decision-making process. Often captured under the rubric of *employee involvement*, direct employee participation may take a variety of forms, such as quality circles, consultative meetings and, possibly the most commonly used example, team working. In contrast, indirect forms rely on the use of employee representatives to articulate the views of the larger body of employees and consequently are often termed *representative participation*, examples of which include collective bargaining and works councils. Representative participation seeks to reduce the extent of management prerogative and make more issues subject to joint negotiation and agreement.

Broadly speaking we can identify four forms of employee participation, each varying in regard to both the level and nature of participation. These are (i) task participation; (ii) equity participation; (iii) representative participation; and (iv) participation through collective bargaining. The characteristic of each of these forms of employee participation is outlined in Figure 12.11 on the next page. Variations in the diffusion of approaches to employee participation may stem from a variety of reasons, such as the structure and development of collective bargaining, the approaches of trade unions or public policy and legislation.

Figure 12.11 Forms of employee participation

Task Participation: Encompasses various initiatives to design jobs and work systems, which allow for greater employee involvement in decisions affecting their jobs and immediate work environment. Such initiatives may take a variety of forms such as autonomous work groups, quality circles and consultative meetings and committees.

Equity Participation: Involves the adoption of mechanisms through which employees can gain an equity share in their organisations through various profit-sharing and share-ownership schemes. Some schemes may have the broad-based objective of increasing employee loyalty, commitment and morale through the closer identification of employee interests with those of the organisation. However, equity participation by itself will not normally allow for a substantial increase in employees' influence, as employees will generally represent a minority of the shareholders. Organisations such as the John Lewis Partnership in the UK and Donnelly Mirrors in Ireland have long been known for their policy of sharing profits with employees, and many companies now offer share options or some other form of profit-sharing.

Representative Participation: This has been the focus of most attention and it applies to institutionalised arrangements that give employees input into management decision-making, sometimes with statutory support. The most obvious example is provision for the election of worker-directors to the boards of management. It also applies to lower-level participation, such as joint consultative committees and works councils. The passing of the *Worker Participation (State Enterprises) Act 1977* introduced board-level participation to seven semi-state companies and these provisions were extended to a number of other state organisations under the terms of the *Worker Participation (State Enterprises) Act 1988*. However, board-level representation has largely been confined to the semi-state companies covered by the legislation.

Participation through Collective Bargaining: This has been the most traditional approach to effecting higher levels of employee participation. The growth of workplace bargaining has greatly facilitated this process with trade unions being the key mechanism for representing and extending employees' rights at workplace level. However, as discussed in the text, this approach is seen as essentially adversarial in nature and as such has attracted the criticism that it is not an effective means of promoting a joint problem-solving approach to employee relations issues.

CONCLUSION

In this chapter we have focused on key areas of ER practice, while also providing some contextual background on factors impacting on the evolution of workplace practice. We specifically considered three key areas of ER practice, viz. collective bargaining, grievance handling and discipline administration. In so doing, we looked in particular at industrial conflict and its manifestations. We also reviewed the issue of employee participation and involvement and its various forms.

In the final chapter we summarily consider the area of employment law, a topic which is of immense relevance in regard to HR practice.

13
Employment Law

This final chapter explores the legal framework within which human resource management (HRM) takes place and details a number of important pieces of legislation that directly affect employment in Ireland. It provides an overview of Irish employment law, but it is not a legal interpretation thereof. Readers are asked to consult with the relevant legislation for more detailed understandings, or to check with online sources for regular updates and useful summaries (see www.citizensinformation.ie, www.wrc.ie, www.cipd.ie, or www.ibec.ie). There are two particular aspects of employment or labour law that are of relevance to HRM:
1. Individual labour law, which concentrates on the relationship between the individual worker and the employer.
2. Collective labour law, which is concerned with regulating the relationship between employers and groups of employees – normally trade unions. The relevant aspects of collective labour law have already been discussed in Chapters 10–12.

The emphasis in this chapter is on documenting the various legislative provisions (statutes) that have particular relevance to the practice of HRM in Ireland. It begins with a brief introduction to the main sources of Irish law with implications for the employment relationship. The formation of a contract of employment is then examined and various statutes affecting employment are discussed.

SOURCES OF IRISH LAW

The Irish legal system comprises a number of sources of law, namely the Constitution, Statute Law and Common Law.
- The *Constitution* is essentially divided into two distinct parts. First, that which sets down fundamental personal rights that are guaranteed to every Irish citizen and that the state is obliged to protect. Second, that which directs the structures and establishment of various institutions such as the Oireachtas, the government and judiciary.
- *Statute Law* consists of the various Acts that have been passed over the years, collectively referred to as legislation. After the Constitution, statute law is the most important source of law. It can be broadly classified according to its subject matter: family law, company law, land law, criminal law, labour law and so forth. A number of pertinent employment statutes are reviewed later in this chapter.
- *Common Law* is an unwritten system that has evolved over the centuries. Often called 'judge-made' law, it consists of the decisions made by the judiciary when cases are decided. In practice, this means that judges refer to similar cases when making their decisions; this is commonly known as following a precedent and it provides for

some element of consistency in the interpretation of the law. Common law implies a number of duties into a contract of employment. Employers' duties specify that all employers must reimburse employees for legitimate expenses and must provide a duty of care, a safe place of work, a safe system of work, safe machinery and competent co-workers. As the employment relationship is a contract of service, it is implied that employees will perform the job personally, work co-operatively, obey all reasonable instructions, give fidelity to the employer, employ reasonable care and skill and avoid conflicts of interest.

FORMATION OF A CONTRACT OF EMPLOYMENT

The contract of employment is the legal basis of the employment relationship and is central to the interpretation and application of statutory rights. As with the basic law of contract, it requires that there must be 'offer and acceptance'; the offer being made by the employer and the acceptance by the employee when s/he agrees to work for the employer. There must also be 'consideration' or remuneration from the employer for work done, and both parties must intend to create legal relations, i.e. both parties must recognise that they have particular rights and obligations that must be observed. The contract of employment may be made either orally or in writing. Normally a contract of employment will specify that it is a contract of service. In the absence of this written specification, common law can be invoked to determine the nature of the contract.

Common law attempts to distinguish between a contract *of* service and a contract *for* service. An employee is someone who is employed under a contract *of* service; this is distinct from an independent contractor, who is employed under a contract *for* services. The distinction is a vital one, for a variety of reasons, not least of which is that only 'employees' can benefit from much of the modern employment legislation granted to workers (Fennell and Lynch 1993). Three tests have been developed to differentiate between contracts of and for service:

1. *The Control Test*: This is based on the principle that the employer has the right to control how work is done. In other words, the employer not only tells the employee what to do but also how to do it. However, this test is difficult to administer in practice, particularly where many contracts of service (employees) have considerable discretion over the work that they do.
2. *The Integration Test*: This is based on the view that an employee is a person whose work is integrated into the business, whereas independent contractors merely work for the business. This test is also difficult to apply today since it fails to take account of work practices such as home working, which can give the appearance of self-employment and thus might be construed as contracts for service.
3. *The Multiple or Economic Reality Test*: Under this test, the entire arrangement between employer and worker is reviewed to determine whether the worker is an employee or an independent contractor. Thus the court would seek information concerning:
    - Whether wages, sick and holiday pay are provided, and who pays them.
    - Whether income tax and social security are deducted under the PAYE and PRSI schemes by the company.
    - Whether the worker shares in the profits or losses of the company.
    - Whether tools and equipment for the job are provided by the company.

- Whether there are specific provisions relating to termination of employment.
- Whether the employer is entitled to exclusive service.

If the person is free to work for other companies, provides his/her own equipment, sets his/her own work pace, and can sub-contract the work to others, then it might generally be assumed that s/he is an independent contractor. However, despite the variety of issues that can be examined in dealing with this question, Fennell and Lynch (1993) suggest that a certain amount of confusion exists about what test should be applied. Table 13.1 outlines the key differences that can be seen to exist between a contract *of* service and a contract *for* service, though as contact types change, and some work becomes more autonomous, it can be harder to make clear distinctions between the two types of contract.

Table 13.1 Key differences between contracts of service and contracts for service

CONTRACTS OF SERVICE	CONTRACTS FOR SERVICE
Employer–employee relationship	Employer–contractor relationship
Usually a continuous relationship	A relationship based on a one-off piece of work
Duty of care owed to employees	Duty of care arising from occupier's liability
Generally liable for the vicarious acts of employees, e.g. any wrong or injury done by an employee while in the course of his or her work	Generally not liable for the vicarious acts of independent contractors
Protective legislation applies to contract	Protective legislation does not apply (apart from *Safety, Health and Welfare at Work Acts*)
Wage or salary payment	Fee payment
Subject of contract is to carry on continuous work	Subject of contract is one-off

Source: Gunnigle, Garavan and Fitzgerald (1992).

EMPLOYMENT LEGISLATION

There is a considerable body of employment protection legislation in Ireland that provides a basic floor of rights for individual employees. Several important Acts have been passed since the 1970s, with many amended since they were originally introduced. Where amendments have occurred, this is reflected in the dates assigned to the Acts here. It is important to note that certain categories of employees are excluded from the protection of some pieces of employment legislation, e.g. members of the Defence Forces, Gardaí, SOLAS trainees, those working for a close relative in the home, and certain public sector categories.

INDIVIDUAL EMPLOYEE LEGISLATION

The following is a brief summary of the main individual rights of employees. Most of the statutory rights (i.e. those granted under the various Acts) are only available to those who have had a specific period of continuous employment with their company or organisation. Legally, this is known as the 'qualifying period', but there is no consistency from one Act to another as differing periods of service apply.

TERMS AND CONDITIONS OF EMPLOYMENT

Written Particulars of Terms of Employment

A contract of employment comes into force as soon as a job offer is made and accepted, whether orally or in writing, and appropriate conditions related to contract formation are adhered to. The *Terms of Employment (Information) Acts 1994–2014* require employers to provide a written statement setting out particulars of the employee's terms of employment within twenty-eight days or to direct employees to where they can find details of their employment. Information to be included in the written statement includes:

- The full names of the employer and employee.
- The address of the employer in the state or, where appropriate, its principal place of business, or the registered address of the employer as registered with the Companies Registration Office (CRO).
- The place of work or, where there is no main place of work, a statement that the employee is required or permitted to work at various places.
- The job title or nature of the work.
- The date of commencement of employment.
- If the contract is temporary, the expected duration of employment.
- If the contract is for a fixed term, the date on which the contract expires.
- The rate of remuneration or method of calculating remuneration.
- Whether remuneration is paid weekly, monthly or otherwise.
- Terms or conditions relating to hours of work (including overtime).
- Terms or conditions relating to paid leave (other than paid sickness leave).
- Terms or conditions relating to incapacity for work due to sickness or injury.
- Terms or conditions relating to pensions and pension schemes.
- Periods of notice which the employee is entitled to receive and required to give on termination of employment; where this cannot be indicated when the written statement is given, the written statement must give the method for determining the period of notice.
- A reference to any collective agreements that affect the terms of employment: where the employer is not a party to the agreement, the written statement must indicate the bodies or institution that made the agreement.

Conditions of Employment

The entitlement of employees to holidays, rest periods and the determination of hours of work is governed by the *Organisation of Working Time Act 1997*. It provides that employees shall not work more than an average of forty-eight hours in each seven-day period. Such an average is calculated over a four-month period, but in certain specified cases a six-month period is permissible.

The Act contains very specific provisions in relation to rest periods, Sunday working and night working. An employee is entitled to at least eleven consecutive hours of rest in each period of twenty-four hours worked. They are also entitled to a rest period of fifteen minutes for working four hours and a rest period of thirty minutes if the working period is six hours. A weekly rest period of twenty-four consecutive hours is also provided for in the Act. This weekly rest period must include a Sunday, unless otherwise provided for in the employee's contract of employment. Where an employee is required to work on Sunday, and this does not form part of the employment contract, the employee is entitled to compensation. This may take the form of the following: time off in lieu, payment of a special allowance, increase in the employee's rate of pay or a combination of both.

Night work is defined under the Act as work carried out between midnight and 7 a.m. A night worker is defined as an employee who works at least three hours of their daily working period during night-time and where the number of hours worked during night-time represents at least 50 per cent of the total hours worked during the year. In order to comply with the Act, employers must ensure that night workers do not work more than an average of eight hours per night, averaged over a two-month period. The Act also sets out quite extensive provisions relating to zero-hour contracts.

The Act provides for the provision of paid holidays. Employees are entitled to:
- Four working weeks in a leave year in which 1,365 hours are worked.
- One-third of a working week for each month in a leave year in which 117 hours are worked.
- Eight per cent of the hours worked in a leave year (to a maximum of four working weeks).

The *Workplace Relations Act 2015* amended the *Organisation of Working Time Act 1997* to provide for the accrual of annual leave during a period of certified sick leave. It also allows workers to retain annual leave they could not take due to illness for up to fifteen months after the end of the year in which it is accrued. Workers who leave their employment within fifteen months of the end of the year in which this annual leave was accrued, are entitled to payment in lieu of this leave which was untaken due to illness. This brings Irish law in line with the European Union Directive and case law which had emerged from the EU Court of Justice on this point.

In the case of public holidays, employees are entitled to one of the following:
- A paid day off on that day.
- A paid day off within a month of that day.
- An additional day of annual leave.
- An additional day's pay.

At present, there are nine public holidays:
- New Year's Day
- St Patrick's Day
- Easter Monday
- May Public Holiday (first Monday in May)

- June Public Holiday (first Monday in June)
- August Public Holiday (first Monday in August)
- October Public Holiday (last Monday in October)
- Christmas Day
- St Stephen's Day

In addition, the Act states that part-time employees must have worked at least forty hours during the five weeks prior to the public holiday to be entitled to the public holiday.

It is recommended that, in addition to being provided with written particulars relating to their contract of employment, all employees are provided with copies of all relevant codes of practices, policies and procedures (or informed of where they can be found), as these also form part of their terms of employment. These may refer to, *inter alia*, company position with respect to handling discipline, grievance, harassment, bullying issues, and use of social media and the internet while at work.

PART-TIME EMPLOYEES

The *Protection of Employees (Part-Time Work) Act 2001* provides labour law protection to all part-time workers, to ensure that part-time employees are not treated less favourably than their full-time equivalents with respect to conditions of work.

The same service requirements apply to part-time as to full-time employees, with respect to qualifying for the provisions of the various Acts.

CONTRACT WORK

The *Protection of Employees (Fixed-Term Work) Act 2003* was introduced to comply with an EU Directive. A fixed-term contract is one that comes to an end on completion of a specific project, after a specified time, or after the occurrence of a specific event. The aim of the Act is to prevent people being employed for years on fixed-term contracts without being offered a permanent position.

For employees on a fixed-term employment contract that commenced after the passing of the Act, where they are employed on two or more continuous fixed-term contracts, the aggregate duration of those contracts may not exceed four years. However, the Act states that the rules do not apply where there are objective grounds justifying the renewal of a contract of employment for a fixed term only.

EMPLOYMENT OF YOUNG PEOPLE

The *Protection of Young Persons (Employment) Act 1996* lays down a number of conditions for the employment of young people. A child is defined under the Act as a person less than fourteen years of age, whereas a young person is regarded as a person between sixteen and eighteen years of age.
- The Act prohibits the employment of children under the age of fourteen and neither children nor young people are permitted to be employed in night work.
- Young people aged between fourteen and sixteen can only be employed with the written permission of parents/guardians and between the hours of 8.00 a.m.–8.00 p.m.
- Young people are allowed to work a maximum of forty hours per week or eight hours in any one day between the hours of 8.00 a.m.–10.00 p.m.

- They must receive a maximum rest period of twelve hours in each twenty-four-hour period and a rest period of two days in each seven-day period.

The Act creates exemptions in relation to the employment of close relations of the employer. Specific provisions are also laid down in the Act in relation to rest periods, rates of pay and the complaints procedure to the Adjudication Service (formerly Rights Commissioner Service).

PAY

The *Payment of Wages Act 1991* provides that no deductions can be made from an employee's wages without their explicit consent. The Act obliges employers to furnish an employee with an itemised pay statement, setting out any deductions from the employee's wages and explaining the nature and amount of the deductions. The Act also allows for the payment of wages in modes other than cash, provided the employee consents to such arrangements.

The *National Minimum Wage Acts 2000–2015* provide a legislative framework establishing the right of employees to a legally enforceable minimum rate of pay for their labour. Significantly, the provisions of the Acts do not apply when the employee is related to the employer, or when the employee is an apprentice. Specific provisions and calculations are also set out under the Act for individuals entering employment for the first time upon reaching the age of eighteen, as well as for individuals undergoing a course of training or study authorised by their employer. However, the provisions of the Acts also extend to individuals employed under a contract for services. The Acts also contain detailed provisions to ensure ease of compliance with the Acts and ease of determination of employee remuneration, taking into account employee working hours and issues of 'reckonable' and 'non-reckonable' pay. The Acts stipulate that employees should be paid for their working hours at an hourly rate of pay that is not less than the minimum hourly rate established by statute. The national minimum wage for an adult worker in Ireland is currently €9.25 per hour.

PENSIONS

The *Pensions Acts 1990–2002* regulate the operation of occupational pension schemes in Ireland. The Pensions Acts are lengthy and complex pieces of legislation which provide a legal framework for the regulation and beneficial tax treatment of pension schemes established by employers for the benefit of employees. They provide that members who have the appropriate length of service and who lose their employment before retirement age are entitled to a preserved benefit. The Acts contain provision for a transfer payment for eligible members and lay down specific provisions relating to the disclosure of information in relation to pension schemes and provisions for the equal treatment of men and women in occupational benefit schemes. The Pensions Board was established under the 1990 Act to carry out the following functions:

- To monitor and supervise the operation of the Act and pensions developments.
- To advise the relevant Minister on pensions matters.
- To issue guidelines on the duties and responsibilities of pension scheme trustees and establish codes of practice.

- To encourage the provision of appropriate training facilities for pension scheme trustees.
- To publish reports (including an annual report).
- To perform other tasks at the Minister's request.

Personal Retirement Savings Accounts (PRSAs) and a Pensions Ombudsman were established in 2002. The function of the Pensions Ombudsman is to investigate and decide on complaints involving occupational pension schemes and the PRSAs (see www.pensionsombudsman.ie).

EMPLOYMENT EQUALITY

Maternity Protection and Maternity Leave

The *Maternity Protection Act 1994* was amended and extended by the *Maternity Protection (Amendment) Act 2004*. The main purpose of the Acts is to provide protection for all pregnant employees and those who have recently given birth, or who are breast-feeding. They do this by giving them certain legal rights, as outlined below:

- The right to twenty-six weeks paid maternity leave.
- The right to up to sixteen weeks' additional unpaid maternity leave.
- The right to return to work.
- The right to paid time off for one set of ante-natal classes, except for the last three classes, for expectant mothers;
- The right to paid time off for fathers to attend the last three ante-natal classes.
- Where breastfeeding facilities are available, the right to breastfeeding breaks for up to one hour per day.
- Where no breastfeeding facilities are available, the right to reduced hours of work by up to one hour per day for breastfeeding purposes.
- The right to health and safety leave in certain circumstances.
- The right to protection of their jobs during maternity leave, additional maternity leave, father's leave, health and safety leave and time off for ante-natal and post-natal care.
- The right to improvement in pay and conditions to which the employee would have been entitled if they were not absent from work.
- The right not to be dismissed for any pregnancy-related reason, from the beginning of pregnancy until the end of maternity leave.
- The right to postpone part of the maternity and/or additional leave should the child be hospitalised.
- The right of the father to certain leave entitlements in the event of the death of the mother.

The Act entitles female employees to a period of maternity leave of twenty-six weeks, if notice is given to the employer in writing at least four weeks before the expected date of birth, together with a medical certificate establishing the fact of pregnancy. There is no qualifying service in order to secure this right. The exact dates of the maternity leave can be chosen by the employee, but the period must cover the two weeks before and the four weeks after the birth. During the period of maternity leave there is no break in the continuity of the employee's service. She is entitled to return to her job after the birth, provided she notifies the employer in writing of her intention at least four working weeks before the expected date of return. Strict compliance with these requirements is essential.

In the event of the death of the mother within sixteen weeks of the birth of a living child, the father of the child is entitled to leave until the end of the sixteenth week. The father is also entitled to 'further leave' of eight weeks. In the event of the death of the mother after sixteen weeks but before twenty-four weeks, the father is entitled to leave up until the end of the twenty-fourth week.

Employers are not obliged to pay women on maternity leave, but women may apply for maternity benefit which is a Department of Social Protection payment. Since January 2014, the standard rate payable is €230.00 per week. In practice, many employers top up the employee's salary to pre-maternity leave levels.

ADOPTIVE LEAVE

Under the *Adoptive Leave Act 1995*, an adopting mother or a sole male adopter who is in employment is entitled to a minimum of ten consecutive weeks' leave from work, beginning on the day of placement of the child, and to up to four weeks' additional leave.

The ten-week period of adoptive leave will attract a social welfare benefit in the majority of cases.

PATERNITY LEAVE

Under the new *Paternity Leave and Benefits Act 2016*, a relevant parent is entitled to two continuous weeks' paid leave in respect of births from September 2016 where the leave is to be used for the sole purpose of looking after the child. The leave can be taken at any time in the twenty-six weeks following the birth of the child (or placement in the case of adoption). Four weeks' notice is required before the leave may be taken, however, there is provision for shorter notice. The Act allows for the postponement of leave in certain circumstances, such as the sickness of a relevant parent and the hospitalisation of the child.

Payment is at the same rate as maternity benefit, subject to a person having the appropriate PRSI contributions. Similar to maternity leave, employers can top up paternity benefit if they wish. Where employers make a top up to female employees, from an equality perspective, they will need to consider a similar approach to paternity benefit for male employees.

A relevant parent is defined as the father of the child or the spouse, civil partner or cohabitant of the mother. In most family circumstances, it will be the father. The leave applies to one person only, except in the case of adoption, whereby a biological father may have already taken paternity leave, so it allows the subsequent adopting father to also take leave.

PARENTAL LEAVE

The *Parental Leave Acts 1998–2006*, in combination with the European Union (Parental Leave) Regulations (Statutory Instrument No. 81 of 2013), provide for an employee to take up to eighteen working weeks' unpaid leave for the purpose of caring for his/her child (under the age of eight years). The new EU Regulations increase the amount of parental leave from fourteen working weeks to eighteen working weeks per parent, per child. The provisions of the Acts apply to the natural or adoptive parents of a child, and both the mother and the father of the child qualify for the leave concerned. In addition, one period of leave may be taken in respect of each natural or adopted child of the employee. However, the Acts stipulate that periods of leave are not transferable between parents (unless both parents work for the same employer and get permission from the employer to transfer up to fourteen weeks from one to the other).

To qualify for the full period of parental leave, the employee must have completed one year's continuous service with the employer from whom the leave is to be taken. Employees wishing to take parental leave must give notice in writing to their employer at least six weeks before the commencement of the period of leave. The eighteen weeks can be taken in one block of eighteen weeks or in blocks of not less than six weeks, with a gap of at least ten weeks between each block. Any other combination requires the agreement of the employer. An employer may postpone parental leave for a period of six months where the taking of parental leave would have a substantial adverse effect on the employer's business. An employee who is on parental leave will still be regarded as working by the employer and, apart from the employee's right to remuneration or superannuation benefits, all other employment rights are preserved.

The Acts also makes provision for *force majeure* leave, when an employee may avail of paid leave where their immediate presence at home or elsewhere is indispensable because of urgent family reasons owing to the injury or illness of certain persons. Force majeure leave may be taken in respect of the following people: a child, a spouse or partner, a person to whom the employee is in loco parentis, a brother or sister, a parent or grandparent, or a person in a relationship of domestic dependency. Such leave should not exceed three days in any twelve-month period or five days in any thirty-six-month period.

CARER'S LEAVE

The *Carer's Leave Act 2001* provides an opportunity to employees with twelve months' continuous service of taking sixty-five weeks' unpaid leave for the purpose of providing full-time care and attention to a person requiring it. It applies to situations where the person involved has a disability that requires the continual supervision and frequent assistance of the employee throughout the day in connection with normal bodily functions, or in order to avoid danger to themselves.

To avail of carer's leave, an employee must apply to the relevant Minister for a decision by a specially appointed deciding officer. Notice of the intention to take carer's leave must be given in writing to the employer at least six weeks before the commencement of such leave. The notice must state:
- The proposal to take carer's leave.
- That an application for carer's leave has been made to the deciding officer.
- The proposed date of commencement of the carer's leave.

The Act also specifies a set of provisions under which an employee may apply for a second consecutive period of carer's leave.

EMPLOYMENT EQUALITY ACTS

The *Employment Equality Acts 1998–2011* have become the cornerstone of Irish employment equality law. They repealed the *Anti-Discrimination Pay Act 1974* and the *Employment Equality Act 1977*. The *Employment Equality Acts 1998–2011* define discrimination as 'the treatment of a person in a less favourable way than another person is, has been, or would be treated in a comparable situation on any of the [nine] grounds', which are:
- Gender
- Civil status
- Family status
- Sexual orientation
- Religious belief
- Age
- Disability
- Race
- Membership of the Travelling community

Discrimination is prohibited in the following areas:
- An employer shall not discriminate against an employee, prospective employee or agency worker in relation to access to employment, conditions of employment, training or experience for or in relation to employment, promotion or regrading or classification of posts.
- Discrimination is outlawed in collective agreements and with regard to equal pay for like work.
- Advertising in relation to employment is prohibited where it indicates (or may be reasonably understood to indicate) an intention to discriminate.
- An employment agency shall not discriminate against any person availing of their services or guidance.
- Instructors or providers of vocational training shall not discriminate in terms of any course offered or provided.
- Professional or trade organisations or vocational bodies shall not discriminate against any person in relation to membership or entry to that profession, vocation or occupation.

The Acts reaffirm the principle that employers are responsible for the actions of their employees, taken in the course of their employment, regardless of whether the employer knew or approved of the actions. The Acts also require an employer to take appropriate measures to accommodate the needs of employees with disabilities, unless the measures would impose a disproportionate burden on the employer. In terms of equality between men and women, the basic principle that men and women should receive equal pay for like work is underlined. In relation to the other grounds of discrimination, the Acts provide that each contract of employment shall be deemed to include a non-discriminatory equality clause. This means that employees are entitled to the same rate of remuneration, despite differences in marital status, family status, sexual orientation, religious belief, age, disability, race and membership of the Travelling community, provided they are engaged in like work for the same or associated employer.

Indirect discrimination is prohibited under the Acts. This relates to a situation where apparently neutral provisions put a group of persons at a particular disadvantage compared with other groups of persons, for example a height requirement for a job would be more likely to disadvantage women than men.

Harassment and sexual harassment are outlawed under the Acts. Harassment is defined as:

> ... any form of unwanted conduct related to any of the discriminatory grounds which has the purpose or effect of violating a person's dignity and creating an intimidating, hostile, degrading, humiliating or offensive environment for the person.
> *Equality Act 2004*

The definition of sexual harassment is the same as harassment, but the former emphasises that unwanted verbal, non-verbal or physical conduct is of a sexual nature. Harassment or sexual harassment may take the form of acts, requests, spoken words, gestures or the production, display or circulation of written words, pictures or other material. An employer will be held responsible for acts of sexual harassment carried out on employees by other employees, clients, customers or other business contacts, regardless of whether the acts take place inside or outside the work environment. Therefore an employer must take 'all reasonable steps' to ensure a harassment-free workplace. Significantly, no remedy is provided under the Acts for same-sex harassment.

Discrimination on the ground of gender is treated differently to discrimination on the other eight grounds in that gender discrimination claims may be brought directly to the Circuit Court, whereas claims on the other grounds must be initiated before the Workplace Relations Commission (WRC).

TERMINATION OF EMPLOYMENT

The *Unfair Dismissals Acts 1977– 2015* provide that within twenty-eight days of offering employment, an employer must give the employee a notice in writing setting out the procedure the employer will observe before and for the purpose of dismissing the employee. If an employee is dismissed, the employer must give a written statement of the reasons within two weeks of the date of dismissal. It is wise to send all such statements by recorded delivery and where related previous correspondence exists – such as warning letters, dismissal letters – to include copies of these as well. Although all such earlier incidents or warnings should have been properly recorded and the employee given copies at the time that they occurred, it is advisable to include copies and refer to them again in the final written reasons for dismissal. An employee may take a case before the Workplace Relations Commission (WRC) if written reasons are refused or if the reasons are perceived to be inadequate.

NOTICE OF TERMINATION

Both the employer and the employee are normally entitled to a minimum period of notice, although either employer or employee may accept pay in lieu of notice. Under

Section 4(1) of the *Minimum Notice and Terms of Employment Act 1973*, an employee who has thirteen weeks' continuous service is entitled to a statutory minimum notice. Section 4(2) of the Act sets out the periods of minimum notice to which employees covered by the Act are entitled:

- Less than two years' continuous service – one week's minimum notice.
- More than two years but less than five years' continuous service – two weeks' minimum notice.
- More than five years but less than ten years' continuous service – four weeks' minimum notice
- More than ten years but less than fifteen years' continuous service – six weeks' minimum notice
- Fifteen years or more continuous service – eight weeks' minimum notice.

These are *minimum* periods: if a contract of employment gives entitlement to a longer period, the longer period will apply. Under Section 6 of the Act the employer in turn is entitled to a period of notice of not less than one week from an employee who has been in continuous employment for thirteen weeks or more. This period does not increase in line with the length of service. However, the contract of employment may specify a period of notice that is required by the employer.

The notice given by the employer must be sufficiently certain and precise, leaving no room for ambiguity or uncertainty. The precise expiry date (date of dismissal) must be clearly specified in writing and the period of notice given must be not less than the minimum statutory period or the formal contractual period of notice. Employees to whom the notice provisions apply are entitled to the same rights during the minimum notice period as they would enjoy but for the notice. Failure by an employer to give notice correctly can affect the effective date of dismissal and therefore the eligibility of an employee's claim of unfair dismissal to be heard by the WRC.

If the employer fails to give the employee the proper period of notice, the employee may claim breach of contract through the courts (common law remedy) or, if s/he is covered by the *Minimum Notice and Terms of Employment Act 1973*, through an action to the WRC. Categories of workers not covered by these provisions include members of the Gardaí, the Defence Forces, local authority employees and civil servants.

UNFAIR DISMISSAL

Under the *Unfair Dismissals Acts 1977–2015*, once an employee has been continuously employed for one year s/he has a right of action if s/he is unfairly dismissed. If an employee has been dismissed and perceives it as being unfair s/he can bring a case to the WRC or to the Adjudication Service (formerly Rights Commissioner Service) within six months of the date of dismissal. The *Unfair Dismissals (Amendment) Act 1993*, provides that, in exceptional circumstances, the time frame within which a case may be brought may be extended to within twelve months of the date of dismissal. The date of dismissal is taken to be the date on which notice of the termination of contract expires. When prior notice is not given, the date of dismissal is taken to be the date on which such notice would have expired if it had been given. (The WRC and the Adjudication Service are discussed in Chapter 10.)

The following categories of employees are not eligible to submit a claim for unfair dismissal.
- Employees who have less than one year's continuous service with the same employer. (If it is shown that a dismissal resulted wholly or mainly from the employee's membership, or proposed membership, of a trade union, or from their activities on behalf of a trade union, the requirement of one year's continuous service does not apply; a woman who claims she was dismissed because of pregnancy may bring an unfair dismissal claim, even though she does not have a year's continuous service with her employer.)
- Employees over the normal retiring age, although this is now being challenged under age descrimination.
- Close relations of the employer who are members of his/her household and work in a private dwelling house.
- Members of An Garda Síochána and the Defence Forces.
- Employees who are employed by or under the state.
- Employees serving apprenticeships.
- Officers of local authorities, health boards and vocational educational committees.

Dismissal is automatically unfair where it is shown that it resulted wholly or mainly from any of the following causes:
- The employee taking part in a strike or other industrial action.
- Following a lockout.
- The employee's trade union membership or activities.
- The employee's religious or political opinions.
- Involvement in legal proceedings against the employer.
- The age of the employee.
- The race or colour of the employee.
- The sexual orientation of the employee.
- The pregnancy of the employee.
- The employee's membership of the Travelling community.
- Unfair selection of the employee for redundancy.

In general, where a dismissal is contested, the burden of proving that the dismissal is fair rests firmly with the employer. However, in constructive dismissal cases, where the employee terminates the employment contract because of the employer's conduct, or because conditions in the organisation make it impossible to stay, the onus is on the employee.

The decision to dismiss must be taken carefully, as the penalties that may be incurred if a dismissal is ruled unfair by the WRC are severe. It is important, therefore, that one should know the conditions under which an employee may be fairly dismissed.

Dismissal for Misconduct

The issue of reasonableness has great significance in the context of dismissal for misconduct. The WRC will consider general industrial standards. There is no absolute definition of reasonableness since it depends on individual circumstances in the company. The WRC has emphasised that misconduct must be measured in the context of the employee's actions and not just the consequences or potential consequences of that behaviour to the employer. It has further decided that in misconduct cases, the employer must, before taking the decision to dismiss, consider whether there were mitigating circumstances, such as a record of good service or personal difficulties experienced by the employee.

In the case of minor misconduct – such as persistent lateness – an employer must show that all the stages in the disciplinary procedure have been followed and that, having exhausted these, they have given written warning that further infringements would lead to dismissal. To prove that the employer had acted properly, it is necessary for them to have kept a written record of all the procedures that had been gone through in the case. If the misconduct was more serious – such as fighting, breaking a work rule, or sleeping on duty – going through every stage of the procedure might be unnecessary. However, the employer would need to observe the *rules of natural justice*, which are:
- The employee has a right to be told the facts of the case against him/her.
- The employee has the right to a hearing (to tell his/her side of the story).
- The employee has the right to representation of his/her choice.
- The employee has the right to appeal to a higher level of his/her choice within the company.

Failure to comply with the rules of natural justice may render a dismissal unfair. An employer should also:
- Enquire into the matter to find out what really happened. If fact-finding is going to take some time it may be necessary to suspend the employee on full pay.
- Interview the employee to get his/her side of the story, advising him/her of the right to be represented if appropriate.
- Decide, on the basis of the information, what action is reasonable in the circumstances. Did the employee know the rule that was broken? Was s/he aware of its significance? Would a clearly stated warning of dismissal for repetition be more reasonable than dismissal for a first-time offence? How have similar cases been treated in the past, i.e. is the employer being consistent with previous 'custom and practice'?
- Make clear to the employee what action is to be taken and how s/he can appeal against the decision if the procedure allows this.

Dismissal for Capability, Competence or Qualifications

The *Unfair Dismissals Acts 1977– 2015* provide that a fair basis for dismissal relates to the capability, competence or qualifications of the employee for performing work of the kind s/he was employed by the employer to do. While it may be fair to dismiss someone for incapability, if a complaint were made an employer would need to convince a tribunal that they had a valid reason for dismissing the person, and that they had acted reasonably in treating that reason as a sufficient cause for dismissal. Capability, as determined by the WRC, usually relates to dismissals arising from illness, injury or similar incapacity. The question of whether the employee was to blame for the illness or incapacity is irrelevant.

In the case of capability the WRC has introduced these exceptions:
1. Where an employee who is incapacitated due to injury or illness could be given lighter work that s/he would have been able to perform, the dismissal may be unfair.
2. Where an employee is absent it is up to the employer to try to find out why. It is not reasonable to assume, without further investigation, that the absence is due to illness that might justify dismissal.

Dismissal for Incapability Because of Ill-Health

Dismissals resulting from incapacity due to ill-health may arise in cases of persistent short-term absenteeism or cases of long-term absence caused by prolonged illness or injury. In both instances, an employer needs to ask how reasonable it is to dismiss an employee who has been off work for an extended period of time. Reasonable action would again consist of being seen to follow fair procedures and securing the fullest possible information. Evidence of fair procedure might include the following:

- Visiting the employee (perhaps on more than one occasion) to find out how likely it is that they will be returning to work, and to make clear to them how long the company can wait.
- If the company cannot wait any longer, obtaining an independent medical report, which would be a useful element in making a decision.
- Considering whether alternative work could be made available.
- Advising the employee of the decision.

In the case of dismissal due to illness-related absence, the High Court has set out the following grounds, placing an onus on employers to prove that the dismissal is fair by showing:
1. It was the employee's ill-health that was the reason for the dismissal.
2. The employee's ill-health was the substantial reason.
3. The employee received fair notice that the question of their dismissal for incapacity was being considered.
4. The employee was afforded an opportunity of being heard.

Dismissal for Incapability Because of Incompetence

Competence issues arise when an employee is alleged to have demonstrated poor work performance, for example failure to meet reasonable targets set by the employer. To act fairly in dismissing someone for this reason, an employer must detail evidence of the alleged incompetence, and must have discussed this with the employee. An employer would also need to establish that they did not contribute to the incompetence by failing to make requirements clear, or by not providing the necessary facilities to allow the job to be done competently.

A warning might be appropriate. If so, it should clearly state what is required of the employee within set time limits. In such instances, an employee must be given a reasonable time period within which to make such improvement and a reasonable work situation within which to concentrate on his/her work defects. In the case of long-serving employees, it might be more reasonable to consider whether a less arduous job could be found. As with misconduct, warnings are not necessary if an employer believes they serve no purpose, but the employer might have to convince a tribunal of this. A case will obviously be much easier to make if an employee has been given warnings and a chance to improve with as much reasonable help as possible from the employer.

Dismissal for Incapability Because of Qualifications

This concept refers primarily to the absence of formal qualifications that are essential to the job, which is another fair reason for dismissal under certain circumstances. This category might include the case of an accountant losing their professional qualifications, or the case of an employee who misled an employer into thinking they had certain qualifications or experience on joining, but in fact did not. It might also arise where the employee did not have the qualifications on joining, has agreed to take steps to obtain them, but who seems unable to obtain them despite repeated attempts and every assistance from the company.

Reasonable dismissal in this category would depend on how critical the qualification is to the job and the duties of the employee in question, and how long the situation is likely to continue. As in other cases, an employer would need to consider whether an alternative job could be offered for which the person was qualified.

Dismissal for Breaking Another Statute

It is fair for an employer to dismiss an employee who could not continue to work without breaking another law. The sales representative who loses his/her driving licence is a clear example. As usual, however, an employer would need to consider alternatives to dismissal. Could the employer offer alternative work? Could other arrangements be made for the period?

Dismissal for Industrial Action

The *Unfair Dismissals Acts 1977–2015* provide that the dismissal of an employee by way of lockout is fair if the employee is offered reinstatement or re-engagement from the date of resumption of work. Section 5(2) provides that the dismissal of an employee for taking part in a strike or other industrial action is unfair if any other employee or employees who took part in the strike were reinstated or re-engaged. Where an employer dismissed all the employees who took part, the onus is still on the employer to prove that they had fair grounds under one of the previous headings or on other substantial grounds. If they cannot do so the dismissal will be deemed unfair.

Dismissal for Other Substantial Grounds

An employer may succeed in termination of employment even if a dismissal does not fall under any of the previous headings, if they can claim that it qualifies on 'other substantial grounds' that are not covered under the Acts. Such cases are atypical, and outcomes are variable depending on the individual circumstances.

REDUNDANCY

The *Redundancy Payments Acts 1991–2014* provide that a dismissal resulting from a redundancy of an employee is not unfair. Redundancy is basically defined as dismissal caused by either the fact that the employer has ceased their business, or that they no longer require the work carried out by the particular employee/s, or they are reducing the scope of their workforce. The onus is on the employer to prove the existence of redundancy. They cannot simply claim that a situation of redundancy exists; they must produce substantial evidence. Even where there is a genuine redundancy, not all dismissals will necessarily be fair. A number of qualifications have been introduced:

1. Where an employee was selected in contravention of a procedure that has been agreed between the employer and the employee or trade union, or that was established by custom and practice and no special reasons are produced for departing from this procedure, the dismissal will be unfair.
2. If the employer had an ulterior motive in selecting the particular employee, the dismissal will be unfair even if there was a genuine redundancy. An employer should not use arbitrary criteria in selecting employees for redundancy. The WRC examines all aspects of an employer's conduct, including the observance of statutory obligations such as the *Protection of Employment Act 1977* (this Act allows for consultation and information relating to mass redundancies). Not only must an employer use proper criteria, but they must also be applied in a fair manner.

REDUNDANCY PAYMENTS

Under the *Redundancy Payments Acts 1967–2014*, employees under a contract of employment or apprenticeship who have had at least two years' continuous service and are aged between sixteen and sixty-six are entitled to a redundancy payment in the event of being made redundant, which is calculated as follows:

- Two weeks' pay per year of service.
- One week's pay (the bonus week).

The statutory redundancy lump sum is subject to a maximum cap of €600.00 per week based on a ceiling on annual reckonable earnings of €31,200 per year. Employees are not entitled to a redundancy payment if they unreasonably refuse an offer of suitable alternative employment with their own employer, or with another company in the same group where continuity of employment can be maintained, provided the alternative employment does not involve a significant reduction in status or conditions.

LEGAL REGULATION FOR REDUNDANCY

Redundancy legislation is very complex and contains many detailed provisions and rules. As a general classification, the Acts fall into two categories:

- Legislation dealing with collective redundancies; this lays down procedural regulations to be observed by employers, and bestows a number of rights on unions.
- Legislation on what constitutes redundancy, the right to a redundancy payment and the calculation of continuous service.

The *Protection of Employment Acts 1977–2007* lay down procedural obligations in the case of collective redundancies, and provide for a redundancy panel to consider proposed collective redundancies. There are a number of specific provisions that a manager will need to be aware of:
1. The Acts apply to a situation where in a period of thirty days a number of employees are dismissed for redundancy. The minimum number required varies, depending on the size of the total workforce.
2. The main obligation on employers is consultation and notification. If a company has a collective redundancy, the Minister must be notified at least thirty days before the final dismissal. The employer must also send a copy of this notice to the employees' representatives.
3. At least thirty days before the dismissal, the employer must enter into consultation with the employee's representatives with a view to reaching agreement on issues such as the numbers to be made redundant, alternative courses of action and the implementation of the redundancies. The Acts do not specify what happens in the event of an agreement not being reached.
4. Employers are also obliged to provide the employees with certain information relating to the redundancy. Examples include the reasons for the redundancy, the number of employees affected and the period during which it is to take place.
5. Employers are also obliged to keep adequate records of the situation.

In the event of a redundancy taking place, the individual employee's situation is governed by the *Redundancy Payments Acts 1967–2014*. Under Section 7 of the 1967 Act as amended, redundancy is defined as follows: '. . . an employee who is dismissed shall be taken to be dismissed by reason of redundancy if the dismissal is attributable wholly or mainly to one of the following':
- Where the employer has ceased or intends to cease to carry on business for the purpose of which the employee was employed.
- Where the requirements of the business do not require the particular type of work which the employee has to offer.
- Where the employer decides to carry on the business with fewer employees.
- Where the employer decides that the work which the employee does is to be done in a different manner.
- Where the employer decides that the work done by the particular employee should from now on be done by a person who is capable of doing other work for which the employee is not sufficiently qualified.

Other important provisions of the *Redundancy Payments Acts 1967–2014* include the following:
- The entitlement to a redundancy payment cannot be waived and any term in a contract of employment that purports to do so is invalid.
- In all redundancies, the employer must give notice in writing to the employee of the proposed dismissal and must send a copy to the Minister thirty days in advance. The employer must also furnish the employee with a redundancy certificate.
- If the employee is offered an alternative job in the organisation, the Acts allow the

employee time off to try out the alternative job to test its suitability. The employee has four weeks in order to assess its suitability.
- Employees eligible for redundancy pay are entitled to reasonable time off work, with pay, to look for another job. An employer may in such circumstances seek evidence that the employee is actually using the time off in the intended manner. If an employer refuses to allow time off, the employee may bring the matter to the WRC.
- An employee who is under notice does not have to work this notice if it is agreed that s/he should receive any due payment in lieu.

However, as mentioned earlier, where the employer terminates the contract of employment, it is also important that they give notice correctly, as this could affect the effective date of dismissal and therefore the eligibility of an employee's claim of unfair dismissal to be heard by the WRC. The effective date of dismissal should be made very clear (in writing) to the employee and any period of notice given must not be less than the minimum statutory period or the formal contractual period of notice.

RETIREMENT

In general, there is no fixed mandatory retirement age in Ireland. Employers are permitted to set their own retirement age, whether by contract, policy or custom and practice. Certain professions do, however, have a statutory retirement age such as the Gardaí, members of the fire service and the defence forces, and others employed in the public sector.

The requirement to retire from employment would normally be contained in the contract of employment. If the employee's contract does not provide for retirement at a given age, then the employee could technically remain employed by the company indefinitely. If forced to retire by the company, the employee could assert unfair dismissal or age discrimination. In the absence of an express contractual retirement age, custom and practice could come into effect. In Ireland the usual retirement age up until recently was sixty-five years, however, the state pension age changed on 1 January 2014 to sixty-six and will increase incrementally to sixty-eight by January 2028.

TRANSFER OF UNDERTAKINGS

The Transfer of Undertakings Regulations (S.I. No. 487 of 2000 and S.I. No. 131 of 2003) provide employees with a series of rights on the transfer of a business. A transfer under the 2003 Regulations means the transfer of an economic entity that retains its identity. Under such circumstances, the employment rights, seniority, continuity of service and representation rights of employees are protected and employers are obliged to consult with their employees in the event of a proposed transfer. An employee may not be dismissed solely by reason of the transfer. The regulations also outline a set of sanctions in the event of non-compliance by employers with the provisions contained therein. Complaints under the 2003 Regulations may be made by an employee, trade union, staff association or excepted body to the Adjudication Service (formerly Rights Commissioner Service), with a right of appeal to the WRC.

HEALTH AND SAFETY AT WORK

Health and safety legislation is a distinct branch of legislation within the broad field of employment related legislation and is governed by a combination of common law, statute law, and over 200 separate Statutory Instruments and Codes of Practice that have legal effect. Together these lay down a number of provisions concerning health and safety in the workplace. A useful classification of the relevant statutes is as follows:
- Those that deal exclusively with the safety, health and wellbeing of workers.
- Those concerned with the regulation of hours of work.
- Those not designed exclusively as worker protection measures, but that nevertheless provide varying degrees of protection.
- Those on the borderline between issues of general environmental pollution and occupational health and safety.

COMMON LAW

Outside all the legislation (statute law) that exists on health and safety at work, an employer may also incur liability under common law. The position is that an employer is legally responsible for any injuries or diseases that occur on the job. Case law has clearly laid down that an employer must exercise reasonable care towards employees and must guard them against any likely injury or disease. If an employer fails to live up to this obligation, liability for negligence will occur if an employee is injured. However, it is important to remember that liability will only arise when an employer's negligence actually caused or contributed to an employee's injury or disease. Furthermore, the incident that occurs must be reasonably foreseeable. The reason for this is simple – common law is not concerned with anticipating damages or setting standards of good behaviour in order to prevent accidents; it only comes into play after the event, and its main function is to compensate employees for any injuries they receive while at work. As well as laying down a general principle of employers' liability for injuries, the courts have gone further and have specified different elements of the employers' duties. This is directly relevant and provides a useful framework within which to evaluate a company's safety effort. The four duties are worth considering in detail.

1. Safe Plant and Equipment

This duty covers machinery, raw materials, tools, and so forth. However, employers will not incur liability if they obtained supplies from a reputable company and had no reason to suspect that they were faulty. Employers must also keep up to date with the potential dangers of new processes and machinery. They will have observed their duty of care if they keep up to date with information that is already known to exist: no liability will arise against a hazard that scientific knowledge is not yet aware of.

2. Competent Fellow Workers

Employers are expected to take reasonable steps to ensure that employees are able to do their jobs. This involves clarifying the personal qualities and skills required to do the particular job, ensuring that one has a systematic recruitment and selection procedure,

and providing the necessary training to do the job and special remedial training where necessary. For an employee to succeed in an action under this heading s/he would have to show two things:
1. That the other worker was unsuitable for the job.
2. That the employer had not been sufficiently careful in appointing or retraining the other worker.

If an employee exhibits quite unpredictable behaviour that causes injury to a fellow employee, the employer will not be held responsible, unless there has been a history of an employee exhibiting such behaviour.

3. Provision of Safety Equipment and Effective Supervision

Employers are under an obligation to provide employees with the necessary protective equipment and clothing required to do the job without exposing them to risk or injury. Proper instructions should also be issued. The courts have also clearly stated that it is not enough for the employer to inform the employee that the equipment is available; they must take reasonable measures to see that the employee uses it. This could include issuing formal warnings for not wearing such personal protective equipment (PPE).

4. Safe Premises and System of Work

Employers must take great care in the way work is laid out and organised. They must not expose employees to risks that could easily be avoided by more careful organisation. They are also expected to maintain their premises in a reasonable state of repair and orderliness. The courts have held that this duty extends to a customer's premises. If an employee is injured while working on a customer's premises they may have a claim against the employer. The employer's responsibility will be less, however, than if it was on the employer's premises. Employers will be liable to their employees for injuries that arise out of defects in the customer's premises that were apparent and that the employer should have taken reasonable precautions against.

Employers will not be liable, as a general rule, for employees on their way to and from work. However, if employers provide a company bus for transporting staff, they must have a competent driver and must ensure that the bus is properly maintained. Furthermore, if an employer allows their employees onto the premises outside working hours, reasonable steps must be taken to ensure that the premises is safe. The law further indicates that employers are vicariously liable for any damage or injury caused by their employees while in the course of their employment. Should a driver employed by a company injure a member of the public whilst driving in the course of their job, the employer may be found liable for the injury to the member of the public.

THE SAFETY, HEALTH AND WELFARE AT WORK ACTS 2005–2007

The *Safety, Health and Welfare at Work Act 2005* and the *Safety, Health and Welfare at Work (General Application) Regulations 2007* are concerned with the prevention of workplace accidents, illnesses and dangerous occurrences and the provision of significantly increased fines and penalties aimed at deterring those who continue to breach health and safety laws. The Acts require every employer to identify the hazards of its workplace, carry out and be in possession of a written risk assessment, and put in place protective and preventative measures to eliminate the hazards or, if that is not possible, to reduce them to the lowest possible level.

Duties Imposed

A number of general and specific duties are imposed by the Acts, on both employers and employees.

Employers
1. To ensure the health, safety and welfare at work of all employees (Section 8). The Acts give examples of some areas that must be considered by employers:
   (a) Design, provision and maintenance of the place of work.
   (b) Safe means of access to and exit from the place of work.
   (c) The provision and maintenance of machinery without risk.
   (d) Safe systems of work.
   (e) The provision of information, instruction, training and supervision.
   (f) Where hazards exist that cannot be controlled or eliminated, the provision and maintenance of suitable protective equipment.
   (g) Adequate and current emergency plans.
   (h) Ensuring safety with regard to articles or substances in use.
   (i) The provision and maintenance of welfare facilities.
   (j) The use of specialist services to provide for the health, safety and welfare of the workforce.
2. To ensure that those not in their employment who may be affected are not exposed to risks to their safety or health (Section 12).
3. To prepare a safety statement (Section 19) which must be brought to the attention of all those who are affected by it. The safety statement must:
   - Specify the manner in which health, safety and welfare shall be secured.
   - Be based on an identification of hazards and an assessment of risks.
   - Include arrangements made and resources provided.
   - Specify the co-operation required from employees.
   - Specify the names of the persons responsible.
4. To consult employees. Employers must consult their employees so that: they can initiate and maintain effective measures; they can co-operate in promoting and developing measures to ensure health and safety; the effectiveness of their arrangements can be ascertained.
5. To take account of employees' views (Section 26). Not only must there be consultation, but employers must take account of representations made by the workforce.

Employees

Section 13 details the general duties of employees while at work.
1. They must take reasonable care for their own safety and that of any other person who may be affected.
2. They must co-operate with their employer to such an extent that all relevant statutory provisions are complied with.
3. They must report any problems of which they become aware that might have an effect on safety, health or welfare.
4. They must not be under the influence of an intoxicant (drugs or alcohol) at the workplace to the extent that they are likely to endanger their own, or another person's, safety, health and welfare.
5. They may be required by their employer to submit reasonable tests for intoxicants by, or under the supervision of, a medical practitioner.
6. They must attend such training and assessment as required by their employer.
7. They must not engage in improper conduct or behaviour.
8. They may be required to undergo a medical assessment of their fitness to perform work activities which give rise to serious risks to health and safety.

COMPLAINTS BY EMPLOYEES

The *Safety, Health and Welfare at Work Act 1989* conferred quite specific rights on employees to make representations to, and to consult their employers on matters of safety, health and welfare in their place of work. Employees and safety representatives now have the right to make a complaint to an Adjudication Officer if they believe they have been penalised for the following:
- Acting in compliance with the legislation.
- Being a safety representative.
- Making a complaint to the safety representative or employer regarding health, safety and welfare at the workplace.
- Leaving a workplace or refusing to return to work while a serious and imminent danger persisted.

Penalisation can include suspension, lay-off, dismissal, demotion, loss of promotion opportunity, transfer of duties, coercion and intimidation. If an Adjudication Officer finds that a complaint is well founded, they may require the employer to take a specific course of action and/or to pay compensation to the employee. Appeals of Adjudication Officers' decisions may be made to the Labour Court.

THE SAFETY REPRESENTATIVE AND SAFETY COMMITTEE

Employees are entitled to appoint a safety representative, whose functions may include the following:
1. To investigate accidents and dangerous occurrences.
2. To investigate complaints relating to health, safety and welfare at work.
3. To accompany an inspector carrying out an inspection of a place of work, not related to an accident.

4. At the discretion of an inspector, to accompany them carrying out an inspection of a place of work related to an accident.
5. At the discretion of an inspector, and at the request of an employee, to attend an interview of an employee by an inspector.
6. To make representations to the employer.
7. To make representations to an inspector on health and safety matters, including the investigation of accidents.
8. To receive advice and information from inspectors.

Employees are also entitled to appoint a safety committee, for the purposes of assisting employers and employees in relation to the legislation. A committee shall consist of not fewer than three people and not more than one for every twenty people employed, or ten, whichever is the fewer.

JOINT SAFETY AND HEALTH AGREEMENTS

A new feature introduced by the *Safety, Health and Welfare at Work Act 2005* is that a trade union of employers and a trade union of employees can negotiate a joint safety and health agreement, which provides practical guidance with respect to safety, health and welfare at work. The parties can then apply to the Health and Safety Authority (HSA) to approve the agreement, and an approved agreement can be taken into account when enforcing the Act.

THE HEALTH AND SAFETY AUTHORITY (HSA)

The Health and Safety Authority is the national statutory body with responsibility for ensuring that all workers, and those affected by work activity, are protected from work-related injury and ill-health. Its main functions are to enforce health and safety laws and regulations, and provide information and advice on health, safety and wellbeing to workplaces.

Breaches of health and safety regulations can result in prosecutions that can range from Circuit Court fines of up to one million euro and/or prison sentences of up to two years. If convicted in the District Court, the employer may be fined up to €5,000 and/or imprisoned for up to twelve months (CIPD 2017). The HSA can also take a range of lesser actions. For example, it may prohibit work where there is serious and imminent danger to health and safety by serving a Prohibition Notice on an employer, or it may, in relation to less serious matters, serve an Improvement Notice.

THE SAFETY, HEALTH AND WELFARE AT WORK REGULATIONS

Since the inception of the original *Safety, Health and Welfare at Work Act 1989*, a series of regulations have emerged to make explicit and operational the provisions implicit in the various Acts. These are commonly referred to as the General Application Regulations, and they deal with seventeen different aspects of work-related health and safety issues, ranging from the condition of the workplace, to the protection to be afforded to pregnant employees, through to specific rules for workplaces with an explosive atmosphere.

Various Codes of Practice have been passed and have legal effect when it comes to terms and conditions of employment. For example, the *Code of Practice for Employers and Employees on the Prevention and Resolution of Bullying at Work (2007)* defines bullying as repeated inappropriate behaviour, direct or indirect, whether verbal, physical or otherwise conducted by one or more persons against another or others, which could reasonably be regarded as undermining the individual's right to dignity at work. As workplace bullying is a pernicious activity that organisations must make every effort to mitigate, all employers are required to have a policy on the prevention of bullying at work, and to make all employees aware of this at the commencement of employment. This works in tandem with the Workplace Relations Commission's Code detailing procedures to address bullying in the workplace and the Equality Authority's Code on sexual harassment and harassment at work.

COLLECTIVE LEGISLATION

Collective labour law establishes the legal framework for employee/industrial relations, and is distinguished from individual labour law in that it is concerned with regulating the relationship between employers and collectives of employees – normally trade unions. Collective legislation has been presented in Chapter 10.

Bibliography

Adams, J. (1965) 'Inequity in social exchange', in L. Berkowitz (ed.) *Advances in Experimental Social Psychology*, 2 London: Academic Press.
Aguinis, H. (2009) 'An expanded view of performance management', in J.W. Smither and M. London (eds.), *Performance management: Putting research into practice* San Francisco: Wiley: 1–43.
Aguinis, H. and Kraiger, K. (2009) 'Benefits of Training and Development for Individuals and Teams, Organizations, and Society', *Annual Review of Psychology* 60: 451–74.
Aguinis, H. Joo, H. & Gottfredson, R.K. (2011: 505) 'Why we hate performance management – and why we should love it', *Business Horizons* 54: 503–507.
Al Ariss, A. Cascio, W.F. & Paauwe, J. (2014) 'Talent management: Current theories and future research directions', *Journal of World Business* 49, 2: 173–179.
Aldag, R. and Brief, A. (1979) *Task Design and Employee Motivation*, New York: Scott, Foreman and Company.
Alderfer, C. (1972) *Existence, Relatedness and Growth*, New York: The Free Press.
Allen, D.G., Bryant, P.C. & Vardaman, J.M. (2010) 'Retaining talent: replacing misconceptions with evidence-based strategies', *Academy of Management Perspectives* 24, 2: 48–65.
Anderson, N. and Shackleton, V. (1993) *Successful Selection Interviewing*, Oxford: Blackwell.
Anderson, N., and Shackleton, V., (1986) 'Recruitment and selection: a review of developments in the 1980s', *Personnel Review* 15, 4.
Anderson, N., Ones, D.S., Sinangil, K. and Visnesvaran, C. (2005) *Handbook of Industrial, Work and Organizational Psychology*, London: Sage.
Angrave, D., Charlwood, A., Kirkpatrick, I., Lawrence, M. and Stuart, M. (2016) 'HR and Analytics: Why HR is set to fail the big data challenge', *Human Resource Management Journal*, 26, 1: 1–11.
Ansari, S., Fiss, P. and Zajak, E. (2010) 'Made to fit: how practices vary as they diffuse', *Academy of Management Review*, 35, 1: 67–92.
Applebaum, E., Bailey, T., Berg, P. and Kalleberg, A. (2000) *Manufacturing Advantage: Why High Performance Work Systems Pay Off*, Washington, D.C.: Economic Policy Institute.
Appelbaum, S. and Shapiro, B. (1991) 'Pay for performance: implementation of individual and group plans', *Journal of Management Development*, 10, 7.
Argote, L. (2012) *Organizational Learning: Creating, Retaining and Transferring Knowledge*, New York: Springer.
Argote, L. and Ingram, P. (2000) 'Knowledge transfer: a basis for competitive advantage in firms', *Organizational Behavior and Human Decision Processes*, 82, 1: 150–169.

Arnold, J., Robertson, I.T. and Cooper, C. (1995) *Work Psychology: Understanding Human Behaviour in the Workplace*, London: Pitman.

Arthur, J. (1992) 'The links between strategy and industrial relations systems in Americal steel minimills', *Industrial and Labor Relations Review*, 45: 488–506.

Arthur, J. (1994), 'Effects of human resource systems on manufacturing performance and turnover', *Academy of Management Journal*, 37, 3: 670–87.

Arthur, J.B. and Boyle, T. (2007) 'Validating the human resource system structure: a level based strategic HRM approach', *Human Resource Management Review*, 17: 77–92.

Arthur, M. and Rousseau, D. M. (eds.) (1996) *The Boundaryless Career: A New Employment Principle for a New Organisational Era*, New York: Oxford University Press.

Atkinson, A. (1984) *Flexible Manning: The Way Ahead*, London: Institute of Manpower Studies.

Bandura, A. (1986) *Social Foundations of Thought and Action*, Englewood Cliffs, NJ: Prentice Hall.

Barends, E., Janssen, B. and Marenco, M (2016) *Rapid evidence assessment of the research literature on the effect of performance appraisal on workplace performance*, London: CIPD.

Barney, J. (1991) 'Firm resources and sustained competitive advantage', *Journal of Management*, 17: 99–120.

Barney, J. (1995) 'Looking inside for competitive advantage', *Academy of Management Executive*, 9: 49–81.

Barrington, T.J. (1980) *The Irish Administrative System*, Dublin: Institute of Public Administration.

Barry, F. (2004) 'FDI and the host economy: a case study of Ireland', in G. Barba Navaretti and A.J. Venables (eds.), *Multinational firms in the world economy*: 187–215, Princeton and Oxford: Princeton University Press.

Barry, F. and O'Mahony, C. (2005) 'Making Sense of the Data on Ireland's Inward FDI.' *Journal of the Statistical and Social Inquiry Society of Ireland*, 34, 1: 28–65.

Batt, R. and Banerjee, M. (2012) 'The scope and trajectory of strategic HR research: evidence from American and British journals', *International Journal of Human Resource Management*, Vol. 23, 9: 1739–1762.

Bean, R. (1976) 'Industrial reactions', in E. Cohen and G. Studdard (eds.), *The Bargaining Context*, London: Arrow.

Beardwell, I. and Holden, L. (1997) *Human Resource Management: A Contemporary Perspective*, London: Pitman.

Beardwell, I. and Holden, L. (2001) *Human Resource Management: A Contemporary Perspective* (3rd edn.), London: Pearson Publishing.

Beattie, R. and McDougall, M. (1998) 'Inside or outside HRM? Locating lateral learning in two voluntary sector organisations', in Mabey, C., Skinner, D. and Clark, T. (eds.), *Experiencing Human Resource Management*, London: Sage: 218–35.

Beaumont, P. (1993) *Human Resource Management: Key Concepts and Skills*, London: Sage.

Becker, B. and Gerhart, B. (1996) 'The impact of human resource management on organizational performance: progress and prospects', *Academy of Management Journal*, 39, 4: 779–801.

Becker, B., Huselid, M., Pickus, P. and Spratt, M. (1997) 'HR as a source of shareholder value: research and recommendations', *Human Resource Management*, 36, 1: 39–47.

Becker, G. (1964) *Human Capital*, New York: Columbia Press.

Beer, M., Spector, B., Lawrence, P., Quinn-Mills, D. and Walton, R. (1984) *Managing Human Assets: The Groundbreaking Harvard Business School Program*, New York: The Free Press.

Beer, M., Spector, B., Lawrence, P., Mills, D., and Walton, R. (1985) *Human Resource Management: A General Manager's Perspective*, New York: The Free Press.

Begley, T.M., Delany, E. and O'Gorman, C. (2005) 'Ireland at a crossroads: Still a magnet for corporate investment', *Organizational Dynamics*, 34, 3: 202–217.

Behan, J. (2014) *Occupational and Labour Market Projections*, Dublin: SOLAS

Behrens, M. and Traxler, F. (2004) 'Employers' organisations in Europe', *European Industrial Relations Observatory* [online].

Bendix, R. (1956) *Work and Authority in Industry: Ideologies of Management in the Course of Industrialization*, New York: Wiley.

Bergin, A., Kelly, E. and McGuinness, S. (2012) 'Explaining Changes in Earnings and Labour Costs during the Recession', *Economic Renewal Series*, Paper 9, Dublin: Economic and Social Research Institute [online]. Available: www.esri.ie/pubs/EC009.pdf.

Bersin, J. (2017) *Bersin by Deloitte Talent Analytics Maturity Model* [online]. Available: www.bersin.com/Lexicon/details.aspx?id=15392.

Blasi, J. and Kruse, D. (2006) 'US high performance work practices at the century's end', *Industrial Relations*, 45, 4: 547–78.

Boon, C., Paauwe, J., Boselie, P. and Den Hartog, D.N. (2009) 'Institutional pressures and HRM: developing institutional fit', *Personnel Review*, 38, 5: 492–508.

Boselie, P., Dietz, G. and Boon, C. (2005) 'Commonalities and contradictions in HRM and performance research', *Human Resource Management Journal*, 15, 3: 67–94.

Boud, D. and Garrick, J. (eds.) (1999), *Understanding Learning at Work*, London: Routledge.

Boxall, P. (1992) 'Strategic human resource management: beginnings of a new theoretical sophistication', *Human Resource Management Journal*, 2, 3: 60–79.

Boxall, P. (2012) 'High-performance work systems: what, why, how and for whom?', *Asia Pacific Journal of Human Resources*, 50, 2: 169–186.

Boxall, P. and Purcell, J. (2003) *Strategy and Human Resource Management*, Basingstoke: Plagrave Macmillan.

Boxall, P. and Purcell, J. (2008) *Strategy and Human Resource Management*, (2nd edn.), Basingstoke: Plagrave Macmillan.

Boxall, P. and Purcell, J. (2000) 'Strategic human resource management: where have we come from and where are we going?', *International Journal of Management Reviews*, 2, 2: 183–203.

Boxall, P. and Purcell, J. (2011) *Strategy and Human Resource Management*, (3rd edn.), London & New York: Palgrave Macmillan.

Brannick, T. and Kelly, A. (1983) 'The Reliability and Validity of Irish Strike Data and Statistics', *Economic and Social Review*, 14, 4: 249–258.

Brannick, T., Doyle, L. and Kelly, A. (1997) 'Industrial Conflict', in T. Murphy and W.K. Roche (eds.), *Irish Industrial Relations in Practice*, Dublin: Oak Tree Press.

Braverman, H. (1974) *Labour and Monopoly Capital: The Degradation of Work in the Twentieth Century*, London: Monthly Review Press.

Breaugh, J.A. (2013) 'Employee Recruitment', *Annual Review of Psychology*, 64: 389–416.

Brewster, C., Mayrhofer, M. and Morley, M. (2000) 'The concept of strategic European human resource management', in C. Brewster, W. Mayrhofer and M. Morley (eds.), *New Challenge for European Human Resource Management*: 3–33.

Brockett, J. (2010). 'See HR as a Professional Services Firm, Says Ulrich', *People Management*, 25 (March): 11.

Brousseau, K., Driver, M., Eneroth, K. and Larsson, R. (1996) 'Career pandemonium: realigning organisations and individuals', *Academy of Management Executive*, 10, 4: 52–66.

Brown, D. (2014). 'The Future of Reward Management: From Total Reward Strategies to Smart Rewards', *Compensation and Benefits Review*, 46, 3.

Brown, K. (2004) 'Human Resource Management in the Public Sector', *Public Management Review*, 6, 3: 303–309.

Buchanan, D. (1979) *The Development of Job Design Theories and Techniques*, London: Saxon House.

Buchanan, D. and McCalman, J. (1989) *High Performance Work Systems: The Digital Experience*, London: Routledge.

Buckingham, M. and Goodall, A. (2015) 'Reinventing Performance Management', *Harvard Business Review*, April, 93: 40–50.

Buckley, M., Ferris, G., Bernardin, H. and Harvey, M. (1998) 'The disconnect between the science and practice of management', *Business Horizons*, 41: 31–8.

Buller, P. and Napier, N. (1993) 'Strategy and human resource management integration in fast growth versus other mid-sized firms', *British Journal of Management*, 4, 2: 77–90.

Byrne, T. (1988) 'IPM in Ireland 1937–1987', *IPM (Institute of Personnel Management) News*, 3, 2: 2–5.

Cafferkey, K. (2007) 'Innovating HRM: an exploration into how HRM facilitates innovation behaviour', *Irish Academy of Management Conference*, Queens University Belfast, 3–4 September.

Campbell, J. P., and Wiernik, B. M. (2015) 'The modeling and assessment of work performance', *Annual Review of Organizational Psychology and Organizational Behavior*, 2: 47–74.

Campion, M.A. (1988) 'Interdisciplinary approaches to job design: a constructive replication with extensions', *Journal of Applied Psychology*, 73:467–81.

Campion, M., Purcell, E. and Brown, B. (1988) 'Structured interviewing: raising the psychometric properties of the employment interview', *Personnel Psychology*, 41: 25–42.

Cappelli, P. (2008a) 'Talent management for the twenty-first century'. *Harvard Business Review*, 86, 3: 74–81.
Cappelli, P. (2008b) *Talent On Demand: Managing Talent in an Age of Uncertainty*, Cambridge, MA: Harvard Business School Publishing.
Cappelli, P. and Keller, J.R. (2014) 'Talent Management: Conceptual Approaches and Practical Challenges', *The Annual Review of Organizational Psychology and Organizational Behavior*, 1:305–31.
Cappelli, P. and Neumark, D. (2001) 'Do "high-performance" work practices improve establishment-level outcomes?', *ILR Review*, 5,44: 737–775.
Carey, A. (1967) 'The Hawthorne Studies: A Radical Criticism', *American Sociological Review*, 32, 3: 403–416.
Carter, C., Stewart, C. and Kornberger, M. (2008) *A Very Short, Fairly Interesting and Reasonably Cheap Book about Studying Strategy*, London: Sage.
Cascio, W. (2015) 'Strategic HRM: Too Important for an Insular Approach', *Human Resource Management*, 54, 3: 423–426.
Central Statistics Office (2006) *Census of Population 2006*, Dublin: Government Publications Office.
Central Statistics Office (2008) Quarterly National Accounts, Quarter 2, [online]. Available: www.cso.ie/releasespublications/documents/economy/2008/qna_q22008.pdf.
Central Statistics Office (2013) *Business in Ireland 2012*, [online]. Available:www.cso.ie/en/media/csoie/releasespublications/documents/multisectoral/2012/businessinireland2012.pdf
Central Statistics Office (2014) *Measuring Ireland's Progress 2012* [online]. Available: www.cso.ie/en/releasesandpublications/ep/p-mip/measuringirelandsprogress2012.
Central Statistics Office (2016) Public Sector Employment by Sub Sector, [online]. Available: www.cso.ie/px/pxeirestat/Statire/SelectVarVal/saveselections.asp.
Central Statistics Office (2010) *Quarterly National Household Survey*, [online]. Available: www.cso.ie/en/media/csoie/releasespublications/documents/labourmarket/2009/qnhsunionmembership_q22009.pdf.
Chasserio, S. and Legault, M.J. (2009) 'Strategic human resources management is irrelevant when it comes to highly skilled professionals in the Canadian new economy', *The International Journal of Human Resource Management*, 20, 5: 1113–1131.
Cherns, A. and Davis, L. (1975) *The Quality of Working Life*, London: Macmillan.
CIPD (2007) *The Changing HR Function*, London: Chartered Institute of Personnel and Development.
CIPD (2009) *Recruitment, Retention and Turnover Survey*, London: Chartered Institute of Personnel and Development.
CIPD (2011) *HR Outlook (Autumn)*, London: Chartered Institute of Personnel and Development.
CIPD (2013) *Talent Analytics and Big Data – The Challenge for HR*, London: Chartered Institute of Personnel and Development.
CIPD (2016) *The Psychological Contract*, CIPD Factsheet [online]. Available: www.cipd.co.uk/hr-resources/factsheets/psychological-contract.aspx.

CIPD (2017) *HR Practices in Ireland: January 2017*, Dublin: Chartered Institute of Personnel and Development in Ireland.

Collings, D.G. and Mellahi, K. (2009) 'Strategic Talent Management: A review and research agenda', *Human Resource Management Review*, 19, 4: 304–313.

Collings, D.G., Gunnigle, P. and Morley, M.J. (2008) 'Between Boston and Berlin, American MNCs and the Shifting Contours of Industrial Relations in Ireland', *International Journal of Human Resource Management*, 19, 2: 242–263.

Colvin, A.J.S. (2003) 'Institutional Pressures, Human Resource Strategies, and the Rise of Non-union Dispute Resolution Procedures', *Industrial and Labor Relations Review*, 56, 3: 375–392.

Combs, J., Liu, Y., Hall, A. and Ketchen, D. (2006) 'How much do high-performance work practices matter? A meta-analysis of their effects on organizational performance', *Personnel Psychology*, 59, 3: 501–528.

Connaughton, M. and Staunton, M. (2017) *HR Practices in Ireland*, Dublin: Chartered Institute of Personnel & Development.

Conner, K. and Prahalad, C. (1996) 'A resource based theory of the firm: knowledge versus opportunism', *Organization Science*, 7: 477–501.

Constitution of Ireland (Bunreacht na hÉireann) (1937) [online]. Available: www.taoiseach.gov.ie/attached_files/Pdf%20files/Constitution%20of%20IrelandNov2004.pdf.

Conway, E. (2004) 'Relating career stage to attitudes towards HR practices and commitment: evidence of interaction effects?', *European Journal of Work & Organizational Psychology*, 13, 4: 417–46.

Conway, E. and McMackin, J. (1997) 'Developing a culture for innovation: what is the role of the HR system?', Dublin City University Business School Research Paper no. 32, Dublin: Dublin City University.

Cook, M. (2016) *Personnel Selection: Adding Value Through People-A Changing Picture*, John Wiley & Sons.

Cooper, C. and Burke, R.J. (2011) *Human Resource Management in Small Business: Achieving Peak Performance*, Cheltenham: Edward Elgar.

Cox, B. and Hughes, J. (1989) 'Industrial relations in the public sector' in *Industrial Relations in Ireland: Contemporary Issues and Developments*, Dublin: University College Dublin.

Coyle-Shapiro, J., Kessler, I. and Purcell, J. (2004) 'Exploring organizationally directed citizenship behaviour: reciprocity or 'it's my job'', *Journal of Management Studies*, 41, 1: 85–105.

Crail, M. (2006) 'HR roles and responsibilities 2006: Benchmarking the HR Function', *IRS Employment Review*, 836 (January).

Cranet E./University of Limerick (1992), *Study of HR Practices in Ireland*, Limerick's Employment Relations Unit, University of Limerick.

Cranet E./University of Limerick (1995), *Study of HR Practices in Ireland*, Limerick's Employment Relations Unit, University of Limerick.

Cranet E./University of Limerick (1999/2010), *Study of HR Practices in Ireland*, Limerick's Employment Relations Unit, University of Limerick.

Crawford, E., LePine, J. and Bruce Louis, R. (2010) 'Linking job demands and resources to employee engagement and burnout: A theoretical extension and meta-analytic test', *Journal of Applied Psychology*, 95, 5: 834–848.
Creaton, S. (2007) *Ryanair: The Full Story of the Controversial Low-Cost Airline*, London: Aurum Press.
Crossan, M.M., Lane, H.W. and White, R.E. (1999) 'An organizational learning framework: from intuition to institution', *Academy of Management Review*, 24, 3: 522–537.
Crossan, M.M., Maurer, C.C. and White, R.E. (2011) 'Reflections on the 2009 AMR Decade Award: do we have a theory of organizational learning?', *Academy of Management Review*, 36, 3: 446–460.
Crouch, C. (1982) *The Politics of Industrial Relations*, London: Fontana.
Crush, P. (2016) 'The end of the annual appraisal: what's next for performance management?', *Personnel Today*, [online]. Available: www.personneltoday.com/hr/end-annual-appraisal-whats-next-performance-management.
Cullinane, N. and Dundon. T. (2006) 'The psychological contract: a critical review', *International Journal of Human Resource Management*, 8, 2: 113–129.
Cunningham, L. (2015) 'In big move, Accenture will get rid of annual performance reviews and rankings', *The Washington Post*, [online]. Available: www.washingtonpost.com/news/on-leadership/wp/2015/07/21/in-big-move-accenture-will-get-rid-of-annual-performance-reviews-and-rankings.
Cunningham, J. and Harney, N. (2010), *Strategy and Strategists*, Oxford: Oxford University Press.
Curran, D. (2014) 'Workplace Mediation in Ireland: Bridging the Research-Practice Gap', *Journal of Mediation and Applied Conflict Analysis*, 2, 1: 15–28.

D'Art, D. and Turner, T. (2002) 'Corporatism in Ireland: a view from below', in D. D'Art and T. Turner (eds.), *Irish Employment Relations in the New Economy*, Dublin: Blackhall Press.
D'Art, D. and Turner, T. (2005) 'Union Recognition and Partnership at Work: A New Legitimacy for Irish Trade Unions', *Industrial Relations Journal*, 36, 2: 121–139.
D'Art, D. and Turner, T. (2007) 'Ireland in Breach of ILO Conventions on Freedom of Association', *Industrial Relations News*, 11, March: 19–21.
D'Art, D. and Turner, T. (2011) 'Irish Trade Unions under Social Partnership: a Faustian bargain?', *Industrial Relations Journal*, 42, 2: 157–173.
Dale, M. (1995) *Successful Recruitment and Selection: A Practical Guide for Managers*, London: Kogan Page.
Daly, B. and Doherty, M. (2010) *Principles of Irish Employment Law*, Dublin: Clarus Press.
Daniel, W. and Millward, N. (1983) *Workplace Industrial Relations in Britain: The DE/PSI/ESRC Study*, London: Heinemann.
Datta, D., Guthrie, J. and Wright, P. M. (2005) 'Human resources management and labour productivity: does industry matter?', *Academy of Management Journal*, 48, 1: 135–46.

Davies, G. and Wilson, T. (2002) 'Implications for reflective HRD practitioners of the influence of life experience on managerial career decisions', in J. McGoldrick, J. Stewart and S. Watson (eds.), *Understanding Human Resource Development: A Research Based Approach*, London: Routledge.

Davis, L. (1966) 'The design of jobs', *Industrial Relations*, 6, 1.

Deery, S. and Walsh, J. (1999) 'The decline of collectivism? A comparative study of white-collar employees in Britain and Australia', *British Journal of Industrial Relations*, 37, 2: 245–269.

Delany, J. and Godard, J. (2001) 'An industrial relations perspective on the high-performance paradigm', *Human Resource Management Review*, 11: 395–429.

Delbridge, R. and Whitfield, K. (2007) 'More than mere fragments? The use of the workplace employment relations survey data in HRM research', *The International Journal of Human Resource Management*, 18(12): 2166–2181.

Deloitte (2017) '*Global Human Capital Trends: Rewriting the rules for the digital age'*, Deloitte University Press: dupress.deloitte.com.

DeNisi, A.S. and Murphy, K.R. (2017) 'Performance appraisal and performance management: 100 years of progress?', *Journal of Applied Psychology*, forthcoming.

Department of Public Expenditure and Reform (2012) 'Government announces plans for a Civil Service wide Human Resources Shared Service Centre (HRSSC)' [online]. Available: www.per.gov.ie/en/government-announces-plans-for-a-civil-service-wide-human-resources-shared-service-centre-hrssc.

Dineen, B.R. and Soltis, S.M. (2011) 'Recruitment: a review of research and emerging directions', in *Handbook of Industrial and Organizational Psychology*, S. Zedeck (ed.), 2: 43–66. Washington, DC: American Psychological Association.

DiRenzo, M.S. and Greenhaus, J.H. (2011) 'Job search and voluntary turnover in a boundaryless world: a control theory perspective', *Academy of Management Review*, 36: 567–89.

Dobbins, T. (2005) 'US Chamber leaves indelible stamp on Employee Consultation Bill', *Industrial Relations News*, 30.

Dobbins, T. (2007) 'Unresolved Union Recognition Question back on Social Partnership Agenda' *Industrial Relations News*, 16: 15–18.

Dobbins, T. (2008) *Tackling the recession: Ireland*, European Restructuring Monitor. Dublin: European Foundation for the Improvement of Living and Working Conditions.

Dobbins, T. (2009) *Annual Review on Industrial Relations Developments 2009: Ireland*, European Industrial Relations Observatory. Dublin: European Foundation for the Improvement of Living and Working Conditions.

Doeringer, P. and Piore, M. (1971) *Internal Labour Markets and Manpower Analysis*, New York: Lexington Books.

Doherty, M. (2012) 'Battered and Fried? Regulation of Working Conditions and Wage-Setting after the John Grace Decision', *Dublin University Law Journal*, 35: 97–120.

Doherty, M. (2013) 'When You Ain't Got Nothin', You Got Nothin'to Lose . . . Union Recognition Laws, Voluntarism and the Anglo Model', *Industrial Law Journal*, 42, 4: 369–397.

Doherty, M. (2015) 'Engagements, Unions and the Law: the 'Re-boot of' Collective Bargaining in Ireland', [online]. Available: http://humanrights.ie/civil-liberties/engagements-unions-and-the-law-the-re-boot-of-collective-bargaining-in-ireland.

Donaghey, J. and Teague, P. (2007) 'The mixed fortunes of Irish Union: living with the paradoxes of social partnership', *International Labor Brief*, 28, 1: 19–41.

Donovan, Lord (Chairman) (1968) *Royal Commission on Trade Unions and Employers' Associations*, 1965–1968, Cmnd 3623, London: HMSO.

Easterby-Smith, M. (1986) *Evaluation of Management, Training and Development*, Aldershot: Gower.

Easterby-Smith, M., Crossan, M. and Nicolini, D. (2000) 'Organizational learning: debates past, present and future', *Journal of Management Studies*, 37, 6: 783–796.

Eby, L. T., Casper, W. J., Lockwood, A., Bordeaux, C. and Brinley, A. (2005) 'Work and family research in IO/OB: Content analysis and review of the literature (1980–2002)', *Journal of Vocational Behavior*, 66, 1: 124–197.

Edwards, P. (1986) *Conflict at work: A materialist analysis of workplace relations*, Oxford: Blackwell.

Edwards, P. K. (1992) 'Industrial Conflict: Themes and Issues in Recent Research', *British Journal of Industrial Relations*, 30, 3: 361–404.

Ehrenberg, R. and Smith, R. (2016) *Modern Labour Economics: Theory and Public Policy*, New York: Routledge.

Eichhorst, W. and Marx, P. (2011) 'Reforming German labour market institutions: A dual path to flexibility', *Journal of European Social Policy*, 21, 1: 73–87.

Elger, T. (2015) 'Dual Labor Market Theories', *The Wiley Blackwell Encyclopedia of Race, Ethnicity and Nationalism*: 1–3.

Elkington, J. (1997) *Cannibals with Forks: The Triple Bottom Line of 21st Century Business*, Oxford: Capstone.

Elliott, R. (1990) *Labour Economics – A Comparative Text*, Berkshire, UK: McGraw Hill.

Eurofound (2010) *Absence in Ireland*, Dublin: European Working Conditions Observatory.

Eurofound (2016) Sixth European Working Conditions Survey – Overview report, Publications Office of the European Union, Luxembourg.

Eurofound [online]: Available: www.eurofound.europa.eu/observatories/eurwork/articles/supreme-court-ruling-will-affect-right-to-bargain-law.

Eurofound [online]: Available: www.eurofound.europa.eu/observatories/eurwork/comparative-information/employers-organisations-in-europe.

Eurofound [online]: Available: www.eurofound.europa.eu/efemiredictionary/trade-union-structureBody.

European Parliament Resolution (2016/2017(INI) 'On creating labour market conditions favourable for work-life balance', Brussels: 13 September.

European Parliament's Committee on Women's Rights and Gender Equality (FEMM)

European Restructuring Monitor (2010) European Restructuring Monitor [online]. Available: www.eurofound.europa.eu/emcc/erm/index.htm.

Eurostat (2010), *Europe in Figures: Eurostat Yearbook 2010*, Brussels, European Commission.

Eurostat (2016), *Educational Attainment Statistics*, Eurostat Press Office: June 2016.

Eurostat News Release 38/2017, Eurostat Press Office: March 6, 2017.
Evenden, R. and Anderson, G. (1992) *Management Skills: Making the Most of People*, Wokingham, UK: Addison-Wesley.

Farndale, E., Pai, A., Sparrow, P. and Scullion, H. (2014) 'Balancing individual and organizational goals in global talent management: A mutual-benefits perspective', *Journal of World Business*, 49, 2: 204–214.
Farnham, D. (1984) *Personnel in Context*, London: Institute of Personnel Management.
Farrelly, R. (2010) 'Kingspan – planned strike action suspended', *Industrial Relations News*, 7, May.
Ferris, G., Hochwarter, W., Buckley, M., Harrell-Cook, G. and Frink, D. (1999) 'Human resources management: some new directions', *Journal of Management*, 25, 3: 385–427.
Festinger, L. (1954) 'A theory of social comparison processes', *Human Relations*, 7, 2: 117–140.
Fine, S.A. and Cronshaw, S.F. (1999) 'Functional Job Analysis', *A Foundation for Human Resource Management*, Mahwah, New Jersey: Lawrence Erlbaum Associates.
Fisher, R., Ury, W. and Patton, B. (2004) *Getting to Yes: Negotiating an Agreement Without Giving In*, London and New York: Random House.
Fitzgerald, T. (1971) 'Why motivation theory doesn't work', *Harvard Business Review*, July–August: 12–19.
Flamholtz, E. and Lacey, J. (1981) *Personnel Management: Human Capital Theory and Human Resource Accounting*, Los Angeles: Institute of Industrial Relations, UCLA.
Flanagan, J. (1954) *The Critical Incident Technique*, Psychological Bulletin, 41: 236–358.
Fleetwood, S. and Hesketh, A. (2008) 'Theorising under-theorisation in research on the HRM-performance link', *Personnel Review*, 37, 2: 126–144.
Fleming, N. and Mills, C. (1992) 'Not Another Inventory, Rather a Catalyst for Reflection', *To Improve the Academy*, 11: 137.
Fombrun, C. (1986) 'Structural dynamics within and between organizations', *Administrative Science Quarterly*, 31: 403–21.
Fombrun, C., Tichy, N. and Devanna, M. (1984) *Strategic Human Resource Management*, New York: Wiley.
Forde, M. and Byrne, A.P. (2009) *Employment Law*, Dublin: Round Hall Press.
Frawley, M. (2002) 'Technology teachers latest group to switch to LRC, Labour Court', *Industrial Relations News*, 24: 14–15.
Fulmer, R., Gibbs, P. and Goldsmith, M. (2000) 'Developing leaders: how winning companies keep on winning', *Sloan Management Review*, 42: 49–59.
Furnham, A. (1997) *The Psychology of Behaviour at Work: The Individual in the Organization*, London: Psychology Press.

Gallardo-Gallardo, E., Dries, N. and González-Cruz, T.F. (2013) 'What is the meaning of 'talent' in the world of work?', *Human Resource Management Review*, 23, 4: 290–300.
Galvin, P. (1988) *Managers for Ireland: The Case for Development of Irish Managers*, Dublin: Advisory Committee on Management Training, Department of Labour.

Garavan, G., Costine, P. and Heraty, N. (1995) *Training and Development in Ireland: Context, Policy and Practice*, Dublin: Oak Tree Press.

Garavan, T., Collins, E. and Brady, S. (2003) *Training and Development in Ireland*, Dublin: Chartered Institute of Personnel and Development.

Geary, J. F. and Roche, W. K. (2001) 'Multinationals and human resource practices in Ireland: A rejection of the new conformance thesis', *International Journal of Human Resource Management*, 12, 1: 109–127.

Geller, L. (1982) 'The Failure of Self-Actualization Theory: A Critique of Carl Rogers and Abraham Maslow', *Journal of Humanistic Psychology*, 22, 2.

Gilliland, S. (1993) 'The perceived fairness of the selection system: an organisational perspective', *Academy of Management Review*, 18: 694–734.

Godard, J. and Delaney, J. (2000) 'Reflections on the 'high performance' paradigm's implications for industrial relations as a field', *Industrial and Labour Relations Review*, 53: 482–502.

Gooderham, P., Morley, M., Brewster, C. and Mayrhofer, W. (2004) 'Human resource management: a universal concept?' in C. Brewster, M. Mayrhofer and M. Morley (eds.), *Human Resource Management in Europe: Evidence of Convergence?*, Oxford: Butterworth-Heinemann.

Grant, A.M. and Parker, S.K. (2009) 'Redesigning work design theories: The rise of relational and proactive perspectives', *Academy of Management Annals*, 3, 1: 317–375.

Gratton, L. (2003) 'The Humpty Dumpty effect: a view of a fragmented HR function', *People Management* (January 5), 18.

Gratton, L. and Scott, A. (2016) *The 100-Year Life: Living and Working in an Age of Longevity*, London: Bloomsbury.

Green, F. (1990) 'Trade union availability and trade union membership in Britain', *The Manchester School*, 58, 4: 378–394.

Green, F. (2006) *Demanding Work. The Paradox of Job Quality in the Affluent Economy*, Woodstock: Princeton University Press.

Green, F. and Whitfield, K. (2009) 'Employees' experience of work', in W. Brown, A. Bryson, J. Forth and K. Whitfield (eds.) *The Evolution of the Modern Workplace*, Cambridge: Cambridge University Press.

Greenberg, J. (1990) 'Organizational justice: Yesterday, today, and tomorrow', *Journal of Management*, 16, 2: 399–432.

Greenhaus, H. and Callanan, G. (1994) *Career Management* (2nd edn.), Forth Worth, TX: Dryden Press.

Greenhaus, J.G. and Kossek. E.E. (2014) 'The Contemporary Career: A Work–Home Perspective', *Annual Review of Organisational Psychology and Organisational Behaviour*.

Griffin, R. and McMahan, G. (1994) 'Motivation through job design', in J. Greenberg (ed.), *Organizational Behaviour: The State of the Science*, Hillsdale: Lawrence Erlbaum.

Grote, D. (1996) *The Complete Guide to Performance Appraisal*, New York: American Management Association.

Guest, D. (1987) 'Human resource management and industrial relations', *Journal of Management Studies*, 24, 5: 503–21.

Guest, D. (1998) 'Combine harvest', *People Management*, 29 October.
Guest, D. (2011) 'Human resource management and performance: still searching for some answers', *Human Resource Management Journal*, 21: 3–13.
Guest, D.E., Michie, J., Conway, N. and Sheehan, M. (2003) Human Resource Management and Corporate Performance in the UK. British Journal of Industrial Relations, 41: 291–314.
Guion, R. (1998) *Assessment, Measurement, and Prediction for Personnel Decisions*, Mahwah, New Jersey: Lawrence Erlbaum Associates.
Guion, R.M. (2011) *Assessment, Measurement, and Prediction for Personnel Decisions*, London: Taylor & Francis.
Gunnigle, P. (1995) 'Collectivism and the management of industrial relations in greenfield sites', *Human Resource Management Journal*, 5, 3: 24–40.
Gunnigle, P. (1998a) 'Human resource management and the personnel function', in W.K. Roche, K. Monks and J. Walsh (eds.) *Human Resource Strategies: Policy and Practice in Ireland*, Dublin: Oak Tree Press.
Gunnigle, P. (1998b) 'More rhetoric than reality: enterprise level industrial relations partnerships in Ireland', *Economic and Social Review*, 28, 2: 179–200.
Gunnigle, P. and Brady, T. (1984) 'The management of industrial relations in the small firm', *Employee Relations*, 6, 5: 21–24.
Gunnigle, P. and McGuire, D. (2001) 'Why Ireland? A qualitative review of the factors influencing the location of US multinationals in Ireland with particular reference to the impact of labour issues', *Economic and Social Review*, 32, 1: 43–67.
Gunnigle, P. and Roche, W.K. (1995) *New Challenges to Irish Industrial Relations*, Dublin: Oak Tree Press/Labour Relations Commission.
Gunnigle, P., Lavelle, J. and McDonnell, A. (2009) 'Subtle but deadly? Union avoidance through "double breasting" among multinational companies', *Advances in Industrial and Labor Relations*, 16: 51–74.
Gunnigle, P., Lavelle, J. and Monaghan, S. (2013) 'Weathering the storm? Multinational companies and human resource management through the global financial crisis', *International Journal of Manpower*, 34, 3: 214–231.
Gunnigle, P., MacCurtain, S. and Morley, M. (2001) 'Dismantling pluralism: industrial relations in Irish greenfield sites', *Personnel Review*, 30, 3: 263–79.
Gunnigle, P., McMahon, G. and Fitzgerald, G. (1999) *Industrial Relations in Ireland: Theory and Practice* (rev. edn.), Dublin: Gill and Macmillan.
Gunnigle, P., O'Sullivan, M. and Kinsella, M. (2002) 'Organised labour in the new economy: trade unions and public policy in the Republic of Ireland', in D. D'Art and T. Turner (eds.), *Irish Employment Relations in the New Economy*, Dublin: Blackhall Press.
Gunnigle, P., Turner, T. and D'Art, D. (1998) 'Counterpoising collectivism: performance-related pay and industrial relations in greenfield sites', *British Journal of Industrial Relations*, 36, 4: 565–79.
Guthrie, J. P., Spell, C. S. and Nyamori, R. O. (2002) 'Correlates and consequences of high involvement work practices: the role of competitive strategy', *International Journal of Human Resource Management*, 13, 1: 183–197.

Guthrie, J., Flood, P., Liu, W. and MacCurtain, S. (2009) 'High performance work systems in Ireland: human resource and organisational outcomes', *International Journal of Human Resource Management*, 20, 1: 112–125.

Hackman, J. (1987) 'The design of work teams', in J. Lorsch (ed.), *Handbook of Organizational Behavior*, New Jersey: Prentice Hall.

Hackman, J. and Oldham, G. (1980) *Work Redesign*, New York: Addison Wesley.

Hall, D. and Moss, J. (1998) 'The new protean career contract', *Organizational Dynamics*, Winter: 22–38.

Hall, P. A. and Soskice, D. (eds.) (2001) *Varieties of Capitalism: The Institutional Foundations of Comparative Advantage*, Oxford: OUP.

Hamann, K., Johnston, A. and Kelly, J. (2013) 'Unions against Governments: Explaining General Strikes in Western Europe, 1980–2006', *Comparative Political Studies*, 46, 9: 1030–1057.

Hamblin, A. (1974) *Evaluation and Control of Training*, Maidenhead: McGraw-Hill.

Hardiman, N. and MacCarthaigh, M. (2008) 'The segmented state: adaptation and maladaptation in Ireland', University College Dublin: Geary Institute, [online]. Available: http://hdl.handle.net/10197/1820.

Harney, B. and Dundon, T. (2006) 'Capturing complexity: developing an integrated approach to analysing HRM in SMEs', *Human Resource Management Journal*, 16, 1: 48–73.

Harney, B. and Jordan, C. (2008) 'Unlocking the black box: line managers and HRM-performance in a call centre context', *International Journal of Productivity and performance Management*, 57, 4: 275–296.

Harney, B. and Monks, K. (2014) *Strategic HRM: Research and Practice in Ireland*, Dublin: Orpen Press.

Harney, B., Heffernan, M. and Monks, K. (2014) 'The Emergence and Status of Strategic HRM in Ireland', in B. Harney & K. Monks (eds.), *Strategic HRM: Research and Practice in Ireland*, Dublin: Orpen Press.

Harney, B. and Nolan, C. (2014) 'HRM in Small and Medium Sized Enterprises' in B. Harney and K. Monks (eds.), *Strategic HRM: Research and Practice in Ireland*, Dublin: Orpen Press.

Harney, N. (2009) 'Theorising HRM and HRM theorising: from normative puzzle solving to theoretical validity', *sixth International Conference of the Dutch HRM network, Capitalising on diversity in HRM research*, The Netherlands: VU University, 13–14 November.

Harrell-Cook, G. (2002) 'Human resources management and competitive advantage: A strategic perspective', in G. Ferris, M. Buckley and D. Fedor (eds.) *Human Resource Management: Perpectives, Context, Functions and Outcomes*, Upper Saddle River, New Jersey: Prentice Hall.

Harrington, D.G., Lawton, T.C. and Rajwani, T. (2005) 'Embracing and Exploiting Industry Turbulence: The Strategic Transformation of Aer Lingus', *European Management Journal* 23, 4: 450–457.

Hay Group (2009) *Hay Group Global Survey April 2009 'Reward in a downturn'* [online]. Available: www.haygroup.com/ww/downloads/details.aspx?ID=15535

Hays Ireland (2015) 'Salary and Recruiting Trends 2015: Employment Insights for a Growing Economy'[online]. Available: www.hays.ie/cs/groups/hays_common/@ie/@content/documents/webassets/hays_1506507.pdf

Heffernan, M. and Dundon, T. (2004) 'High performance work systems and employee outcomes – an organisational justice perspective', HRM Study Group Working Paper Series, International Industrial Relations Association, September.

Heffernan, M., Harney, B., Cafferkey, K. and Dundon, T. (2008) 'People Management and innovation in Ireland', Centre for Innovation and Structural Change (CISC) Working Series, Research Paper No. 27, National University of Ireland, Galway [online]. Available: http://hdl.handle.net/10379/2071.

Heffernan, M., Harney, B., Cafferkey, K. and Dundon, T. (2009) 'Exploring the relationship between HRM, creativity and organisational performance: evidence from Ireland', American Academy of Mangement Conference, Chicago.

Heraty, N. and Garavan, T. (2000/2001) *Training and Development in Ireland*, Dublin: Chartered Institute of Personnel and Development.

Heraty, N. and Morley, M. (1998a) 'In search of good fit: policy and practice in recruitment and selection in Ireland', *Journal of Management Development*, 17, 9: 662–86.

Heraty, N., Morley, M. J., and Cleveland, J. N. (2008) 'Complexities and challenges in the work-family interface', *Journal of Managerial Psychology*, 23, 3: 209–214.

Higgins, C. (2005) 'Chambers HR service offers insurance against losing employment cases', *Industrial Relations News*, 4, January 20.

Higgins C (2009) 'Quarter of larger employers has cut pay – survey', *Industrial Relations News* 43, November 25.

Higgins, C. (2008) 'Civil service unions vote to seek access to Labour Court', *Industrial Relations News*, 19, May 20.

Higgins, C. (2010) 'Review of private sector pay settlements: payment of TA not confined to life sciences', *Industrial Relations News*, 2, January 13.

Higgins, C. (2011a) 'JLC reforms set for end September as five legal cases loom', *Industrial Relations News*, 17, May 4: 10–11.

Higgins, C. (2011b) 'US Chamber Warns on Collective Bargaining, Agency Working' *Industrial Relations News*, 17, May 4: 10–11.

Higgins, C. (2011c) 'Moderate 2% pay hikes the rule in limited re-emergence of local bargaining', *Industrial Relations News*, 43, November 23.

Hill, J. and Trist, E. (1955) 'Changes in accidents and other absences with length of service', *Human Relations*, May 8.

Hillery, B. (1994) 'The institutions of industrial relations', in T. Murphy and W. Roche (eds.), *Irish Industrial Relations in Practice*, Dublin: Oak Tree Press.

Honey, P. and Mumford, A. (1986) 'Learning styles questionnaire, organisational design and development', *HRD Quarterly*, PA.

Hourihan, F. (1997) 'The European Union and industrial relations', in T. Murphy and W. K. Roche (eds.), *Irish Industrial Relations in Practice*, (2nd edn.), Dublin: Oak Tree Press.

Hucznyski, A. and Buchanan, D. (1991) *Organizational Behaviour: An Introductory Text*, Hemel Hempstead: Prentice Hall.

Hunter, J. and Hunter, R. (1984) 'Validity and utility of alternative predictors of job performance', *Psychological Bulletin*, 96: 72–98.

Huselid, M. (1995) 'The impact of human resource management practices on turnover, productivity, and corporate financial performance', *Academy of Management Journal*, 38, 3: 635–72.

Huseman, R., Hatfield, J. and Miles, E. (1987) 'A new perspective on equity theory: the equity sensitivity construct', *Academy of Management Review*, 12: 222–34.

Hutchinson, S. and Purcell, J. (2003) *Bringing Policies to Life: The Vital Role of Front Line Managers in People Management*, London: Chartered Institute of Personnel and Development.

Hyman, R. (1972) *Strikes*, London: Fontana.

Ichniowski, C. (1992) 'Human resource practices and productive labour-management relations', in D. Lewin, O. Mitchell and P. Sherer (eds.), *Research Frontiers in Industrial Relations and Human Resources*, Madison, WI: Industrial Relations Research Association: 239–71.

IDA Ireland (2016) 'FDI Employment Hits New Benchmark of 187,056 People', [online]. Available: www.idaireland.com/newsroom/fdi-employment/.

IMD World Competitiveness Ranking 2016 [online]. Available: www.imd.org/wcc/world-competitiveness-center-rankings/world-competitiveness-yearbook-ranking.

International Labour Organisation (1975) *Collective Bargaining in Industrialised Market Economies*, Geneva: International Labour Organisation.

International Labour Organisation (2016) *ILO Declaration on Fundamental Principles and Rights at Work 1998*, [online]. Available: www.ilo.org/declaration/lang--en/index.htm

Irish Business and Employers Confederation (2009) 'New IBEC survey on pay trends in the economy', [online]. Available: www.ibec.ie/IBEC/Press/PressPublicationsdoclib3.nsf/vPages/Newsroom~new-ibec-survey-on-pay-trends-in-the-economy-15-09-2009?OpenDocument?

Irish Congress of Trade Unions (2016) [online]. Available: www.ictu.ie/about/affiliates.html.

Irish Management Institute (2013) *Survey of MNCs in Ireland 2013*, Dublin: Irish Management Institute and Danske Bank [online]. Available: www.imi.ie/wp-content/uploads/2013/11/2013-IMI-Danskebank-MNC-Survey.pdf.

Jackson, G. (2000) 'Fruit of the Loom to close factory in Derry', Irish Times, November 21 [online]. Available: www.irishtimes.com/business/fruit-of-the-loom-to-close-factory-in-derry-1.1116904.

Jackson, S., Schuler, R. and Jiang, K. (2014) 'An Aspirational Framework for Strategic Human Resource Management', *The Academy of Management Annals*, 8, 1: 1–56.

Jacobsen, D. and Andreosso, B. (1990) 'Ireland as a location for multinational investment', in A. Foley and M. Mulreanny (eds.), *The Single European Market and the Irish Economy*, Dublin: Institute of Public Administration.

Janson, R. (1979), 'Work redesign: a results oriented strategy that works', *S. A. M. Advanced Management Journal*, 44, 1: 21–4.

Jarzabkowski, P. and Spee, A. (2009) 'Strategy-as-practice: A review and future directions for the field', *International Journal of Management Reviews*, 11, 1: 69–95.

Jiang, K., Takeuchi, R. and Lepak, D. (2013) 'Where do we go from here? New perspectives on the black box in strategic human resource management research', *Journal of Management Studies*, 50, 8: 1448–1480.

Kahn, W. A. (1990) 'Psychological conditions of personal engagement and disengagement at work', *Academy of Management Journal*, 33: 692–724.

Kang, S.C. and Snell, S.A. (2009) 'Intellectual capital architectures and ambidextrous learning: a framework for human resource management', *Journal of Management Studies*, 46, 1: 65–92.

Kaplan, R. and Norton, D. (1996) *The Balanced Scorecard: Translating Strategy into Action*, Boston, MA: Harvard Business School Press.

Kaufman, B. (2007) 'The impossibility of a perfectly competitive labour market', *Cambridge Journal of Economics*, 31, 5: 775–787.

Kaufman, B. (2010a) 'SHRM theory in the post-Huselid era: why it is fundamentally misspecified', *Industrial Relations*, 49, 2: 286–313.

Kaufman, B. (2010b) 'A theory for the firm's demand for HRM practices', *Human Resource Management Journal*, 21, 5: 615–36.

Kaufman, B. (2012) 'Strategic Human Resource Management Research in the United States: A Failing Grade After 30 Years?', *Academy of Management Perspectives*, 26, 2: 12–36.

Keegan, A. and Boselie, P. (2006) 'The lack of impact of disensus inspired analysis on developments in the field of human resource management', *Journal of Management Studies*, 43, 7: 1491–1511.

Kelly, A. (1975) 'Changes in the occupational structure and industrial relations in Ireland', *Management*, 22, 6/7: 33–37.

Kelly, A. and Brannick, T. (1988) 'Strike trends in the Irish private sector', *Irish Business and Administrative Research*, 9: 87–98.

Kelly, A. and Brannick, T. (1990) 'The Impact of State Policy and Collective Bargaining Structure on the Character of Industrial Conflict', *International Journal of Conflict Management*, 1, 2: 175–190.

Kelly, J. (1980) 'The costs of job redesign: a preliminary analysis', *Industrial Relations Journal*, 11, 3.

Kerr, A. and Whyte, G. (1985) *Irish Trade Union Law*, Abington: Professional Books.

Kerr, C. (1954) 'Industrial Conflict and Its Mediation', *American Journal of Sociology* 60, 3: 230–245.

Kerr, S. (1995) 'On the folly of rewarding A, while hoping for B', *Academy of Management Executive*, 9, 1: 7–16.

Kersley, B., Alpin, C., Forth, J., Bryson, A.H.B., Dix, G. and Oxenbridge, S. (2006) 'Inside the workplace first: findings from the 2004 workplace employment relations survey', DTI/ESRC/ACAS/PSI.

Keynes, J. (1936) *The General Theory of Employment, Interest and Money*, London: Macmillan.

Kikoski, J. (1999) 'Effective communications in the performance appraisal interview: face-to-face communication for public managers in the culturally diverse workplace', *Public Personnel Management*, 28: 301–23.

Kim, W.C. and Mauborgne, R. (2009) 'Blue ocean strategy, it's now more relevant than ever', *Leadership Exellence*, 1, 62.

Kirkpatick, D. (1959) 'Techniques for evaluating programmes', *Journal of the American Society for Training Directors*, 13.

Kluger, A.N. and DeNici, A. (1996) 'The effects of feedback interventions on performance: a historical review, a meta-analysis, and a preliminary feedback intervention theory', *Psychological Bulletin*, 119, 2: 254.

Kochan, T. and Osterman, P. (1994) *The Mutual Gains Enterprise*, Cambridge, MA: Harvard Business School Press.

Kochan, T., Katz, H. and McKersie, R. (1986) *The Transformation of American Industrial Relations*, New York: Basic Books.

Kolb, D. (1984) *Experiential Learning – Experience as a Source of Learning and Development*, New Jersey: Prentice Hall.

Kopelman, R. (1985) 'Job redesign and productivity: a review of the evidence', *National Productivity Review*, Summer: 237–55.

Labour Relations Commission (2009) *Labour Relations Commission Annual Report 2008*, Dublin: Labour Relations Commission.

Laeven, L. and Valencia, F. (2012) *Systemic Banking Crises Database: An Update* Geneva: International Monetary Fund (IMF) Working Paper WP/12/163.

Lam, A. (2003) 'Organisational learning in multinationals: R&D networks of Japanese and US MNCs in the UK', *Journal of Management Studies*, 40, 3: 673–703.

Lamare, R., Gunnigle, P., Marginson, P. and Murray, G. (2013) 'Union Status and Double-Breasting at Multinational Companies in Three Liberal Market Economies', *Industrial and Labor Relations Review*, 66, 3: 696–722.

Latham, G., Almost, J., Mann, S. and Moore, C. (2005) 'New developments in performance management', *Organizational Dynamics*, 34, 1: 77–87.

Lavelle, J. (2008) 'Charting the contours of union recognition in foreign-owned MNCs in Ireland', *Irish Journal of Management*, 29, 1: 45–64.

Lavelle, J., Gunnigle, P. and McDonnell, A. (2010) 'Patterning employee voice in multinational companies', *Human Relations* 63, 3: 395–418.

Lavelle, J., McDonnell, A. and Gunnigle, P. (2009) *Human Resource Practices in Multinational Companies in Ireland: A Contemporary Analysis*, Dublin: The Stationery Office.

Lavelle, J., Turner, T., Gunnigle, P. and McDonnell, A. (2012) 'The Determinants of Financial Participation Schemes within Multinational Companies in Ireland', *International Journal of Human Resource Management*, 23, 8: 1590–1610.

Law Reform Commission (2010) *Alternative Dispute Resolution: Mediation and Conciliation*, Dublin: Law Reform Commission. [online] Available: www.lawreform.ie/_fileupload/reports/r98adr.pdf.

Lawler, E. (1986) *High Involvement Management: Participative Strategies for Improving Organizational Performance*, San Francisco: Jossey-Bass.

Lawler, E., Mohrman, S. and Ledford, G. (1995) *Creating High Performance Organizations, Practices and Results in Employee Involvement and Total Quality Management in Fortune 1000 Companies*, San Francisco: Jossey-Bass.

Lawler III, E.E. (2010) *Talent: Making people your competitive advantage*, John Wiley & Sons.

Lee, J.J. (1989) *Ireland, 1912–1985: Politics and Society*, Cambridge and New York: Cambridge University Press.

Legge, K. (1978) *Power, Innovation and Problem Solving in Personnel Management*, London: McGraw-Hill.

Legge, K. (1995) *Human Resource Management: Rhetoric and Realities*, London: Macmillan.

Lengnick-Hall, M., Lengnick-Hall, C., Andradem L. and Drake, B. (2009) 'Strategic Human Resource Management: The Evolution of the Field'. *Human Resource Management Review*, 19: 64–85.

Lepak, D. and Shaw, J. (2008) 'Strategic HRM in North America: Looking to the future', *International Journal of Human Resource Management*, 19, 8: 1486–1499.

Lepak, D. and Snell, S. (1999) 'The human resource architecture: toward a theory of human capital allocation and development', *Academy of Management Review*, 24: 31–48.

Lepak, D. and Snell, S. (2002) 'Examining the human resource architecture: the relationship among human capital, employment, and human resource configurations', *Journal of Management*, 28: 517–43.

Lepak, D., Takeuchi, R. and Snell, S. (2003) 'Employment flexibility and firm performance: examining the interaction effects of employment mode, environmental dynamism, and technological intensity', *Journal of Management*, 29: 681–703.

Levy, P. E. and Williams, J. R. (2004) 'The social context of performance appraisal: A review and framework for the future', *Journal of Management*, 30, 6: 881–905.

Lewicki, R.J., Barry, B. andSaunders, D.M. (2010) *Negotiation*, Boston: McGraw-Hill.

Lewin, D. (2001) 'Low Involvement Work Practices and Business Performance', Proceedings of the 53rd Annual Meeting, Industrial Relations Research Association January 3–5: 275–292.

Lewis, R. E. and Heckman, R. J. (2006) 'Talent management: A critical review', *Human Resource Management Review*, 16, 2: 139–154.

Lindbeck, A. and Snower, D.J. (2001) 'Insiders versus Outsiders', *Journal of Economic Perspectives*, 15, 1: 165–88.

Llorens, J. and Battaglio, R. (2010) 'Human Resource Management in a Changing World: Re-assessing Public Human Resource Management Education', *Review of Public Personnel Administration* 30, 1: 112–132.

Lunenburg, F. C. (2011) 'Leadership versus management: A key distinction—at least in theory', *International Journal of Management, Business and Administration*, 14, 1: 1–4.

Lupton, T. (1976) 'Best fit in the design of organisations,' in E. Miller (ed.) *Task and Organisation*, New York: John Wiley.

Lynch-Fannon, I. and Connolly, U. (forthcoming) *Labour Law in Ireland*, Dublin: Gill and Macmillan.

Lyness, K.S., Gornick, J.C., Stone, P. and Grotto, A.R. (2012) 'It's all about control: Worker control over schedule and hours in cross-national context.' *American Sociological Review*, 77, 6: 1023–1049.

Mabey, C. and Salaman, G. (1995) *Strategic Human Resource Management*, Oxford: Blackwell.

MacDuffie, J. (1995) 'Human resource bundles and manufacturing performance: organisational logic and flexible production systems in the world auto industry', *Industrial and Labour Relations Review*, 48, 2: 197–221.

MacMahon, J. (1996) 'Employee relations in small firms in Ireland: An exploratory study of small manufacturing firms', *Employee Relations*, 18, 5: 66 – 80.

Magee, C. (1991) 'Atypical work forms and organisational flexibility', paper presented to the Institute of Public Administration Personnel Management Conference, Dublin, 6 March, 2017.

Marchington, M. and Wilkinson, A. (2005) *Human resource management at work: People management and development*, London: CIPD Publishing.

Marchington, M. and Grugulis, I. (2002) '"Best practice" human resource management: perfect opportunity or dangerous illusion', in P. Gunnigle, M. Morley and M. McDonnell (eds.), *The John Lovett Lectures: A Decade of Developments in Human Resource Management*, Dublin: Liffey Press.

Marchington, M. and Parker, P. (1990) *Changing Patterns of Employee Relations*, Hemel Hempstead: Harvester Wheatsheaf.

Margerison, C. and Leary, M. (1975) *Managing industrial conflicts: the mediator's role*, Bradford: MCB Books.

Markoulli, M., Lee, C., Byington, E. and Felps, W. (2017) 'Mapping Human Resource Management: Reviewing the Field and Charting Future Directions', *Human Resource Management Review* (In Press).

Marler, J. H. and Boudreau, J. W. (2017) 'An evidence based review of HR Analytics', *International Journal of Human Resource Management*, 28, 1: 3–26.

Marsden, D. (1986) *The End of Economic Man? Custom and Competition in Labour Markets*, New York: St Martin's Press.

Marshall, A. (1928) *Principles of Economics* (8th edn.), London: Macmillan.

Maslow, A. (1943) 'A theory of human motivation', *Psychological Review*, 50, 4.

Mayo, G.E. (1945) *The Social Problems of an Industrial Civilization*, Boston: Harvard University, Division of Research, Graduate School of Business Administration.

Mayo, G.E. (1933) *The Human Problems of an Industrial Civilization*, New York: Macmillan.

Mayrhofer, W., Brewster, C. and Morley, M. (2000) 'The concept of strategic European human resource management', in C. Brewster, W. Mayrhofer and M. Morley (eds.), *New Challenges for European Human Resource Management*, London: Macmillan: 3–31.

McCarthy, A. and Pearson, J. (2001) '360° feedback in the global HRM arena and the expatriate management process', in M. Linehan, M. Morley and J. Walsh (eds.), *International Human Resource Management and Expatriate Transfers: Irish Experiences*, Dublin: Blackhall Press.

McCarthy, C. (1984) *Elements in Theory of Industrial Relations*, Dublin: Trinity College Dublin.

McCarthy, J. and Heraty, N. (2017) 'Ageist Attitudes', in E. Parry, and J. McCarthy, (eds.) *The Palgrave Handbook of Age Diversity and Work*, London: Palgrave: 399–422.

McCarthy, J., Cleveland, J. and Heraty, N. (2014) 'Beyond generational differences? Exploring individual and organisational influences on inter-generational work attitudes and experiences', in E. Parry (ed.) *Generational Diversity at Work: New Research Perspectives*. London: Routledge: 164–182.

McClelland, D. (1961) *The Achieving Society*, New York: Van Nostrand.

McDonnell, A., Collings, D.G., Mellahi, K. and Schuler, R. (2017) 'Talent management: a systematic review and future prospects', *European Journal of International Management*, 11, 1: 86–128.

McDonnell, A., Gunnigle, P. and Lavelle, J. (2014) 'Human Resource Management in Multinational Enterprises: Evidence from a Late Industrializing Economy', *Management International Review*, 54, 3: 361–380.

McGinley, M. (1997) 'Industrial Relations in the Public Sector', in T.V. Murphy and W.K. Roche (eds.) *Industrial Relations in Practice, Revised and Expanded Edition*, Dublin; Oak Tree.

McGinnity, F. and Calvert, E. (2009) 'Work-life conflict and social inequality in Western Europe', *Social Indicators Research*, 93,3: 489–508.

McGiver, D., Lengnick-Hall, C.A., Lengnick-Hall, M. L. and Ramachandran, I. (2013) 'Understanding work and knowledge management from a knowledge-in-practice perspective', *Academy of Management Review*, 38: 597–620.

McGrath, P. and Geaney, C. (1998) 'Managing organisational change', in W.K. Roche, K. Monks and J. Walsh (eds.) *Human Resource Strategies: Policy and Practice in Ireland*, Dublin: Oak Tree Press.

McGregor, D. (1960) *The Human Side of Enterprise*, New York: McGraw Hill.

McKersie, R. (1996) 'Labour-management partnerships: U.S. evidence and implications for Ireland', *Irish Business and Administrative Research*, 17, 1: 1–16.

McKinsey & Co. (2009) 'Management Matters in Northern Ireland and the Republic of Ireland', March [online]. Available: www.managementdevelopment.ie.

McMahon, G. and Gunnigle, P. (1994) *Performance Appraisal: How to Get It Right*, Dublin: Productive Personnel Ltd in association with IPM (Ireland).

McNamara, G., Williams, K. and West, D. (1988) *Understanding Trade Unions: Yesterday and Today*, Dublin: O'Brien Educational Press.

McPartlin, B. (1997) 'The Development of Trade Union Organisation', in T.V. Murphy and W.K. Roche (eds.) *Irish Industrial Relations in Practice: Revised and Expanded Edition*, Dublin: Oak Tree Press.

Meriac, J.P., Gorman, C. A. and Macan, T. (2015) 'Seeing the Forest but Missing the Trees: The Role of Judgments in Performance Management', *Industrial and Organizational Psychology*, Cambridge University Press, 8, 1: 102–108.

Meyer, R.D., Dalal, R.S. and Hermida, R. (2010) 'A review and synthesis of situational strength in the organizational sciences', *Journal of Management*, 36: 121–40.

Micheli, P., Schoeman, M., Baxter, D. and Goffin, K. (2012) 'New Business Models for Public Service Innovation', *Research-Technology Management*, 55, 5: 51–57.

Miles, R. and Snow, C. (1978) *Organizational Strategy, Structure and Process*, New York: McGraw Hill.
Miles, R. and Snow, C. (1984) 'Designing strategic human resources systems', *Organisational Dynamics*, Spring: 36–52.
Mintzberg, H. (1978) 'Patterns in strategy formulation', *Management Science*, 24, May: 934–48.
Mintzberg, H. (1987) 'The strategy concept I: five Ps for strategy', *California Management Review*, 30, 1: 11–24.
Mintzberg, M. (1973) *The Nature of Managerial Work*, New York: Harper and Row.
Mitchell, D.B. (1994) 'A Decade of Concession Bargaining', in C. Kerr and P. Stavdohar (eds.) *Labor Economics and Industrial Relations*, Boston: Harvard University Press.
Monks, K. (1992) 'Personnel Management Practices: Uniformity or Diversity? Evidence from some Irish Organisations', *Irish Journal of Business and Administrative Research*, 13, 1: 74-86.
Monks, K. (1993) 'Models of personnel management: a means of understanding the diversity of personnel practices?', *Human Resource Management*, 3, 2: 29–41.
Monks, K. (1997) '60 Years a Growing: The Changing Role of the Personnel Practitioner, 1937–1997', *IPD News*, 4, 1: 3–7.
Monks, K. and McMackin, J. (2001) 'Designing and aligning an HR system', *Human Resource Management Journal*, 11, 2: 57–62.
Montgomery, C. (1996) 'Organization fit as a key to success', *HRM Magazine*, January: 94–6.
Mooney, M. (1988) 'From industrial relations to employee relations in Ireland', unpublished PhD thesis, Trinity College, Dublin.
Morgeson, F.P. and Dierdorff, E.C. (2011) 'Work analysis: from technique to theory', in *APA Handbook of Industrial and Organizational Psychology*, S Zedeck (ed.), 2: 3–41, Washington, DC: Am. Psychol. Assoc.
Morley, M. (1994) 'A team approach to job design', *Irish Business and Administrative Research*, 15, 1: 20–34.
Morley, M. J. (2007) 'Person-organization fit', *Journal of Managerial Psychology*, 22, 2: 109–117.
Mowday, R. (1987) 'Equity theory predictions of behaviour in organisations', in R. Steers and L. Porter, *Motivation and Work Behaviour*, New York: McGraw Hill.
Mulvey, K. (2015) Address by the Director General, Workplace Relations Commission on the Launch of the *Arthur Cox Employment Law Yearbook* 2015[online]. Available: www.arthurcox.com.
Mumford, A. (1986) 'Learning to learn for managers', *Journal of European Industrial Training*, 10, 2: 1–22.
Munro-Fraser, J. (1954) *A Handbook of Employee Interviewing*, London: McDonald and Evans.
Murphy, K. and Cleveland, J. (1991) *Performance Appraisal: An Organizational Perspective*, Needham Heights, MA: Allyn and Bacon.
Myatt, M. (2012) 'The #1 Reason Leadership Development Fails', *Forbes Magazine* [online], December 19.

National Competitiveness Council (2016) WEF Competitiveness Rankings, Competitiveness Bulletin 16–7, September.
Nevin, E. (1963) *Wages in Ireland*, Dublin: Economic and Social Research Institute.
Newell, S. (1995) *The Healthy Organization: Fairness, Ethics and Effective Management*, London: Routledge.
Nierenberg, G. (1968) *The Art of Negotiating*, New York: Cornerstone.
Niven, M. (1967) *Personnel Management 1913–1963*, London: Institute of Personnel Management.

O'Brien, J. (1989) 'Pay determination in Ireland', in *Industrial Relations in Ireland: Contemporary Issues and Developments*, Dublin: University College Dublin.
O'Connell, P.J., Russell, H., Watson, D. and Byrne, D. (2010) *The National Workplace Surveys 2009, Volume 2, The Changing Workplace: A Survey of Employees' Views and Experiences*, Dublin: National Centre for Partnership and Performance.
O'Connor, E. (1995) 'World class manufacturing in a semi-state environment', in P. Gunnigle and W. Roche (eds.), *New Challenges to Irish Industrial Relations*, Dublin: Oak Tree Press in association with the Labour Relations Commission.
O'Higgins, E. (2002) 'Government and the creation of the Celtic Tiger: can management maintain the momentum?', *Academy of Management Executive*, 16, 3: 104–120.
O'Mahony, D. (1958) *Industrial Relations in Ireland*, Dublin: Economic Research Institute.
O'Sullivan, M. and Gunnigle, P. (2009) 'Bearing all the hallmarks of oppression: union avoidance in Europe's largest low cost airline', *Labor Studies Journal*, 34, 2: 252–270.
O'Sullivan, M., Turner, T., McMahon, J., Ryan, L., Lavelle, J., Murphy, C., O'Brien, M. & Gunnigle, P. (2015) 'A *Study on the Prevalence of Zero Hours Contracts among Irish Employers and their Impact on Employees*', Dublin: Department of Jobs, Enterprise and Innovation [online]. Available: www.djei.ie/en/Publications/Publication-files/Study-on-the-Prevalence-of-Zero-Hours-Contracts.pdf.
O'Sullivan, M. & Royle, T. (2014) 'Everything and Nothing Changes: Fast-Food Employers and the Threat to Minimum Wage Regulation in Ireland', *Economic and Industrial Democracy*, 35, 1: 27–47.
OECD (2015) *'Education at a Glance'*, Paris: OECD.
OECD (2016) *'Skills Matter: Further results from the Survey of Adult Skills,'* Paris: OECD.
OECD (Organisation for Economic Co-operation and Development) (1999) *Economic Surveys: Ireland*, Paris: OECD.
OECD (Organisation for Economic Co-operation and Development) (2000) *International Direct Investment Statistics Yearbook*, Paris: OECD.
OECD (Organisation for Economic Co-operation and Development) (2005) *Education at a Glance*, Brussels: OECD.
Orion Partners (2015) 'Ulrich comes of age' – a study of the impact of 18 years of the Ulrich model', [online]. Available: www.orion-partners.com/study-ulrich-comes-age.

Paauwe, J. and Boselie, P. (2005) 'HRM and performance: what next?', *Human Resource Management Journal*, 15, 4: 68–83.

Parker, S. (2014) 'Beyond Motivation: Job and Work Design for Development, Health, Ambidexterity, and More', *Annual Review of Psychology*, 65: 661–91.
Parry, E. and McCarthy, J. (2017) *The Palgrave Handbook of Age Diversity and Work*, London: Palgrave.
Perry, B. (1984) *Enfield: A High-Performance System*, Bedford, MA: Digital Equipment Corporation, Educational Services Development and Publishing.
Personnel Standards Lead Body (1993) *A Perspective on Personnel*, London: Personnel Standards Lead Body.
Peterson, F. (1937) 'Methods used in Strike Statistics', *Journal of the American Statistical Association*, 32, 197: 90–96.
Pfeffer, J. (1994) *Competitive Advantage through People*, Boston: Harvard Business School Press.
Pfeffer, J. (1998a) 'Seven practices of successful organizations', *California Management Review*, 40: 96–124.
Pfeffer, J. (1998b) *The Human Equation: Building Profits by Putting People First*, Boston: Harvard Business School Press.
Pfeffer, J. and Sutton, R. I. (2006) 'Evidence-based management', *Harvard Business Review*, 84.
Pfeffer, J. and Viega, J. (1999) 'Putting people first for organizational success', *Academy of Management Executive*, 13. 37–48.
Phillips, J.M. and Gully, S.M. (2015) 'Multilevel and strategic recruiting: where have we been, where can we go from here?', *Journal of Management*, 41, 5: 1416–1445.
Picardi, C. (2015) 'The effects of multi-rater consensus on performance rating accuracy', *Journal of Strategic Human Resource Management*, 4, 21:361–88.
Pichler, S. (2012) 'The social context of performance appraisal and appraisal reactions: a meta-analysis', *Human Resource Management*, 51, 5: 709–32.
Pil, F. and MacDuffie, J. (1996) 'The adoption of high-involvement work practices', *Industrial Relations*, 35, 3: 423–55.
Piore, M. J. (2002) 'Thirty years later: Internal labor markets, flexibility and the new economy', *Journal of Management and Governance*, 6,4: 271–279.
Pitcher, G. (2008) 'Backlash against HR business partner model', *Personnel Today* (January).
Pollitt, C. and Bouckaert, G. (2004) *Public Management Reform: A Comparative Analysis*, (2nd edn.), Oxford: Oxford University Press.
Poole, M. (1986) 'Managerial strategies and styles in industrial relations: a comparative analysis', *Journal of General Management*, 12, 1: 40–53.
Porter, M. (1980) *Competitive Strategy: Techniques for Analysing Industries and Competitors*, New York: Free Press.
Porter, M. (1985) *Competitive Advantage: Creating and Sustaining Superior Performance*, New York: Free Press.
Porter, M. (1987) 'From competitive advantage to corporate strategy', *Harvard Business Review*, May–June: 43–59.
Porter, M. (1990) *The Competitive Advantage of Nations*, New York: Free Press.

Porter, M. and Siggelkow, N. (2008) 'Contextuality within activity systems and sustainability of competitive advantage', *Academy of Management Perspectives*, 22, 2: 34–56.

Posthuma, R., Campion, M., Masimova, M. and Campion, M. (2013) 'A High Performance Work Practices Taxonomy: Integrating the literature and directing future research', *Journal of Management*, 39,3: 1184–1220.

Prahalad, C. and Hamel, G. (1990) 'The core competencies of the corporation', *Harvard Business Review*, 68: 79–91.

Prendergast, A. (2014) 'Access to State IR bodies for Civil Servants', *Industrial Relations News* 40, November 5.

Pritchard, S. (2010) 'Becoming a HR Strategic Partner: Tales of Transition', *Human Resource Management Journal*, 20, 2: 175–188.

Pritchard, S. (2011) 'Analytics can improve the use of money and staff', *Financial Times*, Connected Business Special Report, April 20.

Pulakos, E. (1997) 'Ratings of job performance', in D. Whetzel and G. Wheaton (eds.), *Applied Measurement Methods in Industrial Psychology*, Palo Alto CA: Davies-Black Publishing.

Pulakos, E.D., Mueller-Hanson, R.A., Arad, S. and Moye, N. (2015) 'Performance management can be fixed: An on-the-job experiential learning approach for complex behavior change', *Industrial and Organizational Psychology: Perspectives on Science and Practice*, 8: 51–76.

Purcell, J. (1987) 'Mapping management styles in employee relations', *Journal of Management Studies*, 24, 5: 533–548.

Purcell, J. (1989) 'The impact of corporate strategy on human resource management', in J. Storey (ed.), *New Perspectives on Human Resource Management*, London: Routledge.

Purcell, J. (1999) 'The search for best practice and best fit in human resource management; chimera or cul de sac?', *Human Resource Management Journal*, 9, 3: 26–41.

Purcell, J. (2004) 'The HRM-performance link: why, how and when does people management impact on organisational performance?', paper presented at the Twelfth Annual John Lovett Memorial Lecture, University of Limerick, March.

Purcell, J. and Hutchinson, S. (2007) 'Front-line managers as agents in the HRM-performance causal chain: theory, analysis and evidence', *Human Resource Management Journal*, 17, 1: 3–20.

Raelin, J.A. (2016) 'Work-Based (Not Classroom) Learning as the Apt Preparation for the Practice of Management', *Management Teaching Review*, 1, 1: 43–51.

Rasmussen, T. and Ulrich, D. (2015) 'Learning from practice: how HR analytics avoids being a management fad', *Organizational Dynamics*, 44, 3: 236–242.

Regan, A. (2013) *The Impact of the Eurozone Crisis on Irish Social Partnership: A Political Economy Analysis*, Working Paper no. 49, Geneva: International Labour Office [online]. Available: www.ilo.org/wcmsp5/groups/public/---europe/---ro-geneva/---ilo-brussels/documents/genericdocument/wcms_195004.pdf

Reilly, R. and Warech, M. (1993) 'The validity and fairness of alternatives to cognitive tests', in L. Wing (ed.), *Employment Testing and Public Policy*, Boston: Kluwer.

Revans, R. (1982) 'Action learning: the skills of diagnosis', *Management Decision*, 21, 2: 46–52.

Rhodes, R. (1994) 'The hollowing out of the state: the changing nature of public service in Britain', *The Political Quarterly*, 65, 2: 138–151.

Roberts, H. (2014) 'Critics of Ulrich model ignore new progress, says Dave Ulrich', HR Magazine [online]. Available: www.hrmagazine.co.uk/article-details/critics-of-ulrich-model-ignore-new-progress-says-dave-ulrich.

Roche, W.K. (1989) 'State strategies and the politics of industrial relations in Ireland since 1945,' in *Industrial Relations in Ireland: Contemporary Issues and Developments*, Dublin: University College Dublin.

Roche, W.K. (1990) 'Industrial relations research in Ireland and the trade union interest', paper presented to the *Irish Congress of Trade Unions Conference* on Joint Research between Trade Unions, Universities, Third-Level Colleges and Research Institutes, Dublin.

Roche, W.K. (1997a) 'The trend of unionisation', in T. Murphy and W. Roche (eds.), *Irish Industrial Relations in Practice*, Dublin: Oak Tree Press.

Roche, W.K. (1997b) 'Pay determination, the state and the politics of industrial relations', in T. Murphy and W. Roche (eds.), *Irish Industrial Relations in Practice*, Dublin: Oak Tree Press.

Roche, W.K. (1999) 'In search of coherent commitment-oriented human resource policies and the conditions which sustain them', *Journal of Management Studies*, 36, 5: 653–78.

Roche, W.K. (2008) 'The Trend of Unionisation in Ireland since the mid-1990s', in Tim Hastings (ed.) *The State of the Unions: Challenges Facing Organised Labour in Ireland*, Dublin: Liffey Press.

Roche, W.K. (2011) 'Irish research throws light on HR's recession', *People Management* (July): 32–35.

Roche, W.K. (2013) 'Human resource management and public service reform' *Administration*, 60, 3: 211–218.

Roche, W.K. (2014) 'HRM in Recession: Managing People in the Private and Public Sectors', in B. Harney and K. Monks (eds.), *Strategic HRM: Research and Practice in Ireland*, Dublin: Orpen Press.

Roche, W.K. and Teague, P. (2011) 'Firms and Innovative Conflict Management systems in Ireland', *British Journal of Industrial Relations*, 49, 3: 436–459.

Roche, W.K. and Teague, P. (2012) 'Business partners and working the pumps: Human resource managers in the recession', *Human Relations*, 65, 10: 1333–1358.

Roche, W.K. and Teague, P. (2015) 'Antecedents of concession bargaining in the Great Recession: evidence from Ireland', *Industrial Relations Journal*, 46, 5–6: 434–445.

Roche, W.K. and Larragy, J. (1989) 'The trend of unionisation in the Irish Republic', in *Industrial Relations in Ireland: Contemporary Issues and Developments*, Dublin: University College Dublin.

Roche, W.K., Monks, K. and Walsh, J. (1998) *Human Resource Strategies: Policy and Practice in Ireland*, Dublin: Oak Tree Press.

Roche, W.K., Teague, P. and Coughlan, A. (2015) 'Employers, trade unions and concession bargaining in the Irish recession', *Economic and Industrial Democracy*, 36, 4: 653–676.

Roche, W.K., Teague, P., Coughlan, A. and Fahy, M. (2011) *Human Resources in the Recession: Managing and Representing People at Work in Ireland*, Dublin: Labour Relations Commission.

Rodger, A. (1952) *The Seven Point Plan*, London: National Institute of Industrial Psychology.

Roethlisberger, F. and Dickson, W. (1939) *Management and the Worker*, Boston: Harvard University Press.

Rollinson, D. (1993) *Understanding Employee Relations: A Behavioural Approach*, Wokingham, UK: Addison-Wesley.

Rose, E. (2008) *Employment Relations*, (3rd edn.), Harlow, Essex: Pearson Education.

Rumelt, R. P. (2009) 'Strategy in a 'structural break', *McKinsey Quarterly*, 1: 35–42.

Russo, G., Rietveld, P., Nijkamp, P. and Gorter, C. (1995) 'Issues in recruitment strategies: an economic perspective', *International Journal of Career Management*, 7, 3: 3–13.

Ryan, A.M and Ployhart, R.E (2014) 'A Century of Selection', *Annual Review of Psychology*, 65: 693–717

Ryan, M. (2016) 'An Explorative Study on how Advances of Big Data and People Analytics relate to HR', Unpublished BA (HRM) Dissertation, University of Limerick.

Rynes, S.L. and Cable, D. M. (2003) 'Recruitment research in the twenty-first century', *Handbook of Psychology: 12, Industrial and Organizatinal Psychology*, New York: John Wiley, 55–77.

Rynes, S.L., Giluk, T.L. and Brown, K.G. (2007) 'The very separate worlds of academic and practitioner periodicals in human resource management: Implications for evidence-based management', *Academy of Management Journal*, 50, 5: 987–1008.

Saks, A. (2006) 'Antecedents and consequences of employee engagement', *Journal of Managerial Psychology*, 21, 7: 600–619.

Salamon, M. (2000) *Industrial Relations: Theory and Practice*, (4th edn.), Hemel Hempstead: Prentice Hall.

Sanchez, J.I. and Levine, E.L (2012) 'The Rise and Fall of Job Analysis and the Future of Work Analysis', *Annual Review of Psychology*, 63: 397–425.

Sanchez, J.I. and Levine, E.L. (1999) 'Is job analysis dead, misunderstood, or both? New forms of work analysis and design', in *Evolving Practices in Human Resource Management*, A. Kraut and A. Korman (eds.): 43–68. San Francisco, CA: Jossey-Bass.

Sanchez, J.I. and Levine, E.L. (2001) 'The analysis of work in the 20th and 21st centuries', in *Handbook of Industrial, Work and Organizational Psychology*, N. Anderson, D.S. Ones, H.K. Sinangil and C Viswesvaran (eds.), 1: 71–89, Thousand Oaks, CA: Sage.

Sanchez, J.I. and Levine, E.L. (2009) 'What is (or should be) the difference between competency modeling and traditional job analysis?', *Human Resource Management Review*, 19: 53–63.

Sandico, C. and Kleiner, B. (1999) 'How to hire employees effectively', *Management Research News*, 22, 12: 33–7.

Schermerhorn, J., Hunt, J. and Osborn, R. (1985) *Managing Organizational Behaviour*, New York: Wiley.

Schuler, R. (1987) 'Personnel and human resource management choices and organizational strategy', *Human Resource Planning*, 10, 1: 1–17.

Schuler, R. (1989) 'Strategic human resource management', *Human Relations*, 42, 2: 157–84.

Schuler, R. (1992) 'Strategic human resource management: linking the people with the strategic needs of the business', *Organisational Dynamics*, 21, 1: 18–31.

Schuler, R. and Jackson, S. (2014) 'Human resource management and organizational effectiveness: yesterday and today', *Journal of Organizational Effectiveness: People and Performance*, 1, 1: 35–55.

Schuler, R. and Jackson, S. (1987a) 'Linking competitive strategies with human resource management practices', *Academy of Management Executive*, 1, 3: 209–13.

Schuler, R. and Jackson, S. (1996) *Human Resource Management: Positioning for the 21st Century*, St Paul, Minneapolis MN: West Publishing Company.

Sheehan B. (2007) 'Supreme Court ruling will affect "right to bargain" law', EurWORK (European Observatory of Working Life).

Sheehan, B. (2009) 'Employers and the traditional industrial relations system; how the bonds have loosened', in T. Hastings (ed.) *The State of the Unions: Challenges Facing Organised Labour in Ireland*, Dublin: Liffey Press.

Sheehan, B. (2010) 'US Chamber: Wage Levels "Unsustainable but Policy Direction Correct"', *Industrial Relations News*, 3: 21–23.

Sheehan, B. (2011) 'Dail answers reveal fees paid to IBEC by some state agencies', *Industrial Relations News*, 20, May 25: 6–7.

Sheehan, B. (2016a) 'First "right to bargain" ruling means "Living Wage" for workers at major employer', *Industrial Relations News*, 22, June 9.

Sheehan, B. (2016b) 'Freshways Food Co & SIPTU conclude collective bargaining agreement', *Industrial Relations News*, 45, December 8.

Sheehan, B. (2016c) 'Rising expectations adds to what is a potent cocktail for IR in 2016', *Industrial Relations News*, 1, January 7.

Sheehan, B., Higgins, C. and Prendergast, A. (2015) 'IRN Review 2015: IR World Reflects Change in Economic Fortunes', *Industrial Relations News*, 46, December 17.

Shuck, B. and Wollard, K. (2010) 'Employee engagement & HRD: A seminal review of the foundations', *Human Resource Development Review*, 9, 1: 89–110.

Skinner, B. (1938) *The Behaviour of Organisations*, New York: Appleton-Century-Cross.

Skrovan, D. (1983) *Quality of Work Life*, Reading, MA: Addison-Wesley.

Small Firms Association (2014) *Absenteeism Report 2014*, Dublin: Small Firms Association.

Smith, C. and Turner, S. (2016) *The Millennial majority is transforming your culture*, Deloitte: 1–15, [online]. Available: www2.deloitte.com/content/dam/Deloitte/us/Documents/about-deloitte/us-millennial-majority-will-transform-your-culture.pdf.

Smith, P. and Kendall, L. (1963) 'Retranslation of expectations: an approach to the construction of unambiguous anchors for rating scales', *Journal of Applied Psychology*, 47: 149–55.

Smither, J., London, M. and Reilly, R. (2005) 'Does performance improve following multisource feedback? A theoretical model, meta-analysis and review of empirical findings', *Personnel Psychology*, 58, 1: 33–66.

Snell, S. (2005) 'HR strategy and organizational learning: extending the architecture in an era of competitive potential', Thirteenth Annual John Lovett Memorial Lecture, University of Limerick, April.

Snell, S. and Youndt, M. (1995) 'Human resource management and firm performance: testing a contingency model of executive controls', *Journal of Management*, 21: 711–37.

Steers, R. and Mowday, R. (1987) 'Employee turnover in organisations' in R. Steers and L. Porter (eds.), *Motivation and Work Behaviour*, New York: McGraw-Hill.

Steers, R. and Porter, L. (1987) *Motivation and Work Behaviour*, New York: McGraw Hill Publishing Company.

Steers, R. and Rhodes, S. (1978) 'Major influences on employee attendance: a process model', *Journal of Applied Psychology*, 63: 391–407.

Steiber, N. (2009) 'Reported levels of time-based and strain-based conflict between work and family roles in Europe: A multilevel approach.' *Social Indicators Research*, 93, 3: 469–488.

Stiles, P. and Kulvisaechana, S. (2003) *Human capital and performance: A literature review*, DTI.

Stone, K. (1999) 'Employment Arbitration under the Federal Arbitration Act', in Adrienne E. Eaton and Jeffrey H. Keefe (eds.) *Employment Dispute Resolution and Worker Rights in the Changing Workplace*, Madison, WI: Industrial Relations Research Association.

Storey, J. (1989) *New Perspectives on Human Resource Management*, London: Routledge.

Storey, J. (1989) 'Management development: a literature review and implications for future research part 1', *Personnel Review*, 18: 2–15.

Subramony, M. (2009) 'A meta-analytic investigation of the relationship between HRM bundles and firm performance', *Human Resource Management*, 48, 5: 745–768.

Swift, G. (2012) 'Human Resource Service Delivery', in S. Taylor and C. Woodhams (eds.) *Managing People and Organisations*, London: Chartered Institute of Personnel and Development.

Tansey, P. (1998) *Ireland at Work: Economic Growth and the Labour Market 1987–1997*, Dublin: Oak Tree Press.

Taylor, F. W. (1911) *The Principles of Scientific Management*, New York: Harper and Row.

Taylor, F. W. (1947) *Scientific Management*, New York: Harper and Row.

Taylor, P. (2011) 'Human Resources goes Technical' *Financial Times*, Connected Business Special Report, April 20 [online]. Available: http://im.ft-static.com/content/images/d5afead0-68ab-11e0-81c3-00144feab49a.pdf.

Taylor, S. and Armstrong, M. (2014) *Armstrong's Handbook of Human Resource Management Practice*, (13th edn.), London: Kogan Page.

Teague, P. and Doherty, L. (2011) 'Conflict Management Systems in Subsidiaries of Non-Union Multinational Organisations located in the Republic of Ireland', Research Paper, Labour Relations Commission [online]. Available:

www.workplacerelations.ie/en/Publications_Forms/Reference_Materials/Conflict_Management_Systems_in_Subsidiaries_of_Non-Union_Multinational_Organisations_located_in_the_Republic_of_Ireland.pdf.

Teague, P. and Donaghey, J. (2009) 'Why has Irish social partnership survived?' *British Journal of Industrial Relations*, 47, 1:55-78.

Teague, P. and Roche, W.K. (2014) 'Recessionary bundles: HR practices in the Irish economic', *Human Resource Management Journal*, 24, 2: 176–192.

Teague, P. and Roche, W.K., Gormley, T. and Currie, D. (2015a) *Managing Workplace Conflict: Alternative Dispute Resolution in Ireland*, Dublin: Institute of Public Administration.

Teague, P., Roche, W.K. and Hann, D. (2012) 'The diffusion of alternative dispute resolution practices in Ireland', *Economic and Industrial Democracy*, 33, 4: 581–604.

Teague, P., Roche, W.K., Gormley, T. and Currie, D. (2015b) 'The Changing Pattern of Workplace Conflict in Ireland', Innovations in Conflict Management (Research Paper 2), Labour Relations Commission.Terpstra, D., Mohamed, A. and Kethley, R. (1999) 'An analysis of federal court cases involving nine selection devices', *International Journal of Selection and Assessment*, 7, 1: 26–34.

Thelen, H.A. and Withall, J. (1949) 'Three frames of reference: the description of climate', *Human Relations*, 2, 2: 159–176.

Thomason, G. (1984) *A Textbook of Industrial Relations Management*, London: Institute of Personnel Management.

Thompson, P. (1983), *The Nature of Work – an Introduction to Debates on the Labour Process*, London: Macmillan.

Tiernan, S. and Morley, M. (2013) *Modern Management: Theory and Practice for Students in Ireland*, (4th edn.), Dublin: Gill and Macmillan.

Toegel, G. and Conger, J. (2003) '360-degree assessment: time for reinvention', *Academy of Management Learning and Education*, 2: 297–311.

Tonidandel, S., King, E. and Cortina, J. (2015) *Big Data at Work: The Data Science Revolution and Organizational Psychology*, New York: Routledge.

Traxler, F. (2008) 'Employer organisations', in P. Blyton, E. Heery, E., N. Bacon, and J. Fiorito (eds.) *The Sage Handbook of Industrial Relations*, London: Sage: 225–238.

Tregaskis, I. and Heraty, N. (2011) 'Human Resource Development: National Embeddedness', in C. Brewster& W. Mayrhofer (eds.) *Handbook of Research on Comparative Human Resource Management*, Cheltenham: Edward Elgar Publishing.

Turnbull, P. and Sapsford, D. (1992) 'A Sea of Discontent: The Tides of Organised and 'Unorganised', Conflict on the Docks', *Sociology* 26, 2: 291–309.

Turner, T. and O'Sullivan, M. (2013) 'Economic Crisis and the Restructuring of Wage Setting Mechanisms for Vulnerable Workers in Ireland', *Economic and Social Review*, 44, 2: 197–219.

Turner, T., D'Art, D. and O'Sullivan, M. (2013) *Are Trade Unions Still Relevant? Union Recognition 100 Years On*, Dublin: Orpen Press.

Tyson, S. (1987) 'The management of the personnel function', *Journal of Management Studies*, 24, 5: 523–532.

Tyson, S. and Fell, A. (1986) *Evaluating the Personnel Function*, London: Hutchinson.

Tyson, S., Witcher, M. and Doherty, N. (1994) *Different Routes to Excellence*, Human Resource Research Centre, Cranfield School of Management.

Ulrich, D. (1997) *Human Resource Champions: The Next Agenda for Adding Value and Delivering Results*, Boston: Harvard Business School Press.

Ulrich, D. (2012) [online]. Available: www.hrmagazine.co.uk/article-details/critics-of-ulrich-model-ignore-new-progress-says-dave-ulrich.

Ulrich, D. and Dulebohn, J. (2015) 'Are we there yet? What's next for HR?', *Human Resource Management Review*, 25, 2: 188–204.

Ulrich, D., Younger, J. and Brockbank, W. (2008) 'The twenty-first-century HR organization', *Human Resource Management*, 47, 4: 829–850.

Vaara, E. and Whittington, R. (2012) 'Strategy as Practice: Taking Social Practices Seriously', *Academy of Management Annals*, 6,1: 285–336.

Vaill, P. (1982) 'The purpose of high performing systems', *Organizational Dynamics*, Autumn: 23–39.

Vaughan–Whitehead, D. (2013) *Public Sector Shock: The Impact of Policy Retrenchment in Europe*, Cheltenham: Edward Elgar.

Vera, D., Crossan, M. and Apaydin, M. (2011) 'A framework for integrating organizational learning, knowledge capabilities, and absorptive capacity', in M. Easterby-Smith and M.A. Lyles (eds.), *Handbook of Organizational Learning and Knowledge Management*, Hoboken, NJ: John Wiley & Sons.

Vroom, V. (1964) *Work and Motivation*, New York: Wiley.

Wahba, M. and Bridwell, L. (1976) 'Maslow reconsidered: A review of research on the need hierarchy theory', *Organizational Behavior and Human Performance*, 15,2: 212–240.

Waldman, D., Atwater, L. and Antonioni, D. (1998) 'Has 360 degree feedback gone amok?', *Academy of Management Executive*, 12, 2: 86–94.

Walker, C. and Guest, R. (1952) *The Man on the Assembly Line*, Boston: Harvard University Press.

Wall, T. (1982) 'Perspectives on job redesign', in J. Kelly and C. Clegg (eds.), *Autonomy and Control at the Workplace: Context for Job Redesign*, London: Croom Helm.

Wall, T. and Wood, S. (2005) 'The romance of human resource management and business performance, and the case for big science', *Human Relations*, 58, 4: 429–62.

Wallace, J. (1988a) 'Unofficial strikes in Ireland', *Industrial Relations News*, no. 8, February 15.

Wallace, J. (1988b) 'Workplace aspects of unofficial strikes', *Industrial Relations News*, no. 9, March 3.

Wallace, J. and O'Shea, F. (1987) *A Study of Unofficial Strikes in Ireland*, Dublin: Stationery Office.

Wallace, J., O'Sullivan, M., Gunnigle, P. and McMahon, G.V. (2013) *Industrial Relations in Ireland*, (4th edn.), Dublin: Gill and Macmillan.

Walsh, F. and Strobl, E. (2009) 'Recent trends in Trade Union membership in Ireland', *Economic and Social Review*, 40, 1: 117–138.

Walsh, F. (2015) 'Union membership in Ireland since 2003', *Journal of the Statistical and Social Inquiry Statistical Society of Ireland*, 44: 86–100.

Walton, J. (1999) *Strategic Human Resource Development*, London: Prentice Hall.

Walton, R. (1973) 'Quality of working life: what is it?', *Sloan Management Review*, 15, Fall: 11–21.

Walton, R. (1985) 'From control to commitment in the workplace', *Harvard Business Review*, 63, 2: 77–84.

Wang, D. and Chen, S. (2013) 'Does intellectual capital matter? High-performance work systems and bilateral innovative capabilities', *International Journal of Manpower*, 34: 8: 861–879.

Way, S. and Johnson, D. (2005) 'Theorizing about the impact of strategic human resource management', *Human Resource Management Review*, 15: 1–19.

Way, S. and Johnson, D. (2001) 'The evaluative process model: a multiple stakeholder framework for strategic human resource management research', paper read to the Washington meeting of the Academy of Management, August 2017.

Wiesner, W. and Cronshaw, S. (1988) 'A meta-analytic investigation of the impact of interview format and degree of structure on the validity of the employment interview', *Journal of Occupational Psychology*, 61: 275–90.

Wilkinson, A., Godfrey, G., and Marchington, M. (1997) 'Bouquets, brickbats and blinkers: total quality management and employee involvement in practice', *Organization Studies*, 18, 5: 799–819.

Williams, S. and Adam-Smith, D. (2010) *Contemporary Employment Relations*, Oxford: Oxford University Press.

Williamson, O. E. (1978) *Markets and Hierarchies: Analysis and Anti-Trust Implications*, Glencoe: Free Press.

Williamson, O. E. (1981) 'The economics of organization: The transaction cost approach', *American Journal of Sociology*, 87, 3: 548–577.

Workplace Relations Commission (2006) *Code of Practice on Grievance and Disciplinary Procedures*, [online]. Available: www.workplacerelations.ie/en/Good_Workplace_Relations/codes_practice/COP3.

Workplace Relations Commission (2016) *Workplace Relations Commission Annual Report 2015* [online]. Available: www.workplacerelations.ie/en/Publications_Forms/WRC-Annual-Report-2015-English.pdf.

Wright, P. and Ulrich, M. (2017) 'A Road Well Travelled: The Past, Present and Future Journey of Strategic Human Resource Management'. *Annual Review of Organizational Psychology and Organizational Behavior*, 4: 45–65.

Wright, P. and McMahon, G. (1992) 'Theoretical perspectives for strategic human resource management', *Journal of Management*, 18, 2: 295–320.

Wright, V. and Brading, L. (1992) 'A balanced performance', *Total Quality Magazine*, October.

Wrzesniewski, A. and Dutton, J. E. (2001) 'Crafting a job: Revisioning employees as active crafters of their work', *Academy of Management Review*, 26. 2: 179–201.

Yeates, P. (2000) *Lockout: Dublin 1913*, Dublin: Gill and Macmillan.

Index

Note: Figures are denoted by an italic *f* following the page number, tables by *t* and boxes by *b*.

ability tests 126, 127*t*, 130
absenteeism 111–112, 315
Accenture 190
accountability 176, 177*t*
accumulation strategy 58, 59*t*
acquired needs theory 141, 164
adjudication officers 271, 272, 273, 274, 278, 348
Adjudication Service (formerly Rights Commissioner Service) 268, 271, 277, 331, 337, 344
Adobe 190
adoptive leave 333
Adoptive Leave Act 1995 333
adult education 219, 238
adversarialism, partnership and 322–324
advertising jobs 117, 122*t*, 335
Aer Lingus 11, 41*t*
affiliation need 141
age profile of workforce 112–113
Agricultural & Technical Instruction (IRL) Act 1898 215*t*
agricultural employment 12, 39
airlines 11, 57
Alderfer, C., existence–relatedness–growth theory 140
Aldi 57
alternative dispute resolution (ADR) 278, 317, 321
Amalgamated Society of Engineers 249
Amdahl 160
American Chamber of Commerce 288
AMICUS 250
analyser organisations 61, 62
AnCO (An Chomhairle Oiliuna) 32, 216*t*
annual hours contract 180–181
annual leave 274, 303, 329
Anti-Discrimination Pay Act 1974 29, 335
appeals 193, 268, 272, 273, 274, 348
Apple 160
application forms 107, 123, 129
appraisal interviews 206–210
  errors in 208–210*t*
  styles 207

appraisals *see* performance appraisal
Apprenticeship Act 1931 215*t*
Apprenticeship Act 1959 216*t*
apprenticeships 215, 216*t*, 220*t*, 248, 249
  redundancy and 342
  reorganisation in 1992 217*t*
  unfair dismissal and 338
arbitration 266, 267, 278, 279–280, 290, 304
alternative dispute resolution (ADR) 278, 317, 321
  ICTU and 254
  legally binding 277
Arbitration Board 279–280
assessment centres 126, 128*t*, 206
Association of Secondary Teachers Ireland (ASTI) 251
autonomous work groups (AWGs) 161
AXA 41*t*

'balanced score card' 71
ballots, secret 254
Baltimore Technologies 40
banking sector 40, 43
bargained corporatism 266, 267
bargaining process 289, 305, 306, 307
Bausch and Lomb 41*t*
behaviour, cause-effect models of 235
behavioural science movement 26–27
behaviourally anchored rating scales (BARS) 204–205
belief statements 7*t*
benchmarking
  jobs 174
  labour turnover 108
  pay 18
benefits 165, 168, 179–187
  fringe benefits 12, 165, 166, 167, 188–189, 289
  see also reward packages
Bersin, J., talent analytics maturity model 48*f*
'best fit' (contingency) HRM 56–63
  criticism of approaches to 62–63
  Fombrun's 'strategy implementation' model 58–61

Miles and Snow's 'strategy-HR fit' model 61–62
Schuler's 'strategy-employee behaviour' model 58
'best practice' (universalistic) HRM 46, 64–68
  criticisms of 66–68
  Pffeffer's seven key HRM practices 65t
Bethlehem Steel Company 26
big data 47, 48, 49, 113
'big idea' 75–76
'Bill of Rights for Workers' 246
Black, Angela 277
'black box' of HRM 52, 56, 82
bonus schemes *see* reward packages
Bord na Móna 160–161
British Airways 11
broadbanding 185–187
Building and Allied Trades' Union (BATU) 249
bundling HR practices 65, 69, 71
business information, sharing with employees 65t
business interest associations 283
business partners 20, 21, 22, 43
business strategy 44, 53, 54, 56, 58, 63
  decisions on 9
  external environment and 11
  and HRM policy 37, 51
  and identification of learning/training needs 226
  linking to HRM 58, 59f, 61–62f, 82
  reward system and 17
  study of 5–6, 35–36
  see also strategic management

capability, dismissal and 339–340
capitalism 46, 88
career breaks 188
career development 94, 116, 224, 231, 232–233
career management 231
career portfolios 233
careers, contemporary career perspectives 233f
carer's leave 334
Carer's Leave Act 2001 334
cause-effect models of behaviour 235
Celtic tiger 38, 41, 254, 289
centres of excellence/expertise 20, 21, 45, 46
CERT (Council for Education, Recruitment and Training) 216t
certification, of knowledge and skills 241

Chambers Ireland (formerly Chambers of Commerce Ireland) 287
Charter of Fundamental Social Rights of Workers (the Social Charter) 13
Chartered Institute of Personnel and Development (CIPD) 6, 73, 221, 288
  education courses 32
  membership of 33
  survey on HR practices in Ireland 51, 109, 123, 131, 132, 133
Cheard Comhairle, An 216t
childcare services 95, 188
children, employment of 330
choice, strategic 9
Circuit Court 336, 349
Civil and Public Service Union (CPSU) 251
coaching 228t, 234
Coca-Cola 41t
Codes of Practice 350
  on Disputes in Essential Services 277
  on the Duties and Responsibilities of Employee Representatives 251
  for Employers and Employees on the Prevention and Resolution of Bullying at Work 2007 350
  on Grievance and Disciplinary Procedures 315
  on Voluntary Dispute Resolution 259
cognitions 214t
cognitive tests 131
collaboration HR configuration 80b
collective agreements 274, 292, 298, 299
  discrimination and 335
  negotiations with trade unions 2
  procedural 297
  substantive 297
  and terms of employment 297, 328
collective bargaining 244, 248, 266, 267, 288, 297–303
  advantages of 298
  adversarial 265
  approaches to 295
  'best fit' HRM and 63
  broadbanding and 187
  centralised 29, 299–300
  conditions 298
  contemporary developments 301–303
  Donovan Report and 29
  employee participation through 324f
  by employers' associations 284, 287, 289–290, 292

collective bargaining, *continued*
  establishment-level 299
  formalised 291
  in Ireland 300–301
  JICs and 275
  JLCs and 276
  legal context 259–261
  levels of 299–300
  local 303
  multi-employer 285, 299, 300
  multi-establishment 299
  national-level 299–300
  negotiations 303–308
  with trade unions 2, 17, 28, 172, 246, 247
  see also pay
collective labour law 325, 350
collectivism, liberal 266, 267
Commission on Industrial Relations 1981 279
common law 246, 318, 325–326, 345–346
communications technology (ICT) sector 39–40
Communications Workers' Union (CWU) 251
communities of practice 239
competence
  -based job evaluation 177–178
  dismissal for 339–340
  or skill-based pay 185
competencies 214t
core 94
competitive advantage 15, 21, 49, 51, 163, 265
  human capital and 74
  means of establishing 34
  research on 56–57
  sources of 73, 91, 223
  strategic decision-making and 55
competitive strategy 15–16, 56–58, 61, 63, 67, 78
  analysers 61, 62
  'best fit' 61
  business-level 53
  cost leadership 57, 58
  defenders 61, 62
  differentiation strategy 57, 58
  focus 57, 58
  prospectors 61, 62
competitiveness 17, 40, 212
compliance HR configuration 80b
comprehensive needs analysis 226
concession bargaining 40, 42, 44
conciliation 254, 267, 268, 269–270
  and arbitration (C&A) schemes 279–280

conditioning 235
conditions of employment 328–330
Confederation of Irish Industry (CII) 286
configurations, and strategy 77–82
conflict, industrial 294, 308–315
conflict resolution 315–320
  handling disciplinary issues in the workplace 317–320
  handling grievances in the workplace 315–317
  in Ireland 321t
Congress of Irish Unions 253
Constitution of Ireland 259, 277, 325
construction industry 299
Construction Industry Federation (CIF) 286, 287, 299
contingency theory 57
contract of employment 328, 329, 330, 335, 337
  fixed-term 83, 94, 328, 330
  formation of 325, 326–327
  job description and 116
  job offer as 131
  redundancy payments and 342, 343
  requirement to retire and 344
contract work 330
contracting 17, 249, 274t, 275
core competencies 94
Cork Master Butchers Association 286
corporate belief statements 7
corporate-level strategy 53
corporation tax 288
corporatism 266, 267
cost leadership strategy 57, 58, 59f
cost, of employee benefits 189
craft unions 248–249
Cranet surveys 131–132, 186, 188, 210, 211, 240–241
critical HR goals (performance domains) 70–73
  labour productivity 70–71
  organisational flexibility 71
  social legitimacy 71
critical incident appraisal technique 203–204, 301, 302
'Croke Park Agreement' 2010–2014 281
Culliton report 217t
curriculum vitae (CV) 122t, 123, 129

decision-making, strategic 5, 37, 51, 53, 54
  and HRM 55–56, 57, 58

levels of 53f
market performance and 12
upstream and downstream 55f
workforce management and 36
defender organisations 61, 62
Dell Computers 15, 30, 41t
Deloitte 48, 190, 197, 242
demarcation 33, 94, 249, 274t
Demarcation Tribunal 254
Department of Education and Skills (DES) 218t, 220t
deskilling 88
differentiation strategy 57, 58, 59f
Digital 160
disciplinary interviews 320
disciplinary issues 317–320
disciplinary procedures 317, 318, 319f, 320–322
disciplinary rules 317
discretionary employee behaviour 73, 74–75
discrimination 113, 335–336
dismissals 274t, 318
  for breaking another statute 341
  for capability, competence or qualifications 339–340
  for incapability because of incompetence 340–341
  for incapability because of qualifications 341
  for incapacity because of ill-health 340
  for industrial action 341
  for misconduct 338–339
  for other substantial grounds 341
  see also termination of employment; unfair dismissals
disputes
  in employment relations 315–320
  resolution and wage setting institutions 268–272
  see also industrial conflict
distributive bargaining 303, 322
District Court 270, 272, 349
divide and conquer strategy 89
Donnelly Mirrors 324f
Donovan Report on industrial relations in Britain (1968) 29
dot.com downturn 39, 67
downsizing 11, 40, 44
Dropbox 30
dual-factor theory 137, 141–143, 164
Dublin Airport Authority 41t, 291
Dublin Lockout (1913) 28, 246, 250, 314

Duffy, Kevin 273
Dunnes Stores 15, 63

e-learning 50, 229
eBay 30
Ebeon 40
economy
  from the 1980s to the global financial crisis 38–39
  economic activity 11, 12, 33, 40, 52, 309
  HRM in the 'great recession' 39–44
  role of multinational companies in the 30, 262
education 213t
  and the human resource profession 32–33
  participation in 102–103
  and training by employers' associations 290
  see also training
Eir (formerly Telecom Éireann) 11
Electricity Supply Board (ESB) 11
Element Six 41t
Emergency Powers Orders 28
emigration 38, 98, 172, 311
  see also migration
employee absenteeism 111–112, 315
employee development 3t, 12, 60, 61, 80, 178
  see also education; learning; training
employee forums 264
employee participation 65, 157, 297, 323–324
employee performance 164, 190
  assessment of 197
  evaluation of 170, 198
  monitoring 17
  performance-related pay/performance by results systems 18
  see also performance appraisal; performance management
Employee Representative Committees (ERCs) 260
employee satisfaction 68, 164, 309
employee share ownership 184, 186
employee stock ownership schemes (ESOPs) 180
employees
  health and safety complaints by 348
  individual legislation 328–336
  involvement in decision-making 60
  Safety, Health and Welfare at Work Act 1989 348
  safety representative and safety committee 348–349

employees, *continued*
 training 65t
 see also training
employers
 duties 326, 345
 Safety, Health and Welfare at Work Acts 2005–2007 347
employers' associations 299
 Chambers Ireland (formerly Chambers of Commerce Ireland) 287
 collective bargaining 289–290
 comparability with other firms 292
 Construction Industry Federation (CIF) 286, 287, 299
 economic objectives 284t
 education and training 290
 ER/HRM style of a firm 292
 functions of 285
 in Ireland 285–288
 Irish Business and Employers Confederation (IBEC) *see* IBEC (Irish Business and Employers Confederation)
 Irish Hotels Federation 286, 287
 Irish Small and Medium Enterprises Association (ISME) 277, 288
 Licensed Vintners' Association 286, 287
 membership of 290–292
 objectives of 284t
 public sector organisations 290–291
 Quick Service Food Alliance (QSFA) 287
 research and advisory services 289
 role of 283–285
 services 289–290
 Society of the Irish Motor Industry 286, 287
employment
 flexibility and alternative forms of 92–95
 and occupation trends in Ireland 98–102
 termination of 336–344
 terms and conditions of 328–330
 written particulars of terms of 328
 see also labour market
employment agencies 335
Employment Appeals Tribunal (EAT) 268, 277
employment citizenship 71
employment contract 79, 80, 239, 330, 338
employment equality 105, 289, 332–333
Employment Equality Act 1977 29, 335
Employment Equality Acts 1998–2011 335–336
employment law *see* law
employment legislation *see* law

employment regulation orders (EROs) 276–277
employment relations 17, 244–281, 297–324
 achievement of satisfactory returns for the owners 282
 bargained corporatism 266, 267
 collective bargaining 297–303
 conflict resolution 315–320
 corporate control 266
 diffusion of grievance and disciplinary procedures 320–322
 dispute resolution and wage setting institutions 268–272
 effective utilisation of human resources 283
 employer and management approaches to 282–296
 employers' objective in 282–283
 establishment and maintenance of satisfactory management–employee relations 283
 forms of 267
 industrial conflict 308–315
 Labour Court *see* Labour Court
 liberal collectivism 266, 267
 main parties 245f
 maintenance of control and authority in decision-making 283
 management approaches to 292–295
 market individualism 266
 negotiations 303–308
 partnership and adversalialism in Irish employment relations 322–324
 pluralist tradition 265
 preservation and consolidation of the private enterprise system 282
 role of employers' associations 283–285
 role of the state in 265–268
 state approaches to employment relations in Ireland 265–268
 in the state sector 278–281
 trade unions *see* trade unions
 voluntarist tradition 266, 267
 see also industrial relations
employment rights 273–274
employment security 65t
engagement 133
equality 105, 289, 332–333
Equality Authority 274, 350
Equality Tribunal 268, 277
equity participation 323, 324f
equity theory 146–147, 195
European Union (EU) 13
 labour market 101t

work–life balance 95
evaluating jobs *see* job evaluation
evaluating performance *see* performance appraisal
existence-relatedness-growth (ERG) theory 140
expectancy theory 144–146
experiential learning 235–236
Expert Group on Future Skills Needs (EGFSN) 218t
externalisation 94

Facebook 13, 30, 113
facilitation strategy 58
factory system 24, 245
fairness, and performance 196
family-friendly work practices 95
Farm Apprenticeship Board 216t
FÁS (Foras Áiseanna Saothair) 32n, 217t, 218t, 220t
FDI (foreign direct investment) 13, 30–32
Federated Workers Union of Ireland (FWUI) 250
Federation of Irish Employers (FIE) 286
feedback
    360-degree 205–206
    intervention theory 195
    and performance 195–196
FETAC (Further Education and Training Awards Council) 218t, 221
financial crisis *see* global financial crisis (great recession)
financial/pay flexibility 93
financial services sector 251, 262
First World War 25, 28
Fitzgerald, Thomas 134
fixed-term contracts 83, 94, 328, 330
flat rate pay schemes 180–181
flexible firm model 92–93
focus strategy 57, 58, 59f
Foley, Kevin 273
Fombrun, Charles 35
    strategy implementation model 58–61
force majeure leave 334
forecasting human resource planning model 107–113
    absenteeism 111–112
    age profile of workforce 112–113
    demand for labour 107–108
    labour turnover 108–111
    supply of labour 108–113
foreign direct investment (FDI) 13, 30–32

Forum on the Workplace of the Future 219t
frames of reference, managerial 293–294
free-form appraisal technique 199t, 200
freedom of association 259, 298
fringe benefits 12, 165, 166, 167, 188–189, 289
front line managers (FLMs) 76, 77b, 77t
Fruit of the Loom 12–13
frustration–regression principle 140
functional flexibility 93
functional-level strategy 53
Further Education and Training Act 2013 220t
Further Education and Training Awards Council (FETAC) 218t, 221

gain-sharing schemes 184–185
Galvin report 217t
Gap 190
Gateway 39
General Application Regulations 349
General Strike (1926) 28
general unions 249–250
generalists *see* business partners
Global Competitiveness Report 212
global financial crisis (great recession) 11, 12, 18, 30, 55, 265
    HRM in the 39–44
    impact of 257, 278, 281, 292, 301
go slow industrial conflict 314
'going rate' concept 18
Google 13, 30
Government White Paper on Human Resource Development (HRD) (1997) 218t
grievances 315–317, 320–322
gross domestic product (GDP) 40
gross misconduct 319f
group bonus schemes 183
guild system 215

Hackman and Oldham, job characteristics model 153–155
halo/horns effect 129, 208
harassment 336, 350
hard HRM 36, 44, 45f
Harvard Business School (HBS) model 34–35, 64
'Hawthorne effect' 27
Hay method 176, 177f
health and safety at work 345–350
    common law 345–346
    complaints by employees 348
    Health and Safety Authority (HSA) 285, 349

health and safety at work, *continued*
  joint safety and health agreements 349
  Safety, Health and Welfare at Work Acts 2005–2007 346–348
  safety, health and welfare at work regulations 349–350
  safety representative and safety committee 348–349
Health and Safety Authority (HSA) 285, 349
HETAC (Higher Education and Training Awards Council) 218t
Hewlett Packard 15, 62
hierarchy of needs 137–140
High Court 340
high-involvement (people-centric) work system 68
high-performance work systems (HPWS) 65–66, 157–163
  models in Ireland 162–163f
  organisational characteristics of 159–160f
historical development of HRM 24–33
holidays, paid 329
home-working 94, 326
HPWS *see* high-performance work systems (HPWS)
HR *see* human resource (HR)
HRM *see* human resource management (HRM)
human assets, complexity of managing 79
human capital 34, 74f, 78, 79, 90, 212
  advantage 74
  anticipating needs in 105
  global trends 242
  human resource (HR)
  activities 2, 3t
  advantage 74
  analytics 47–49, 113
  architecture 79, 80, 81f, 94
  bundles, for different occupational categories 77b
  configurations 80b
  emergence of the role of 24–26
  functions of 4f
  Human Resource Development White Paper (1997) 218t
  industrial/employment relations 17
  models 20–22
  policies 16–22, 77t
  recruitment and internal HR flow practices 18
  roles in Ireland 20t
  size of HR function in Ireland 20t
  specialist HR function 18–22
  three-legged stool model 20, 21f, 22, 46
  work systems and 16–17
Human Resource Information Systems (HRIS) 44, 46
human resource management (HRM)
  in the 1980s 33–37
  'best fit' (contingency) approaches to 56–63
  business strategy and 5–6
  from a competitive perspective 86–87
  competitive pressures impacting on 10t
  competitive strategy 15–16
  contrasting personnel management and 36–37
  established practices and traditions 16
  external environment 10–14
  as generalist management 1, 2
  historical development of 24–33
  influence of managerial values and ideology on 14–15
  from an institutional perspective 88
  internal environment 14–16
  multinational influences on 30–32
  nature of 1–5
  organisational approaches to 9
  and organisational scale 3–5
  and performance 52–53
  policies 7, 8t
  procedures 8
  professional model 19
  from a radical perspective 89
  as specialist management 1–2
  statements of corporate beliefs in 7t
  strategy 6
  strategy implementation model 58–61
  in the US in the 1980s 34–36
  workforce profile 16
  see also management
human resource planning 105–114
  forecasting demand for labour 107–108
  forecasting supply of labour 108–113
  implementation of plan 114
  model of 106f
  purpose of 105
  stocktaking 107
human resource shared service centres (HRSSCs) 21, 44, 45–46
Hyman, Richard 309

IBEC (Irish Business and Employers Confederation) 42, 277, 285, 286, 287, 288

analysis of industrial training 218t
employers' associations and 299
fees paid to 291, 292
MNCs members of 290
role in collective bargaining 289
services 286
training for members 290
withdrawal from the terms of the Transitional Agreement 301
IBM 48
IBOA the Finance Union (formerly the Irish Bank Officials Association) 251
ICT *see* technology
ICTU (Irish Congress of Trade Unions) 253–254, 301
IDA Ireland 30, 40
ill-health, and dismissal 340
ILO Declaration on Fundamental Principles and Rights at Work 298
IMD World Competitiveness Yearbook 212
immigration 98
IMPACT (Irish Municipal Public and Civil Trade Union) 251, 260
in-house courses 228t
incapability 339–341
incentives 165, 166, 168, 179–187
    financial 168
    issues in implementing 186
    use in Ireland 187t
    see also reward management
incompetence, and dismissal 340–341
Independent News and Media 41t
individual bargaining 263, 298
individual difference hypothesis 123
individual employee legislation
    adoptive leave 333
    carer's leave 334
    contract work 330
    employment equality 332–333, 335–336
    employment of young people 330–331
    force majeure leave 334
    parental leave 333–334
    part-time employees 330
    paternity leave 333
    pay 331
    pensions 331–332
    terms and conditions of employment 328–330
individual labour law 325, 350
individual learning and development 235–240
individual needs analysis 226
individualism 265, 266

induction 18, 41, 122, 131, 147–148t
    crisis 110
industrial action 308
    dismissal for 341
industrial conflict 294, 308–315
    absenteeism 315
    all-out-pickets 254
    collective conflict 309
    explicit (organised) 308, 309
    forms of 314–315
    go slows 314
    implicit (unorganised) 308, 309
    individual conflict 309
    labour turnover 314
    lockout 314
    official and unofficial strikes 313
    overtime bans 314
    pilferage 314
    sabotage 314
    sit-in 314
    strike activity in Ireland 309–312, 313t
    work to rule 314
industrial disputes *see* industrial conflict
industrial relations 17, 27–30, 31, 37t, 39, 273
    see also employment relations
Industrial Relations Act 1946 272
Industrial Relations Act 1990 247
Industrial Relations Act 2001 260, 261
Industrial Relations Act 2004 260, 261
Industrial Relations Act 2012 277
Industrial Relations Act 2015 261
Industrial Relations (Amendment) Act 2001 259, 260
Industrial Relations (Amendment) Act 2012 276, 287
Industrial Relations (Amendment) Act 2015 261, 275
Industrial Relations (Miscellaneous Provisions) Act 2004 259
Industrial Relations News 291, 301
Industrial Relations Officer 269
Industrial Revolution 24, 134, 245
Industrial Training Act 1967 216t
industrialisation 215
information and communications technology (ICT) sector 39, 45, 164
Institute of Industrial Welfare Workers 25
Institute of Personnel and Development (IPD) 33
Institute of Personnel Management (IPM) 32, 33

Institute of Public Administration (IPA) 221
integrated talent management suites (ITMS) 48
Intel 13, 57
internal labour market 108–113, 131
International Airlines Group (IAG) 11
International Labour Organization (ILO) 298
interviews 128–129, 130t, 132
   functions of 127t
   structured 126
   types of interview questions 130t
INTO (Irish National Teachers' Association) 251
Ireland
   from the 1980s to the global financial crisis 38–39
   age distribution of population of 96f
   collective bargaining in 300–301
   common law 325–326
   conflict management practices in 321t
   Constitution 325
   employers' associations in 285–288
   employment and occupation trends in 98–102
   L&D practices in 240–243
   management development in 241
   migration and 98
   models of high-performance work systems in 162–163f
   performance management in 210–211
   population 96–97
   sources of Irish law 325–326
   statute law 325
   strike activity in 309–312
   unemployment rates 99
Irish Airline Pilots Association (IALPA) 260
Irish Business and Employers Confederation *see* IBEC (Irish Business and Employers Confederation)
Irish Commercial Horticultural Association 286
Irish Congress of Trade Unions *see* ICTU (Irish Congress of Trade Unions)
Irish Congress of Trade Unions (ICTU) 253–254
Irish Dental Association 248
Irish Hospital Consultants Association 248
Irish Hotels Federation 286, 287
Irish Human Rights and Equality Commission 285
Irish Institute of Training and Development (IITD) 221

Irish Management Institute (IMI) 221
Irish Municipal Public and Civil Service Union (IMPACT) 251, 260
Irish National Teachers' Organisation (INTO) 251
Irish Nurses and Midwives Organisation (INMO) 251, 253
Irish Pharmacy Union 286
Irish Printing Federation 286
Irish Small and Medium Enterprises Association (ISME) 277, 288
Irish Trade Union Congress 253
Irish Transport and General Workers' Union (ITGWU) 28, 250
ISME (Irish Small and Medium Enterprises Association) and 277, 288
isomorphism 87

Jacobs 25
Jaguar 75
job advertisements 110, 116, 119, 121
job analysis 115–121, 226
job appraisal *see* performance appraisal
job characteristics 133, 153–155
job classification 174
job crafting 149
job description 116–117, 118t, 119–120t
job design 151, 164
job enlargement 152–153
job enrichment 143, 152, 153, 167
job evaluation 172–178
   analytical schemes 173, 175–178
   choosing and introducing 179
   competence- or skill-based 177–178
   criticisms of 178–179
   Hay method (plan) 176, 177f
   job classification 174
   job ranking 173–174
   non-analytical schemes 173–175
   paired comparison 174–175
job grades 172, 174
job hierarchies 91, 173
job interviews *see* interviews
job offers 131
job performance *see* performance management
job ranking 173–174
job rotation 228t
job satisfaction 143
job security 42, 93, 156, 167, 257, 314
John Lewis Partnership 324f
Joint Industrial Councils (JICs) 274, 275, 287

Joint Labour Committees (JLCs) 274, 276–277, 287

Kemmy Business School surveys 131, 186, 210, 211, 240
Kilcommins, Gerard 288
Kingspan 41*t*
knowledge and skills 90
knowledge flows 78
knowledge management 214*t*
knowledge, skills and attitudes (KSAs) 104, 105
knowledge stocks 78
Kolb's learning cycle 235–236

Labour Court 259–260, 262, 267, 272–278, 279, 317
  issues and challenges of the 277
  and wage setting institutions 274–277
labour, forecasting supply of 108–113
labour market 12, 38, 39, 68, 84–103
  atypical 39, 94
  characteristics 89–95
  competitive model of the 85–87
  external 60
  institutional model of the 87
  internal 60, 91–92, 122, 243
  pay and the 171–172
  perspectives on HRM and the 84–89
  profile of the Irish 96–103
  radical model of the 88–89
  segmented 90–91
  skilled workers 87
  unskilled workers 86
  wage rigidities 90
  see also unemployment
labour, productivity 70–71
Labour Relations Commission (now Workplace Relations Commission) 259
labour scarcity 72
Labour Services Act 1987 217*t*
labour turnover 108–111, 131, 314
laissez-faire ideology 266*t*
Larkin, Jim 28, 250
law 13, 29, 325–350
  adoptive leave 333
  carer's leave 334
  collective labour law 325, 350
  contract work 330
  employment equality 332–333, 335–336
  employment of young people 330–331
  formation of a contract of employment 326–327
  health and safety at work 345–350
  individual employee legislation 325, 328–336
  parental leave 333–334
  part-time employees 330
  paternity leave 333
  pay 331
  pensions 331–332
  redundancy 342–344
  retirement 344
  sources of Irish law 325–326
  termination of employment 336–344
  terms and conditions of employment 328–330
  transfer of undertakings 344
  unfair dismissal 337–341
  see also individual employee legislation
Law Reform Commission 267–268
lead indicators 68
leadership development 234, 235*f*
learning 213*t*
  evaluation of 230–231
  factors influencing 239
  identifying learning needs 225–227
  individual learning and development 235–240
  lifelong 219*t*, 220*t*, 231
  organisational 214*t*
  transfer of 229–230
  VARK model of 238
  see also education; workplace learning and development (LT&D)
'Learning for Life' White Paper on Adult Education (2000) 219*t*
learning gap 225
learning styles 237*t*, 240
Leaving Certificate 102
legislation *see* law
levy/grant scheme 216*t*, 217*t*
liberal collectivism 266, 267
Licensed Vintners' Association 286, 287
Lidl 57
Lincoln Electric 62
line management 1–2, 5, 19, 37, 46
  and ER workplace issues 304, 315
  HR responsibility of 3
LinkedIn 113
loan book 43
lockouts 314
  Dublin Lockout (1913) 28, 246, 250, 314

low-involvement (structure-centric) work system 68
LT&D *see* workplace learning, training and development (LT&D)

management
  career 231
  line management *see* line management
  by objectives (MBO) 203
  prerogative 294
  top/senior *see* top/senior management
  values and ideology 14–15
  and work design 149
  see also human resource management (HRM); performance management
management development 234, 241
Management Development Council (MDC) 219*t*, 241
management styles 28, 136, 143, 149, 159, 164
  authoritarian 28, 246
  in employment relations 294–295
managerial frames of reference 293–294
managerial values 9, 14, 15
managers
  assumptions about employees 143
  development of 234
Mandate 250
Manpower Policy White Paper 217*t*
manual workers 28–29, 210
market-based HR configuration 79, 80*b*
market individualism 266
market performance 12, 89, 291
Marks and Spencer 15
Marxism 88
Maslow's hierarchy of needs theory 137–140
'matching' process 51
maternity benefit 188, 333
maternity leave 188, 332–333
Maternity Protection Act 1994 271, 332
Maternity Protection (Amendment) Act 2004 332
Mayo, Elton 27
McGregor's theory X, theory Y 143–144
mediation 266, 290, 304, 317, 321
  conciliation and 267–268
  WRC 269, 270, 278
Medtronic 190
mentoring 90, 228*t*, 234, 242
Merck 70
'Michigan School' 35
Microsoft 120*t*, 190

migration 12, 22, 39, 96, 97, 98
  see also emigration
Miles and Snow, strategy-HR fit model 61–62
Minimum Notice and Terms of Employment Act 1973 337
minimum wages 276, 331
misconduct
  dismissal for 338–339
  gross misconduct 319*f*
MNCs *see* multinational corporations (MNCs)
money 146, 166, 167
  see also pay
motivation 133–148
  acquired needs theory 141
  to attend work 111
  content model of 137
  dual-factor theory 141–143
  equity theory 146–148
  existence-relatedness-growth (ERG) theory 140
  expectancy theory 144–146
  extrinsic outcomes 136
  factors influencing 136*f*
  features of 136
  intrinsic outcomes 136
  to learn 238
  Maslow's hierarchy of needs theory 137–140
  McGregor's theory X, theory Y 143–144
  measuring 135
  pay and 166–168
  process model of 137
  worker 72, 74
  see also work design
Motorola 39
multi-rater assessment *see* feedback
multi-sourced assessment *see* feedback
multinational corporations (MNCs) 13, 14, 30–32, 39, 262–263, 288
  HRIS among 46
  membership of employers' associations 290
  performance-based incentive pay trend 187
  trade union recognition in 263*f*
  unionised 42
Mulvey, Kieran 268
mutual gains 322

National Bus and Rail Union (NBRU) 253
National Centre for Partnership and Performance (NCPP) 219*t*
National Economic and Social Council (NESC) 219*t*, 285

National Employment Rights Authority
    (NERA) 268, 277
National Framework of Qualifications (NFQ)
    221, 222t
National Manpower Service 32n
National Minimum Wage Act 2000 271
National Minimum Wage Acts 2000–2015 331
National Qualifications Authority of Ireland
    (NQAI) 218t
National Skills Strategy 2025 220t
National Training Fund (NTF) 218t, 290
National Understandings 267
National Union of Sheet Metal Workers of
    Ireland 249
national wage agreements 29, 267
National Workplace Strategy 219t
National Workplace Survey 42, 184
natural justice 318, 339
negotiations 303–308
negotiations, employment relations 303–308
    adjournments 306
    agreements 306
    bargaining 304t, 306–307
    breakdown in 306
    distributive bargaining 303
    fall-back position 305
    ideal settlement point 305
    integrative (co-operative) bargaining 303
    post-negotiations 304t, 308
    preparation 304t, 305–306
    realistic settlement point 305
New Public Management (NPM) 280
'new unionism' 27, 283
night work 329, 330
Nike 57
numerical flexibility 72–73, 93

O'Connor, Edward 161
OECD 38, 94, 102, 212, 222, 288
    Education at a Glance report 103
    report on vocational education and training
        (VET) in Ireland 220t
    trade union density in selected countries
        258t
onboarding 131
online recruitment 123
open door management 321, 322
operational measures 68
Operative Plasterers and Allied Trades Society
    of Ireland (OPATSI) 249
opportunity to perform 74

organisation change 16, 72
Organisation of Working Time Act 1997 274,
    328–329
organisation process advantage 74
organisational behaviour 34, 167
organisational capital 74, 78
organisational culture 57
organisational development 167
organisational flexibility 70, 71
organisational learning 213, 214t
organisational needs analysis 226
organisational performance 1, 51, 64, 67,
    69–73, 74
    'black box' between HRM practices and 82
    high pay and 65t
    human capital and 84
    improving 35–36, 49, 54, 158, 187
    leadership development and 234
    linkage between HRM and 52, 66
    maximising 282
    reward management and 165
    workplace learning and development and
        223
organisations
    size 14, 184
    structure 14
outsourcing 40, 232, 280
overtime bans 40, 309, 314

paired comparison 174–175
parental leave 95, 188, 333–334
Parental Leave Acts 1998–2006 333–334
part-time employees 274, 330
part-time work 39, 94–95, 99, 101t, 330
Partnership 2000 300t
partnership, and adversalialism 322–324
paternity leave 188, 333
Paternity Leave and Benefits Act 2016 333
pay 165, 168, 179–187, 331
    and economic climate 171
    equity 172
    and government policy 172
    high pay and organisational performance 65t
    and the labour market 171–172
    as a motivator 166–168
    and trade unions 172
    see also collective bargaining; money;
        performance-related pay (PRP)
pay cuts 42, 44, 281, 300, 301, 302
pay freezes 42, 43, 281, 300, 301
pay movements 18, 41, 246, 303

pay negotiations 41, 253, 303, 305f, 306
pay schemes 143, 167, 168, 169, 180–187
   flat rate 180–181
   performance-based incentive schemes 181–187
Payment of Wages Act 1991 271, 331
payroll 3
PDForra 253
Peninsula (Chambers Ireland HR service) 287
pension levy 42
pensions 43, 331–332
Pensions Acts 1990–2002 331
Pensions Board 331–332
Pensions Ombudsman 332
people and performance model 75–76
performance 52–53, 69
   communication 194t
   counterproductive work behaviour 195t
   dimensions of 194–195t
   employee 164, 170
   evaluation 60
   feedback and 195–196
   HR and 73–82
   initiative, persistence and effort 194t
   management performance 195t
   market to book 81
   measurement of 193–195
   peer/team member management performance 195t
   perceived fairness and performance 196
   return on equity 81
   supervisory, management, and/or executive leadership 194t
   technical 194t
   worker 74, 75, 137
performance appraisal 191, 198–210
   360-degree feedback 205–206
   appraisal interview 206–210
   assessment centres 200t, 206
   behaviourally anchored rating scales (BARS) 204–205
   critical incident 199t, 203–204
   errors in appraisal process 208–210t
   form for employees 202t
   free-form 199t, 200
   methods of 199–206
paired comparison 199t
performance/objectives-oriented systems 199t
plan for managers 201t
   ranking 199t
   rating 199t, 200–202

results-oriented schemes 203
self-assessment 200t
uses of data from 211
see also employee performance; performance management
performance-based incentive systems 181–187
   broadbanding 185–187
   for clerical/administrative grades 186
   competence/skill-based pay 185
   flat rate plus group-based 183–184
   flat rate plus individual 183
   gain-sharing and share ownership schemes 184–185
   piecework 184
performance management 190–211
   benefits of 192t
   characteristics of an ideal system for 192–193t
   complexity of 193–196
   in Ireland 210–211
   process of 197–198
   rationale for 191–193
   see also employee performance; performance appraisal
performance outcomes 73, 161, 163, 165, 194
performance process 194
performance-related pay (PRP) 18, 31, 43, 181–182, 186, 211
   growth in 187
   individual 66, 180
   see also pay
performance/work sample tests 131
person–organisation fit 105, 129
person specification 116, 117–121, 123, 124, 125, 132
personal retirement savings accounts (PRSAs) 332
personality tests 127t, 128t, 130, 131
personnel management 34
   contrasting HRM and 36–37
   'reactive/operational' 159
   'traditional' 24
Pfeffer J., key HRM practices 64–65
Pfizer 41t, 70
pharmaceutical sector 45, 70
picketing 246, 254
piecework 184
pilferage 314
placements 16, 62, 131, 228t
pluralism 15
points rating 175–176

policy statements 7, 8t
principle of freedom of association 259
private sector 257, 279, 280, 321
   collective bargaining 300
   external environment and 10, 11
   gain-sharing and share ownership schemes 184
   growth in employment in 221
   HR shared service centres (HRSSCs) 21
   pay agreements for 301
   pay bargaining in 303
   pay freezes 42
   skills shortages 132
   strike activity in 312, 313t
   union membership 254
   wage rigidities 90
probation periods 131
procedure statements 8t
product innovation strategy 169
product market performance 12
professional workers 77b, 77t
profit sharing 43, 72, 180, 184, 186
Programme for Competitiveness and Work 300t
Programme for Economic and Social Progress 300t
Programme for National Recovery 300t
Programme for Prosperity and Fairness 300t
Prohibition Notice, on an employer 349
prospector organisations 61, 62
Protection of Employees (Fixed-Term Work) Act 2003 13, 330
Protection of Employees (Part-Time Work) Act 2001 13, 274, 330
Protection of Employment Act 1977 342
Protection of Employment Acts 1977–2007 343
Protection of Young Persons (Employment) Act 1996 330–331
PRP *see* performance-related pay (PRP)
PRSAs (Personal Retirement Savings Accounts) 332
Psychiatric Nurses Association (PNA) 253
psychological contracts 36, 37t, 60, 92
psychology 235
psychometric tests 69, 127t, 132, 206
public holidays 329–330
public management reform 280
public policy 11, 13, 14, 288, 324
public sector 4, 28, 251, 277, 279, 290–291
   agreements 301, 302

   C&A schemes 280
   development 221
   employment 278
   employment relations 279
   HR shared service centres 21
   pay cuts 42
   pension levy 42
   reform 280, 281, 288
   retirement 344
   strike activity 312, 313t
   trade union density 42, 254
   wage rigidities 90
Public Sector Agreements 2010-2018 281
Public Service Agreement 2010–2014 ('Croke Park Agreement') 301, 302
Public Service Stability Agreement 2012–2016 ('Haddington Road Agreement') 301, 302
Public Service Stability Agreement 2013–2018 ('Lansdowne Road Agreement') 301, 302
Public Services Executive Union (PSEU) 251
punishment, and rewards 166
Purcell, John 73

Quakers 25
qualifications
   dismissal for capability, competence or 339–340
   dismissal for incapability because of 341
Qualifications (Education and Training) Act 1999 218t
quality
   circles 157, 323
   of working life movement 156–157
questions, for interviews 129, 130t
Quick Service Food Alliance (QSFA) 287

Rabbitte, Pat 250
rating scales
   behaviourally anchored 204–205
   performance appraisal 200–202
RBV (resource-based view) 73–74, 78, 79, 82
realism hypothesis 122–123
recessions
   1970s and 1980s 216t
   impact on HR function 43
   see also global financial crisis (great recession)
recruitment and selection 114–132
   candidate assessment techniques 127–128t
   direct applications 122t
   errors and biases in 129

recruitment and selection, *continued*
  external labour market 122*t*
  flow diagram of 115*f*
  individual difference hypothesis 123
  instruments 126
  internal HR flow practices 18
  internal labour market 122*t*
  interview efficiency 128–129
  in Ireland 131–132
  job analysis phase 115–121
  methods of 122*t*
  online recruitment 123
  placement, onboarding and follow-up 131
  realism hypothesis 122–123
  recruitment phase 121–125
  reliability of selection decision 126
  screening and short-listing 123–125
  selection phase 125–131
  structured interviews 126
  suitability of a candidate 125
  targeted selection 65*t*
  unsolicited applications 122*t*
  validity of selection method 125
recruitment freezes 90
redundancy 40, 342–344
Redundancy Payments Acts 1967–2014 342, 343–344
reference checks 132
Regional Newspapers and Printers Association of Ireland 286
registered employment agreements (REA) 274, 275
remuneration *see* pay
representative participation 90, 324*f*
research and advisory services 289
resource-based view of the firm (RBV) 51, 73–74, 78, 94
rest periods 328, 329, 331
results-oriented schemes 200, 203
retirement 344
reward management 165–189
  choosing and introducing the job evaluation scheme 179
  criticisms of job evaluation 178–179
  determination of relative value of jobs 171–172
  effective reward system 169–171
  fringe benefits 188–189
  job evaluation approaches 172–178
  pay as motivator 166–168
  reward package 179–187

scope of 168–169
reward packages 17–18, 165
  broadbanding 185–187
  competence- or skill-based pay 185
  components of 170*f*
  effective 169–171
  employee stock ownership schemes (ESOPs) 180
  flat rate plus group-/team-based performance-based 183–184
  flat rate plus individual performance-based 183
  flat rate systems 180–181
  fringe benefits 188–189
  gain-sharing schemes 180, 184–185
  group incentive schemes 180
  individual incentive schemes 180
  pay, incentives and benefits 179–187
  performance-based incentive systems 181–187
  piecework 184
  profit-sharing schemes 180
  share ownership schemes 184–185
  skill-based pay schemes 180
reward systems *see* reward packages
Rights Commissioners Service *see* Adjudication Service (formerly Rights Commissioner Service)
Ryanair 11, 13, 15, 57, 260–261

sabotage 314
Safety, Health and Welfare at Work Act 1989 348, 349–350
Safety, Health and Welfare at Work Act 2005 346–347, 349
Safety, Health and Welfare at Work (General Application) Regulations 2007 346–348
safety representative and safety committee 348–349
safety statement 347
Schuler, Randall, strategy-employee behaviour model 58
scientific management 25–26, 88, 151
screening and short-listing 123–125
Second World War 28, 311
secret ballots 254
sectoral employment orders (SEO) 273, 274, 275, 276, 311
selection *see* recruitment and selection
selection interviews *see* interviews
selection tests 130–131

self-actualisation 138, 139, 144
self-employment 39, 101t
Selfridges 75
senior management *see* top/senior management
September 11, impact of 39, 67
Services, Industrial, Professional and Technical Union *see* SIPTU (Services, Industrial, Professional and Technical Union)
services sector 22, 67, 101, 244, 250, 303
sexual harassment 336, 350
share ownership schemes 184–185
shop stewards 29, 251
short-listing, in recruitment 123–125
short-time working 114
Single European Act 1987 13
SIPTU (Services, Industrial, Professional and Technical Union) 217t, 250, 253, 262
sit-ins 314
skill-based pay schemes 180, 185
skill shortages 12, 18, 132, 222, 241
   HR planning and 107
   unemployment and 90
skills profiles 125
Skillsnet programme 218t, 290
Social Action Programme 13
social capital 74
social changes 11
Social Charter 13
social comparison theory 195
social legitimacy 70, 71, 82
social partnership 13, 41–42, 257, 288
   agreements 38, 90, 267, 289, 301
Society of the Irish Motor Industry 286, 287
soft HRM 34, 64, 70, 83, 86, 88
   market performance and 12
   in recessions 44, 45f
Southwest Airlines 57
specialisation of tasks 88
specialist human resource management 18–22
staff associations 248, 264, 279, 297, 344
status differentials 65t
stock option schemes 184
stocktaking, human resources 107
strategic behaviour 61
strategic capability 78, 79
strategic choice 9, 35, 60
strategic decision-making 5, 58, 60, 224, 283
   competitive strategies and 57
   downstream (second-order) 55
   and HRM 36, 37, 51, 55–56
   levels of 53f

   market performance and 12
   third-order 55
   upstream (first-order) 55, 56
strategic human resource management (SHRM) 51, 56, 90
strategic management 53–54, 60
Strategic Management Initiative (1994–2007) 280, 281
strategic partners *see* business partners
strategic planning 14, 29, 58, 78
strategic tensions 72, 82
'strategy as practice' perspective 54
strategy content 54
strategy process 54
strike activity 309–312
Sunday working 278, 329
Superquin 15
supervision 112, 150, 151, 156, 172, 185
survival curve 109–111
Sustaining Progress 300t

talent 104, 121
   management 104, 214t, 231–234
   trends 233f
target setting 198, 203
Task Force on Lifelong Learning 219t
task participation 323, 324f
task specialisation 149, 151–152
Taylor, F.W. 26
Taylorism 25–26, 88, 151
Teachers' Union of Ireland (TUI) 251
teamwork 66, 157, 165, 171, 183, 185
Technical, Electrical and Engineering Union (TEEU) 249
technology 45–49
   developments in 11–12
   HR analytics 47–49
   influence on L&D 229
   used in the delivery of HR services 45–46
termination of employment 336–344
   dismissal for breaking another statute 341
   dismissal for capability, competence or qualifications 339–340
   dismissal for incapability because of ill-health 340
   dismissal for incapability because of incompetence 340–341
   dismissal for incapability because of qualifications 341
   dismissal for industrial action 341
   dismissal for misconduct 338–339

termination of employment, *continued*
  dismissal for other substantial grounds 341
  notice of termination 336–337
  redundancy 342–344
  unfair dismissal 337–341
terms and conditions 121, 328–330
Terms of Employment (Information) Acts 1994–2014 328
Texas Instruments 62
theory X, theory Y 143–144
TNA (training needs analysis) 225
top/senior management 5, 6, 9, 19, 64
  handling ER and industrial conflict 315
  success in 141
Towards 2016: Review and Transitional Agreement 2008–2009 41, 300, 301
trade associations 283, 285
trade disputes 246, 272, 273
Trade Disputes Act 1906 ('Bill of Rights for Workers') 246
Trade Union Act 1941 247, 260, 285–286
Trade Union Act 1971 247
trade union movement 24, 27, 245, 246, 253, 261
trade unions 33, 187, 245–254, 298
  alternatives to 263–264
  annual delegate conference (ADC) 251, 253
  branch 252
  branch committee 252–253
  branch secretary 253
  and collective bargaining 172
  craft unions 248–249
  definition of 247
  density of 42, 255–257, 258f
  general unions 249–250
  law and practice 258–263
  legal context 259–262
  management approaches to 294
  membership 28, 254–255
  membership fees 253
  multinational context 262–263
  national executive 253
  negotiating licence 247, 248
  negotiations with 13
  objectives and legal status 246–248
  perspectives on training 217t
  reasons workers join 254–255
  section committee 251
  shop stewards 29, 251
  structure of 251–253
  for teachers 251
  types of 248
  white-collar unions 250–251
  and work design 149
traditional personnel management 24, 36, 37
training 213t
  calls for reform from the mid-1990s 217t
  computer-based 228t
  IBEC analysis of industrial 218t
  identifying training needs 225–227
  institutional reform to support 216t
  trade unions perspectives on 217t
  voluntarism in 216t
  see also education; learning
training needs analysis (TNA) 225
transaction cost theory 90
transfer
  of learning 229–230
  of undertakings 344
Transitional Agreement 301
'triple bottom line' 71
turnover of labour 108–111

unemployment 11, 12, 18, 86, 89–90, 113
  in the 1980s 33
  in 2017 40, 99
  during the 'Celtic tiger' 38
  after the First World War 25
  and strike activity in Ireland 309
  see also labour market
unfair dismissals 318, 320, 337–341, 344
Unfair Dismissals Acts 1977–2015 29, 318, 336, 337, 339, 341
Unfair Dismissals (Amendment) Act 1993 337
Union of Construction Allied Trades and Technicians (UCATT) 249
unions *see* trade unions
unitarism 308
UNITE 250
United States of America 30, 83
Universal Social Charge 42
University of Bath, people and performance model 75–76
utilisation HRM strategy 58

valence 145
vertical loading 153
Vocational Education Act 1930 215t
Vocational Education Colleges (VECs) 215t
vocational training 335
voluntarism in training 216t
'voluntarist' tradition 13, 266, 267

wage agreements 29, 267
'wage–effort' bargain 72
wage rigidities 86, 90
wage rounds 28, 29
wage setting institutions 274–277
   employment regulation orders (EROs) 276–277
   joint industrial councils (JICs) 275
   joint labour committees (JLCs) 276–277
   registered employment agreements (REA) 275
   sectoral employment orders (SEO) 276
Wages Standstill Order 311
wastage 108, 109, 110, 154
websites, recruitment 119
welfare officers 25
welfare tradition 25, 26
Welfare Workers' Association 25, 33
Welfare Workers' Institute 25
white-collar unions 29, 215, 248, 250–251
Women's Rights and Gender Equality (FEMM) 95
work design 148–163
   autonomy 154
   client relationships 154f
   combining tasks 154f
   enriched jobs 154–155f
   feedback 154, 155f
   Hackman and Oldham's job characteristics model 153–155
   high-performance work systems (HPWS) 157–163
   job enlargement 152–153
   model of job characteristics 155f
   natural work units 154f
   quality of working life movement 156–157
   restructuring of jobs 149, 150f
   skill variety 154
   task identity 154
   task significance 154
   task specialisation 151–152
   vertical expansion of jobs 155f
   see also motivation
work doing 26
work examples 128t
work-family conflict 95
work-life balance 95
work organisation 164
work planning 26
work systems 16–17, 26, 35, 164, 214, 322
   changes to 155
   employee influence in design of 156
   high-performance *see* high-performance work systems (HPWS)
   restructuring 152
work to rule industrial action 309, 314
worker ability 74
worker-directors 324f
Worker Participation (State Enterprises) Act 1977 324f
workers
   HR bundles for 77b
   HR policies linked to 77t
workforce
   in Europe in 2015 101f
   innovation 161, 162f, 163
   management 36
   profile of 16, 101t, 112–113
working life, 'quality of working life' movement 156
working week 180, 329
workplace learning and development (LT&D) 212–243
   career development 232–233
   career management 231–233
   communities of practice 239
   competencies 214t
   design and delivery of 227–229
   development 213t
   education 213t
   evaluation of effectiveness of 241
   evaluation of learning 230–231
   external courses 228t
   feedback 239
   human resource development (HRD) 214t
   identifying learning/training needs 225–227
   individual learning and development 235–240
   institutional and regulatory context of 215–222
   involvement of the learner 239
   in Ireland 240–243
   knowledge management 214t
   leadership development 234
   learning process 213t
   learning/training philosophies and policies 223–225
   learning transfer 229–230
   meaningfulness of the material 239
   methods of 227–228t
   motivation to learn 238
   off-the-job methods 228t

workplace learning and development, *continued*
   on-the-job methods 227–228*t*
   organisational learning 214*t*
   organisational processes of 223
   process of 223–229
   reinforcement of learning 239
   stages 215–220*t*
   talent management 214*t*, 231–234
   terminology of 213–214
   training 213*t*
   transfer of learning 229–230
workplace learning, training and development (LT&D) 41
Workplace Relations Act 2015 268, 271, 272, 329
Workplace Relations Commission (WRC) 267, 268–272, 279, 317, 336, 337
   adjudication service 268, 271, 277, 331, 337, 344
   advisory service 269
   conciliation service 269–270
   dismissal for misconduct 338–339
   early resolution service (ERS) 270
   inspection service 271–272
   jurisdiction of 277
   mediation service 270
   procedures to address bullying in the workplace 350
   redundancy and the 342
workplace mediation service 270
workplace teams and decentralisation 65*t*
works councils 264, 323
workshops 228*t*
World Competitiveness Report 40, 212
World Economic Forum (WEF)'s Global Competitiveness Report 212

young people 96, 102
   employment of 330–331
Youth Employment Agency 32*n*